Lecture Notes in Computer Science 15929

The series Lecture Notes in Computer Science (LNCS), including its subseries Lecture Notes in Artificial Intelligence (LNAI) and Lecture Notes in Bioinformatics (LNBI), has established itself as a medium for the publication of new developments in computer science and information technology research, teaching, and education.

LNCS enjoys close cooperation with the computer science R & D community, the series counts many renowned academics among its volume editors and paper authors, and collaborates with prestigious societies. Its mission is to serve this international community by providing an invaluable service, mainly focused on the publication of conference and workshop proceedings and postproceedings. LNCS commenced publication in 1973.

Vasilios Andrikopoulos · Cesare Pautasso ·
Nour Ali · Jacopo Soldani · Xiwei Xu
Editors

Software Architecture

19th European Conference, ECSA 2025
Limassol, Cyprus, September 15–19, 2025
Proceedings

Editors
Vasilios Andrikopoulos
University of Groningen
Groningen, The Netherlands

Cesare Pautasso
University of Lugano
Lugano, Switzerland

Nour Ali
Brunel University London
Uxbridge, UK

Jacopo Soldani
University of Pisa
Pisa, Italy

Xiwei Xu
Data61, CSIRO
Eveleigh, NSW, Australia

ISSN 0302-9743 ISSN 1611-3349 (electronic)
Lecture Notes in Computer Science
ISBN 978-3-032-02137-3 ISBN 978-3-032-02138-0 (eBook)
https://doi.org/10.1007/978-3-032-02138-0

This Springer imprint is published by the registered company Springer Nature Switzerland AG
The registered company address is: Gewerbestrasse 11, 6330 Cham, Switzerland

Preface

The European Conference on Software Architecture (ECSA) is the premier European software architecture conference, providing researchers, practitioners, and educators with a platform to present and discuss the most recent, innovative, and significant findings and experiences in the field of software architecture research and practice.

The theme for the 19th edition of ECSA was "Impactful Software Architecture". The software architecture discipline has a critical role in shaping robust, scalable, and maintainable systems. ECSA 2025 aimed to explore software architecture principles and practices, emerging trends, and case studies highlighting strategic architectural choices that can lead to enhanced performance, improved collaboration, and long-term sustainability. The overarching question is how these architectural principles and practices, both well-established and emerging, are making an impact in real-world systems, and how that impact is being felt across various domains, from enterprise systems to more novel areas such as AI-driven or autonomous applications. ECSA 2025 provided participants with insights into impactful software architecture principles and practices, solutions from and for industry to architect software, and methods for evaluating the suitability of the software architecture for its intended application. Furthermore, ECSA 2025 covered research and practical experiences in building impactful software architectures across diverse application domains.

This edition of ECSA was held during September 15–19, 2025, as an in-person conference in the beautiful city of Limassol (Cyprus). The core technical program included sessions that blended contributions from the research, industry, journal-first, and tools & demonstration tracks, plus two keynote talks. Moreover, ECSA 2025 offered a doctoral symposium track and six workshops, i.e., the 1st International Workshop on *AI-Assisted Software Architecting* (AISA), the 5th International Workshop on *Agility with Microservices Programming* (AMP), the 1st International Workshop on *Architecting Digital Twin of an Organization* (ArchDTO), the 12th Workshop on *Adaptive and Reconfigurable Systems and Architectures* (AROSA), the 8th International Workshop on *Context-Aware, Autonomous and Smart Architectures* (CASA), and the 1st International Workshop on *Software Architecture for Data-Intensive Systems* (SADIS).

For ECSA 2025, we received 76 submissions for the Research track and 15 submissions with 1 withdrawn for the Industry track. For the fourth time, this year's ECSA Research track followed a double-blind review process. After desk-rejecting 10 papers, each paper submitted to the Research track received at least three reviews. Based on the discussions and recommendations of the Program Committee, we accepted 22 papers to the Research track (namely, 13 full research, 3 experience report and 6 short papers). Additionally, each paper in the Industry track was reviewed by three reviewers representing both industrial and academic perspectives. We accepted 2 full papers, 2 short papers, and 1 full paper as a short paper. The selected papers span various domains—automotive, automation, agriculture, and assistive technologies—demonstrating how software architecture enables scalability, maintainability, and innovation across sectors.

The conference attracted papers authored by researchers, practitioners, and academics from 35 countries (Argentina, Australia, Austria, Belgium, Brazil, Canada, Chile, China, Colombia, Cyprus, Czechia, Denmark, Egypt, Finland, France, Germany, Greece, India, Ireland, Italy, Japan, Lebanon, Netherlands, New Zealand, Poland, Portugal, Russia, Spain, Sweden, Switzerland, Thailand, Tunisia, Ukraine, the UK, and the USA).

Following the successful initiative started in 2024, ECSA 2025 explicitly encouraged authors to support Open Science. More precisely, we encouraged all contributing authors to disclose (anonymized and curated) data/artifacts to increase reproducibility. Authors were encouraged to share artifacts in a Zenodo community for the ECSA conference series (https://zenodo.org/communities/ecsa/). However, sharing research artifacts was not mandatory for submission or acceptance.

The main ECSA program featured three keynotes by Eoin Woods, Catia Trubiani, and Elisabetta Di Nitto, on topics related to the main theme of the conference.

We are grateful to the members of the Program Committee for their valuable and timely reviews, as well as for the positive discussions, which contributed to a high-quality technical program for ECSA 2025. Furthermore, we would like to thank the members of the Organizing Committee for successfully organizing the event with several tracks, as well as the workshop organizers, who made significant contributions to this year's event. We thank our sponsor Springer, which funded the best paper award of ECSA 2025 and supported us by publishing the proceedings in the *Lecture Notes in Computer Science* series. Finally, we thank the authors of all the ECSA 2025 submissions and the attendees of the conference for their participation.

July 2025

Nour Ali
Vasilios Andrikopoulos
Cesare Pautasso
Jacopo Soldani
Xiwei Xu

The original version of the book has been revised. A correction to this book can be found at https://doi.org/10.1007/978-3-032-02138-0_28

Organization

Steering Committee

Nour Ali	Brunel University London, UK
Vasilios Andrikopoulos	University of Groningen, The Netherlands
Paris Avgeriou	University of Groningen, The Netherlands
Thais Batista	Federal University of Rio Grande do Norte, Brazil
Stefan Biffl	TU Wien, Austria
Tomas Bures	Charles University, Czech Republic
Laurence Duchien	University of Lille, France
Carlos E. Cuesta	Rey Juan Carlos University, Spain
Matthias Galster	University of Canterbury, New Zealand
Ilias Gerostathopoulos	Vrije Universiteit Amsterdam, The Netherlands
Paola Inverardi	Gran Sasso Science Institute, Italy
Andrea Janes	Free University of Bozen/Bolzano, Italy
Patricia Lago	Vrije Universiteit Amsterdam, The Netherlands
Grace Lewis	Carnegie Mellon University, USA
Ivano Malavolta	Vrije Universiteit Amsterdam, The Netherlands
Raffaela Mirandola	Politecnico di Milano, Italy
Henry Muccini	University of L'Aquila, Italy
Elisa Yumi Nakagawa	University of São Paulo, Brazil
Elena Navarro	University of Castilla-La Mancha, Spain
Flavio Oquendo	University of Southern Brittany, France
Ipek Ozkaya	Carnegie Mellon University Software Engineering Institute, USA
Cesare Pautasso	Università della Svizzera italiana, Switzerland
Patrizia Scandurra	University of Bergamo, Italy
Jacopo Soldani	University of Pisa, Italy
Davide Taibi	University of Oulu, Finland
Bedir Tekinerdogan	Wageningen University & Research, The Netherlands
Chouki Tibermacine	University of Southern Brittany, France
Catia Trubiani	Gran Sasso Science Institute, Italy

Research Track

Program Chairs

Nour Ali	Brunel University London, UK
Jacopo Soldani	University of Pisa, Italy

Program Committee

Michel Albonico	Universidade Tecnológica Federal do Paraná, Brazil
Nuha Alshuqayran	Imam Mohammad Ibn Saud Islamic University, Saudi Arabia
Jesper Andersson	Linnaeus University, Sweden
Paolo Arcaini	National Institute of Informatics, Japan
Hernán Astudillo	Universidad Andrés Bello, Chile
Paris Avgeriou	University of Groningen, The Netherlands
Rami Bahsoon	University of Birmingham, UK
Steffen Becker	University of Stuttgart, Germany
Justus Bogner	Vrije Universiteit Amsterdam, The Netherlands
Jim Buckley	University of Limerick, Ireland
Matteo Camilli	Politecnico di Milano, Italy
Jan Carlson	Mälardalen University, Sweden
Filipe Correia	University of Porto, Portugal
Martina De Sanctis	Gran Sasso Science Institute, Italy
Khalil Drira	LAAS-CNRS, France
Amr Elsayed	University of Arizona, USA
Matthias Galster	University of Canterbury, New Zealand
David Garlan	Carnegie Mellon University, USA
Ilias Gerostathopoulos	Vrije Universiteit Amsterdam, The Netherlands
Alfredo Goldman	University of São Paulo, Brazil
Eduardo Guerra	Free University of Bozen-Bolzano, Italy
Robert Heinrich	Karlsruhe Institute of Technology, Germany
Sören Henning	Johannes Kepler University Linz, Austria
Ahmad Ibrahim	University of Birmingham - Dubai, UAE
Paola Inverardi	Gran Sasso Science Institute, Italy
Anne Koziolek	Karlsruhe Institute of Technology, Germany
Patricia Lago	Vrije Universiteit Amsterdam, The Netherlands
Van-Hoang Le	University of Newcastle, Australia
Valentina Lenarduzzi	University of Oulu, Finland
Grace Lewis	Carnegie Mellon University, USA

Ivano Malavolta	Vrije Universiteit Amsterdam, The Netherlands
Nabor Mendonca	University of Fortaleza, Brazil
Tommi Mikkonen	University of Jyväskylä, Finland
Raffaela Mirandola	Politecnico di Milano, Italy
Angelika Musil	TU Wien, Austria
Elisa Yumi Nakagawa	University of São Paulo, Brazil
Elena Navarro	University of Castilla-La Mancha, Spain
Evangelos Ntentos	University of Vienna, Austria
Pablo Oliveira Antonino	Fraunhofer IESE, Germany
Flavio Oquendo	University of Southern Brittany, France
Patrizio Pelliccione	Gran Sasso Science Institute, Italy
Diego Perez	Linnaeus University, Sweden
Ana Petrovska	TU Munich, Germany
Francisco Ponce	University of Pisa, Italy
Jennifer Perez	Universidad Politécnica de Madrid, Spain
Elvinia Riccobene	University of Milan, Italy
António Rito Silva	Universidade de Lisboa, Portugal
Salah Sadou	University of Southern Brittany, France
Riccardo Scandariato	TU Hamburg, Germany
Patrizia Scandurra	University of Bergamo, Italy
Bradley Schmerl	Carnegie Mellon University, USA
Stefan Schulte	TU Hamburg, Germany
Lionel Seinturier	University of Lille, France
Romina Spalazzese	Malmö University, Sweden
Christos Tsigkanos	University of Athens, Greece
Dimitri Van Landuyt	KU Leuven, Belgium
Roberto Verdecchia	University of Florence, Italy
Rainer Weinreich	Johannes Kepler University Linz, Austria
Anna Wingkvist	Linnaeus University, Sweden
Andrzej Zalewski	Warsaw University of Technology, Poland
Uwe Zdun	University of Vienna, Austria

Additional Reviewers

Yosr Baccari
Adam Bachorek
Ismael Bouassida Rodriguez
Chiara Braghin
Rodrigo Falcão
Samuele Giussani
Hamideh Hajiabadi
Tobias Hey
Ezdehar Jawabreh
Joran Leest
Haoyu Liu
Iyed Nasra
Sara Pettinari
Lotfi Souifi
Karim Zarour
Thomas Zimmermann

Industrial Track

Industry Chair

Xiwei Xu	CSIRO Data61, Australia

Program Committee

Marion Wiese	University of Hamburg, Germany
Federico Ciccozzi	Mälardalen University, Sweden
Heiko Koziolek	ABB Corporate Research, Germany
Dhanunjaya Rao Gorrle	Western Digital Technologies, Inc., USA
Klara Borowa	Warsaw University of Technology, Poland
Tommi Mikkonen	University of Helsinki, Finland
Remco de Boer	ArchiXL, The Netherlands
Turgay Çelik	Turkish Aerospace Industries, Turkey
Carlos E. Cuesta	Rey Juan Carlos University, Spain
Qinghua Lu	CSIRO Data61, Australia
Abhay Paroha	Schlumberger, Ltd., USA
Elisa Yumi Nakagawa	University of São Paulo, Brazil
Mario Benitez	Carnegie Mellon University, USA
Thomas Kuhn (Scientist)	Fraunhofer IESE, Kaiserslautern, Germany
Antonino Sabetta	SAP Security Research, France
Mirko D'Angelo	Ericsson Research, Sweden
Uwe Zdun	University of Vienna, Austria
James Ivers	Carnegie Mellon University, USA
Vijay Govindarajan	Expedia Group, USA
Dawen Zhang	CSIRO Data61, Australia
Olaf Zimmermann	University of Applied Sciences of Eastern Switzerland, Switzerland
Ian Gorton	Northeastern University, USA
Pablo Oliveira Antonino	Fraunhofer IESE, Germany
Antero Taivalsaari	Nokia Technologies, Finland
Henry Muccini	University of L'Aquila, Italy
Damian Andrew Tamburri	University of Sannio, Italy
Andrei Furda	Hitachi Rail STS, Australia
Jens Knodel	Caruso GmbH, Germany
Xabier Larrucea	University of the Basque Country (UPV/EHU), Spain

Organizing Committee

General Chairs

Vasilios Andrikopoulos — University of Groningen, The Netherlands
Cesare Pautasso — USI Lugano, Switzerland

Workshops Chairs

Tommi Mikkonen — University of Jyväskylä, Finland
Jennifer Perez — Universidad Politécnica de Madrid, Spain

Tools and Demos Chairs

Mohamed Soliman — Paderborn University, Germany
Uwe Zdun — University of Vienna, Austria

Tutorials Chairs

Tomas Bures — Charles University, Czech Republic
Martina De Sanctis — Gran Sasso Science Institute, Italy

Doctoral Symposium Chairs

Henry Muccini — University of L'Aquila, Italy
Elena Navarro — University of Castilla-La Mancha, Spain

Journal-First Chairs

Jesper Andersson — Linnaeus University, Sweden
Romina Spalazzese — Malmö University, Sweden

MIP Chairs

Raffaela Mirandola — Karlsruhe Institute of Technology, Germany
Remco de Boer — ArchiXL & Vrije Universiteit Amsterdam, The Netherlands

Open Science Chair

Valentina Lenarduzzi — University of Oulu, Finland

Proceedings Chairs

Domenico Bianculli — University of Luxembourg, Luxembourg
Hassan Sartaj — Simula Research Laboratory, Norway

Web Chair

Christos Therapontos — Easyconferences, Cyprus

Local Chair

George Angelos Papadopoulos — University of Cyprus, Cyprus

Contents

Architectures for MLOps

An Approach for Integrated Development of an MLOps Architecture 3
Petra Heck, Jacco Snoeren, Merel Veracx, and Manon Peeters

MLOps in Practice: Requirements and a Reference Architecture from Industry 20
Indika Kumara, Rowan Arts, Renato Cordeiro Ferreira, Dario Di Nucci, Rick Kazman, Damian Andrew Tamburri, and Willem-Jan van den Heuvel

HarmonE: A Self-adaptive Approach to Architecting Sustainable MLOps 38
Hiya Bhatt, Shaunak Biswas, Srinivasan Rakhunathan, and Karthik Vaidhyanathan

Large Language Models in Software Architecture

Using Incremental LLM Context for Cost Reduction in LLM-Driven IoT Applications 59
Aashna Sofat and Balwinder Sodhi

Automated Software Architecture Design Recovery from Source Code Using LLMs 73
Domenico Amalfitano, Marco De Luca, Tiziano Santilli, Patrizio Pelliccione, and Anna Rita Fasolino

Exploring Architectural Smells Detection Through LLMs 90
Claudio Tessa, Matteo Bochicchio, and Francesca Arcelli Fontana

LLMs for Software Architecture Knowledge: A Comparative Analysis Among Seven LLMs 99
Mohamed Soliman, Elia Ashraf, Kamel M. K. Abdelsalam, Jan Keim, and Ashwin Prasad Shivarpatna Venkatesh

LLM-Based Quality Assessment of Software Architecture Diagrams: A Preliminary Study with Four Open-Source Projects 116
Glauber Queiroz de Oliveira and Nabor C. Mendonça

Architectures for Embedded Systems

Nanosatellite Flight Software: A Rigorous Software Architecture Perspective 127
Christoforos Vasilakis, Alexandros Tsagkaropoulos, Angelos Motsios, Christos Tsigkanos, and Dionysios Reisis

Towards Mixed-Criticality Software Architectures for Centralized HPC Platforms in Software-Defined Vehicles: A Systematic Literature Review 144
Lucas Mauser, Eva Zimmermann, Pavel Nedvědický, Tobias Eisenreich, Moritz Wäschle, and Stefan Wagner

Runtime Monitor Synthesis for Automotive Software Architectures 161
Fazli Faruk Okumus, João-Vitor Zacchi, Maike Salfeld, Markus Schweizer, Núria Mata, and Stefan Kugele

Self-adaptive, Secure and Federated Learning Systems

Model-Based Proactive Self-adaptation for Cloud Systems 181
Raphael Straub, Sarah Stieß, Steffen Becker, and Matthias Tichy

SAFER-D: A Self-adaptive Security Framework for Distributed Computing Architectures 197
Marco Stadler, Michael Vierhauser, Michael Riegler, Daniel Waghubinger, and Johannes Sametinger

SURE! A Catalog of Uncertainties and RELAXed Requirements for Self-adaptive Systems 214
Claudia Raibulet, Ilias Gerostathopoulos, and Osman Abdelmukaram

Architecting Federated Learning Systems: A Requirement-Driven Approach 224
Luciano Baresi, Livia Lestingi, and Iyad Wehbe

Microservice Architecture

Centrality Change Proneness: An Early Indicator of Microservice Architectural Degradation 243
Alexander Bakhtin, Matteo Esposito, Valentina Lenarduzzi, and Davide Taibi

A Comparative Analysis of Monolith vs Microservices Energy Consumption 260
Roberta Capuano, Eoan O'Dea, and Henry Muccini

Data-Driven Understanding of Design Decisions in Pattern-Based Microservices Architecture 276
J. Andres Diaz-Pace, Catia Trubiani, and David Garlan

Software Architecture Practices, Perspectives and Evolution

Architectural Design Decisions and Best Practices for Fast and Efficient CI/CD Pipelines 297
Francesco Urdih, Theodoros Theodoropoulos, and Uwe Zdun

From Lab to Market: Architectural Evolution in Open Source Transition 306
Sven Thielen, Björn Salgert, and Thomas Franz

How Do Practitioners Perceive the Relevance of Software Architecture Research? 323
Everton Cavalcante, Elisa Yumi Nakagawa, Rick Kazman, and Thais Batista

Towards Legal Knowledge Transfer Based on Software Architecture 332
Nicolas Boltz, Janne Wagner, Leonie Sterz, Oliver Raabe, and Christopher Gerking

Industry Papers

WebAssembly with wasi-nn for Edge Machine Learning Inference: Experiences and Lessons Learned 343
Joshua Bachmeier, Vladimir Yussupov, Jörg Henß, and Heiko Koziolek

Software Architecture for a Robust, Multithreaded, Realtime, Control System Used on an Adaptive Racecar 360
Harry George Direen, Randal Hugh Direen, George York, James Edward Direen, Vernon Joseph Brabec, and Shanjay Kailayanathan

Asynchronous Interoperability Description and Authentication:: Addressing Challenges in a Webhook-Based Event-Driven Architecture 367
Jean-Philippe Gouigoux, Dalila Tamzalit, and Khaoula Jbari

Variant Management Impact on Architectural Maintainability in Embedded Systems – A Case Study 378
Bengt Haraldsson and Miroslaw Staron

AI-Driven Machine Learning Architecture for Scalable Irrigation Detection in Precision Agriculture: A Case Study with CropX 389
Jakub Ozimek, Matan Yakobovich, Henk-Jan Hoving, and Andrea Capiluppi

Correction to: Software Architecture C1
Vasilios Andrikopoulos, Cesare Pautasso, Nour Ali, Jacopo Soldani, and Xiwei Xu

Author Index 407

Architectures for MLOps

An Approach for Integrated Development of an MLOps Architecture

Petra Heck(✉), Jacco Snoeren, Merel Veracx, and Manon Peeters

Fontys University of Applied Sciences, Eindhoven, The Netherlands
{p.heck,j.snoeren,m.veracx,m.peeters}@fontys.nl

Abstract. Many publications elaborate on the so-called AI engineering or MLOps (Machine Learning Operations) processes, also from an architecture point of view. However, it remains a challenge to translate this into a practical approach for designing an MLOps architecture from the very beginning of a project.

In this paper, we define an integrated approach to develop an MLOps architecture (including data, models and software) based on Google's MLOps maturity levels and publications on architectural design decisions for machine learning. We demonstrate this approach on a real-life machine learning project, where we designed a streaming wearable data platform for detecting stress.

The approach we took and the lessons learned are valuable for practitioners working on similar projects. Furthermore, the challenges we encountered in our project can serve as future research directions.

Keywords: software architecture · MLOps · AI engineering · ADDs

1 Introduction

Amershi et al. [1] were the first to describe the workflow of a machine learning (ML) project. Since then, many publications have elaborated on so-called AI engineering [3] or MLOps [17,24] processes. Kreuzberger et al. [12] present "an end-to-end MLOps architecture and workflow with functional components and roles". They end their paper by stating: "The results ... will hopefully assist researchers and professionals in setting up successful ML projects in the future." In the industry and research projects we collaborate with, we do however see that it remains a challenge to translate these published processes to a practical approach for designing an MLOps architecture.

In this paper we describe the development of one such project: a wearables platform that detects stress in a healthcare setting. For this project we developed an MLOps architecture that fulfils the social, technical and legal requirements of all stakeholders. We needed an integrated approach for developing such architecture: 1) including data, models and software; 2) supporting both the training phase and the inference phase.

V. Andrikopoulos et al. (Eds.): ECSA 2025, LNCS 15929, pp. 3–19, 2026.
https://doi.org/10.1007/978-3-032-02138-0_1

Based on our practical and theoretical experience with software engineering, AI engineering and MLOps, we outlined a semi-structured approach for the project, consisting of the following main steps:

1. Collect system requirements from all stakeholders, including ML-related quality requirements [8];
2. Define the required MLOps maturity level [5];
3. Make important ML-related architectural choices, using ML Architectural Design Decisions (ADDs) [21,22];
4. Implement the architecture based on ADDs and requirements;
5. Validate against system requirements;

Although the main steps are presented sequentially, in practice there will be a constant iteration between requirements, design, development and testing like in any agile project.

Our approach and the lessons learned are valuable for researchers and practitioners working on similar projects. While our focus is on stress detection, the challenges and methodologies presented can be applicable to any project involving an interdisciplinary context, continuous data streams that require complex processing, and ML integration. Furthermore, the challenges we encountered in our project can serve as future research directions.

The remainder of this paper is organized as follows. Section 2 describes background on MLOps and architectures for ML systems. Section 3 describes the stress detection project and its stakeholders. Section 4 till Sect. 8 describe how each of the five steps in our approach is executed for the design of the stress detection platform. Section 9 discusses the approach and the lessons learned for practitioners and applied researchers. The paper concludes by summarizing our contributions and future work.

2 Background and Related Work

2.1 MLOps and AI Engineering

Kreuzberger et al. [12] define MLOps as a "paradigm, including aspects like best practices, sets of concepts, as well as a development culture when it comes to the end-to-end conceptualization, implementation, monitoring, deployment, and scalability of machine learning products. Most of all, it is an engineering practice that leverages three contributing disciplines: machine learning, software engineering (especially DevOps), and data engineering. MLOps is aimed at productionising machine learning systems by bridging the gap between development (Dev) and operations (Ops). Essentially, MLOps aims to facilitate the creation of machine learning products by leveraging these principles: CI/CD [Continuous Integration and Continuous Deployment] automation, workflow orchestration, reproducibility; versioning of data, model, and code; collaboration; continuous ML training and evaluation; ML metadata tracking and logging; continuous monitoring; and feedback loops."

Google [5] provides a technical view on this, by defining three maturity levels for automating the monitoring and improvement of the ML system:

- MLOps Level 0: manual integration and deployment of the model;
- MLOps Level 1: both model and training pipeline are deployed - allowing for Continuous Training (CT);
- MLOps Level 2: Upon any change the ML pipeline will automatically build, test, and deploy - allowing for CI/CD.

See Table 1 for a more detailed list of requirements per MLOps Level. We included the MLOps Levels from Google in our approach because we already had hands-on experience with it from earlier projects.

Table 1. MLOps requirements [5], Level 2 in Italic

ID	MLOps Requirement
ML1a	System shall handle version control for models
ML1b	System shall handle version control for (training) data sets
ML1c	System shall automate data processing and model training on that data
ML1d	System shall automate model validation
ML1e	System shall automate model deployment
ML1f	System shall automatically retrain the model in production using fresh data based on live pipeline triggers
ML2a	*System shall collect statistics on the model performance based on live data*
ML2b	*System shall automate the deployment of an ML pipeline that can automate retraining and deployment of new models*
ML2c	*System shall automatically run tests on the pipeline before deployment*
ML2d	*System shall first be deployed in a testing (and staging) environment before going to production*

According to Bosch et al. [3], AI Engineering is "an engineering discipline that is concerned with all aspects of the development and evolution of AI systems, i.e. systems that include AI components". In this way the MLOps paradigm and the AI engineering paradigm overlap, and in our view can be considered synonyms. Both MLOps and AI engineering, are engineering practices that aim to build production-ready ML systems. In this paper we present an approach on designing such an ML-based software system using the MLOps (AI engineering) paradigm.

Several case studies have been conducted on MLOps [4,13,16]. Our project mostly resembles the case study by Grote and Bogner [7], as they also set a goal to develop a production-ready AI-based system. They present a case study where they applied AI engineering practices to develop a stock trading system. However, their case study was a technical prototype to demonstrate certain practices (focused on model training), where our project aims to develop a production-ready stress detection platform, involving the end users of the platform, in the actual context they will use it in (environment, workflow, ethical/legal considerations, infrastructure, etc.).

2.2 Architectures for ML Systems

In 2021, Muccini and Vaidhyanathan [14], describe the lessons learned and a research agenda based on a case study where they had to architect an ML system. In there discussion of the architecting process they describe challenges similar to our project. In 2023, Gorton et al. [6] published a book chapter, with an update on the state of the practice, and future research areas for AI-based software systems architectures. Again, they identify a lack of practices and processes. We offer a possible solution in the form of our semi-structured approach. Furthermore, we extend upon the discussion, by not just considering software architectures for ML systems, but presenting it as an integrated MLOps architecture, that includes data, software, and models.

Jansen and Bosch [9] consider software architectures as a composition of a set of explicit design decisions. Although we did not use their formal Archium meta-model to describe our decisions, we did follow the same line of reasoning in our approach. With regards to design decisions for ML systems, Warnett and Zdun [21,22] extracted 16 Architectural Design Decisions (ADDs) from gray literature (including the MLOps manifesto from Google [5]). We use their ADDs to guide our architecture design, thereby validating the usefulness of the ADD catalogue in a practical ML project. Table 2 lists the 16 ADDs they extracted (refer to their work for the answer options for each question), (partially) mapped to the MLOps Requirements from Table 1. Whereas Warnett and Zdun [21] present MLOps as a deployment decision ("MLOps is a complex domain in its own right, it lies outwith the scope of this study"), we present an integrated approach where the MLOps principles form the base for our project from the start.

3 Project Description: An MLOps Platform for Stress Detection

The functionality that the stakeholders expect from the stress detection platform is relatively simple, see Table 3. Algorithms to detect stress from Electro-Dermal Activity (EDA) have been validated in lab settings, showing their potential [11]. The challenge in this project lies in building a stress detection platform that fulfils all user requirements, while at the same time being compliant with legislation, and easy to maintain.

The stress detection platform had to be designed for two specific user groups: 1) persons with dementia and challenging behaviour living in a nursing home; 2) physiotherapists treating clients with Persistent Physical Symptoms (PPS). For both groups it might help the treatment when stress can be detected from wearable data: persons with dementia cannot communicate their own stress, and persons with PPS are often not aware of their own stress. This leads to a diverse group of stakeholders for the project: elderly people with dementia, nurses, behavioural experts, nursing home innovation managers, informal caregivers, physiotherapists, and clients with PPS. Stress is a personal experience,

Table 2. Architectural Design Decisions ML [21,22] linked to the MLOps requirements from Table 1; ( ) means partial mapping

ID	ADD	ID
ADD1	How to automatically process the data used for model building?	ML1c
ADD2	Which data processing tasks can be performed by a data processing pipeline or component?	ML1c
ADD3	How to persist and provide access to features?	ML1c
ADD4	Should data be processed in batches or in real-time?	ML1c
ADD5	How to ingest data into ML projects or applications?	ML1c
ADD6	How to trigger a machine learning pipeline or orchestrator?	(ML1f)
ADD7	How to perform model building in an ML project?	ML1c ML1d
ADD8	Which tasks can be performed by a model building pipeline or component?	ML1c ML1d
ADD9	When and how to train the model?	ML1c
ADD10	Should AutoML be used and if so where?	ML1c
ADD11	How to approach deployment of machine learning models?	ML1e
ADD12	How to automate integration and delivery in a machine learning context?	ML1e
ADD13	Which tasks can be performed by a delivery pipeline or component?	ML1e
ADD14	How to version data?	ML1b
ADD15	Which model versions should be deployed and how?	(ML1a)
ADD16	Should MLOps be applied and, if so, when?	(All)

and also the way individuals want to see their own stress, or another individual's stress, differs per person. We wanted to design the system as generic as possible, to also be applicable for other use cases, thus leading to the requirement for a highly flexible and personalisable user interface.

Because the platform contains biometric data and uses medical devices (instead of consumer-grade wearables), our solution is highly regulated. That is why we involved legal experts from the beginning of the project to collect all legal requirements.

The project aimed at implementing MLOps Level 1 [5]. In the following sections we will present the approach we took to design the MLOps architecture for the project.

4 Step 1: ML-Related Requirements for the Stress Detection Platform

As said in Sect. 3, the functionality of the platform is fairly simple. However, we realized that the non-functional or quality requirements for this platform are

Table 3. Data platform system requirements, collected through focus groups and interviews

ID	System Requirement
SR1	User shall be able to register a wearable
SR2	System shall receive raw streaming data from wearables
SR3	System shall process raw streaming data
SR4	System shall visualize processed streaming data
SR5	System shall detect a stress moment
SR6	System shall visualize stress moments
SR7	User shall be able to alter the sensitivity of their stress level indications
SR8	User shall be able to annotate a stress moment
SR9	System shall handle multiple wearable types

not so straight-forward, especially since we are using ML to detect stress and are working with highly sensitive user data in a health care setting.

To identify ML-related quality requirements we used the AI quality model from [8] as a dictionary of possibly relevant criteria: model correctness, model robustness, reproducibility, explainability, collaboration effectiveness, controllability, human autonomy, privacy, and fairness. All stakeholders (legal experts, healthcare experts, IT experts, data scientists, end users) were involved in defining and iteratively detailing the requirements. Table 4 shows the most important quality requirements for our project.

Eliciting requirements for the quality criterion "Model Correctness" forced us to explicitly state what is meant by detecting stress. This resulted in statements like: "The system shall detect 90% of the stress periods that last longer than 5 min and 95% of the stress periods that last longer than 10 min".

In our experience using a quality model as a standard dictionary for defining ML-related quality requirements is a crucial step in any AI engineering project. The model we used also nicely ensures the 'human-in-the-loop' [11] quality aspects such as collaboration effectiveness, controllability and human autonomy (extending the traditional notion of usability). Furthermore it emphasizes that model correctness is not the holy grail in AI projects, but should be balanced with robustness, reproducibility, compliance, privacy, fairness and explainability according to the needs of the project.

5 Step 2: MLOps-Related Requirements for the Stress Detection Platform

Since we use ML to detect stress in the EDA signal, we also need to define how we would like to include the data and the models into the overall software architecture. We call this overall architecture "the MLOps architecture" for the

Table 4. Most important ML-related quality requirements

ID	ML-related Quality Requirement
QR1	**Reproducibility** The system and its development process shall comply with EU regulations for both medical and AI-based software
QR2	**Robustness** The model shall be resilient against artefacts that may occur during measurement of physiological signals
QR3	**Explainability** The system shall make use of published algorithms to detect stress peaks or publish any new algorithm it uses
QR4	**Collaboration Effectiveness** The system shall present real-time stress peaks with a delay of 15 min at most
QR5	**Collaboration Effectiveness** The user shall be able to select different visualizations (time-frame, features/data streams, combined graphs, etc.) of the stress peaks, overlayed on the wearables data
QR6	**Collaboration Effectiveness** The system shall present historical stress peaks for the past 30 d
QR7	**Privacy** The wearable data shall only be visible for authorized caregivers/medical professionals to whom the person wearing the wearable has given written permission
QR8	**Privacy** The wearable data should be stored separately from the personal data
QR9	**Privacy** The system shall store as little personal data as needed
QR10	**Fairness/Bias** The stress detection method should work for all ages, sexes and ethnicities, or state explicitly which groups are excluded
QR11	**Human Autonomy** The user shall not be hindered in his or her daily activities by the system
QR12	**Human Autonomy** The system shall not be the cause of additional stress perceived by the user

stress detection platform. So for us, MLOps is a starting point (integrating data, models and code in a collaborative workflow), and not one of the ADDs.

Before defining the MLOps architecture, we need to decide on the level of automation for data and model pipelines. For this, we use the MLOps maturity levels as defined by Google [5]. As mentioned, this project aimed at implementing MLOps level 1. See requirement ML1a till ML1f in Table 1 for more details on what this entails.

6 Step 3: Architectural Design Decisions for the Stress Detection Platform

Starting from the goal to implement MLOps Level 1 [5] for our stress detection platform, we can now discuss the fifteen other ADDs from Table 2 for a more detailed choice on how to implement each of the six MLOps Level 1 requirements from Table 1.

6.1 ADD1 Till ADD5: Data Processing

MLOps Level 1 [5] requires automated data processing (**ML1c**). For processing data coming from the wearables we decided to use data pipelines (ADD1), that execute all data processing tasks from data extraction to feature engineering (ADD2). We experimented with different pre-processing pipelines as there are several known algorithms (QR3) to separate the raw EDA signal into components (e.g., tonic, phasic) that can be analysed with machine learning. Furthermore, we needed a normalization step in the data pipelines, since different wearables (SR9) have different ways of representing the EDA signal, e.g., different frequencies. Lastly, an important part of data processing is also the removal of artefacts, e.g., physically impossible values for the biometric data (QR2).

We decided not to use a dedicated feature store (ADD3) for our first design, since we were analysing time series data, thus making it a good fit for a time series database (InfluxDB in our case) to store raw and processed data (our 'features').

The goal of our stress detection platform was to detect personalized stress (near) real-time (QR4), so we needed a real-time data processing pipeline (ADD4). At the same time, the system should also be able to handle batch uploads, e.g., when users have been disconnected from the internet for a while. The wearables we use all have capacity to store data on device and upload when ready. And some wearables require downloading data (with or without API) from the cloud environment of the supplier. This means the system should support all forms of data ingestion: streaming, by request, in batches or even manual (ADD5).

6.2 ADD6 till ADD10: Model Building

MLOps Level 1 [5] requires automated retraining of the ML model based on some trigger (**ML1f**, ADD6). Furthermore, it requires automated model building (**ML1c**). For this we decided to use a separate ML orchestrator (ADD7) that can also automatically validate the model (**ML1d**) and perform all other model building tasks (ADD8). There are multiple such tools available [18]. We decided not to use a cloud-based ML platform like AzureML since we did not want to be tied to a specific cloud provider with our platform. Based on our previous experience we chose MLFlow, combined with Whylogs for model monitoring (not included in MLFlow). In the future we could also add Optuna for hyper-parameter tuning, but we left that out of scope in our first architecture design.

Since our system needs to support personalized stress detection, and models (even the underlying algorithms) may differ per person, the system needs to support both batch-based learning and incremental learning (ADD9). For the moment, we decide not to use AutoML (ADD10).

6.3 ADD11 till ADD13: Model Deployment

MLOps Level 1 [5] requires automated deployment of the ML models (**ML1e**, ADD11). We decided to have the integration and delivery of the models handled by the same orchestrator used for automated model building, in our case MLFlow (ADD12, ADD13).

6.4 ADD14 and ADD15: Version Control

MLOps Level 1 [5] requires version control for both models (**ML1a**) and data (**ML1b**). Our training data consisted of an open source dataset [20], and a few short-duration datasets collected from real-life measurements. Those anonymous, static datasets could easily be stored in code version control (ADD14). For production data we store historical data (QR6) in our InfluxDB, thus we do not need separate data version control systems like DVC (ADD14).

For model version control, we heavily rely on the model registry in MLFlow, to be able to have multiple versions of the same model or multiple different models in production at the same time (ADD15). We need this because our hypothesis is that we need different models or different hyper-parameters per person to accurately detect stress.

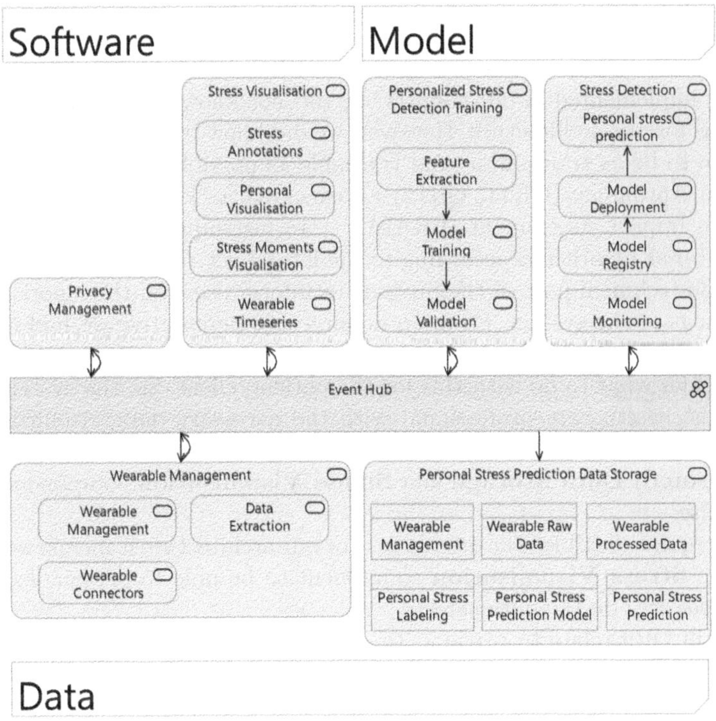

Fig. 1. MLOps application architecture of the stress detection platform

7 Step 4: MLOps Architecture for the Stress Detection Platform

Now that we have discussed all architectural decisions, we can define the overall MLOps architecture for the stress detection platform.

7.1 MLOps Architecture

The overall MLOps architecture combines the results from step 1 (requirements), step 2 (MLOps level) and step 3 (ADDs). Figure 1 shows the overall architecture, including data processing (ADD1 till ADD5), the model building pipeline and model monitoring (ADD6 till ADD10), the model registry (ADD14 and ADD15), and the model deployment (ADD11 till ADD13). The following section describes how the architecture supports the ML-related quality requirements.

7.2 ML-Related Quality Requirements

QR2 till QR4 and QR6 have already been discussed in the previous section related to the ADDs for ML.

QR1 (see Table 4) requires compliance with the EU AI Act. Since this act is not yet implemented in our country, we did not know the full details of what this means for our architecture. However, we did know it would probably require the design to be as transparent and traceable as possible. From the perspective of Human Autonomy (QR11, QR12) we executed a "Fundamental Rights and Algorithm Impact Assessment (FRAIA)"[1], an instrument that can be used to assess high-risk algorithms according to the EU AI act. This led to many advises for the non-technical part of the project, to inform users on the algorithms and the workings of the system. From an architecture perspective we had to ensure the 'human-in-the-loop' [11]: the system detects stress but the health care professional decides what to do with this for the patient/client. So, the system should provide the health care professional with the necessary data/visualizations to base his/her decision or treatment on. This results in the need for a highly flexible (**Personal**) **Data Storage** and **Stress Visualisation** components in our architecture.

QR5 requires flexible user interfaces. For our architecture it means we created a separate **Stress Visualisation** component to be able to personalize what a specific user sees on the data screen.

QR7 till QR9 relate to privacy. To ensure full compliance with privacy regulations (GDPR) we executed a so-called "Data Protection Impact Assessment (DPIA)"[2]. A DPIA is an assessment of what the impact on privacy is and where these risk factors may occur when processing personal data. This resulted in a list of (security) measures to be implemented in our platform to prevent the

[1] https://www.government.nl/documents/reports/2022/03/31/impact-assessment-fundamental-rights-and-algorithms.

[2] https://business.gov.nl/regulation/data-protection-impact-assesment-dpia/.

biggest privacy risks. Wearable data is stored based on a unique wearable ID. User data is kept minimal (user ID, name, year of birth), and a separate table in the platform contains the link between user ID and wearable ID. The architecture has separate **Privacy Management** and **Wearable Management** components for this.

QR10 relates to the stress detection algorithm being fair to all user groups. Previous research on this has not given rise to concerns on discrimination, but we should keep evaluating the platform and its algorithms with end users on this aspect.

8 Step 5: System Validation

To validate the architecture we implemented an MVP (Minimal Viable Product) of the stress detection platform. With this MVP we could demonstrate the desired (MLOps) capabilities of the platform. We also performed scenario-based architecture analysis [10], to have a second way of validating the architecture.

Our goal with the project was to hand-over the platform to a third-party that can put the system in production, so we did not have access to a production environment to do a real-life validation. Future work remains to perform extensive testing on real-life data, including user experience testing and security testing. From an MLOps point of view we can only have a true validation (e.g., for the model monitoring) when working with real-life data and adding more and more users (wearables) to the platform.

9 Discussion and Lessons Learned

This section discusses our approach and the application to the stress detection platform with lessons learned for practitioners and applied researchers.

9.1 Lessons Learned

Legal Requirements. Because our ML platform falls under the EU Medical Device Regulation (MDR), it automatically falls under high-risk in the EU AI act. While waiting for standardization of what this means in practice, as said, we already executed a FRAIA and a DPIA (see Sect. 7) early in the project. Both assessments helped us to define any legal requirements on our solution and also forced us to describe our data and model design in an early stage. Involving legal expertise early in the project, working together with the software engineers, is crucial when dealing with personal data and models based on that data.

Security. One important aspect of the DPIA was to analyse possible risks for the data in the system. For this we could reuse the threat- and impact analysis executed by one of our DevOps engineers specializing in cyber security (based on the NIST guide for Risk Assessments [19] and the OWASP Top Ten[3]). This type of threat- and impact analysis is good to carry out early in the project such that necessary mitigation measures can be taken in the architecture.

Transdisciplinary. Next to legal experts the project also included allied health professionals (AHPs), all researching different aspects of the project. Through the AHPs there was a consortium of physiotherapy practices and nursing homes involved that recruited physiotherapists, nurses and their clients to test our prototypes (i.e., non-academic stakeholders). This transdisciplinary approach was crucial for defining an integrated MLOps architecture fulfilling all legal, social and technical requirements.

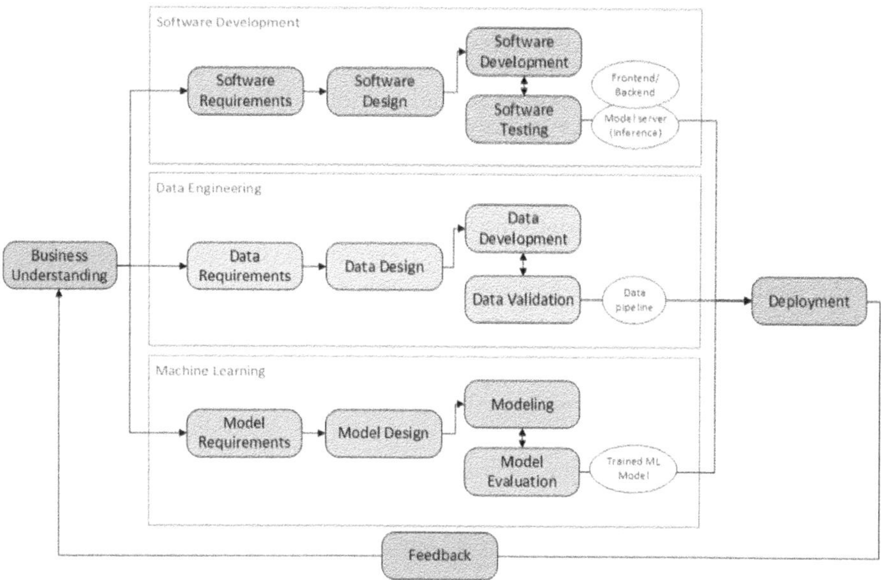

Fig. 2. MLOps is a parallel process, synchronizing software, data and model engineering

9.2 An Integrated MLOps Approach

The most important realization we had in this project is that we should not wait with designing the MLOps architecture (code, models and data) until after we had a successful stress detection model. That is why we aimed for an approach that allowed us to define all requirements, including the desired MLOps level [5], early in the project. Even though we did not have a working ML model yet, we

[3] https://owasp.org/www-project-top-ten/.

already designed the overall architecture of the stress detection platform and implemented an MVP. This allowed us to, e.g., try out tools like MLFlow, or ensure that the data pipeline(s) in production output the data format that is needed for model inference.

Our approach really benefited from this integrated design of ML models, data pipelines and software (backend and frontend). That this is not so obvious, has also been experienced by Grote and Bogner: "At first, we designed and implemented the overall system based on our initial idea of the best way, and only then started to develop the ML component. This turned out to be a huge mistake..." [7].

Compared to Grote and Bogner we focused more on the design phase of the project, realizing that there are requirements for both software, models and data. Our approach was not sequential, as depicted in other case studies, e.g., Grote and Bogner [7] and Amershi et al. [1]. We learned from our experience that to have a truly integrated MLOps approach (and architecture), you need to co-develop your software, models and data, starting from the same common ground, and working towards integration at the end. This is an iterative process, requiring a lot of synchronization and monitoring and evaluation. We have depicted this collaborative process in Fig. 2. Note that for reasons of simplicity we have only drawn one big iteration. In reality, many arrows would be going back and forth both horizontally (i.e., smaller iterations) and vertically (i.e., synchronizations).

9.3 Architectural Design for ML Systems

This section discusses our findings on the architectural design of ML systems from several perspectives, and points to areas for future research.

ADDs. The ADDs as described by Warnett and Zdun [21,22] give good guidance on how to implement Google's MLOps level 1 [5]. However, we propose to merge the ADDs into one list (see Table 2), because it is a big risk to postpone the deployment decisions until later in the project. Next to that we also propose to remove "using MLOps" as a separate ADD. We claim that all projects should use an MLOps approach to developing production-ready ML systems, even if they do everything manually (Google's MLOps level 0 [5]).

When comparing the MLOps requirements to the ADDs (see Table 2), two more things stand out. Firstly, there is not a separate ADD for model versioning (MLOps requirement ML1a). Model versioning is only indirectly addressed in ADD15 (see Table 2). We propose to add a separate ADD "How to version models?", analogue to ADD14 "How to version data?". In our project it was one of the more important decisions, since we designed the platform to have multiple models running in production, so version control should be well taken care of. Secondly, there is also not a separate ADD for monitoring (MLOps requirement ML1f). Monitoring is indirectly addressed by ADD6 ("How to trigger a machine learning pipeline"). We propose to add two separate ADDs for monitoring ML models and production data, where of course a choice could also be "no monitoring". See Table 5 for our updated list of ADDs.

Table 5. Updated Architectural Design Decisions ML from Table 2

ID	ID	ADD
ML1f	ADD17*	How to monitor data ingested into ML projects or applications?
ML1f	ADD18*	How to monitor the model?
ML1a	ADD19*	How to version the model?
(All)	~~ADD16~~	~~Should MLOps be applied and, if so, when?~~

Design Patterns. Already in 2020, Washizaki et al. [23] published about design patterns for ML systems. Most publications are about collecting patterns from existing publications or systems, not about integrating design patterns and their underlying choices in the approach for designing new ML architectures. In our approach, we used ADDs for guidance on the architecture design, but design patterns could have been a good extension or alternative for this. Future work remains to integrate the design and architecture patterns with the ADDs, based on the MLOps level one wants to achieve. This might even lead to new ADDs being added to the list.

MLOps Level 2. We currently have an MVP of our system. To take the next step, we would need a test environment for extensive testing and probably also need to include A/B testing of models/algorithms. For this it would be wise to move to MLOps level 2 [5], to profit from full CI/CD on machine learning pipelines, including testing. What stands out is that the current ADDs we have, are a perfect fit for MLOps level 1, but do not seem to cover MLOps level 2. Thus open research remains to extend the list of ADDs for MLOps level 2.

A good starting point for this could be a recent mapping study by Najafabadi et al. [2] on MLOps architectures. From 43 primary studies they identified 35 different MLOps architecture components and four+ architecture variants. In our opinion their variants are close to the Google MLOps levels. So, one could define variants that comply to Google MLOps level 2, comprising of the necessary components, and then described which ADDs are related to those components.

9.4 From MLOps to DataOps

Grote and Bogner [7] stated "Regarding our encountered challenges, most of them and also the ones perceived as most critical were related to acquiring suitable data and training an effective ML model for the use case at hand...". We had a similar experience in our project. Although we did find some online training data [20], we are still working on collecting a real-life labelled dataset with EDA signals and known stress moments to validate our models with. Furthermore, our platform needs to connect multiple data sources (wearables) that will stream data, so we needed to design for that as well. E.g., how to detect 5 min stress periods, when the data is coming in real-time?

Another big challenge we had in the project, was to get from raw signals (EDA values in microSiemens), to features that could be used for machine learning. We quickly realized that we should not only focus on the model pipeline, but also pay attention to the data pipelines, especially since we also plan to train models on multiple biosignals (not just EDA). There are many data processing steps involved, e.g., normalize data coming from different wearables or filter out artifacts. Currently, we are working on detailing the data-related components in our architecture. However, we did not find any publications on ADDs for data pipelines specifically, so this remains an area open for research.

We learned from our project that it is crucial to involve the data engineering stream from the beginning, and synchronize with the software engineering and the model building stream (see Fig. 2). This application of DevOps principles to data engineering is often called DataOps [15]. An open area for research is how to integrate DataOps and MLOps when dealing with ML systems. Our integrated approach to design an MLOps architecture is a good starting point for this. Future work remains to extend it with more specific DataOps requirements and DataOps-related ADDs.

10 Conclusion

This paper describes an integrated approach to develop an MLOps architecture. This approach is demonstrated on a real-life ML system to detect stress in signals from wearables. In this paper we make the following contributions:

- we present an approach to design an **integrated MLOps architecture**;
- we demonstrate this approach for a **real-life ML system**;
- we add three **ADDs** to the list from Warnett and Zdun [21,22];
- we emphasize the need for **DataOps** in production-ready ML systems;
- we present **lessons learned** for practitioners and applied researchers.

Future work remains to extend the MVP of our stress detection platform, validate with real-life data and improve the stress detection models and user interface. At the same time we work on extending our approach for an integrated MLOps architecture with new ADDs, and more guidance and tooling for practitioners wanting to implement it.

Acknowledgments. This research has been co-financed by "Regieorgaan SIA", part of the "Nederlandse Organisatie voor Wetenschappelijk Onderzoek (NWO)". The authors would like to thank Sebas Bakker for his invaluable contribution to this project.

Data Availability. Details can be requested from the first author.

References

1. Amershi, S., et al.: Software engineering for machine learning: A case study. In: 2019 IEEE/ACM 41st International Conference on Software Engineering: Software Engineering in Practice (ICSE-SEIP), pp. 291–300. IEEE (2019)

2. Amou ch1Najafabadi, F., Bogner, J., Gerostathopoulos, I., Lago, P.: An analysis of mlops architectures: a systematic mapping study. In: Software Architecture: 18th European Conference, ECSA 2024, Proceedings, pp. 69–85. Springer-Verlag (2024). https://doi.org/10.1007/978-3-031-70797-1_5
3. Bosch, J., Olsson, H.H., Crnkovic, I.: Engineering AI systems: A research agenda. Artifi. Intell. Paradigms Smart Cyber-Phys. Syst., 1–19 (2021)
4. Faubel, L., Schmid, K.: Mlops: a multiple case study in industry 4.0. In: 2024 IEEE 29th International Conference on Emerging Technologies and Factory Automation (ETFA), pp. 01–08. IEEE (2024)
5. Google: MLOps: Continuous delivery and automation pipelines in machine learning. online, https://cloud.google.com/architecture/mlops-continuous-delivery-and-automation-pipelines-in-machine-learning
6. Gorton, I., Khomh, F., Lenarduzzi, V., Menghi, C., Roman, D.: Software architectures for ai systems: State of practice and challenges. In: Software Architecture: Research Roadmaps from the Community, pp. 25–39. Springer (2023). https://doi.org/10.1007/978-3-031-36847-9_2
7. Grote, M., Bogner, J.: A case study on ai engineering practices: developing an autonomous stock trading system. In: IEEE/ACM 2nd International Conference on AI Engineering (CAIN 2023), pp. 145–157. IEEE (2023)
8. Heck, P., Schouten, G.: Defining quality requirements for a trustworthy AI wildflower monitoring platform. In: IEEE/ACM 2nd International Conference on AI Engineering (CAIN 2023), pp. 119–126. IEEE (2023)
9. Jansen, A., Bosch, J.: Software architecture as a set of architectural design decisions. In: 5th Working IEEE/IFIP Conference on Software Architecture (WICSA 2005), pp. 109–120. IEEE (2005)
10. Kazman, R., Abowd, G., Bass, L., Clements, P.: Scenario-based analysis of software architecture. IEEE Softw. **13**(6), 47–55 (1996)
11. Klimek, A., Mannheim, I., Schouten, G., Wouters, E.J., Peeters, M.W.: Wearables measuring electrodermal activity to assess perceived stress in care: a scoping review. Acta Neuropsychiatrica, 1–11 (2023)
12. Kreuzberger, D., Kühl, N., Hirschl, S.: Machine learning operations (mlops): Overview, definition, and architecture. IEEE Access (2023)
13. Lwakatare, L.E., Raj, A., Bosch, J., Olsson, H.H., Crnkovic, I.: A taxonomy of software engineering challenges for machine learning systems: an empirical investigation. In: Kruchten, P., Fraser, S., Coallier, F. (eds.) XP 2019. LNBIP, vol. 355, pp. 227–243. Springer, Cham (2019). https://doi.org/10.1007/978-3-030-19034-7_14
14. Muccini, H., Vaidhyanathan, K.: Software architecture for ml-based systems: What exists and what lies ahead. In: 2021 IEEE/ACM 1st Workshop on AI Engineering-Software Engineering for AI (WAIN), pp. 121–128. IEEE (2021)
15. Munappy, A.R., Mattos, D.I., Bosch, J., Olsson, H.H., Dakkak, A.: From ad-hoc data analytics to dataops. In: Proceedings of the International Conference on Software and System Processes, pp. 165–174 (2020)
16. Paleyes, A., Urma, R.G., Lawrence, N.D.: Challenges in deploying machine learning: a survey of case studies. ACM Comput. Surv. **55**(6), 1–29 (2022)
17. Raffin, T., Reichenstein, T., Werner, J., Kühl, A., Franke, J.: A reference architecture for the operationalization of machine learning models in manufacturing. Procedia CIRP **115**, 130–135 (2022)
18. Recupito, G., Pecorelli, F., Catolino, G., Moreschini, S., Di Nucci, D., Palomba, F., Tamburri, D.A.: A multivocal literature review of mlops tools and features. In: 2022 48th Euromicro Conference on Software Engineering and Advanced Applications (SEAA), pp. 84–91. IEEE (2022)

19. Ross, R.S.: Guide for conducting risk assessments (2012)
20. Schmidt, P., Reiss, A., Duerichen, R., Marberger, C., Van Laerhoven, K.: Introducing WESAD, a multimodal dataset for wearable stress and affect detection. In: Proceedings of the 20th ACM international conference on multimodal interaction, pp. 400–408 (2018)
21. Warnett, S.J., Zdun, U.: Architectural design decisions for machine learning deployment. In: 2022 IEEE 19th International Conference on Software Architecture (ICSA), pp. 90–100. IEEE (2022)
22. Warnett, S.J., Zdun, U.: Architectural design decisions for the machine learning workflow. Computer **55**(3), 40–51 (2022)
23. Washizaki, H., Uchida, H., Khomh, F., Guéhéneuc, Y.G.: Machine learning architecture and design patterns. IEEE Softw. **8**, 2020 (2020)
24. Zeller, M., Waschulzik, T., Schmid, R., Bahlmann, C.: Toward a safe mlops process for the continuous development and safety assurance of ml-based systems in the railway domain. AI and Ethics **4**(1), 123–130 (2024)

MLOps in Practice: Requirements and a Reference Architecture from Industry

Indika Kumara[1(✉)], Rowan Arts[1], Renato Cordeiro Ferreira[1], Dario Di Nucci[2], Rick Kazman[3], Damian Andrew Tamburri[4], and Willem-Jan van den Heuvel[1]

[1] Jheronimus Academy of Data Science, Tilburg University, 's-Hertogenbosch, The Netherlands
{i.p.k.weerasinghadewage,rowan.aarts,r.cordeiroferreira, w.j.a.m.v.d.heuvel}@uvt.nl

[2] University of Salerno, Salerno, Italy
ddinucci@unisa.it

[3] University of Hawaii, Honolulu, USA
kazman@hawaii.edu

[4] Eindhoven University of Technology, Eindhoven, The Netherlands
d.a.tamburri@tue.nl

Abstract. Machine Learning Operations (MLOps) streamline the lifecycle of machine learning (ML) models in production. In recent years, the topic has attracted the interest of practitioners, and consequently, a considerable number of tools and gray literature on architecting MLOps environments have emerged. However, this has created a new problem for organizations: selecting the most appropriate tools and design options to implement their MLOps environments. To alleviate this problem, this paper proposes a reference architecture and 32 requirements for MLOps by systematically reviewing 59 articles in the industrial gray literature. Furthermore, we used a survey and conducted semi-structured interviews with six MLOps experts to validate, refine, and extend our findings. This reference architecture, derived from the current state of practice, will enable organizations to make informed design and technology choices when embarking on their MLOps journey, while providing a technology-independent baseline for further MLOps research.

Keywords: MLOps · Machine Learning Operations · Requirements · Reference Architecture · Gray Literature · Interviews

1 Introduction

Organizations are increasingly adopting machine learning (ML) in their businesses to extract value from their raw business data. However, achieving productive ML solutions is tough, due to the challenges of maturing an ML model—developed by data scientists who are typically not skilled software engineers—into production and keeping it operating at scale [18]. For example, according

V. Andrikopoulos et al. (Eds.): ECSA 2025, LNCS 15929, pp. 20–37, 2026.
https://doi.org/10.1007/978-3-032-02138-0_2

to Algorithmia [1], only 22% of the organizations that use ML have successfully deployed a model into production. *MLOps* has emerged as a discipline to help bridge the gap between the development of ML models and their (continuous, resilient, scalable) operations [15,22]. MLOps aims to provide a set of practices and tools to automate and integrate processes between model development and model operations, thus accelerating the delivery of models [2,22].

MLOps has garnered the attention of commercial technology providers and the open-source community, and the MLOps landscape is rapidly expanding with many tools and platforms [11,19,22]. With numerous diverse technology options available, organizations must select the most suitable options and build or assemble an MLOps environment that best serves their needs. To help address this problem, we (a) distilled the typical minimum requirements—a set of 32 degrees of freedom to be addressed in MLOps-type pipelines—and (b) synthesized a reference architecture. An organization can use this reference architecture as a template for designing its MLOps systems. MLOps should be agnostic of language, tool/platform, and infrastructure [22]; a reference architecture and a standard set of requirements could facilitate this objective.

To identify the two key contributions above, we employed a systematic review of the gray literature on MLOps, confirming our results and analyses with semi-structured interviews with six MLOps practitioners.

We considered the gray literature, as we are interested in learning about practitioner perspectives, and there is limited academic literature on designing MLOps solutions that draws from industrial experience [11,24]. In addition, we observe that practitioners (*e.g.*, tool developers and data scientists) are increasingly publishing their MLOps experiences. Moreover, the requirements identified from industrial sources can help researchers identify MLOps research issues relevant to practitioners, thereby making a significant industrial impact.

The paper is organized as follows. Section 2 presents the research methodology and Sect. 3 discusses our findings. Section 4 reviews the related studies and Sect. 5 discusses the threats to validity. Section 6 concludes the paper.

2 Methodology

Our methodology includes a systematic gray literature review (SGLR) on MLOps and an expert-based validation of its results.

SGLR. We adopted standard guidelines for systematically reviewing gray and multi-vocal literature [5,9,14,17]. As we aim to identify requirements and architectures for MLOps, we used the following search query: *(machine learning operations OR mlops) AND (architecture(s) OR requirement(s) OR feature(s) OR component(s))*.

We ran the query in the Google search engine in incognito mode, scanning each resulting page to saturation (i.e., we stopped our search when no new relevant articles emerged from the search results [5,17]). Specifically, for relevance, we considered textual sources such as articles, blogs, white papers, and slides that explicitly outline or discuss MLOps pipelines in practice. Following such a relevance clause, we identified 257 sources and applied inclusion/exclusion and quality assessment criteria to select 58 sources. For inclusion criteria, we considered the focus of the study, articles in English, and accessibility of the full text [9]. The quality assessment of the sources used criteria such as the publisher's reputation and the author's expertise, which we also applied in existing systematic gray literature studies [5,17]. The first two authors of this article independently selected and evaluated the quality of the sources. We measured Cohen's kappa coefficient [10] to determine the inter-rater reliability, which was 0.74, indicating substantial agreement. We resolved all discrepancies through discussion and chose 58 articles for further analysis.

To extract data from selected sources, we used structural and descriptive coding to establish codes, groups, and categories [25]. The codes were derived from our research objectives. The first author coded all the sources, and the second author reviewed those codes. We resolved all the discrepancies via discussion. We also analyzed the architectural designs in the sources to identify components in MLOps environments. The results of our gray literature review included 30 requirements and a reference architecture for MLOps environments.

To focus our work on preparing a reference architecture for practical use, we provide design decisions corresponding to the logical component(s) responsible for each identified requirement. At the same time, there may be alternative implementation options for each requirement, and each such architecture option may need multiple components to be subjected to more classical architecture trade-off analysis [13]. For example, an implementation of model monitoring may require multiple components to gather various metrics, utilize the collected data to detect different types of model drifts (degradation of model performance over time), visualize them, and diagnose the root causes of the drifts. There are many studies on these individual concerns (including surveys), for example, drift detection and adaptation [3]. The analysis of all academic and gray literature related to each requirement is beyond the scope of this study.

Expert-Based Refinement and Validation. We then conducted a study with MLOps practitioners to validate our findings from the gray literature review. We applied *purpose sampling* [8] to select participants with relevant experience and varied points of view on MLOps. The candidates had at least five years of experience designing ML-enabled systems. To identify potential candidates, we searched for industry practitioners within the authors' professional network on LinkedIn. We contacted nine candidates, and six agreed to participate in the study. Table 1 provides information about the participants.

We followed a two-step research protocol. First, we sent a questionnaire to the participants. For each requirement, we asked how often participants think about it while developing and producing ML-enabled systems. The answers were on a Likert scale with five values: "Never", "Rarely", "Sometimes", "Often", and "Always". Next, we conducted semi-structured interviews with the same participants to explore their choices for each requirement. We also asked them to suggest missing requirements. The reference architecture was also presented to get their opinions. We conducted all interviews virtually and took notes during the interviews, summarizing key takeaways. We used the interview protocol refinement framework [6] to develop our interview protocol. On average, each participant took 7.5 min to respond to the questionnaire and then participated in a 45 min interview.

Table 2 summarizes the answers to the survey question. For 28 out of 32 requirements, three or more participants stated that they consider those requirements "Always" or "Often" in their MLOps projects. The subsequent interviews revealed that all participants consider all requirements relevant, but do not necessarily think about some requirements because they are embedded into the tools/platforms used. In general, the interview participants agreed with our findings from the literature, suggesting minimal refinements. In particular, they proposed splitting an existing requirement into two (R26 and R27) and introducing a new requirement (R30). No changes were suggested for the reference architecture and pipelines. However, they provided valuable information about how to support some requirements in their MLOps environments.

Table 1. Interviewed Experts. YE - Years of Experience

Expert ID	Industry	Specialty	Country	YE	
P1	e-Commerce	DS	BR	5	**DS**: Data Scientist
P2	FinTech	DS, DE, ME, DPM	NL	6	**DE**: Data Engineer
P3	Marketing	DS, DE, ME	BR	5	**ME**: ML Engineer
P4	Software	ME	NL	8	**DPM**: Data Product Manager
P5	Software	ME, DPM	US	20	
P6	e-Commerce	DS, DE, ME, DPM	BR	7	

Table 2. Interviewed Experts – Answers to Questionnaire

	1	2	3	4	5	6	7	8	9	10	11	12	13	14	15	16	17	18	19	20	21	22	23	24	25	26	27	28	29	30
P1	5	4	5	4	5	4	5	1	1	4	4	5	5	5	4	4	4	5	4	5	4	4	4	4	1	1	4	5	4	4
P2	2	1	4	1	5	5	5	2	5	1	2	4	2	5	5	5	5	5	4	4	1	5	1	1	1	4	1	5	5	5
P3	5	2	5	5	5	1	4	2	5	1	5	5	1	5	5	1	4	5	2	1	5	5	5	5	4	1	5	5	5	5
P4	4	5	4	1	5	5	5	5	5	1	1	4	4	1	4	1	4	1	1	2	2	1	5	5	5	1	5	5	1	5
P5	1	5	5	5	5	4	5	2	4	5	5	5	2	5	2	5	5	5	1	4	5	5	5	5	5	5	5	2	5	5
P6	4	1	5	1	5	5	5	1	5	1	2	1	1	5	4	4	4	4	4	4	4	4	1	1	1	5	4	4	5	1

1 Never   2 Rarely   3 Sometimes   4 Often   5 Always

The replication package[1] of this study includes the list of sources, qualitative analysis of sources, extracts from sources, the survey questionnaire and results, interview notes, and ethical approval for conducting interviews.

3 Reference Architecture and Requirements

MLOps processes occur on a compute stack with the necessary development and operations capabilities. We identified the requirements (see Table 3) and developed a reference architecture (see Fig. 1) for such an MLOps environment. They reflect the consolidated findings of both the gray literature and expert feedback. The reference architecture consists of three horizontal layers and two vertical cross-cutting modules. The horizontal layers present the key capabilities and responsibilities of infrastructures, platforms, and applications (*i.e.*, MLOps pipelines). The vertical modules, *i.e.*, automation and governance, capture the key functionalities relevant to each horizontal layer. This section discusses each layer and requirement based on the information extracted and consolidated from the gray literature and interviews. Table 3 provides the references to the gray literature used for each requirement. As in comparable studies using gray literature [17,23,24], we do not refer to each source in the text.

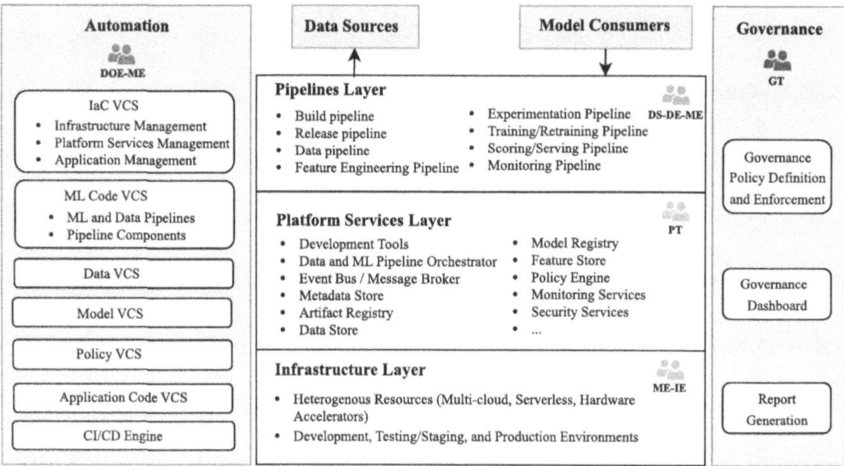

Fig. 1. Layered Reference Architecture for MLOps. DS: Data Scientist, ME: ML Engineer, DE: Data Engineer, DOE: DevOps Engineer, PT: Platform Team, DE: Data Engineer, GT: Governance Team, VCS: Version Control System.

[1] https://doi.org/10.6084/m9.figshare.28661342.v1.

Table 3. Requirements for an MLOps Environment

Category	Requirements		Sources
Infrastructure	R1	Portability, reproducibility, and versionability	S2, S4, S12, S15, S18, S35
	R2	Auto-scaling and use of GPU and hardware accelerators	S3, S5, S19, S28, S35, S37, S38, S44, S52, S53
	R3	Cater for different environments (e.g., test and production)	S3, S2, S6, S17, S27
	R4	Manage the infrastructure using IaC (Infrastructure as Code)	S7, S12, S22, S54
Pipeline Development, and Execution	R5	Create, publish, discover, use, and customize pipelines	S3, S5, S17, S26, S29, S28, S32, S33, S34, S35, S42, S44, S47, S49, S53, S56, S58
	R6	Modular and reusable pipelines and components	S3, S14, S17, S19, S32, S41, S49, S58
	R7	Execution of pipelines via orchestration or choreography	S2, S7, S10, S26, S52, S53, S58
Experimentation, Training, and Testing	R8	Export experimental code from notebooks into pipelines	S4, S17, S22, S49
	R9	Record and query experiments and training runs	S7, S9, S16, S22, S23, S25, S30, S33, S38, S53, S58
	R10	Apply training scaling strategies such as model check-pointing, distributed training, use of hardware accelerators, and training with data set slices	S2, S3, S4, S8, S9, S10, S23, S24, S36, S38, S53
	R11	Use automated machine learning tools	S7, S10, S11, S16, S29, S58
	R12	Validation tests for all ML assets (e.g., model, code, and data)	S3, S4, S5, S9, S24, S25, S33, S39, S45, S47, S58
	R13	Prioritization and scheduling of validation tests and training jobs	S3, S4, S33
Model Deployment and Serving	R14	Ensure the compatibility of the model with the target infrastructure	S17, S22, S44, S58
	R15	Use open model formats for portable and flexible deployments	S7, S9, S10, S16, S24, S35, S38, S40, S57
	R16	Package models for ease of deployment, integration, and testing	S3, S17, S28, S48, S49
	R17	Support different patterns of deploying, releasing, and serving models	S1, S2, S7, S9, S17, S23, S24, S26, S28, S31, S33, S34, S35, S51, S58
Monitoring and Feedback Loops	R18	Monitoring of and alerting for various issues in models, data, pipelines, and infrastructure	S1, S2, S3, S4, S7, S10, S11, S13, S15, S16, S17, S19, S20, S23, S25, S26, S28, S29, S31, S32, S33, S34, S35, S43, S44, S48, S52, S54, S57, S58
	R19	Triggering of corrective actions for alerts	S1, S2, S16, S17, S25, S35
	R20	Creating custom actionable dashboards for models	S2, S3, S10, S34, S40, S54
	R21	Support different pipeline triggering models	S2, S3, S4, S5, S7, S9, S17, S19, S20
ML Asset Life Cycle Management and Governance	R22	ML asset storage and marketplace	S1, S2, S3, S9, S16, S17, S18, S19, S21, S23, S26, S35, S50, S51, S53, S56, S58
	R23	Version control and lineage tracking for ML assets	S2, S4, S5, S7, S9, S20, S22, S23, S26, S25, S31, S33, S34, S35, S41, S45, S57, S58
	R24	ML asset metadata management	S9, S14, S16, S17, S24, S35, S49, S58
	R25	Access control, governance, and regulatory compliance for ML assets	S2, S5, S7, S10, S11, S12, S24, S28, S54, S56, S58
	R26	Ensure interpretability of models	S2, S7, S19, S22, S24, S34, S41, S43, S54, S58
	R27	Ensure adversarial robustness of models	S10, S24, S47, S48, S54

continued

Table 3. continued

Category		Requirements	Sources
General Platform Services	R28	Support for general data platform services such as data catalog, data storage, data discovery, data exploration, data augmentation/labeling, and data fusion	S7, S10, S11, S19, S23, S24, S31, S33, S36, S38, S50, S53, S58
	R29	Support for general ML platform services such as feature engineering, model exploration, model selection, hyper-parameter tuning, and model validation	S2, S4, S6, S9, S26, S33, S58, etc. (most articles)
Standardization and Automation	R30	Establishing standards and practices for MLOps processes	S9, S24, S28
	R31	Treat ML assets as first-class citizens in DevOps processes	S1, S2, S3, S4, S5, S7, S8, S9, S22, S25, S27, S29, S31, S32, S35, S45, S55, S57
	R32	Integrate unit, integration, and other tests of ML assets to CI/CD pipelines	S8, S9, S24, S25, S26, S33, S53, S58

3.1 Infrastructure Layer

This layer provides computing resources to host and execute platform services, MLOps pipelines, governance applications, and CI/CD automation services. The infrastructure needs to be flexible and portable to prevent vendor lock-in and enable rapid pipeline (re)deployment (**R1**). A reproducible and versionable infrastructure supports auditing and debugging infrastructure changes and allows switching between different versions of platform services, pipelines, and ML models. However, preventing vendor lock-in can be problematic as most organizations select and adopt a specific cloud provider or data/ML platform and prioritize time-to-market over flexibility and portability (participant **P5**). On the other hand, adopting open-source tools can help avoid lock-in (**P2**).

The infrastructure layer should also support multicloud, auto-scalability, and hardware accelerators (**R2**). Multi-cloud support allows different teams in an organization to use the best possible cloud and tools to build and deploy their models. Auto-scaling enables scaling up and down training pipelines and models (serving components) automatically to cope with fluctuating data and serving requests. Hardware accelerators may be necessary to speed up pipeline execution during experimentation and (re)training, and to improve real-time serving latency. However, a few ML projects (e.g., computer vision) may need GPUs (participants **P2, P6**), while most training jobs do not need auto-scaling since their workload is stable and their resource usage is predictable (**P3**).

An MLOps environment can include separate development, staging, and production environments (**R3**). The configurations of these environments (*e.g.*, tools and hardware resources) may exhibit variations. Infrastructure as code (IaC) [17] can be used to automate the provisioning and management of such environments while preserving their reproducibility and auditability (**R4**). Platform teams generally develop IaC scripts, and data scientists use them (participant **P2**). However, an ML platform tool used by an organization may support the automatic and transparent provisioning of resources to execute pipelines and hosting models, avoiding the need to use IaC scripts (participants **P4, P6**).

3.2 Platform Services Layer

This layer facilitates applying platform thinking [7,23] to build a *self-serve* MLOps platform to empower different actors involved in creating, deploying, and maintaining ML models. It supports managing the entire lifecycle of models and related assets, such as data and ML code. This section presents the platform capabilities we synthesized from the gray literature and expert interviews.

Pipeline Development and Execution. The pipelines implement ML processes such as data preprocessing, feature engineering, (re)training, and prediction. A pipeline consists of steps that must be executed in a specific order. The platform should empower developers to publish, share, and reuse pipelines to enable fast development and automated (re)deployment of pipelines (**R5**). In addition, pipeline steps must be implemented as modular containerized components that can be easily reused and composed (**R6**). The pipeline execution can adopt a choreography model or an orchestration model (**R7**). The former needs an event bus to facilitate the event/message-driven coordination of pipeline steps. The latter defines the pipeline as a workflow model that a workflow engine can execute centrally. The interview participants stated that all these requirements are supported by the ML platforms they use. Although they practice the modular development of pipelines to reduce complexity and improve maintenance, reusability is not a primary goal for them.

Experimentation, Training, and Testing. Experimentation with a pipeline requires its deployment, execution, and debugging, followed by the analysis and interpretation of the assets produced (*e.g.*, models and features). Notebooks are commonly used for experiments. However, they are not recommended in production due to the difficulties of versioning, instrumentation, and automated execution. All interview participants strongly agree with this recommendation. Hence, the platform should provide services to export executable ML pipelines from notebooks used in the development environment, for example, to convert a Python-based pipeline to a workflow definition file that can be executed by an ML workflow engine (**R8**). Moreover, the platform needs to offer a service to record and query the metadata of each ML experiment to enable reproducing and troubleshooting them (**R9**). Typical metadata includes, but is not limited to, code and data versions, configuration files, output assets, and performance metrics. A production ML pipeline may reuse only parts of different experiments, e.g., by copying the source code from experiment notebooks (**P5**).

Platform services for training may improve the performance and reliability of training jobs through strategies such as model check-pointing, distributed model training, exploitation of specific heterogeneous hardware (*e.g.*, GPU and TPU accelerators), AutoML (Automated Machine Learning), prioritizing training activities, and training on a slice of the data set (**R10 and R11**). Check-pointing enables incremental model training using more iterations and recovery from failures during the training. Distributed training needs specific middleware capable of running a training job elastically on multiple compute nodes.

A scheduler service can queue and prioritize training jobs, enabling policing training activities, for example, capping the data used by training or preventing long-running jobs from blocking critical tasks such as deploying security or bug fixes. Finally, AutoML can simplify and accelerate the build of ML models and reduce the barriers for domain experts to develop models from their data.

Although these training optimization strategies are desirable, their inclusion in a platform should consider the potential uses of ML in the organization (participants **P3, P6**). For example, in most use cases, only deep learning pipelines may need GPUs (participant **P3**). Moreover, due to the infrequency of training jobs, using a compute node with higher resources is sufficient (participant **P4**).

All ML assets must be tested appropriately; the key testable assets are data, code, and models (**R12**). Data tests can verify that input data and features do not exhibit data quality issues such as malformed data, anomalies, and mismatches with the expected schemas and distributions. Such tests can prevent training-serving skew, namely differences in model performance during training and serving, which can be caused by differences between training data and serving data. Similarly to the testing of conventional software applications, source code tests can assess the quality of the ML code, *e.g.*, violation of best practices, the existence of known defects, and the efficiency of training tasks resources. Tests can verify model properties, e.g., fairness and consistency.

As model training and data processing can be expensive and time-consuming, the execution of tests needs to be prioritized and scheduled appropriately, for example, running a subset of tests or long-running testing during off-hours and training on small datasets (**R13**). Including these capabilities in the platform helps data scientists be effective in their tasks, i.e., model experimentation and development (participants **P2, P5**).

Deployment and Serving. When deploying a model to the target serving environment, it is necessary to ensure its compatibility with the infrastructure regarding compute resources (e.g., hardware accelerators and edge devices), software dependencies, and model formats (**R14**). As ML libraries may use specific formats for their models, a model translation service may be necessary to convert models into an open model format (e.g., Open Neural Network Exchange) for portable and flexible deployments (**R15**). However, many ML libraries support widely used model formats such as Joblib or Pickle (**P3**). Moreover, some ML use cases may not benefit from open model formats (**P5**).

A platform can also offer an image-building service to package models, scoring scripts, and dependencies into container images (**R16**). In this way, the operational team can quickly deploy a model in staging and production environments, test it, and integrate it with the applications that need to consume the predictions from the model. There exist model deployment engines that can simplify deployments by automating this end-to-end process (**P4**).

The platform must support different strategies for deploying and serving models (**R17**). Common deployment approaches include shadow, canary, and black/green. A shadow deployment does not immediately release the new model to users; instead, it uses production traffic to test the model. A canary deployment releases the new model incrementally to users. In contrast, a black/green deployment immediately deploys and releases the new model to users.

Common patterns from serving predictions from a model include *model-as-service*, *precompute*, and *model-as-dependency*. Model-as-service exposes the model as a web service/API or a messaging endpoint. Precompute pattern computes predictions for a batch of input data and stores them to serve clients later. In the model-as-dependency pattern, the application embeds the model as a binary and loads it at runtime to make predictions. The application can also download the model at runtime from a model registry. Serving methods can also be classified into offline and online serving. Each method may require specific platform services, such as data processing and event streaming engines, to run batch and stream data processing pipelines and ingest data streams.

Monitoring and Feedback Loops. The platform layer should monitor various quality issues in the models and data at runtime, generating alerts and triggering corrective actions (**R18**). Two typical quality issues are data drift and concept drift, which refer to changes to the statistical properties of the model input and the target variable, respectively. Both can contribute to the degradation of the model performance over time, *i.e.*, *model drift* [3]. The metrics related to the stability of the model need to be continuously monitored to detect drifts. The model needs to be re-trained regularly in response to drift alerts to address the model drift. Pipelines should also be monitored, as their failures can prevent updating models. The logs of a pipeline can be collected and analyzed to gauge its health. Common metrics such as resource usage, execution time, and throughput should also be collected for pipelines and inference services. They can be used to trigger auto-scaling services to scale pipelines and models up and down.

Platform services should support the generation of alerts based on the data collected from the MLOps environment and the implementation of corrective actions to alleviate these issues and their impacts (**R19**). For example, the developer should be able to develop and run a monitoring pipeline that can process logs and metrics from the MLOps environment, generate alerts, and define the rules to trigger actions on alerts. In addition, a platform service can support the creation of interactive dashboards that allow the monitoring of models, pipelines, and infrastructure and the troubleshooting of suspicious or poorly performing models and failed ML/data pipelines (**R20**). Model performance reports can also serve the same purpose.

The platform also needs to support common approaches to trigger training pipelines (**R21**): *metrics-driven*, *schedule-driven*, *event-driven*, and *ad-hoc manual*. In the metrics-driven approach, data and model performance metrics are measured and used to determine pipeline (re)execution. The schedule-driven strategy triggers the pipelines at a specified time or regularly. In the event-driven model, events, such as changes to the model's source code and the availability of a new training data set, trigger pipelines. A human operator can also manually execute a pipeline.

The interview participants generally considered all the requirements related to the monitoring and feedback loops relevant. Participant **P4** stated that they use ML platforms that support these requirements. Monitoring models/data and triggering corrective actions may not have real-time constraints in practice, as diagnosing an issue and finding a resolution often require human intervention (**P3**). Implementing self-healing may also be problematic, as interventions are usually complex and ad-hoc (**P5**). Alerts are generally sufficient, allowing developers to roll back a faulty model to a previous version and fix it later (**P3**).

Lifecycle Management and Governance Services. ML assets and metadata must be versioned, stored, and managed to support their reproduction, discovery, auditing, and reuse (**R22-24**). Different assets may need specific storage components, *e.g.*, a model registry for models, a feature store for features, a pipeline store for data/ML pipelines, and a source code repository for ML and IaC scripts. Artifact metadata (*e.g.*, schemas, hyperparameters, and model metrics) can also be placed in the data store or in a separate metadata store.

The platform should provide services to enforce policies that govern the life cycle of ML assets, for example, identity and access management services to implement access control policies and privacy preservation mechanisms (*e.g.*, data anonymization and federated learning) to enforce data privacy compliance (**R25**). Moreover, practitioners may need tools to write, test, and observe policies that enforce constraints on metrics such as model accuracy, fairness, and data privacy. Platform services can empower pipeline developers to use the *policy-as-code* approach for automating policy enforcement. For example, access control policies for controlling data and model access can be embedded into the stages of data and ML pipelines using a policy authoring service. Those policies can then be tested when pipelines are developed using a policy testing service and observed and enforced during their execution using a policy engine service and model/data monitoring services.

Models should be resilient to model attacks such as membership inference attacks, adversarial attacks, and model inversion attacks (**R26**). Moreover, model decisions must be explainable and interpretable (**R27**). Hence, practitioners need platform services to test models for their vulnerability to potential attacks and to generate and visualize explanations for model behaviors.

The interview participants generally agree with the above requirements. Participant **P1** stated that the compliance requirements are primarily related to raw data, which may contain sensitive data (compared to model output). Moreover, all participants mentioned that they often consider the interpretability of a model but rarely test its robustness to model attacks.

General Platform Services. Developers use data pipelines to turn raw historical and online data from multiple sources into features for their ML models. A data pipeline typically considers tasks such as data ingestion, storage, discovery, standardization, labeling, cleaning, and transformation (**R28**). The platform should offer services to simplify the implementation of these tasks, *e.g.*, a messaging service for data ingestion and a data catalog service for data inventory and discovery. Similarly, an ML pipeline involves tasks such as feature engineering, model exploration, model selection, hyperparameter tuning, and model validation. Hence, the platform should offer tools and libraries/APIs to perform these tasks (**R29**). In addition, the platform should also provide tools for building, testing, orchestrating, monitoring, and managing data/ML pipelines.

3.3 Pipelines Layer

This layer comprises pipelines that can be built, tested, and executed using platform services and CI/CD automation tools. From the gray literature, we identified eight major pipeline types in an MLOps environment: build, release (and deployment), data, feature engineering, experimentation, training, scoring/serving, and monitoring. Build and release pipelines are CI/CD pipelines. The first pipeline builds the code, performs tests to verify code quality, and publishes the produced assets. The second pipeline operationalizes and promotes the assets in different environments (*e.g.*, staging and production) to enable their consumption and testing. When building ML and data pipelines, the source codes are pipeline models (*e.g.*, workflow configurations) and pipeline components (*e.g.*, Python programs). The pipeline models are generally published on the platform services of pipeline coordinators/engines as endpoints to enable their execution via API calls and other triggers. In addition, the pipeline components are containerized and stored in a container image registry. The same processes apply to platform services and scoring/prediction services.

Figure 2 shows the pipelines and an essential subset of their interconnections. Developers create and test pipelines and platform services, potentially reusing existing relevant implementations. Deploying pipelines and platform services may require provisioning and configuring compute stacks, which can be automated using Infrastructure as Code (IaC). All source codes should be version-controlled. Changes in the code can trigger build pipelines, which can result in publishing ML/data pipelines and container images. Consider the first-time execution of the training process. A data pipeline extracts raw data sets from multiple sources, cleans, standardizes, and stores them in a data store. A feature engineering pipeline creates, selects, and stores features in a feature store. Finally, the training pipeline builds and tunes a model and publishes it to the model registry, which triggers the model release pipeline, which builds and deploys serving pipelines/services. A deployed model may serve client requests using batch, event-driven, or real-time serving methods. The logs from the execution of each step of the training and serving processes are continuously collected. Monitoring pipelines can analyze such logs and generate alerts indicating quality issues in models, data, pipelines, and infrastructure. Alerts can trigger the re-execution of the training process and, consequently, the deployment of a new model.

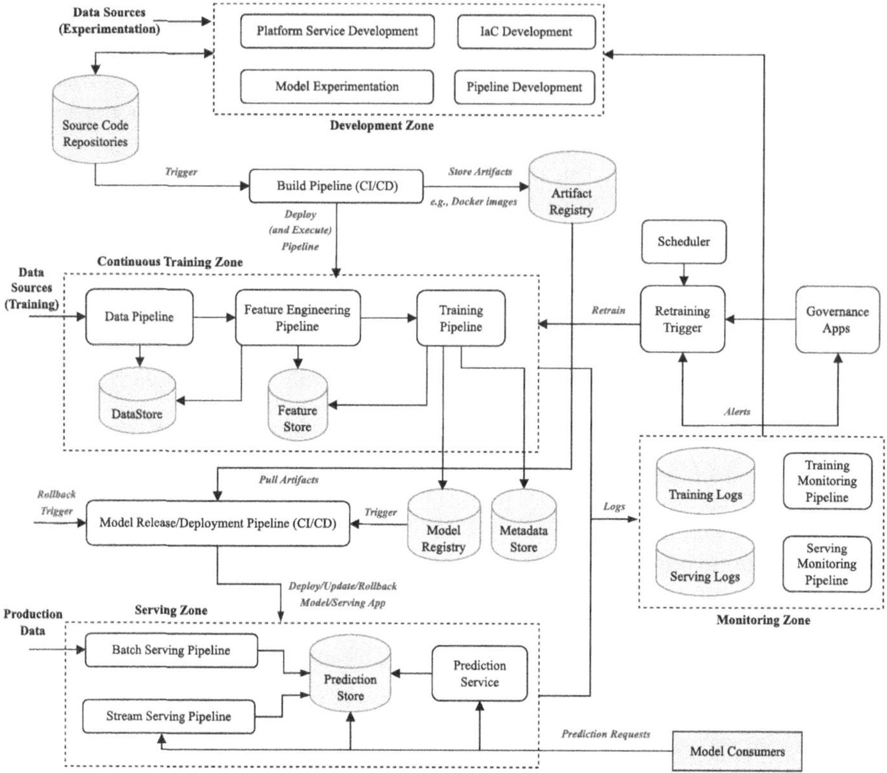

Fig. 2. MLOps Pipelines and their Relationships.

3.4 Governance and Automation Cross-Cutting Modules

Governance needs the ability to consistently specify, configure, observe, and enforce policies for all ML assets and MLOps processes (*e.g.*, model approval and data collection/sharing). This module comprises components such as policy definition and enforcement, model/data governance dashboards, and report generation (e.g., model performance and data quality reports). These can be built using the services provided by the platform layer, e.g., a model registry for storing models and a workflow engine for running model approval processes.

Governance can also establish standards and practices for MLOps processes (**R30**). They can improve the quality and interoperability of ML assets and the usability of platform services. For example, best practices for collecting data can improve data quality and compliance, and standards for storing models and data can improve their interoperability and reusability. These standards and practices may emerge when MLOp processes in organizations become mature (**P2**).

Automation applies CI/CD techniques and processes to automate the provisioning and configuration of infrastructure resources in target environments and the building, testing, deploying, and configuring of components such as platform services, pipelines, serving apps, and governance apps (**R31-32**). The relevant assets are stored in version control repositories, and their CI-CD pipelines can be triggered in various ways, *e.g.*, manual, event-driven, or scheduled.

3.5 Roles and Responsibilities

From the gray literature, we identified three key roles for MLOps team members: *data engineer*, *data scientist*, and *ML engineer*. Data engineers build, test, deploy, execute, and manage data pipelines that extract raw data from various sources, validate, clean, and standardize it, and make the curated data accessible to data scientists in a secure and timely manner. Data scientists analyze a business problem that needs a data science solution and then build ML models that address the business problem. They typically work in an experimentation environment. ML engineers are responsible for operationalizing models developed by data scientists.

An MLOps team must interact with various individuals and groups, including business analysts, DevOps engineers, application developers, and infrastructure engineers. Our proposed reference architecture introduces two new teams: the platform team and the governance team. The former builds, tests, deploys, and manages platform services. The latter defines and enforces governance policies by utilizing the services provided by the platform.

The interview participants also agreed with these roles. Participant **P5** advocated the separation of concerns in the platform services based on these roles and responsibilities. Participants **P2** and **P5** stated that their workplaces have platform teams, and platform users such as data scientists and ML engineers often provide the requirements for platform services.

4 Related Work

Kolltveit and Li [15] reviewed 25 academic articles on MLOps, focusing on tooling and infrastructure aspects. John et al. [12] synthesized a maturity model for the adoption of MLOps, using the findings of the gray and academic literature. They also proposed an MLOps framework consisting of three main pipelines (*i.e.*, data, modeling, and release) and a governance layer. Warnett and Zdun [24] systematically reviewed 35 articles in the gray literature to identify design decisions for model deployment, where MLOps is a specific design option.

Symeonidis et al. [20] surveyed the tools that support various tasks in MLOps, such as model deployment and experiment tracking. They also identified several MLOps challenges, including pipeline development, retraining, and monitoring. Idowu et al. [11] compared 17 tools to manage ML assets such as data, models, pipelines, and experiments. Recupito et al. [19] studied 13 MLOps tools selected from a multivocal literature review, comparing them over a catalog of 32 features found among them. Berberi et al. [4] compared 16 open-source MLOps platforms with 10 features, compiling a flow chart to choose these tools based on their capabilities. They focused on comparing MLOps platforms rather than providing a technology-agnostic reference architecture for ML-enabled systems.

Testi et al. [21] established a taxonomy to classify MLOps projects, based on the academic literature available between 2015 and 2022. They proposed three categories: *ML-based software systems*, *ML use case applications*, and *ML automation frameworks*. The authors provided a general description of nine components found in MLOps pipelines. The pipelines presented in Fig. 2 include similar components with more granularity, including their relationship, pipeline triggers, and data flow.

Kreuzberger et al. [16] reviewed 27 academic articles and conducted semi-structured interviews with eight specialists. They proposed an end-to-end architecture for MLOps, which depicts multiple workflows to indicate the order in which tasks should be executed. Their workflows are similar to the pipelines we identified from the gray literature (see Fig. 2).

Najafabadi et al. [2] mapped 43 academic studies in the literature. They described 35 unique architectural components. Since some components are optional, each combination describes a different architecture variant. Furthermore, the authors used these components to catalog the features of 18 tools and frameworks mentioned in the literature. Our proposed reference architecture focuses on structuring and grouping logical components that implement the 32 MLOps requirements identified from the gray literature. Additionally, our pipeline architecture organizes the eight workflows within an MLOps environment, all of which are derived from the gray literature.

Overall, unlike the work above, our objective was to identify the requirements for and components of a reference architecture for a complete MLOps stack (from infrastructure to applications) by systematically reviewing the gray literature. Additionally, we conducted a qualitative study involving six MLOps practitioners to validate and refine our findings, thereby strengthening their industrial relevance.

5 Threats to Validity

The internal validity [25] in our study concerns the validity of the methods used to collect and interpret data from the gray literature and practitioners. To reduce bias in selecting and interpreting articles, as mentioned in Sect. 2, we applied the guidelines used in systematic literature reviews, particularly inclusion and exclusion criteria, quality assessment criteria, and inter-rater reliability assessment using Cohen's Kappa coefficient. Another threat to internal validity is bias in the selection of participants. Although we used our professional networks to contact candidates, we opted for those with more than 5 years of ML production experience to limit the selection bias.

Threats to external validity [25] exist in terms of the generalizability of the results of this study. The interview participants may not reflect the entire population of MLOps practitioners. The limited number of participants may also threaten external validity. As mentioned above, our participants had extensive

MLOps experience and represented different types of organizations from three different countries and continents. Although the sample size of six practitioners is insufficient for a deeper quantitative analysis, we believe that it is sufficient to qualitatively assess and refine the results of the gray literature study, which is the key intention of this work.

6 Conclusion

Organizations are adopting MLOps to accelerate the deployment and delivery of high-quality ML models and pipelines to production. Not surprisingly, there has been a rapid proliferation of gray literature on MLOps driven by the needs of practice. This paper investigated the requirements and architectures for MLOps proposed in the gray literature. By systematically analyzing 58 sources, we distilled a catalog of 30 requirements and proposed a reference architecture for MLOps environments. A qualitative study involving six MLOps experts validated and refined these findings, resulting in 32 enhanced requirements. The requirements and reference architecture can provide a research framework for MLOps and guide identifying key research challenges in bringing ML models into widespread use. They can also help practitioners build or assemble an MLOps environment, select and adapt an existing one, and choose or develop tools to support various tasks within an MLOps environment.

In future research, we aim to conduct a similar study on the operationalization of large language models (i.e., LLMOps). We also plan to study the effectiveness of LLMs in extracting requirements and architectural components from gray and academic literature.

Acknowledgments. This research has received funding from the European Union's Horizon research and innovation program under the grant agreement No. 20506018 (MARIT-D). It has also been partially supported by the EMELIOT national research project, which has been funded by the MUR under the PRIN 2020 program (Contract 2020W3A5FY).

References

1. Algorithmia: 2020 state of enterprise machine learning. Technical report, Algorithmia (2020)
2. Amou Najafabadi, F., Bogner, J., Gerostathopoulos, I., Lago, P.: An analysis of MLOps architectures: a systematic mapping study. In: Galster, M., Scandurra, P., Mikkonen, T., Oliveira Antonino, P., Nakagawa, E.Y., Navarro, E. (eds.) ECSA 2024. LNCS, vol. 14889, pp. 69–85. Springer, Cham (2024). https://doi.org/10.1007/978-3-031-70797-1_5
3. Bayram, F., Ahmed, B.S., Kassler, A.: From concept drift to model degradation: an overview on performance-aware drift detectors. Knowl.-Based Syst. **245**, 108632 (2022)
4. Berberi, L., et al.: Machine learning operations landscape: platforms and tools. Artif. Intell. Rev. **58**, 167 (2025)

5. Butijn, B.J., Tamburri, D.A., Heuvel, W.J.v.d.: Blockchains: a systematic multivocal literature review. ACM Comput. Surv. (CSUR) **53**(3), 1–37 (2020)
6. Castillo-Montoya, M.: Preparing for interview research: the interview protocol refinement framework. Qual. Rep. **21**(5), 811–831 (2016)
7. Dehghani, Z.: Data Mesh: Delivering Data-Driven Value at Scale. O'Reilly Media Inc, Farnham (2022)
8. Etikan, I., Musa, S.A., Alkassim, R.S., et al.: Comparison of convenience sampling and purposive sampling. Am. J. Theor. Appl. Stat. **5**(1), 1–4 (2016)
9. Garousi, V., Felderer, M., Mäntylä, M.V.: Guidelines for including grey literature and conducting multivocal literature reviews in software engineering. Inf. Softw. Technol. **106**, 101–121 (2019)
10. Gisev, N., Bell, J.S., Chen, T.F.: Interrater agreement and interrater reliability: key concepts, approaches, and applications. Res. Social Adm. Pharm. **9**(3), 330–338 (2013)
11. Idowu, S., Strüber, D., Berger, T.: Asset management in machine learning: a survey. In: 2021 IEEE/ACM 43rd International Conference on Software Engineering: Software Engineering in Practice (ICSE-SEIP), pp. 51–60 (2021)
12. John, M.M., Olsson, H.H., Bosch, J.: Towards MLOps: a framework and maturity model. In: 2021 47th Euromicro Conference on Software Engineering and Advanced Applications (SEAA), pp. 1–8 (2021)
13. Kazman, R., Klein, M., Barbacci, M., Longstaff, T., Lipson, H., Carriere, J.: The architecture tradeoff analysis method. In: Proceedings. 4th IEEE International Conference on Engineering of Complex Computer Systems, pp. 68–78 (1998)
14. Kitchenham, B., Charters, S., et al.: Guidelines for performing systematic literature reviews in software engineering. Technical report (2007)
15. Kolltveit, A.B., Li, J.: Operationalizing machine learning models - a systematic literature review. In: 2022 IEEE/ACM 1st International Workshop on Software Engineering for Responsible Artificial Intelligence (SE4RAI), pp. 1–8 (2022)
16. Kreuzberger, D., Kuhl, N., Hirschl, S.: Machine learning operations (MLOps): overview, definition, and architecture. IEEE Access **11**, 31866–31879 (2023)
17. Kumara, I., et al.: The do's and don'ts of infrastructure code: a systematic gray literature review. Inf. Softw. Technol. **137**, 106593 (2021)
18. Paleyes, A., Urma, R.G., Lawrence, N.D.: Challenges in deploying machine learning: a survey of case studies. ACM Comput. Surv. (2022)
19. Recupito, G., et al.: A multivocal literature review of MLOps tools and features. In: Proceedings - 48th Euromicro Conference on Software Engineering and Advanced Applications, SEAA 2022, pp. 84–91 (2022)
20. Symeonidis, G., Nerantzis, E., Kazakis, A., Papakostas, G.A.: MLOps - definitions, tools and challenges. In: 2022 IEEE 12th Annual Computing and Communication Workshop and Conference (CCWC), pp. 0453–0460 (2022)
21. Testi, M., et al.: MLOps: a taxonomy and a methodology. IEEE Access **10**, 63606–63618 (2022)
22. Thoughtworks: Guide to evaluating MLOps platforms. Technical report (2021)
23. Van Eijk, T., Kumara, I., Di Nucci, D., Tamburri, D.A., Van den Heuvel, W.J.: Architectural design decisions for self-serve data platforms in data meshes. In: 2024 IEEE 21st International Conference on Software Architecture (ICSA), pp. 135–145 (2024)

24. Warnett, S.J., Zdun, U.: Architectural design decisions for machine learning deployment. In: 2022 IEEE 19th International Conference on Software Architecture (ICSA), pp. 90–100 (2022)
25. Wohlin, C., Runeson, P., Höst, M., Ohlsson, M.C., Regnell, B., Wesslén, A.: Experimentation in Software Engineering. Springer, Heidelberg (2012). https://doi.org/10.1007/978-3-662-69306-3

$\mathcal{H}armonE$: A Self-adaptive Approach to Architecting Sustainable MLOps

Hiya Bhatt[1(✉)], Shaunak Biswas[1], Srinivasan Rakhunathan[2], and Karthik Vaidhyanathan[1]

[1] Software Engineering Research Centre, IIIT Hyderabad, Hyderabad, India
{hiya.bhatt,shaunak.biswas}@research.iiit.ac.in,
karthik.vaidhyanathan@iiit.ac.in

[2] Microsoft, Hyderabad, India
srrakhun@microsoft.com

Abstract. Machine Learning Enabled Systems (MLS) are becoming integral to real-world applications, but ensuring their sustainable performance over time remains a significant challenge. These systems operate in dynamic environments and face runtime uncertainties like data drift and model degradation, which affect the sustainability of MLS across multiple dimensions: technical, economical, environmental, and social. While Machine Learning Operations (MLOps) addresses the technical dimension by streamlining the ML model lifecycle, it overlooks other dimensions. Furthermore, some traditional practices, such as frequent retraining, incur substantial energy and computational overhead, thus amplifying sustainability concerns. To address them, we introduce $\mathcal{H}armonE$, an architectural approach that enables self-adaptive capabilities in MLOps pipelines using the MAPE-K loop. $\mathcal{H}armonE$ allows system architects to define explicit sustainability goals and adaptation thresholds at design time, and performs runtime monitoring of key metrics, such as prediction accuracy, energy consumption, and data distribution shifts, to trigger appropriate adaptation strategies. We validate our approach using a Digital Twin (DT) of an Intelligent Transportation System (ITS), focusing on traffic flow prediction as our primary use case. The DT employs time series ML models to simulate real-time traffic and assess various flow scenarios. Our results show that $\mathcal{H}armonE$ adapts effectively to evolving conditions while maintaining accuracy and meeting sustainability goals.

Keywords: Self-Adaptation · MLOps · Sustainability · Green AI

1 Introduction

Machine Learning Enabled Systems (MLS) are increasingly being deployed in real-world settings such as intelligent transportation [4], healthcare [21], and

H. Bhatt and S. Biswas—Equal contribution.

V. Andrikopoulos et al. (Eds.): ECSA 2025, LNCS 15929, pp. 38–55, 2026.
https://doi.org/10.1007/978-3-032-02138-0_3

industrial automation [20]. As these systems become integral to everyday applications, ensuring their sustainability has emerged as a critical challenge. Sustainability is recognized as a multi-dimensional quality attribute [2], encompassing *technical* (e.g., model accuracy and maintainability), *environmental* (e.g., energy consumption and emissions), *economic* (e.g., cost-efficiency and resource usage), and *social* (e.g., user trust and long-term impact) dimensions [17]. However, current ML practices often neglect sustainability, given that ML models have evolved to become more computationally intensive over time. In response, the Green AI movement emphasizes resource efficiency and environmental responsibility in AI research and practice [22]. Despite these efforts, recent surveys indicate that approximately half of ML models fail to transition from prototype to production [7], possibly due to sustainability issues like operational complexity, high resource demands, and long-term maintainability challenges [24]. This highlights the importance of explicitly incorporating sustainability into ML deployment practices. Machine Learning Operations (MLOps), which automates the lifecycle of an ML model, has improved technical robustness of MLS but often overlooks environmental and economic impacts. For instance, retraining large models like BERT can consume over 1,500 kWh, emit more than 700 lbs of CO_2, and cost upwards of \$12,000, highlighting the significant sustainability trade-offs involved [25]. Recent literature has considered self-adaptation as a strategy to improve sustainability across all dimensions of MLOps pipelines [3]. By enabling systems to autonomously monitor their internal state and external environment, self-adaptive mechanisms can respond to runtime uncertainties such as data drift, performance degradation, or energy overuse. However, existing approaches typically rely on instantaneous reactions, leading to aggressive adaptations that can increase operational overhead [14,28].

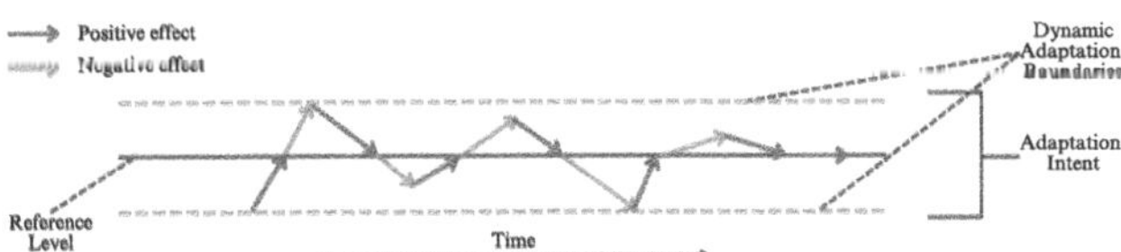

Fig. 1. Adaptation explained as a sustainability goal

To overcome these limitations, we propose $\mathcal{H}armonE$, an architectural approach that integrates self-adaptive capabilities into MLOps pipelines through the MAPE-K loop [13], with the goal of supporting long-term sustainability. $\mathcal{H}armonE$ continuously monitors metrics such as prediction accuracy, energy consumption, and data distribution shifts, aligning adaptations with sustainability goals established at design time. Prior work has represented adaptation intent as a sustainability goal, defined by maintaining system quality within adaptation boundaries [9]. Drawing inspiration from this, we introduce a control-theoretic mechanism centered around a fixed *reference level*, near which the system is expected to operate over time. This enables the system to tolerate temporary deviations, both positive and negative, without triggering immediate adaptation. It allows the *dynamic adaptation boundaries* to evolve gradually based on the cumulative effect of deviations. As illustrated in Fig. 1, adaptation is only triggered when deviations approach these evolving boundaries, allowing for more deliberate, context-aware responses that ensure the sustainability of the system over time. We demonstrate $\mathcal{H}armonE$'s effectiveness using a traffic flow prediction scenario within a Digital Twin (DT) of an Intelligent Transportation System (ITS). This realistic environment evaluates how $\mathcal{H}armonE$ maintains predictive performance and achieves sustainability goals under dynamic real-world conditions. Our results indicate that $\mathcal{H}armonE$ effectively balances short-term performance and long-term sustainability objectives across multiple dimensions.

2 Use Case: DT for ITS

As part of an ongoing collaborative effort between *IIIT Hyderabad, India* and *Middlesex University, London* under the *DigIT* project, a DT is being developed for ITS [4]. The DT is intended to support a wide range of urban mobility functionalities, including real-time simulation, monitoring, and control of traffic infrastructure. One of the key system requirements, identified by stakeholders, is the ability to predict the flow of traffic. These predictions will drive downstream tasks such as adaptive traffic re-routing and congestion management within the DT environment. To fulfill this requirement, the system employs an ML-enabled prediction layer integrated into an MLOps pipeline in the DT architecture. The pipeline automates data ingestion from road sensors, preprocessing, model training and validation, deployment, and continuous performance monitoring. Due to the dynamic and non-stationary nature of traffic patterns, which is affected by factors such as time-of-day, accidents, and seasonal variations, the prediction models must be frequently updated to retain accuracy over time. However, this retraining process is computationally intensive, leading to increased energy consumption and associated operational costs. In the early development phase, the Performance Measurement System (PeMS) dataset from Californias highway sensor network (Refer Sect. 9) was used to benchmark the prediction performance of several ML models under varying conditions. During this evaluation, the high energy cost and computational overhead of frequent retraining raised concerns about the long-term environmental and economic sustainability of the DTs predictive capabilities. To address this challenge, we develop $\mathcal{H}armonE$, a self-adaptive framework designed to balance model accuracy with energy efficiency. The PeMS dataset, which includes high-frequency readings from over 40,000 sensors, provides real-world traffic data. For this use case, we use a single sensor node and extract traffic flow aggregated at 5-min intervals. Predictive models are trained on this data to support traffic forecasting within the DT. This setting enables us to examine how adaptation strategies can contribute to the long-term sustainability of the DTs predictive layer under real-world variability. We refer to this use case throughout the paper to contextualize $\mathcal{H}armonE$.

3 *HarmonE*

HarmonE is an architectural approach that integrates self-adaptive capabilities into MLOps pipelines to manage runtime uncertainties while aligning with sustainability goals using MAPE-K loop [13]. The overall architecture of *HarmonE* is illustrated in Fig. 3, which outlines the interaction between its three main components: (1) the *Managed System*, representing the MLS under adaptation; (2) the *Managing System*, which monitors the MLS and its environment, detects uncertainties, and plans and executes adaptations; and (3) the *Decision Map* [17], which captures sustainability concerns at design time to guide runtime adaptation.

3.1 Managed System

The *Managed System* encompasses the operational elements of the MLOps pipeline and consists of two key components:

1. **Training Subsystem**: This subsystem is responsible for training and retraining models when explicitly triggered by the *Managing System* in response to runtime uncertainties such as data/model drift, or sustained performance degradation. After retraining, the new model, along with its corresponding training data, is forwarded to the *Managing System* for versioning. This ensures that previous models and their corresponding training data are preserved for future reference, reproducibility, and comparison.
2. **Inference Subsystem**: It performs real-time predictions using a model deployed in the system. The selection of this model is made at runtime by the *Managing System* based on current operating conditions and sustainability goals.

3.2 Decision Map

A Decision Map (DM), as shown in Fig. 2, is a visual representation of sustainability concerns across the Social, Environmental, Technical and Economic dimensions [17]. At design time, the system architect defines key system functionalities, identifies their associated sustainability concerns, and captures their relationships in the DM. Adaptation boundaries are then set based on sustainability goals to guide runtime decisions.

Figure 2 shows the DM for our DT use case, which is designed for ITS as explained in Sect. 2. Although the DT encompasses multiple functionalities, such as simulation and monitoring of traffic conditions, this DM specifically addresses sustainability concerns related to the traffic flow prediction component. For the predictive component of the DT to remain sustainable, it needs to continuously meet its sustainability goals: (a) Reducing energy consumption; (b) Improving prediction accuracy and model performance; (c) Minimizing operational costs; (d) Enhancing overall system performance; (e) Ensuring system maintainability. To achieve these goals, the DM identifies three functionalities: **model retraining**, **data and model versioning**, and **model switching**. Each functionality affects distinct sustainability dimensions, guiding runtime adaptations through explicit boundaries stored in the *Knowledge Base* of the MAPE-K loop. **Model Retraining** happens whenever changes in traffic patterns due to events like road closures or festivals are identified. Retraining models ideally improves predictive accuracy, positively impacting system performance, but also negatively influences environmental and economic sustainability by increasing energy consumption and operational costs (see Fig. 2). An example of an adaptation boundary here is setting a threshold for allowable data distribution drift (e.g., maximum acceptable KL divergence [16]) before retraining is triggered. These boundaries ensure retraining is performed only when necessary, balancing model accuracy against resource utilization. **Data and Model Versioning** involves storing trained models along with their corresponding training datasets. This functionality positively affects system maintainability by allowing the reuse of existing models whenever similar traffic conditions reoccur, such as regular rush hours or predictable seasonal variations. However, it negatively impacts operational costs due to additional storage requirements. Hence, an adaptation boundary defined here could be the maximum allowable storage capacity, ensuring the versioning process remains sustainable without excessive overhead. Lastly, **Model Switching** allows dynamic selection among pre-trained models based on runtime observations, guided by adaptation boundaries set for metrics like energy consumption and inference accuracy. For instance, in the DT for ITS scenario (refer Sect. 2), if a highly accurate model surpasses an energy consumption threshold defined in the DM, the system switches to a more energy-efficient model, even if it is less accurate, to preserve environmental sustainability. The system can later revert to the more accurate model when conditions permit, ensuring long-term balance across sustainability goals.

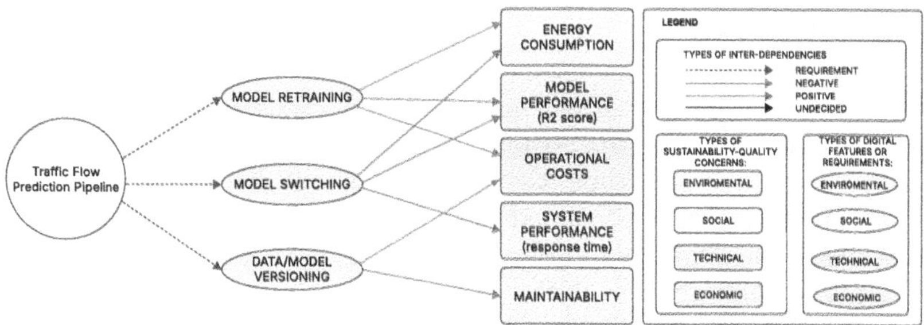

Fig. 2. A decision map for a traffic flow prediction pipeline

3.3 Managing System

The *Managing System* is responsible for monitoring the *Managed System* and its environment, detecting uncertainties at runtime, planning, and executing adaptations. It is composed of several components:

1. **Knowledge Base**: The *Knowledge Base* serves as the central repository of design-time knowledge, enabling self-adaptive capabilities in the MLS to make informed decisions at runtime. It consists of five key components as shown in Fig. 3. First, the **Data Repository** stores the incoming sensor data along with the corresponding model predictions from the *Inference Subsystem*, enabling drift detection, ongoing performance assessment, and informed model selection during adaptation. Second, the **Sustainability Goals Repository** stores the sustainability goals defined by the system architect. These goals are translated into measurable thresholds for metrics such as accuracy, energy consumption, and cost. Derived from the systems DM, these thresholds define the acceptable operational boundaries within which the system is expected to function. Third, the **Tactics Repository** includes a library of predefined adaptation strategies for managing sustainability trade-offs. During runtime, these strategies are evaluated and selected by the $\mathcal{P}lanner$ based on the current system state. A detailed list of the tactics used in our implementation is presented in Table 1. Fourth, the **Current Model Repository** maintains a predefined set of n models $\mathcal{M} = \{M_1, M_2, \ldots, M_n\}$ available for deployment during inference. These models are characterized by different trade-offs between accuracy and resource efficiency and are used by the *Managing System* to adaptively select the most suitable model at runtime. Finally, the **Versioned Model Repository** (VMR) stores retrained versions of models from $\mathcal{M}$, along with the data distributions on which they were trained. Whenever a model from the current repository is retrained due to drift or performance degradation, the resulting model-data pair is archived here. This enables the system to match incoming data distributions with previously seen ones and reuse past models when appropriate, avoiding redundant retraining and supporting long-term sustainability.

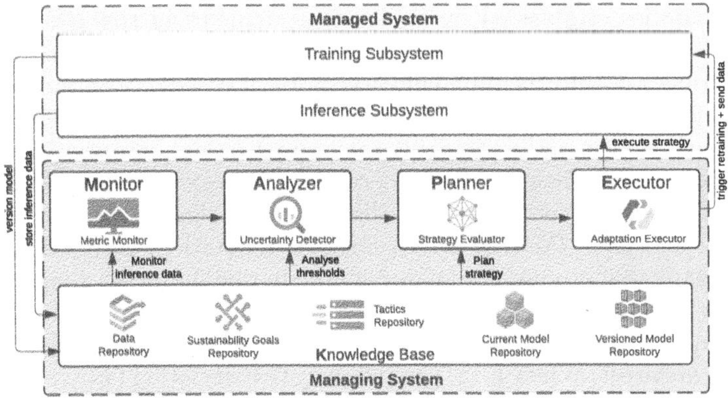

Fig. 3. HarmonE Architecture

2. **Monitor**: $\mathcal{M}onitor$ consists of a *Metric Monitor* as shown in Fig. 3. It observes system behaviour during inference by periodically aggregating runtime

metrics at intervals predefined by the system architect. At each interval i, metrics are aggregated over all new timesteps received since the last monitoring interval. Key metrics include prediction accuracy, energy usage of the system, and data distribution shifts. The specific formulation of prediction accuracy can vary across application domains, for example, R^2 score in regression tasks or confidence scores in classification settings. To capture energy efficiency, the system computes a normalized energy value $\bar{E}_i$ at each interval i, calculated by dividing the current interval's energy consumption by the maximum energy usage observed in the training data. These two metrics are combined into a performance score: $S_i = \beta A_i + (1 - \beta)(1 - \bar{E}_i)$, where A_i is the accuracy metric (e.g., R^2 score), $\bar{E}_i$ is normalized energy, and $\beta \in [0, 1]$ is a design-time weight, balancing accuracy and efficiency linearly. To smooth short-term fluctuations, an Exponential Moving Average (EMA) of S_i is maintained:

$$\text{EMA}(S_i) = \gamma S_i + (1 - \gamma)\text{EMA}(S_{i-1}), \tag{1}$$

where γ is a smoothing factor that determines the sensitivity to recent performance. To monitor distributional shifts in the data, a suitable divergence measure is used based on the task domain. For instance, in regression settings, KL Divergence $\mathcal{D}$ is computed between the data distribution of recently observed true values P_t and a reference distribution P_r, as demonstrated in [19]. All metrics computed by the *Metric Monitor* are passed to $\mathcal{A}nalyzer$ as inputs to guide adaptation decisions. For instance, in the DT use case described in Sect. 2, these metrics are derived from real-time traffic data captured by a sensor node within Californias highway network.

3. **Analyzer**: $\mathcal{A}nalyzer$ consists of an *Uncertainty Detector* that evaluates system performance metrics received from $\mathcal{M}onitor$ to determine whether runtime adaptation is necessary. Uncertainty is defined as a violation of adaptation boundaries established by the system architect in the DM (Sect. 3.2). For performance-based adaptation, $\mathcal{A}nalyzer$ compares $\text{EMA}(S_i)$, computed by $\mathcal{M}onitor$ using Eq. 1, to the minimum acceptable threshold S_{min} which is stored in the *Knowledge base*. If $\text{EMA}(S_i) < S_{\text{min}}$, $\mathcal{A}nalyzer$ identifies a potential performance degradation and triggers $\mathcal{P}lanner$ to select an appropriate adaptation strategy. For energy efficiency, if the normalized energy consumption $\bar{E}_i$ at any interval i exceeds a dynamic energy threshold τ_{E_i}, $\mathcal{A}nalyzer$ flags this as an uncertainty and calls $\mathcal{P}lanner$ which triggers adaptation. Inspired by control theory principles [8], we use the following update rule for τ_{E_i} to adapt to persistent energy deviations: $\tau_{E_{i+1}} = \tau_{E_i} + \delta \cdot (\bar{E}_{\text{ref}} - \bar{E}_i)$, where $\bar{E}_{\text{ref}}$ is a design-time reference energy level and $\delta \in (0, 1)$ is a decay factor, both defined in the DM by the system architect. When $\bar{E}_i > \bar{E}_{\text{ref}}$, the negative deviation $(\bar{E}_{\text{ref}} - \bar{E}_i)$ reduces τ_{E_i} to a lower $\tau_{E_{i+1}}$, tightening the adaptation boundaries to enforce stricter energy constraints. Conversely, if $\bar{E}_i < \bar{E}_{\text{ref}}$, the positive deviation increases τ_{E_i} to $\tau_{E_{i+1}}$, loosening the adaptation boundaries to accommodate transient energy spikes while maintaining efficiency. For drift-based adaptation, $\mathcal{A}nalyzer$ evaluates the distribution shift metric $\mathcal{D}$, computed by $\mathcal{M}onitor$, against a predefined threshold τ_{drift} specified by the system architect. If $\mathcal{D} > \tau_{\text{drift}}$, an uncertainty

is detected, and $\mathcal{P}lanner$ is invoked to mitigate this drift-related violation. For example, in the DT use case, a sudden change in traffic patterns may increase $\mathcal{D}$ beyond the acceptable limit, prompting $\mathcal{A}nalyzer$ to initiate appropriate drift-handling adaptations.

Table 1. Self-Adaptation Uncertainties, Tactics, and Strategies for Sustainable MLOps

Uncertainty	Concern	Impact			Tactics	Strategy
		Immediate	Enabling	Systemic		
1. Model Drift	Technical	Reduced prediction quality	Reduced user trust	Reduced social benefits	**1. Model switch 2. Retrain**	a. Switch to better-fit model from VMR b. Retrain via Incremental/Transfer Learning/Full retraining
2. Data Drift	Technical	Degraded due to data shifts	Inaccurate predictions	Trust loss, low relevance	**1. Model switch 2. Retrain**	a. Switch to better-fit model from VMR b. Retrain with resampled/augmented data
3. High Energy Consumption	Environmental	Increased costs	Environmental impact	Lower competitiveness	**1. Model switch 2. Model Compression**	a. Switch to lighter model b. Quantize current model
4. Model performance degradation	Technical	Decline in predictive accuracy	Increased need for *frequent* retraining	Reduced maintainability	**1. Model switch 2. Retrain**	a. Switch to a model with higher accuracy b. Retrain the model

4. **Planner**: $\mathcal{P}lanner$ consists of a *Strategy Evaluator*, as shown in Fig. 3, which is responsible for selecting and initiating the appropriate adaptation strategy whenever $\mathcal{A}nalyzer$ detects a runtime uncertainty. These strategies are derived from the set of predefined tactics [12,18] associated with each type of uncertainty, as outlined in Table 1, and are stored in the Tactics Repository within the *Knowledge Base* (see Fig. 3). The table also categorizes the impact of each uncertainty as *immediate* (direct operational effects), *enabling* (mid-term consequences on resource use or retraining), and *systemic* (long-term or structural implications) [17]. Thus, the *Strategy Evaluator* makes decisions based on the current runtime context and accumulated historical performance metrics. For performance-based adaptation, the *Strategy Evaluator* retrieves the model-specific EMA scores from the *Knowledge Base* and selects from the spectrum of models, excluding the currently active one, the model that yields the highest EMA(S_i) (refer to Eq. 1). An ϵ-greedy exploration strategy is used, wherein with probability ϵ, the *Strategy Evaluator* randomly selects a model from the *current model repository* $\mathcal{M}$ in the Knowledge Base. For energy-based adaptation, if the normalized energy consumption $\bar{E}_i$ for interval i exceeds the dynamic threshold τ_{E_i}, $\mathcal{P}lanner$ is triggered to reassess the deployed model. When an energy violation occurs, the *Strategy Evaluator* selects the model with the best EMA(S_i) among those excluding the currently active model, thereby addressing environmental sustainability concerns without compromising predictive performance. In case of drift-based adaptation, if the distribution shift metric $\mathcal{D}$ exceeds the drift threshold τ_{drift}, the planner compares the current data distribution with the stored training distributions of versioned models stored in the VMR in the *Knowledge Base* (see Fig. 3). If a suitable match is found, the system switches to that versioned model; otherwise, $\mathcal{E}xecutor$ is triggered for full retraining. This planning mechanism allows the system to adapt dynamically to runtime uncertainties while preserving long-term sustainability goals. For instance, in the DT

use case discussed in Sect. 2, if a sudden traffic disruption leads to reduced accuracy or increased energy usage, the planner may decide to switch from an LSTM model to a lighter linear model until stability is restored.

5. **Executor**: $\mathcal{E}xecutor$ is responsible for enacting the adaptation strategies determined by the $\mathcal{P}lanner$. When the selected strategy involves retraining, $\mathcal{E}xecutor$ calls the *Training Subsystem* to initiate the process. Once training is complete, $\mathcal{E}xecutor$ versions the trained model and its associated data in the VMR in the *Knowledge Base*. If the strategy involves switching to a different model, either from the VMR or from the predefined spectrum of models $\mathcal{M}$, $\mathcal{E}xecutor$ updates the model used by the *Inference Subsystem* accordingly. In doing so, it ensures that subsequent predictions are made using the model selected by the $\mathcal{P}lanner$.

4 Experiment Design

We assess the effectiveness and efficiency of $\mathcal{H}armonE$ by answering these Research Questions (RQ):

RQ1: To what extent does $\mathcal{H}armonE$ ensure the long-term environmental sustainability of MLS?
RQ2: To what extent does $\mathcal{H}armonE$ manage the trade-off between energy consumption and predictive accuracy compared to baseline approaches?
RQ3: How efficient are the adaptation decisions made by $\mathcal{H}armonE$ in terms of their frequency and resource usage?

Next, we describe the setup and design of the experiments to evaluate our system.

4.1 Experimental Setup

To evaluate $\mathcal{H}armonE$, we design an experimental setup that reflects the challenges and operational dynamics of sustainability-aware inference in real-world systems. As described in the use case (Sect. 2), we utilize traffic flow (`Vehicles/5min`) data collected from sensor nodes deployed as part of the California PeMS platform (see Sect. 9). For forecasting, we structure the data in a supervised learning format where each model receives the previous 5 timesteps (i.e., 25 min of sensor readings) as input to predict the traffic flow for the 6th timestep (i.e., the 30th minute). This setup allows us to evaluate the models' ability to learn short-term temporal dependencies while operating under energy and latency constraints. Further, we construct a spectrum of models that vary in both predictive accuracy and computational cost:

- **Linear Regression (LR)**: Lightweight and fast but less expressive. It serves as the most energy-efficient model [29].
- **Support Vector Machine (SVM)** [10]: Balances moderate accuracy with intermediate inference time and energy consumption.
- **Long Short-Term Memory (LSTM)** [10]: Offers highest accuracy but comes with the highest energy and latency overhead.

We conducted a pilot experiment over a short interval and observed that while LSTM generally provides higher accuracy, LR and SVM models often yield satisfactory performance at significantly lower energy cost. This supports their inclusion in the inference setup to enable more energy-efficient predictions when appropriate. All models are trained on a fixed-size historical dataset to ensure uniform comparison. After training, they are deployed in the *Inference Subsystem* for real-time inference on incoming sensor data. During inference, the system logs key metrics such as prediction output, ground truth, inference time, and energy consumption. The coefficient of determination R^2 is used to evaluate predictive accuracy. Energy consumption is measured using the `pyRAPL`[1] library, which provides high-resolution energy profiling at the system level. The models were implemented using the Python libraries `scikit-learn` for Linear Regression and SVM, and `PyTorch` for LSTM. For details of the implementation, please refer to our Github repository[2].

4.2 Baselines Setup

To systematically evaluate the sustainability and effectiveness of $\mathcal{H}armonE$, we compare it against the following baselines:

- **LR**: Inference using Linear Regression model
- **LR+PRT**: Linear Regression with periodic retraining.
- **SVM**: Inference using Support Vector Machine.
- **SVM+PRT**: Support Vector Machine with periodic retraining.
- **LSTM**: Inference using Long Short-Term Memory.
- **LSTM+PRT**: Long Short-Term Memory with periodic retraining.
- **Switch**: Switching among LR, SVM, and LSTM based on uncertainties detected by the Managing System (see Sect. 3); however, no retraining is performed.
- **Switch+PRT**: **Switch** with periodic retraining.
- $\mathcal{H}armonE$: Our approach, as explained in Sect. 3

We divide the dataset into three parts: 80% (1200 samples) is used for training, 20% (240 samples) for validation, and a separate test set of 14,500 samples is used for inference and evaluation. All models are trained using the same training-validation split to ensure consistency across approaches. Retraining, whether periodic or triggered ($\mathcal{H}armonE$), is performed using 1200 samples, consistent with the original training window size, with periodic retraining triggered uniformly every 3200 timesteps. To ensure consistent and reliable results, each baseline experiment is repeated independently five times, following established guidelines for empirical software engineering [30]. Additionally, a cooldown period of 20 min is introduced between consecutive runs to stabilize hardware conditions and ensure accurate energy profiling. All experiments are conducted in a controlled simulation environment, enabling reproducibility and fair comparisons. The performance of these approaches is summarized in Table 2.

[1] https://pypi.org/project/pyRAPL/ (last accessed March 28, 2025).

[2] https://github.com/sa4s-serc/HarmonE (last accessed June 10, 2025).

4.3 Drift Induction

To evaluate $\mathcal{H}armonE$'s performance in the presence of real-world uncertainties, we simulate distribution drift in the test dataset. This is done to mimic scenarios where external factors, such as traffic rerouting due to roadblocks or unexpected events like accidents, cause abrupt changes in data patterns. Specifically, we induce controlled data drift by applying a consistent scale-and-shift transformation twice to designated segments of the test data. Our drift induction method, inspired by [19], ensures the changes are measurable and representative of natural concept drift, thereby enabling meaningful evaluation of $\mathcal{H}armonE$ s adaptation capabilities. By repeating the same transformation, we simulate a scenario where the data distribution first diverges and later realigns with a previously seen pattern. This enables $\mathcal{H}armonE$ to demonstrate both drift detection and effective model reuse by identifying similarity with historical distributions stored in the VMR.

4.4 System Specifications

All experiments were conducted on a system with the following specifications: Debian GNU/Linux 12 (Bookworm) operating system with kernel version 6.1.0-32-amd64, running on a 12th Gen Intel i5-1240P processor at 4.40 GHz. The system had 8 GB RAM, an integrated Intel Alder Lake-P GPU, and utilized the GNOME 43.9 desktop environment. The consistent hardware configuration ensured fair comparisons and reproducible energy profiling across all experiments.

5 Results

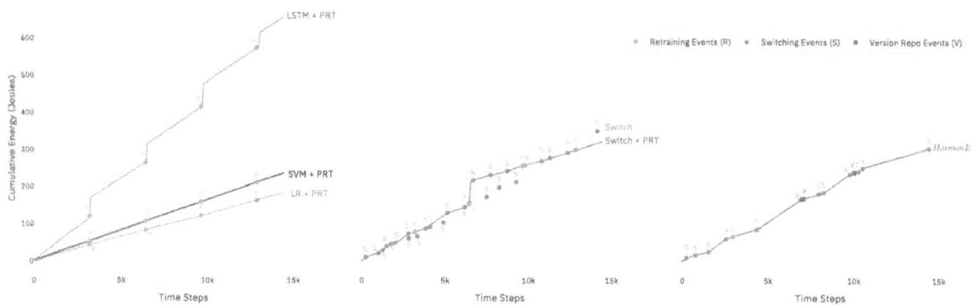

Fig. 4. Adaptation strategies activated by $\mathcal{H}armonE$ during execution

This section presents the experimental results of our proposed approach, $\mathcal{H}armonE$, in comparison to eight baseline approaches. Figure 4 illustrates the adaptation strategies triggered by $\mathcal{H}armonE$ throughout execution. Non-adaptive baselines: LR, SVM and LSTM are excluded, as they do not trigger any adaptation events. The temporal distribution of switching (S), retraining (R), and version repository access (V) events reflects how $\mathcal{H}armonE$ responds to evolving conditions while balancing adaptation costs. To ensure reliability, we conducted five independent runs for each approach and averaged the energy consumption. As shown in Fig. 5, results are consistent across runs, with minor variation in Switch+PRT due to stochastic model selection during retraining. Despite this, the relative performance trends remain stable, supporting the reproducibility of our findings.

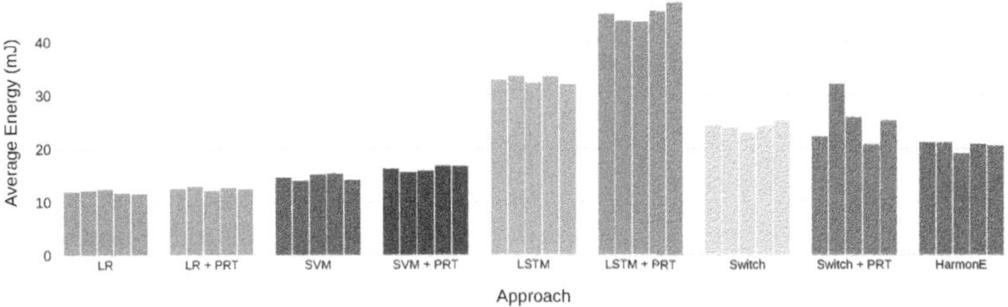

Fig. 5. Average energy consumption (mJ) across five runs for all nine approaches

RQ1: To what extent does $\mathcal{H}armonE$ ensure the long-term environmental sustainability of MLS?

> $\mathcal{H}armonE$ ensures long-term sustainability by maintaining energy consumption below threshold constraints. It consumes **54.5%** less energy compared to high-performing LSTM+PRT.

To analyze environmental sustainability, we examine cumulative energy consumption over time steps (Fig. 6) for all approaches. $\mathcal{H}armonE$ consistently maintains its energy consumption below the reference energy level (red dotted line) defined by the system architect at design time using the DM (refer 3.2), by dynamically adapting whenever this boundary is violated. Comparatively, approaches like LR, LR+PRT, SVM, and SVM+PRT show consistently low energy use but significantly underperform in predictive accuracy (discussed further in the section). In contrast, approaches like LSTM, LSTM+PRT significantly surpass $\mathcal{H}armonE$ s energy consumption. Approaches like Switch, Switch+PRT perform better than single models but still exhibit higher energy consumption than $\mathcal{H}armonE$. It is observed that all the approaches with PRT, retrain models after fixed intervals regardless of necessity thus consuming more energy, whereas $\mathcal{H}armonE$ only retrains the models whenever drift is detected (refer Sect. 3) thus significantly reducing the energy consumption. Quantitatively, $\mathcal{H}armonE$ consumes 20.62 mJ, representing a 54.5% reduction compared to LSTM+PRT (45.35 mJ) and an 18.6% reduction compared to Switching+PRT (25.32 mJ).

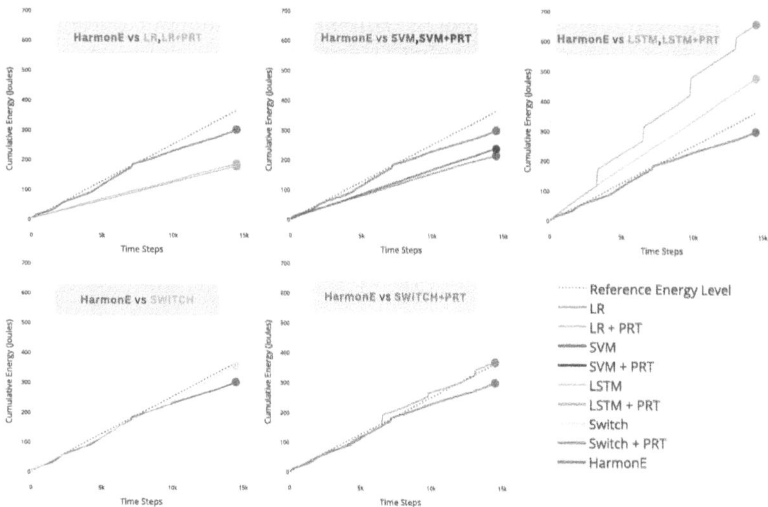

Fig. 6. Cumulative energy consumption over time for different approaches

RQ2: To what extent does *HarmonE* manage the trade-off between energy consumption and predictive accuracy compared to baseline approaches?

> *HarmonE* effectively manages the trade-off between energy consumption and predictive accuracy. It achieves **95.0%** of LSTM+PRT's accuracy while consuming only **45.5%** of its energy and improves inference time by **53.4%**.

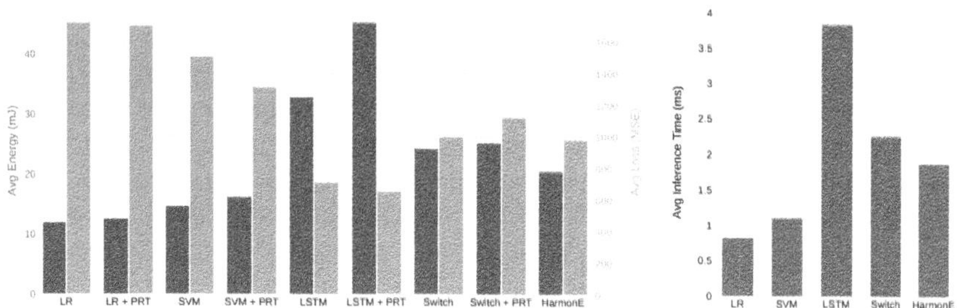

Fig. 7. Energy vs. prediction error (MSE) across approache—lower is better on both axes (on left). Inference time comparison excluding retraining—lower is better (on right)

To address RQ2, we analyze how different approaches balance predictive accuracy, energy consumption, and inference speed using the results summarized in Fig. 7 and Table 2. LR and SVM-based approaches achieve minimal energy consumption (12.1157-16.3304 mJ), but exhibit significantly higher prediction errors (1315-1723 MSE), Fig. 7) and lower predictive accuracy (R^2 scores ranging from 0.7597 to 0.8167). Conversely, LSTM-based approaches deliver lower prediction errors (657713 MSE) and higher predictive accuracy ($R^2 = 0.9005$ and 0.9085) at the expense of substantial energy consumption (32.9147–45.3517 mJ) and inference latency (3.8475 ms). Periodic retraining, irrespective of necessity, further escalates these energy and latency costs. The Switch approach, despite aiming for balance, defaults to the heavier LSTM model without retraining smaller models when drift occurs, resulting in higher average energy usage (24.3218 mJ) without achieving LSTM-level accuracy ($R^2 = 0.8445$). In contrast, $\mathcal{H}armonE$ dynamically manages model selection, selective retraining, and versioned model reuse, achieving an R^2 score of 0.8627–95.0% of LSTM+PRT accuracyat only 45.5% of its energy cost. Additionally, $\mathcal{H}armonE$ attains faster inference times (1.89 ms), reducing latency by 53.4% compared to LSTM+PRT (4.05 ms). These results highlight $\mathcal{H}armonE$'s ability to efficiently balance energy and accuracy, significantly outperforming baseline approaches.

RQ3: How efficient are the adaptation decisions made by $\mathcal{H}armonE$ in terms of their frequency and resource usage?

$\mathcal{H}armonE$ makes highly efficient adaptation decisions, with the decision-making process itself consuming only 1.3660% of total system energy while enabling strategic resource optimization through context-aware adaptation mechanisms.

To address RQ3, we analyze the frequency of adaptation decisions and their resource consumption (Refer Table 2). Our experiments reveal that $\mathcal{H}armonE$'s adaptation decisions are highly efficient in terms of both frequency and resource usage. The adaptation logic (MAPE-K loop) executes swiftly, averaging 17.899 ms per invocation, thereby imposing negligible runtime overhead. The energy consumed by the MAPE-K loop accounts for only 1.3660% of the total energy usage of the system. This extremely low overhead demonstrates that $\mathcal{H}armonE$'s decision-making mechanism itself is highly energy-efficient. Periodic retraining approaches (LR+PRT, SVM+PRT, LSTM+PRT, Switch+PRT) conduct retraining at fixed intervals (4 per run), regardless of necessity, leading to redundant resource usage. In contrast, purely switching-based adaptation (Switch) triggers frequent model switches (average of 13 per run) without retraining, often defaulting to heavier models due to degraded performance in lighter models. $\mathcal{H}armonE$ addresses these inefficiencies by selectively performing adaptations, either switching, retraining, or reusing versioned models, only when required by system conditions (as shown in Fig. 4). This significantly reduces unnecessary resource consumption while maintaining predictive performance.

6 Threats to Validity

A threat to *internal validity* arises from the consistency of results across repeated experimental runs, as energy consumption and performance metrics can be

Table 2. Performance comparison of different approaches

Approach	Energy(mJ)	R^2	Inference Time(ms)	# Adaptations
LR	12.1157	0.7597	0.8306	–
LR + PRT	12.6987	0.7624		4
SVM	14.7649	0.7897	1.1134	–
SVM + PRT	16.3304	0.8167		4
LSTM	32.9147	0.9005	3.8475	–
LSTM + PRT	45.3517	0.9085		4
Switch	24.3218	0.8445	2.2656	13
Switch + PRT	25.3176	0.8435		17
HarmonE	**20.6203**	**0.8628**	**1.8887**	**12**

affected by background processes and runtime fluctuations. To mitigate this, all experiments were repeated independently five times for each approach, and average results were reported to ensure consistency. Additionally, a cooldown period of 20 min was enforced between consecutive runs to allow system conditions, particularly energy usage and temperature, to stabilize before the next experiment. A threat to *Construct Validity* could be that the energy measurements in our experiments were collected using the `pyRAPL` library, Python package specifically designed for assessing the energy consumption and power usage of software applications running on Intel processors. While the absolute energy values may differ when using alternative measurement tools or hardware platforms, we believe that the relative patterns and trends in adaptation behaviour would remain consistent. A threat to *external validity* concerns the generalizability of our findings beyond the specific use case of traffic flow prediction. Although this represents a realistic and dynamic application, it may not fully reflect the characteristics of other domains such as computer vision or natural language processing. Additionally, our evaluation focuses on a single task type and a limited set of models. To mitigate this, we employed a spectrum of models with varying complexity and resource requirements to simulate diverse operational conditions. While further validation is needed in other domains, *HarmonE* is designed to be domain-agnostic and can be extended to different MLS through appropriate domain knowledge.

7 Related Work

There has been substantial progress in developing MLOps frameworks to automate the ML model lifecycle, as seen in works such as [1,23,26], but these primarily emphasize maintainability, scalability, and reliability, without addressing sustainability as an architectural concern. Notable efforts have been made to employ self-adaptation in MLS, such as [15], which proposes dynamic model switching strategies using MAPE-K loops to balance Quality of Service (QoS) metrics at runtime, yet remain limited to inference and do not incorporate energy, retraining cost, or long-term sustainability trade-offs. EcoMLS [28] introduces energy-aware switching during inference, marking a shift toward integrating sustainability at runtime, but it is too restricted in scope and does not address sustainability across the full ML lifecycle, including training and continuous evolution. Work in software sustainability, including [9,17], advocates architectural DM and the expression of adaptation intent as sustainability goals, but lacks integration with runtime MLOps adaptation to handle uncertainties typical in MLS. In parallel, the "Green AI" community focuses on efficient model architectures [5,11], offering energy savings at the algorithmic level, but these methods are typically static and disconnected from lifecycle or runtime MLOps concerns. Work such as [27] articulates the organizational and architectural challenges in achieving sustainable MLOps, while others like [18] explore architectural tactics to support evolvability in ML pipelines, though without mechanisms to operationalize these decisions adaptively. [6] highlights the absence of integrated, end-to-end architectural support for environmental sustainability in ML system engineering through a systematic mapping study. While these efforts lay essential groundwork, a lack of approaches that operationalize sustainability across the ML lifecycle by adaptively managing runtime uncertainties and evolving trade-offs remains. To address this, we present $\mathcal{H}armonE$, an architectural approach that enables self-adaptive capabilities in MLOps pipelines via the MAPE-K loop. $\mathcal{H}armonE$ dynamically balances predictive performance and energy consumption throughout the ML lifecycle.

8 Conclusion

This paper presented $\mathcal{H}armonE$, a self-adaptive architectural approach that integrates the MAPE-K loop within MLOps pipelines to address long-term sustainability challenges in MLS deployments. $\mathcal{H}armonE$ dynamically adjusts system configurations through strategies such as model switching, selective retraining, and versioned model reuse, rather than relying on fixed-interval retraining. These design choices allow the system to continuously balance energy consumption and predictive accuracy. Experimental results obtained using a DT of an ITS demonstrate that $\mathcal{H}armonE$ maintains environmental sustainability over extended periods. Specifically, $\mathcal{H}armonE$ reduces energy consumption by 54.5% compared to LSTM+PRT while preserving 95% of its predictive accuracy. The approach outperforms periodic retraining methods by triggering adaptations only when sustainability boundaries are reached, thereby reducing unnecessary resource expenditure and mitigating long-term operational overhead. Future work will focus on validating $\mathcal{H}armonE$ in more diverse and complex real-world environments, including domains such as computer vision and natural language processing. In particular, we aim to evaluate its applicability in LLM/SLM-enabled systems where the sustainability trade-offs of model selection, fine-tuning, and inference are more pronounced, further extending its relevance to a broader class of MLS deployments.

Acknowledgements:. This research was funded by the ANRF Prime Minister Early Career Research Grant (ANRF/ECRG/2024/003379/ENS). We would also like to thank the UKIERI-SPARC project titled DigITDigital Twins for Integrated Transportation Platform (UKIERI-SPARC/01/23) for their support.

Data Availability. The traffic flow data used in this study is publicly accessible via the California Performance Measurement System (PeMS) website at https://pems.dot.ca.gov/. For reproducibility and verifiability, the source code and configurations for implementing $\mathcal{H}armonE$ are available at https://github.com/sa4s-serc/HarmonE. Additional resources, updates, and documentation are maintained on the project website at https://sa4s-serc.github.io/HarmonE/

References

1. Amershi, S., et al.: Software engineering for machine learning: a case study. In: 2019 IEEE/ACM 41st International Conference on Software Engineering: Software Engineering in Practice (ICSE-SEIP) (2019)
2. Becker, C., et alC.: Sustainability design and software: The karlskrona manifesto. In: 2015 IEEE/ACM 37th IEEE International Conference on Software Engineering, vol. 2 (2015)
3. Bhatt, H., Arun, S., Kakran, A., Vaidhyanathan, K.: Towards architecting sustainable mlops: a self-adaptation approach. In: ICSA-C (2024)
4. Bhatt, H., Sahil, Vaidhyanathan, K., Biju, R., Gangadharan, D., Trestian, R., Shah, P.: Architecting digital twins for intelligent transportation systems. In: 2025 IEEE 22nd International Conference on Software Architecture Companion (ICSA-C) (2025)
5. Cai, H., Gan, C., Wang, T., Zhang, Z., Han, S.: Once-for-all: Train one network and specialize it for efficient deployment. arXiv preprint arXiv:1908.09791 (2019)
6. Chadli, K., Botterweck, G., Saber, T.: The environmental cost of engineering machine learning-enabled systems: a mapping study. In: Proceedings of the 4th Workshop on Machine Learning and Systems. EuroMLSys 2024. Association for Computing Machinery
7. Costello, K., Rimol, M.: Gartner identifies the top strategic technology trends for 2021
8. Franklin, G., Powell, J., Workman, M.: Digital Control of Dynamic Systems (2022)
9. Gerostathopoulos, I., Raibulet, C., Lago, P.: Expressing the adaptation intent as a sustainability goal. In: Proceedings of the ACM/IEEE 44th International Conference on Software Engineering: New Ideas and Emerging Results (2022)
10. Goodfellow, I., Bengio, Y., Courville, A.: Deep Learning. MIT Press (2016)
11. Han, S., Mao, H., Dally, W.J.: Deep compression: compressing deep neural networks with pruning, trained quantization and huffman coding (2015)
12. Järvenpää, H., Lago, P., Bogner, J., Lewis, G., Muccini, H., Ozkaya, I.: A synthesis of green architectural tactics for ml-enabled systems. In: Proceedings of the 46th International Conference on Software Engineering: Software Engineering in Society, ICSE-SEIS 2024. Association for Computing Machinery, New York (2024)
13. Kephart, J.O., Chess, D.M.: The vision of autonomic computing. Computer **36**(1) (2003)

14. Kulkarni, S., Marda, A., Vaidhyanathan, K.: Towards self-adaptive machine learning-enabled systems through qos-aware model switching. In: 2023 38th IEEE/ACM International Conference on Automated Software Engineering (ASE). IEEE (2023)
15. Kulkarni, S., Marda, A., Vaidhyanathan, K.: Towards self-adaptive machine learning-enabled systems through qos-aware model switching. In: 2023 38th IEEE/ACM International Conference on Automated Software Engineering (ASE) (2023)
16. Kullback, S., Leibler, R.A.: On information and sufficiency. Annals Math. Statist. **22**(1) (1951)
17. Lago, P.: Architecture design decision maps for software sustainability. In: 2019 IEEE/ACM 41st International Conference on Software Engineering: Software Engineering in Society (ICSE-SEIS). IEEE (2019)
18. Leest, J., Gerostathopoulos, I., Raibulet, C.: Evolvability of machine learning-based systems: an architectural design decision framework. In: 2023 IEEE 20th International Conference on Software Architecture Companion (ICSA-C). IEEE (2023)
19. Lewis, G.A., Echeverría, S., Pons, L., Chrabaszcz, J.: Augur: a step towards realistic drift detection in production ml systems. In: 2022 IEEE/ACM 1st International Workshop on Software Engineering for Responsible Artificial Intelligence (SE4RAI) (2022)
20. Maschler, B., Weyrich, M.: Deep transfer learning for industrial automation: a review and discussion of new techniques for data-driven machine learning. IEEE Indust. Electr. Mag. **15**(2) (2021)
21. Miotto, R., Wang, F., Wang, S., Jiang, X., Dudley, J.T.: Deep learning for healthcare: review, opportunities and challenges. Briefings Bioinform. **19**(6) (2018)
22. Schwartz, R., Dodge, J., Smith, N.A., Etzioni, O.: Green ai. Commun. ACM **63**(12) (2020)
23. Shankar, S., Garcia, R., Hellerstein, J.M., Parameswaran, A.G.: Operationalizing machine learning. University of California, Berkeley
24. Shivashankar, K., Martini, A.: Maintainability challenges in ml: a systematic literature review. In: 2022 48th Euromicro Conference on Software Engineering and Advanced Applications (SEAA) (2022)
25. Strubell, E., Ganesh, A., McCallum, A.: Energy and policy considerations for modern deep learning research. Proceedings of the AAAI Conference on Artificial Intelligence (09)
26. Symeonidis, G., Nerantzis, E., Kazakis, A., Papakostas, G.A.: Mlops - definitions, tools and challenges. In: 2022 IEEE 12th Annual Computing and Communication Workshop and Conference (CCWC) (2022)
27. Tamburri, D.A.: Sustainable mlops: Trends and challenges. In: 2020 22nd International Symposium on Symbolic and Numeric Algorithms for Scientific Computing (SYNASC)
28. Tedla, M., Kulkarni, S., Vaidhyanathan, K.: Ecomls: A self-adaptation approach for architecting green ml-enabled systems. arXiv preprint arXiv:2404.11411 (2024)
29. Verdecchia, R., Cruz, L., Sallou, J., Lin, M., Wickenden, J., Hotellier, E.: Data-centric green ai an exploratory empirical study. In: 2022 International Conference on ICT for Sustainability (ICT4S) (2022)
30. Wohlin, C., Runeson, P., Höst, M., Ohlsson, M., Regnell, B., Wesslén, A.: Experimentation in software engineering. Springer Science & Business Media (2012)

Large Language Models in Software Architecture

Using Incremental LLM Context for Cost Reduction in LLM-Driven IoT Applications

Aashna Sofat and Balwinder Sodhi(✉)

Department of Computer Science and Engineering, IIT Ropar, Rupnagar 140001, PB, India
sodhi@iitrpr.ac.in

Abstract. The LLM driven IoT applications need to handle time-sensitive information and dynamically evolving data. For example, the sensors in IoT systems send real-time data that must be taken into consideration by the LLM-driven application. The traditional architectures store such real-time IoT data in a database and re-prompt the LLM by suitably incorporating the new information on each request (or at designated time). Such an approach becomes inefficient especially when:
(1) Data arrives at a high rate, e.g., streaming updates, large volumes of logs. (2) Only some fraction of updates are relevant to the user's current question or context. (3) The application must preserve the conversation flow in a manageable size while still allowing new data to "flow in."
In this paper we present an architecture that addresses these challenges by maintaining a lightweight "timeline" of recent and relevant "events". This design ensures that the LLM always sees a relevant snapshot of the most critical information at each step, **without needing** to ingest the entire stream of events every time. An important element in our architecture is the "event relevance scoring" module which allowed us to maintain a "sliding window" of the most crucial recent incoming sensors data. Our experiments show that, compared to the baseline, the proposed approach's response time is 15.41% faster and it generates 65.16% fewer tokens, which reduces token-based costs significantly. On average, it uses 5.41% less GPU and consumes 5.13% less CPU.

Keywords: LLM in IoT · Ephemeral LLM context · LLM-driven application · Software Architecture

1 Introduction

Large Language Models (LLMs) and Small Language Models (SLMs) have begun to play a significant role in IoT applications, though their adoption is still evolving. LLMs and SLMs are transforming IoT applications by enhancing natural language interactions, improving anomaly detection, and optimizing smart infrastructure. For example, the traditional IoT interfaces involve structured

V. Andrikopoulos et al. (Eds.): ECSA 2025, LNCS 15929, pp. 59–72, 2026.
https://doi.org/10.1007/978-3-032-02138-0_4

commands and predefined interactions. LLMs introduce natural language processing (NLP), enabling users to interact with IoT systems conversationally. Users can describe tasks in natural language, and an LLM translates them into structured IoT commands. Of course, there are more complex use cases too such as the ones where IoT networks generate continuous streams of telemetry data, and LLMs help analyze these logs and detect unusual patterns in real-time.

Effective integration of LLMs into IoT applications pose significant challenges for the software architects. One of the most significant challenge is handling time-sensitive information and dynamically evolving data that is common in IoT systems. In traditional architectures, the dynamic events/data is stored in a database and is used (after appropriate 'scrubbing' and transformation) to re-prompt the LLM with the entire knowledge base or conversation history on each request. The problem is that such approach becomes inefficient or unwieldy, especially if:

- Data arrives at a high rate (e.g., streaming updates, large volumes of logs).
- Only some fraction of updates are relevant to the user's current question or context.
- The use cases require us to preserve the conversation flow in a manageable size while still allowing new data to "flow in"

1.1 Problem Statement

Traditional architectures store IoT data in databases and re-prompt LLMs with updated information on each request. This approach leads to issues such as exponential growth of prompt size. For example, when the application appends data from every exchange in the user conversation, the prompt can ultimately become very large. This quickly runs into token limits (especially for GPT-style models). Even if the LLM can handle large contexts, performance and cost can degrade significantly as the conversation gets longer. Another issue is that many "old" messages or irrelevant data might be included in the prompt even if they are not critical for answering the current question. This increases API usage (costs) and can slow down responses. Repetitive retrieval of the entire knowledge base is yet another problem here. When the application has a knowledge base or domain data that is large (e.g., hundreds of pages of documentation or thousands of user records), repeatedly embedding large portions of it in the prompt is not feasible. Even if one does partial retrieval, this approach can still be wasteful. Furthermore, over time, the application logic that decides "which parts of the knowledge base or conversation history to include" becomes complicated, often involving manual heuristics or partial retrieval. Such designs fail to scale. Finally, if new data arrives frequently (e.g., sensor readings, real-time transaction logs, etc.), re-prompting with the entire dataset on every query can be slow or easily exceed context windows.

1.2 Contributions

This paper introduces an architecture that employs:

1. A lightweight timeline to maintain recent, relevant events.
2. An event summarization module that also prioritizes critical data dynamically.
3. A sliding window technique ensuring efficient context management.
4. The proposed approach reduces response time by 15.41% and it generates 65.16% fewer tokens. On average, it uses 5.41% less GPU and consumes 5.13% less CPU.

2 Related Work

We looked at mainly two aspects of existing work related to the design and development of LLM-driven applications: (a) how they addressed performance and cost issues across application domains, and (b) specifically for the IoT domain applications, how are those issues tackled.

In general, it appears (e.g. see [2]) that the design and development of LLM-driven applications is faced with several challenges and one of the chief issues that remains inadequately addressed is performance and cost optimization. Furthermore, the commonly available guidance (e.g., see [1][Ch. 3]) on building LLM-driven applications does not adequately address these challenges either.

Specifically for IoT domain, we note that the current methods often rely on databases for storing IoT data, requiring frequent re-prompting of LLMs. This leads to inefficiencies when handling high-volume or non-essential updates. Recent approaches have explored static prompt templates but lack dynamic context management. A recent example is PestGPT [12] which proposes a framework that integrates IoT and LLMs to provide users with accurate and customised pest management recommendations based on environmental information from edge IoT devices. Similarly, this [11] work aims to create event records from raw sensor readings and merge the logs from multiple IoT sources into a single event log suitable for further Process Mining applications. Another example is ChatIoT [4], a large language model (LLM)-based IoT security assistant that disseminates IoT security and threat intelligence. ChatIoT integrates the advanced language understanding and reasoning capabilities of LLM with fast-evolving IoT security information. We also examined the relevant projects (e.g., [3] [7], etc.) on GitHub that were tagged [5] with 'LLM' to learn how such systems propose to address these issues.

Gaps in Current Designs: Existing solutions can do better to efficiently manage dynamic, real-time data streams and maintain conversation flow effectively. A common feature of these systems is that they treat the LLM almost like a stateless text transformer in the sense that for each user query, the application:

- Collects historical data (conversation logs, domain knowledge, updated events records, etc.) from a database.
- Appends that data (sometimes all of it, sometimes large chunks) to the user's current prompt.
- Sends the combined text to the LLM, which returns a response.

– Stores the new user query and LLM response back into the database thus continuing to grow the history.

This design leads to the problems already discussed in §1.1. Our work addresses these gaps by introducing a lightweight, dynamic approach to event handling.

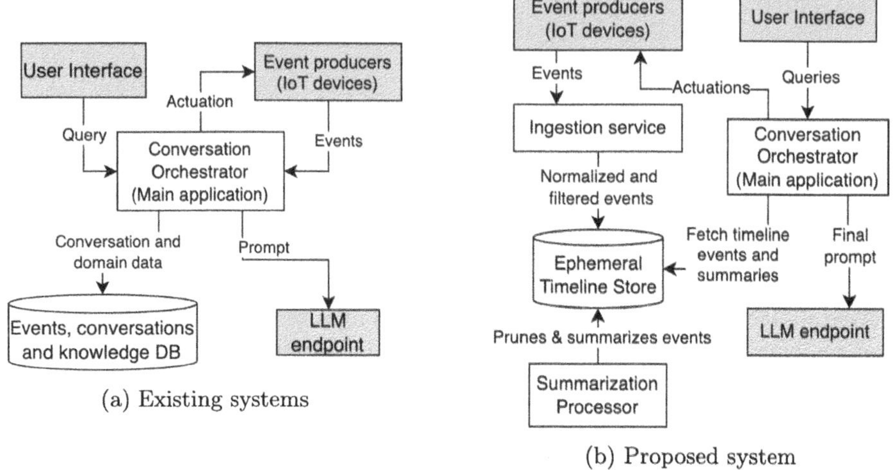

Fig. 1. High-level architectures (The shaded items remain the same in both.)

3 Proposed Architecture

The central ideas in our design are:

1. We maintain an "Ephemeral Timeline" of structured records of small, discrete events or data snippets that accumulate as time progresses. Such records of events look like:
   - `At 10:01AM the humidity sensor in location E543J reported anomalous reading.`
   - `At 11:48PM the door actuator at location in location K721P was overridden manually.`

   These snippets are short, self-contained pieces of information that could be relevant to the conversation or the LLM's reasoning. Each snippet is time-stamped (or versioned) and stored in chronological order.
2. We prune the events based on age and relevance. Each new event can be scored or tagged (e.g., "actuation failure", "sensor anomaly", "policy update"). The system can keep only the top-N most relevant recent events for the user's query or for the general conversation context. Further, the events that are older than a certain threshold (e.g., 24 h) might be compressed or summarized to keep the timeline lightweight. If a new event supersedes an older event (e.g., "Manual ovrride threshold for access control sensors updated"), we mark the older one as outdated or archive it.

As such, the timeline doesn't grow unbounded; it maintains a "sliding window" or "compressed summary" of the most crucial recent data. The important modules of the architecture are shown in Fig. 1b, and described in the following subsections.

3.1 Event Producers

These are mostly IoT devices or systems that generate events or data relevant to the LLM-based application. The examples include: **User actions** such as manual overriding of some actuators; **System actions** such as switching on the lights when occupancy sensor reports presence; **External data feeds** such as energy prices in the market. These producers typically emit small, discrete messages containing: **Timestamp** or other ordering key (e.g., an incrementing sequence number). **Event type** (e.g., "SENSOR_DATA", "USER_ACTION"), and **Payload** (the data relevant to the event).

3.2 Ingestion Service

This module listens to events from all Event Producers and writes them into the Ephemeral Timeline Store (described shortly). It converts raw events into a uniform schema so they can be sorted, filtered, and retrieved easily. It performs filtering and tagging of events. Filtering allows us to discard/deprioritize the events that may be irrelevant to the LLM e.g., a noisy internal system heartbeat. Event tagging allows for partial summarization of events. Also, if events contain PII or restricted data, the ingestion service can redact or anonymize them before storing. Finally, it writes each normalized event into the Ephemeral Timeline Store with the necessary metadata such as timestamp, type, user/session ID, etc.

3.3 Ephemeral Timeline Store (ETS)

This module is the database or data structure that holds the short-lived, time-ordered events that we have discussed above. It indexed the events data by event type and user context for quick filtering. A typical implementation choice is a specialized time-series database such as InfluxDB or TimescaleDB etc. (we used TimescaleDB).

3.4 Summarization and Relevance Processor

This module periodically runs a query on ETS to fetch events older than a certain threshold (e.g., 24 h) or beyond a certain count (e.g., the 100 most recent events). It then summarizes these events using the LLM (one may also use another summarization approach), producing a short textual summary (e.g., *Over the past 24 h, door actuator E4543 has been overridden 4 times, 3 anomalies were detected for temperature sensors, and one policy update.*). This summary is stored back into the timeline in ETS as a single "summary event", while archiving or deleting the raw events. The summary event might look like:

```
{
  "timestamp": 1678889999, "type": "SUMMARY",
  "content": "4 door override actions, 3 anomalies, one
     policy published. Locations involved K781P, T65W2."
}
```


It ensures that critical events (like a brand new policy that's still in effect) remain or are re-injected into the summary if needed.

We note that all events are not of same relevance. Therefore, we incorporate a scoring or classification step for effective event filtering. The key factors influencing IoT event's relevance often include:

- How well the event's data matches the user's recent query history. For example, for a query (at 2:30PM) like "Show me all manual override alerts today" the event "Pump room door lock overridden at 2:15 PM" will have high relevance.
- Contextual relevance inferred from the user's environment and preferences. As an example, a temperature alert might be more relevant if the user recently queried about "HVAC issues".
- Recent events are often more relevant. A water leak alert from 2 min ago is more urgent than one from 5 d ago.
- Criticality or Severity – events classified as urgent, warning, or info can affect their relevance score. That is, a fire alarm should score higher than a routine sensor reading.
- Proximity or importance of the device may affect relevance. For example, "Exhaust pipe clogged" might score higher than "Inspection drone charging complete" if the user is indoors.

Therefore, if an event's relevance score drops below a **threshold** Θ (due to the factors like those mentioned above), the system might skip including it in the prompt. The orchestrator can dynamically recalculate relevance by analyzing the user's current query and the data pertaining to the factors listed above. We would like to note that our emphasis was more on summarization than the relevance scoring in our application. As such, we used a simpler heuristics based relevance scoring function.

Furthermore, summaries can be stored at different levels of detail (e.g., daily, weekly, or per important milestone), and possibly even vectorized for efficient query and comparison etc. (this is our future plan). If an event is crucial (like a manual override of a sensor/actuator), we might keep it in raw form for compliance etc.

3.5 Conversation Orchestrator

It encapsulates the main orchestration logic that constructs prompts for the LLM and returns answers to the user or triggers further actions. Its key steps include:

1. **New Request:** The user or another system triggers a question or command that requires an LLM response.
2. **Fetch from Timeline:** The orchestrator queries the ETS to retrieve the top N recent or relevant events for that user/session/context. Could also filter by event type depending on the question.
3. **Summarize if needed:** If the returned set is too large, the orchestrator might do a quick summary pass. This can either be done by the LLM or a separate summarization step. Note that this summarization is different from the periodic summarization described in §3.4.
4. **Inject into prompt:** The orchestrator appends the curated set of timeline snippets (plus any high-level conversation instructions, user query, etc.) into a single LLM prompt.
5. **LLM call:** Sends the prompt to the LLM endpoint.
6. **Response handling:** Receives the LLM's answer. Optionally logs the result as a new "assistant response" event in the timeline.
7. **Return to user:** Sends the final answer back or triggers next steps.

3.6 Processing Use Case Example

We now show the flow of steps in our system when handling a simple use case of our industrial IoT application which monitors sensors in a factory. The system tracks changes in temperature, vibration, and other readings from various sensors:

1. Event Producer sends an event for Sensor #12 (a temperature sensor):

```
{"type": "SENSOR_READING", "sensor_id": 12, "timestamp
    ": 1678889000, "reading": 82.5, "units": "F"}
```

   Ingestion Service receives this event, normalizes it (if needed), and writes it to the ETS.
2. The same sensor or another sensor might emit a new event:

```
{"type": "SENSOR_READING", "sensor_id": 12, "timestamp
    ": 1678889300, "reading": 90.2, "units": "F"}
```

   The same or possibly a different sensor triggers an alarm:

```
{"type": "ALERT", "sensor_id": 12, "timestamp": 167888
    9400, "alert_level": "HIGH_TEMP"}
```

   Ingestion Service writes each event to the ETS.
3. User submits a question like: *Has Sensor #12 been overheating in the last hour?* Then, the Conversation Orchestrator does the following:
   (a) Identifies which timeline(s) to query (e.g., session_id = "sensor_12").
   (b) Pulls recent events from the ETS (e.g., the last hour's readings plus any relevant summary events).
   (c) Retrieves events like the ones above (SENSOR_READING at 82.5, 90.2, plus an ALERT).

   (d) The orchestrator might further summarize if there are too many readings or if the user's question is high-level.
4. If the timeline has dozens of readings, the orchestrator might do a quick summarization step. It is done by asking the LLM: *Summarize the last hour of temperature readings for Sensor #12.* The system might then produce a short text snippet: *Sensor #12 had readings from 82.5F to 90.2F, triggered a high-temp alert at 1678889400.* The orchestrator either uses that snippet or merges it with the raw event content.
5. The orchestrator constructs the final prompt for the LLM: *Sensor #12 recent timeline: 1) 1678889000, SENSOR_READING, 82.5F 2) 1678889300, SENSOR_READING, 90.2F 3) 1678889400, ALERT, "HIGH_TEMP" User question: "Has Sensor #12 been overheating in the last hour?" Please provide a concise answer and recommended next steps.* The orchestrator calls the LLM API with this prompt.
6. LLM Responds: *Yes, Sensor #12's temperature rose from 82.5F to 90.2F, triggering a high temperature alert at 1678889400. It appears to be overheating. Recommended action: verify cooling system or reduce workload.* The orchestrator may store this assistant answer in the ephemeral timeline as a type: "ASSISTANT_MESSAGE", or in a separate conversation log.

Table 1. Hardware and software details for testbed

Server hardware	NVIDIA Quadro RTX 5000, Intel i9-10900 @2.8GHz 20 Cores, RAM 32GB, 1TB SSD
Server OS	Ubuntu 22.04 LTS
LLM setup	Ollama [9] 0.5.7 with Phi4:latest 14B model [8]
Testing software	Python3, JMeter
Development stack	TimescaleDB, Python3, JMeter

4 Experiments and Results

We implemented our approach and compared it with an implementation of the traditional architecture (source code for both are provided for easily reproducing our results). The architecture of the testbed is shown in Fig. 2 and the details of the hardware and software elements are shown in Table-1.

By setting up both architectures side-by-side and using the same data volume and query patterns, we were able to empirically measure:

1. **Response time differences:** Time from user query until LLM response is fully returned. It is the sum of (data retrieval time) + (prompt construction) + (LLM API latency).

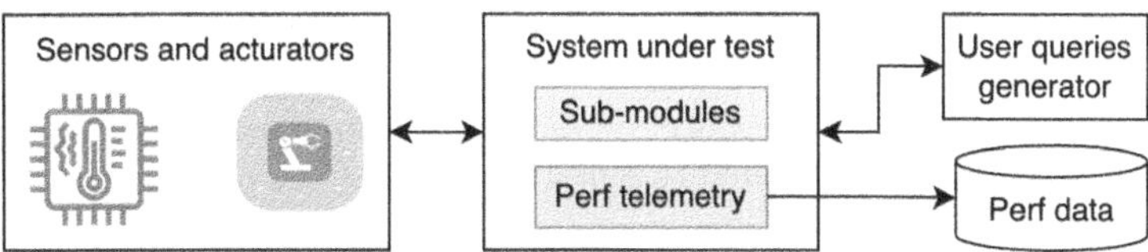

Fig. 2. Testbed setup

2. **Token usage/cost differences:** How many tokens are being sent per request to the LLM. Monitored through LLM logs/stats.
3. **Resource consumption:** The CPU/GPU, IO, memory, etc. usage in the system hosting our implementation.
4. **Correctness w.r.t the baseline:** For a given question, we took the answer produced by traditional approach as the source of truth. Therefore, an important goal for us was to check if the proposed approach produced a divergent answer to the same question.

4.1 Testing Methodology

We evaluated the following performance metrics outlined above. Following are the steps of our test procedure:

Data loading: The data is ingested in two stages: a) When we run a script to add suitable sensors and events data at the time of creating the time series database container,and b) We run our sensor simulator service for the necessary period to populate the DB with sensor events.

Warm-Up Phase: To avoid artificial "Cold Start" bias, we let the ingestion services run for sometime so the state for summaries and pruning is stablized.

Testing: We use a python script to issue a variety of queries (summary, comparison, alert investigation). We use a set of 100 different questions that target a randomly chosen set of sensors in our system. Then we record the metrics mentioned above, and compare the observations for the two approaches.

Answer similarity with baseline: For a given question, the answer produced in case of both traditional (baseline) and the proposed approach is compared for similarity. This was achieved by using the LLM itself. The prompt used for it included: **(a)** the brief about the IoT application, **(b)** the question under consideration, **(c)** summary (generated by the LLM) of each of the two answers, and finally **(d)** a query asking the LLM to give the similarity score for the answers on a scale of 1–10 where 1 indicates totally different and 10 indicates identical.

4.2 Sample Data Generation

Table-2 shows the dataset details for our experiments. It mimics our actual industrial IoT deployment. The schema for the events is Listing-1.1 and alerts

Table 2. Dataset details for experiments

Number of Sensors	1000 sensors of types: temperature sensors, vibration sensors, humidity sensors, etc.
Event Frequency	Each sensor posts a reading once per minute. That is, $1000 \times 60 = 60000$ events/hour
Alert Frequency	Randomly, 5% of readings trigger an "alert event" (like "HIGH_TEMP"), leading to 3000 alerts per hour

is shown in Listing-1.2. We used a data generator script that, for each sensor generates random readings within a plausible range relevant for a sensor (e.g., temperature between 70-90F, with occasional spikes). It injects periodic anomalies or outliers that might trigger an "alert". The events and alerts are supplied to the ingestion service at a rate that mimics real-time streaming.

Code Listing 1.1. Schema for events

```
{
  "sensor_id":   "<string or numeric ID>",
  "timestamp":   "<epoch or ISO8601>",
  "reading":     "<numeric value>",
  "units":       "e.g., C, F, g-force, ...",
  "metadata":    {"... optional fields, e.g. location ..."
      }
}
```

Code Listing 1.2. Schema for alerts

```
{
  "sensor_id":   "<string or numeric ID>",
  "timestamp":   "<epoch or ISO8601>",
  "alert_type":  "HIGH_TEMP | HIGH_VIBRATION | ...",
  "severity":    "CRITICAL | WARNING | ..."
}
```

To measure how each architecture handles typical user queries, we designed mainly three types of questions: **a) Summary Queries** such as: "What happened with Sensor #123 in the last hour? Did it overheat?" **b) Multi-Sensor Comparison** such as: "Which sensors on line A have had the most alerts in the last 24 h?" **c) Alert Investigation** such as: "Sensor #500 triggered a high vibration alert. Show me the last 10 readings and any relevant maintenance records."

These queries simulate a user or operator wanting to see recent data or diagnosing issues. For our experiments we used 100 different questions.

4.3 Results and Discussion

We now analyse and compare the important performance metrics observed for the two approaches. We look at mainly the following four aspects: (a) Compute resource utilization, (b) Response and generation efficiency, (c) Complexity of prompt handling, (d) Cost implications, and (e) Similarity of answer to the baseline truth.

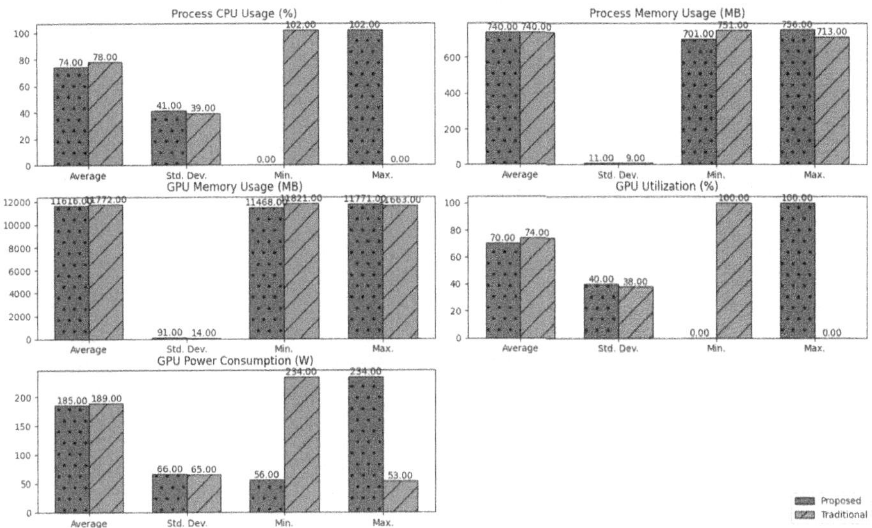

Fig. 3. Server Performance Metrics

Compute Resource Utilization: Observed trends are shown in Fig. 3. CPU Usage: The traditional approach has a slightly higher average CPU usage (78% vs. 74%) but with lower variability, suggesting that it may be using CPU more efficiently. However, higher CPU usage increases costs because CPU time is billed directly. GPU Usage: The traditional approach also consumes more GPU memory (11,772 MB vs. 11,616 MB) and more GPU power (189 W vs. 185 W), indicating higher GPU cost. Higher GPU utilization (74% vs. 70%) means that the traditional approach requires more expensive GPU instances.

Response and Generation Efficiency: Figure 4 shows the trends observed in our experiments. Response Size: Traditional approach generates significantly more tokens per response (7835 vs. 2730), which means more processing per request – driving up token-based costs (common in LLM billing models). The proposed approach produces smaller responses, which will reduce per-token costs if billing is based on token output. Response Time: Traditional approach takes longer to generate responses (10.71s vs. 9.06s), which means higher compute time per request. The proposed approach processes more requests in the same time frame, leading to better throughput and lower operational costs.

Complexity of Prompt Handling: Prompt Evaluation: Traditional approach ends up processing much more complex prompts (1603 prompt evaluations vs. 203), suggesting that it is generating more complex prompts for the same user query, and thus also resulting in greater compute demand. The higher prompt evaluation time for the traditional approach (1.56s vs. 0.08s) increases overall processing time and costs. Given that query complexity remains consistent, the proposed approach is cheaper since it results in simpler final prompts for the same user query and handles it more efficiently.

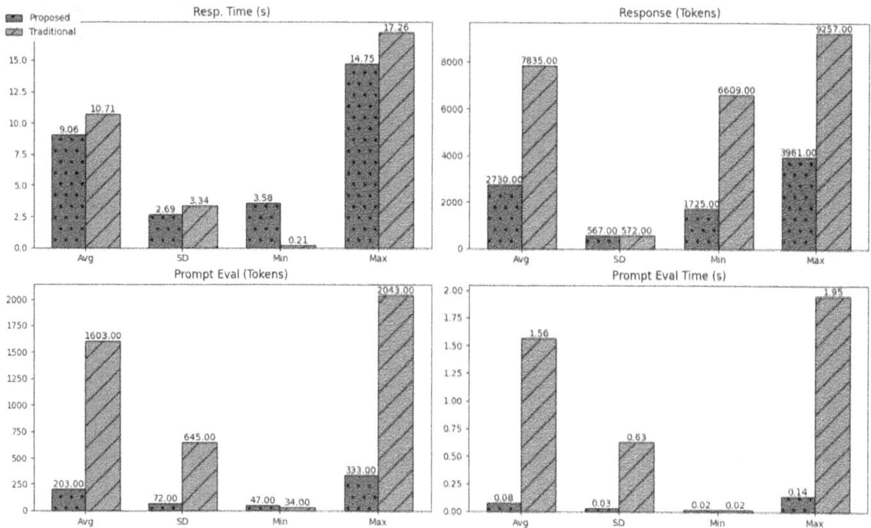

Fig. 4. LLM Performance Metrics.(SD=Standard Deviation, Avg.=Average)

Billing Implications: Since the billing is often based on the number of input and output tokens, the proposed approach will be significantly cheaper due to its smaller token count. Compute-Based Costs: The proposed approach's faster processing and smaller token counts translates to lower costs, especially in environments with per-second billing for GPU/CPU time. For the proposed approach, Response Time is 15.41% faster, it generates 65.16% fewer tokens, which reduces token-based costs significantly. On average, it uses 5.41% less GPU and consumes 5.13% less CPU.

Overall, we notice there is not a huge difference ($\approx 5\%$) from server resource consumption perspective. However, the real significant benefit of our approach is in the response generation ($\approx 15\%$ faster) and prompt handling ($\approx 65\%$ lower) related costs.

To estimate real-world savings, we can define a typical usage scenario by assuming: a) Request volume to be 1 million requests per month for the IoT system, and b) Token-based billing at \$0.002 per 1,000 tokens (OpenAI's GPT-4 Turbo rate [10] as a reference, as of Feb 2025. Google Gemini would be similar [6]).

Since our approach reduces average token count by 65.16%, and average token count per request with traditional approach to be 7835 (assuming similar scenario as our experiments), the savings attributed only to the tokens cost would be: $7835 - 7835 \times (1 - 0.6516) \approx 5105$ tokens/request, giving a total monthly savings of $\frac{5105}{1,000} \times 0.002 \times 1000,000 = 10210$ USD.

Answer Similarity to Baseline: The approach we used for measuring this aspect has already been discussed in §4.1. We did not find any surprises here. As expected, we did not find any question for which the two approached produced completely divergent or identical answers. The minimum score was roughly 5, average score was 6.97 and maximum was 8.9 with standard deviation of roughly 1.3.

5 Conclusions

The proposed architecture significantly enhances the efficiency of LLM-driven IoT applications by addressing key challenges associated with real-time data processing. By implementing a lightweight, time-ordered queue system and an event relevance scoring module, our approach ensures that only pertinent information is processed at each step. This results in faster response times (15.41% improvement), reduced token generation (65.16% fewer tokens), and lower resource consumption (5.41% less GPU and 5.13% less CPU usage). These optimizations streamline the processing of high-rate data streams and also maintain conversational flow without overwhelming system resources. It demonstrates an improved performance over traditional architectures in managing dynamically evolving IoT data. The findings underscore the potential for the proposed architecture to be adopted in LLM-driven applications that are similar to the one considered in our work, leading to more efficient and cost-effective solutions. In a practical scenario with 1 million requests per month and token-based billing at \$0.002 per 1,000 tokens, the proposed approach offers substantial savings of approximately \$10,210 monthly in token-related costs alone.

Data Availability. To allow reproducing the results that we have presented in this paper, we have shared the relevant artifacts for our experimental setup. It can be accessed at the following link: https://bit.ly/3FmIZ0u. You will find there a README.md file containing the instructions for how to use the artifacts.

References

1. Auffarth, B.: Generative AI with LangChain: Build large language model (LLM) apps with Python, ChatGPT, and other LLMs. Packt Publishing Ltd. (2023)
2. Chen, X., Gao, C., Chen, C., Zhang, G., Liu, Y.: An empirical study on challenges for LLM application developers. ACM Trans. Softw. Eng. Methodol. (2025). https://doi.org/10.1145/3715007
3. Dify AI: Dify – an open-source LLM app development platform (2025). https://github.com/langgenius/dify, Retrieved 3 Oct 2025
4. Dong, Y., Aung, Y.L., Chattopadhyay, S., Zhou, J.: ChatIoT: Large language model-based security assistant for internet of things with retrieval-augmented generation arXiv:2502.09896 (2025)
5. GitHub Website: Public repositories tagged LLM on github (2025). https://github.com/topics/llm?o=desc&s=stars, Retrieved 3 Oct 2025
6. Google: Gemini developer api pricing (2025). https://ai.google.dev/gemini-api/docs/pricing, Retrieved 3 Oct 2025
7. MetaGPT: Metagpt – an open-source multi-agent framework (2025). https://github.com/geekan/MetaGPT, Retrieved 3 Oct 2025
8. Microsoft: Phi-4: A 14b parameter, state-of-the-art open model from microsoft. (2025). https://ollama.com/library/phi4, Retrieved 3 Oct 2025
9. Ollama Project: Get up and running with llama 3.3, deepseek-r1, phi-4, gemma 3, and other large language models (2025). https://github.com/ollama/ollama. Retrieved 3 Oct 2025
10. OpenAI Inc.: OpenAI API princing (2025). https://openai.com/api/pricing/, Retrieved 3 Oct 2025
11. Shirali, M., Sani, M.F., Ahmadi, Z., Serral, E.: LLM-based event abstraction and integration for IoT-sourced logs arxiv:2409.03478 (2024)
12. Yuan, Z., et al.: PestGPT: leveraging large language models and IoT for timely and customized recommendation generation in sustainable pest management. IEEE Internet of Things Mag. **8**(1), 26–33 (2025). https://doi.org/10.1109/IOTM.001.2400036

Automated Software Architecture Design Recovery from Source Code Using LLMs

Domenico Amalfitano[2], Marco De Luca[2](✉), Tiziano Santilli[1], Patrizio Pelliccione[1], and Anna Rita Fasolino[2]

[1] Gran Sasso Science Institute, L'Aquila, Italy
{tiziano.santilli,patrizio.pelliccione}@gssi.it
[2] University of Naples "Federico II", Naples, Italy
{domenico.amalfitano,marco.deluca2,fasolino}@unina.it

Abstract. Recent advancements in Large Language Models (LLMs) offer promising opportunities for automating software architecture recovery (SAR). In this study, we assess the effectiveness of state-of-the-art general-purpose LLMs when used as off-the-shelf tools by practitioners seeking architectural insights from source code. We evaluate four models across three key tasks: (i) identifying implementation-level class diagrams, (ii) identifying architectural and design patterns, and (iii) identifying architectural styles. The experiment adopts a realistic usage setting, combining prompt engineering with a Self-Reflection mechanism to simulate how users iteratively refine queries. Results show that LLMs can support SAR activities, particularly in identifying structural and stylistic elements, but they struggle with complex abstractions such as class relationships and fine-grained design patterns. In addition to performance evaluation, we analyze the types of errors made by the models and assess the impact of Self-Reflection in refining their outputs, offering deeper insights into LLM behavior and highlighting implications for future research and practice.

Keywords: Software Architecture · Large Language Models · Architecture Recovery · Prompt Engineering

1 Introduction

The importance of software architecture has long been recognized [30], including in agile development contexts [3,26]. Architecture spans the entire development process [32,33], with some decisions made upfront and others emerging incrementally. To capture these evolving aspects, architecture documentation must be continuously updated. However, inconsistencies between documentation and implementation remain common [33], often leading to architecture erosion [2,27], drift [18], or architectural debt [17]. Maintaining up-to-date architecture documentation is critical for system quality and maintainability, yet it is often

V. Andrikopoulos et al. (Eds.): ECSA 2025, LNCS 15929, pp. 73–89, 2026.
https://doi.org/10.1007/978-3-032-02138-0_5

neglectedespecially in iterative and legacy systems. Descriptive architectural elements [9,13] can be partially recovered from source code, but the process remains largely manual and time-consuming.

Recent advances in Large Language Models (LLMs) open new possibilities for automating architectural recovery. Trained on large volumes of software-related data, LLMs show potential in extracting architectural knowledge directly from source code, thus helping bridge the gap between implementation and documentation. Architecture design relies on well-known abstractionsarchitectural styles, architectural patterns, and design patterns [7,11]which can serve as reference points in this recovery process.

This work evaluates the effectiveness of LLMs in addressing three architecture recovery tasks, each focusing on a different architectural perspective:

- *Task 1* (T1): identifying implementation-level class diagrams from Java source code;
- *Task 2* (T2): identifying architectural and design patterns from Java projects;
- *Task 3* (T3): identifying architectural styles from the source code of different software architectures.

Task 1 focuses on recovering class diagrams, which serve as the structural foundation of a system. While often considered low-level, they support architectural reasoning by capturing key components, relationships, and modular decompositions [11,23,31]. In this study, Task 1 complements Task 2 and Task 3 to provide a multi-layered evaluation of LLM capabilities in architecture recovery.

To systematically assess LLM performance, we define a Research Question (RQ) for each task:

- *RQ1*: To what extent can LLMs identify detailed code-level class diagrams from source code?
- *RQ2*: To what extent can LLMs identify architectural and design patterns from source code?
- *RQ3*: To what extent can LLMs identify architectural styles from source code?

Our approach combines prompt engineering with a Self-Reflection mechanism, where LLMs are asked to reassess and refine their initial outputs. While results demonstrate that LLMs can support software architects in code analysis, they also highlight limitations in abstraction and consistency. Nevertheless, this study contributes to understanding how LLMs can be leveraged in architecture recovery, laying the groundwork for future developments.

The paper is structured as follows: Sect. 2 introduces related work, Sect. 3 describes the research methodology, Sect. 4 presents the results and addresses the research questions, Sect. 5 discusses further findings and implications, Sect. 6 outlines threats to validity, and Sect. 7 concludes the paper and outlines future research directions.

2 Related Work

This section presents related work on Large Language Models (LLMs) in software engineering tasks and their emerging application to software architecture recovery (SAR).

Large Language Models (LLMs) have significantly advanced both natural language processing and software engineering tasks, owing to their ability to understand and generate human-readable content. Recent work highlights their strong performance in code generation and bug detection [14,15]. Studies have also shown that, when guided by well-designed prompts, LLMs can support more specialized tasks, including design pattern identification and class diagram generation [29]. Prompt-based learning has thus emerged as a key paradigm, enabling models to adapt to new tasks by reformulating them as textual instructions. The effectiveness of this approach heavily relies on prompt engineering, which involves designing structured input prompts to guide LLM behavior. A recent contribution in this space is a taxonomy of prompt engineering techniques organized by application domain, offering a framework for adapting prompts to diverse software engineering contexts [21].

In software architecture recovery (SAR), prior research has addressed the challenge of reconstructing a systems architecture from source code, often through the analysis of components, their interactions, and recurring organizational patterns [10]. This process is especially critical in the case of architectural erosion, decay, or drift, where systems diverge from their intended design over time [2,18]. While prior work has demonstrated the usefulness of LLMs in code summarization, repair, and even high-level architecture comprehension from textual descriptions [4,12,34], their application to direct extraction of architectural artifacts from source code remains underexplored. Early findings suggest that while LLMs show promise, they also face limitations in tasks that require accurate structural modeling, such as generating UML diagrams or identifying non-trivial design patterns [6].

This study builds on these previous efforts by evaluating how general-purpose LLMs perform on three representative SAR tasks: recovering class diagrams, identifying architectural and design patterns, and retrieving architectural styles. In doing so, it expands the understanding of LLM capabilities in architecture recovery and offers insights into their potential integration into software engineering workflows.

3 Research Methodology

In this section, we describe the methodology used in this study. Specifically, we present the evaluation metrics, selected models, study objects, experimental procedure, and validation approach.

Metrics. To evaluate the correctness of LLM-generated output we refer, for each task, to a different Ground-Truth (GT) and count the following type of errors, each one designed to capture a distinct kind of discrepancy concerning the GT:

- *Hallucination*: number of elements identified by the LLM that are not present in the GT.
- *Mistake*: number of elements incorrectly identified by the LLM with respect to the GT.
- *Missing*: number of elements not identified by LLM that are present in the GT.

LLMs Selection. We evaluated four widely adopted LLMs: GPT-4o, Gemini 1.5 Pro, Claude 3.5 Sonnet, and Mistral Large, hereafter referred to as ChatGPT, Gemini, Claude, and Mistral [1,8]. These models were selected based on their state-of-the-art performance in code understanding and generation [22,25], their availability through web-based interfaces, and their representation of diverse architectures and providers. By focusing on general-purpose, commercially available LLMs, we aimed to simulate real-world usage conditions and provide a balanced assessment of their capabilities in recovering architectural knowledge from source code, without relying on domain-specific fine-tuning or proprietary integrations.

We excluded Copilot due to its tight integration with Microsoft tools and overlap with GPT-4. Additionally, we excluded Llama from our study due to accessibility constraints, as it was not available in our country at the time of the experiment[1]. We are also aware of tailored LLMs, such as ReVa[2] and ReverserAI[3], but we excluded them from our study. In particular, ReVa was excluded because it is based on the GPT-4o model, which is already included in our evaluation, while ReverserAI was excluded as it is still in beta and not yet suitable for practical use.

Objects Selection. In the following, we present the objects used in our empirical comparison and their selection criteria. We chose the objects separately for each task. Table 1 provides an overview of the size and characteristics of each object, detailing the samples used in the analysis.

T1 Sample Definition. For T1, we adopted a convenience sampling strategy, selecting Java projects developed by students as part of an Object-Oriented Programming course taught by one of the authors at the University of Naples "Federico II". This choice ensured direct access to the source code and ground truth class diagrams. As shown in Table 1, these projects are relatively small, averaging six classes and around 350 lines of code (LOC), making them suitable for evaluating LLMs in a controlled, educational setting.

T2 Sample Definition. For T2, we assembled a diverse set of real-world Java projects containing architectural and design patterns. We filtered GitHub repositories by language (Java) and randomly selected 30 repositories. Two authors manually reviewed them, retaining only those with fewer than 1,000 LOC. This

[1] Experiments were conducted in November 2024.

[2] ReVa: https://github.com/cyberkaida/reverse-engineering-assistant.

[3] ReverseAI: https://github.com/mrphrazer/reverser_ai.

Table 1. Characterization of the samples used in the experiment

Task 1				Task 2				Task 3			
ID	#LOC	#Class	#Package	ID	#LOC	#Class	#Package	ID	#LOC	#Files	Language
T1C1	339	6	1	T2C1	122	5	4	T3C1	242	10	java
T1C2	229	6	1	T2C2	176	6	4	T3C2	325	14	java
T1C3	414	6	1	T2C3	173	4	4	T3C3	87	4	java
T1C4	390	6	1	T2C4	112	4	4	T3C4	533	18	python
T1C5	434	9	1	T2C5	482	11	9	T3C5	166	3	javascript
T1C6	388	8	1	T2C6	546	16	4	T3C6	434	11	javascript
				T2C7	336	8	5	T3C7	600	22	python, solidity
				T2C8	213	4	7	T3C8	36	1	python
								T3C9	651	1	python
								T3C10	552	7	kotlin
								T3C11	292	5	go, shell
								T3C12	758	5	shell, python
								T3C13	491	6	python

constraint was adopted following preliminary tests indicating that Claude has stricter input size limits compared to other models[4]. To ensure comparability across all LLMs under the same input conditions, we applied this threshold uniformly. The final set includes projects ranging from 112 to 546 LOC, typically distributed across multiple packages. This selection provides a realistic but manageable testbed for evaluating LLM performance in pattern recognition.

T3 Sample Definition. For T3, we again used convenience sampling, leveraging the dataset provided by *Migliorini et al.* [24], which includes open-source projects that were manually labeled by the authors with their corresponding architectural styles. These curated labels made the dataset well-suited for evaluating LLMs in the context of architectural style inference. From this dataset, we selected a subset of repositories with fewer than 1,000 LOC to comply with LLM input limits. Unlike T1 and T2, this task includes multi-language projects. As summarized in Table 1, the selected samples span Java, Python, JavaScript, Go, and Kotlin. We characterized each object by the number of files, total LOC, and programming language to reflect the diversity and structure of real-world software architectures.

Ground-Truth Definition. For each task, we constructed a dedicated ground truth (GT) to serve as a reference for evaluating the LLM-generated outputs during the validation phase.

T1 GT Definition. For T1, the GT consisted of class diagrams corresponding to the Java code used as objects in this task. These diagrams represented the intended design of each project and were originally provided by the course teacher as reference solutions for the students' exam implementations.

T2 GT Definition. For T2, we constructed the GT manually by analyzing the source code of the selected GitHub repositories. Two authors independently

4 https://support.anthropic.com/en/articles/7996848-how-large-is-claude-s-context-window.

reviewed the code to identify design patterns (e.g., Singleton, Observer, Factory) and architectural patterns (e.g., Model-View-Controller, Layered Architecture). A third author cross-validated their findings and resolved any discrepancies to ensure consistency. The final GT was a curated list of design and architectural patterns identified in each repository.

T3 GT Definition. For T3, we used as a starting point the architectural style labels provided in the dataset by *Migliorini et al.* [24], where each repository was categorized based on its documented architecture (e.g., Client-Server, Event-Driven, Microservices, SOA). Since such documentation may be outdated or incomplete, two authors independently analyzed the source code to validate and possibly extend the initial labels. A third author then reviewed their annotations to ensure consistency. The final GT consisted of an updated list of architectural styles assigned to each repository.

3.1 The Experimental Process

Our experimental process systematically evaluates the ability of LLMs to extract architectural information from source code across the three defined *architecture recovery tasks* (T1, T2, and T3). Each step is aligned with a specific *Research Question (RQ)* to ensure accurate, complete, and unbiased results. We followed an iterative *LLM Prompt Execution* strategy, where each model was prompted in two steps to refine its understanding of the software architecture.

The experimental dataset was selected based on the specific needs of each task, ensuring structural and conceptual diversity. Each LLM was given code under controlled conditions to ensure consistency across models. The process began with an initial task-specific prompt (*Prompt 1*): for *T1 (RQ1)*, we asked LLMs to generate a class diagram from the code; for *T2 (RQ2)*, to identify architectural and design patterns within the code; and for *T3 (RQ3)*, to determine the architectural style from the code. The output was labeled *"Architectural Design Insights"* as the models first attempt.

A second prompt (*Prompt 2*) was then issued to encourage self-assessment and refinement. Early experiments showed that a single prompt often led to incomplete results, while a self-reflective follow-up produced more accurate and detailed outputs. The revised output was labeled *"Refined Architectural Design Insights"*, reflecting the improvement. This iterative prompting is inspired by Self-Reflection techniques [28], echoing how developers refine architectural understanding through iteration.

Since LLMs retain conversational memory, we processed each sample in isolation: starting a new session, clearing context, and resetting the browser cache. This ensured that each interaction was independent, avoiding any influence from previous prompts and improving reliability. To replicate real-world usage, we interacted with the web-based versions of each LLM. This allowed us to evaluate the latest model versions and reflect actual developer workflows.

Prompt 1 Definition (Task-Specific Queries). Preliminary testing revealed that basic queries often led to incomplete or generic responses, lacking the level of detail needed for architectural analysis. To improve accuracy and completeness, we crafted *Prompt 1* using three complementary prompting strategies: Role Prompting, Zero-shot Prompting, and Emotion Prompting. Role Prompting assigns a professional identity to the LLM (e.g., *"Act as an expert software architect"*) to shape its perspective [16]. Zero-shot Prompting assesses the models ability to perform the task without prior examples or templates [20]; in our setup, LLMs received only the code and the prompt, simulating a realistic zero-shot scenario. Emotion Prompting introduces emphatic cues (e.g., *"It is crucial"*) to highlight the importance of completeness and encourage more structured output [19]. Each version of *Prompt 1* was tailored to its respective task and is reported below, with Role Prompting and Emotion Prompting highlighted.

> ***Prompt 1 for T1:*** Act as an expert software architect. *I will provide you with a Java code snippet. Your task is to analyze the code and provide me a class diagram in PlantUML code with the following details: Classes, including their names, attributes, and methods (distinguishing between public and private members); Relationships between classes, including Relationship type, role multiplicity, role navigation, and role name.* It is crucial *that you base your analysis strictly on the code provided, without making any assumptions or inferences beyond what is explicitly present.* Please *ensure maximum completeness in your reconstruction.*

Prompt 2 Definition (Self-reflection Mechanism). To further improve response completeness, we introduced a second prompt based on the Self-Reflection technique [28], where we asked the LLM to evaluate the correctness of its previous answer. This approach has been shown to enhance reasoning by encouraging the model to revisit and revise its initial output. Our *Prompt 2* was intentionally concise to maintain generality across tasks and was applied uniformly after each *Prompt 1* to promote consistency in evaluation. The prompt is shown below:

> ***Prompt 2:*** *Are you sure you correctly identified the information I requested in the provided code?*

Prompt Development and Refinement.

Prompt 1 and *Prompt 2* were developed through an *iterative refinement process* to ensure clarity, completeness, and effectiveness in guiding LLMs to extract architectural information. Instead of defining the prompts arbitrarily, we employed a three-step structured evaluation approach:

Parallel Testing Across Multiple LLMs. We initially tested candidate prompts on all four models (e.g., GPT-4o, Gemini 1.5 Pro, Claude 3.5 Sonnet, Mistral Large) to observe how each responded. This allowed us to observe *how different architectures responded* to the same queries, identifying common issues such as incomplete answers, overgeneralization, or hallucinations.

Iterative Refinement. Refinements were carried out on a separate set of representative code samples, distinct from the final experimental dataset. We refined the prompts to improve specificity, *reduce ambiguity*, and ensure *consistency across models.* Prompts were tuned to emphasize structural details, recurring patterns, and high-level styles, with constraints like *"Do not infer beyond the provided code"*. While this generally improved response quality, in some cases, excessive detail led to hallucinations or misinterpretations, highlighting the trade-off between precision and overfitting.

Final Standardization. Once a set of prompts produced *consistently high-quality responses* across all LLMs, we adopted them for the experiments. This methodology ensured that the prompts were *not optimized for a single LLM*, preventing bias toward a specific models response behavior. By refining the prompts iteratively across multiple LLMs and using a controlled but independent dataset, we ensured a fair comparison of their performance without inadvertently favoring one over the others.

3.2 Validation

To evaluate the performance of LLMs across the three recovery tasks, we compared their outputs against task-specific Ground Truths (GTs), identifying and quantifying errors as defined in Sect. 3. Validation was conducted in two stages: two authors independently classified discrepancies in the LLM-generated outputs, followed by a third author who reviewed and resolved any conflicts to ensure consistency and accuracy.

For T1, validation focused on core elements of class diagrams, including classes, relationships, inheritance, and associations [5]. We labeled errors as hallucinations (nonexistent elements), mistakes (naming or semantic issues), and missing elements (omitted elements present in the GT). In T2, we classified discrepancies as missing elements when architectural or design patterns were not recognized, hallucinations when patterns were detected but absent in the GT, and mistakes when an architectural pattern was incorrectly labeled as a design pattern or vice versa. For T3, we applied the same classification: missing for undetected architectural styles, hallucinations for styles not present in the GT, and mistakes for incorrect style labeling.

4 Results of the Empirical Comparison

In this section, we present and discuss the results of our study on using LLMs to recover software architectural artifacts from source code, providing evidence for answering the research questions of our experiment. All raw experimental data, as well as their aggregation and analysis, are provided as supplemental material at this link[5].

RQ1: To what extent can LLMs correctly identify detailed code-level class diagrams from source code? Fig. 1 shows the distribution of total errors made by the four LLMs in recovering class and relationship information. A closer look at class-level errors revealed frequent omissions or misrepresentations of nested classes, and difficulties distinguishing abstract classes or interfaces, which were often treated as regular classes. LLMs also tended to

[5] Supplemental Material: https://tinyurl.com/4cy9s9nt.

omit methods in classes with many methods, likely due to output length constraints or simplification heuristics. In relationship recovery, all LLMs struggled to capture correct semantics, particularly with nested or complex associations. Common issues included missing role multiplicity, role names, and navigability detailskey aspects of accurately modeling associations. In some cases, aggregation was incorrectly shown on both sides of a relationship, indicating further confusion in relationship semantics. Overall, LLMs showed better performance in identifying individual class details (e.g., names, attributes, methods) than in capturing inter-class relationships like inheritance and associations. Among the evaluated models, Gemini and Mistral performed best, with Gemini achieving the lowest total error count across both class and relationship recovery. *In response to RQ1, LLMs demonstrate a reasonable ability to identify structural elements such as classes and their members, especially in simpler codebases. However, they often struggle with accurately identifying relationships between classessuch as inheritance or aggregationhighlighting limitations in understanding the overall class structure and interdependencies.*

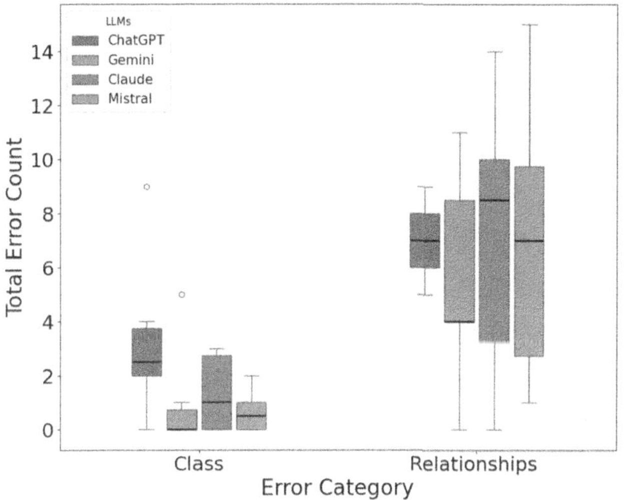

Fig. 1. Boxplot of Class and Relationship Errors in T1 for each LLM

RQ2: To What Extent can LLMs Correctly Identify Architectural and Design Patterns from Source code? Fig. 2 shows the box-plots of the number of errors made by the four LLMs when identifying architectural and design patterns. LLMs generally performed better on architectural patterns than on design patterns. Architectural patterns such as *MVC* and *Layered* were identified with relatively few errors, particularly by Claude and Mistral. However, some models struggled to detect more nuanced patterns like *Repository*, suggesting that certain architectural concepts remain challenging to interpret. Design pattern recognition proved more difficult. While patterns such as *DAO*, *Singleton*, *Factory Method*, and *Dependency Injection* were often correctly identified, others like *DTO* and *Observer* were frequently missed or misclassified. In this task, ChatGPT and Mistral showed the most consistent results, outperforming the other models. *Regarding RQ2, LLMs exhibit solid performance in identifying common architectural patterns, benefiting from their familiarity with recurring high-level structures. In contrast, their effectiveness declines when recognizing design patterns, which require a more nuanced and implementation-aware analysis of class responsibilities and interactions.*

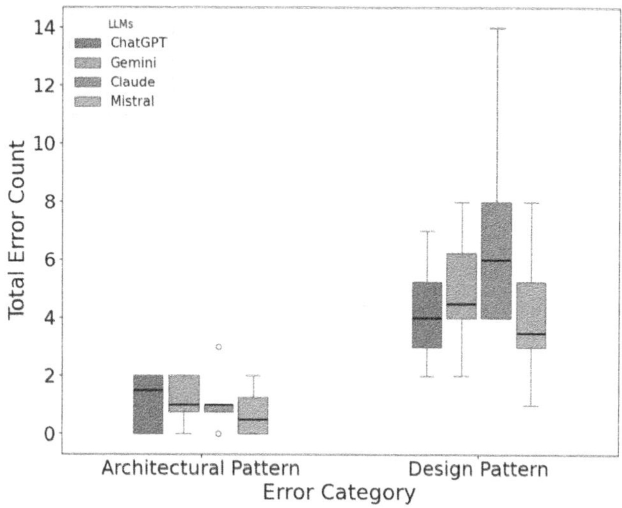

Fig. 2. Boxplot of Architectural and Design Pattern errors in T2 for each LLM

RQ3: To What Extent can LLMs Correctly Identify Architectural Styles from Source Code? The boxplot in Fig. 3 illustrates the total number of errors made by the four LLMs in identifying architectural styles, enabling a direct comparison between models. Analysis shows that all models were generally able to recognize widely adopted styles such as *Client-Server*, *SOA*, and *Microservices*. In contrast, they encountered difficulties with less conventional styles, particularly *Publish-Subscriber*, which were often misclassified or missed altogether. Among the models, Mistral exhibited the highest accuracy and most consistent behavior, reporting the fewest errors. Claude achieved similar median results but showed greater variability, indicating occasional inconsistencies in its outputs. *As for RQ3, LLMs show consistent reliability in identifying architectural styles, particularly when those styles follow well-known conventions. Their performance, however, tends to decrease in the presence of abstract or less explicitly defined styles, indicating the need for improved handling of edge cases and non-standard architectural configurations.*

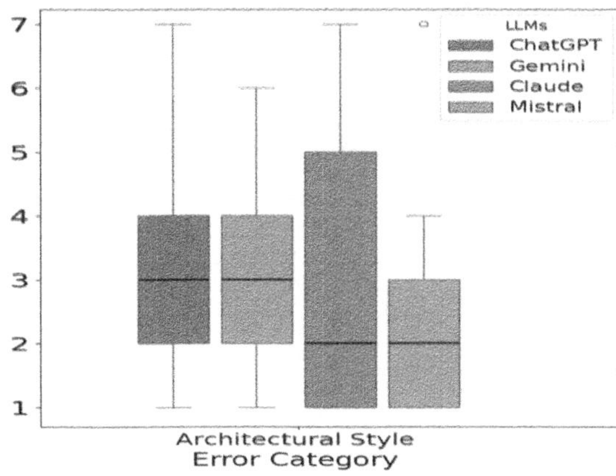

Fig. 3. Boxplot of Architectural Style errors in T3 for each LLM

5 Further Discussion

This section expands on the results of the experiment by analyzing the types of errors observed across the three recovery tasks and discussing the role of Self-Reflection prompts in improving LLM performance. We also reflect on the broader implications of these findings for software architecture recovery research and practice.

Error Type Analysis. The types of errors produced by LLMs across the three architecture recovery tasks were analyzed and categorized into three types presented in Sect. 3, i.e., *Missing* (key information omitted), *Mistake* (misinterpretation of the input), and *Hallucination* (generation of non-existent information). Table 2 summarizes the frequency of each error type across the evaluated tasks and models. Overall, *Missing* errors were the most frequent, especially in tasks requiring the identification of structured elements such as class relationships or complete pattern instances. These errors often involved omitted return types, visibility modifiers, or inheritance relations. *Mistake* errors, while less common, occurred primarily in tasks requiring semantic interpretation, such as distinguishing architectural from design patterns. *Hallucination* errors were relatively rare in structural recovery (T1), but more evident in pattern and style recognition (T2 and T3), where models sometimes generated concepts not present in the code. The quantitative data confirms that error distribution is influenced both by task complexity and by the type of abstraction required. While syntactic-level elements are often handled with moderate reliability, higher-level reasoning continues to pose a challenge for general-purpose LLMs.

Self-reflection Prompts on LLM Outputs. The impact of Self-Reflection (*Prompt 2*) on LLM performance in architectural recovery was also examined, focusing on its ability to reduce errors and refine the quality of the generated architectural outputs. Table 3 compares total errors made using *Prompt 1*

Table 2. Total Errors Count divided per type. **Legenda:** C: Class, R: Relationship, DP: Design Pattern, AP: Architectural Pattern, AS: Architectural Style

		LLM	Missing				Hallucination				Mistake			
			Avg	Std	Min	Max	Avg	Std	Min	Max	Avg	Std	Min	Max
Task 1	C	ChatGPT	2,33	2,66	0	7	0,00	0,00	0	0	1,00	0,89	0	2
		Gemini	0,17	0,41	0	1	0,00	0,00	0	0	0,83	1,60	0	4
		Claude	0,17	0,41	0	1	0,00	0,00	0	0	1,17	1,33	0	3
		Mistral	0,50	0,55	0	1	0,17	0,41	0	1	0,00	0,00	0	0
	R	ChatGPT	3,17	1,47	2	6	0,17	0,41	0	1	3,67	2,25	2	7
		Gemini	3,30	3,20	0	9	0,33	0,82	0	2	1,83	1,60	0	4
		Claude	5,17	4,17	0	11	0,33	0,52	0	1	1,67	1,37	0	3
		Mistral	5,17	3,19	1	9	0,00	0,00	0	0	1,83	3,54	0	9
Task 2	DP	ChatGPT	2,25	1,00	1	4	1,88	1,36	0	4	0,13	0,35	0	1
		Gemini	4,13	1,80	2	8	0,88	0,83	0	2	0,13	0,35	0	1
		Claude	2,25	1,00	1	4	4,50	4,20	1	12	0,13	0,35	0	1
		Mistral	2,25	1,59	0	5	1,88	1,36	1	5	0,00	0,00	0	0
	AP	ChatGPT	0,63	0,74	0	2	0,38	0,52	0	1	0,13	0,35	0	1
		Gemini	1,00	0,76	0	2	0,13	0,35	0	1	0,00	0,00	0	0
		Claude	0,63	0,74	0	2	0,38	0,52	0	1	0,00	0,00	0	0
		Mistral	0,63	0,74	0	2	0,13	0,35	0	1	0,00	0,00	0	0
Task 3	AS	ChatGPT	1,00	0,91	0	3	1,39	1,44	0	4	0,70	0,85	0	3
		Gemini	0,85	0,55	0	2	1,00	1,63	0	5	1,15	0,90	0	3
		Claude	1,15	0,55	0	2	0,77	1,70	0	6	1,15	1,57	0	4
		Mistral	0,92	1,03	0	3	0,46	0,78	0	2	1,23	1,17	0	4

(#EP1) and *Prompt 2* (#EP2), with $\Delta = \#EP1 - \#EP2$ indicating improvement (higher values mean fewer errors with *Prompt 2*). Overall, *Prompt 2* reduced errors in complex tasks like relationship recovery in T1 (e.g., ChatGPT: $\Delta = +15$) and architectural style identification in T3 (e.g., Claude: $\Delta = +33$), showing the value of Self-Reflection in refining outputs.

Table 3. Differences of the Total Error Count between Prompt 1 and Prompt 2. **Legenda:** C: Class, R: Relationship, DP: Design Pattern, AP: Architectural Pattern, AS: Architectural Style, CG: ChatGTP, G: Gemini, CL: Claude, M: Mistral

	Task 1								Task 2								Task 3			
	C				R				DP				AP				AS			
LLM	CG	G	CL	M	CG	G	CL	M	CG	G	CL	M	CG	G	CL	M	CG	G	CL	M
#EP1	24	14	9	7	57	37	39	43	33	40	60	35	8	9	7	7	41	35	73	40
#EP2	20	6	8	4	42	33	43	42	34	40	56	33	9	9	8	6	40	39	40	34
Δ	+4	+8	+1	+3	+15	+4	-4	+1	-1	0	+4	+2	-1	0	-1	+1	+1	-4	+33	+6

In T1, all models improved in class recovery, with Gemini achieving the largest gain ($\Delta = +8$). Relationship recovery also improved, except for Claude, which showed a slight increase ($\Delta = -4$), indicating variability in model behavior. For T2, improvements were minimal. Some models even performed worse in architectural pattern recognition (e.g., ChatGPT and Claude: $\Delta = -1$), suggesting Self-Reflection has limited benefit for identifying nuanced patterns.

Gemini, for instance, showed no change in design pattern errors. In T3, Self-Reflection proved highly effective, especially for Claude, which showed the largest overall errors reduction. This suggests that high-level, standardized concepts like architectural styles benefit most from reflective refinement. In summary, Self-Reflection helps reduce errors in tasks involving structural and conceptual abstractions (T1 and T3), but offers limited value in tasks requiring fine-grained pattern recognition (T2). It holds promise for improving LLM-driven architecture recovery, particularly at higher levels of abstraction.

Implications for Software Architecture Recovery Research and Practice. This study provides several key takeaways for researchers and practitioners in software architecture. From a research perspective, our results demonstrate that general-purpose LLMs, even without domain-specific training, can recover elements of architectural knowledge across various abstraction levels. However, the performance variation across tasks reveals limitations in abstraction, consistency, and contextual understanding. These findings highlight opportunities for future research, such as combining LLMs with static or dynamic analysis tools, improving prompt engineering tailored to architecture, and fine-tuning models with architecture-specific datasets. For practitioners, LLMs already show potential in supporting architecture-related tasks, especially in documentation, early design analysis, and pattern recognition in small to mid-sized systems. However, their use must be approached with caution due to accuracy issues and the risk of hallucinated or misleading outputs. While not yet suitable for fully automated architecture recovery in critical environments, LLMs can effectively complement human-driven efforts.

6 Threats to Validity

In this section, we outline the potential threats to the validity of our study and the strategies adopted to mitigate them.

Construct Validity. This threat relates to the chosen prompting strategies (e.g., Role, Zero-shot, and Emotion Prompting) which, while intended to improve model output, may introduce bias or inconsistency in interpretation. To mitigate this, prompts were designed to be clear and grounded in the provided source code. Future work may explore more neutral prompts and test model behavior across different instructions.

Internal Validity. Response variability may stem from how LLMs interpret prompts or from model-specific behavior. The Self-Reflection step in Prompt 2 may also introduce inconsistencies. To reduce these effects, we reset the model's memory before each query, ensuring independent responses. Future studies could explore additional models or configurations to assess consistency.

Sample Validity. Our code samples are smaller than large-scale industrial systems, ranging from hundreds to a few thousand LOC. However, they still reflect meaningful architectural patterns and styles, especially in mid-sized or embedded systems. Token limitations of LLMs also necessitated compact samples. To address this, we selected a diverse mix of projects, including both academic and real-world repositories, representing various domains and architectural styles. While not covering very large systems, this work lays the foundation for future scalability studies.

Validation Validity. Manual Ground-Truth construction may introduce bias, especially in classifying design and architectural patterns. We mitigated this by employing a two-stage validation process: two authors performed independent labeling, followed by a review and resolution of conflicts by a third. Future work could benefit from automated validation tools or broader reviewer participation.

External Validity. Our evaluation was limited to four general-purpose LLMs, excluding tailored models (e.g., ReVa, ReverseAI), which may perform differently. Future research should include a wider variety of LLMs, including specialized ones, and test them on more diverse and complex software systems to generalize findings.

Statistical Conclusion Validity. Variability in responsesespecially after Self-Reflectionmay affect the reliability of conclusions. To control for this, we tested all models under identical conditions and compared them against Ground-Truth. Future studies may include multiple runs per model and broader metric sets to strengthen the robustness of the evaluation.

7 Conclusion and Future Works

In this paper, we investigated the use of LLMs for software architecture recovery, focusing on three core tasks: class diagram extraction, design and architectural pattern recognition, and architectural style identification. We evaluated four leading general-purpose LLMs (e.g., GPT-4o, Gemini 1.5 Pro, Claude 3.5 Sonnet, and Mistral Large 2) by comparing their outputs against task-specific Ground-Truth data. To enhance performance, we employed prompt engineering and introduced a Self-Reflection mechanism that encouraged models to reassess and improve their initial responses.

Our findings indicate that LLMs can assist in recovering architectural knowledge, especially in identifying broad and well-defined structures such as classes and architectural styles. However, they struggled with more detailed aspects, including relationship recovery in class diagrams and the nuanced identification of design patterns. The most common issue was missing information, while hallucinations, though less frequent, were more likely in abstract or high-level tasks. Variability among model outputs, particularly from ChatGPT and Claude, highlighted inconsistency as a key limitation. Despite these challenges, the study confirms the potential of LLMs to support software architects in architecture-related tasks.

Future work will focus on enhancing prompt design using more contextual or few-shot strategies and evaluating domain-specific LLMs trained on software artifacts to determine if specialization leads to performance gains. We also plan to increase the number and diversity of samples, incorporating multiple programming languages, a wider range of design and architectural patterns, and more architectural styles. A key direction involves assessing LLMs on larger codebases and exploring strategies like modular decomposition or hierarchical analysis to overcome input limitations. Moreover, integrating LLMs with existing architecture recovery tools could bridge the gap between experimental use and practical adoption. Retrieval-Augmented Generation (RAG) techniques may help overcome token constraints by allowing dynamic retrieval of relevant code fragments. Finally, we aim to investigate structured and multi-step prompting strategies to improve the models accuracy in recovering detailed architectural relationships. Addressing these challenges will help LLMs evolve into more reliable and scalable tools for architecture recovery, paving the way for broader adoption of AI-driven techniques in software engineering.

References

1. What's the most popular LLM?. https://www.thisisdefinition.com/insights/most-popular-llm
2. De Silva, L., Balasubramaniam, D.: Controlling software architecture erosion: a survey. J. Syst. Softw. **85**, 132–151 (2012)
3. Abrahamsson, P., Babar, M.A., Kruchten, P.: Agility and architecture: can they coexist? IEEE Softw. **27**, 16–22 (2010)
4. Ahmed, T., Pai, K.S., Devanbu, P., Barr, E.: Automatic semantic augmentation of language model prompts (for code summarization). In: Proceedings of the IEEE/ACM 46th International Conference on Software Engineering (2024)
5. Camara, J., Troya, J., Burgueño, L., Vallecillo, A.: On the assessment of generative AI in modeling tasks: an experience report with ChatGPT and UML. Softw. Syst. Model. **22**, 781–793 (2023)
6. Camara, J., Troya, J., Montes-Torres, J., Jaime, F.J.: Generative AI in the software modeling classroom: an experience report with ChatGPT and unified modeling language . IEEE Softw. **41**, 73–81 (2024)
7. Cervantes, H., Kazman, R.: Designing Software Architectures: A Practical Approach (2016)
8. Chen, K., Yang, Y., Chen, B., Hernández López, J.A., Mussbacher, G., Varró, D.: Automated domain modeling with large language models: a comparative study. In: 2023 ACM/IEEE 26th International Conference on Model Driven Engineering Languages and Systems (MODELS) (2023)
9. Eliasson, U., Heldal, R., Pelliccione, P., Lantz, J.: Architecting in the automotive domain: Descriptive vs prescriptive architecture. In: 2015 12th Working IEEE/IFIP Conference on Software Architecture (2015)
10. Garcia, J., Ivkovic, I., Medvidovic, N.: A comparative analysis of software architecture recovery techniques. In: 2013 28th IEEE/ACM International Conference on Automated Software Engineering (ASE), pp. 486–496 (2013)
11. Garlan, D., et al.: Documenting Software Architectures: Views and Beyond. Addison-Wesley Professional, 2nd edn. (2010)
12. Gustrowsky, B., Villarreal, J.L., Alférez, G.H.: Using generative artificial intelligence for suggesting software architecture patterns from requirements. In: Intelligent Systems and Applications (2024)

13. Heldal, R., Pelliccione, P., Eliasson, U., Lantz, J., Derehag, J., Whittle, J.: Descriptive vs prescriptive models in industry. In: Proceedings of the ACM/IEEE 19th International Conference on Model Driven Engineering Languages and Systems, pp. 216–226. MODELS 2016, Association for Computing Machinery, New York, NY, USA (2016)
14. Jiang, J., Wang, F., Shen, J., Kim, S., Kim, S.: A survey on large language models for code generation (2024)
15. Jin, M., et al.: InferFix: end-to-end program repair with LLMS. In: Proceedings of the 31st ACM Joint European Software Engineering Conference and Symposium on the Foundations of Software Engineering (2023)
16. Kong, A., et al.: Better zero-shot reasoning with role-play prompting (2024)
17. Kruchten, P., Nord, R.L., Ozkaya, I.: Technical debt: From metaphor to theory and practice. IEEE Softw. **29**(6), 18–21 (2012)
18. Le, D.M., Link, D., Shahbazian, A., Medvidovic, N.: An empirical study of architectural decay in open-source software. In: 2018 IEEE International Conference on Software Architecture (ICSA) (2018)
19. Li, C., et al.: Large language models understand and can be enhanced by emotional stimuli (2023)
20. Li, Y.: A practical survey on zero-shot prompt design for in-context learning. In: Proceedings of the 14th International Conference on Recent Advances in Natural Language Processing (2023)
21. Liu, P., Yuan, W., Fu, J., Jiang, Z., Hayashi, H., Neubig, G.: Pre-train, prompt, and predict: a systematic survey of prompting methods in natural language processing. ACM Comput. Surv. **55**(9), 1–35 (2023)
22. Liu, Z., Tang, Y., Luo, X., Zhou, Y., Zhang, L.F.: No need to lift a finger anymore? Assessing the quality of code generation by ChatGPT. IEEE Trans. Softw. Eng. 50, 1548–1584 (2024)
23. Matzko, S., Clarke, P., Gibbs, T., Malloy, B., Power, J., Monahan, R.: Reveal: a tool to reverse engineer class diagrams (2002)
24. Migliorini, S., Verdecchia, R., Malavolta, I., Lago, P., Vicario, E.: Architectural views: the state of practice in open-source software projects. In: European Conference on Software Architecture (ECSA)
25. Nejjar, M., Zacharias, L., Stiehle, F., Weber, I.: LLMS for science: usage for code generation and data analysis. J. Softw. Evol. Process **37**, e2723 (2023)
26. Pelliccione, P., et al.: Automotive architecture framework: the experience of Volvo cars. J. Syst. Archit. **77**, 83–100 (2017)
27. Perry, D.E., Wolf, A.L.: Foundations for the study of software architecture (1992)
28. Renze, M., Guven, E.: Self-Reflection in LLM agents: effects on problem-solving performance. arXiv e-prints (2024)
29. Sahoo, P., Singh, A., Saha, S., Jain, V., Mondal, S., Chadha, A.: A systematic survey of prompt engineering in large language models: techniques and applications (2024)
30. Shaw, M., Clements, P.: The golden age of software architecture. IEEE Softw. **23**, 31–39 (2006)
31. Sutton, A., Maletic, J.I.: Recovering UML class models from c++: A detailed explanation. Inf. Softw. Technol. **49**(3), 212–229 (2007). 12th Working Conference on Reverse Engineering
32. Taylor, R., Medvidovic, N., Dashofy, E.: Software Architecture: Foundations, Theory, and Practice. Wiley (2009)

33. Wohlrab, R., Eliasson, U., Pelliccione, P., Heldal, R.: Improving the consistency and usefulness of architecture descriptions: guidelines for architects. In: 2019 IEEE International Conference on Software Architecture (ICSA) (2019)
34. Zhang, L., Zou, Q., Singhal, A., Sun, X., Liu, P.: Evaluating large language models for real-world vulnerability repair in C/C++ code. In: Proceedings of the 10th ACM International Workshop on Security and Privacy Analytics (2024)

Exploring Architectural Smells Detection Through LLMs

Claudio Tessa, Matteo Bochicchio(✉), and Francesca Arcelli Fontana

University of Milano-Bicocca, Milan, Italy
c.tessa@campus.unimib.it, {matteo.bochicchio,francesca.arcelli}@unimib.it

Abstract. Architectural smells (AS) are design flaws in software systems that, if left unaddressed, can negatively impact maintainability and system evolution. This preliminary study investigates the use of Large Language Models (LLM) for detecting and explaining an AS called Hub-like Dependency (HL), a critical smell type characterized by components with numerous incoming and outgoing dependencies. The research leverages Google's Gemini 1.5 Pro, comparing its performance to Arcan, a specialized AS detection tool. The study analyzes 135 AS across 39 open-source Java projects, including 100 Hub-like Dependency smells with varying severity levels and 35 non-Hub-like Dependency smells. Results show that the LLM achieves 100% recall but varying precision, with more detailed prompts improving detection performance from 64% to 82% for lower-severity smells. However, the model's ability to generate human-understandable explanations remains limited, with only 49% of the generated explanations rated as satisfactory. These findings highlight both the potential and current limitations of one specific LLM in HL smell detection, suggesting the importance of prompt design in enhancing its capabilities.

Keywords: Architectural Smells detection · LLM · Hub-like Dependency smell · Architectural Smells explainability

1 Introduction

Architectural Smells (AS) are patterns or structures within software systems that violate design principles, and therefore negatively impact design quality. If not addressed, these smells can accumulate over time, leading to poor maintainability [6] and technical debt [16]. For this reason, early detection and resolution of AS is crucial. In this study, we focus our attention on one frequent and critical AS, the Hub-like Dependency (HL) smell. This smell arises when an abstraction has a large number of both incoming and outgoing dependencies with other abstractions, making the dependency graph look like a hub [16]. The more traditional approaches to detecting AS rely usually on rule-based systems. However, these methods can miss architectural issues that require a deeper understanding of the system's design [5]. This is where Large Language Models (LLMs) could

V. Andrikopoulos et al. (Eds.): ECSA 2025, LNCS 15929, pp. 90–98, 2026.
https://doi.org/10.1007/978-3-032-02138-0_6

offer a promising solution. LLMs can process and analyze large amounts of code and have already shown promising potential in supporting code maintenance activities, such as detecting test smells [11], code smells [19], and vulnerabilities [12]. However, to the best of our knowledge, no study to date has specifically focused on the detection of AS using LLMs. This preliminary study will analyze how HL smells can be detected with the use of LLMs, in particular Google's Gemini 1.5 Pro[1], and compare its performance to Arcan, a specialized tool for AS detection [3]. Furthermore, we will examine whether LLMs could be useful in explaining the identified smells, i.e., providing insights into the underlying causes of the AS and possible refactoring suggestions. All the data is publicly available on Zenodo [17].

2 Related Work

The detection of AS in software systems has been an area of active research within the field of software engineering, as outlined in the works below. Traditional approaches to detecting these smells have largely relied on static analysis tools. Recently, the advent of Machine Learning (ML) and LLMs has opened new avenues for analyzing and understanding such smells. Tools like Arcan[2] and SonarQube[3] analyze source code to detect architectural or code smells, relying on manually curated rules and metrics like coupling, cohesion, and complexity. These methods are highly effective in detecting well-known smells, however, they often struggle with contextual nuances and cannot easily adapt to modern software architectures, as noted by Ernst et al. [5]. To address the limitations of static tools, ML methods have emerged. Supervised ML models have achieved impressive results, with Arcelli et al. [2] reporting up to 99% accuracy in detecting code smells like Data Class. Additionally, unsupervised methods such as Self-Organizing Maps have been applied to anomaly detection, achieving 90%-94% accuracy without requiring labeled data [7]. Despite these advances, ML-based methods have largely focused on code smells rather than AS. More recently, LLMs have also been evaluated for code smell detection, with ChatGPT reaching up to 70% accuracy on test smells [11,15], especially when using detailed prompts. Moreover, LLMs have been applied to technical debt explanations [12], though their performance on AS remains underexplored and is an ongoing area of investigation.

3 Study Design

Our goal is to evaluate LLMs (in particular, Google's Gemini 1.5 Pro) performance in the detection and explainability of HL smells. We elaborated the following research questions (RQ):

[1] See https://deepmind.google/technologies/gemini/.
[2] See https://arcan.tech.
[3] See https://www.sonarsource.com/products/sonarqube/.

RQ1: *To what extent can LLMs detect HL smells in Java code?*

RQ1.1: *How does a HL smell's severity affect the LLM's ability to detect it?*

The answers to these questions can help us understand some LLM limitations (in particular, of Gemini 1.5 Pro) and whether there are biases in identifying smells with varying degrees of criticality (severity). We compare the LLM detection performance with that of the Arcan tool.

RQ2: *How effective are LLMs in providing human-understandable explanations for the identified AS?*

Providing meaningful explanations can help developers understand the underlying causes and potential consequences of having AS in their codebase. Moreover, these explanations could also be useful for refactoring the smell.

Architectural Smells. We decided to use the tool Arcan (the first version of the tool has been developed at our lab [3]) able to detect several AS and provide a graph representation of each smell, useful to understand and remove the smell[4]. Moreover, the tool has been used in several previous studies (such as in [1,8,14]). In this paper, we focus our attention on the Hub-like Dependency smell (HL), which arises when a component has a high number of incoming and outgoing dependencies, becoming a central point of control. We decided to focus our attention on this smell, since an HL is generally bad for the project maintainability, as changes to the central "hub" component can have a cascading effect on all the other modules that depend on it or that it depends on [16]. An AS can arise at both the package level and at the class level. In this preliminary study, we focus only on class-level smells, as package-level smells often contain too much code to be analyzed by the considered LLM. HL smells are classified by Arcan with varying levels of severity (1–10), which indicate the complexity, criticality of the smell. For our study, we selected only the smells with severity levels 6 and 7 (the most common ones), in order to verify whether the model is capable of handling sufficiently complex and non-trivial smells. An example of a HL dependency graph of severity 7 is provided in the replication package [17].

Analyzed Projects. For our evaluation, we chose 39 open-source projects from GitHub. according to a set of prerequisites: (1) the project must have a code base written for at least 30% in the Java programming language; (2) be actively maintained, with the latest updates being no more than 2 years ago; (3) have at least 100 stars on GitHub, indicating that it has a certain level of interest within the developer community; (4) be analyzable by Arcan; (5) have at least one severity-6 or severity-7 HL smell, as classified by Arcan. According to these constraints, we were able to analyze a total of 100 HL smell instances. We then individuated from these projects 35 more AS that are not HL smells, considering the same requirements as above, except the last one. These instances will serve to evaluate false positives.

[4] https://www.arcan.tech/.

Selection of the LLM and Prompts. In this study, we used Google Gemini 1.5 Pro because it has a declared context window of one million tokens, which is sufficiently large for our work. This extensive context length made it feasible to analyze HL smells, which often consist of tens of thousands of Lines of Code (LOC) and hundreds of thousands of tokens. Before this decision, we evaluated other alternative LLMs, both open-source and proprietary (see [17]).

Different *prompting techniques* have been studied to try and increase LLMs performance on specific tasks. The ones we used to construct our prompts are Zero-shot [4], Role-Play [9], and Chain-Of-Thought (COT) prompting [18]. We identified Prompts 1 and 2 to evaluate how the detection performance differs from each prompt style, and one Prompt 3 to assess the model's reasoning capabilities in explaining the AS using the COT prompting technique. For the details of the prompts see the replication package [17].

Prompt 1. No definition was given on what an HL smell is, but it was given all the Java code involved in the smell.

Prompt 2. It was given the definition of the HL smell [16] and the Java code involved in the smell.

Prompt 3. It was given all the Java code involved in the smell and asked to explain it. We evaluated the model's capabilities in explaining HL smells and give some suggestions on refactoring. We used COT prompting to give the model an example of what we were expecting and the thought process behind our answer.

Each AS was given to the model with every prompt, each in a separate new chat. This ensured that the previous context of the chat did not affect the model's performance. For each smell, all the comments from the Java code were removed. This not only reduced the token count (and thus the complexity of the prompt) but it also ensured that the model did not receive any hints from self-admitted technical debt in the comments.

Evaluation Methods. Given the probabilistic nature of LLMs, the output may vary considerably across interactions, even when provided with identical input. To reduce the impact of stochastic variability and ensure the robustness of our evaluation, each unsuccessful prompt was tested *up to three times*, with each attempt performed in a separate, newly initialized chat session. A prompt was considered successful if the model produced the correct response within these three attempts [11]. Once a correct response was obtained, no further trials were conducted. To evaluate the performance of the model in detecting HL smells, we used three metrics often used in ML and information retrieval: *Precision*, *Recall* and *F-Measure* [13]. While to evaluate the performance of the model in the explainability of the given AS, we consider the following three criteria, proposed by Mao et al. [12]: 1 - *Correctness*: the explanation must be factually correct and describe how the smell came to be there in the first place, and which insights the developers can gain from the model's response; 2 - *Clarity*: the explanation must be given in a concise way and be understandable by a software developer; 3 - *Refactoring suggestions*: the explanation must contain a high-level description of how to remove the HL smell, or how to reduce its impact.

We evaluated the responses manually and rated them with the predefined rating scale and criteria, although the subjectivity of this evaluation poses significant challenges to its validity. The evaluations have been done by the three authors expert of this context, with a particularly deep attention of the first author. Based on the aforementioned judging criteria, the rating scale is the following: a score is given and it can be either **1** - indicating satisfaction or **0** - indicating non-satisfaction. An arithmetic average of the results was then calculated to obtain a representative value of the overall performance. Finally, we divided the results into two groups, based on the severity level of the smells, severity-6 and severity-7, to evaluate if there is a correlation between the severity level of the smells and the model's performance.

4 Results

Detection Performance to Answer RQ1 and RQ1.1. Table 1 shows the detection results of the smells divided by severity level and prompt used. To address **RQ1** we designed experiments employing two different prompts: Prompt 1 with a basic level of information, and Prompt 2 with a more detailed definition of the HL smell. Although both prompts achieve perfect recall (1.00) across severity levels, meaning they successfully identify all true instances, there is a notable difference in precision. Prompt 2 outperforms Prompt 1 in precision, indicating that it reduced the number of false positives. In answering **RQ1.1** we observed that the detection performance deteriorates as the severity of the smell increases. This is particularly evident in Severity-7 precision score, where Prompt 1 achieves only 0.50 precision, compared to 0.71 in Prompt 2. A more comprehensive overview of these results can be obtained by looking at the F-measure score, which combines both precision and recall. For both Prompt 1 and Prompt 2, the F-measure drops substantially when going from Severity-6 to Severity-7. For the model, it is more difficult to understand more complex smells or smells with more LOC (see Table 1). Overall, while some of these results may seem promising for LLMs, especially for Prompt 2, it is important to note that the dataset is unbalanced. As mentioned before, the non-Hub-like smells only comprise about 26% of our dataset, which may inflate recall.

Table 1. Detection results on Prompt 1 and Prompt 2 and LOC statistics.

Severity	Prompt	Precision	Recall	F-measure	Avg LOC	Median LOC
6	1	0.64	1.00	0.78	4 163	3 305
7	1	0.50	1.00	0.67	9 113	4 177
6	2	0.82	1.00	0.90	4 163	3 305
7	2	0.71	1.00	0.83	9 113	4 177

Explainability Performance to Answer RQ2. We evaluated the answers of the model giving a score of either 0 (not satisfactory) or 1 (satisfactory) [12], and then calculated the percentage of satisfactory answers[5]. A Likert scale will be used in future works. The percentage of satisfying explanations is **0.53%** for *severity-6* smells and **0.41%** for *severity-7* smells, resulting in an overall rate of 0.49% satisfactory responses. These results suggest that while the model shows promise in generating understandable explanations for AS, its performance varies according to complexity. Higher severity smells may involve more intricate dependencies (and, therefore, a more complex dependency graph) that the model is not properly able to understand.

According to RQ2 and the answers received from Prompt 3, in Table 2 we summarize the most frequent suggested refactorings (for the complete table, please refer to [17]). These suggestions align with best practices for reducing coupling and improving modularity in software architecture. Among the design patterns recommended by the model, the Façade pattern (56 occurrences) and the Observer pattern (13 occurrences) were suggested more frequently, likely because they help encapsulate dependencies and promote better separation of concerns. Other patterns such as Strategy, Mediator, and Factory were also occasionally proposed, but with significantly lower frequency. These findings highlight that the LLM, while capable of suggesting various refactoring techniques, tends to rely on a core set of well-known remedies, particularly those aimed at reducing dependency complexity at the class level rather than restructuring the system's architecture at a higher level.

Table 2. Most suggested refactorings (from Prompt 3)

Proposed remedy	Number of times proposed
Introduce interfaces or abstract classes	46
Decompose classes	68
Dependency injection	71
Strategy pattern	10
Observer pattern	13
Façade pattern	56
Mediator pattern	11

5 Threats to Validity

Several factors may affect the validity of this study. Evaluation metrics for AS detection (precision, recall, F-measure) depend on dataset size and balance; a

[5] See the rep. package [17] for examples of satisfactory answers and prompt responses.

small, skewed dataset may inflate recall. However, the data includes AS of varying severities, sizes, and projects to reflect real-world diversity. Subjective rating of LLM-generated explanations introduces potential bias, despite predefined criteria. Standardized evaluation could yield different results. LLM stochasticity also adds variability; prompts were run three times to reduce this, though some randomness remains. The study is limited to HL smells at class level detected using the Arcan tool in open-source Java projects. Therefore, the findings may not be generalizable to other types of AS, programming languages, industrial systems, or AS detection tools. Additionally, the focus on severity-6 and -7 smells may further reduce the representativeness of the results. The LLM was tested with default settings to assess general-purpose performance. Larger models like Qwen2.5-Coder and Code LLaMA were excluded due to hardware limits and insufficient context windows for AS up to 700k tokens.

6 Conclusions and Future Work

The findings of this study highlight both the opportunities and limitations of integrating LLMs into software maintenance workflows. According to **RQ1** and **RQ1.1**, a key insight is the significant influence of prompt design on detection performance. Providing contextual information, such as a formal definition of HL smells, improved precision by 1520%, while recall remained stable. Additionally, the model's performance varied with the severity of AS: higher-severity smells (severity-7) posed greater challenges, especially in terms of precision and explanation quality. COT prompting improved reasoning slightly but did not fully mitigate performance drops on more complex smells. According to **RQ2**, the analysis of the explainability results shows that while the LLM is capable of producing understandable explanations for simpler HL smells, its effectiveness decreases notably as complexity increases. On average, only 49% of the explanations were rated satisfactory, with lower performance observed on more severe smells. Nevertheless, when successful, the model consistently suggests well-known refactoring strategies that align with best practices for reducing coupling and improving modularity. This indicates that the LLM can effectively support developers by reinforcing established design principles, particularly in less complex scenarios or when supplemented by clear, domain-specific prompts. Different improvements of this study can be considered: model fine-tuning on domain-specific datasets and the adoption of emerging techniques like Retrieval Augmented Generation (RAG) [10], which could enhance the model's capacity to provide accurate explanations by leveraging external knowledge sources, consider different types of AS, other programming languages, and additional LLM architectures. Investigating alternative prompting strategies, such as few-shot prompting, could also yield better performance. Finally, a more extended evaluation framework involving multiple experts or real-world validation in collaboration with developers could provide more reliable insights into the practical utility of LLM-generated explanations.

Data Availability. All analyses conducted with Arcan, along with all the code involved in the smells, the prompts used, and the obtained results, are publicly available in the replication package on Zenodo [17].

References

1. Arcelli, F.F., Locatelli, F., Pigazzini, I., Mereghetti, P.: An architectural smell evaluation in an industrial context. In: ICSEA 2020, pp. 68–74 (2020)
2. Arcelli Fontana, F., Mäntylä, M.V., Zanoni, M., Marino, A.: Comparing and experimenting machine learning techniques for code smell detection. Empir. Softw. Eng. **21**, 1143–1191 (2016)
3. Arcelli Fontana, F., Pigazzini, I., Roveda, R., Zanoni, M.: Automatic detection of instability architectural smells. In: ICSME 2016, pp. 433–437. IEEE Computer Society (2016). https://doi.org/10.1109/ICSME.2016.33
4. Dang, H., Mecke, L., Lehmann, F., Goller, S., Buschek, D.: How to prompt? Opportunities and challenges of zero- and few-shot learning for human-AI interaction in creative applications of generative models. In: ACM CHI Conference - Workshops (2022). https://www.hciai.uni-bayreuth.de/pool/docs/workshops%5fCHI22.pdf
5. Ernst, N.A., Bellomo, S., Ozkaya, I., Nord, R.L.: What to fix? Distinguishing between design and non-design rules in automated tools. In: 2017 ICSA, pp. 165–168 (2017). https://doi.org/10.1109/ICSA.2017.25
6. Garcia, J., Popescu, D., Edwards, G., Medvidovic, N.: Identifying architectural bad smells. In: 2009 13th CSMR, pp. 255–258 (2009). https://doi.org/10.1109/CSMR.2009.59
7. Gupta, R., Kumar, N., Kumar, S., Kumar Seth, J.: Unsupervised machine learning for effective code smell detection: a novel method. J. Commun. Softw. Syst. **20**(4), 307–316 (2024)
8. Herold, S.: An initial study on the association between architectural smells and degradation. In: Jansen, A., Malavolta, I., Muccini, H., Ozkaya, I., Zimmermann, O. (eds.) ECSA 2020. LNCS, vol. 12292, pp. 193–201. Springer, Cham (2020). https://doi.org/10.1007/978-3-030-58923-3_13
9. Kong, A., et al.: Better zero-shot reasoning with role-play prompting. In: NAACL-HLT (2024)
10. Lewis, P., et al.: Retrieval-augmented generation for knowledge-intensive NLP tasks. Adv. Neural. Inf. Process. Syst. **33**, 9459–9474 (2020)
11. Lucas, K., Gheyi, R., Soares, E., Ribeiro, M., Machado, I.: Evaluating large language models in detecting test smells. arXiv preprint arXiv:2407.19261 (2024)
12. Mao, Q., Li, Z., Hu, X., Liu, K., Xia, X., Sun, J.: Towards effectively detecting and explaining vulnerabilities using large language models. arXiv preprint arXiv:2406.09701 (2024)
13. Naidu, G., Zuva, T., Sibanda, E.M.: A review of evaluation metrics in machine learning algorithms. In: Silhavy, R., Silhavy, P. (eds.) CSOC 2023. LNNS, vol. 724, pp. 15–25. Springer, Cham (2023). https://doi.org/10.1007/978-3-031-35314-7_2
14. Sas, D., Avgeriou, P., Arcelli Fontana, F.: Investigating instability architectural smells evolution: an exploratory case study. In: IEEE ICSME 2029, pp. 557–567 (2019). https://doi.org/10.1109/ICSME.2019.00090
15. Silva, L.L., Silva, J.R.d., Montandon, J.E., Andrade, M., Valente, M.T.: Detecting code smells using chatGPT: initial insights. In: Proceedings of the 18th ESEIW (2024)

16. Suryanarayana, G., Samarthyam, G., Sharma, T.: Refactoring for Software Design Smells: Managing Technical Debt. Morgan Kaufmann (2014)
17. Tessa, C., Bochicchio, M., Arcelli Fontana, F.: Dataset: exploring architectural smells detection through LLMs (2025). https://doi.org/10.5281/zenodo.15488631
18. Wei, J., Wang, X., Schuurmans, D., Bosma, M., Xia, F., Chi, E., Le, Q.V., Zhou, D., et al.: Chain-of-thought prompting elicits reasoning in large language models. Adv. Neural. Inf. Process. Syst. **35**, 24824–24837 (2022)
19. Wu, D., et al.: iSMELL: assembling LLMs with expert toolsets for code smell detection and refactoring. In: Proceedings of the 39th ASE, pp. 1345–1357 (2024)

LLMs for Software Architecture Knowledge: A Comparative Analysis Among Seven LLMs

Mohamed Soliman[1(✉)], Elia Ashraf[1], Kamel M. K. Abdelsalam[3], Jan Keim[2], and Ashwin Prasad Shivarpatna Venkatesh[1]

[1] Universität Paderborn, Paderborn, Germany
{mohamed.soliman,elia.ashraf,ashwin.prasad}@uni-paderborn.de
[2] Karlsruhe Institute of Technology (KIT), Karlsruhe, Germany
jan.keim@kit.edu
[3] Ain Shams University, Cairo, Egypt
kamelmk@sci.asu.edu.eg

Abstract. Software developers require extensive architectural knowledge (AK) to effectively maintain and extend existing software systems. Recently, Large Language Models (LLMs) have demonstrated promising capabilities in learning from vast datasets, including software repositories, to provide insightful answers about existing software systems. With the development of various LLMs, each characterized by distinct sizes, architectures, and vendors, there is potential for these models to assist developers in addressing architectural queries related to AK. Despite the advancements, there is a limited understanding of the comparative performance of different LLMs, particularly regarding the accuracy and similarity of their responses to architectural questions. This paper aims to bridge this gap by evaluating seven diverse LLMs, including GPT, Mistral, LLaMA, and DeepSeek, focusing on their ability to accurately and consistently respond to queries about the AK of the open-source system, Hadoop HDFS. Our study reveals significant variations in the performance of these LLMs, highlighting differences in the accuracy and similarity of their responses. These findings provide valuable insights for software developers and researchers, guiding the selection and utilization of LLMs for architectural knowledge tasks in software development.

Keywords: Software architecture · Architectural design decisions · Architectural knowledge · LLMs · GPT · DeepSeek · LLaMA

1 Introduction

Software engineers need *Architectural knowledge (AK)* to develop and maintain software systems. This encompasses three *AK concepts* [27]: (i) *Components and connectors* (e.g., layers, remote calls) [3], (ii) *Quality solutions* (e.g., patterns [8], tactics [3]) that ensure attributes like maintainability and availability, and

V. Andrikopoulos et al. (Eds.): ECSA 2025, LNCS 15929, pp. 99–115, 2026.
https://doi.org/10.1007/978-3-032-02138-0_7

(iii) *Rationale behind design decisions* [38]. Each *AK concept* is important for software engineers: AK on *components and connectors* assists in understanding the structure and behavior of a system, AK on *quality solutions* supports quality improvements, and *design rationale* [38] facilitates making new design decisions.

Despite the importance of AK, retrieving AK for existing software systems remains a challenge due to its distribution. No single source holds complete AK, requiring software engineers to integrate information from various repositories (e.g., Git) [20], issue trackers [5,32], mailing lists [33], forums (e.g., Stack Overflow [11]), and blog articles [35]. This manual aggregation from these sources is complex and time-consuming and remains an open challenge.

To tackle this challenge, software architecture researchers (e.g., [13,15,18,19]) are now exploring the potential of Large Language Models (LLMs), such as GPT [30] and LLaMA [39], to automate AK extraction and integration. Due to advanced architectures and large-scale training on diverse datasets, LLMs demonstrate strong capabilities in text processing, code analysis, and documentation understanding [9,29,42]. For example, GPT-3 [7] was trained on over 1 TB of filtered internet data, including open-source repositories (e.g., GitHub, Jira) and developer discussions from forums like Stack Overflow. This extensive training allows LLMs to consolidate knowledge from multiple sources into a single model.

Given their accessibility and effectiveness, LLMs offer software engineers a promising tool to efficiently retrieve AK. For instance, engineers can directly query LLMs for AK about open-source systems, reducing the need for manual integration and improving the overall understanding of software architectures. However, the number of LLMs, their vendors, and sizes have increased significantly in the last year, showing many options for software engineers to select from. Furthermore, we know little about the differences between the different LLMs, especially regarding the accuracy of their answers and similarities among their responses to questions about the AK of existing software systems. In our prior state-of-the-art work [37], we evaluated only on GPT-3.5, without considering more recent LLMs such as DeepSeek-R1, LLaMA 3.3, or GPT-4o. Therefore, in this paper, we **aim** to *compare different LLMs regarding the accuracy and similarity of their responses to questions about the architectural knowledge of an open-source system embedded in their models.*

To achieve our goal, we selected seven prominent LLMs with different sizes and vendors. We then evaluated the accuracy of the selected LLMs using our existing dataset from previous work [36] consisting of 229 questions written by software engineers on the AK of the open-source system, Hadoop HDFS. Furthermore, we compared the responses of the different LLMs with each other to determine which LLMs provide similar responses. In summary, we have the following contributions:

1. *An empirical evaluation on the accuracy of different LLMs to answer questions about the AK of an open-source system embedded in their models.* We focus on assessing the precision and recall in responding to queries related to various *AK concepts*, including components and connectors, quality solu-

tions, and the rationale of decisions. Our experiments compare various LLMs in terms of their accuracy in addressing questions about the AK concepts embedded within software systems.
2. *An empirical evaluation regarding the similarities of responses among the different LLMs.* Our work identifies which LLMs provide similar or distinct responses to architectural questions. Additionally, we determine which LLMs share correct or false answers.

With our contributions, we aim to determine if LLMs have differences regarding their accuracy and responses and if these differences are related to the size or vendor of the LLMs. This knowledge can support practitioners and researchers in deciding on suitable LLMs to answer questions on the AK of an existing system.

The remainder of the paper is structured as follows: Sect. 2 details our study design, while Sect. 3 and Sect. 4 present our findings. In Sect. 5, we discuss our results, and we discuss threats to validity in Sect. 6. In Sect. 7, we tackle related work. Finally, Sect. 8 concludes the paper.

2 Study Design

To achieve our aim (see Sect. 1), we ask the following research questions (RQs). (***RQ1***) *How accurate are the answers provided by different LLMs regarding the architectural knowledge of an existing system embedded in their models?*

With the increasing number of LLMs and lack of information about their accuracy, researchers and practitioners struggle to select one or more LLMs to answer architectural questions. This RQ aims to determine accuracy variations among LLMs across different AK concepts. We seek to determine if certain LLMs excel in specific AK concepts, such as components, connectors, or quality solutions. Accordingly, researchers and practitioners could better decide on the most accurate LLM for their questions.
(***RQ2***) *How similar are the responses of the different LLMs to questions about the architectural knowledge of an existing system embedded in their models?*

Different LLMs may produce similar or divergent responses to the same architectural questions, potentially sharing correct or incorrect answers. This RQ explores whether LLMs provide similar responses and if they share the same correct or incorrect answers. Response similarity could benefit researchers and practitioners combining multiple LLMs to query AK of existing systems, supporting effective usage of various LLMs for architectural questions.

To answer the research questions (RQs), we followed three steps, depicted in Fig. 1 and detailed in the following sections. In Step 1, we selected seven prominent LLMs and submitted 229 architectural questions from an existing dataset, which served as our ground truth. In Step 2, we analyzed the LLMs' responses, extracting answers and comparing them to the ideal answers in the ground truth to evaluate the accuracy of LLMs for RQ1. In Step 3, we measured the similarity between LLMs' responses, including correct and incorrect answers, to address RQ2.

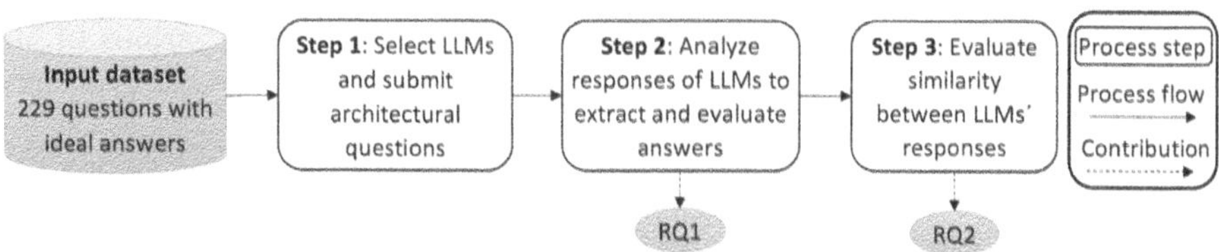

Fig. 1. Overview on the research process

Input Dataset

For the input dataset, we use the dataset from our previous work [36,37] with questions about the AK concepts and answers about the AK of Hadoop HDFS that we can use for our evaluation. Furthermore, the questions in the dataset are written independently by software engineers, along with their ground truth answers. The participants could freely articulate the questions and use direct questions (i.e., zero-shot) without providing examples or applying other prompting techniques, which aligns with how software engineers would commonly use LLMs. The dataset overall consists of 229 questions, distributed as follows: 80 questions about components and connectors, 81 questions about quality attribute solutions, and 68 questions about the rationale of design decisions. Sample questions include: (i) How do the architectural components in SPS (Storage Policy Satisfier) depend on each other? (ii) What are the security tactics used to improve security in the implementation of the SPS? (iii) For the SPS, what alternative solution was used prior or considered as an alternative solution?

Step 1: Select LLMs and Submit Architectural Questions

Table 1. The selected LLMs, their vendors, parameters, and training sizes. B stands for billions, and T stands for trillions tokens.

ID	Vendor	Model Name	Parameters	Training Size	Ref.
Q	Alibaba	Qwen2-Instruct	72B	7T	[43]
DS	DeepSeek	DeepSeek-R1-Distill-Llama	70B	14T	[12]
G4	OpenAI	gpt-4o	–	–	–
GM		gpt-4o-mini	–	–	–
LL	Meta	Llama-3.3-Instruct	70B	15T	[23]
TL		TinyLlama-Chat-v1.0	1.1B	3T	
M	Mistral	Mistral-Large-Instruct-2407	123B	–	[1]

To address our RQs, we selected various LLMs from different vendors with distinct sizes of parameters and training datasets. Table 1 lists each LLM's ID, vendor, model name, parameters, and training size. The IDs of the LLMs will be referenced in Sect. 3 and Sect. 4. We chose these prominent models due to their widespread application in software engineering tasks [16]. While all LLMs use the decoder architecture, some are tailored for specific purposes or employ unique training techniques. For example, DeepSeek-R1-Distill undergoes a distillation process, fine-tuning the model from the larger DeepSeek-R1.

To retrieve responses for the architectural questions, we submitted the same questions from the input dataset to each LLM, ensuring a fair comparison of accuracy and answers. We used the Hugging Face transformers Python interface to run open LLMs on our hardware, providing a flexible and efficient environment for managing inference tasks across multiple models. All models were run in 4-bit quantization mode to accommodate hardware constraints, ensuring efficient inference without significant performance loss. Responses from all LLMs, except those from OpenAI, were retrieved using Hugging Face transformers. For OpenAI models, we used the OpenAI interface with the Langchain Python module. All experiments were conducted on the following hardware: 1xNVIDIA H100-80C GPU, 16xIntel(R) Xeon(R) Platinum 8462Y+ CPUs, and 78 GB RAM. This process returned responses from all LLMs in Table 1 to all 229 questions, totaling 1603 responses. All responses and scripts are available online [34].

Step 2: Analyze Responses of LLMs to Extract and Evaluate Answers

Table 2. Example for a question and responses of LLMs, answers are in *italic*

	Question: How has the Performance of QJournal within Hadoop HDFS been improved through implemented tactics ?
LL	...several tactics have been implemented: 1. **_Data Striping_**: QJournal uses a striping approach to store data across multiple DataNodes... 2. **_Async Writes_**: QJournal uses asynchronous writes... 3. **_Batching_**: ... 4. **_Caching_**:... 5. **_Data Compression_**: ... 6. **_Parallelization_**: QJournal uses parallelization techniques, such as multi-threading and parallel processing, to improve performance... 10. **_Monitoring and Tuning_**:...
DS	<think> Okay, so I'm trying to understand how the performance of QJournal... has been improved through implemented tactics...</think>The performance of QJournal...has been enhanced through several strategic implementations...: 1. **_Data Writing Efficiency_**: - **_Batching Writes_**: Aggregating multiple log entries into a single write... - **_Efficient Serialization_**: Utilizing formats like Avro or Protobuf... 2. **_File Management_**: - **_Concatenation ..._**:...
M	Here are some key strategies that have been implemented to enhance QJournal performance: 1. **_Efficient Data Replication_**: - **_Pipeline Optimization_**: ...- **_Parallel Replication_**: ... 2. **_Improved Write Path_**: - **_Batch Writes_**:...- **_Asynchronous Writes_**:... 3. **_Metadata Management_**: - **_Efficient Metadata Storage_**:...
TL	here are some tactics...: 1. *Implementing a distributed journaling mechanism*: qjournal uses a distributed journaling mechanism... 2. *Implementing a write-ahead log (wal)*: qjournal uses a write-ahead log (wal) to write data to the disk...

In this step, we analyze the responses of the LLMs to extract answers and compare them to the ideal answers in the ground truth. We note that each response involves multiple answers for the submitted question. Table 2 provides examples for different responses of LLMs and the *answers* in each response. When comparing answers to the ground truth, we classify answers among:

- *True positive (TP)* generated answers that match the ground truth.
- *False positive (FP)* generated answers that do not match the ground truth.
- *False negative (FN)* answers from the ground truth that are not generated.

Given the large number of responses, manually analyzing all 1603 responses to extract answers and compare them to the ground truth was not feasible. We opted for semi-automatic analysis as the analysis is time-consuming, as also reported in our previous work [37]. Initially, we aimed for a fully automated analysis but encountered obstacles in accurately extracting and classifying answers from the LLMs' responses. Specifically, we followed three steps:
1. **Determine formats of responses and extract answers**: One obstacle in extracting answers from LLMs' responses is their diverse formats. Table 2 illustrates these differences. For instance, LLaMA provides a numerical list using the format ***Answer***, while DeepSeek and Mistral use hierarchical lists with numbers and dashes. To address this, we identified common formats in each LLM's responses and developed a script (available online [34]) to extract answers.
2. **Compare answers to the ground truth**: To evaluate the extracted answers, we compared them with the ground truth. One challenge was the varied terminology used by LLMs for the same answer. For instance, concurrency appears as *parallelization* in LLaMA and *parallel replication* in Mistral (Table 2). Exact string matching would miss these variations. To overcome this, we applied fuzzy string matching [10] using the difflib Python library[1]. This method allowed us to classify answers as TP, FP, or FN. Fuzzy matching requires a threshold to determine similarity. We experimented with thresholds between 0.9 and 0.5 on a random sample of 400 responses, finding 0.65 to be the most precise with a precision of 0.92. Using fuzzy matching, we compared all extracted answers to the ground truth and stored them for manual verification.
3. **Manual verification and corrections**: Certain answers contained synonymous that fuzzy matching could not identify correctly, such as *parallel processing* as a synonym for *parallelization.* To ensure accurate classification, two authors manually reviewed all FP answers to detect and correct misclassified answers. This step required significantly less effort than manually checking full responses, as we focused on specific answers. All answers are shared online [34].
4. **Calculate precision and recall**: Using TP, FP, and FN counts, we calculated $Precision = \frac{TP}{TP+FP}$ and $Recall = \frac{TP}{TP+FN}$ for each LLM response to answer RQ1. To identify significant differences in *Precision* and *Recall* among LLMs, we conducted significance tests on their distributions across all questions and pairs of LLMs. Specifically, we used the t-test for normalized data and the Mann-Whitney-U-Test for skewed data. The results are presented in Sect. 3. Also, all values of precision, recall, and significance test results are online [34].

[1] https://docs.python.org/3/library/difflib.html.

Step 3: Evaluate Similarity Between LLMs' Responses
To answer RQ2, we compared responses to the same questions across all pairs of LLMs using the following two approaches:
• **Compare full responses of LLMs using BERTScore**: In this approach, we measure the similarity between full responses from different LLMs to the same questions using BERTScore [44]. We chose BERTScore over other methods (e.g., BLEU) because it captures semantic similarity. Using the BERTScore library[2], we evaluated the similarity among responses of all combinations of LLM pairs (21 pairs) from the 7 LLMs in Table 1. The results include precision, recall, and F-score values, indicating the similarity between two responses. The average F-score values are presented in Table 4, and further values are online [34].
• **Compare answers using fuzzy matching and manual analysis**: BERTScore does not differentiate between true and false answers in a response. Therefore, in this approach, we separately compare the identified TP and FP answers (from Step 2) to determine which LLMs provide similar correct or incorrect answers for the same questions. We applied fuzzy matching to the TP and FP answers separately, using the steps described in Step 2 to determine the fuzzy threshold (0.6) with the best precision. Evaluating the results, we found that matching similar TP answers had a high precision of 0.95, while matching FP answers had a low precision of 0.5. This low precision is due to the hallucination behavior of LLMs, which produce FP answers with varied terms that fuzzy matching cannot capture. To ensure accurate similarity between FP answers, two authors manually verified all FP answers among the different LLMs. After determining similar answers, we calculated the *ratio of similar answers* in a response with each of the other LLMs. The average ratios are presented in Sect. 4, and ratios for all questions are available online [34].

To determine significant similarities, we executed the same significance tests as RQ1. Tests were executed separately among the BERTScores and ratios. Detailed results of the significance tests are available online [34].

3 RQ1: Accuracy of LLMs

Figure 2 shows the precision and recall distributions for each LLM and AK concept. Generally, all LLMs achieve low precision for AK concepts, with quality attribute solutions having the lowest precision. Conversely, most LLMs exhibit higher recall for all AK concepts. These findings align with our previous work [37] on GPT-3.5, indicating that LLMs tend to provide all possible answers for architectural questions, resulting in high false positives. Therefore, researchers and practitioners must filter out false positives, especially for quality attribute solutions like patterns or tactics.

Regarding the differences in precision and recall among LLMs, Table 3 presents the results of our significance tests. We observe the following:

[2] https://pypi.org/project/bert-score/.

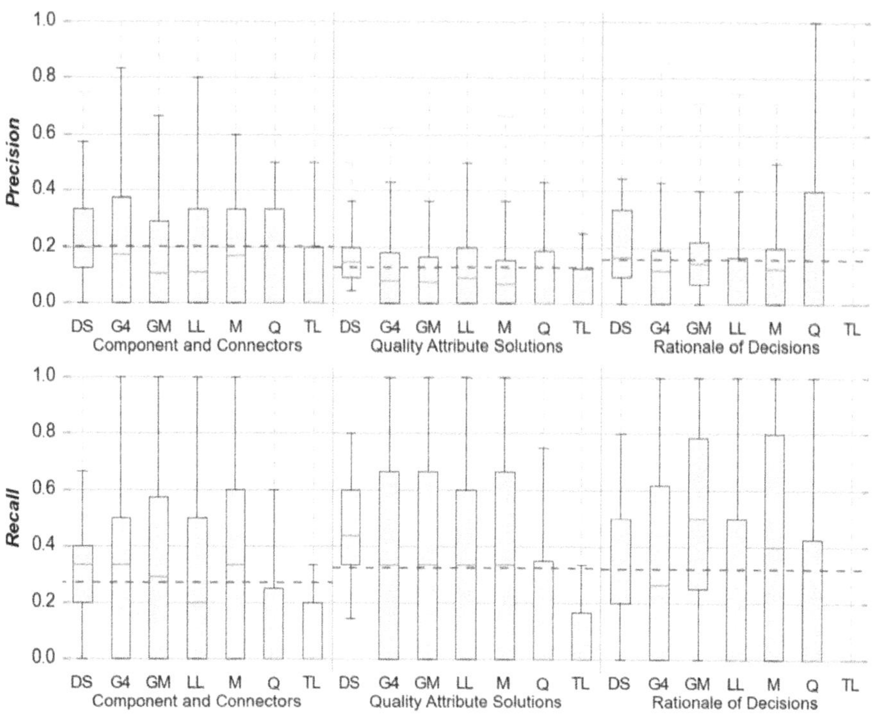

Fig. 2. Precision and recall of different LLMs and AK concepts

- For *components and connectors*, most LLMs show similar precision and recall but with different distributions. TinyLLaMA has significantly lower precision and recall, and Qwen has significantly lower recall than other LLMs. Therefore, for questions on components and connectors, practitioners and researchers can choose among the LLMs in Table 1, except for TinyLLaMA and Qwen.
- For *quality attribute solutions*, most LLMs show very low precision, with DeepSeek having significantly better precision than all other LLMs except Large LLaMA. TinyLLaMA has the significantly worst precision. Most LLMs show high recall, except for TinyLLaMA and Qwen. DeepSeek has the best recall, but it is only significantly better than GPT-4o and GPT-4 mini. Thus, for questions on quality attribute solutions, DeepSeek is recommended.
- For *rationale of decisions*, LLMs show varying precision and recall. DeepSeek and GPT-mini achieve the best precision, significantly outperforming all other LLMs. For recall, GPT-mini leads significantly better than others, except DeepSeek and Mistral. TinyLLaMA and Qwen have the worst precision and recall. Thus, for questions on the rationale of design decisions, practitioners and researchers should use DeepSeek and GPT-mini for their superior precision and recall.

Table 3. Results of significance tests for precision and recall, and among all pairs of LLMs. Given the set of LLMs in Table 1, we specify significance. We use $X >> Y$ to indicate that the LLM X is significantly better than the LLM Y for the metric, and $X << Y$ to show that X is significantly worse than Y

AK concept	Metric	Significant results
Components and connectors	Precision	$TL << x, \quad \forall x \in LLMs \setminus \{Q\}, \quad G4 >> Q$
	Recall	$x >> TL, Q \quad \forall x \in LLMs \setminus \{TL, Q\}$
Quality attribute solutions	Precision	$DS >> x \quad \forall x \in LLMs \setminus \{LL\}, \quad TL << x \quad \forall x \in LLMs \setminus \{Q\}, \quad LL >> Q$
	Recall	$TL, Q << x \quad \forall x \in LLMs, \quad DS >> G4, GM$
Rationale of design decisions	Precision	$DS >> x \quad \forall x \in LLMs \setminus \{GM\} \quad GM >> LL, TL << x \quad \forall x \in LLMs$
	Recall	$TL << x \quad \forall x \in LLMs, \quad GM >> Q, LL, G4, DS, M >> Q, LL$

RQ1 key takeaways:

- LLMs achieve *low precision but higher recall* for architectural questions.
- *DeepSeek* achieves better results than larger models like GPT-4 and Mistral for questions on quality solutions and rationale of decisions.
- *TinyLLaMA and Qwen* achieve the worst precision and recall overall.

4 RQ2: Similarities Among LLMs

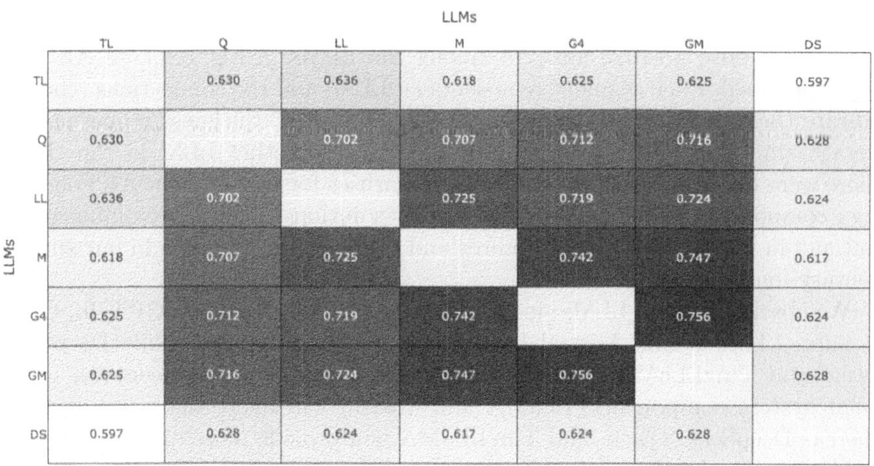

Fig. 3. Average BERTScore (F_{BERT}) for the LLMs' response similarities

Figure 3 shows a heatmap with the average F-score from the BERTScore (F_{BERT}) among the used LLMs (see Fig. 1) for all AK concepts combined. There were no significant differences in similarities between different AK concepts. The LLMs exhibit high and close similarities in their responses, ranging from 0.597 to 0.756. The highest similarities are among GPT-4o, GPT-4o mini, and Mistral, followed by LLaMA and Qwen. In contrast, DeepSeek and TinyLLaMA have the lowest similarities with other LLMs. Therefore, from Fig. 3, when asking multiple LLMs, more than half of a response of an LLM will be similar to other LLMs.

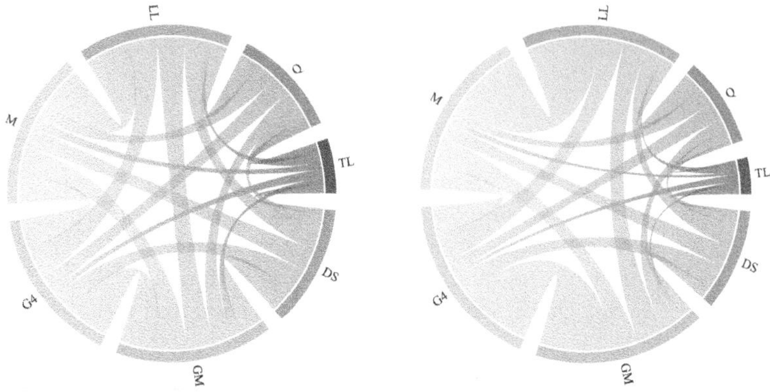

Fig. 4. Similarity ratios of true positive and false positive answers

The BERTScore in Fig. 3 does not differentiate between true and false positive answers. Figure 4 shows a chord diagram illustrating the similarity ratios in true and false positive answers among the LLMs in Fig. 1 for all AK concepts combined. Each segment represents an LLM, and the connections (chords) indicate their similarities with other LLMs. The cords' thickness represents the average similarity ratio of an LLM's answers to another LLM in the chord. There were no significant differences in similarities for the different AK concepts (e.g., components and connectors vs. quality solutions). Thus, we combined AK concepts in Fig. 4, with further figures and exact ratios available in our supplementary material [34].

We observe that all LLMs share both true and false answers. GPT-4o, GPT-4o mini, LLaMA, and Mistral have the highest similarities, while DeepSeek, Qwen, and TinyLLaMA have the lowest. For example, if engineers ask LLMs about system components, LLaMA and Mistral will likely share components, whereas DeepSeek, Qwen, and TinyLLaMA will provide more different ones.

Comparing the similarities among true and false positive answers in Fig. 4a and Fig. 4b, we see that false positive answers have higher similarities than true positive answers, especially between GPT-4o and GPT-4o mini and between Mistral and LLaMA. DeepSeek, Qwen, and TinyLLaMA show even smaller similarities for false positives than true positives. These observations may be due to similarities in the training datasets or architectures of LLMs, causing their models to produce similar or different hallucinations of false positives. For example, if software engineers ask GPT-4o and GPT-4o mini about security tactics, they might receive responses with similar false security tactics.

RQ2 key takeaways:

- *All LLMs share at least half of their responses with other LLMs.* This includes true and false positive answers to architectural questions.
- *GPT-4o, GPT-4o mini, LLaMA, and Mistral* have the biggest similarity among their responses and answers, while *DeepSeek, Qwen, and TinyLLaMA* have the smallest similarities among their responses and answers.

5 Discussion

Implications for Researchers

The results of RQ1 confirm our previous findings [37] that zero-shot LLMs achieve low precision and high recall, providing many false positives. This suggests that standard LLMs, with their current architecture and training datasets, are not yet suitable for architectural questions without further customization. Researchers should explore approaches to customize LLMs, such as using advanced prompting techniques (e.g., Chain-of-Thought) or fine-tuning.

RQ1 results also show that the parameters size, training dataset and methodology of LLMs significantly impact their precision and recall. TinyLLaMA and Qwen, the smallest model and smallest training datasets, have the worst precision and recall. Very large models like GPT-4o and Mistral show saturation, with no significant improvement over mid-sized models like GPT-4 mini and LLaMA. Interestingly, DeepSeek, a mid-sized LLM with a different training methodology through distillation, outperforms larger models, indicating that methodologies of training play a crucial role in achieving better precision and recall. Thus, researchers should focus on improving the methodologies of LLM training and architectures over expanding parameter sizes.

RQ2 results can guide researchers in combining LLMs to answer architectural questions more accurately. For instance, a voting mechanism could be used to find the correct answers. However, since some LLMs share false positive answers, researchers should select LLMs with the least similarity in false positives for this approach. DeepSeek and Mistral, which have the least similarity ratios of false positives, could be good candidates for a voting mechanism.

Implications for Practitioners

The results of RQ1 indicate that LLMs should be used cautiously for architectural questions due to the high number of false positives. Practitioners can use LLMs to create initial architectural documentation and provide preliminary answers, but these answers should be filtered and verified for accuracy.

For components and connectors, different LLMs (except TinyLLaMA and Qwen) have similar performance, giving practitioners flexibility in their choice.

For other architectural questions, DeepSeek or GPT-4 mini are recommended for their superior performance for quality solutions and rationale of decisions.

The results of RQ2 guide practitioners on which combinations of LLMs to use for architectural questions. To obtain a higher variety of answers and information, practitioners should ask LLMs with less similar responses. For example, DeepSeek and GPT-4o have lower similarity and high accuracy, making them good choices to cover the most correct and varied answers.

6 Threats to Validity

External Validity
One threat to external validity is that our evaluation of LLMs was based on the AK of a single software system, Hadoop HDFS, as has been provided in the ground truth [37]. This may limit the generalizability of our findings to other open-source systems, which might have more or less resources about their software architecture in the training datasets of LLMs. However, researchers frequently analyzed Hadoop HDFS for its software architecture [25,32], due to its extensive resources on AK. Therefore, we believe our results could apply to other open-source systems with similar AK resources.

Another threat to external validity is that we evaluated seven specific LLMs. Our findings may not be generalizable to other models of varying sizes and datasets. Nevertheless, our results can serve as a baseline and hypothesis regarding the accuracy and similarities of LLMs to answer architectural questions related to existing systems.

Construct Validity
One threat to construct validity is due to the applied textual comparison technique (see Sect. 2) to compare the responses of the LLMs to the ground truth, and among responses, which might involve mistakes. However, we have utilized fuzzy string matching to cover the most variations and adjusted the threshold of fuzzy matching to achieve the best accuracy. Furthermore, we followed a semi-automated approach with manual verification.

Reliability
One threat to reliability arises from the variability of LLMs. These models typically incorporate a random element in their output to enhance text diversity. For instance, when the same question is posed multiple times, an LLM might generate slightly different responses each time due to this stochastic nature. This randomness can make it challenging to replicate results. However, we share the responses of LLMs and scripts [34] to facilitate replication of the research process.

Another threat to reliability is using a semi-automated approach to analyze responses and extract answers. The manual analysis might involve bias. However, two authors analyzed and discussed the data. Also, we limited the manual analysis to specific answers (e.g., only false positives), where each answer has few terms. The small size of manual analysis reduced the chance for disagreements.

7 Related Work

This section discusses related work on AK and other related work that utilizes LLMs for software architecture.

7.1 Architectural Knowledge

Early work (e.g., [27,38]) explored AK concepts and proposed manual documentation tools (e.g., [21]). More recent studies have explored AK within software repositories, such as issue trackers [4,28,32] and mailing lists [33], as well as on the Web through forums [6], technical documentation [22], and blogs [35]. Additionally, researchers investigated design decisions for specific domains, such as quantum [2] and machine learning systems [41]. However, these studies do not utilize or evaluate LLMs, which sets them apart from our research aim.

Researchers applied machine learning techniques to classify design decisions from issue trackers [4] and mailing lists [17]. However, these approaches do not incorporate or evaluate LLMs, setting them apart from this study.

7.2 Language Models for Software Architecture

Software engineers started to use LLMs for different tasks [24,40], and software architecture researchers also started to evaluate LLMs.

Some work utilizes BERT for different architectural tasks, such as classifying design decisions in documentation [26] and mailing lists [33]. However, these works do not use or evaluate advanced LLMs like GPT and LLaMA, which offer different capabilities (e.g., prompting) than BERT.

Dhar et al. [13,14] use GPT and T5 to recommend design decisions. The authors evaluate different prompting techniques and fine-tuning. Similarly, Díaz-Pace et al. [15] propose approaches to recommend and document design decisions, in which the authors use GPT combined with retrieval-augmented generation. However, the goal of these works is different, as they aim to propose and document new design decisions, whereas our study evaluate seven LLMs to answer questions about the AK of existing systems.

Rukmono et al. [31] propose an approach to perform conformance checks between code and architectural components. The proposed approach use prompting techniques in LLMs, and specifically chain-of-thoughts. However, this work is different than ours, because it focus on conformance checks, whereas our study explore AK in existing systems without having a design specification.

Fuchß et al. [18] apply LLMs for traceability between architecture documentation and code. They also explore in another work [19] the usage of LLMs to generate simple architecture models that can be used as intermediate artifacts in transitive traceability. However, these works are different as they focus on traceability rather AK.

In our previous work [36,37], we evaluated the accuracy, quality and trustworthiness of GPT-3.5 to answer architectural questions on Hadoop HDFS. However, in this paper, we evaluate seven different LLMs and analyze the similarity of their generated answers.

8 Conclusion

In this study, we compared the accuracy and similarity of various LLMs in addressing architectural questions. Our findings show that all LLMs achieve higher recall than precision. Additionally, we observed significant differences in accuracy among the LLMs, with certain models performing better on specific architectural knowledge concepts. Despite these differences, LLMs show high similarity in their responses, including both correct and incorrect answers.

Future work involves extending this evaluation to other software systems. Furthermore, we plan to develop new approaches to improve the accuracy of LLMs for answering questions about the architectural knowledge of an existing system. Our planned approaches will use recent prompting techniques, fine tuning and combining the results of LLMs to improve accuracy.

Acknowledgements. This work was funded by the Topic Engineering Secure Systems of the Helmholtz Association (HGF) and supported by KASTEL Security Research Labs, Karlsruhe.

Data Availibility. All data and artifacts are available online [34].

References

1. Large Enough — Mistral AI. https://mistral.ai/news/mistral-large-2407
2. Aktar, M.S., Liang, P., et al.: Architecture decisions in quantum software systems: an empirical study on stack exchange and GitHub. Inf. Softw. Technol. **177**, 107587 (2025). https://doi.org/10.1016/j.infsof.2024.107587
3. Bass, L., Clements, P., Kazman, R.: Software Architecture in Practice, 3rd edn. Addison-Wesley (2012)
4. Bhat, M., Shumaiev, K., Biesdorf, A., Hohenstein, U., Matthes, F.: Automatic extraction of design decisions from issue management systems: a machine learning based approach. In: Lopes, A., de Lemos, R. (eds.) ECSA 2017. LNCS, vol. 10475, pp. 138–154. Springer, Cham (2017). https://doi.org/10.1007/978-3-319-65831-5_10
5. Bhat, M., et al.: An expert recommendation system for design decision making: who should be involved in making a design decision? IEEE 15th ICSA, pp. 85–94 (2018). https://doi.org/10.1109/ICSA.2018.00018
6. Bi, T., Liang, P., Tang, A., Xia, X.: Mining architecture tactics and quality attributes knowledge in Stack Overflow. J. Syst. Softw. (2021). https://doi.org/10.1016/j.jss.2021.111005
7. Brown, T., Mann, B., Ryder, N., et al.: Language models are few-shot learners. In: Advances in Neural Information Processing Systems, vol. 33, pp. 1877–1901. Curran Associates, Inc. (2020). https://proceedings.neurips.cc/paper_files/paper/2020/file/1457c0d6bfcb4967418bfb8ac142f64a-Paper.pdf
8. Buschmann, F., Meunier, R., Rohnert, H., Sommerlad, P., Stal, M.: Pattern-Oriented Software Architecture: A System of Patterns, 1 edn. Wiley (1996)

9. Chen, L., et al.: A survey on evaluating large language models in code generation tasks (2024). arXiv:2408.16498
10. Crochemore, M., Rytter, W.: Jewels of stringology: text algorithms. World Sci. (2002). https://doi.org/10.1142/4838
11. de Dieu, M.J., Liang, P., et al.: Characterizing architecture related posts and their usefulness in stack overflow. J. Syst. Softw. **198**, 111608 (2023). https://doi.org/10.1016/j.jss.2023.111608
12. DeepSeek-AI, Guo, D., Yang, D., Zhang, H., et al.: DeepSeek-R1: incentivizing reasoning capability in LLMs via reinforcement learning (2025). https://doi.org/10.48550/arXiv.2501.12948
13. Dhar, R., Vaidhyanathan, K., Varma, V.: Can LLMs generate architectural design decisions? - an exploratory empirical study. In: IEEE 21st ICSA, pp. 79–89. IEEE (2024). https://doi.org/10.1109/ICSA59870.2024.00016
14. Dhar, R., Vaidhyanathan, K., Varma, V.: Leveraging generative AI for architecture knowledge management. In: IEEE 21st ICSA Companion, pp. 163–166 (2024). https://doi.org/10.1109/ICSA-C63560.2024.00034
15. Díaz-Pace, J.A., Tommasel, A., Capilla, R.: Helping novice architects to make quality design decisions using an LLM-based assistant. In: Galster, M., Scandurra, P., Mikkonen, T., Oliveira Antonino, P., Nakagawa, E.Y., Navarro, E. (eds.) ECSA 2024. LNCS, vol. 14889, pp. 324–332. Springer, Cham (2024). https://doi.org/10.1007/978-3-031-70797-1_21
16. Fan, A., et al.: Large language models for software engineering: survey and open problems. In: IEEE/ACM ICSE: Future of Software Engineering, pp. 31–53 (2023). https://doi.org/10.1109/ICSE-FoSE59343.2023.00008
17. Fu, L., Liang, P., Li, X., Yang, C.: A machine learning based ensemble method for automatic multiclass classification of decisions. In: ACM EASE, pp. 40–49 (2021). https://doi.org/10.1145/3463274.3463325
18. Fuchß, D., et al.: LiSSA: toward generic traceability link recovery through retrieval-augmented generation. In: ICSE (2025). https://doi.org/10.1109/ICSE55347.2025.00186
19. Fuchß, D., Liu, H., Hey, T., Keim, J., Koziolek, A.: Enabling architecture traceability by LLM-based architecture component name extraction. In: 22nd IEEE ICSA (2025). https://doi.org/10.5445/IR/1000179830
20. Garcia, J., Ivkovic, I., Medvidovic, N.: A comparative analysis of software architecture recovery techniques. In: IEEE/ACM ASE, pp. 486–496 (2013). https://doi.org/10.1109/ASE.2013.6693106
21. Gerdes, S., Soliman, M., Riebisch, M.: Decision buddy: tool support for constraint-based design decisions during system evolution. In: International WS on FoSADA, pp. 13–18. ACM, New York (2015). https://doi.org/10.1145/2751491.2751495
22. Gorton, I., Xu, R., Yang, Y., Liu, H., Zheng, G.: Experiments in curation: towards machine-assisted construction of software architecture knowledge bases. In: IEEE/IFIP ICSA 2017, pp. 79–88 (2017)
23. Grattafiori, A., Dubey, A., Jauhri, A., et al.: The Llama 3 Herd of Models (2024). https://doi.org/10.48550/arXiv.2407.21783
24. Hou, X., et al.: Large language models for software engineering: a systematic literature review. TOSEM (2024). https://doi.org/10.1145/3695988
25. Kazman, R., Goldenson, D., Monarch, I., Nichols, W., Valetto, G.: Evaluating the effects of architectural documentation: a case study of a large scale open source project. IEEE Trans. Software Eng. **42**(3), 220–260 (2016). https://doi.org/10.1109/TSE.2015.2465387

26. Keim, J., Hey, T., Sauer, B., Koziolek, A.: A taxonomy for design decisions in software architecture documentation. In: Batista, T., Bureš, T., Raibulet, C., Muccini, H. (eds.) ECSA 2022. LNCS, vol. 13928, pp. 439–454. Springer, Cham (2023). https://doi.org/10.1007/978-3-031-36889-9_29
27. Kruchten, P., Lago, P., van Vliet, H.: Building up and reasoning about architectural knowledge. In: Hofmeister, C., Crnkovic, I., Reussner, R. (eds.) QoSA 2006. LNCS, vol. 4214, pp. 43–58. Springer, Heidelberg (2006). https://doi.org/10.1007/11921998_8
28. Maarleveld, J., Dekker, A., Druyts, S., Soliman, M.: Maestro: a deep learning based tool to find and explore architectural design decisions in issue tracking systems. In: ECSA Tools Tracks (2023)
29. Naveed, H., et al.: A comprehensive overview of large language models (2024). arXiv:2307.06435
30. Radford, A., Narasimhan, K., Salimans, T., Sutskever, I.: Improving language understanding with unsupervised learning (2018). https://web.archive.org/web/20230318210736/https://openai.com/research/language-unsupervised
31. Rukmono, S.A., Ochoa, L., Chaudron, M.: Deductive software architecture recovery via chain-of-thought prompting. In: ICSE-NIER (2024). https://doi.org/10.1145/3639476.3639776
32. Soliman, M., Galster, M., Avgeriou, P.: An exploratory study on architectural knowledge in issue tracking systems. ECSA (2021). https://doi.org/10.1007/978-3-030-86044-8_8
33. Soliman, M.: Exploring architectural design decisions in mailing lists and their traceability to issue trackers. In: Galster, M., Scandurra, P., Mikkonen, T., Oliveira Antonino, P., Nakagawa, E.Y., Navarro, E. (eds.) ECSA 2024. LNCS, vol. 14889, pp. 307–323. Springer, Cham (2024). https://doi.org/10.1007/978-3-031-70797-1_20
34. Soliman, M., Ashraf, E., Abdelsalam, K.M.K., Keim, J., Venkatesh, A.P.S.: Supplementary material for 'LLMs for Software Architecture Knowledge: A Comparative Analysis Among Seven LLMs'. https://doi.org/10.5281/zenodo.15584019
35. Soliman, M., Gericke, K., Avgeriou, P.: Where and what do software architects blog?: An exploratory study on architectural knowledge in blogs, and their relevance to design steps. In: IEEE ICSA, pp. 129–140 (2023). https://doi.org/10.1109/ICSA56044.2023.00020
36. Soliman, M., Keim, J.: Supplementary material for 'Do Large Language Models Contain Software Architectural Knowledge? An Exploratory Case Study with GPT'. https://doi.org/10.5281/zenodo.14512761
37. Soliman, M., Keim, J.: Do large language models contain software architectural knowledge? An exploratory case study with GPT. In: IEEE ICSA. IEEE (2025). https://doi.org/10.5445/IR/1000178724
38. Tang, A., Jin, Y., Han, J.: A rationale-based architecture model for design traceability and reasoning. JSS **80**(6), 918–934 (2007). https://doi.org/10.1016/j.jss.2006.08.040
39. Touvron, H., et al.: Llama: open and efficient foundation language models (2023). arXiv:2302.13971
40. Venkatesh, A.P.S., Sabu, S., Mir, A.M., Reis, S., Bodden, E.: The emergence of large language models in static analysis: a first look through micro-benchmarks. In: FORGE (2024). https://doi.org/10.1145/3650105.3652288
41. Warnett, S.J., Zdun, U.: Bridging the gap between MLOps and RLOps: an industry 4.0 case study on architectural design decisions in practice. In: IEEE ICSA (2025). http://eprints.cs.univie.ac.at/8343/

42. Xuanfan, N., Piji, L.: A systematic evaluation of large language models for natural language generation tasks. In: 22nd Chin. Nat. Conf. on Comp. Linguistics, Harbin, China, pp. 40–56 (2023). https://aclanthology.org/2023.ccl-2.4
43. Yang, A., Yang, B., Hui, B., et al.: Qwen2 Technical Report (2024). https://doi.org/10.48550/arXiv.2407.10671
44. Zhang, T., Kishore, V., Wu, F., Weinberger, K.Q., Artzi, Y.: BERTScore: evaluating text generation with BERT (2020). arXiv:1904.09675

LLM-Based Quality Assessment of Software Architecture Diagrams: A Preliminary Study with Four Open-Source Projects

Glauber Queiroz de Oliveira and Nabor C. Mendonça(✉)

Post Graduate Program in Applied Informatics, University of Fortaleza, Fortaleza, CE, Brazil
nabor@unifor.br

Abstract. This works explores the feasibility and challenges of using a Large Language Model (LLM) to automatically assess the quality of software architecture diagrams. Our approach is based on a structured prompt that guides the LLM to evaluate architecture diagrams and their accompanying descriptions according to five core quality criteria: clarity, consistency, completeness, accuracy, and level of detail. Preliminary experimental results using OpenAI's ChatGPT-4o in four open-source projects suggest that LLMs can provide valuable feedback and detect diagrammatic inconsistencies, often in alignment with human expert evaluations. However, the LLM also struggled with context-specific design choices, sometimes misjudging deliberate omissions or the appropriate level of detail, indicating that human oversight remains indispensable. To guide researchers and practitioners, we further recommend practical guidelines for data preparation, prompt construction, and result interpretation, aiming to maximize the reliability and utility of LLM-based architectural evaluations.

Keywords: Software architecture assessment · Large language models · Open-source projects

1 Introduction

Architecture diagrams are essential tools for communicating the structure and behavior of complex software systems [3,12]. They help diverse stakeholders understand and refine technical design decisions [2,19]. However, many diagrams are created in an *ad hoc* manner, lacking standardization and often suffering from inconsistencies, visual clutter, and ambiguous semantics [5,18]. A recent large-scale study by Migliorini *et al.* [15] confirmed that most architecture diagrams in open-source projects are informal, relying on basic shapes and arrows rather than formal notations like UML.

As systems grow in complexity, maintaining clear and accurate diagrams becomes more difficult. In this context, Large Language Models (LLMs) have

V. Andrikopoulos et al. (Eds.): ECSA 2025, LNCS 15929, pp. 116–123, 2026.
https://doi.org/10.1007/978-3-032-02138-0_8

emerged as powerful tools in software engineering [7,8,17], yet their potential for assessing the quality of software architecture diagrams remains underexplored [6]. This paper presents a preliminary empirical study investigating whether an LLM can help identify quality issues in architecture diagrams.

We address the following research questions:

RQ1: How effectively can an LLM assess software architecture diagrams across multiple quality criteria compared to a human expert?
RQ2: What are the main challenges in using an LLM for this purpose, and how can these be mitigated?

To explore these questions, we designed a structured prompting strategy based on five quality criteria: clarity, consistency, completeness, accuracy, and level of detail. We applied this approach using OpenAI's ChatGPT-4o on diagrams from four open-source projects [15], and compared the LLM's assessments to those of a software architecture expert.

Our findings show that LLMs can reliably detect some types of quality issues, especially inconsistencies or missing elements, but also tend to overestimate omissions or misinterpret design choices without context. These limitations reinforce the importance of human oversight. We also offer practical guidelines for improving prompt design and interpretation of LLM-generated evaluations.

In summary, this work (i) proposes a structured prompt for LLM-based architecture diagram assessment; (ii) evaluates its effectiveness in a small-scale study; and (iii) identifies key limitations and guidelines to inform future use of LLMs in software architecture quality assurance.

2 Background and Related Work

Software architecture documentation plays a key role in communicating design decisions to stakeholders. Standards such as ISO/IEC/IEEE 42010 [9] emphasize qualities like consistency, completeness, and stakeholder relevance. Classical models [3,12,19] promote multi-view representations tailored to specific concerns. Nonetheless, diagrams are often informal and inconsistent in practice [15], highlighting the need for better assessment methods.

Although methods like SAAM [11] and ATAM [10] assess architectural decisions, they rely on clear, accurate diagrams. Studies on UML clarity and comprehension [5,18] reinforce the importance of attributes such as visual clarity, semantic accuracy, and completeness [13]. These criteria form the basis of our evaluation framework.

Recent work has explored LLMs for architectural decision support [4], design tasks [1], and conformance checking [20]. While promising, these applications often focus on code or textual artifacts. Esposito *et al.* [6] identify the lack of validation methods for GenAI outputs in architecture tasks. Our work addresses this gap by focusing on automated quality assessment of architecture diagrams, a largely unexplored problem with distinct challenges related to visual representation, context, and stakeholder intent.

Architecture Assessment Prompt

Objective: Evaluate the quality of the attached architecture diagram, considering both the diagram and its description below.

[*Insert diagram here*]

Description: [*Insert textual description here*]

Evaluation Criteria:
1. *Clarity*: The diagram should be understandable to both technical and non-technical stakeholders. Assess whether the symbols, labels, and information flow are clear. Provide suggestions for improving clarity, if necessary (e.g., using more accessible language, improving labeling, simplifying the explanation of key components, providing a clearer description).
2. *Consistency*: Check whether symbols, styles, and terms are used uniformly throughout the diagram. If there is inconsistency (e.g., symbols representing the same type of component are different), highlight this and recommend a standard set of symbols or styles. Also, check for consistency between the architecture diagram and its description (e.g., are both communicating the same content? Are there any discrepancies or omissions in either the diagram or the description? Provide suggestions for improvement if needed).
3. *Completeness*: The diagram should present all relevant components of the architecture, including any interactions between them. Note any missing components or interactions and suggest what should be added to provide a comprehensive view.
4. *Accuracy*: Ensure that the diagram accurately reflects the described architecture. Highlight any discrepancies between the diagram and the text (e.g., if a component described in the text is missing in the diagram or vice versa). Provide recommendations to resolve any inaccuracies.
5. *Level of Detail*: Evaluate whether the level of detail is appropriate for the target audience. Technical diagrams may require more details for developers, while high-level diagrams for stakeholders should simplify complex concepts. If the diagram is too detailed or too vague for the intended audience, suggest changes to meet the audience's needs.

Evaluation Instructions:
For each criterion, rate the diagram as follows:
Meets Expectations: No significant changes needed.
Partially Meets Expectations: Minor improvements needed (explain what they are).
Does Not Meet Expectations: Significant issues need to be addressed (explain what they are and provide specific suggestions for improvement).

Use this structure to ensure that the evaluation is thorough and specific. Justify your rating for each criterion and provide suggestions for improvement where necessary.

Fig. 1. Prompt template to assess the quality of software architecture diagrams

3 Methodology

Our methodology comprises five stages: defining quality criteria, designing a structured prompt, selecting an LLM, preparing the dataset, and reviewing outputs with human feedback.

We evaluate diagrams using five criteria drawn from standards and literature [9,13]: *clarity*, *consistency*, *completeness*, *accuracy*, and *level of detail*. While clarity and consistency concern the diagram's internal presentation, the other criteria require comparison with a textual description. Thus, both diagram and description are evaluated together to ensure a complete understanding of the architecture.

To elicit structured responses, we developed a prompt template guiding the LLM through the five criteria, requesting both ratings and justifications (Fig. 1). The design applies prompt engineering techniques such as zero-shot, chain-of-thought, and role prompting [14].

We used ChatGPT-4o [16] for its advanced visual and reasoning capabilities. Experiments were conducted via the models' web interface in late 2024. We selected four open-source projects from Migliorini *et al.*'s dataset [15], covering diverse domains such as e-readers, health APIs, and middleware integration. The selected projects are:

- **Readium (P1):** a toolkit for building Web/mobile readers that support ebooks, audiobooks and comics.[1]
- **HyperTrack Live App (P2):** a live location sharing application for Android.[2]
- **FHIR Reference Client (P3):** a reference implementation for a client application that uses the NVSS Fast Healthcare Interoperability Resources (FHIR) API.[3]
- **Integration Service (P4):** a Linux tool that enables communication among an arbitrary number of middleware protocols that speak different languages.[4]

For each project, we extracted one architecture diagram and a textual description. These were verified for clarity and completeness before being submitted to the LLM using our prompt.

A software architecture expert independently reviewed the LLM's outputs and evaluated their accuracy and relevance per criterion. In cases of disagreement, the expert judgment was considered ground truth. This validation step was essential to identify limitations in the LLM's reasoning and assess its reliability for architecture quality assessment.

4 Results

Table 1 summarizes the LLM's assessments for each of the four projects, compared against the human expert's judgments across the five quality criteria. Overall, the LLM's evaluations aligned well with expert judgment, particularly for clarity and consistency. The most common issues identified were mismatched symbols and vague labels. Ratings diverged most in the level of detail, where the LLM sometimes assumed a broader stakeholder audience than justified. Completeness and accuracy often fluctuated together, typically due to omitted elements in the diagrams that were mentioned in the textual description. These gaps were flagged by the LLM and partially confirmed by the expert.

Figure 2 shows the architecture diagram for the Integration Service project (P4). The architecture centers on a core component that translates across middleware protocols using system handles. The diagram is relatively simple but omits several functional details found in the textual description. Table 2 summarizes ChatGPT-4o's and the expert's evaluations of the that architecture diagram and its accompanying textual description. Both partially agree on issues of clarity, consistency, and completeness, noting that unclear flows, inconsistent symbols, and omitted components reduce overall quality. On accuracy, the LLM flags mismatches between text and diagram, which the expert confirms, though suggests the LLM should be more specific. For level of detail, the LLM recommends tailoring views to different audiences, while the expert disagrees, arguing the system primarily targets developers.

[1] https://github.com/readium.
[2] https://github.com/hypertrack/live-app-android.
[3] https://github.com/nightingaleproject/Reference-Client.
[4] https://github.com/eProsima/Integration-Service.

Table 1. LLM and expert evaluation of the four projects' architecture diagrams

	Quality Criteria Evaluation (LLM/Human Expert)				
Project	**Clarity**	**Consistency**	**Completeness**	**Accuracy**	**Lev. Detail**
P1	😐 / 👍	😐 / 👍	☹️ / 👍👎	😐 / 👍	😐 / 👍
P2	😐 / 👍	☹️ / 👍	😐 / 👍	😐 / 👍	🙂 / 👍
P3	😐 / 👍	☹️ / 👍	😐 / 👍👎	😐 / 👍	🙂 / 👍
P4	😐 / 👍	😐 / 👍👎	😐 / 👍👎	☹️ / 👍👎	😐 / 👎

Legend:

🙂 Meets Expectations — 👍 Agrees
😐 Partially Meets Expectations — 👍👎 Partially Agrees
☹️ Does Not Meet Expectations — 👎 Disagrees

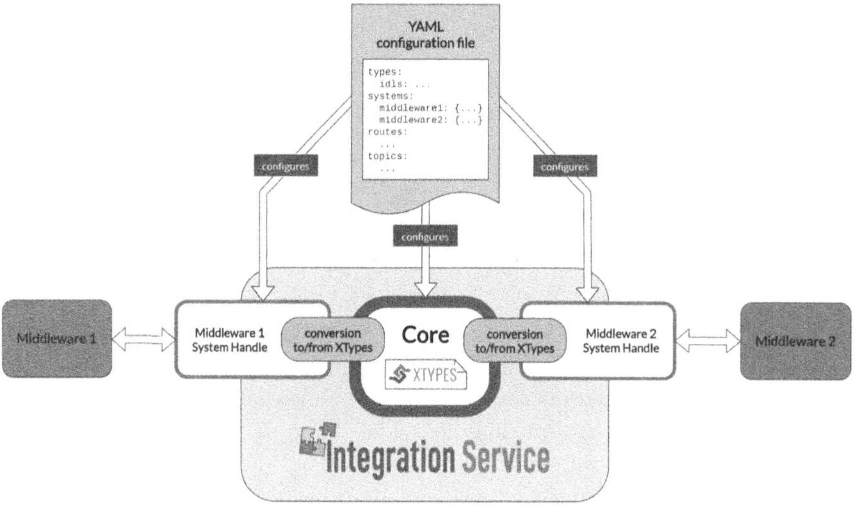

Fig. 2. Architecture diagram of Integration Service (P4). Source: https://github.com/eProsima/Integration-Service

5 Discussion and Guidelines

Our findings indicate that LLMs like ChatGPT-4o can successfully detect relevant quality issues in software architecture diagrams, especially concerning clarity, consistency, and completeness. In many cases, their assessments closely mirrored those of a human expert, suggesting that LLMs can provide useful initial

Table 2. LLM and expert assessments of Integration Service's architecture diagram

	ChatGPT-4o	Human Expert
Clarity:	*Partially Meets Expectations*	*Agrees*
While the diagram includes labels and use some standardized symbols, certain aspects lack clarity. For example, the flow of information between components isn't immediately evident in all cases. **Suggestions:** Enhance labeling with more descriptive text or tooltips to explain key components. Use arrows or lines consistently to represent data flow or interactions. Consider simplifying the layout for improved readability, especially for non-technical stakeholders.		
Consistency:	*Partially Meets Expectations*	*Partially Agrees*
The diagram uses a mix of symbols and styles, leading to potential confusion. For instance, similar components are represented differently. Additionally, there are slight mismatches between the diagram and its textual descriptions (e.g., a component described in the text may appear differently in the diagram or might be missing). **Suggestions:** Adopt a standardized set of symbols and styles. Ensure description and diagram align by conducting a thorough review to check for mismatches or omissions.		The model could have been more specific by naming the components that are represented differently or inconsistently with the textual description.
Completeness:	*Partially Meets Expectations*	*Partially Agrees*
The diagram generally covers key components but fails to include certain interactions or auxiliary components mentioned in the description. For example, supporting systems or middleware mentioned in the text are absent in the diagram. **Suggestions:** Include all critical components and their interactions as described in the text. Clearly represent auxiliary systems or middleware that contribute to the architecture.		Idem.
Accuracy:	*Does Not Meet Expectations*	*Partially Agrees*
There are notable discrepancies between the diagram and its description. Some elements mentioned in the text are missing from the diagram, and the role of certain components is inaccurately portrayed. **Suggestions:** Cross-reference the diagram with the text to ensure accuracy. Update the diagram to include all components and interactions as described in the textual explanations.		Idem.
Level of Detail:	*Partially Meets Expectations*	*Disagrees*
The diagram attempts to strike a balance between technical detail and simplicity but often leans too heavily in one direction depending on the target audience. **Suggestions:** Tailor the level of detail in the diagram to the intended audience. For example, provide high-level diagrams for stakeholders and detailed ones for developers. Consider layering information, where users can drill down into details if needed.		It's unreasonable to consider other types of stakeholders for a middleware integration tool rather than distributed applications developers.

feedback during architecture reviews. However, we also observed limitations: LLMs sometimes misinterpret design intent, misjudge omissions as errors, or overgeneralize the level of detail required. These behaviors reinforce the importance of human oversight and contextual awareness in architectural analysis.

This preliminary study has clear limitations. It was conducted using a single, albeit advanced, LLM and relied on one expert for human evaluation. Furthermore, the dataset was restricted to four open-source projects, and while selected for diversity, these examples may not reflect the range and complexity of architecture diagrams encountered in industrial settings. These constraints limit generalizability and emphasize the need for broader replication involving multiple experts, varied LLMs, and more diverse architectural artifacts.

Despite these limitations, the results open promising avenues for practice. LLMs could be integrated into architecture-centric development workflows to support tasks such as early-stage diagram review, consistency checking, and documentation refinement. Their ability to identify missing or unclear elements makes them potential allies in improving stakeholder communication and ensuring alignment between visual and textual architectural representations. To that end, we distill our experience into a set of practical guidelines that may enhance the effectiveness of LLMs in this context:

- **Consolidate artifacts:** Provide the architecture diagram and its accompanying description in a single input. Fragmented or partial context can reduce the LLM's ability to cross-reference components accurately.
- **Use high-quality images:** Low-resolution diagrams with small or blurry labels hinder the model's visual parsing. Ensure diagrams are sharp and readable, especially when labels convey architectural roles.
- **Prompt explicitly:** LLMs often prioritize text over visuals. Instruct them to consider both the diagram and the textual description explicitly to mitigate text-only bias.
- **Encourage step-by-step reasoning:** Chain-of-thought prompts, such as asking the model to summarize the diagram before assessing it, improve interpretability and coherence by guiding the model through visual-textual alignment.

6 Conclusion and Future Work

This paper presented a preliminary study on using a state-of-the-art LLM, ChatGPT-4o, to assess the quality of software architecture diagrams. Our results show that LLMs can highlight useful design issues, particularly related to clarity and consistency, but often require expert oversight to account for context and intent. We also proposed practical guidelines for improving prompt quality and result interpretation. As future work, we plan to expand the dataset, evaluate other more advanced LLMs (e.g., o3, Gemini 2.5, DeepSeek-R1), and explore integration of LLM-based diagram review into real-world architecture workflows.

Acknowledgments. ChatGPT, Gemini, and GitHub Copilot were used to assist in structuring and revising portions of this paper. Nabor C. Mendona is partially supported by the Brazilian National Council for Scientific and Technological Development (CNPq) under grant 313558/2023-0.

Data Availability. All data artifacts collected and generated during this research are available at https://gitlab.com/my-anonymous-repos/LLM-Architecture-Assessment-ECSA2025

References

1. Ahmad, A., et al.: Towards human-bot collaborative software architecting with ChatGPT. In: Proceedings of the 27th International Conference on Evaluation and Assessment in Software Engineering (EASE), pp. 279–285 (2023)
2. Bass, L., Clements, P., Kazman, R.: Software Architecture in Practice, 3rd edn. Addison-Wesley (2012)
3. Clements, P., et al.: Documenting Software Architectures: Views and Beyond. Addison-Wesley, Boston (2002)
4. Dhar, R., Vaidhyanathan, K., Varma, V.: Can LLMs generate architectural design decisions? an exploratory empirical study. arXiv preprint arXiv:2403.01709 (2024)
5. Dobing, B., Parsons, J.: How UML is used. Commun. ACM **49**(5), 109–113 (2006)
6. Esposito, M., et al.: Generative AI for software architecture. Applications, trends, challenges, and future directions. arXiv preprint arXiv:2503.13310 (2025)
7. Fan, A., et al.: Large language models for software engineering: survey and open problems. In: 2023 IEEE/ACM International Conference on Software Engineering: Future of Software Engineering (ICSE-FoSE), pp. 31–53. IEEE (2023)
8. Hou, X., et al.: Large language models for software engineering: a systematic literature review. ACM Trans. Softw. Eng. Methodol. (2023)
9. ISO/IEC/IEEE: ISO/IEC/IEEE 42010:2022 Software, systems and enterprise – Architecture description. International Standard (2022)
10. Kazman, R., Klein, M., Clements, P.: ATAM: method for architecture evaluation. Technical report. CMU/SEI-2000-TR-004, Software Engineering Institute, Carnegie Mellon University (2000)
11. Kazman, R., et al.: SAAM: a method for analyzing the properties of software architectures. In: Proceedings of 16th International Conference on Software Engineering (ICSE), pp. 81–90. IEEE (1994)
12. Kruchten, P.: Architectural blueprints—the "4+1" view model of software architecture. IEEE Softw. **12**(6), 42–50 (1995)
13. Lange, C., Chaudron, M.: Managing model quality in UML-based software development. In: 13th IEEE International Workshop on Software Technology and Engineering Practice (STEP), pp. 7–16. IEEE (2005)
14. Liu, P., et al.: Pre-train, prompt, and predict: a systematic survey of prompting methods in natural language processing. ACM Comput. Surv. **55**(9), 1–35 (2023)
15. Migliorini, S., et al.: Architectural views: the state of practice in open-source software projects. In: Galster, M., Scandurra, P., Mikkonen, T., Oliveira Antonino, P., Nakagawa, E.Y., Navarro, E. (eds.) ECSA 2024. LNCS, vol. 14889, pp. 396–415. Springer, Cham (2024). https://doi.org/10.1007/978-3-031-70797-1_27
16. OpenAI: GPT-4O system card (2024). https://openai.com/index/gpt-4o-system-card/
17. Ozkaya, I.: Application of large language models to software engineering tasks: opportunities, risks, and implications. IEEE Softw. **40**(3), 4–8 (2023)
18. Purchase, H., Colpoys, L., McGill, M., Carrington, D.: UML class diagram syntax: an empirical study of comprehension. In: Proceedings of the 2001 Asia-Pacific Symposium on Information Visualisation (APVis), pp. 113–120 (2001)
19. Rozanski, N., Woods, E.: Software Systems Architecture: Working with Stakeholders Using Viewpoints and Perspectives, 2nd edn. Addison-Wesley (2012)
20. Rubei, R., Salle, A.D., Bucaioni, A.: LLM-based recommender systems for violation resolutions in continuous architectural conformance. In: 4th International Workshop on Model-Driven Engineering for Software Architecture (MDE4SA) (2025)

Architectures for Embedded Systems

Nanosatellite Flight Software: A Rigorous Software Architecture Perspective

Christoforos Vasilakis(✉), Alexandros Tsagkaropoulos, Angelos Motsios, Christos Tsigkanos, and Dionysios Reisis

University of Athens, Athens, Greece
christof-v@phys.uoa.gr

Abstract. Engineering of flight software architectures for nanosatellite missions presents significant challenges due to constrained on-board computational resources, stringent reliability requirements and complex, mission-specific operational demands. Despite the advancements of the New Space era, designs and architectural documentation are seldomly available, largely due to intellectual property restrictions. To address this gap, this paper illustrates the flight software architecture for a nanosatellite mission as per the 4+1 view model. By deconstructing the on-board software system into its physical, logical, development, process and scenario views, we offer an in-depth analysis of the architectural decisions, trade-offs, and design rationales that guided development. The design presented extends beyond typical reliability and safety to emphasize deployability, integrability, modifiability, and testability design drivers. This experience report intends to advocate rigorous software architecture principles in software engineering for space software, by sharing insights and providing detailed architectural documentation with the overall goal of advancing a novel research agenda within the community.

Keywords: Flight Software · Architectural Views · Experience Report

1 Introduction

The engineering of flight software (FSW) architectures for nanosatellite missions involves a constellation of complex challenges inherent to the domain of on-board space systems. Constraints imposed by limited on-board computational resources, the imperative for high reliability in the unforgiving space environment, and intricate operational demands of each mission require sophisticated and well thought-out architectural designs—while software size and complexity are further typical constraints [7]. The body of knowledge spanning architecture, requirements, specification and implementation of software on spacecraft and their payloads [10] is vast and such engineering know-how has long been a core component of specialized teams within institutional space organizations. Recently, the emergence of low-cost, powerful on-board computers on contemporary small-scale flight- and space- craft [33], has led to wide availability of

V. Andrikopoulos et al. (Eds.): ECSA 2025, LNCS 15929, pp. 127–143, 2026.
https://doi.org/10.1007/978-3-032-02138-0_9

platforms and lowered the barrier to entry, often referred to as *New Space* [23]. However, designs and architectural documentation are often not available to the research community due to intellectual property restrictions that inhibit the dissemination of detailed design information across the aerospace industry.

We seek to address this gap by providing a comprehensive perspective of the FSW of the ERMIS3 mission from a software architecture lens and in particular through Kruchten's 4+1 architectural view model [20]. The ERMIS3 mission, a component of Greece's inaugural nanosatellite constellation, is designed to demonstrate high-throughput laser optical downlinking achieving data rates of up to 1 Gbps and hyperspectral imaging for Earth observation. By deconstructing the on-board software system into its Physical, Logical, Development, Process, and Scenario views, we report an in-depth analysis of our experience; namely the architectural decisions, trade-offs, and design rationale that inform the development process of the flight software architecture at hand.

Naturally, FSW engineering for a space mission is tied to (and begins with—also due to the waterfall process typical in the domain) particular mission requirements. However, broad design goals do apply and guide the architecture development, reliability and safety being at the forefront due to the criticality of the space domain. As such, the design we present is crafted to satisfy certain design goals beyond mission requirements—we select in particular *deployability*, *integrability*, *modifiability*, and *testability* as design drivers. By leveraging the principle of modularity and sticking to standardized interfaces, the FSW facilitates efficient deployment and seamless integration with the various subsystems on-board (such as sensors, payloads, etc.). We advocate loose coupling and high cohesion within the architecture to support straightforward code modifications, accommodating often evolving mission objectives with minimal impact on existing components. Comprehensive testability is achieved through embedded testing interfaces, utilization of automated build and simulation environments, and adherence to rigorous verification protocols, something typical in the aerospace domain. We work on top of F Prime (F') [2], a cutting-edge open-source framework developed by the Jet Propulsion Laboratory. Our choice is motivated by its notable real-world applications [4,19], and rigorous application of software engineering practices (e.g., components with typed port connections, and object-oriented design). Supplementary artifacts consist of further documentation of the software architecture as open-source assets.

In this paper, we seek to bring the attention of the community to space software, by presenting detailed architectural documentation. Specifically, our contributions are as follows:

- We advocate a rigorous approach for applying software architecture principles to the design of a nanosatellite software architecture;
- We report in-depth our experience including architectural decisions, trade-offs, and rationale that informed the design;
- We present detailed architectural documentation of the software design, following Kruchten's 4+1 view model.

The rest of this paper is structured as follows. Section 2 outlines the design drivers for the FSW architecture. Section 3 describes the architectural design per the 4+1 view model, while Sect. 4 elaborates on design rationale and trade-offs including in particular a reflection on the design drivers informing the architecture. Related work is considered in Sect. 5, and Sect. 6 concludes the paper along with an outlook to a research agenda.

2 Flight Software Design Drivers

Naturally, numerous software requirements are identified as part of any space mission, in typically extensive requirements processes involving high stakeholder engagement. In the following, we maintain a birds-eye view—excluding mission particularities—and distill design goals that drive the architectural design. Those comprise essentially quality attributes, functionality and constraints, and were identified with the following methodological steps:

1. Key quality attributes were identified through consultations with mission partners, hardware-providers and stakeholders.
2. An iterative feedback loop was used to refine these to design drivers, ensuring alignment with institutional oversight and mission partners.
3. The 4+1 View Model was selected for representation due to its clarity and effectiveness in supporting both technical validation and team on-boarding.
4. The flight software system was deconstructed and mapped to the views to clearly represent structure and behavior, and used for validating the design.

The methodological steps above yielded design drivers (as architectural goals), selected to the stringent and particular operational demands of our working context—the FSW must not only function correctly but also adapt to evolving mission parameters and potential anomalies.

(D1) Deployability. The FSW design shall be deployable in terms of appropriate allocation of the software to on-board compute elements, as the runtime execution environments that support integration with various subsystems.

(D2) Integrability. The FSW design shall ensure that its software elements can interact and function together in a cohesive manner.

(D3) Modifiability. The FSW design shall support modifiability in order to support software changes with minimal risk, in order to accommodate updates or addition of new functionality.

(D4) Testability. The FSW design shall support testability in order to ensure that functions behave as expected and meet the appropriate space mission reliability and safety requirements.

Observe that each driver addresses a specific concern. Deployability (D1) ensures efficient allocation across heterogeneous on-board computing resources, vital for resource-constrained environments and redundancy demands (aligning with flexibility in ISO/IEC 25010). Integrability (D2) aims for seamless interaction between software elements, minimizing interface errors that can propagate system-wide failures (interoperability per 25010). Modifiability (D3) addresses the need for in-flight updates and feature enhancements, crucial for extending mission lifecycles or responding to unforeseen circumstances, while minimizing regression risks. Testability (D4) is naturally paramount for validating adherence to reliability and safety of a specific class of mission [11].

3 Architectural Views as per 4+1

In the following, we elaborate on the architecture using the 4+1 architectural view model [20]. Our selection of 4+1 stems from its long-recognized ability to comprehensively address the multifaceted nature of complex software systems. This structure supports thorough analysis and promotes clear communication across interdisciplinary teams, which are typical in scientific missions. Additionally, it aids on-boarding by presenting the system in accessible, role-specific views. Although the model's merits have been long-recognized in the community, we note the absence of a comprehensive FSW architectural design in the public domain. For elaborating a FSW architecture, we believe that it is highly appropriate in its provision of multiple perspectives. In our case, perspectives are tailored to specific concerns (from on-board compute elements, to development, to fault management techniques), ensuring that the architecture is understood and validated from various angles. Accordingly, we detail the architecture according to the following views:

1. **Physical**: Representing the system engineer's perspective, this view describes the on-board hardware topology and the various execution environments of the FSW.
2. **Logical**: Representing the end-user perspective, this view describes the organization of on-board software components and their functionalities.
3. **Development**: From the programmer's perspective, this view concerns the arrangement of modules in a topology as well as the development workflow.
4. **Process**: From the integrator's perspective, this view illustrates task interactions and execution flows within the FSW system.

The Scenario View serves as the "+1" component, integrating the four primary views through a series of scenarios that demonstrate key system functionalities—to illustrate such a scenario, we select particularly a fragment of the *fault detection and isolation* mechanism [17]—often deemed cross-cutting as it involves activations of different parts of the software architecture. We adopt UML2 diagrams to illustrate the 4+1 views [25].

3.1 Physical View

The Physical View illustrated in Fig. 1 consists of two primary components: the ground segment and the space segment, reflecting the typical perspective of space system engineers. Communication between the ground station and the nanosatellite is facilitated by each segment's transceivers, which ensure data

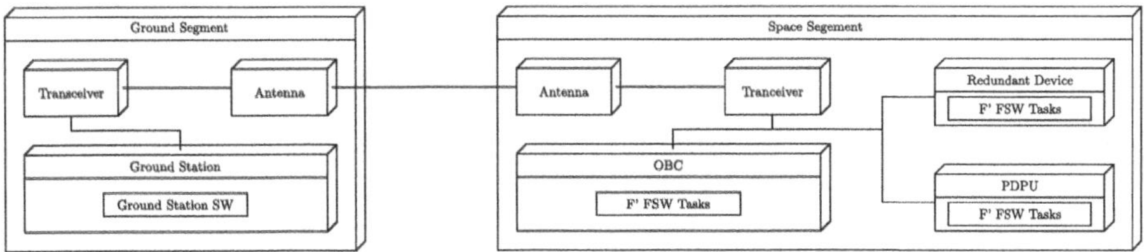

Fig. 1. Deployment diagram illustrating the hardware aspects of the system and software modules running on each hardware component

exchange through the ground and satellite antennas, establishing a communication link between the segments during 5-min windows that occur every 12 h.

In the ground segment, the primary interface for operators comprises the ground software[1]. Its core functions include monitoring the satellite's health by collecting telemetry beacon data and issuing operational commands controlling the spacecraft. Within the space segment, onboard communication between subsystems takes place over a shared Controller Area Network (CAN) bus. The mission's FSW operates on two processing units: the On-Board Computer (OBC), specifically the GOMspace Nanomind A3200, which utilizes an Atmel AVR32 microcontroller unit (MCU), and the Payload Data Processing Unit (PDPU), the Nanomind HP MK3, which integrates a Xilinx Zynq 7000 system-on-chip.

The FSW deployed on these processing units is responsible for executing mission specific tasks, including system configuration, command execution, event logging, telemetry management, health monitoring, and task scheduling. Due to the limited duration of the communication windows with the ground station, the software is designed for autonomous operation, transmitting collected data only on request when the satellite is within range of the ground station's antennas. Additionally, the PDPU handles the compression of data acquired from the mission's on-board hyperspectral camera and transmits the processed output to a high-speed laser communication system.

Observe that in the design presented, both the OBC and the PDPU function in a multi-master configuration, where the OBC serves as the primary system controller. While the OBC is the primary execution context of the FSW as is typical in missions, we highlight an important deployment aspect of the developed architecture: All FSW components are also deployed on the PDPU to ensure continued operation in the event of an OBC failure, demonstrating the system's deployability and fault tolerance. This redundancy is illustrated in Fig. 1, where the redundant device represents the OBC functionalities that the PDPU can assume, in addition to its nominal role in managing payload operations.

[1] We treat ground software as out of scope in this paper, as it involves axiomatically different architectural drivers, decisions and operational context.

3.2 Logical View

The Logical View of the proposed FSW architecture focuses on realizing its functional requirements. We opted for the class diagram of Fig. 2 to describe the objects of the architecture and the static relationships that exist among them. It is divided into functionality areas [25] that encompass classes providing the same functionality.

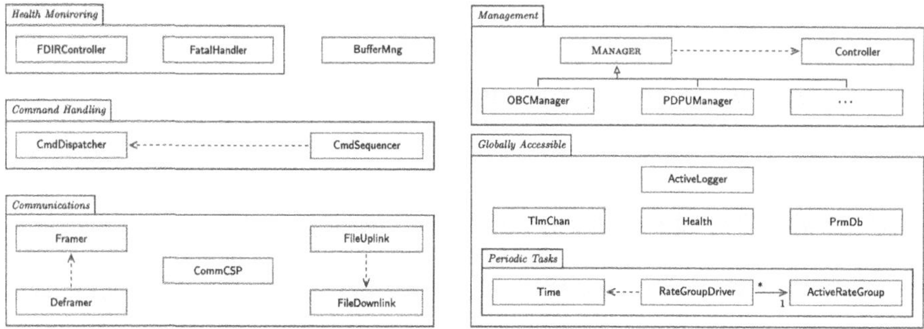

Fig. 2. Class diagram representing the Logical View of the FSW architecture—it categorizes classes based on their functional areas and explicitly illustrates significant relationships among them. Dashed arrows express dependency, solid arrows denote association and solid hollow arrows indicate generalization, following UML2 notation

The *Communications* area facilitates the communication with other satellite subsystems and the ground station uniformly (D2). The CubeSat Space Protocol (CSP) is a proven low-footprint and modular choice [21] that encapsulates networking information (D3). The CommCSP class encapsulates the networking functionality: it receives (or forwards) packets' content from the Framer class (or the Deframer class). The Framer class undertakes the encryption of the payload of the packet that results from the issuance of a command or file transfer. The Deframer decrypts the packet's payload and either routes commands to the CmdDispatcher class or forwards the file contents to the FileUplink class. The FileUplink class assembles parts to complete a file, while the FileDownlink class is responsible for fragmenting file contents into CSP packets.

Following the third (3rd) rule proposed by Hinchey [18], the BufferMng class manages memory statically to mitigate the unpredictability of dynamic allocation, something typical in critical flight software. The centralized memory management allows: (a) straightforward modification of memory allocation strategy without impacting other classes of the FSW (D3); (b) controlled testing scenarios and more robust verification of memory usage (D4).

The *Command Handling* area consists of two classes, the CmdDispatcher and the CmdSequencer. The CmdDispatcher handles the routing of issued commands to their destination and the return of their status to the source after completion. Moreover, it encapsulates how the class instances communicate with commands in the runtime environment using the mediator design pattern [12]. The CmdSequencer class complements the functionality of the CmdDispatcher class by supporting in-order execution and scheduling of command groups.

Certain classes provide functionality globally accessed by all components. The *Periodic Tasks* sub-area consists of three classes: Time, RateGroupDriver and ActiveRateGroup. The Time class shares the system's time with other classes and can synchronize the system's time to that of the ground station. The time can be retrieved from either GPS, FRAM RTC or the MCU's system clock. The RateGroupDriver handles periodic signaling of the ActiveRateGroup by sourcing its timing information from the Time class. When the ActiveRateGroup gets signaled, it will perform sequentially the actions with which it has been configured. Although the RateGroupDriver is a singleton [12] class, the ActiveRateGroup supports multiple instances. The PrmDB class utilizes non-volatile memory storage to persist configuration parameters, while the TlmChan class is responsible for storing telemetry in non-volatile memory (ROM) in a serialized form suitable for downlink to ground. The ActiveLogger class stores the generated events from the FSW components in a non-volatile memory (ROM/FRAM); using configurable filtering functionality (D3), it forwards filtered events to FDIRController and fatal ones to FatalHandler. The Health class implements a software watchdog timer tailored for FSW components, effectively realizing the Ping/Echo architectural tactic described in [1]. If a periodic ping sent from the Health class is not returned in a timely manner, a fatal event will be raised. Note that both telemetry and events are optionally and periodically downlinked.

The *Health Monitoring* area comprises classes that handle and respond to events from the ActiveLogger class. The FDIRController class reacts to filtered events with pre-configured and tested procedures. It enables early mitigation of predefined high-risk events to ensure quick system response and prevent mission failure. The FatalHandler class manages fatal events and reboots the system after a configurable amount of time if one is received. Section 4 elaborates on the reasoning behind these two classes that handle events.

Spacecraft operation typically involves several so-called *modes*, which encompass the various planned phases of the mission. Each mode has specific objectives and operational requirements, and the *nominal* mode is the standard state with all systems functional. When significant anomalies occur, the spacecraft may autonomously enter *safe* mode, a minimal configuration focused on survival. *Critical* mode signifies a severe failure demanding immediate action to prevent mission loss. The *Satellite's Management* area includes the subsystem's managers and the operational mode management. The *Manager* abstract class provides the basic common interface, used by concrete manager classes to realize their own. Each satellite subsystem—OBC, Attitude Determination and Control System (ADCS), Electrical Power System (EPS), etc.—is assigned a dedicated manager. The basic common interface includes: (a) tracking the subsystem's state, (b) managing peripherals, and (c) validating the operational mode to execute the corresponding command that was received. The Controller class encapsulates the spacecraft modes and the transitions between them through a hierarchical structure of Finite State Machines (FSMs). A top-level FSM manages the mode of operation (e.g., nominal, safe, critical), while each is further decomposed into substates, implemented as nested sub-FSMs, to capture more granular system behavior. The class also provides entry, exit and guard functions at each mode and an interface to change the mode from ground or other FSW component.

3.3 Development View

The development process includes two phases: the initial project setup and the component-based decomposition. The setup phase establishes foundational elements including compilers, build systems, hardware drivers, and the Operating System Abstraction Layer (OSAL). Subsequently, the development process decomposes the system into modular components. The design of these components targets their generic functionality and their reusability. We opted to present the Development View using two UML diagrams: (i) a package diagram (Fig. 3) illustrating the fundamental building blocks, and (ii) a component diagram (Fig. 4) detailing the interconnection of the framework components. These are known as Service Components (Svc) and mission-specific Components and are designed to meet the functionality specifications of the OBC FSW. To maximize reuse of flight-proven code we leverage F' facilities as much as possible [2].

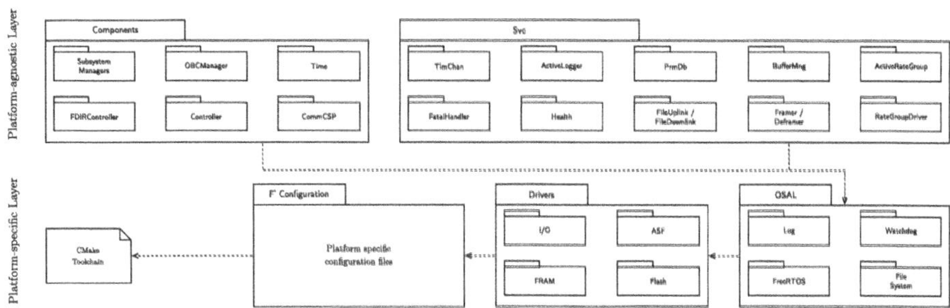

Fig. 3. Package diagram illustrating the platform-specific layer (bottom) and platform-agnostic layer (top). Arrows denote dependency, following the UML2 notation.

Platform Porting: Porting is essential and requires adaptation of the component-based workflow, involving cross-compilation of the framework in the AVR32 toolchain[2]. Platform-specific constraints and capabilities such as the number of buffers, their size and the maximum number of concurrent commands, are specified in the F' Configuration. The F' platform layer also includes Drivers needed for the hardware of the A3200 board like the NOR Flash, FRAM and I/O interfaces, while the platform specific development concludes with the OSAL,

[2] https://nasa.github.io/fprime/v3.4.3/UsersGuide/dev/porting-guide.html.

which consists of the RTOS, the File System, Watchdogs and Log format of the system[3]. After configuring the platform-specific layer, later component development is hardware-agnostic, enabling the same FSW codebase to be deployed across different platforms (D1); observe that components such as Health and FatalHandler are connected to hardware and the OSAL of the architecture, pointing to additional platform-specific adaptation. Figure 3 distinguishes the upper layer as platform-specific and the lower layer as platform-agnostic.

Component Architecture: For an effective modular system, the FSW design relies on building blocks termed components, which encapsulate discrete portions of the system's functionality. This component-based architectural principle enhances testability significantly by enabling independent unit testing and integration testing through scenario-based evaluation, typically employed at final process stages in the domain (D4). We use F' ports to create communication channels between components; F' ports are base classes that represent well-defined interfaces (D2) and are categorized as either input (receiving data) or output (invoking an input port by sending data to it). Components and ports collectively form the core functionality of the FSW, enabling the system to execute its intended mission objectives, as illustrated in Fig. 4.

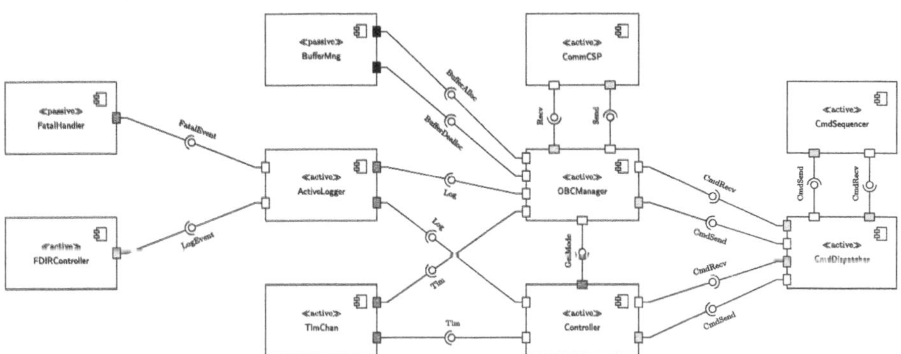

Fig. 4. Fragment of a Component diagram of the FSW architecture. The ports are type-designated: (a) output ports in white; (b) asynchronous ports in light gray; (c) synchronous ports in dark; (d) guarded ports in black. The complete Component diagram is available in the anonymized accompanying material

3.4 Process View

From the integrator's perspective, FSW components can be classified as either active or passive. Active components include their own execution thread and

[3] https://nasa.github.io/fprime/v3.4.3/UsersGuide/dev/os-docs.html.

contain a queue to store incoming data prior to processing. In contrast, passive components operate within the context of the caller's thread. The communication ports between the components are categorized as either asynchronous or synchronous. Asynchronous ports enable non-blocking communication by operating independently on the thread of execution of their component. Conversely, synchronous ports function akin to traditional function calls, executing their functionality within the thread of the invoking component. A subtype of synchronous ports, known as guarded ports, ensures single-threaded access, thereby preventing race conditions among calling threads. The BufferMng component exemplifies the practical utility of guarded ports in ensuring thread-safe operations. This component is responsible for managing the system's limited pool of statically allocated buffers. To prevent race conditions during buffer transmission and reception—which could otherwise compromise system stability—the component exclusively utilizes guarded ports for synchronization and safe access control. As a result, active components may include both synchronous and asynchronous ports, whereas passive ones which do not correspond to a thread of their own, are limited to synchronous ports. Figure 4 illustrates the classification of ports within our architecture alongside the corresponding component types.

Figure 5 depicts a representative example of process communication; it illustrates the Process View of the mode change mechanism. In short, inherent functionality in Fig. 5 entails the following. The CmdDispatcher thread is responsible for forwarding mode change commands to the Controller component, which controls the satellite's operational mode. The CmdDispatcher thread places the command in the queue of the Controller component. As an active component, the Controller has a dedicated execution thread. Once the command is dequeued, the Controller thread first issues an acknowledgment of its reception. It then evaluates whether the requested transition is permissible. This evaluation step is crucial for ensuring system stability, preventing unsafe mode transitions, thus maintaining operational constraints. The assessment considers factors such as the current subsystem states, ongoing mission tasks, and predefined mode transition rules—all of which are encapsulated within the Controller's logic. If the transition is evaluated as valid, the Controller thread enqueues the new mode data into the queue of the PrmDb component. As an active component, PrmDb processes the new mode data using its execution thread to update the parameter representing the current operational mode in FRAM storage; it then notifies the Controller thread of the result of the mode change. Subsequently, the Controller thread suspends execution until the ActiveLogger task completes logging the event in the ROM and FRAM. Since the input port of ActiveLogger is a synchronous port, it operates within the execution context of the calling thread—in this case, the Controller thread. Upon a successful mode transition, any additional commands required for execution are forwarded to the CmdDispatcher thread, which routes them to the appropriate components as part of the new mode's entry function. Conversely, if the mode change request is evaluated as invalid, the Controller component logs an event and takes no further action.

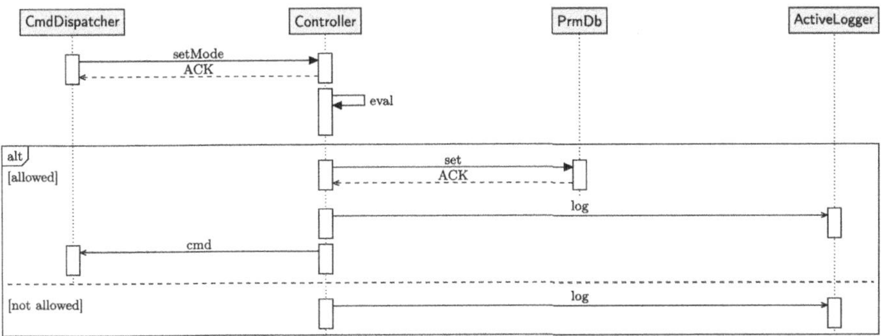

Fig. 5. Sequence diagram presenting the Process View of the mode change mechanism. Filled arrows indicate asynchronous calls, unfilled arrows denote synchronous calls and alternative (alt) frame models conditional execution, following UML2 notation.

3.5 Scenario View

To complete the Kruchten's view model and showcase the combination of the primary 4 views, in the following paragraph we present the critical scenario of Fault Detection, Isolation, and Recovery (FDIR) [17]. The FDIR mechanism onboard a spacecraft is a critical autonomous system that identifies anomalies, pinpoints their source, and executes pre-programmed actions to restore nominal operations. It ensures mission survival by mitigating effects of hardware or software failures through rapid response and corrective measures, minimizing downtime and potential damage. As such, we select a fragment of FDIR, particularly because it involves different parts of the overall architecture.

The (use case) scenario in Fig. 6 demonstrates a high-level view on the system's autonomous fault management capability. The procedure begins when a subsystem manager (OBCManager, EPSManager, etc.) component raises an event. Such events are collected by the ActiveLogger component, which categorizes them based on severity. Lower-severity events (trace, debug, info) are logged for later inspection by ground operators, whereas higher-severity events (warning, error) are both logged and forwarded to the dedicated FDIRController component. The response of the FDIRController component depends on the satellite's mode of operation. As an example, if the satellite operates in `image_capture` mode and the EPS battery level falls below a critical threshold, the system will deactivate the hyperspectral camera unit. In the other case, if the same battery event occurs in `compression` mode, the PDPU unit will be deactivated (instead of the hyperspectral camera). To determine the appropriate action, the FDIRController component queries the Controller component for the current operational mode and sends the required command to the CmdDispatcher for routing to the relevant component. In the case of the previous example, the EPSManager component receives a command to cut the power of the activated payload. Additionally, if a change in the spacecraft's mode of operation is required, the corresponding command will be sent to the Controller to save the new mode. This autonomous monitoring and response process operates continuously at runtime, ensuring that the system detects and reacts to critical conditions.

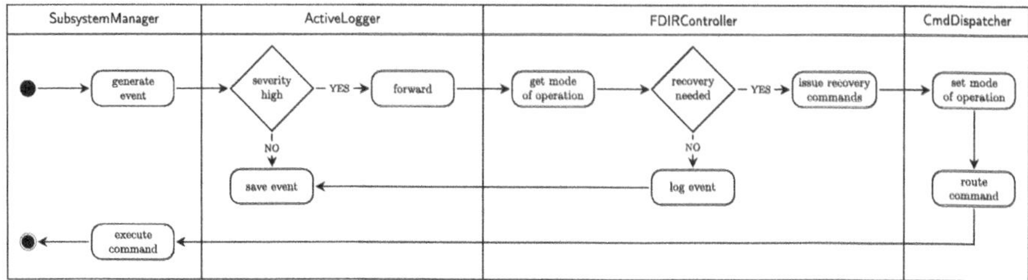

Fig. 6. Activity diagram illustrating the FDIR use case scenario, following UML2

4 Discussion and Lessons Learned

The FSW architecture presented in this paper is the result of a series of deliberate design decisions and trade-offs aimed at satisfying the stringent requirements of the mission at hand. Our experience in designing this architecture has led us to several key observations and insights, which we detail below.

Among the primary design drivers was the need for *deployability* in order to ensure efficient allocation of software across the heterogeneous on-board compute hosts (OBC/PDPU) and meet the redundancy demands of the mission. Beyond the flight environment, deployability was also critical to the development workflow, particularly in supporting continuous integration (CI) processes, where build and testing (at unit, integration, and harware-in-the-loop levels) are supported across various pipeline stages. Given that these activities occur on different hardware architectures,—i.e., development on x86, testing on x86/AVR/hardware-in-the-loop, and deployment on AVR—deployability was deemed important to be seamless, despite the inherent complex technicalities.

Integrability was another key focus, aiming to minimize interface errors that could propagate system-wide failures, as exemplified in the FDIR use case. This was achieved by limiting dependencies, promoting encapsulation, and defining narrow interfaces with ports serving as the sole communication channels between components. To dictate the execution flow, these components are categorized into active and passive types. This separation allows certain operations to progress concurrently, while others executed on the caller's thread of control lead to a finer-grained management and monitoring of the system's state. Additionally, the architecture emphasizes loose coupling and high cohesion, e.g., as exemplified by the CmdDispatcher; this component employs the mediator pattern to prevent others from sending direct commands to each other, thereby ensuring that command dispatching is mediated through a centralized entity. Finally, careful resource management was achieved through static allocation with the BufferMng serving as an intermediary entity enforcing, prioritization, safety, and fairness in memory—a critical and scarce resource.

Modifiability was also a crucial consideration, as in-flight updates and feature enhancements are often necessary to extend the mission lifecycle or respond to unforeseen circumstances. By adhering to loose coupling and high cohesion principles, we ensured that modifications could be implemented with minimal risk of regression. For instance, the Time class encapsulates the system's time source, allowing straightforward time source modifications. Additionally, the proposed architecture balances flexibility and efficiency in fault handling by incorporating both a FatalHandler and an FDIRController. While the FDIRController is an active component requiring a thread context switch and incurring greater overhead; the FatalHandler is passive and executes on the caller's thread with minimal delay. More broadly, the modularity of the proposed architecture enhances modifiability by enabling component updates and replacements with minimal effort, thereby streamlining both development and maintenance.

Finally, *testability* was paramount, as it is essential for validating adherence to the stringent reliability and safety standards of space missions. This was achieved by incorporating dedicated testing interfaces, leveraging F' primitives and workflows to facilitate structured validation, and utilizing automated simulation environments alongside continuous integration to streamline testing across different stages of development. Additionally, rigorous verification protocols inspired by common practice [11] were followed to ensure the system meets its requirements, further enhancing reliability and robustness.

The trade-offs of the proposed design reflect the balance between the four competing requirements and the constraints of development time and resources. These time limitations are inherent in the overall endeavor given a relatively short mission timeline of a few months from the project's start to launch typical in *New Space* nanosatellite missions [5,26]. Our design rationale was guided by a combination of mission requirements, industry best practices, and lessons learned from hitherto space software development efforts. These lessons include:

- Although meeting the mission's redundancy demands introduced a level of managerial and technical complexity that was initially underestimated, the adoption of standardized interfaces and modularity as principles were essential for realization.
- The interdisciplinary nature of the mission requiring collaboration among different fields (e.g., physics, computer science, aerospace engineering) highlighted the need for architecture and process phases capable of accommodating diverse domain-specific concerns and various approaches to solutions. The architecture's inherent modifiability was instrumental in supporting this adaptability, especially given the mission's accelerated development timeline.
- Due to the mission-critical implications of fatal events, the software system was designed to preserve error state information promptly and initiate timely reboots to prevent further damage. This capability was made possible through the use of a dedicated passive component (FatalHandler), to enable error state preservation and system recovery with minimized overhead.

- The decision of following component-based design was also instrumental. While loose coupling introduces additional complexity in terms of inter-component communication, it supports key non-functional requirements such as modifiability and integrability.
- Similarly, although loose coupling supports integrability and modifiability, it can impact performance at runtime, e.g., due to increased function calls and higher memory usage which requires careful design and assessment.

However, we underline that the approach of following a rigorous architectural design through the 4+1 model provided a comprehensive and multifaceted representation of the system, supported stakeholder communication and enabled architecture understanding and validation from various angles.

5 Related Work

We advocated a FSW architecture and described our experience in its design; consequently, we classify related work into two major categories. First, we discuss software architectures in other spacecraft contexts, positioning our work within a major application area. Subsequently, we consider other, but architecturally-relevant works from a wider software engineering perspective.

Forms of layered and component-based architectures are typical in FSW architectures, often largely comprising of the operating system abstraction, communication/interfaces, middleware, and functional software [6,8,32]. Often cited as key goals include availability, extensibility, flexibility, reusability and reliability [21,27]. The utilization of component-based architectures emerges as a prominent trend—lately including adoption of F'. Rosemurg et al. [29] detail the integration of the Interplanetary Overlay Network mission with F', demonstrating its adaptability and test-related component-level features. Rizvi et al. [28] further highlight the reusability and modularity of F' components through their deployment on the Lunar Flashlight and NEA Scout missions. Eshaq et al. [9] propose a ground-up FSW design emphasizing modularity and reusability through an app-based, service-oriented architecture with a command-line interface and script engine, an approach that aligns with the principle of abstraction as a cornerstone of robust FSW design. Latest endeavors have employed model-based engineering and adoption of UML (or variants, such as SysML)—see [16] for a notable approach. A taxonomy of architecture styles is outlined in [24] with respect to the CubETH satellite.

Advanced software engineering techniques have also seen use in spacecraft missions—in the following, we highlight key ones that we deem architecture-relevant for our context. Wang et al. [30]'s decomposition of system requirements into distinct architectural layers, coupled with the implementation of heterogeneous backup modes, exemplifies a systematic approach to addressing complex mission objectives. Similarly, the LADEE mission FSW [14] highlights MBSE from requirements to automated code generation—we highlight the emphasis on performance-related test drivers and formal verification techniques. Advanced requirements techniques such as goal modeling are developed in GOPRIME [22], a framework for monitoring a goal model (from individual requirements to satisfaction of higher-level goals) integrated within the FSW architecture with according executable instrumentation. Due to the modularity inherent in the architecture presented and use of F', integration of such reasoning could be a conceptual next step in our design and highly relevant to FDIR activities. Gonzalez et al. [13] apply software visualization techniques for FSW quality monitoring illustrated over the SUCHAI satellite series along with a FSW architecture based on the command design pattern, while also adopting fuzz testing [15]. Fuzz testing is also employed for automated vulnerability analysis in [31] with an empirical analysis over the FSW for ESTCube-1, OPS-Sat, and Flying Laptop, without over-reliance on extensive human expertise.

6 Conclusions and an Emerging Research Agenda

In this paper, we illustrated the FSW architecture for the ERMIS3 nanosatellite mission as per the 4+1 architectural view model. By deconstructing the on-board software system into its Physical, Logical, Development, Process and Scenario Views, we highlighted the architectural description and distilled architectural decisions, trade-offs, and design rationales that guided development. This experience report intends to advocate rigorous software architecture principles in software engineering for space software, by sharing insights and providing detailed architectural documentation with the overall goal of advancing a novel research agenda within the community. Thereupon, we identify key directions that comprise an emerging research agenda.

Firstly, development of a comprehensive reference software architecture as per ISO/IEC WD4 42010, similarly to those that have been proposed in similar contexts but for FSW is highly desirable; drawing inspiration from established architectures, this has potential to consolidate state-of-the-art research of the community in a common platform. For instance, the architecture presented implements fault tolerance at the architectural level to the scale required by the standards of the class of mission; considerations of other classes may dictate other mechanisms. Secondly, formal verification at the FSW architecture layer, with techniques such as model checking that can be embedded at the architectural (i.e., versus code) level can aim for guaranteeing correctness and reliability especially with respect to component interactions and interfacing (which yield runtime behaviors) over a variety of properties [3]. Finally, we believe a careful assessment of which variation points in the architecture should be reconsidered in order to enable architectural technology transfers to other on-board space systems can provide a systematic way forward to architectural developments by the community.

Acknowledgements. Partially supported by HFRI Project 15706/RV4THINGS and the ERMIS 3 project 4000140732/23/NL/ND.

Data Availability Statement. Further architectural documentation can be accessed at: https://software.aerospace.uoa.gr/ecsa25-ermis-arch.

References

1. Bass, L., Clements, P., Kazman, R.: Software Architecture in Practice, 3rd edn. Carnegie Mellon University, Software Engineering Institute's Digital Library (2012)
2. Bocchino, R., Canham, T., Watney, G., Reder, L., Levison, J.: F': an open-source framework for small-scale flight software systems. In: 31st AIAA Space Conference (2017)
3. Bögli, R., Rohani, A., Studer, T., Tsigkanos, C., Kehrer, T.: Temporal logics meet real-world software requirements: a reality check. In: 13th International Conference on Formal Methods in Software Engineering (FormaliSE) (2025)
4. Canham, T.: The mars ingenuity helicopter - a victory for open-source software. In: 2022 IEEE Aerospace Conference (AERO), pp. 01–11 (2022)
5. De, R., Abegaonkar, M.P., Basu, A.: Enabling science with CubeSats—trends and prospects. IEEE J. Miniaturization Air Space Syst. (2022)
6. de Souza, K., Bouslimani, Y., Ghribi, M.: Flight software development for a cubesat application. IEEE J. Miniaturization Air Space Syst. (2022)
7. Dvorak, D.: NASA study on flight software complexity. In: Infotech Aerospace Conference American Institute of Aeronautics and Astronautics (2009)
8. El Allam, A.K., Jallad, A.H.M., Awad, M., Takruri, M., Marpu, P.R.: A highly modular software framework for reducing software development time of nanosatellites. IEEE Access **9** (2021)
9. Eshaq, M., Al-Midfa, I., Al-Shamsi, Z., Atalla, S., Al-Mansoori, S., Al-Ahmad, H.: Flight software design and implementation for a CubeSat. In: Advances in Science and Engineering Technology International Conferences (ASET) (2023)
10. European Cooperation for Space Standardization: ECSS-E-HB-40A: Software engineering handbook (2011)
11. European Cooperation for Space Standardization: ECSS-E-ST-40C: Space Engineering - Software (2009)
12. Gamma, E. (ed.): Design Patterns: Elements of Reusable Object-Oriented Software. Addison-Wesley, Boston (2011)
13. Gonzalez, C.E., Rojas, C.J., Bergel, A., Diaz, M.A.: An architecture-tracking approach to evaluate a modular and extensible flight software for cubesat nanosatellites. IEEE Access **7**, 126409–126429 (2019)
14. Gundy-Burlet, K.: Validation and verification of LADEE models and software. In: 51st Aerospace Sciences. American Institute of Aeronautics and Astronautics (2013)
15. Gutierrez, T., Bergel, A., Gonzalez, C.E., Rojas, C.J., Diaz, M.A.: Systematic fuzz testing techniques on a nanosatellite flight software for agile mission development. IEEE Access **9**, 114008–114021 (2021)
16. Halvorson, M., Dale Thomas, L.: Architecture framework standardization for satellite software generation using MBSE and F'. In: IEEE Aerospace (2022)
17. Hanmer, R.: Patterns for Fault Tolerant Software. Wiley Publishing (2007)
18. Hinchey, M.: The power of ten—rules for developing safety critical code. In: Software Technology: 10 Years of Innovation in IEEE Computer. IEEE (2018)
19. Kolhof, M., Rawson, W., Yanakieva, R., Loomis, A., Lightsey, E.G., Peet, S.: Lessons learned from the GT-1 1U cubesat mission. In: 35nd AIAA/USU Conference on Small Satellites (2021)
20. Kruchten, P.: The 4+1 View Model of architecture. IEEE Software **12**(6) (1995)
21. Latachi, I., Rachidi, T., Karim, M., Hanafi, A.: Reusable and reliable flight-control software for a fail-safe and cost-efficient cubesat mission: design and implementation. Aerospace **7**(10), 146 (2020)

22. Li, J., Tsigkanos, C., Li, N., Tei, K.: Instrumenting runtime goal monitoring for F' flight software. In: 2024 IEEE 48th Annual Computers, Software, and Applications Conference (COMPSAC), pp. 1300–1309 (2024)
23. Martin, G.: Newspace: the emerging commercial space industry (2017). NASA Ames Research Center
24. Mavridou, A., Stachtiari, E., Bliudze, S., Ivanov, A., Katsaros, P., Sifakis, J.: Architecture-based design: a satellite on-board software case study. In: Formal Aspects of Component Software, pp. 260–279 (2017)
25. Muchandi, V.: Applying 4+1 View Architecture with UML 2. Technical, FCG Software Services (FCGSS) (2007)
26. Osman, D.A.M., Mohamed, S.W.A.: Hardware and software design of onboard computer of ISRASAT1 CubeSat. In: 2017 International Conference on Communication, Control, Computing and Electronics Engineering, pp. 1–4 (2017)
27. Quiros-Jimenez, O.D., d'Hemecourt, D.: Development of a flight software framework for student CubeSat missions. Revista Tecnología en Marcha **32**(8) (2019)
28. Rizvi, A., Ortega, K.F., He, Y.: Developing lunar flashlight and near-earth asteroid scout flight software concurrently using open-source F prime flight software framework. In: Small Satellite Conference (2022)
29. Rosemurgy, P., Gao, J., DeBaun, S., Starch, M., Levison, J., Castano, R.: Enabling DTN in spaceflight systems: integration of ION with the F prime flight software framework. In: 2024 IEEE Aerospace Conference, pp. 1–8 (2024)
30. Wang, W., et al.: Software system design and implementation of remote sensing SAR satellite. In: IEEE 11th Joint International Information Technology and Artificial Intelligence Conference (2023)
31. Willbold, J., et al.: Scaling software security analysis to satellites: automated fuzz testing and its unique challenges. In: 2024 IEEE Aerospace Conference (2024)
32. Yao, Y., Chang, L., Yu, X., Zhang, H.: Application-oriented on-board software management system for micro-nano satellite. In: IEEE International Geoscience and Remote Sensing Symposium (2024)
33. Yost, B., et al.: State-of-the-art small spacecraft technology. Technical report, Small Spacecraft Systems Virtual Institute, Ames Research Center, 2021 (2021)

Towards Mixed-Criticality Software Architectures for Centralized HPC Platforms in Software-Defined Vehicles: A Systematic Literature Review

Lucas Mauser[1(✉)], Eva Zimmermann[2], Pavel Nedvědický[2], Tobias Eisenreich[2], Moritz Wäschle[1], and Stefan Wagner[2]

[1] Daimler Truck AG, Leinfelden-Echterdingen, Germany
lucas.mauser@daimlertruck.com
[2] Technical University of Munich, Heilbronn, Germany

Abstract. Centralized electrical/electronic architectures and High-Performance Computers (HPCs) are redefining automotive software development, challenging traditional microcontroller-based approaches. Ensuring real-time, safety, and scalability in software-defined vehicles necessitates reevaluating how mixed-criticality software is integrated into centralized architectures. While existing research on automotive SoftWare Architectures (SWAs) is relevant to the industry, it often lacks validation through systematic, empirical methods. To address this gap, we conduct a systematic literature review focusing on automotive mixed-criticality SWAs. Our goal is to provide practitioner-oriented guidelines that assist automotive software architects and developers design centralized, mixed-criticality SWAs based on a rigorous and transparent methodology. First, we set up a systematic review protocol grounded in established guidelines. Second, we apply this protocol to identify relevant studies. Third, we extract key functional domains, constraints, and enabling technologies that drive changes in automotive SWAs, thereby assessing the protocol's effectiveness. Additionally, we extract techniques, architectural patterns, and design practices for integrating mixed-criticality requirements into HPC-based SWAs, further demonstrating the protocol's applicability. Based on these insights, we propose an exemplary SWA for a microprocessor-based system-on-chip. In conclusion, this study provides a structured approach to explore and realize mixed-criticality software integration for next-generation automotive SWAs, offering valuable insights for industry and research applications.

Keywords: Software engineering · Software architecture · Software-defined vehicle · HPC platform · Mixed-criticality system · Virtualization · Systematic literature review

V. Andrikopoulos et al. (Eds.): ECSA 2025, LNCS 15929, pp. 144–160, 2026.
https://doi.org/10.1007/978-3-032-02138-0_10

1 Introduction

Today's emerging technologies in automotive, such as powertrain electrification, computing-power-intensive autonomous driving, bandwidth-hungry infotainment systems, enhanced connectivity, and the resulting need for cybersecurity, challenge the component-, domain-oriented development of distributed, embedded Electrical/Electronic (E/E) architectures [8]. Within these, system properties such as busload, computing power, fault rate, modularity, and flexibility are reaching their limits [29]. The Software-Defined Vehicle (SDV) and its centralized E/E architecture promise to address these limitations as an enabler to accelerate innovation, reduce time-to-market of features, and revolutionize business models [10,44]. It will enable original equipment manufacturers to continuously develop, integrate, and deploy software faster and more flexible [34].

Traditional, component-oriented development in the automotive industry resulted in embedded and distributed E/E architectures with over 100 Electronic Control Units (ECUs) [39]. By now, there has been an evolution towards partially consolidated, domain-oriented E/E architectures [8]. To differentiate from the competition, key features have been integrated into more powerful domain controllers with the target of developing customer-perceivable application software in-house [39]. Still, the domain-oriented E/E architecture is characterized by a large number of ECUs widely distributed in the vehicle and hardware-dependent functions, often called logical SoftWare Components (SWCs) [8,29].

Today, automotive E/E architectures evolve towards centralized, zonal E/E architectures, as discussed in our previous work [29,30], and by various researchers [8,21,27,28,41]. Centralization is based on functional consolidation into a few, powerful High-Performance Computers (HPCs). Functional decomposition as an exemplary method helps abstract a system and its functionalities to extract SWCs and allocate them to central HPCs [42]. This separation of computing and Input/Output (I/O) forms the basis for centralized E/E architectures of SDVs. Here, centralization helps overcome today's distributed system limitations such as busload, computing power, and updateability [29]. While most logic resides in the HPCs, zonal gateway controllers aggregate distributed, smart I/Os to reduce overall vehicle wiring and weight [21]. More details on the different types of E/E architectures shown in Fig. 1 can be found in literature [8,21,30,45].

Functional consolidation within an HPC brings new challenges to its HardWare (HW) and SoftWare (SW) Architecture (SWA). The growing demand for computing power – driven not only by functional consolidation, but also by emerging technologies such as AI-based algorithms – is driving a shift from microcontroller-based (µC-based) to microprocessor-based (µP-based) architectures [10]. The global development partnership AUTOSAR introduced the µC-based platform, AUTOSAR Classic, in 2003, evolving it into a widely adopted SWA for real-time and time-critical applications [6]. The AUTOSAR Adaptive platform was introduced in 2017 to support the aforementioned paradigm shift to meet the demands of service-oriented, high-performance, µP-based SWAs [5]. AUTOSAR Adaptive is not intended to replace AUTOSAR Classic. Rather,

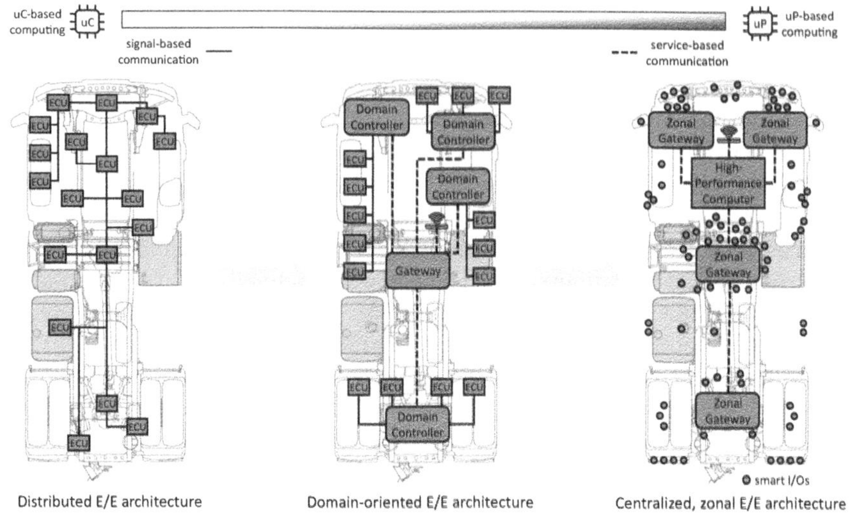

Fig. 1. Evolution of automotive E/E architectures

both platforms will coexist, depending on the specific area of application [45]. In modern vehicles, HPCs integrate consolidated µC and µP partitions, designed as System-on-Chip (SoC) solutions, offering advantages such as reduced external communication [10] while backbone networks approach bandwidth limitations [37,46]. This consolidation of real-time applications with service-oriented, event-driven applications into one single SWA comprises a Mixed-Criticality System (MCS) [13]. MCSs integrate functionalities of different criticality levels. In the automotive context, these are categorized as Automotive Safety Integrity Levels (ASILs) according to the ISO 26262 (QM, ASIL A to D) [13]. Meeting the diverse requirements of real-time systems and emerging performance technologies within a centralized SWA leads to our primary research question:

RQ: *How are automotive, centralized SWAs designed to incorporate mixed-criticality requirements of SDVs?*

Addressing the research question, this paper assists SW architects and developers in consolidating mixed-criticality functions within centralized SWAs of HPC platforms, leveraging the advantages of SDVs. Focusing on technical and methodical enablers, the study bridges academic research and industry practices.

The paper is organized as follows: We review related work to contextualize our research and highlight its added value in Sect. 2. In Sect. 3, we outline the research method used for the Systematic Literature Review (SLR). The results are presented and discussed in Sect. 4. Addressing the threats to validity in Sect. 5, we conclude and provide an outlook for future research in Sect. 6.

2 Related Work

This section reviews related work to position our contributions. While previous studies have examined automotive SWAs, no comprehensive SLR has specifically addressed mixed-criticality architectures for centralized HPC platforms in SDVs. Aleti et al. [2] conducted an SLR on SWA optimization methods, presenting a taxonomy to assist architects in selecting techniques. However, since their 2013 study focused on embedded systems, their scope differs from ours, as we propose a centralized, HPC-based SWA rather than optimizing existing ones. Other SLRs have a narrower focus than our goal of a universal, in-vehicle SWA for centralized HPC platforms. Banijamali et al. [9] analyzed SWAs for IoT-cloud convergence, discussing attributes, such as portability and maintainability, and Service-Oriented Architectures (SOAs) – key considerations for SDVs [29,30]. However, it does not specifically address in-vehicle architectures. Similarly, Avci et al. [7] studied big-data architectures across industries, identifying automotive use cases offloaded to the cloud rather than in-vehicle architectures, as explored in our research [29]. Beyond SLRs, several Systematic Mapping Studies (SMSs) provide broader overviews of automotive SWA research. However, their general scope limits their relevance to the specific challenges of centralized HPC platforms in SDVs. For example, Haghighatkhah et al. [19] analyzed literature on Automotive Software Engineering (ASE), identifying "system/software architecture and design, qualification testing, and reuse" as the three most frequently studied areas. Their findings highlight the critical role of SWA and design in academia and industry, as evidenced by the leading ASE research institutions spanning companies and public organizations. The review highlights research with high industrial relevance but low scientific rigor. Here, we derive and conclude, in alignment with the conclusion of Haghighatkhah et al., the need for practitioner-oriented "guidelines for selecting existing solutions, technologies, and practices" based on a rigorous SLR satisfying scientific expectations.

3 Research Method

We conducted an SLR to answer the research question to address the identified need for systematic research. This section highlights the key milestones of the three phases of planning, conducting, and reporting to ensure the key characteristics of a credible SLR according to Kitchenham et al. [22]: comprehensiveness, reproducibility, and transparency. The working products of these key milestones are documented and publicly available on GitHub and Zenodo.

3.1 Research Question

Kitchenham et al. [22] emphasize the importance of the research question as the essential part of a systematic review. Thus, we applied the PICOC (Population, Intervention, Comparison, Outcomes, Context) criteria presented within the guidelines to refine and reframe the research question. The PICOC criteria determine the research scope, ensure the consideration of different viewpoints, and help reduce bias.

P: Automotive SWAs – **I:** Centralized HPC SWA – **C:** Real-time, embedded SWA – **O:** Mixed criticality SWAs – **C:** Technological transformation in automotive industry.

With these, we substantiate our research question: *How are automotive, centralized SWAs designed to incorporate mixed-criticality requirements of SDVs?*

3.2 Review Protocol

Three performance indicators guide the selection of our SLR protocol: recall, precision, and F-measure. Recall ensures the review's comprehensiveness by minimizing the risk of missing relevant studies, while precision ensures identified studies contribute to answering the research question. The F-measure, the harmonic mean of precision and recall, balances both metrics. [31] For this study, we selected an SLR based on a Scopus database search, which has demonstrated high precision in evaluations by Mourão et al. [31]. This approach prioritizes relevance over recall, avoiding the lower precision seen in databases like Google Scholar [31]. Threats to validity of the protocol will be discussed in Sect. 5.

3.3 Search String

For the Scopus search, we constructed the following search string based on the PICOC criteria:

TITLE-ABS-KEY ("software architecture*" AND (vehicle OR automotive) AND ("mixed critical*" OR hpc OR "High*Performance Comput*" OR "central*" OR "functional domain*"))

The search string is applied to titles, abstracts, and keywords in Scopus (TITLE-ABS-KEY). We discussed, reviewed, and modified the search string in review sessions with all authors to ensure plausibility and reduce overlooks of a single author. The search string is intended to answer the research question by identifying modern, mixed-criticality automotive SWAs in recent literature.

3.4 Inclusion and Exclusion Criteria

To produce the seed set of studies from the database search, we defined the inclusion and exclusion criteria in Table 1. These include content-related criteria and quality-related criteria for achieving a certain level of quality, as discussed in the guidelines of Kitchenham et al. [22]. For a study to be included, content-related and quality-related criteria must be valid. The exclusion of non-peer-reviewed publications ensures the inclusion of high-quality studies. For the same reasons, we exclude books or sections from books, as peer review is not guaranteed. Based on the identified literature and the evolution of automotive E/E architectures described in Sect. 1, the SDV approach, which separates computing and I/O, gained momentum in the mid-2010s. This can also be confirmed by analyzing the search results by publication year. As a result, we exclude studies from the HW-driven and ECU-oriented era of E/E architectures before 2010. The study language is limited to English and German, in which the authors are proficient.

Table 1. Inclusion and exclusion criteria

A study is included if	A study is excluded if
IC1: the title, abstract, and keywords clearly demonstrate a contribution to the research question	**EC1**: the study does not meet any of the inclusion criteria
IC2: the abstract tends to answer the aspects of data extraction derived from the research question	**EC2**: the study is not peer-reviewed
	EC3: the study is either a book or a section from a book
	EC4: the study is published before 2010 or after December 2024
	EC5: the study is not written in English or German
	EC6: the study is not accessible

We use the tool Rayyan to efficiently document and perform the inclusion/exclusion process [33]. Each study's inclusion and exclusion criteria are documented, with references to the short names of the corresponding criteria and a detailed rationale. The first four authors reviewed each study from the Scopus database search. This process served as a pilot to establish a common understanding and consensus on the inclusion/exclusion criteria while reducing the potential for bias from a particular author. Any initial disagreements, discussions, and resolutions have been documented in the SLR report.

3.5 Data Extraction

For data extraction of the included papers, we broke down the research question into Data Extraction Criteria (DEC) to further explore the particular aspects. The criteria facilitate data extraction and the subsequent synthesis of the study outcomes.

- DEC1 Which functional domain(s) does the study analyze and/or modify in relation to SWA changes?
- DEC2 Which constraint(s) does the study identify as drivers for SWA changes?
- DEC3 Which technologies does the study identify as enablers or catalysts for changes in the SWA?
- DEC4 How does the study technically address the integration of diverse SW requirements (real-time, non-real-time, safety-critical, etc.) within a centralized automotive SWA?

DEC5 Which architectural patterns or design practices are proposed to systematically support mixed-criticality in centralized automotive SWAs?

To effectively divide the work of data extraction while minimizing bias, only the first author reviewed all of the literature in the seed set. Authors 2, 3, and 4 each reviewed one-third of the seed set. The extracted data were compared between the first author and the other reviewers. Agreement on the results was required, and any ambiguities have been resolved.

3.6 Data Synthesis

The data synthesis is designed based on the extraction criteria. DEC1, DEC2, and DEC3 provide context on why SWAs are facing change. For DEC1, we conducted a quantitative, deductive coding to highlight functional domains according to the domain taxonomy Vehicle Signal Specification (VSS) V5.0 by the COVESA community [15]. For DEC2 and DEC3, we conducted an explorative, qualitative open coding by extracting and grouping identified constraints and technologies from the literature without applying weightings. DEC4 and DEC5 answer the research question. We conducted a qualitative content analysis using open coding for both: DEC4 to discuss technical implementations and approaches, and DEC5 to examine architectural patterns and design practices. The results of the data extraction and synthesis are presented and discussed in the following section.

4 Results and Discussion

The search string applied in the database Scopus resulted in 97 identified studies. The inclusion/exclusion criteria application resulted in 21 studies included in the final set. The data extraction of these 21 studies is the basis for the results in this section. While we discuss each of the included studies below, we list them here in a preliminary manner to provide a central overview: [1,4,11,12,14,16–18,20,23–26,32,35–38,40,43,46].

4.1 Providing Context

Figure 2 illustrates the key functional domains driving change in automotive SWAs. The three most influential domains are: Advanced Driver Assistance Systems (ADASs), particularly its autonomous subcategory; powertrain, driven by electrification; and cabin, driven by infotainment. ADASs and autonomous vehicles demand high computing power to support computer vision algorithms, pushing embedded, µC-based ECUs and their SWAs to their limits [14]. In the powertrain domain, electrification expands the design space, increasing the complexity of SW implementations and necessitating a fundamental rethinking of embedded SWAs [40]. The evolution of high-performance digital displays challenges Instrument Cluster (IC) and In-Vehicle Infotainment (IVI) systems, not only by increasing HW and SW complexity but also by requiring integration of safety-critical and non-safety-critical applications within a single, centralized SWA [20].

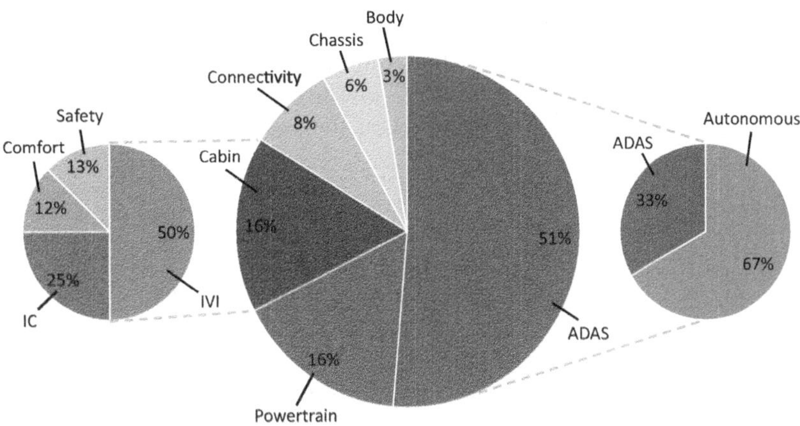

Fig. 2. DEC1 - Functional domains driving change in SWAs according to Vehicle Signal Specification (VSS) V5.0 [15]

Such constraints of today's SWAs, identified in the literature by DEC2, and technologies as enablers and catalysts for changes in SWAs, identified in the literature by DEC3, are illustrated by the word clouds in Fig. 3.

(a) Constraints driving change

(b) Technologies driving change

Fig. 3. Word clouds DEC2 (left) and DEC3 (right)

With these extracted and synthesized data providing context, we want to focus on the research question of Sect. 1. To answer the research question, we set up DEC4 and DEC5, the results of which we will discuss qualitatively below.

4.2 Answering the Research Question

We analyze DEC4 and DEC5 inspired by the AUTOSAR structure and its layers, starting from the HW layer, through HW-near SW layers, the operating system layer, the middleware layer as so-called basic SW in AUTOSAR Classic, to the application SW layer [5,6]. Based on the following discussion, we integrated the findings into the exemplary SWA shown in Fig. 4 illustrating key aspects for realizing mixed-criticality SWAs for HPC platforms. Details and the derivation will be elaborated in the following, based on the analysis of DEC4 and DEC5.

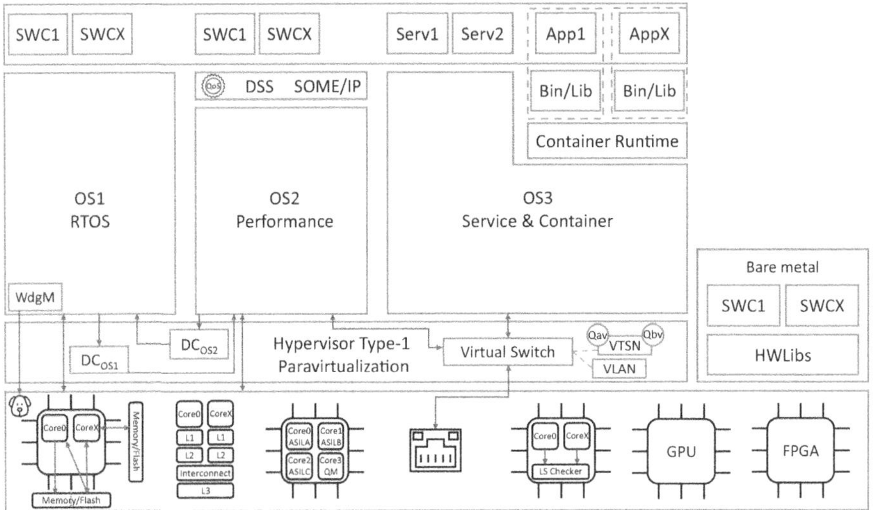

Fig. 4. SoC-based, mixed-criticality SWA

HW Layer: High-performance SoC HW forms the foundation of centralized HPC platforms [4,20,26]. Literature suggests multi-core and SoC designs to allocate SWCs with similar properties, such as criticality class, to the same core or SoC semiconductor partition [14,36,40]. Placing dedicated SWC sets on individual cores facilitates space partitioning and ensures Freedom from Interference (FFI) [4,18,37]. For highly parallel workloads, many-core processors optimize specific computational aspects, often at the expense of other performance trade-offs [12]. Similarly, Field-Programmable Gate Arrays (FPGAs) are increasingly used in automotive HPC platforms as energy-efficient, reconfigurable HW accelerators with low-latency processing [18]. Private memory and cache HW partitions improve timing predictability and FFI, but at the same limit parallelization and timing gains due to static (design-time) core allocation in comparison to dynamic (run-time) core allocation [4,12,17]. Mode-based dynamic core allocation can further improve performance by adapting to varying criticality levels and environmental changes in real-time, ensuring optimal resource utilization and scalability for ADASs [4,36]. To improve fault tolerance, lock-step operation modes distributed across available cores can detect failures in HW components and increase system reliability [16]. Redundant flash memory partitions are identified to enhance the system's robustness and consistency [32]. Figure 4 illustrates these capabilities for extensive resource partitioning and redundancy approaches at HW layer as the foundation for a centralized, mixed-criticality SWA.

HW-Near SW Layer: At the HW-near SW layer, HW resources must be allocated and managed efficiently. The literature suggests virtualization via hypervisors as a key approach [4,20,25,26,36]. Hypervisors enable the creation of Virtual Machines (VMs), each running a required Operating System (OS), or even bare-metal applications [18,20]. There are two commonly used types of hypervisors. Type 1 (bare-metal) hypervisors run directly on the HW, providing exclusive and static resource management, leading to higher efficiency, performance, and strongest FFI. Type 2 hypervisors run on a host OS, making HW access less efficient and introducing a risk of failure if the host OS crashes [4,18,25]. Additionally, virtualization can be classified as full or paravirtualization. Full virtualization emulates HW components, allowing unmodified guest OSs to run as if on physical HW. Paravirtualization requires guest OS modifications to interact more efficiently with the hypervisor, improving performance. The literature confirms paravirtualization offers higher performance than full virtualization, which incurs overhead due to HW emulation [18,25]. Virtualization is also seen as having "cost, reliability, availability, and adaptability" benefits while guaranteeing spatial and temporal isolation [18,36]. In summary, virtualization enables the separation of SW logic from HW and mixed OS environments as a prerequisite for SDVs [24].

OS Layer: At the OS layer, Ferraro et al. [18] propose a Real-Time OS (RTOS) for actuation and a Linux OS for performance-intensive object detection. Additionally, Robot Operating System 2 (ROS2), based on Data Distribution Service (DDS), is used in self-driving applications to enhance scalability [18]. Similarly, Lee and Wang [24] split sensing/actuation-heavy SW and processing-heavy SW. Niedballa and Reuss [32] employ an RTOS for safety- and time-critical tasks and system monitoring, while Linux OS handles computing-intensive application logic.

Middleware Layer: At the middleware layer, various methods and protocols support the coexistence of mixed-criticality OSs and applications. With increasing cross-domain communication [37,46] and dependencies [14], a key challenge is ensuring FFI as centralized HPC platforms consolidate multiple domains [37,46]. Holstein and Wietzke [20] address this risk for inter-VM communication by introducing architectural approaches such as the *clear separation approach*, *layers of interconnections*, and *minimalistic approach* with its one-way/read-only Data Containers (DCs) illustrated in Fig. 4. To maintain data integrity in mixed-criticality environments, key enablers include memory management and stack monitoring mechanisms such as isolated communication channels, access control mechanisms, signed communication data, consistency checks, redundant memory, multiple memory copies, and checksums [17,20,32]. For both communication and isolation, a Virtual Local Area Network (VLAN) enables FFI by creating virtualized network segments [18]. Also, Virtual Time-Sensitive Networking (VTSN) extends Quality-of-Service (QoS) capabilities to VMs using TSN schedulers Qav (bandwidth reservation based on criticality or priority) and Qbv (communication separation into fixed-duration periodic cycles) [18]. Although Qbv achieves lower end-to-end latency, Ferraro et al. [18] suggest combining both approaches to improve reliability and robustness. Ensuring that both functional and non-functional requirements are met at runtime is critical to meeting QoS requirements [38]. Similarly, DDS is proposed as middleware to ensure "reliable, scalable, and efficient real-time communication" [35]. Additionally, time partitioning can enhance predictability and reliability in program execution, which Watchdog Managers (WdgMs) can monitor [37,40]. Furthermore, self-diagnostic capabilities can enhance software-sided redundancy, enabling hot-switching between redundant components to mitigate failures and maintain system continuity [1]. In general, the literature identifies a shift from statically configured, signal-oriented communication towards a more flexible, scalable, and updateable service-oriented communication [11,37,46]. This evolution is exemplified by the publisher-subscriber mechanism implemented in the automotive communication protocol Scalable service-Oriented MiddlewarE over IP (SOME/IP) [11,24], which decouples communication between applications [37]. However, this approach introduces timing uncertainties, which can be managed using the previously mentioned mechanisms, such as TSN, DDS, and other timing-aware solutions [11]. This evolution lays the foundation for centralized, data-centric Automotive Service-Oriented Architectures (ASOAs), enabling the SDV approach to update vehicles post-production in a more flexible manner and thus to evolve over time in response to new customer needs, while also reducing time to market [4,18,35,38]. Several frameworks support these advancements at the middleware layer, including: SOAFEE [20] providing real-time guarantees in SOAs by integrating cloud-native practices with automotive requirements; Time-Sensitive Autonomous Architecture (TSAA) [18] leveraging TSN protocols to support mixed-criticality SDVs; Brain Centralized Electronic and Electrical Architecture (BCEA) [26] enabling HW-SW decoupling, facilitating offloading to cloud computing; Hypervisor-based Fault tolerance approach for heterogeneous Automotive Real-time systems (HyFAR) [25] enabling mixed-criticality via virtualization technology; and AUTOSAR Adaptive as a middleware (see Sect. 1) introducing ASOAs with enhanced updateability [12,25] for centralized HPCs with high computing power and high-speed communication demand [26].

Application SW Layer: At the application SW layer, Lee and Wang [24] advocate for microservice architectures to enhance evolvability and accelerate software development and release, addressing the growing complexity of automotive software [43]. This aligns with broader recommendations in the literature to design loosely coupled SWCs that maximize HW independency, improving transferability and scalability [24,26,37]. Li et al. [26] highlight HW-SW decoupling as a critical enabler for cloud computing, facilitating computational offloading while maintaining compatibility with HPC-based architectures. To further enhance portability, isolation, and deployment flexibility, containerization is proposed as a lightweight alternative to full virtualization. In automotive HPC platforms, containers are typically deployed atop a hypervisor, combining the strong isolation of VMs with the efficiency of containers. This setup enables multiple guest OSs to run separate containerized applications, ensuring scalability, modularity, and rapid software updates while preserving FFI between mixed-criticality applications [11]. Additionally, Kugele et al. [23] propose architectural patterns, such as the *User Shadow Learning Pattern*, for integrating AI-driven personalization into automotive software architectures. These patterns enhance the application software layer by enabling adaptive, context-aware functions that personalize vehicle behavior while maintaining safety constraints.

We conclude the section with the exemplary mixed-criticality SWA shown in Fig. 4, which incorporates these findings. While evidence emphasizes SWAs as "one of the most critical success factors for the design and development of complex software systems" [12], Fig. 4 illustrates its strong relation to the HW layer beneath. The literature often discusses and explores architecture as a whole, considering the close relationship between HW and SW from the very beginning [12,14,16]. Lee and Wang [24] even highlight HW as the design driver for automotive architectures. While the SDV approach aims to decouple SW functions from HW [24], the SWA and its requirements still depend on the HPC HW it runs on, and close co-design can help to solve this multiobjective problem [14].

The following section discusses threats to validity related to our SLR.

5 Threats to Validity

We evaluate our study's quality by discussing the three main threats to validity in secondary software engineering studies as identified by Ampatzoglou et al [3]: *threats to study selection*, *threats to data collection*, and *threats to research validity*.

5.1 Threats to Study Selection

Our study omits snowballing due to the balanced F-measure of Scopus searches, as detailed in Sect. 3.2. While some relevant papers were excluded due to access restrictions or language barriers, such as Chinese-language papers and SAE reports, the high precision of Scopus ensured a comprehensive seed set to answer our research question. We acknowledge potential publication bias and propose a search strategy for snowballing with our seed set as a basis to explore additional methodological and technical approaches in the outlook section. Additionally, industry insights may be outdated due to limited disclosure. Including gray literature or industry expert interviews could enhance understanding and identify current practices but conflicts with our focus on peer-reviewed studies. Concluding, we want to emphasize the potential threat by variability in evaluating loose inclusion criteria wordings as "clearly demonstrate" and "tend to answer".

5.2 Threats to Data Collection

We mitigated data extraction bias by using commonly agreed-upon data extraction criteria, with each study independently reviewed by two authors. Disagreements were resolved through discussion and consensus-building. Pre-piloting of the extraction criteria ensured a common understanding. As the study neither applies snowballing nor includes gray literature, it persists the threat of publication bias related to the data collected. To still ensure validity of the related study and reduce publication bias, we considered quality-related inclusion criteria (see Table 1) as proposed by Kitchenham et al. [22]. Furthermore, the diversity of journals and conferences from which the included publications were drawn helps to mitigate the threat of publication bias.

5.3 Threats to Research Validity

To minimize research bias, the first four authors collaboratively designed and refined the review protocol, aligning with established guidelines. The first three authors specialize in automotive SW engineering, while the fourth focuses on AI integration into SWAs. The fifth and sixth authors – experts in functional safety and SW engineering, respectively – reviewed the protocol to further reduce bias. Disagreements on protocol, data extraction, and synthesis were resolved within the core group or escalated to the reviewers. To enable repeatability, all review discussions, protocol changes, and inclusion/exclusion decisions are documented and made publicly available on GitHub and Zenodo. This study focuses on automotive SWAs and may have limited applicability to other domains due to industry-specific constraints. Future research could explore cross-industry approaches, such as avionics systems (see IMA and ARINC standards [37]), or IT and cloud-based architectures, to identify transferable best practices.

6 Conclusion and Outlook

In this paper, we systematically reviewed existing research on mixed-criticality SWAs for centralized HPC platforms in SDVs. To ensure methodological rigor and transparency in our analysis, we employed a structured research protocol grounded in established literature review practices. Through this protocol, we identified key functional domains, constraints, and enabling technologies that shape modern automotive SWAs. Furthermore, we extracted architectural patterns and design practices that support the integration of mixed-criticality requirements within centralized automotive SWAs. Our findings provide practitioner-oriented insights to aid SW architects and developers in designing HPC-based SWAs.

However, our study also revealed limitations and open challenges. The lack of publicly available industry data hinders validating recent advancements in automotive SWAs. Moreover, the transferability of best practices from other domains, such as avionics or cloud-based SWAs, requires further investigation.

Future work can build on the review protocol and expand the empirical findings with the hybrid search strategy *Scopus + BS——FS* based on its consistent high F-measure values as analyzed by Mourão et al. [31]. Our study delivers the seed set for parallel Backward Snowballing (BS) – which increases recall by identifying references cited within a study – and Forward Snowballing (FS) – which improves precision by identifying newer studies citing a given publication [31]. In addition, the study of cross-industry approaches could reveal transferable design principles for automotive applications. To capture the latest advances, the inclusion of gray literature and an empirical interview study with industry experts could uncover emerging approaches and technologies.

Acknowledgments. This research was partially supported by the German Federal Ministry of Education and Research in the project AutoDevSafeOps (01IS22087R) and the Incentive Fund of TUM Campus Heilbronn.

Disclosure of Interests. The authors declare that they have no known competing financial interests or personal relationships that could have appeared to influence the work reported in this paper.

References

1. Akkaya, S., et al.: A modular five-layered v-shaped architecture for autonomous vehicles. In: 2019 11th International Conference on Electrical and Electronics Engineering (ELECO), pp. 850–854. IEEE (2019). https://doi.org/10.23919/ELECO47770.2019.8990402
2. Aleti, A., et al.: Software architecture optimization methods: a systematic literature review. IEEE Trans. Software Eng. **39**(5), 658–683 (2012). https://doi.org/10.1109/TSE.2012.64
3. Ampatzoglou, A., et al.: Identifying, categorizing and mitigating threats to validity in software engineering secondary studies. Inf. Softw. Technol. **106**, 201–230 (2019). https://doi.org/10.1016/j.infsof.2018.10.006
4. Askaripoor, H., et al.: E/e architecture synthesis: challenges and technologies. Electronics **11**(4), 518 (2022). https://doi.org/10.3390/electronics11040518
5. AUTOSAR: Autosar adaptive platform (2024). https://www.autosar.org/standards/adaptive-platform. Accessed 07 Mar 2025
6. AUTOSAR: Autosar classic platform (2024). https://www.autosar.org/standards/classic-platform. Accessed 07 Mar 2025
7. Avci, C., et al.: Software architectures for big data: a systematic literature review. Big Data Anal. **5**(1), 5 (2020). https://doi.org/10.1186/s41044-020-00045-1
8. Bandur, V., et al.: Making the case for centralized automotive E/E architectures. IEEE Trans. Veh. Technol. **70**(2), 1230–1245 (2021). https://doi.org/10.1109/TVT.2021.3054934
9. Banijamali, A., et al.: Software architectures of the convergence of cloud computing and the internet of things: a systematic literature review. Inf. Softw. Technol. **122**, 106271 (2020). https://doi.org/10.1016/j.infsof.2020.106271
10. Bauer, T., et al.: Reference architectures for automotive software. In: Nakagawa, E.Y., Oliveira Antonino, P. (eds.) Reference Architectures for Critical Domains: Industrial Uses and Impacts, pp. 73–111. Springer, Cham (2022). https://doi.org/10.1007/978-3-031-16957-1_5

11. Bordoloi, U., et al.: Autonomy-driven emerging directions in software-defined vehicles. In: 2023 Design, Automation & Test in Europe Conference & Exhibition (DATE), pp. 1–6. IEEE (2023). https://doi.org/10.23919/DATE56975.2023.10136910
12. Bucaioni, A., et al.: Modelling centralised automotive e/e software architectures. Adv. Eng. Inform. **59**, 102289 (2024). https://doi.org/10.1016/j.aei.2023.102289
13. Cinque, M., et al.: Certify the uncertified: towards assessment of virtualization for mixed-criticality in the automotive domain. In: 2022 52nd Annual IEEE/IFIP International Conference on Dependable Systems and Networks Workshops (DSN-W), pp. 8–11. IEEE (2022). https://doi.org/10.1109/DSN-W54100.2022.00012
14. Collin, A., et al.: Autonomous driving systems hardware and software architecture exploration: optimizing latency and cost under safety constraints. Syst. Eng. **23**(3), 327–337 (2020). https://doi.org/10.1002/sys.21528
15. COVESA: Vehicle signal specification (2025). https://covesa.github.io/vehicle_signal_specification/introduction/index.html. Accessed 07 Mar 2025
16. Druml, N., et al.: Time-of-flight 3D imaging for mixed-critical systems. In: 2015 IEEE 13th International Conference on Industrial Informatics (INDIN), pp. 1432–1437. IEEE (2015). https://doi.org/10.1109/INDIN.2015.7281943
17. El-Bayoumi, A.: An enhanced algorithm for memory systematic faults detection in multicore architectures suitable for mixed-critical automotive applications. Int. J. Saf. Secur. Eng. **10**(4), 467–474 (2020). https://doi.org/10.18280/ijsse.100405
18. Ferraro, D., et al.: Time-sensitive autonomous architectures. Real-Time Syst. **59**(4), 568–608 (2023). https://doi.org/10.1007/s11241-023-09404-2
19. Haghighatkhah, A., et al.: Automotive software engineering: a systematic mapping study. J. Syst. Softw. **128**, 25–55 (2017). https://doi.org/10.1016/j.jss.2017.03.005
20. Holstein, T., Wietzke, J.: Contradiction of separation through virtualization and inter virtual machine communication in automotive scenarios. In: Proceedings of the 2015 European Conference on Software Architecture Workshops, pp. 1–5 (2015). https://doi.org/10.1145/2797433.2797437
21. Kadry, H.M., et al.: Electrical architecture and in-vehicle networking: Challenges and future trends. In: 2022 IEEE International Symposium on Circuits and Systems (ISCAS), pp. 1009–1013. IEEE (2022). https://doi.org/10.1109/ISCAS48785.2022.9937481
22. Kitchenham, B., et al.: Guidelines for performing systematic literature reviews in software engineering. Technical report, ver. 2.3 ebse (2007)
23. Kugele, S., et al.: Architectural patterns for cross-domain personalised automotive functions. In: 2020 IEEE International Conference on Software Architecture (ICSA), pp. 191–201. IEEE (2020). https://doi.org/10.1109/ICSA47634.2020.00026
24. Lee, J., Wang, L.: A method for designing and analyzing automotive software architecture: a case study for an autonomous electric vehicle. In: 2021 International Conference on Computer Engineering and Artificial Intelligence (ICCEAI), pp. 20–26. IEEE (2021). https://doi.org/10.1109/ICCEAI52939.2021.00004
25. Lex, J., et al.: Hyfar: a hypervisor-based fault tolerance approach for heterogeneous automotive real-time systems. J. Syst. Architect. **156**, 103263 (2024). https://doi.org/10.1016/j.sysarc.2024.103263
26. Li, Y., et al.: Key technology and standardization route for new electronic and electrical architecture of intelligent and connected vehicles. In: 2023 3rd International Conference on Electrical Engineering and Control Science (IC2ECS), pp. 323–328. IEEE (2023). https://doi.org/10.1109/IC2ECS60824.2023.10493525

27. Lu, S., et al.: A comparison of end-to-end architectures for connected vehicles. In: 2022 Fifth International Conference on Connected and Autonomous Driving, pp. 72–80. IEEE (2022). https://doi.org/10.1109/MetroCAD56305.2022.00015
28. Maier, J., Reuss, H.C.: Design of zonal E/E architectures in vehicles using a coupled approach of k-means clustering and Dijkstra's algorithm. Energies **16**(19), 6884 (2023). https://doi.org/10.3390/en16196884
29. Mauser, L., Wagner, S.: Centralization potential of automotive E/E architectures. J. Syst. Softw. 112220 (2024). https://doi.org/10.1016/j.jss.2024.112220
30. Mauser, L., et al.: Methodical approach for centralization evaluation of modern automotive E/E architectures. In: Batista, T., Bureš, T., Raibulet, C., Muccini, H. (eds.) ECSA 2022. LNCS, vol. 13928, pp. 165–179. Springer, Cham (2022). https://doi.org/10.1007/978-3-031-36889-9_13
31. Mourão, E., et al.: On the performance of hybrid search strategies for systematic literature reviews in software engineering. Inf. Softw. Technol. **123**, 106294 (2020). https://doi.org/10.1016/j.infsof.2020.106294
32. Niedballa, D., Reuss, H.C.: MPSOC-based platform for fail-operational control of an automated research vehicle. J. Tongji Univ. (Nat. Sci.) **50**(S1), 151–155 (2024). https://doi.org/10.11908/j.issn.0253-374x.23717
33. Ouzzani, M., et al.: Rayyan—a web and mobile app for systematic reviews. Syst. Rev. **5**, 1–10 (2016). https://doi.org/10.1186/s13643-016-0384-4
34. Pelliccione, P., et al.: Automotive architecture framework: the experience of volvo cars. J. Syst. Architect. **77**, 83–100 (2017). https://doi.org/10.1016/j.sysarc.2017.02.005
35. Püllen, D., et al.: A security process for the automotive service-oriented software architecture. IEEE Trans. Veh. Technol. **73**(4), 5036–5053 (2023). https://doi.org/10.1109/ETFA.2019.8868957
36. Savithry, J., et al.: Design of criticality-aware scheduling for advanced driver assistance systems. In: 2019 24th IEEE International Conference on Emerging Technologies and Factory Automation (ETFA), pp. 1407–1410. IEEE (2019). https://doi.org/10.1109/ETFA.2019.8868957
37. Sommer, S., et al.: Race: a centralized platform computer based architecture for automotive applications. In: 2013 IEEE International Electric Vehicle Conference (IEVC), pp. 1–6. IEEE (2013). https://doi.org/10.1109/IEVC.2013.6681152
38. Stähle, H., et al.: Towards the deployment of a centralized ICT architecture in the automotive domain. In: 2013 2nd Mediterranean Conference on Embedded Computing, pp. 66–69. IEEE (2013). https://doi.org/10.1109/MECO.2013.6601320
39. Staron, M.: Automotive Software Architectures. Springer, Cham (2021). https://doi.org/10.1007/978-3-030-65939-4
40. Sundharam, S.M., et al.: Software architecture modeling of autosar-based multi-core mixed-critical electric powertrain controller. Modelling **2**(4), 706–727 (2021). https://doi.org/10.3390/modelling2040038
41. Surjekar, N.N., et al.: A case study on migrating towards functionally safe zonal architecture using MBSE. In: INCOSE International Symposium, vol. 33, pp. 1403–1417. Wiley Online Library (2023). https://doi.org/10.1002/iis2.13089
42. Vogelsang, A.: Feature dependencies in automotive software systems: extent, awareness, and refactoring. J. Syst. Softw. **160**, 110458 (2020). https://doi.org/10.1016/j.jss.2019.110458
43. Wallin, P., et al.: Problems and their mitigation in system and software architecting. Inf. Softw. Technol. **54**(7), 686–700 (2012). https://doi.org/10.1016/j.infsof.2012.01.004

44. Xie, G., et al.: Recent advances and future trends for automotive functional safety design methodologies. IEEE Trans. Industr. Inf. **16**(9), 5629–5642 (2020). https://doi.org/10.1109/TII.2020.2978889
45. Zerfowski, D., Lock, A.: Functional architecture and E/E-architecture – a challenge for the automotive industry. In: Bargende, M., Reuss, H.C., Wagner, A., Wiedemann, J. (eds.) 19. Internationales Stuttgarter Symposium, pp. 909–920. Springer, Wiesbaden (2019). https://doi.org/10.1007/978-3-658-25939-6_70
46. Zhou, X., et al.: Development of vehicle domain controller based on ethernet. In: Journal of Physics: Conference Series, vol. 1802, p. 022065. IOP Publishing (2021). https://doi.org/10.1088/1742-6596/1802/2/022065

Runtime Monitor Synthesis for Automotive Software Architectures

Fazli Faruk Okumus[1], João-Vitor Zacchi[2], Maike Salfeld[3], Markus Schweizer[3], Núria Mata[2], and Stefan Kugele[1(✉)]

[1] AImotion Bavaria, Technische Hochschule Ingolstadt, Ingolstadt, Germany
{FazliFaruk.Okumus,Stefan.Kugele}@thi.de
[2] Fraunhofer-Institut für Kognitive Systeme, Munich, Germany
{joao-vitor.zacchi,nuria.mata}@iks.fraunhofer.de
[3] Dependable Systems, Robert Bosch GmbH, Renningen, Germany
{Maike.Salfeld,Markus.Schweizer}@de.bosch.com

Abstract. *Background:* The automotive industry's shift towards automated driving introduces new safety, reliability, and real-time challenges. While Service-oriented Architectures offer modular and scalable solutions, they struggle to meet stringent safety requirements. *Aim:* This work enhances the reliability and safety of automated driving systems by introducing a taxonomy of monitoring aspects and a runtime monitoring synthesis approach, both tailored to Service-oriented Architectures. *Method:* A monitoring taxonomy is developed using Contract-based Design, extending Service-oriented Architectures by explicitly formalising service behaviours as contracts. This enables runtime verification against well-defined expectations and facilitates the automated synthesis of runtime monitors. *Results:* The approach is evaluated in the CARLA simulator using a Construction Zone Assist use case, demonstrating its effectiveness in realistic driving scenarios. Additionally, the scalability and performance are assessed through resource utilisation. *Conclusion:* Combining the taxonomy with runtime monitor synthesis provides a robust framework for ensuring that safety-critical automotive systems meet operational standards, fostering innovation without compromising safety.

Keywords: Runtime monitor synthesis · Service-oriented architecture · Automotive · Contract-based design

1 Introduction

Modern vehicles at higher levels of automation (levels 3 to 5, SAE J3016 [1]) demand robust safety and reliability to manage increasing complexity and interconnectivity. Although much effort is invested in early-stage verification to ensure

This work has been funded by the Federal Ministry of Education and Research (BMBF) as part of MANNHEIM-AutoDevSafeOps (01IS22087).

V. Andrikopoulos et al. (Eds.): ECSA 2025, LNCS 15929, pp. 161–177, 2026.
https://doi.org/10.1007/978-3-032-02138-0_11

correct and safe operation, not all scenarios can be foreseen. These uncertainties stem from the complexity of challenging urban and rural driving situations, unpredictable road users and functional insufficiencies (*Safety of the Intended Functionality* (SOTIF), ISO 21448 [2]), and the inherent uncertainties within technical systems. Also, potential component failures, such as electronic control units (ECUs), contribute to these uncertainties. Despite comprehensive safety cases and type approvals, unforeseen traffic scenarios and edge cases can still emerge in real-world conditions. To address these limitations, *runtime monitors* continuously verify compliance with predefined *contracts* during operation, enabling the real-time detection and mitigation of faults. The recent ISO PAS 8800 [12] standard, "Road vehicles – Safety and artificial intelligence," acknowledges this need by mandating field data monitoring.

Service-oriented Architectures (SoA) promise modularity, scalability, adaptability, and reusability for complex systems-of-systems by facilitating communication through well-defined services. Particular implementations in the automotive domain are AUTOSAR Adaptive [4] or *Robot Operating System 2* (ROS 2) [15]. While automotive SoA enhances functional suitability, it also introduces challenges related to timing, security, safety, and reliability, marking a fundamental shift from component-based to service-oriented development in the automotive domain, as noted by Kugele et al. [14].

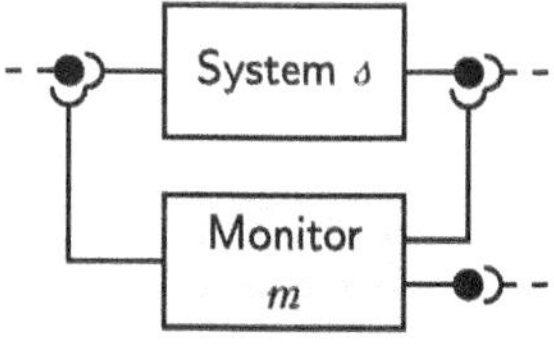

Fig. 1. Monitor m observes system $\mathscr{s}$.

Contract-based Design (CbD) has its roots in the fundamental early work of Tony Hoare, including Hoare logic [11]. CbD is a promising approach for developing complex cyber-physical systems. Building upon CbD, this work proposes a taxonomy of monitoring aspects that systematically decomposes runtime monitoring into measurable units. Additionally, it presents an approach for the automated synthesis of runtime monitors for SoA-based systems. The system $\mathscr{s}$ in Fig. 1 includes a publish-subscribe service interface monitored at runtime by m. By embedding safety contracts throughout the system lifecycle, our approach bridges the gap between safety concept specifications and practical implementations, enabling more robust and reliable automotive SoAs.

This paper utilises ROS 2, a flexible and robust platform for integrating system components. Its used core concepts are: (i) *nodes*, (ii) *topics*, and (iii) the *publish-subscribe communication model*. *Nodes* are the fundamental execution units, supporting distributed and modular development while enabling seamless integration into existing architectures. *Topics* act as communication channels for data exchange between nodes, promoting organised and efficient interaction. The *publish-subscribe* model further enhances this process by decoupling data publisher (*talker*, —●) from subscriber (*listener*,)—), ensuring adaptability to complex and dynamic architectures.

Contributions: We provide the following contributions:

(i) we extend SoA with CbD by linking interface assertions to contracts;

(ii) we propose a taxonomy of monitoring aspects for SoA designs, where each monitoring aspect is systematically derived from contracts;
(iii) we introduce an automated procedure to synthesise and integrate runtime monitors into existing SoA-based systems.

2 Related Work

Guissouma et al. [10] propose a contract-based monitoring approach for evolving systems with learning-based components. While they support assessment during component evolution, our method offers a more general, architecture-integrated solution. By operating at the interface level, our monitors remain valid despite component updates and enable re-integration during architectural changes. Ameller and Franch [3] present SALMon, a non-intrusive monitoring framework for service-based systems based on service-level agreements. While this suggests contract awareness, it lacks formal interface-level contracts and structured behavioural assertions. In contrast, our approach supports fine-grained runtime verification by explicitly encoding formal contracts and architectural context, enabling automated synthesis of component-specific monitors. Watanabe et al. [19] apply runtime monitoring in automotive systems using Signal Temporal Logic (STL) within a CbD framework. Giannakopoulou et al. [9], Perez et al. [17], and Pike et al. [18] present domain-specific languages (DSLs) based monitoring framework. These methods provide precise control over monitor behaviour, especially for verifying internal semantics. However, they require learning sophisticated languages (e. g., FRETISH), which increases specification errors and integration efforts. In contrast, our taxonomy enables monitor synthesis from intuitive specifications, providing an accessible solution. While DSL-based monitors may be more expressive for tightly controlled internal systems, our method is especially suited for third-party or black-box components, where internal logic is unknown and quick integration is needed.

3 Definitions

We employ the FOCUS notation introduced by Broy and Stølen [6], with adaptations for automotive applications as proposed by Kugele et al. [14]. However, we have introduced modifications and extensions to these definitions to better align with our specific requirements. These refinements include adjusting existing formulations and adding new elements, ensuring a more comprehensive representation tailored to our framework. We will first review the necessary formalisms and definitions to facilitate a clear understanding of our work. In this notation, a system $s \in \texttt{SYSTEM}$ is fully characterised by its *syntactic* and *semantic* interfaces. The syntactic interface comprises typed channels $c \in \texttt{CHANNEL}$, which enable interaction with the system's environment. $\texttt{SYSTEM}$, $\texttt{CHANNEL}$, and $\texttt{MESSAGE}$ represent the set of all systems, channels, and messages, respectively.

Definition 1 (Syntactic Interface). *Let $I \subseteq$ `CHANNEL` be a set of typed input channels and $O \subseteq$ `CHANNEL` be the set of typed output channels with $I \cap O = \emptyset$. The pair (I, O) characterises the* syntactic interface *of a (sub)system. The syntactic interface is denoted by $(I \triangleright O)$.*

Messages m are exchanged discretely over time, forming a *timed stream.*

Definition 2 (Timed Stream). *Let $M \subseteq$ `MESSAGE` be a set of messages of the same type $T \in$ `TYPE`. A* timed stream s *of type T is a function* $\mathsf{s}\colon \mathbb{N}^+ \rightarrow M \cup \{\bot\}$.

In a timed stream s, exactly one message $\mathsf{s}(t)$ is transmitted per discrete time interval $t \in \mathbb{N}^+$. If no message is transmitted in time interval t, we write $\mathsf{s}(t) = \bot$.

We denote with $\mathsf{s} \downarrow t$ the *prefix* of length $t \in \mathbb{N}$ of stream s and with $\mathsf{s} \uparrow t$ the *tail* without its first t time intervals, respectively. The number of copies of messages $m \in$ `MESSAGE` of stream s is obtained using $m\#\mathsf{s}$.

For channels, we define a *channel history* $\hbar$, which is a mapping of streams to channels: $\hbar\colon \mathtt{CHANNEL} \rightarrow (\mathbb{N}^+ \rightarrow (\mathtt{MESSAGE} \cup \{\bot\}))$. We denote the set of all channel histories for the channel set $C \subseteq$ `CHANNEL` by $\vec{C}$. The semantic interface defines the behaviour.

Definition 3 (Semantic Interface). *The logical and temporal behaviour, i. e., the* semantic interface *of a system $\mathcal{s}$ with syntactic interface $(I \triangleright O)$ is given by the function: $f\colon \vec{I} \rightarrow \wp(\vec{O})$*

The semantic interface provides a high-level logical description of the system's expected behaviours, thus capturing the logical constraints over the interface assertions (cf. Sect. 4), which directly correspond to monitoring aspects in the taxonomy. The runtime monitor verifies system compliance by evaluating whether the semantic interface remains valid under these assertions during execution. On the other hand, the syntactic interface defines a system's interaction points. Through *abstraction*, it is simplified to the *service interface*, which focuses on the services provided and consumed, such as producing, consuming, or manipulating data, rather than detailed interactions.

Definition 4 (Service, Service Interface). *A* service $\mathfrak{s}$ *is characterised by its syntactic interface $(I^{\mathfrak{s}} \triangleright O^{\mathfrak{s}})$ and its semantic interface given by the behaviour function f, with $I^{\mathfrak{s}} \subseteq I$ and $O^{\mathfrak{s}} \subseteq O$, where $(I \triangleright O)$ is the syntactic interface of the system $\mathcal{s}$ providing the service $\mathfrak{s}$. The set of services of a system $\mathcal{s}$ is denoted by $\mathfrak{S}$. The* service interface *of a (sub)system $s \in$ `SYSTEM` is denoted by $(P, C)^{\#}_{s}$, where P denotes the set of* published *and C the set of* consumed *services.*

Subsystems, their interactions, and associated interface assertions constitute the *architecture specification* of a system.

Definition 5 (Architecture Specification). *An* architecture specification *$\mathcal{A}$ for a system $\mathcal{s} \in$ `SYSTEM` is a triple $S, \multimap, Q$ where $S \subseteq$ `SYSTEM` is the set of contained subsystems, $\multimap \subseteq (\mathfrak{S} \times \mathfrak{S})$ is the set of all* publish/subscribe relationships *between subsystems, and Q is the set of* interface assertions.

4 Runtime Monitor Synthesis

Two steps are essential to synthesise runtime monitors: (1) identifying the target component or service and (2) specifying the properties to monitor. The following section illustrates and explains the proposed synthesis process.

Architecture. Software architecture is crucial for ensuring the safety of automated systems, particularly when integrating methods such as deep learning, which are central to modern automated vehicles. Effective architectures must ensure seamless component interactions, rigorously enforce safety constraints, and incorporate robust monitoring and redundancy mechanisms to detect and mitigate unpredictable behaviours. Structuring the architecture to isolate and manage risks significantly enhances safety, reliability, and predictability, even with evolving algorithms. In developing automated systems, we adopt the established *Sense-Plan-Act* control loop from robotics, combined with the *Monitor-Actuator* pattern [8]. This approach organises system functionality into distinct components, clearly separating perception, decision-making, and execution. Such separation enhances modularity, simplifies integration of complex components, and improves scalability and maintainability, providing a solid foundation for ensuring safety in dynamic and uncertain environments.

Architectural Contracts. The interface behaviour of a system $\mathscr{s}$ can be specified as a predicate logic formula, with channel identifiers from $(I \cup O)$ as free variables representing streams of the respective types.

[$\mathscr{s}$]
in I
out O
Q

The interface assertion Q defines constraints on the *interface behaviour* $f_{\mathscr{s}}$, semantic interface, of system $\mathscr{s}$ with the syntactic interface $(I \triangleright O)$. For input and output channel histories $x \in \vec{I}$ and $y \in \vec{O}$, we also write $q(x, y)$. The semantic interface $f_{\mathscr{s}}$ fulfils the specification of system $\mathscr{s}$ with interface assertion $q(x, y)$ if $\forall x \in \vec{I}, y \in \vec{O} \colon y \in f_{\mathscr{s}}(x) \implies q(x, y)$. An interface assertion is an *invariant* that must always be satisfied. A commonly used paradigm is that of *assume/guarantee* (A/G), i. e., the interface assertion Q can be written as $Q \equiv A \implies G$, where A and G are the predicates describing the *assumption* and *guarantee*, respectively. A set of interface assertions is canonically represented as a logical expression by logically conjoining the individual interface assertions.

Bridging the Gap from Logical to Technical Execution. Using FOCUS requires bridging the gap between an idealised logical model and a real-time system operating on a physical platform, where finite resources and natural constraints prevail. Maintaining semantic consistency between these models, particularly concerning time and resource constraints, is crucial. FOCUS follows a discreetly ticked logical zero-time model. Mapping these ticks to real-time durations (e. g., one tick = 1 ms) is use case-specific; however, we assume this fixed duration for ticks in this paper. FOCUS employs idealised data types like $\mathbb{N}$ (natural numbers) that require no memory. While suitable for logical specifications, practical implementations approximate these types (e. g., using 32-bit integers). Furthermore, bounded data structures do not account for memory consumption, assuming unlimited resources such as memory, bandwidth, and energy. To ensure unified modelling and specification, we extend FOCUS to explicitly define *resource requirements*, enabling compliance with resource constraints specific to the execution platform (e. g., SRAM, Flash, or CPU time).

Definition 6 (Timed Resource Requirement). *Let $\rho \in \texttt{RESOURCE}$ denote an arbitrary resource as described above, and let θ represent the corresponding threshold, i. e., the maximum allowable usage of that resource. A* timed resource requirement *is a stream associating each time and resource a threshold, i. e.,* $\mathsf{c}\colon \mathbb{N}^{+} \times \texttt{RESOURCE} \rightarrow \mathbb{R} \cup \{\bot\}$. *Note that $\bot$ allows for an unbounded resource at a given time. We assume that the timed resource requirements are given.*

4.1 Taxonomy of Contractual Aspects

We present a taxonomy that systematically organises complex requirements into well-defined monitoring aspects—time, resource, plausibility, and liveliness—as summarised in Table 1. It offers a structured approach to decomposing high-level requirements into measurable units, forming the basis for contracts that specify expected component behaviour and support automated runtime monitoring. The taxonomy is based on our mapping study [16], which surveyed a broad range of works on CbD. We identified recurring categories of monitoring aspects, particularly in the context of CbD-based runtime monitoring. These categories were refined in collaboration with industry partners. While not exhaustive, the taxonomy captures the most prevalent runtime monitoring needs observed in practice. Table 1 summarises the formalised monitoring aspects.

Requirements to Contracts. Monitoring aspects allow us to assess whether assurances are upheld and, if not, identify necessary corrective measures. Requirements are usually expressed in natural language. Instead, we encode requirements in a structured JSON format compatible with the synthesiser's formal specifications. For instance, consider the following requirement: *"The system shall detect and classify objects within the perception component with a maximum latency of 100 ms to ensure real-time responsiveness in automated driving scenarios,"* which is formalised in FOCUS and encoded in JSON as follows:

[perception_service]

in $I = \{i\}$ **out** $O = \{o\}$

$$\forall i \in \vec{I}, o \in \vec{O}, \forall t_i \in \mathbb{N}^{+}\,.\ \exists\, t_o \in \mathbb{N}^{+}, t_o \leq t_i + 100\colon i(t_i) \neq \bot \Rightarrow o(t_o) \neq \bot$$


```
{
 "service": "perception_service",
 "monitoring_aspects": {"temporal": "response_time": "100ms"}
}
```

Table 1. Parameterised monitoring aspects, subaspects, and contracts.

Aspect	Description	Contract
Temporal Monitoring	Checks whether the time from input reception to output generation does not exceed τ.	**Response Time** (τ) **in** $I = \{i\}$ **out** $O = \{o\}$ $\forall i \in \vec{I}, o \in \vec{O}, \forall t_i \in \mathbb{N}^+ .\ \exists t_o \in \mathbb{N}^+, t_o \leq t_i + \tau \colon i(t_i) \neq \bot \Rightarrow o(t_o) \neq \bot$
Temporal Monitoring	The rate (frequency in Hz) of messages with $\ell = 1/f$.	**I/O Rates** (f) **in** $I = \{i\}$ **out** $O = \{o\}$ $\forall i \in \vec{I}, o \in \vec{O}, \forall t \in \mathbb{N}^+ \colon i(t) \neq \bot \Rightarrow o(t) \neq \bot \wedge m\#((i \uparrow t) \downarrow \ell) = m\#((o \uparrow t) \downarrow \ell)$ with $m \neq \bot$
Plausibility Monitoring	Checks whether an in-/output value is within a given range $[l, u]$.[1]	**Range Check** ($[l, u]$) **out** $O = \{o\}$ $\forall o \in \vec{O}, \forall t \in \mathbb{N}^+ \colon o(t) \in [l, u]$
Plausibility Monitoring	Checks whether an in-/output value satisfies a relational condition $\circ \in \{<, \leq, >, \geq, =\}$ w.r.t. a given threshold θ.	**Threshold Check** ($\circ, \theta$) **out** $O = \{o\}$ $\forall o \in \vec{O}, \forall t \in \mathbb{N}^+ \colon o(t) \circ \theta$
Plausibility Monitoring	Verifies whether data values remain consistent over time, constrained by physical laws (e. g., velocity, acceleration). Two approaches: (i) bounded deviation ϵ over time interval Δt or (ii) deviation ϵ relative to the mean within a sliding window of length Δt.	**Temporal Consistency Check** ($\Delta t, \epsilon$) **out** $O = \{o\}$ $\forall o \in \vec{O}, \forall t \in \mathbb{N}^+ \colon$ (i) $\lvert o(t + \Delta t) - o(t) \rvert \leq \epsilon$ or (ii) $\left\lvert o(t) - 1/\Delta t \sum_{i=1}^{\Delta t} o(t - i) \right\rvert \leq \epsilon$ w/ $\Delta t \leq t$
Plausibility Monitoring	Verifies whether different data sources consistently describe the same phenomenon (e. g., distance) based on a similarity measure S, even when time-shifted by τ.	**Cross-Data Consistency Check** (τ, θ) **in** $I = \{i_1, i_2\}$ For $i_1, i_2 \in \vec{I}, \forall t \in \mathbb{N}^+ \colon S(\tau_{max}) \geq \theta$ with $\tau_{max} = \arg max_{\eta \in [-\tau, \tau]} S(\eta)$ and $S(\tau) = \frac{i_1(t) \cdot i_2(t-\tau)}{\sqrt{i_1(t)^2 + i_2(t-\tau)^2}}$
Res. Mon.	Verifies whether resource usage ρ exceeds defined thresholds θ. Resources include $\rho \in \texttt{RESOURCE} = \{Flash, SRAM, EEPROM, DRAM, CPU, time, Energy\}$	**Resource Usage Check** (ρ, θ) $\forall t \in \mathbb{N}^+, \rho \in \texttt{RESOURCE}.\ \hat{\rho}(t) \leq c(t, \rho)$ if $c(t, \rho) \neq \bot$, $\hat{\rho}(t)$ is the resource usage of ρ at time t.
Liv. Mon.	Checks whether s is responsive, i. e., messages are sent within an interval Δt and tolerance ϵ.	**Liveliness Check** ($\Delta t, \epsilon$) **out** $O = \{o\}$ $\forall o \in \vec{O}, \forall k \in \mathbb{N}^+\ \exists t_k \in \mathbb{N}^+ \colon o(t_k) \neq \bot \wedge \Delta t - \epsilon \leq (t_{k+1} - t_k) \leq \Delta t + \epsilon$

[1] Aspects applying to both inputs and outputs are shown for outputs only, without loss of generality.

Safety engineers and system architects can define requirements as structured JSON files based on system design and constraints, refining them through simulation and real-world validation feedback. Unlike natural language, which is often ambiguous and inconsistent, our approach ensures clarity and automation by translating requirements into a machine-readable format. This standardised representation streamlines specification, enhances accessibility for diverse stakeholders, and enables direct synthesis into runtime monitors.

4.2 Monitor Synthesis

We adopt a black-box approach when creating monitors, focusing solely on the I/O relationship. This approach offers high automation, as it does not require internal modifications to the system. Moreover, many off-the-shelf components integrated as third-party products are difficult to instrument. Knowledge about the architecture and the contracts in the form of requirements that need to be fulfilled is necessary to synthesise runtime monitors. First, requirements need to be written by engineers, system architects, or safety experts by filling out the JSON file, as mentioned in Sect. 4.1. Also, the architectural description can be given in the same JSON file. Before code generation, the conflict check phase is essential for validating the consistency and feasibility of the interface assertions. Each interface assertion is analysed during this phase to ensure compatibility with others. For example, if a ROS 2 node must publish fresh data every second, its response time must not exceed one second. Addressing such potential conflicts upfront allows the generated monitors to enforce requirements effectively, ensuring reliable monitoring without compromising system performance.

After passing the checks, a complete ROS 2 package is created including all necessary build files (e. g., `package.xml`, `CMakeLists.txt`) and the monitor node's source code. It automatically resolves message types and inserts required dependencies to enable a correct subscription and evaluation of the defined assertions. The generated monitor code is built using the standard ROS 2 build process. Once compiled, the monitor can be launched either alongside the system or independently at runtime. It connects directly to the specified topics defined in the contract (e. g., input/output channels of a node) and observes the message streams for *runtime verifica-*

Algorithm 1: Monitor Synthesis

Input: $\mathcal{A} = (S, -\!\bullet\!\succ\!-, Q)$
Output: $\widehat{\mathcal{A}} = (\widehat{S}, \widehat{-\!\bullet\!\succ\!-}, Q)$ w/ monitors
$\widehat{\mathcal{A}} \leftarrow \mathcal{A}$
if centralised **then**
  Let m be $(I_m \rhd \{o\})$ and $(\{\mathfrak{s}_m\}, C_m)^{\#}_m$
  foreach $s \in S$ *with* $(I_s \rhd O_s)$ *and* $(P_s, C_s)^{\#}_s$ **do**
    $I_m \leftarrow I_m \cup (I_s \cup O_s) \quad C_m \leftarrow C_m \cup (P_s \cup C_s)$
    $\widehat{-\!\bullet\!\succ\!-} \leftarrow \widehat{-\!\bullet\!\succ\!-} \cup \bigcup_{\mathfrak{s} \in \mathfrak{S}_s = P_s \cup C_s} (\mathfrak{s}, \mathfrak{s}_m)$
  Let $f_m \colon \vec{I_m} \rightarrow \wp(\{\vec{o}\})$ be s.t.
  if $\forall s \in S, x \in \vec{I_s}, y \in \vec{O_s}, t \in \mathbb{N}^+ : y \in f_s(x) \Rightarrow Q(x, y)$ **then** $o(t) \leftarrow$ true **else** $o(t) \leftarrow$ false
  $\widehat{S} \leftarrow \widehat{S} \cup \{m\}$
else
  foreach $s \in S$ *with* $(I_s \rhd O_s)$ *and* $(P_s, C_s)^{\#}_s$ **do**
    Let m be $(I_m \rhd \{o\})$ and $(\{\mathfrak{s}_m\}, C_m)^{\#}_m$
    foreach $\mathfrak{s} \in \mathfrak{S}_s = P_s \cup C_s$ **do**
      $I_m \leftarrow I_m \cup (I_s \cup O_s) \quad C_m \leftarrow C_m \cup (P_s \cup C_s)$
      $\widehat{-\!\bullet\!\succ\!-} \leftarrow \widehat{-\!\bullet\!\succ\!-} \cup \{(\mathfrak{s}, \mathfrak{s}_m)\}$
    Let $f_m \colon \vec{I_m} \rightarrow \wp(\{\vec{o}\})$ be s.t.
    if $\forall x \in \vec{I_s}, y \in \vec{O_s}, t \in \mathbb{N}^+ : y \in f_s(x) \Rightarrow Q(x, y)$ **then** $o(t) \leftarrow$ true **else** $o(t) \leftarrow$ false
    $\widehat{S} \leftarrow \widehat{S} \cup \{m\}$
return $\widehat{\mathcal{A}}$

---

tion. The monitor is fully decoupled and passive, ensuring non-intrusive integration.

The procedure, detailed in Algorithm 1, for synthesising runtime monitors uses architectural specifications (containing contracts as interface assertions) as input. In this process, each ROS 2 node is treated as an independent service within a SoA, where nodes communicate through well-defined interfaces (i. e., over topics). This aligns with the FOCUS framework, enabling runtime verification through formal contracts. These systems provide or consume various services, including each service's syntactic and semantic interfaces. This setup effectively captures the inputs and outputs that need to be monitored. The architectural specification outlines the relationships between subsystems, establishing rules for connectivity and hierarchy while ensuring that services interact according to interface assertions, describing the specific aspects detailed in Table 1. The synthesis process supports both centralised and decentralised monitoring modes, allowing flexibility in how runtime monitoring is implemented. In decentralised mode, each ROS 2 node is assigned an independent monitor responsible for verifying the compliance of its local input-output interactions. Alternatively, in centralised mode, a single global monitor evaluates interface assertions system-wide, ensuring a comprehensive system-wide verification. This mode selection allows the framework to adapt to different performance and scalability requirements. Upon execution, the synthesiser processes the architectural specifications to create monitoring code that complies with ROS 2 automatically for our use case. Like all other system components, the monitor is a (sub)system, following the definitions introduced in Sect. 3. To generate a suitable runtime monitor m, both the *syntactic* and *semantic interface* of the monitor for the observed system s must be described. This will be done in the following.

Definition 7 (Runtime Monitor). *Let* $m = (s, O_m)$ *be a* runtime monitor *for system* s *with the syntactic interfaces* $(I_s \triangleright O_s)$ *and* $(I_m \triangleright O_m)$*, respectively, with* $I_m = I_s \cup O_s$ *and* O_m *being the set of output channels. The monitor observes the fulfilment of the system's interface assertions* Q*, i. e., contracts, defined in the architectural specification* $\mathcal{A}$.

5 Evaluation

Evaluation Planning. To assess the scalability and applicability of our approach, we employ two complementary strategies: (1) We examine two distinct *architectural paradigms*: a centralised monitor overseeing multiple system components and a federated approach with individual monitors for each component (cf. Figs. 2 and 3). These paradigms are tested under simulated load in terms of memory and CPU. Evaluating centralised and federated monitoring approaches reveals their distinct trade-offs in performance, scalability, and architecture. By comparing both paradigms, we can assess how the proposed synthesis framework adapts to different system topologies and resource constraints, which is crucial for its practical deployment in diverse automotive platforms. The two contrasting approaches can be elegantly combined within a zonal E/E architecture using a central intra-zone and a federated inter-zone monitoring strategy. (2) We test the approach in a realistic driving scenario using CARLA, focusing on a *Construction Zone Assistance* (CZA) system. This validates the framework under complex, high-fidelity conditions.

All evaluations were conducted on a Ubuntu 20.04 machine (Intel i7-13850HX, 32 GiB RAM, RTX 2000 Ada), using Python 3.10 and the default ROS Humble configuration, with *reliability policy* set to *reliable* and the *depth* of 10.

Scalability Benchmark. This benchmark evaluates the approach's efficiency by measuring performance metrics under varying scales: (i) *CPU utilisation*: The ratio of time spent by the CPU executing a process to the actual elapsed clock time. (ii) *Memory consumption*: Measured as Proportional Set Size (PSS), which includes a ROS 2 node's private and a fraction of its shared memory.

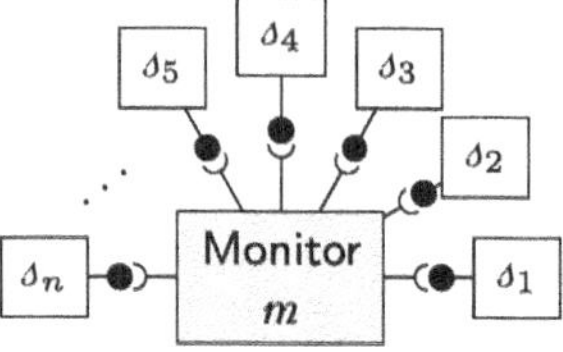

Fig. 2. Centralised monitor

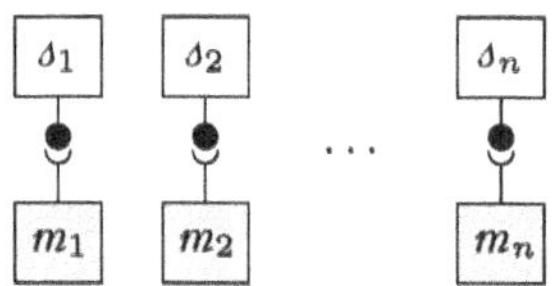

Fig. 3. Federated monitors

Scalability testing assesses how efficiently the framework adapts as the system scales from small to large. This involves evaluating the framework's ability to handle increasing numbers of nodes, message rates, and payload sizes. For realistic benchmarks and topic count definition, we referred to simulation environments [7,20] and ROS 2-based automated driving stacks [13], which typically operate with 50–100 topics plus additional packages. To stress-test our framework, we expanded this range to 1–200 topics. The message rate range of 1–100 Hz reflects realistic automotive system behaviour, where cameras stream data at 30–60 Hz, LiDAR sensors at 10–20 Hz, and GNSS at 1–10 Hz. Control algorithms generally run at 20–100 Hz, with platforms like Apollo [5] operating at 100 Hz. We employ the runtime monitor to verify the output rate of *talker* nodes publishing `UInt8MultiArray` messages with specified payloads and message rates. LiDAR point clouds and compressed camera frames typically range from 100 KiB to 10 MiB. Therefore, we varied the payload size between 1 KiB and 10,000 KiB to represent different message types.

Figure 4 shows the performance comparison, where the charts present average values across repeated runs and shaded areas indicate variability and configuration stability. In Figs. 4(a) and 4(b), memory usage is measured at 100 Hz, as higher message rates had a negligible effect in preliminary tests. A fixed frequency was used for clarity. The centralised setup shows higher memory variability, especially at the largest payload (10.000 KiB), while the federated setup displays a stable, near-linear profile with variability dropping around 120 topics. Adjusting the *depth* (e.g., to 50) changed this behaviour, and beyond 100 topics, communication became dysfunctional. Regarding CPU usage (Figs. 4(c) and 4(d), 1.000 KiB payload), federated monitoring consumes more CPU at low

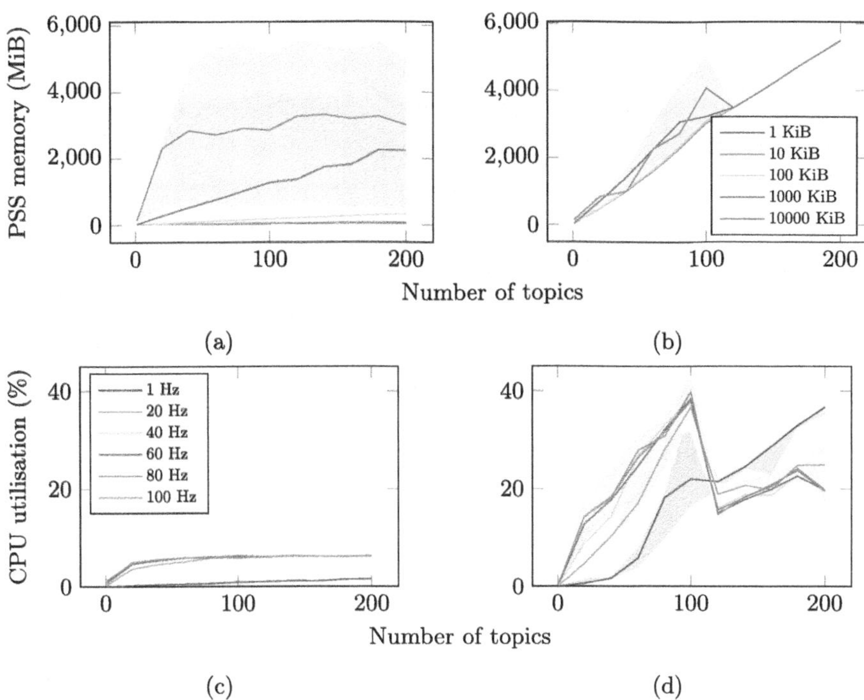

Fig. 4. Memory usage vs. number of topics (100 Hz): (a) central, (b) federated; CPU usage vs. number of topics (1000 KiB payload): (c) central, (d) federated.

topic counts due to multi-node overhead. Message dropouts appear beyond 100 listener nodes, causing a dramatic decrease in CPU utilisation due to middleware or OS-level limitations. Payload size has little effect on CPU usage in the federated setup, whereas in the centralised case, CPU usage increases with topic count (for 100 KiB), indicating scalable load handling. However, with 1.000 KiB payload, CPU usage plateaus around 40 topics, suggesting a performance ceiling from data-handling bottlenecks.

Use Case. We demonstrate our approach using the CZA developed by Zacchi et al. [20], an ADAS designed for the reliable detection of highway construction zones. We focus on the perception component, which must address challenges from irregular road layouts, temporary signage, and static and dynamic obstacles like machinery and workers. CZA enables automated vehicles to navigate complex, dynamic environments. Figure 5 presents a high-level SoA of the *monitored* perception stack. The

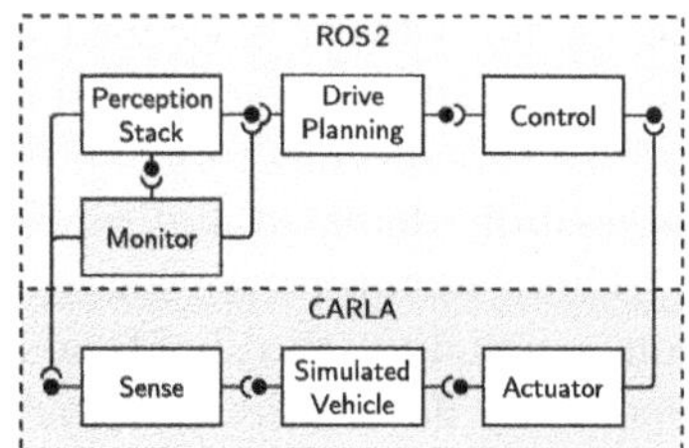

Fig. 5. High-level functional SoA of the CZA.

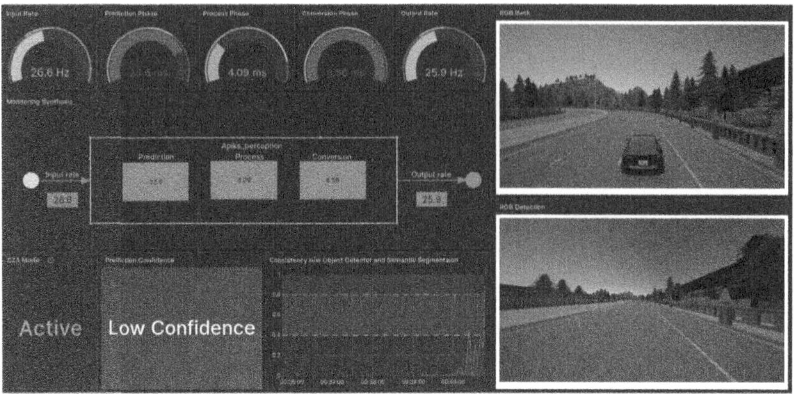

Fig. 6. Safety dashboard and CARLA simulator

simulation environment combines CARLA [7], a ROS bridge, our ROS 2-based implementations, and a dashboard, all within separate Docker containers. The simulator executes predefined construction zone scenarios simulating real-world conditions, as shown in Fig. 6.

During the simulation, a synthesised runtime monitor continuously observes and evaluates the perception system's performance. This monitor is automatically generated from predefined requirements specified as monitoring aspects and architectural specifications (`Apiks_perception`, comprising `Prediction`, `Process`, and `Conversion`; cf. Fig. 6), provided in JSON format. Requirements are first checked for consistency to prevent conflicts, followed by automated monitor generation. The monitor is then seamlessly deployed within the simulation environment, streamlining the workflow from specification to execution. For this application, we define temporal and plausibility requirements for the perception system. Temporal constraints include response time limits for prediction, processing, and conversion modules and I/O rate limits at a higher architectural level than the individual perception components in $\mathscr{A}$. Plausibility checks include thresholds on prediction confidence and cross-data consistency of cone positions from object detection and semantic segmentation. These values are continuously monitored and visualised in the dashboard (Fig. 6), ensuring alignment between specification and runtime behaviour in dynamic scenarios like CZA. During the execution of the CZA scenario, every deviation from the specified constraints (e. g., threshold violations or cross-data inconsistencies) was successfully detected and reported by the synthesised monitors.

These monitors are based on simple, yet formally defined, concrete assertions, including thresholds and response time bounds, which enable them to report any deviations deterministically. Since the monitors rely on definite conditions, statistical detection metrics (e. g., precision or recall) are not applicable in this context. Instead, whenever a contract is violated during execution, the corresponding monitor reliably reports it. This demonstrates both the functional validity and operational applicability of the proposed monitoring framework.

6 Discussion

Evaluation Results. In Sect. 5, we compared two architectural paradigms. Centralised monitoring is more efficient for small payloads but exhibits significant memory variability with large ones (Fig. 4(a)), raising concerns for high-data-rate sources like cameras. Federated monitoring, while requiring more memory for fewer topics and small payloads, offers a stable and predictable memory pattern (Fig. 4(b)), supporting better scalability. Message drops and anomalies beyond 100 topics indicate an evaluation platform limitation. A similar trend appears in CPU usage. Federated monitoring is more resource-intensive at low topic counts but scales better under high throughput until it reaches system-level saturation. The sharp CPU decline beyond 100 topics suggests resource exhaustion, likely due to middleware or OS constraints rather than monitoring logic. This highlights the need to fine-tune system settings for large-scale deployment. Conversely, centralised monitoring shows plateauing CPU usage under high payloads but scales well for lower payloads (e. g., 100 KiB). Under heavy loads, it encounters earlier saturation, potentially leading to latency and underutilisation of computational resources.

These results stress the need for context-aware architecture selection. Federated setups suit high-payload, high-topic scenarios up to 100 topics, where isolation and predictability are key. Centralised setups may fit lightweight, tightly-coupled systems. Variability and performance ceilings suggest resource and middleware limitations. However, deploying a distributed electrical and electronic architecture requires additional considerations. A single central monitor increases bus load and risk of failure, while per-ECU monitoring avoids this but fails if the monitor and target system share the same ECU. This underlines the need for case-specific or hybrid setups, such as *zonal architectures*, i. e., intra-zone centralised and inter-zone federated monitoring.

The CZA use case provides a concrete scenario featuring challenges like irregular road layouts, temporary signage, and dynamic obstacles to evaluate the runtime monitoring framework in realistic conditions. This application demonstrated the framework's capacity to ensure operational correctness for safety-critical systems by using monitoring aspects such as temporal and plausibility checks. Temporal monitoring verified component responsiveness, essential for timely detection and reaction to sudden obstacles, such as cones appearing on the road. Plausibility monitoring ensured consistency and reliability of perception outputs, preventing erroneous sensor data from leading to unsafe decisions, particularly in environments with irregular and temporary layouts.

Usability, Integration, and Safety Argumentation. The proposed monitoring framework emphasises usability by enabling easy integration of runtime monitors by directly translating architectural specifications $\mathscr{A}$, including interface assertions, into runtime monitors. Its modular SoA setup allows monitors to be integrated without interrupting the system, which is especially beneficial in adaptive environments where configurations evolve during runtime. Unlike prior approaches requiring manually formalised specifications, our framework provides an automated synthesis pipeline. Monitoring aspects are specified as modular assertions, making the process accessible to engineers without formal methods expertise. This automated synthesis minimises misalignment risks, ensuring that monitors consistently enforce specified requirements and bridge the gap between design-time specifications and runtime assurance. Safety assurance is enhanced through: (i) formal methods for specifying safety concepts, with validation checks providing evidence of suitability prior to implementation and testing; (ii) code generation for implementing safety requirements, ensuring alignment between specifications and implementation, and reducing reliance on tests and reviews.

Because of the aforementioned usability and integration characteristics, the proposed framework is particularly well-suited for modular, safety-critical systems such as those found in automated driving. It is most effective in scenarios involving third-party or learning-based components whose internal implementations are inaccessible or not fully understood. In such cases, intrusive instrumentation is often impractical or impossible. By operating solely at the interface level, the monitors can verify system behaviour without altering internal logic, making it effective for validating black-box components. It offers a practical and effective usage for systems subject to regular changes or unpredictable behaviours. Furthermore, the framework enables early detection of requirement violations, making it valuable for runtime and design-time assurance.

Limitations and Future Work. In addition to scalability-related limitations, the proposed taxonomy introduces inherent constraints. It was designed to categorise monitoring aspects in safety-critical systems, help engineers in specifying runtime contracts without requiring formal methods expertise. However, the taxonomy is general-purpose and does not capture domain-specific semantics or application-level logic. As the method is based on this taxonomy, it also inherits its limitations. Unlike prior DSL- or STL-based approaches that support expressive, domain-specific specifications, our framework prioritises simplicity, modularity, and ease of integration. Additionally, it does not support inter-aspect or inter-component relationships, which restricts the ability to define context-sensitive or risk-combined conditions. Future work will aim to enhance expressiveness and diagnostics. We plan to support mode-aware contracts that are activated by system states (e. g., ROS 2 lifecycle), and to extend the taxonomy with inter-aspect/component relationships for more context-sensitive monitoring. Additionally, we intend to utilise Large Language Models (LLMs) to interpret contract violations in relation to system architecture and component behaviour, supporting automated diagnosis and explanation generation.

Threats to Validity. 1) *Internal Validity:* The reliability of results depends on assumptions in the contracts and monitoring framework. Undetected anomalies may occur if these do not reflect real-world complexities. To reduce this risk, we validated contract specifications against system requirements and designed the experimental environment using both measurement- and simulation-based evaluations. 2) *External Validity:* Evaluation was conducted using CARLA with a single CZA use case, which may limit generalisability. To address this, we used widely adopted platforms (ROS 2, CARLA) and conducted scalability tests to simulate diverse conditions. 3) *Construct Validity:* Metrics such as CPU and memory usage may not fully capture runtime constraints. To address this, we included qualitative assessments of system responsiveness and compliance with safety requirements, supported by real-time visualisation for runtime behaviour analysis. 4) *Conclusion Validity:* Biases in simulation or monitor synthesis may affect results. To reduce this, we performed reproducible experiments with automated tests and cross-validation between centralised and federated paradigms.

7 Conclusion

In this paper, we presented a runtime monitoring framework designed for automotive SoA. By integrating CbD with automated monitor synthesis, the approach ensures operational correctness. In contrast to prior works, our approach enables the direct synthesis of runtime monitors from structured requirements, eliminating the need for manual formalisation or specification language expertise. The framework is particularly effective in modular and safety-critical systems, especially when dealing with third-party or learning-based components where internal behaviour is unknown. By monitoring interfaces, it enables non-intrusive verification during both runtime and development. The framework was evaluated across different architectural paradigms and use case simulations, demonstrating scalability, efficiency, and adaptability to real-world challenges. These evaluations confirmed the framework's effectiveness in addressing runtime constraints while integrating seamlessly with existing systems. Future work will focus on supporting mode-aware contract activation, inter-aspect/component relationships, and leveraging LLMs to interpret contract violations.

Data Availability Statement. Due to intellectual property constraints, a complete framework and simulation, developed in collaboration with academic and industrial partners, cannot be released. Nonetheless, to support transparency and reproducibility, a modified version of the synthesised monitor used for scalability experiments, along with evaluation results and test scripts, is available at: https://doi.org/10.5281/zenodo.15464461.

References

1. Taxonomy and Definitions for Terms Related to Driving Automation Systems for On-Road Motor Vehicles (SAE J3016), April 2021. https://www.sae.org/standards/content/j3016_202104/. Version April 2021
2. Road vehicles – Safety of the intended functionality (2022). https://www.iso.org/standard/70939.html
3. Ameller, D., Franch, X.: Service level agreement monitor (salmon). In: 7th International Conference on Composition-Based Software Systems, ICCBSS 2008, pp. 224–227. IEEE CS (2008). https://doi.org/10.1109/ICCBSS.2008.13
4. AUTomotive Open System ARchitecture: AUTOSAR Adaptive Platform Specification (2023). https://www.autosar.org/standards/adaptive-platform/
5. Baidu Apollo Team: Apollo: Open source autonomous driving (2017). https://github.com/ApolloAuto/apollo. Accessed 26 Mar 2025
6. Broy, M., Stølen, K.: Specification and Development of Interactive Systems – Focus on Streams, Interfaces, and Refinement. Monographs in Computer Science. Springer (2001). https://doi.org/10.1007/978-1-4613-0091-5
7. Dosovitskiy, A., Ros, G., Codevilla, F., López, A.M., Koltun, V.: CARLA: an open urban driving simulator. In: 1st Annual Conference on Robot Learning, CoRL 2017. Proceedings of Machine Learning Research, vol. 78, pp. 1–16. PMLR (2017). http://proceedings.mlr.press/v78/dosovitskiy17a.html
8. Douglass, B.P.: Real-Time Design Patterns: Robust Scalable Architecture for Real-Time Systems. Addison-Wesley Professional (2002)
9. Giannakopoulou, D., Pressburger, T., Mavridou, A., Schumann, J.: Automated formalization of structured natural language requirements. Inf. Softw. Technol. **137**, 106590 (2021). https://doi.org/10.1016/J.INFSOF.2021.106590
10. Guissouma, H., Zink, M., Sax, E.: Continuous safety assessment of updated supervised learning models in shadow mode. In: 2023 IEEE 20th International Conference on Software Architecture Companion (ICSA-C), pp. 301–308 (2023). https://doi.org/10.1109/ICSA-C57050.2023.00069
11. Hoare, C.A.R.: An axiomatic basis for computer programming. Commun. ACM **12**(10), 576–580 (1969). https://doi.org/10.1145/363235.363259
12. International Organization for Standardization: ISO/PAS 8800:2024 – Road vehicles — Safety and artificial intelligence (2024). https://www.iso.org/standard/83303.html. Accessed 15 Mar 2025
13. Kato, S., et al.: Autoware on board: enabling autonomous vehicles with embedded systems. In: Proceedings of the 9th ACM/IEEE International Conference on Cyber-Physical Systems, ICCPS 2018, pp. 287–296. IEEE CS/ACM (2018). https://doi.org/10.1109/ICCPS.2018.00035
14. Kugele, S., Obergfell, P., Broy, M., Creighton, O., Traub, M., Hopfensitz, W.: On service-orientation for automotive software. In: 2017 IEEE International Conference on Software Architecture, ICSA 2017, pp. 193–202. IEEE Computer Society (2017). https://doi.org/10.1109/ICSA.2017.20
15. Macenski, S., Foote, T., Gerkey, B., Lalancette, C., Woodall, W.: Robot operating system 2: design, architecture, and uses in the wild. Sci. Robot. **7**(66), eabm6074 (2022). https://doi.org/10.1126/scirobotics.abm6074
16. Okumus, F.F., Ramic, A., Kugele, S.: A systematic mapping study on contract-based software design for dependable systems. CoRR abs/2505.07542 (2025). https://doi.org/10.48550/arXiv.2505.07542

17. Perez, I., Mavridou, A., Pressburger, T., Goodloe, A., Giannakopoulou, D.: Automated translation of natural language requirements to runtime monitors. In: 28th International Conference on Tools and Algorithms for the Construction and Analysis of Systems, TACAS 2022, Proceedings, Part I. LNCS, vol. 13243, pp. 387–395. Springer (2022). https://doi.org/10.1007/978-3-030-99524-9_21
18. Pike, L., Wegmann, N., Niller, S., Goodloe, A.: Copilot: monitoring embedded systems. Innov. Syst. Softw. Eng. **9**(4), 235–255 (2013). https://doi.org/10.1007/S11334-013-0223-X
19. Watanabe, K., Kang, E., Lin, C., Shiraishi, S.: Runtime monitoring for safety of intelligent vehicles. In: 55th Annual Design Automation Conference, DAC 2018, pp. 31:1–31:6. ACM (2018). https://doi.org/10.1145/3195970.3199856
20. Zacchi, J., Clementi, E., Mata, N.: APIKS: a modular ROS2 framework for rapid prototyping and validation of automated driving systems. CoRR abs/2502.20507 (2025). https://doi.org/10.48550/ARXIV.2502.20507

Self-adaptive, Secure and Federated Learning Systems

Model-Based Proactive Self-adaptation for Cloud Systems

Raphael Straub[1(✉)], Sarah Stieß[2], Steffen Becker[2], and Matthias Tichy[1]

[1] Institute of Software Engineering and Programming Languages, Ulm University, James-Franck-Ring, 89075 Ulm, Germany
{raphael.straub,matthias.tichy}@uni-ulm.de

[2] Institute of Software Engineering, University of Stuttgart, Universitätsstraße 38, 70569 Stuttgart, Germany
{sarah.stiess,steffen.becker}@iste.uni-stuttgart.de

Abstract. Context: Self-adaptive systems in the cloud domain leverage dynamic adaptations to meet their service level objectives (SLOs) under changing environments, e.g., varying load or VM failures. This can be realized by defining scaling policies (adaptations) that reactively trigger when SLOs are violated. An alternative way to achieve this is for the system to predict the impact of adaptations as well as future environmental changes, thus enabling proactive reconfigurations.

Objective: This paper introduces a framework that leverages model-based analysis to optimize reconfiguration plans proactively. It aids developers in constructing proactive reconfigurations at design time.

Method: This paper presents a state exploration-based methodology for optimizing reconfiguration plans to maximize system utility with respect to predefined SLOs. We use the Palladio Component Models (PCM) to simulate the self-adaptive system using Slingshot, generating a state graph where transitions represent different adaptation rules or environment changes. For each state, we calculate a utility value that reflects how well the state satisfies the SLOs. The optimal reconfiguration plan is identified by finding the path from the root node to any leaf node that maximizes cumulative utility.

Results: We show the effectiveness of our approach on a simple exemplary system where the state exploration allows the system to find a reconfiguration plan that outperforms a purely reactive approach.

Conclusion: Our approach is a promising method for optimizing reconfiguration behavior in self-adaptive cloud systems. This approach outperforms a purely reactive approach, showing the potential of our methodology.

Keywords: Self-adaptive Systems · Proactive Reconfiguration · Cloud Computing · Model-based Analysis · Performance Prediction

V. Andrikopoulos et al. (Eds.): ECSA 2025, LNCS 15929, pp. 181–196, 2026.
https://doi.org/10.1007/978-3-032-02138-0_12

1 Introduction

In cloud computing, self-adaptive systems have become indispensable for managing the inherently dynamic and evolving environment in which they operate. These systems must continuously achieve predefined Service Level Objectives (SLOs) despite fluctuations in workload, resource availability, and other environmental changes. The systems require the ability to adapt dynamically to maintain optimal performance and ensure pivotal user satisfaction.

However, achieving resource-efficient self-adaptation poses significant challenges. For example, predicting the impact of potential adaptations and anticipating future environmental changes early in the development cycle is challenging. Additionally, the defined SLOs must appropriately capture the desired end-user quality requirements. The scaling policies that guide the adaptations must be carefully selected, with appropriate degrees of freedom, to allow the desired adaptions and balance resource utilization with performance targets.

Most industry approaches use reactive mechanisms, where the system responds to changes after their occurrence. For example, when the response time of a service exceeds a predefined threshold, the system scales out the service to handle the increased load. While reactive strategies can address immediate issues, they may not be sufficient for achieving long-term performance goals. Reactive approaches might act myopically, focusing on the immediate problem without considering the broader context. Hence, they are unable to utilize strategies of combined adaptations and other more sophisticated actions.

To address these limitations, we propose a novel state-exploration-based methodology designed to optimize reconfiguration plans proactively during design time. Our approach performs model-based simulations to evaluate the potential outcomes of different adaptation strategies, each defined as a sequence of adaptations and the specific times they are applied, prior to their execution. We systematically explore these adaptation strategies by aggregating the simulation results into a state graph. The state graph represents various system configurations and transitions, each corresponding to specific adaptation rules. Currently, model-based simulations for proactive reconfigurations have not been investigated yet as shown in current taxonomies for auto-scaling and elasticity [1,15].

We use Palladio, a modeling tool for performance prediction in software architectures, to create models of (existing) self-adaptive cloud systems. These models are then simulated using the slingshot simulator, which generates the state graph needed for our exploration. Each state within the graph is assessed using a utility function that quantifies how well it satisfies the SLOs, allowing us to identify not just feasible but optimal adaptation paths for different future system evolutions.

To demonstrate the efficacy of our methodology, we apply it to the espresso system, a minimal accounting example. Our results indicate that our state-exploration-based approach outperforms a purely reactive strategy.

The remainder of this paper is structured as follows. Section 2 provides the background for our approach. Then, we present our approach in Sect. 3, detailing the simulation, exploration, and planning components, and evaluate the approach in Sect. 4, where we compare it to a reactive approach. Finally, we discuss the results of the evaluation in Sect. 5, followed by a discussion of related work in Section Sect. 6. We conclude the paper in Sect. 7.

2 Background

A self-adaptive system [10] adapts itself to achieve certain goals in spite of changing environments. Such goals may be described as service level objectives (SLO) and the likes, e.g., "The total response time must be less than 5 s.". In an unchanging world, a system will always achieve such goals, once it is correctly configured. However, when faced with changes in the environment, such as an increased number of incoming requests, the system might violate its goals. Thus, the system must adapt to handle the increasing number of requests, while keeping the total response time below 5 s.

Self-adaptive system can be differentiated considering three aspects. First, adaptations can be reactive or proactive. Second, the adaptations are either uncoordinated or coordinated. And third, decision about adaptations are made either based on a real system, or based on models.

Our approach is proactive, coordinated and model based. Further more, our approach uses rule-based adaptations. I.e., possible adaptations are described in terms of rules, and the adaptations cover addition and deletion of resources only.

The Palladio approach [16] is for quantitative design time analysis of component-based software systems. The initial intention was to analyze static systems. However, the recently added Slingshot approach [8] adds a view point for self-adaptivity, such that dynamically changing system can be analyzed as well. Both approaches are model-based [8,16]. The Palladio approach [16] provides a set of meta-models – the Palladio Component Model (PCM) – for modelling the static structure of a system. The Slingshot approach [8] provides an additional meta-model – the Scaling Policy Definition language – for modelling the elasticity aspects of the system as rules [13] for rule-based adaptations. Notably, with the given models, we can also model a system's service level objectives and the cost of the resources.

3 Approach

In this section, we present our approach for proactive application of reconfiguration rules to a self-adaptive system. The approach centralizes the reconfiguration decisions. An overview of the approach is depicted in Fig. 1. It encompasses three vital components: simulation, exploration, and planning, which are discussed in more detail in the following subsections.

Simulation is responsible for creating single states, while exploration processes the states into a graph and directs the simulation to create additional states. Planning is responsible for planning reconfigurations based on the graph provided by Exploration. Planning and Exploration work in parallel, i.e. the plan might be updated based on new exploration insights.

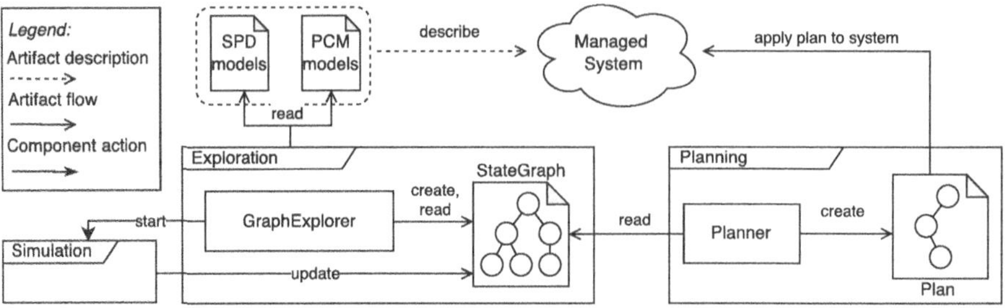

Fig. 1. System architecture overview

3.1 Simulation

The simulations of the states are done by the Slingshot simulator [8], which we extended with additional plugins to facilitate the exploration of different future states.

In the original simulator, each new simulation run starts at point in time $t = 0$ s, without any request in the system. However, the additional plugin enable the simulator to resume where the previous run left off. This is necessary for simulating new node for the state graph. For example, when the predecessor state ends at $t = 42$ s, the simulation run for the successor node starts at that very point in time, with the exact same request already in the system.

Slingshot operates using an event-oriented worldview paradigm where each event constitutes an entity. For example, a simulated user request enqueues an event on the target resource. The resource calculates the required processing time and schedules a subsequent event, indicating that the request was processed, at a specific future point. When the simulation advances to this point, the subsequent event can be processed as well.

This approach offers significant advantages over process-oriented tools such as SimuLizar [5]. In an event-oriented worldview a snapshot of the current state can be created by copying the currently scheduled events. A snapshot can be used to continue the simulation multiple times from the same point. Conversely, copying and reusing processes in a process-oriented paradigm would be considerably more challenging. In practice, restarting the simulation in Slingshot is slightly more complex due to dependencies on prior event knowledge. However, a detailed discussion of the technical details is beyond the scope of this paper.

3.2 State Exploration

The state exploration controls the simulation runs and collects their results as a state graph. In case of multiple possible futures, e.g., a future where an adaptation rule is applied to the system and one where no rule is applied, the explorer starts simulations for both futures. In such a case, the exploration component will simulate both the system with the reconfiguration applied and the system without the reconfiguration applied. If multiple reconfigurations are possible, the exploration will simulate all possible combinations of reconfigurations. We later use the results of the state space exploration to plan the optimal adaption strategy.

The state graph consists of nodes and transition. Each node consists of the state of the simulated system, i.e., the Palladio models, the currently processed requests, and the measurements collected while simulating it.

Each transition signifies an adaptation of the simulated system or lack thereof. Figure 2 shows an excerpt of a state graph.

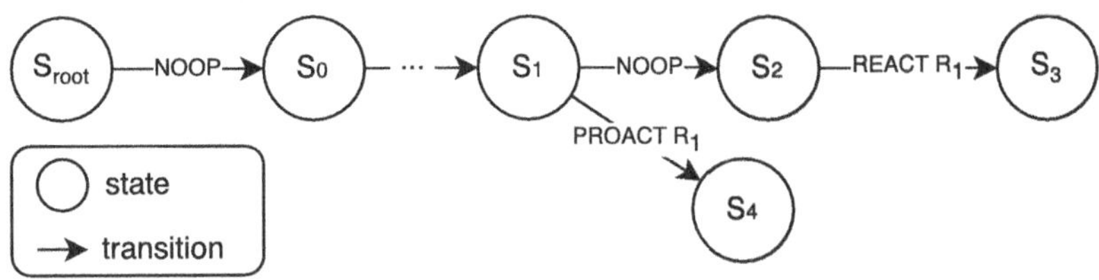

Fig. 2. Excerpt of a state graph.

S_{root} is the root node. It has zero duration and no measurements attached. The nodes S_0 to S_4 result from different simulation runs. After each simulation run, the explorer computes future changes and puts them into a prioritized fringe. Possible changes are applying a reconfiguration rule, either reactively (`REACT`) or proactively (`PROACT`), or doing nothing (`NOOP`).

As an example, during the simulation run for S_2 rule R_1 triggered. The explorer detects this, stops the run before R_1 is applied, saves the results as S_2 to the state graph, and creates new changes. Afterwards the explorer selects a change from the fringe and starts the next simulation run.

In Fig. 2, S_2, and S_4 are results of the changes created after S_1, while S_3 is the result of an adaptation rule R_1 applied after S_2. As R_1 triggered at the end of S_2, the application is reactive. The simulation run for S_2 continues S_1, but applies no adaptations. The simulation run for S_4 also applies R_1, but continues S_1. S_1 is the predecessor of S_2, thus this application of R_1 is proactive.

Given the necessary circumstance, the explorer back propagates a reconfiguration rule over multiple predecessor nodes, i.e., also applies R_1 to the predecessor of S_2 and so on. If possible, the explorer also creates new changes by combining adaptations. E.g., assuming S_2 stopped because a rule R_1 triggered, the explorer might attempt to proactively apply R_1 after S_1. If an outgoing transition for R_2 would already exists at S_1, the explorer might also create a change that combines R_2 and R_1, i.e., applies both.

3.3 Planning

Once the state graph is computed, we use it to find the optimal reconfiguration plan for the managed system. To do this, we calculate a utility value for every state based on the SLO fulfillment and the cost of the components:

$$U = \int_{t_0}^{t_d} \frac{\sum_{i=1}^{n} G(SLO_i(t))}{\sum_{j=0}^{m} C_j(x)} dt$$

The utility value of the SLO fulfillment is calculated by using a grading function, $G(SLO_i(t)) \in [0, 1]$ on the SLO related measurements $SLO_i(t)$. We choose to use the established SLO grade function available in the Palladio SLO addon [6]. The sum of graded SLOs, $SLO_1, \ldots, SLO_n$ is normalized by the aggregated cost of all components $C_1, \ldots, C_m$. The final utility value is the integral of this fraction from the start time of the state, t_0, to the end time of the state, t_d. Currently, each SLO contributes equally. However, if the SLOs importance differs, a weighted sum could be used instead.

Once the utility values are computed, we find the path from the root node to any leaf node that maximizes the cumulative utility.

The adaption rules represented in this path then form the reconfiguration plan. The managed system applies the adaption rules in this order at the time of the state transition in the graph.

The extension of the state graph can lead to the discovery of new paths that are more efficient than the current reconfiguration plan. In this case, the reconfiguration plan is updated to reflect the new insights.

In practice, the exploration results in a large number of possible futures that should be simulated. However, simulating all of them is not possible in a reasonable amount of time, especially as we need to be ahead of the managed system. To cope with this problem at design time, we limit the evaluation of a system by defining a maximum number of nodes that should be explored. For optimal results, we need to prioritize the most promising nodes to expand and explore their futures. Therefore, in every iteration, we use the utility value and explore the planned transition that maximizes the priority function:

$$P(n) = \frac{n_{totalUtility} + n_{utility}}{C(n_{depth})} \cdot \beta^{n_{policy}}$$

By using both the sum of the utility of all states in the path from the root to the current node, $n_{totalUtility}$, and the local utility, $n_{utility}$, we prioritize deeper nodes, as the utility is monotonically increasing, while also prioritizing promising nodes with a high utility. The division by the number of nodes in the graph with the given depth, $C(n_{depth})$, ensures that we do not focus solely on deeper nodes but also grow the width of the graph. Finally, $\beta^{n_{policy}}$ with the discount factor $0 < \beta \leq 1$ prioritizes transitions with a small amount of simultaneous adaptation policies, n_{policy}, to avoid exploring all combinations of adaptations at a single highly promising node instead of exploring the rest of the graph. For our evaluation we choose $\beta = 0.75$ as discount factor. However, systems employing a larger set of adaptation rules require a lower β to mitigate combinator complexity.

4 Evaluation

In this section, we evaluate our approach by comparing it to a reactive baseline approach. To ensure comparability, we also simulated the reactive baseline with the Slingshot simulator.

4.1 Evaluation Methodology

We evaluate our approach by comparing the performance of our approach with a baseline in terms of utility. The baseline is a reactive approach, where the system only applies reconfiguration rules when the SLOs are violated and the SPD rule triggers. In the reactive approach, it is possible for no adaptation to occur even if the SLOs are violated, for example when the SPD rule is on cooldown. We use Slingshot to perform this simulation with the same models as the exploration. Therefore, the null hypothesis is that both approaches perform equally well, resulting in the same utility. The alternative hypothesis is that our approach outperforms the baseline. In addition to utility, we also analyze the cost and SLO related measurements to gain a deeper understanding of the systems performance and the impact of the reconfiguration approach.

As these simulations use the same PCM models, it is a fair assumption, that they will yield very similar results, although the simulations are not deterministic. When a real system is managed, it is essential to correctly model the system and user behavior to ensure that the simulations of the exploration are similar enough. In practice, when the divergence between the states of the exploration and the managed system becomes too large, the exploration needs to be restarted, potentially with adapted models.

4.2 Evaluation Model

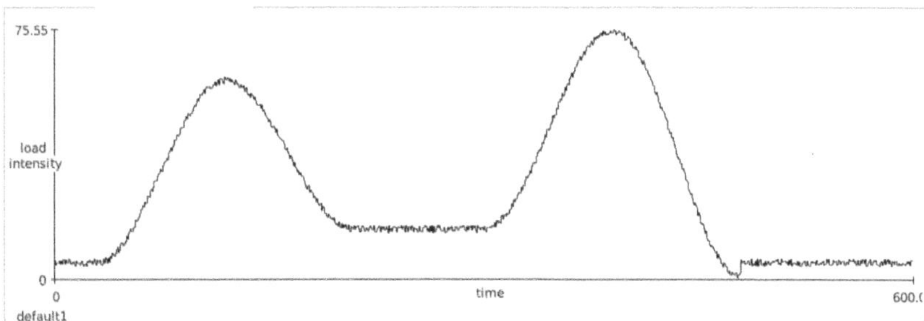

Fig. 3. Load intensity for Espresso Accounting example over one workday (10 h/600 min). First peak after 2 h. Second, slightly higher, peak after 6 and a half hours.

We evaluate our approach on the Espresso Accounting example from the Palladio example models. We continue with a description of this system, focusing on the environment, the components, the adaptions they offer, as well as the SLOs we defined. For the possible adaptions, we describe the condition that triggers the adaption rule. These triggers are used for the reactive approach that serves as baseline, but also impact the proactive approach, as described in Sect. 3.2.

Environment: The system's usage evolves over one workday, with two peaks in load intensity, as shown in Fig. 3. In other words, in the morning and afternoon, more users place orders, leading to higher load intensity.

Components: The system has a straightforward architecture consisting of a single service for processing the accounting of an espresso order.

Adaptations: We either scale out or in the service based on the response time of the espresso accounting component. The scale out is triggered when the response time exceeds 3 s, and the scale in is triggered when the response time falls below 0.1001 s. When a service is added, we assign it to a new resource equal to the resource of the existing instances. Each service is assigned to a single core CPU.

SLOs: For this evaluation, we define a single SLO targeting the response time of the entire system. This SLO has a hard threshold on 6 s and a soft threshold on 3 s. These two thresholds impact the grade assigned to the measurements, which we use in the utility calculation as discussed in Sect. 3.3.

For this system, no real-world counterpart exists. However, it is used as a Palladio example model[1]. Unfortunately, the provided models are limited to the core PCM instances. Our approach requires additional models to enable self-adaption. Therefore, we defined the adaptation rules (SPD) and SLO as described above.

4.3 Results

The goal of our evaluation is to show that the alternative hypothesis, which states that we outperform the reactive baseline approach in terms of utility, holds. The utility value describes how well the system performs in terms of the SLOs and the cost of the components, as described in Sect. 3.3. We evaluate this by comparing the cumulative utility over time for both approaches.

The cumulative utility of our approach and of the reactive baseline are displayed in Fig. 4. Until $t = 225$, both approaches resulted in a similar cumulative utility. From this point on, our approach begins to slightly outperform the reactive baseline. Especially starting from $t = 475$, the utility of our approach is considerably higher.

As discussed in Sect. 3.3, the utility depends on both the SLO fulfillment and system cost. Our model assumes a linear relationship between instance count and system cost, and defines a single SLO for overall system response time. Figure 5, compares our approach and the reactive baseline regarding instance count and

[1] See https://github.com/PalladioSimulator/Palladio-Example-Models/tree/0e347e695609484cfb795d20dbe0dfc0988f3ee2/Minimum_Project_Example.

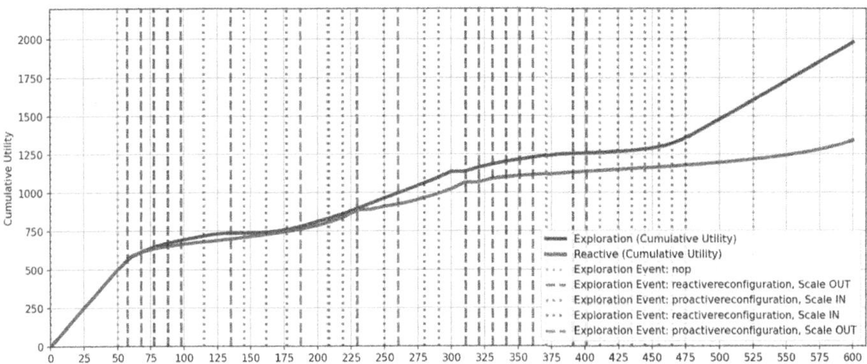

Fig. 4. Cummulative Utiltiy of our approach (blue) and the reactive baseline (red). The vertical lines represent the reactive (green) and proactive (pink) reconfiguration executed by our approach. (Color figure online)

response time. These two metrics directly determine the utility, as they represent cost and SLO adherence, respectively.

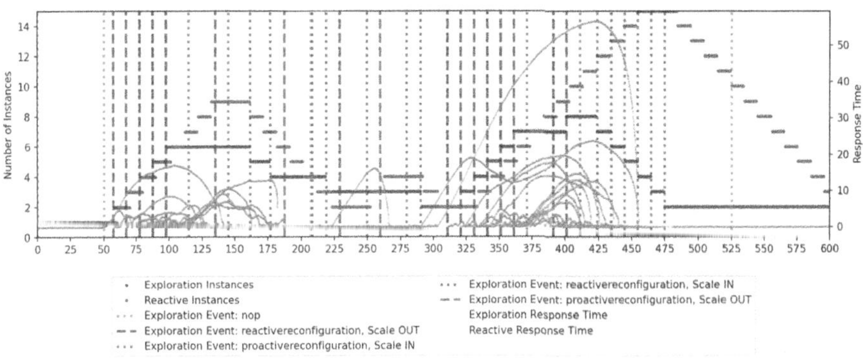

Fig. 5. The number of instances (left axis) and the response time (right axis) of our approach (blue) and the reactive baseline (red). (Color figure online)

By comparing the number of instances over time, we can see, that our approach overall had a smaller number of instances, resulting in reduced costs. So our approach did not just produce a higher utility than the reactive baseline, but it did so while also lowering the overall costs.

When analyzing the response time measurements, we first notice that there appears to be multiple lines for each case. The reason for this is simple: Incoming user request are assigned to one of the available instances. Although the load-balancer attempts to balance the workload, the instances still need to complete their current queue of pending requests, resulting in varying response times per instance despite similar performance capabilities.

From $t = 325$ to $t = 450$ the workload is generally too high for the system. Both, our approach and the reactive case are unable to appropriately adapt themselves, resulting in a maximum response time of 23 s for our approach and 57 s for the reactive baseline. By proactively adapting earlier, our approach allowed for a better distribution of user request, which allowed it to handle the situation more efficiently, although a smaller number of instances were deployed. Furthermore, the adaptation rules in our example are configured with a 10 s cooldown. The reactive case took a long time to scale back after the high workload because of that. Meanwhile, our approach did not scale out that far, which is why the scale in happened faster. This resulted in a larger utility gain at the end, because the cost were smaller, while both approaches achieved great response times.

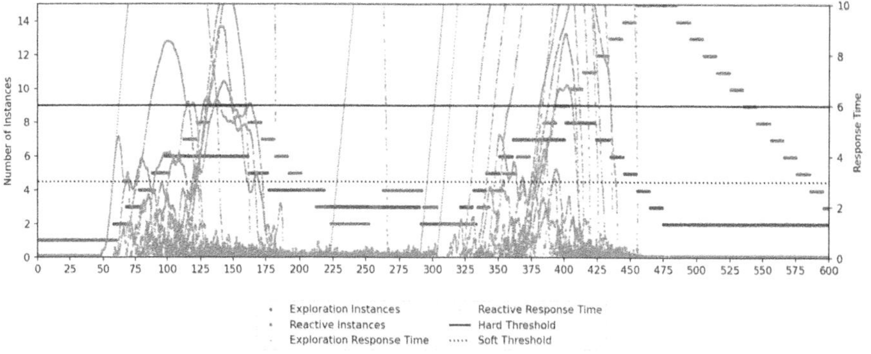

Fig. 6. The number of instances (left axis) and the response time (right axis) of our approach (blue) and the reactive baseline (red) with the response time limited to 10 s. The SLO thresholds are represented as horizontal lines (black). The soft threshold at 3 s also represents the trigger for the reactive Scale OUT rule. (Color figure online)

The response time of both our approach and the reactive baseline exceeded the hard threshold of the SLO we defined. In Fig. 6 we only show the measured response time of up to 10 s and included the two thresholds of the SLO. This reaffirms the previous observation that the reactive baseline achieved a minimal response time after $t = 450$ but was limited in its ability to scale in. Furthermore, in Sect. 3.3 we explained that we use the grading function from the Palladio SLO addon to grade the response time values for calculating the utility. If the measurement is above the hard threshold, the grading function will always return 0. Therefore, although our approach performed better than the reactive baseline when the workload is intense, this is not reflected in the utility we calculated. Overall, our approach had lower costs compared to the reactive baseline and had a lower maximum response time. While our approach also struggled to minimize the response time when the demand was high, the results overall indicate an improvement over the reactive baseline, although this is not completely reflected in the utility we calculate.

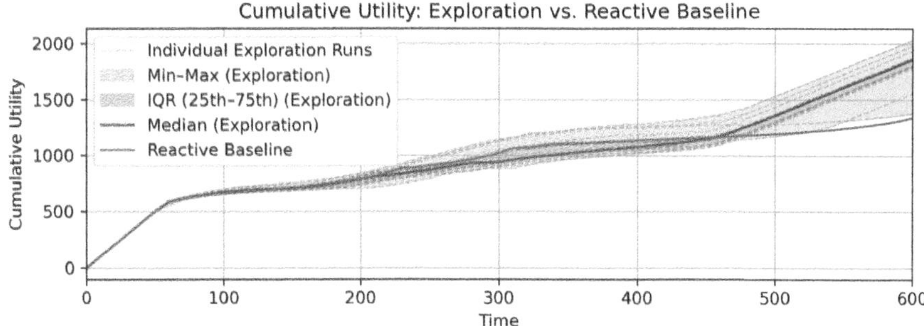

Fig. 7. Cumulative utility over time for multiple exploration runs (light dotted lines) and their distribution (lightblue min–max band, lightgreen interquartile range, and blue median line). The red line indicates the reactive baseline. (Color figure online)

As our approach is not deterministic, it is essential to demonstrate that these results are reproducible across multiple runs. Therefore, we executed the exploration 16 times and compare the results in Fig. 7. While there is some variety across the different runs, we outperform the reactive baseline in every run. However, between $t = 200$ and $t = 450$ our approach usually performed worse than the reactive baseline, although that is compensated when $t > 450$. The narrow interquartile range indicates that our approach generally performs consistently, despite occasional higher variability evident in the minimum and maximum values.

4.4 Threats to Validity

We had to create SPD and SLO models for the Espresso Accounting example. This is a threat to internal validity, as the models might not accurately represent the real system. For example, the models might not capture all possible reconfiguration rules, artificially limiting the state space, which would be beneficial for our approach, therefore, making it seem more effective than it actually is. Furthermore, we depend on the accuracy of Slingshot, which was adapted to our needs. If slingshot does not accurately simulate the system or user behavior, the results of our approach might be skewed.

A significant threat to external validity in our study is the fact that we used the same slingshot simulation for the exploration and the managed system. This completely removes the need for measuring the divergence between the exploration and the managed system. Furthermore, for the same reason, the user behavior never changes and the usage model never needs to be replaced.

Therefore, the system never needs to be restarted, like it would be necessary in a real-world scenario. Frequent or late divergences leading to restarts could significantly impact system performance.

In addition, the generalizability of our approach is limited by the fact that we only evaluated it on the Espresso Accounting example. On other systems, the results could be different, especially when the system is more complex and allows for a wider range of reconfiguration rules. In this scenario, the explorer would have to explore a much larger state space. This could lead to a significant increase in the time needed to find the optimal reconfiguration plan, making it hard or even impossible to compute and consider all the relevant paths in the state graph.

5 Discussion

In this section, we discuss our results: We discuss the state exploration, the utility and priority functions guiding the exploration, and the models used to simulate the system.

5.1 State Exploration

When performing the evaluation, we observed that the state graph grew to be huge. This happened although we only had the minimal amount of two adaptation rules. On a larger system with more adaptation rules the graph would grow even faster, resulting in more possible futures to explore.

Independent of the prioritization function we chose, this will limit the amount of possible futures we can consider. At runtime, the real system could catch up to exploration. When that happens and the number of rules is large, we might only be able to consider a minor amount of future states before the managed system requires an adaptation decision. However, the performance of our approach depends on the size of the state graph.

In our preliminary testing, we noticed that some priority functions are able to halt the progression of the state graph entirely. For example, once we explored for multiple hours without progressing past 200 s, although we used the espresso model with only two adaptation rules.

5.2 Utility and Prioritization

The results of our evaluation show, that the utility function does not accurately capture the desired system behavior. For example, both a response time of 10 s and 500 s would result in a utility value of 0. This might misguide our exploration as states with this response times would be prioritized equally.

When the response time is below the soft threshold, the grade function always returns 1. In our example, this would produce the same utility for 0.1 s as it would for 3 s. Conversely, altering it may over-emphasize response time, producing a plan with lower response time but higher cost.

The prioritization function not just depends on the utility, but also on the structure of the state graph as well as the number of adaptations per transitions. While our concrete function was chosen based on the results of preliminary tests, it is unclear how different priority functions would impact the exploration. We only tested a small amount of priority functions beforehand and did not perform a proper evaluation with them. A more refined priority function could lead to better results and help with the combinatorial complexity.

5.3 Models

In our evaluation, the reactive baseline was unable to scale in fast enough after the high workload was over. This indicates a problem with scaling policies: We could reduce the cooldown to allow for faster adaptation or create a scaling policy that removes multiple instance at once. In our approach, the proactive adaptations are able to ignore the cooldown constraint. However, a proactive adaptation may only continue at the end of an existing state. Because of that, our approach also took some time to scale in after the high workload was over. This shows how dependent our approach is on the existing adaptation rules. To improve this, an engineer might perform multiple exploration at design time to refine the existing adaptation rules.

6 Related Work

According to existing secondary literature [1,15] our approach uses a horizontal scaling method with homogeneous resource clusters and rule-based resource estimation. Also, our scaling is automatic, more specifically proactive and uses queuing theory, at least in so far that Slingshot simulates a system's resources as queues. The purpose of our approach is to improve performance while minimizing costs. As such, our approach relates to [9] due to the proactive use of rule-based adaptions and to [2,20] and [23] due to the proactiveness and the use of queuing theory. All of them differ from our approach with regard to how they come to their proactive decisions. Compared to [2], our modeling language is more expressive than simple queuing models, supporting diverse types of SLOs beyond just response time. [9,20] and [2] base proactive reconfigurations on predictions about workload and [23] base them on the analytical solution of a queueing model, but neither uses simulation to build a state graph as we do.

Considering state graphs, Smit and Stroulia [18,18] also construct graphs from simulation results, with performance measurements and degrees of satisfaction for service level objectives. They aim to find unsatisfactory states that indicate the need for an adaptation. In constrast to our work, they do not model the user behavior and focus solely on the system and performance metrics. However, their work appears to be discontinued.

Bauer *et al.* [4] and Urgaonkar *et al.* [19] focus on reactive and predictive techniques to coordinate adaptations. They predict future workload and make coordinated scaling decisions based on queuing models. Unlike our approach, their adaptations are not rule-based. Also Bauer et al. [4], and others [21], do a forecast on the arrival rates to act proactively, while we explore multiple futures, also considering futures, that may be omitting short term benefit in favor of improved system utility later on. Others attempt to coordinate adaptation but only in a reactive way [7,17].

Arcelli explore a multi-objective optimization technique to optimize performance in self-adaptive architectures that are modeled using queuing networks [3]. Their approach suggest near-optimal alternative architectures for different operation modes like *normal* and *critical*. More specifically, they focus on solving the *Controller Selection Policy* problem by finding these near-optimal architectures.

Oliveira and Barbosa presents a coordination-targeted reconfiguration framework for formal verification of architectural requirements [12]. Their approach uses a model that plans reconfiguration strategies at design time and use this model to perform reconfigurations at runtime. The main focus of their work is the performance prediction problem at the coordination level.

Palm, Metzger, and Pohl proposed an online reinforcement learning approach that addresses the uncertainties in self-adaptive systems by dynamically learning and updating its adaptation behavior at runtime [14]. In general, reinforcement learning approaches in the self-adaptive system domain require manual finetuning of the exploration rate, limiting their usefulness. Palm, Metzger, and Pohl tackle this problem by exploring a policy-based reinforcement learning approach, which chooses adaptions from a probability distribution over possible adaptions, that is constantly updated to reflect the expected utility of the adaptions.

Metzger *et al.* consider a similar problem: If the adaption space is large, the learning might be slow, leading to suboptimal adaptions in the beginning. They use a feature model to represent the adaption space and then guide the exploration by leveraging the structure of the feature model [11]. This is especially useful for a discrete adaption space, which is typical for self-adaptive systems. Furthermore, Metzger *et al.* also show that this approach strongly increases the learning rate in a system evolution scenario.

Zhang *et al.* introduce a meta-reinforcement learning approach that aims to quickly adapt to changing environments by learning meta-policies over multiple models [22]. These models represent different aspects of the environment-system dynamics and are often created by domain experts. Then, the models are synthesized into dynamic models which are used to learn a meta-policy offline. At runtime, the meta-policy is used initially to guide the adaption, but online learning is used to finetune the policy.

7 Conclusion

In conclusion, our approach is a promising alternative to a purely reactive approach. Our evaluation has shown that we are able to outperform a purely reactive approach in terms of cost and response time. Nonetheless, our approach was not able to perfectly adapt the system to the environment either. Furthermore, there are major challenges we have to consider in future work.

Our approach foucses on the design time of the system. However, we plan to extend it to a runtime scenario in the future. The exploration would progress while the real system is running, while the plan would be created starting from a state in the graph that represents the current system. Such an extension comes with various challenges that need to be addressed. For example, it is possible that the user behavior changes while the system is running. Even if the user behavior initially was modeled correctly, for our approach to work, the usage model has to be replaced by a version that accurately captures their behavior.

The State Exploration produces a large number of states to explore. We employed a priority function to select and explore the most promising states. However, this prioritization can be further improved. This is especially important for larger systems with more possible adaptations. In future work, we need to explore how a larger adaptation space impacts this prioritization and how the combinatorial complexity impacts the exploration.

Our evaluation has also shown that the utility function does not accurately capture performance differences in high-workload situations. This does not just impact the evaluation, but also the exploration, as the priority function uses the calculated utility. Future work should explore how different utility functions impact the exploration and how a utility function can accurately capture the system goals, especially when multiple SLOs need to be balanced.

Acknowledgment. This work was partially funded by the Deutsche Forschungsgemeinschaft (DFG, German Research Foundation) - 453895475.

Data Availability. The reproducibility package including the data is publicly available at zenodo: https://doi.org/10.5281/zenodo.15591036.

References

1. Al-Dhuraibi, Y., Paraiso, F., Djarallah, N., Merle, P.: Elasticity in cloud computing: state of the art and research challenges. IEEE Trans. Serv. Comput. **11**(2), 430–447 (2018). https://doi.org/10.1109/TSC.2017.2711009
2. Ali-Eldin, A., Tordsson, J., Elmroth, E.: An adaptive hybrid elasticity controller for cloud infrastructures. In: NOMS 2012, pp. 204–212 (2012). https://doi.org/10.1109/NOMS.2012.6211900
3. Arcelli, D.: A multi-objective performance optimization approach for self-adaptive architectures. In: ECSA 2020, pp. 139–147 (2020)
4. Bauer, A., Lesch, V., Versluis, L., Ilyushkin, A., Herbst, N., Kounev, S.: Chamulteon: coordinated auto-scaling of micro-services. In: ICDCS 2019 (2019). https://doi.org/10.1109/ICDCS.2019.00199
5. Becker, M., Becker, S., Meyer, J.: SimuLizar: design-time modeling and performance analysis of self-adaptive systems. In: SE 2013 (2013)
6. Becker, M.W.: Engineering self-adaptive systems with simulation-based performance prediction. Ph.D. thesis, Universität Paderborn (2017)
7. Beltrán, M.: Automatic provisioning of multi-tier applications in cloud computing environments. J. Supercomput. **71**(6), 2221–2250 (2015). https://doi.org/10.1007/s11227-015-1380-5

8. Klinaku, F., Stieß, S.S., Hakamian, A., Becker, S.: An architectural view type for elasticity modeling and simulation—the slingshot approach. J. Syst. Softw. (2025)
9. Loff, J., Garcia, J.: Vadara: predictive elasticity for cloud applications. In: 2014 IEEE 6th International Conference on Cloud Computing Technology and Science, pp. 541–546 (2014). https://doi.org/10.1109/CloudCom.2014.161
10. Macías-Escrivá, F.D., Haber, R., del Toro, R., Hernandez, V.: Self-adaptive systems: a survey of current approaches, research challenges and applications. Expert Syst. Appl. **40**(18), 7267–7279 (2013). https://doi.org/10.1016/j.eswa.2013.07.033
11. Metzger, A., Quinton, C., Mann, Z.Á., Baresi, L., Pohl, K.: Realizing self-adaptive systems via online reinforcement learning and feature-model-guided exploration. Computing **106**(4), 1251–1272 (2024)
12. Oliveira, N., Barbosa, L.S.: Self-adaptation by coordination-targeted reconfigurations. J. Softw. Eng. Res. Dev. **3**, 1–31 (2015)
13. MISC
14. Palm, A., Metzger, A., Pohl, K.: Online reinforcement learning for self-adaptive information systems. In: CAiSE 2020, pp. 169–184 (2020)
15. Qu, C., Calheiros, R.N., Buyya, R.: Auto-scaling web applications in clouds: a taxonomy and survey. ACM Comput. Surv. **51**(4) (2018). https://doi.org/10.1145/3148149
16. Reussner, R.H., et al.: Modeling and Simulating Software Architectures —The Palladio Approach. MIT Press (2016)
17. Sharma, U., Shenoy, P., Towsley, D.F.: Provisioning multi-tier cloud applications using statistical bounds on sojourn time. In: ICAC 2012, pp. 43–52 (2012). https://doi.org/10.1145/2371536.2371545
18. Smit, M., Stroulia, E.: Autonomic configuration adaptation based on simulation-generated state-transition models. In: SEAA 2011, pp. 175–179 (2011). https://doi.org/10.1109/SEAA.2011.36
19. Urgaonkar, B., Shenoy, P., Chandra, A., Goyal, P.: Dynamic provisioning of multi-tier internet applications. In: ICAC 2005 (2005). https://doi.org/10.1109/ICAC.2005.27
20. Urgaonkar, B., Shenoy, P., Chandra, A., Goyal, P., Wood, T.: Agile dynamic provisioning of multi-tier internet applications. ACM Trans. Auton. Adapt. Syst. **3**(1) (2008). https://doi.org/10.1145/1342171.1342172
21. Wu, S., Li, B., Wang, X., Jin, H.: HybridScaler: handling bursting workload for multi-tier web applications in cloud. In: ISPDC 2016, pp. 141–148 (2016). https://doi.org/10.1109/ISPDC.2016.26
22. Zhang, M., Li, J., Zhao, H., Tei, K., Honiden, S., Jin, Z.: A meta reinforcement learning-based approach for self-adaptive system. In: ACSOS 2021, pp. 1–10 (2021)
23. Zhang, Q., Cherkasova, L., Smirni, E.: A regression-based analytic model for dynamic resource provisioning of multi-tier applications. In: ICAC 2007, p. 27 (2007). https://doi.org/10.1109/ICAC.2007.1

SAFER-D: A Self-adaptive Security Framework for Distributed Computing Architectures

Marco Stadler[1](✉), Michael Vierhauser[2], Michael Riegler[3], Daniel Waghubinger[1], and Johannes Sametinger[1]

[1] LIT Secure and Correct Systems Lab/Institute of Business Informatics – Software Engineering, Johannes Kepler University Linz, Linz, Austria
{Marco.Stadler,Daniel.Waghubinger,Johannes.Sametinger}@jku.at

[2] Department of Computer Science, University of Innsbruck, Innsbruck, Austria
michael.vierhauser@uibk.ac.at

[3] Information Security, ENGEL Austria GmbH, Schwertberg, Austria
michael.riegler@engel.at

Abstract. The rise of the Internet of Things and Cyber-Physical Systems has introduced new challenges on ensuring secure and robust communication. The growing number of connected devices increases network complexity, leading to higher latency and traffic. Distributed computing architectures (DCAs) have gained prominence to address these issues. This shift has significantly expanded the attack surface, requiring additional security measures to protect all components – from sensors and actuators to edge nodes and central servers. Recent incidents highlight the difficulty of this task: Cyberattacks, like distributed denial of service attacks, continue to pose severe threats and cause substantial damage.

Implementing a holistic defense mechanism remains an open challenge, particularly against attacks that demand both enhanced resilience and rapid response. Addressing this gap requires innovative solutions to enhance the security of DCAs.

In this work, we present our holistic self-adaptive security framework which combines different adaptation strategies to create comprehensive and efficient defense mechanisms. We describe how to incorporate the framework into a real-world use case scenario and further evaluate its applicability and efficiency. Our evaluation yields promising results, indicating great potential to further extend the research on our framework.

1 Introduction

The hype surrounding the Internet of Things (IoT) and Cyber-Physical Systems (CPSs) drives a surge in Internet-connected devices. Managing this many devices requires careful organization, often achieved through diverse architectural styles and patterns [9]. Instead of a centralized infrastructure, distributed computing architectures (DCAs) are used to provide reduced latency, real-time

V. Andrikopoulos et al. (Eds.): ECSA 2025, LNCS 15929, pp. 197–213, 2026.
https://doi.org/10.1007/978-3-032-02138-0_13

analysis, high scalability, low operational cost, and improved quality of service [9]. Although distributed computing helps operators deal with complexity, it affects the attack surface of these architectures. The sheer number of devices and their convolution, heterogeneity, diversity, interoperability, portability, mobility, location, topology, and distribution of objects cause an increase in attack surface and make the architecture susceptible to cyberattacks (details in [26]). In particular, interoperability and interdependency are crucial factors in this context [22]. A failure caused by an attacker to one subsystem can lead to cascading failures, rendering the whole DCA inoperable [4]. Particularly on critical infrastructure, a successful cyberattack can cause severe harm [6,24,29], ranging from compromised databases to human injury. Recent incidents, such as the record-breaking 5.6 Tbps Distributed Denial of Service (DDoS) attack targeting Cloudflare's infrastructure [35], highlight the tangible risks faced by the industry. Studies [6,24,29] demonstrate that the scientific community recognizes these threats, emphasizing the urgent need for resilient security strategies in DCAs.

The reasons for such incidents still occurring are manifold. Security measures often only provide isolated and passive defense mechanisms, severely limiting their effectiveness [34]. Passive mechanisms usually rely on predefined rules. For example, they may block network packets based on known signatures [23]. They follow a "detect then patch" philosophy, meaning they are only effective after an attack. As a result, they cannot adapt proactively and respond to threats in real-time [34]. – As a result, the question of securing DCAs with a holistic and active security solution to efficiently adapt to the evolving threat landscape remains. In this paper, we propose a novel idea of combining self-adaptive architectural patterns to improve the security of DCAs. More specifically, we leverage, among others, hierarchical adaptation strategies [33], adaptation strategies used in Systems of Systems (SoS) [32], and the concept of security levels (cf. Sect. 3.2) to enhance the overall resilience of DCAs in the event of attacks. To the best of our knowledge, no prior work combines hierarchical, collaborative, and decentralized adaptation strategies to ensure self-adaptive security under partial system failure. Our framework addresses this gap through its dual-loop architecture and adaptation modes. As part of this, we claim the following contributions:

- Novel, Secure Adaptive Framework for Efficient Resilience in Distributed computing architectures (SAFER-D) that allows for security adaptations at the architectural level, even when under attack.
- Prototypical implementations using real-world edge computing architectures for component reuse.
- Evaluation of applicability and efficiency of SAFER-D, based on realistic security use case scenarios.

2 Motivating Architectural Challenges

In an increasingly interconnected world, the ability to dynamically adapt to emerging threat scenarios is becoming ever more critical. Adaptive threat monitoring focuses on continuously observing systems for unusual or suspicious activities and adjusting responses based on evolving contexts. This adaptability is vital in defending against cyberattacks targeting CPSs/IoT systems where static approaches are insufficient. Intrusion Detection Systems (IDS) [19] often leverage an adaptive approach to detect and withstand cyberattacks. An IDS commonly monitors network or system activities, detects potential security threats, and executes appropriate countermeasures or sends alerts. – This process largely aligns with the MAPE-K (Monitor, Analyze, Plan, Execute on a shared Knowledge base) loop [16], a foundational pattern for self-adaptive system architectures.

Consider the following DCA example, which will serve as our running case: Edge computing, combined with fog and cloud computing, places substantial computing and storage resources at the (physical) outer "edges," where data is generated. The system processes data directly, forwards only aggregated data to fog computing components, aggregates it again, and then sends only the relevant data to the next central server, continuing this pattern [5]. An IDS applied to one of the edge devices of such an edge computing architecture *monitors*, for instance, the network traffic on the device, *analyzes* the data to identify anomalies or suspicious patterns (e.g., a DDoS flooding attack), *plans* appropriate responses (e.g., block a specific Internet Protocol (IP) address), and *executes* the countermeasures (append IPs to a blocklist) or generates alerts, all supported by a *knowledge* base to enhance detection accuracy and adaptability. In the following, we highlight **Architectural Challenges (ACs)** concerning a self-adaptive security framework for DCAs. These challenges are informed by our industry collaborations and supported by academic literature, based on recurring needs identified in regular technical meetings and through a structured review of recent research on self-protective and adaptive systems.

AC 1 - Managing Adaptation in Complex and Large-Scale DCAs Using a Single MAPE-K Loop is Insufficient: Weyns *et al.* formalized a series of architectural patterns comprising multiple interconnected MAPE-K loops to deal with large, complex, and heterogeneous systems [33]. Among others, they introduced the hierarchical control pattern. This pattern manages the complexity of self-adaptation by establishing a layered separation of concerns through a hierarchy of MAPE-K loops. Loops at lower layers operate on a short time scale, ensuring that the portion of the system under their direct control adapt promptly. Higher levels operate on a more global/strategic scale over an extended period. Ultimately, the MAPE-K loop at the system's summit determines the system's overarching adaptation objectives. Applying the hierarchical MAPE-K pattern to our aforementioned example implies that, for instance, the fog nodes in the edge computing architecture use the monitoring data of multiple underlying edge devices for the adaptation loops and then roll out a collective adaptation strategy for all devices associated with the respective fog node.

AC 2 - Hierarchical Adaptation Strategies Break When Intermediate Nodes are Compromised: In our example, the edge computing architecture follows a hierarchical organization, which creates dependencies. Suppose fog node in the hierarchy is compromised and unavailable, e.g., due to a successful attack.

In that case, the underlying edge devices will not receive adaptation updates and thus remain susceptible to subsequent cyberattacks. Regarding security, individual system components must be independent from an operational and managerial viewpoint, exhibiting SoS characteristics [7,32]. Self-adaptive architectural patterns for SoS have been frequently studied [32]. One of them, the *Collaborative Adaptations* style, allows for adaptations on a control-theoretic level. Additionally, the architecture allows for interactions among the managed systems, supporting collaboration between the subsystems. Using this pattern, the SoS can adapt comprehensively while considering each component [32]. Subsystems can then coordinate locally and continue adaptation without relying on the compromised node.

AC 3 - Security Mechanisms Must Remain Effective Even When Parts of the System are Already Compromised: The Risk of an attacker compromising a system is defined as follows [15]:

$$R = \{s_i, p_i, x_i\}, \qquad i = 1, 2, ..., N \tag{1}$$

where R represents the risk; s an undesirable event scenario description; p the probability of the scenario; x the potential damage caused by the scenario; and N the number of possible scenarios that may cause damage to a system. It is important to note that p and x are not constants but rather evolve over the time of an attack, serving here as a conceptual model to illustrate this dynamic. In our edge computing example, if an attacker compromises one edge device, the probability that they successfully compromise another edge device increases (i.e., p in Eq. (1) evolves). If attackers can circumvent security mechanisms once, they can reproduce the attack on other devices with the same security mechanisms. Similarly, once a publicly available proof of concept exploit exists for a known vulnerability, the probability of reproduction increases. A compromised single system can also influence the "neighbors" communicating with the device. Depending on the type of attack, the attackers move laterally [12] and propagate [1] to the controlling (managing) systems [17], i.e., in the best case (from an attacker's perspective), up the hierarchy to attain more and more control. Security solutions are required to respond promptly to attacks and must be able to cope with already compromised system components.

AC 4 - Security Adaptations Must Consider the Evolving Criticality and Impact of Threats Over Time: Not only does the probability evolve, but also the potential damage (cf. x in Eq. (1)). For instance, if the running example's edge computing system supports autonomous driving, it must prioritize safety to protect human lives [20]. A collision becomes more likely if the vehicle malfunctions (due to an attack). Autonomous vehicles must slow down, or even shut down entirely, after detecting malicious activity. To cope with these evolving factors, security mechanisms must support means of criticality.

3 The SAFER-D Framework

In the following, our novel SAFER-D framework addresses the architectural challenges (**AC 1–4**).

3.1 Core Components

Figure 1 depicts a high-level overview of SAFER-D. The core idea is that SAFER-D is deployed on every single subsystem of the DCA. In the running case, this implies server, fog, and edge computing subsystems each run an instance of SAFER-D. Naturally, these instances must be tailored to the respective hardware capabilities, meaning that resource-intensive tools may only be available on more powerful subsystems, while lightweight variants are deployed on constrained edge devices. `Subsystem` *n* represents one of N subsystems in the computing architecture, e.g., a single edge device, where the SAFER-D instance communicates with other SAFER-D instances deployed on the rest of the architecture (i.e., the `Subsystems of Interest`). With the term "subsystem," we refer to a single independent computing node. As part of SAFER-D, we use two types of MAPE-K loops: First, `Local MAPE-K` represents the "traditional" adaptation loop commonly found in a self-adaptive system, running locally and only internally on each subsystem. Second, the adaptation loop `Global MAPE-K` has a dedicated communication channel to other subsystems in the architecture, i.e., other edge and fog devices running a SAFER-D instance.

`Local MAPE-K`: The `Local Runtime Monitor` gathers data from the `Managed system` and forwards it to the `Local Adaptation Middleware`. The `Local SL Manager` (SL: Security Level) plans an appropriate security level (cf. Sect. 3.2). Finally, a `Local Execution Adapter` executes the planned adaptations on the `Managed system` (M ⇒ A ⇒ P ⇒ E).

`Global MAPE-K`: This adaptation loop serves two purposes: (*i*) The loop allows for holistic adaptations together with other subsystems (cf. **AC 1**) and (*ii*) ensures a prompt response in the event of an attack (cf. **AC 3**).

(*i*) The `Global SL Monitor` forwards adaptation information from the other `Subsystems of Interest`. In our running case for a fog subsystem, the subsystems of interest are the superordinate server subsystems and the subordinate edge subsystems. The adaptations, i.e., the security levels of other computing systems, are then forwarded to the `Local Adaptation Middleware`. The `Local MAPE-K` can then, besides the local monitoring data, also take comprehensive information from other connected systems into account for performing adaptations (M/M ⇒ A ⇒ P ⇒ E).

(*ii*) Security incidents can lead to isolated subsystems, disrupting their integration into the `Subsystems of Interest` (cf. SoS in **AC 2**). When this happens, it is critical to ensure prompt adaptation times to prevent other subsystems from being compromised. Disruptions can cause delays in the adaptation time, e.g., due to unanswered requests during an attack (cf. **AC 3**). The `Global MAPE-K` takes these disruptions into account by adapting the `Managed API`

(Application Programming Interface). The API configuration uses two operational modes: Full Adaptation (FA) when all other subsystems are available and Partial Adaptation (PA) when at least one subsystem of interest is not reachable. In both modes, the `Global MAPE-K` will be executed, and the **`Managed API`** adapts continuously. The difference lies in the number of **`Subsystems of Interest`** checked for adaptation updates (cf. details in Sect. 3.3). The switch between these modes is decided within the `Global MAPE-K`: The **`Managed API`** gathers the *Global SL Adaptations* and forwards the *Network Status Data* to the **`Global Network Monitor`**. The **`Global Adaptation Middleware`** checks the connections to other subsystems and detects if a subsystem in the **`Subsystems of Interest`** is unresponsive. The **`Global Config Manager`** then triggers the respective mode, and the **`Global Execution Adapter`** carries out the adaptation by reconfiguring the **`Managed API`** (Ⓜ ⇒ Ⓐ ⇒ Ⓟ ⇒ Ⓔ).

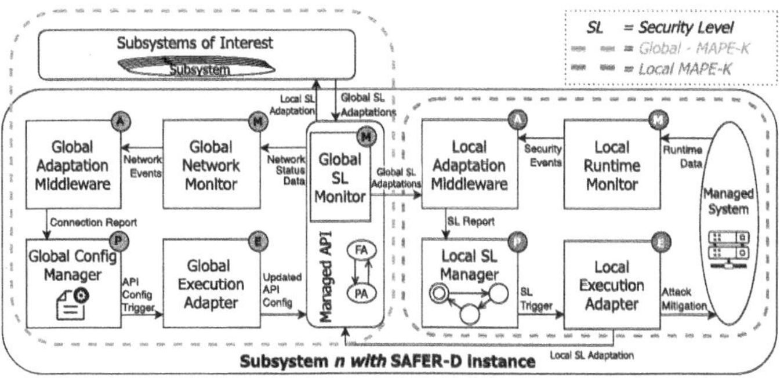

Fig. 1. High-level Overview of SAFER-D.

3.2 Security Levels

Security (criticality) levels (SLs) in SAFER-D represent varying degrees of protective measures specifically tailored to the current risk and criticality of a system (cf. **AC 4**). The concept is inspired by so-called "readiness levels," found, for instance, in the US military's DEFense readiness CONdition (DEFCON) stages [30]. They enable dynamic adaptation of security mechanisms, ensuring system can escalate or de-escalate their defenses based on evolving threats or environmental conditions. We introduce SLs as part of SAFER-D's **`Local SL Manager`** to adjust security based on dynamic changes (cf. x and/or p in Eq. (1)). For example, in our running case, under normal conditions, an edge device operates at DEFCON 5. If unusual behavior suggests a potential attack, it escalates to DEFCON 4, increasing the monitoring of system load, as sudden spikes may indicate a DDoS attack. The DEFCON level continues to adapt as risks rise. The highest escalation is DEFCON 1 in critical cases (e.g., a confirmed DDoS attack) where the system may even shut down. The discrete SL design encourages security engineers to define clear, scenario-specific countermeasures per threshold, though we acknowledge this limits flexibility in multi-threat situations; addressing such conflicts will be a focus in future iterations of the framework.

The `Local Adaptation Middleware`, and the subsequent `Local SL Manager`, consider two sources when deciding on the appropriate SL. The local *Security Events* provided by the `Local Runtime Monitor` (M) and the *Global SL Adaptations* of the other `Subsystems of Interest` in the architecture forwarded by the `Global SL Monitor` (M). SAFER-D supports a human-in-the-loop approach for returning to less restrictive security levels.

3.3 Full and Partial Adaptation Mode

The `Global MAPE-K` leverages two distinct operational modes to speed up the global adaptation loop (cf. Sect. 3.1): *Full Adaptation (FA)* and *Partial Adaptation (PA)*. In both modes, SAFER-D tries to gather adaptation information from other `Subsystems of Interest`.

In a perfect world, a single subsystem can always communicate with the other subsystems of interest. Consider the example in Fig. 2a, showing a conceptual edge computing architecture with server, fog, and edge computing subsystems. For instance, `#2` communicates updates to its superordinate server subsystem `#1` and its subordinate subsystems `#6` and `#4`. During FA, full adaptation within the DCA is possible, and every subsystem can receive respective adaptation updates from every other subsystem. For the example in Fig. 2a, the subsystems adapting and exchanging data consists of all subsystems: [`#1, #2, #3, #4, #6, #7, #5, #8`].

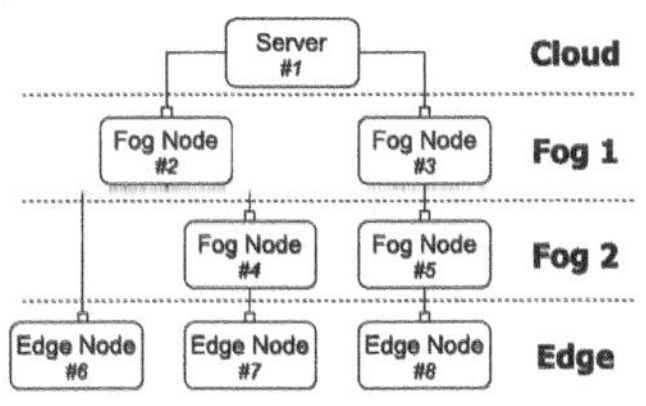

(a) Architecture during *FA*.

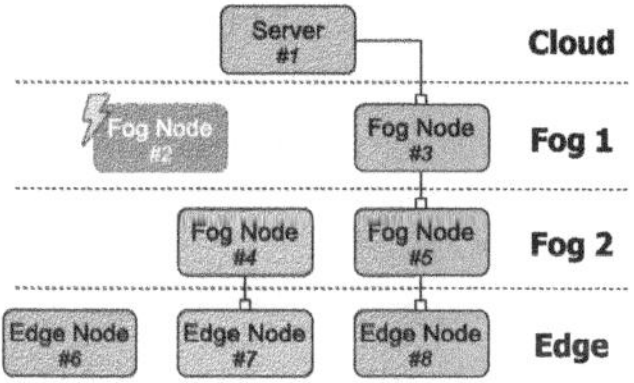

(b) Successful attack at subsystem #2 and resulting *PA* adaptation subgroups.

Fig. 2. Edge computing architecture in the use case scenario.

In practice, a subsystem of interest can become unresponsive or unavailable due to an attack. In such a case, fast and timely adaptation becomes one of the most important properties for preventing and potentially repelling attacks on other uncompromising subsystems. The unavailable subsystem interferes with this goal. For instance, when subsystem A sends a request to the unresponsive subsystem B. A cannot continue the adaptation until it reaches a timeout, thereby delaying the adaptation loop. The problem is exacerbated when more than one subsystem is already compromised. – In such a case, SAFER-D uses the PA mode, displayed in Fig. 2b. In the example, subsystem #2 is unresponsive due to an attack. As part of SAFER-D's Global MAPE-K loop, the remaining (still available) subsystems form adaptation subgroups based on the availability of connections. In the example in Fig. 2b, the architecture is split into three adaptation subgroups: [#1, #3, #5, #8], [#4, #7], and [#6]. Splitting the architecture and excluding the unresponsive subsystem #2 helps maintain adequate adaptation times. The splitting (i.e., the mode switch) in SAFER-D is performed by reconfiguring the **Managed API** and dictating which subsystems of the **Subsystems of Interest** should be requested for adaptation updates (i.e., contribute to the *Global SL Adaptations*) and which are ignored. As part of the Global MAPE-K loop, a recovery strategy is in place to check the responsiveness of unavailable subsystems, similar to a heartbeat function. Once a subsystem is up and running again, the subsystem is reintegrated into the adaptation set until the system can switch back to the FA mode.

In the following, we further describe the interplay of the two MAPE-K loops. SAFER-D is efficiently greedy in the sense of how it conducts adaptations. The more subsystems are available, the more information can be used. SAFER-D always tries to connect to the other **Subsystems of Interest** as part of the Global MAPE-K. When this is impossible, it still uses its PA mode to receive as many timely adaptations as possible. In the worst case, no other subsystems are available (i.e., Ⓜ is exhausted). In this case, SAFER-D can at least adapt locally (i.e., Ⓜ is the only source for adaptations). The interplay of the loops is also visualized in Fig. 3. The novelty of SAFER-D lies in its flexibility in different situations. SAFER-D is capable of dealing with interruptions and can, whenever necessary, adapt so that two MAPE-K loops are always running efficiently: One to adapt the **Managed System**, and one to adapt the **Managed API**. This flexibility directly adheres to the resilience of the architecture SAFER-D is deployed to and marks the main contribution of our framework.

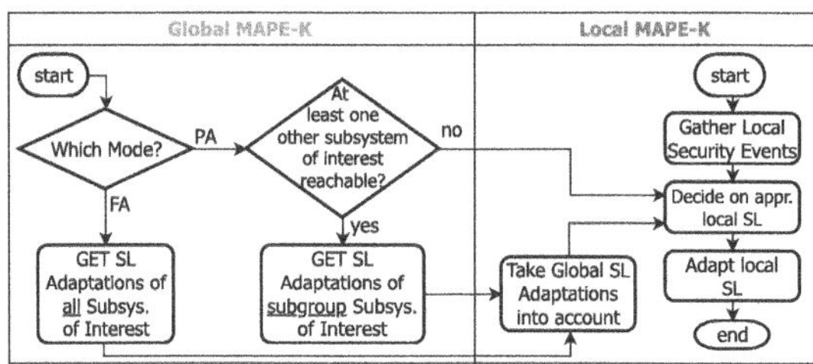

Fig. 3. Simplified flowchart illustrating Global MAPE-K's influence on the Local MAPE-K.

4 Evaluation

We executed a series of rigorous experiments. We evaluated the *Feasibility* and *Security* in an earlier framework version [28] here, we focus on *Applicability* and

Efficiency to evaluate our framework's general applicability and efficiency. In this section, we first describe the research questions, use case scenarios, evaluation setup, results, and finally, the answers to our research questions.

RQ1: *(Applicability) To what extent can SAFER-D be applied to execute security adaptations, and what is the integration effort when embedding it into existing system architectures?* With this first research question, we aim to qualitatively evaluate the applicability of SAFER-D. Applicability is essential to bridge theory and practice, and we try to approach an answer by addressing some of the key factors used in similar evaluation setups (see [18]). For measuring the integration effort, we report on the reusability of components and the required resources to use SAFER-D in a given scenario, i.e., the time and Lines of Code (LoC) it takes to configure and run SAFER-D.

RQ2: *(Efficiency) To what extent can SAFER-D be used to execute security adaptations efficiently?* With the second research question, we quantitatively determine the efficiency of SAFER-D. Since a timely adaptation is paramount during an attack (cf. [8] and **AC 3**), short adaptation times are a crucial indicator of SAFER-D's efficiency. We assess the *Time to Adapt* (*TtA*) on the deployed architecture of all MAPE-K loops. First, we measure the *Time to Adapt for Security Levels* (TtA_{SL}) to evaluate the adaptation times of Ⓜ/Ⓜ $\Rightarrow$ Ⓐ $\Rightarrow$ Ⓟ $\Rightarrow$ Ⓔ. Hence, the adaptations from one SL to another. Second, we measure the *Time to Adapt for Global Adaptations* (TtA_G) to measure the switch between PA and FA to form adaptation subgroups. Hence, TtA_G reflects the time it takes for a Ⓜ $\Rightarrow$ Ⓐ $\Rightarrow$ Ⓟ $\Rightarrow$ Ⓔ loop configuration to take effect on the `Managed API`.

4.1 Use Case Scenario

Our use case is motivated by a real-world example provided by our industry partner ENGEL Austria GmbH. The company is a large machine manufacturing enterprise operating in over 80 countries worldwide, with several thousand employees. The company is one of the leading manufacturers of industrial injection molding machines. With its globalized status, the company provides multiple large edge computing architectures distributed worldwide for its customers. Machine data (e.g., production cycles, usage data) is collected and distributed to central cloud computing nodes via a hierarchically structured edge computing architecture. This data is used, among other things, for predictive maintenance, remote support, and data analysis to increase production efficiency and reduce energy consumption and scrap. Multiple machines are connected via edge devices, which are again connected to fog computing nodes and ultimately report to a central cloud server. Although the machines can be operated standalone, downtime of the edge computing architecture due to a security incident or a cyberattack can impede normal operation and cause financial losses. With its underlying edge computing architecture and security requirements, the company provides an excellent example for evaluating the different aspects of SAFER-D. For the evaluation, we focused on DDoS attacks on the edge computing architecture [34]. More specifically, we used SAFER-D to adapt in the event of an Internet Control Message Protocol (ICMP) flood attack. In such an attack, an excessive number of ping requests are sent to the target, thereby clogging up its resources, such as network bandwidth and processing capabilities. The use case's goal is to dictate security-level adaptations among the edge computing subsystems during an ICMP flood attack. If a system becomes unavailable due to the attack, the respective subsystems shall switch into the PA mode to allow for respective adaptations within the remaining adaptation subgroup.

4.2 Evaluation Setup

Based on the conceptual framework above, we created a prototype implementation in Python to conduct the evaluation. In the following, we provide a brief overview of SAFER-D's instantiation (see details in suppl. material). The industry partner provided us with edge devices (hardware) utilized on-site at their manufacturing plants. We use these devices to replicate a typical edge computing architecture for the evaluation. The evaluated architecture is depicted in Fig. 2a and consists of four layers: one cloud, two fog, and one edge layer.

RQ1: The `Local Runtime Monitor`[1], `Local Execution Adapter` *(together 96 LoC)*, and the initial *Architecture Configuration* (*47 LoC*) are use-case-specific; the remaining implementation is reusable for other use cases (*approx. 3* h). We created three use-case-specific SLs with increasing measures for a potential ICMP flood attack. The levels are implemented using the Python state machine package [21] (*70 LoC, approx. 1.5* h) and are defined as follows: Level 3 – Normal Readiness, Regular monitoring; Level 2 – Moderate Readiness, Rate limiting; Level 1 – Maximum Readiness, Block entirely. Each SL represents a state in the state machine. In the event of an attack, the `Local MAPE-K` triggers state transitions from one state to another. The stepwise transitions are in place for control and dependency management. SAFER-D fully supports configurable SL transitions (e.g., skipping a SL) when needed, which can be enabled by modifying the state machine definition. At runtime, each subsystem periodically issues heartbeat requests to check for the SLs of the other connected subsystems. For instance, `#2` sends a heartbeat every ten seconds (interval aligns with typical machine cycle times, allowing heartbeats to be sent alongside operational data), requesting the SLs of `#1`, `#6`, and `#4`. If one of the connected subsystems of interest responds with a higher criticality level than the one currently used for `#2`, `#2` adapts, i.e., transitions to the most critical SL. We prioritize the most restrictive SL to ensure rapid and effective response in high-impact scenarios like DoS attacks; in less time-critical contexts, incorporating human-in-the-loop decision-making can offer a more balanced trade-off between security and functionality. Furthermore, RESTful communication allows us to easily identify whether a device is unresponsive: If a request times out, the prototype adapts accordingly using global adaptations. The global adaptations are implemented by adding functionality to the periodic heartbeat checks. Each system sends out a tree traversal (REST calls), checking which subsystems are still reachable.

[1] The specificity concerns the selection of monitored properties, not the underlying mechanism. Industrial systems often expose extensive metrics (e.g., Netdata), allowing the `Local Runtime Monitor` to function as a configurable filter or bridge.

RQ2: We evaluated TtA_{SL} by monitoring our deployed framework operating on top of the edge computing architecture. Adaptations are checked every ten seconds via a heartbeat (i.e., `Local MAPE-K` and `Global MAPE-K` are periodically triggered). The goal is to capture the time from the beginning of an adaptation cycle (i.e., the start of the heartbeat) until an adaptation is detected (monitored), analyzed, processed, and executed. For instance, when considering Fig. 2a, `#1` is before the adaptation heartbeat in *Level 3*. `#2` is under attack and, therefore, in *Level 2*. For TtA_{SL}, we measure the time from the beginning of the heartbeat from `#1` until `#1` completes the adaptation to *Level 2*. – We chose `#1` as the monitored subsystem to control the influence of network depth: The closer the attacked subsystem is to the one monitored (in our case `#1`), the faster it can adapt. For instance, `#2` is closer to `#1` than `#8`. Since the heartbeat adaptation checks occur sequentially, network depth matters. Therefore, `#1` provides the best-case and worst-case scenario. It has systems connected directly (e.g., `#2`) and, at the same time, exhibits the longest depth to traverse. During the evaluation, we seeded predefined SL triggers for each system depicted in Fig. 2a. We measured the TtA_{SL} and validated that the adapted SLs were correct according to our seed, i.e., checking if `#1` transitions to *Level 2* when it is supposed to. We repeated this process for every subsystem $N = 100$ (i.e., a total of 700 SL adaptations). We employed a similar procedure for TtA_G. We randomly terminated components in Fig. 2a. The rest of the edge computing architecture had to respond accordingly and globally adapt to the PA mode. We measured the time again from the start of a heartbeat cycle until the system transitioned to the PA mode (i.e., all adaptation subgroups were formed). We chose `#1` again as our monitored component to control for network depth. Every subsystem in Fig. 2a is randomly terminated $N = 50$ times (350 in total).

4.3 Evaluation Results

RQ1: As a first step, we validated that every SL adaptation was carried out correctly as expected. Each change in the SL of an attacked subsystem in the architecture resulted in the expected change of `#1`. For the global adaptations, we can also confirm that SAFER-D's implementation executed correct adaptations in the architecture every time. Regarding the integration effort, we identified the components that would need re-implementation and counted the LoC and the time it took us to implement them. A total of 213 LoC are use-case-specific, which took us approximately 4–5 h. Since every subsystem runs the same instance of SAFER-D, the development and configuration effort must be invested once. The code is pulled via version control on every subsystem and is ready to run without further configuration. Considering that the majority of SAFER-D's components can be reused for other use cases, 213 LoC and 4.5 h of effort represent a considerably low effort with respect to the benefits SAFER-D can bring to such an architecture.

RQ2: Figure 4a and b show the boxplots of our quantitative analysis. One can notice the considerably long adaptation times for TtA_G, especially compared to

TtA_{SL}. However, 3 s of the values in TtA_G can be attributed to the initial HTTP timeout. An HTTP request always waits 3 s (the time an SL adaptation would take additionally) for a response during the heartbeat. After the waiting period, the system is deemed unresponsive. Therefore, these numbers always contain a fixed constant of 3000 ms. The adaptation times for the TtA_{SL} remain consistent across runs (cf. distribution in Fig. 4a). The average median of TtA_{SL} is 344.86 ms (roughly comparable to the 333 ms in [25]). Therefore, most of TtA_{SL} are considerably lower than half a second. Similarly, for TtA_G, the average median adaptation time is 4543.29 ms, which means 1543.29 ms (total minus 3 s timeout) solely for the adaptation. However, adaptation times are still longer compared to TtA_{SL}. The reason is that once a subsystem is unresponsive, the system again traverses through the tree to determine the subgroup. The traversal takes time, as shown in TtA_G. The distribution of adaptation times among the subsystems can be considered equally stable for all subsystems for TtA_{SL}. For TtA_G, the distribution is dense for `#6`, `#4`, `#5`, and `#8`. `#2` and `#3` yielded a rather loose distribution, although their median is similar to the other subsystems.

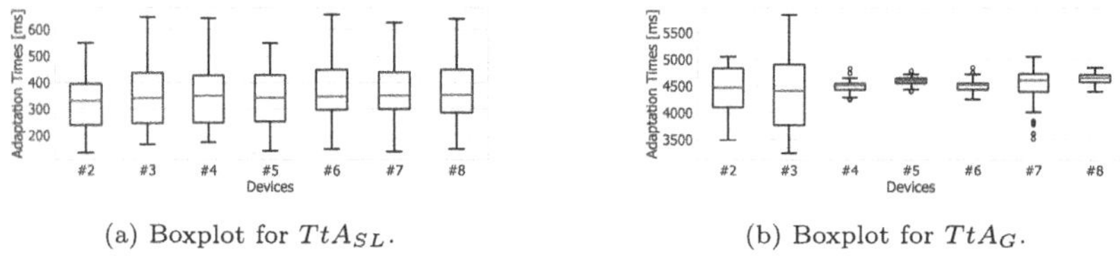

(a) Boxplot for TtA_{SL}.

(b) Boxplot for TtA_G.

Fig. 4. Boxplots of TtA_{SL} & TtA_G.

4.4 Answers to Research Questions

Answer to RQ1: The use case was inspired by a real-world industrial example. SAFER-D was successfully implemented within the edge computing architecture similar to the one utilized by the partnering company. This application validated the framework's capability to address practical challenges in an industry-relevant context. Although not discussed here, due to space constraints, we deployed SAFER-D to a second use case focused on web authentication, further showcasing SAFER-D's adaptability to different domains and highlighting its ability to cater to security requirements in diverse settings (details can be found in the supplemental material; cf. data availability). Both prototypical implementations are publicly available, enabling users to explore and leverage the adaptation mechanisms provided by SAFER-D. The implementation effort for SAFER-D's adaptation components in our scenario offers a first indication of manageable integration (considering time and LoC), though further validation is needed. A total of 21h were invested to implement `Global MAPE-K` components and the `Local Adaptation Middleware` and `Local SL Manager` (i.e., the reusable parts of

SAFER-D); the `Local Runtime Monitor` and `Local Execution Adapter` are use-case-specific and took us approx. 4.5h. We found the PA mode particularly helpful during development since even a network misconfiguration immediately resulted in respective global adaptations. For this reason, we find SAFER-D's global adaptations helpful not only in the event of a security incident but also in maintenance or operational malfunctions. In summary, through these applications, we demonstrated SAFER-D's applicability in real-world scenarios. The initial results indicate that integration is feasible; however, a more comprehensive evaluation is required for general claims.

Answer to RQ2: We comprehensively evaluated SAFER-D's efficiency by quantitatively analyzing data from our use case, measuring adaptation times for SL adaptations (TtA_{SL}) and global adaptations (TtA_G). Adaptation times were sufficiently efficient for the given scenarios. Our analysis suggests that the centrality of the subsystem being considered influences adaptation times across the architecture (cf. Fig. 4a). In general, top-level systems require longer adaptation times compared to low-level systems. Optimized implementation strategies can improve performance, such as parallel tree traversal for adaptation checks. While our findings highlight areas with potential for further optimization, the prototypical implementations provide a proof of concept. The results affirm that SAFER-D delivers promising efficiency, making it a viable framework for dynamic system adaptations in distributed computing systems.

5 Threats to Validity

Like any study, our work faces threats to validity. For conclusion validity, we used quantitative metrics TtA_{SL} and TtA_G and repeated runs to ensure consistency, though relying solely on time-based measures limits insight into securityâĂŞ-functionality trade-offs; broader quantitative applicability metrics could offer a more comprehensive picture. Regarding internal validity, we controlled the experimental setup to isolate the framework's effect on adaptation times, minimizing the influence of hardware/network factors, although real-world deployments may introduce unforeseen variables. For external validity, our use cases and metrics (e.g., time, LoC) serve as a foundation for generalization; however, further validation in diverse environments is necessary to confirm broader applicability.

6 Related Work

Multi-level Adaptation: In their work, Jahan *et al.* [13] propose a framework for dynamically maintaining functional and security concerns in autonomous systems, ensuring coordination between multiple MAPE-K feedback control loops. An additional MAPE-SAC loop is introduced that emphasizes security-related adaptations. Similarly, also employing a multi-feedback loop approach, Vromant *et al.* [31] relied on intra-loop and inter-loop coordination of multiple MAPE-K loops to perform coordinated adaptation actions. Braberman *et al.* [3]

present MORPH, a reference architecture for self-adaptation based on the MAPE-K loop. MORPH consists of three layers for goal management, strategy management, and strategy enactment with different reconfiguration strategies. Ben Halima *et al.* [2] introduce a set of MAPE-K design patterns tailored for decentralized control in self-adaptive CPSs. Gerostathopoulos *et al.* [11] propose IRM-SA, an Invariant Refinement Method for Self-Adaptation, tailored to ensure dependability and adaptivity in software-intensive CPSs.

Security Adaptation: Fotohi *et al.* [10] propose an Agent-based Self-Protective method (ASP-UAVN) inspired by the human immune system to enhance secure communication in Unmanned Aerial Vehicle Networks. Riegler *et al.* [25] introduce DSEC4IoT, a distributed MAPE-K framework for self-protective IoT devices, enabling local and centralized monitoring, analysis, planning, and execution of security measures. Jones *et al.* [14] present Crispy, a CRISPR-inspired (bacterial adaptive immune system) resiliency mechanism to protect N-variant systems from DoS attacks by leveraging automatic attack signature generation. Finally, Skandylas [27] presents an approach for enhancing adaptive security in software-intensive systems by equipping them with self-protective capabilities, including runtime threat modeling, proactive adaptation, and decentralized trust-based mechanisms.

Table 1. Overview of Related Work; [ ] = Aspect absent, [○] = Aspect mentioned, [◑] = Aspect partially addressed, [●] = Aspect fully addressed

	[13]	[31]	[3]	[2]	[11]	[10]	[25]	[14]	[27]	SAFER-D
Multi-System	◑	◑	○	●	●	◑	●		●	●
Security Focus	●			○		●	●	●	●	●
Failure Resilience		●	◑	○	●	◑	●	●		●
Loop Interaction	●	●	●	●	●	◑	◑	○		●
Decentral Coordination		◑		●	●	◑	○		●	●

We provide an overview of the addressed contents of related work and how it compares to SAFER-D in Table 1. The table reveals that SAFER-D is closely related to Fotohi *et al.* [10] and Riegler *et al.* [25]. – Fotohi *et al.* [10] focus on *securing communication* between UAVs, relying on detecting network-layer attacks and isolating malicious nodes. In contrast, SAFER-D *protects the devices themselves* through hierarchical coordination (vs. purely peer-to-peer) and adaptive security levels (vs. strict isolation), enabling graded and context-aware responses. Unlike Riegler *et al.* [25], who rely on a central "Managing Server" to coordinate security adaptation across independently operating devices, SAFER-D enables fully decentralized coordination among autonomous subsystems. Moreover, DSec4IoT supports a fixed two-level structure (server and devices) while SAFER-D introduces a multi-level hierarchy where adaptation decisions can propagate and adjust across layers. Therefore, in case of connection loss, SAFER-D can adapt within subgroups while DSec4IoT adapts only locally.

7 Conclusion

In this paper, we presented SAFER-D, a novel self-adaptive security framework for DCAs. SAFER-D integrates diverse adaptation strategies to enable security adaptations, even in the event of system failures caused by attacks. Our evaluation using a realistic use case scenario has confirmed that SAFER-D can be used in practice and that the adaptations are efficiently carried out. As part of our ongoing and future work, we aim to extend our adaptation strategies, improve performance and scalability for large-scale architectures, and incorporate advanced runtime threat modeling techniques.

Acknowledgments. This work has partially been supported by the LIT Secure and Correct Systems Lab funded by the State of Upper Austria.

Data Availability. Supplemental material on GitHub: Edge computing use case/ WebAuthn use case.

References

1. Acarali, D., Rajesh Rao, K., Rajarajan, M., Chema, D., Ginzburg, M.: Modelling smart grid IT-OT dependencies for DDoS impact propagation. COSE **112**, 102528 (2022)
2. Ben Halima, R., Hachicha, M., Jemal, A., Hadj Kacem, A.: MAPE-K patterns for self-adaptation in cyber-physical systems. J. Supercomput. **79**(5), 4917–4943 (2023)
3. Braberman, V., D'Ippolito, N., Kramer, J., Sykes, D., Uchitel, S.: MORPH: a reference architecture for configuration and behaviour self-adaptation. In: Proceedings of the 1st International Workshop on Control Theory for Software Engineering, August 2015, pp. 9–16 (2015)
4. Buldyrev, S.V., Parshani, R., Paul, G., Stanley, H.E., Havlin, S.: Catastrophic cascade of failures in interdependent networks. Nature **464**(7291), 1025–1028 (2010)
5. Cao, K., Liu, Y., Meng, G., Sun, Q.: An overview on edge computing research. IEEE Access **8**, 85714–85728 (2020)
6. Carlo, A., Obergfaell, K.: Cyber attacks on critical infrastructures and satellite communications. Intl. J. Crit. Infrastruct. Prot. **46**, 100701 (2024)
7. Chambers, T., Cleland-Huang, J., Vierhauser, M.: Self-adaptation of loosely coupled systems across a system of small uncrewed aerial systems. In: International Workshop on Software Engineering for SoS and Software Ecosystems, August 2024, pp. 37–44 (2024)
8. Coppolino, L., D'Antonio, S., Nardone, R., Romano, L.: A self-adaptation-based approach to resilience improvement of complex internets of utility systems. Environ. Syst. Decis. **43**(4), 708–720 (2023)
9. El-Sayed, H., et al.: Edge of Things: the big picture on the integration of Edge, IoT and the Cloud in a distributed computing environment. IEEE Access **6**, 1706–1717 (2018)
10. Fotohi, R., Nazemi, E., Shams Aliee, F.: An agent-based self-protective method to secure communication between UAVs in unmanned aerial vehicle networks. Veh. Commun. **26**, 100267 (2020)

11. Gerostathopoulos, I., et al.: Self-adaptation in software-intensive cyber-physical systems: from system goals to architecture configurations. JSS **122**, 378–397 (2016)
12. He, D., Gu, H., Zhu, S., Chan, S., Guizani, M.: A comprehensive detection method for the lateral movement stage of APT attacks. IEEE IoT J. **11**(5), 8440–8447 (2024)
13. Jahan, S., et al.: MAPE-K/MAPE-SAC: an interaction framework for adaptive systems with security assurance cases. Fut. Gener. Comp. Sys. **109**, 197–209 (2020)
14. Jones, J., Hiser, J.D., Davidson, J.W., Forrest, S.: Defeating denial-of-service attacks in a self-managing N-variant system. In: Proceedings of the 14th International on SEAMS, May 2019, pp. 126–138 (2019)
15. Kaplan, S., Garrick, B.J.: On the quantitative definition of risk. Risk Anal. **1**(1), 11–27 (1981)
16. Kephart, J., Chess, D.: The vision of autonomic computing. Computer **36**(1), 41–50 (2003)
17. Larkin, R.D., Lopez, J., Butts, J.W., Grimaila, M.R.: Evaluation of security solutions in the SCADA environment. SIGMIS Database **45**(1), 38–53 (2014)
18. Leszczyna, R.: Aiming at methods' wider adoption: applicability determinants and metrics. Comput. Sci. Rev. **40**, 100387 (2021)
19. Liao, H.J., Richard Lin, C.H., Lin, Y.C., Tung, K.Y.: Intrusion detection system: a comprehensive review. J. Netw. Comput. App. **36**(1), 16–24 (2013)
20. Liu, S., Liu, L., Tang, J., Yu, B., Wang, Y., Shi, W.: Edge computing for autonomous driving: opportunities and challenges. Proc. IEEE **107**(8), 1697–1716 (2019)
21. Macedo, F.: fgmacedo/python-statemachine, December 2024. https://github.com/fgmacedo/python-statemachine
22. Momoh, J.: Smart Grid: Fundamentals of Design and Analysis. Wiley, March 2012
23. Otoum, Y., Nayak, A.: AS-IDS: anomaly and signature based IDS for the Internet of Things. J. Netw. Syst. Manage. **29**(3), 23 (2021)
24. Palleti, V.R., Adepu, S., Mishra, V.K., Mathur, A.: Cascading effects of cyber-attacks on interconnected critical infrastructure. Cybersecurity **4**(1), 8 (2021)
25. Riegler, M., Sametinger, J., Vierhauser, M.: A Distributed MAPE-K framework for self-protective IoT devices. In: Proceedings of the 18th International Conference on SEAMS, May 2023, pp. 202–208. IEEE (2023)
26. Sadhu, P.K., Yanambaka, V.P., Abdelgawad, A.: Internet of Things: security and solutions survey. Sensors **22**(19), 7433 (2022)
27. Skandylas, C.: Design and analysis of self-protection: adaptive security for software-intensive systems. In: Companion Proceedings of the 15th European Conference on Software Architecture: ECSA 2021 Companion. CEUR-WS (2021)
28. Stadler, M., Riegler, M., Sametinger, J.: Cyber-resilient edge computing: a holistic approach with multi-level MAPE-K loops. In: 2024 IEEE 21st International Conference on Software Architecture Companion (ICSA-C), June 2024, pp. 79–83. IEEE (2024)
29. Thakur, K., Ali, M.L., Jiang, N., Qiu, M.: Impact of cyber-attacks on critical infrastructure. In: 2016 IEEE BigDataSecurity, HPSC, and IDS, pp. 183–186 (2016)
30. Theisen, T.: DEFCON Levels, January 2023. https://www.military.com/military-life/defcon-levels.html
31. Vromant, P., Weyns, D., Malek, S., Andersson, J.: On interacting control loops in self-adaptive systems. In: Proceedings of the 6th International Conference on SEAMS, pp. 202–207 (2011)
32. Weyns, D., Andersson, J.: On the challenges of self-adaptation in systems of systems. In: Proceedings of the First International Workshop on Software Engineering for Systems-of-Systems, July 2013, pp. 47–51 (2013)

33. Weyns, D., et al.: On patterns for decentralized control in self-adaptive systems. In: Software Engineering for Self-Adaptive Systems II, pp. 76–107 (2013)
34. Xiao, Y., Jia, Y., Liu, C., Cheng, X., Yu, J., Lv, W.: Edge computing security: state of the art and challenges. Proc. IEEE **107**(8), 1608–1631 (2019)
35. Yoachimik, O., Pacheco, J.: Record-breaking 5.6 Tbps DDoS attack and global DDoS trends for 2024 Q4, January 2025. https://blog.cloudflare.com/ddos-threat-report-for-2024-q4/

SURE! A Catalog of Uncertainties and RELAXed Requirements for Self-adaptive Systems

Claudia Raibulet[1](✉), Ilias Gerostathopoulos[2], and Osman Abdelmukaram[2]

[1] DISCo-Dipartimento di Informatica, Universita' degli Studi di Milano-Bicocca, Sistemistica e Comunicazione, Viale Sarca 336, Milan, Italy
claudia.raibulet@unimib.it

[2] Computer Science Department, Vrije Universiteit Amsterdam, De Boelelaan 1111, 1081 HV Amsterdam, The Netherlands
i.g.gerostathopoulos@vu.nl

Abstract. In software engineering of self-adaptive systems, uncertainties arise from the inherent complexity of these systems (i.e., the limitation to foresee all aspects related to their development and operation) and the unpredictability of the execution environments (i.e., the limitation to predict all the events), among other sources. Several taxonomies and specification languages have been proposed for uncertainties. However, they remain at a theoretical level and are hardly applied in practice. There is a lack of best practices and concrete examples of how to apply taxonomies and languages in real systems. To address this gap, we contribute a catalog of uncertainties. All the uncertainties in the catalog have been extracted from concrete artifacts. Each uncertainty is described using the same template and associated with requirements specified in the RELAX language. Our objective is to provide an initial version of a catalog (to be further extended) of uncertainties and requirements that can be (re)used as prototypical examples in different application domains.

Keyword: uncertainty, catalog, RELAX language, self-adaptive systems

1 Introduction

As software engineering evolves, there is a need to complement *well defined* requirements with specifications concerning *expected* and *unexpected* uncertainties [1,2] that software systems may deal with at runtime (without interrupting their operation and continuing to provide their functionality with a discrete level of quality). Uncertainties should be explicitly considered and addressed from the early software analysis and design stages. This has been outlined in

V. Andrikopoulos et al. (Eds.): ECSA 2025, LNCS 15929, pp. 214–223, 2026.
https://doi.org/10.1007/978-3-032-02138-0_14

various research papers for several years, e.g., [3] underlines the need for dealing with uncertainty in early software architecture and proposes GuideArch - a framework for evaluating architectural solution space under uncertainty, [4] cites uncertainty as one of the main causes of architecture changes and introduces a framework for the management of uncertainty in software architecture, while the recent [5] notices that design decisions may be made based on unproven premises or false assumptions because uncertainty is not considered explicitly and presents ArchHypo - a framework that uses hypothesis engineering to manage uncertainties related to software architecture. In general, in the attempt to address uncertainties, various approaches considering different aspects of software engineering/development have been proposed: self-adaptive systems (SAS) based on control feedback loops, reference architectural models, runtime models, and verification and evaluation mechanisms among many others [2].

This paper proposes a catalog of uncertainties (called SURE! - Software Uncertainty REpository) that can be collocated at the requirements specification phase. Uncertainties should be explicitly considered from the beginning when requirements are identified. This way, they will be addressed in the design and implementation, during testing and validation, and eventually at runtime.

Uncertainties in our catalog were identified in actual SAS artifacts[1]. We have grouped identical and/or similar uncertainties from different artifacts together and defined generalized uncertainties (i.e., uncertainty patterns) that are independent of any specific artifact or application domain.

To describe each uncertainty, the taxonomy proposed in [6] has been adopted. This taxonomy describes the sources of uncertainties based on a template inspired by the well-known template for design patterns. Uncertainties are divided into three groups based on the phases of development life cycle when they occur: requirements, design, and runtime. We have slightly revised this template and extended it including the degree of severity and evaluation of each uncertainty.

Our catalog currently contains 30 uncertainties, all described in full detail (compared to [6] catalog - called DAS - where 26 uncertainties are presented and one uncertainty per group is described using the template) - see Fig. 1. 13 out of the 30 uncertainties in our SURE! catalog, are new in that they are not included in DAS. Moreover, we have used the RELAX language [7] to explicitly and rigorously specify the requirements concerning the identified uncertainties.

In this paper, our objective is to provide an initial version of a catalog of uncertainties that can be used, reused, and continuously extended. This will enable researchers and practitioners to consider uncertainties explicitly during the development of software systems. For self-adaptive systems, it will become a starting point to associate the uncertainties with the adaptation strategies [8] used to address them, and hence create a catalog of such strategies, too.

The contribution of our paper can be summarized as follows:

- A revised taxonomy for uncertainties based on the one proposed in [6].

[1] SAS: https://www.hpi.uni-potsdam.de/giese/public/selfadapt/exemplars/.

- A catalog of 30 uncertainties divided into three categories based on their sources (i.e., requirements, design, and runtime).
- 76 requirements (each uncertainty may be translated into one or more requirements) and 219 RELAX specifications covering all the uncertainties and their related requirements in the catalog (each requirement may have associated one or more RELAX specifications).

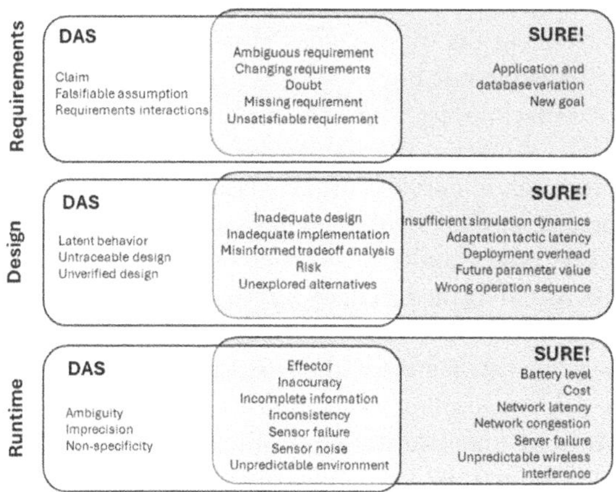

Fig. 1. DAS and SURE! Uncertainties

2 Related Work

Taxonomies for Uncertainties: Ramirez et al. [6] presented a comprehensive classification of uncertainties within SAS. They proposed a taxonomy to classify the sources of uncertainties according to the development phases of their occurrence: *requirements* (e.g., unresolved issues), *design* (e.g., inadequate design), and *run-time* (e.g., unpredictable environmental interactions). Concrete uncertainties for each of these sources are indicated (see Fig. 1). Furthermore, it offers a descriptive template for uncertainties (see Table 1). Weyns' book [2] (see Chap. 8) classified the sources of uncertainties in four main groups from a holistic perspective: *system*, *goals*, *context*, and *humans*. Walker et al. [9] proposed a classification for modeling uncertainty encompassing three dimensions: *location* (area where the uncertainty is observed), *level* (degree of our understanding/knowledge of the uncertainty), and *nature* (distinguishes whether the source of uncertainty arises from inadequate knowledge or the inherent variability of the phenomenon in question). It was adopted by Perez-Palacin et al. [10].

Specification Languages for Uncertainties: In SAS, the RELAX language [7] enriches the keywords used for requirements specification (e.g., MoSCoW -

must, should, could, want to have) with operators to express uncertainty. Operators express modal, temporal, and ordinal aspects, and are complemented by uncertainty factors, e.g., environmental and system-monitored properties. Alternatively, FLAGS [11], a derivative of the KAOS model [12], offers another means to identify requirements for SAS. It serves as a goal model and treats requirements sd run-time entities.

Our approach uses the taxonomy and template proposed in [6]. It extends the list of uncertainties in [6]. It adopts RELAX [7] to describe uncertainties.

3 The SURE! Catalog

This section presents our SURE! catalog, which consists of:

- 30 uncertainties, all extracted from concrete artifacts;
- 76 requirements corresponding to the 30 uncertainties;
- 219 RELAX specifications concerning the 76 identified requirements.

The catalog is linked via its Github repository available at https://github.com/iliasger/SURECatalog. Upon selecting the uncertainties on the first table in this application, another table with the related requirements appears below.

For the description of the uncertainty structure, we have adopted the template proposed in [6]. We have revised the template as follows. We substituted *Mitigation Strategies* and *Related Sources* with *Degree of Severity* and *Evaluation*. We consider that *Mitigation Strategies* is a vast topic we plan to address in the next steps. Strategies can hardly be indicated as a field in this template due to their complexity. *Related Sources* are to some degree overlapping with *Context* or *Sample Illustration*. Instead, we consider *Degree of Severity* relevant to quantify the level of impact of the uncertainties in a system, even if it may be influenced significantly by the application domain. Degrees of severity range from *low* (uncertainty incites minor operational impairment), *medium* (the system exhibits noticeable side effects), and *high* (uncertainty drives the system into a potential critical or even non-operational state). *Evaluation* indicates the benefits and costs of addressing the uncertainty. It assesses the effect of self-adaptation in managing uncertainty and may be used to compare this effect with situations where self-adaptation is not employed. Table 1 provides a full-blown example of an uncertainty specification using our template.

For the description of the requirements structure, we have used the operators and uncertainty factors of the RELAX specification language. In general, the keywords most applied to requirements specification in software engineering are summarized by the MoSCoW prioritization template: Must, Should, Could, and Want to Have. The traditional approach to defining requirements encounters limitations when applied to SAS, e.g., lack of conciseness in expressing the changing hierarchical order of objectives at run-time, the potential for completely omitting certain objectives – particularly in critical situations, the challenge of addressing unidentified objectives, or the specification of the allowed variability. RELAX [7] has been developed to overcome such limitations and establish a

Table 1. Example of Uncertainty Description in SURE!

Name	Unsatisfied Requirements
Classification	Requirements
Context	Arises when a system fails to meet a specific requirement due to changes in its environment. Changes may be internal, e.g., alterations in system components/processes, or external, e.g., shifts in user needs, regulatory standards, environmental conditions
Impact	Can be significant, potentially compromising the system's functionality and its ability to achieve its intended goals. This can lead to partial or complete system dysfunction, rendering the system ineffective or even useless in certain cases. The degree of impact largely depends on the nature of the unfulfilled requirement and its relevance to the system's core functionality
Degree of Severity	MEDIUM TO HIGH, depending on the nature and importance of the unfulfilled requirement. If the requirement is essential to the system's core functionality or safety, its non-fulfillment can lead to serious consequences, potentially rendering the system impractical or unreliable. On the other hand, if the requirement is not critical, its non-fulfillment may only result in partial loss of functionality
Sample Illustration	AMELIA - Consider a requirement that states, "Each hospital has a taxi less than 10 min away." This requirement ensures that if there is a person who needs emergency treatment and requires a taxi to reach the hospital, the taxi must arrive within 10 min. If this requirement is unsatisfied, patients may miss out on timely treatment, putting their lives at risk and causing a negative impact DRAGONFLY - Consider a scenario where the system experiences widespread connection issues in the area, resulting in a poor connection for a certain time. In normal operation, the drone would initiate the "Return to Home" function due to the poor connection, indicating that the package delivery cannot be completed. This failure to fulfill the requirement results in an incomplete delivery. However, if the connection issue is temporary or limited to a specific location, and the drone waits for instructions, it could successfully deliver the package, thereby fulfilling the requirement. To address such situations, the *glide* function was developed to increase the chances of payload delivery while waiting for the connection to recover.
Evaluation	SAS equipped with mechanisms to adapt to unanticipated events and environmental changes, are able to address this uncertainty by monitoring system state and property values over time, recognizing potential requirement non-fulfillment, and execute mitigation strategies to meet the requirements.
Also Known As	Non-compliant Requirements, Unaccomplished Requirements

uniform method for declaratively defining requirements in SAS. It introduces a comprehensive set of operators (e.g., modal, temporal, ordinal) and clauses to express requirements in a flexible and adaptable manner. The key feature of the RELAX language is its ability to handle uncertainty and variability, allowing for the 'relaxation' of requirements under certain conditions. This flexibility enables

Table 2. RELAX specifications of System Resilience requirement associated with Unsatisfied Requirements uncertainty.

RS1:	The system SHALL maintain optimum operational functionality AS CLOSE AS POSSIBLE TO its ideal state, when encountering unexpected environmental changes that could lead to unsatisfied requirements. MONITOR: Environmental changes, functionality. ENVIRONMENT: Dynamic and unpredictable environment
RS2:	EVENTUALLY, the system SHALL recover from any disruptions that lead to unsatisfied requirements, ensuring a return to operational functionality. MONITOR: Disruptions, recovery speed, functionality. ENVIRONMENT: Operational environment with potential disruptions.
RS3:	The system SHALL adapt its core functionalities to maintain operational capacity AS EARLY AS POSSIBLE AFTER experiencing significant changes leading to unsatisfied requirements. MONITOR: Significant changes, adaptation speed. ENVIRONMENT: Dynamic and changing environment.

the specification of system behavior under varying conditions. As an example, the 'System Resilience' requirement associated with the uncertainty of Table 1 can be specified as indicated in Table 2. The same can be seen in the online catalog by selecting the 'Unsatisfied Requirements' uncertainty in the first table.

4 How to Use SURE!

This section shows how to use our SURE! catalog to specify the RELAX requirements concerning a new SAS exemplar or extensions of an existing exemplar to address a new uncertainty. Target users of our catalog are requirement engineers and business analysts who need to specify the requirements of a SAS. For our illustration, the analyst chooses the Tele Assistance System (TAS) [13]. We assume they want to extend it with the 'Unpredictable Environment' uncertainty.

The main steps are summarized in Fig. 2 through a UML activity diagram. The first step is to understand when the uncertainty may occur: during the requirements, design, or runtime phase. Once established that Unpredictable Environment occurs at runtime, the analyst looks for it in the SURE! catalog by filtering for uncertainties with classification attribute set to 'Run-time'. Then, the analyst reads the entire description of the uncertainty they are interested in to understand if it suits their needs. If this is the case, then they identify its related RELAX specification. Our catalog associates three requirements for the 'Unpredictable Environment' uncertainty: 'Adaptability', 'Response to Unforeseen Events', and 'Exception Handling'. Let us suppose they are interested in the response to unforeseen events. In this case, they look at its related RELAX requirements. These requirements may be used as they are or be personalized for the TAS system. The analyst decides to perform only minor modifications in the requirements RUE1, RUE2, and RUE3 as in Fig. 3.

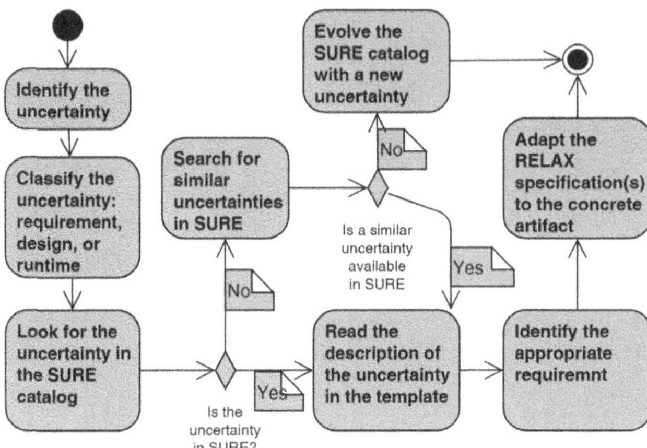

Fig. 2. Main steps to specify the RELAX requirements for an uncertainty using SURE!

RUE1	Upon detection of an unforeseen event, ~~the system~~ TAS SHALL initiate a predetermined safety procedure AS EARLY AS POSSIBLE. MONITOR: frequency of unforeseen events, time to initiate safety procedures. ENVIRONMENT: conditions leading to unforeseen events.
RUE2	EVENTUALLY, ~~the system~~TAS SHALL invoke an alarm service and recover from an unforeseen event, returning to a safe state. MONITOR: time to recover, frequency of unforeseen events. ENVIRONMENT: aftermath conditions of unforeseen events.
RUE3	~~The system~~TAS SHALL minimize the number of AS MANY unforeseen events AS POSSIBLE by incorporating predictive measures. MONITOR: number of unforeseen events, effectiveness of predictive measures. ENVIRONMENT: factors leading to unforeseen events.

Fig. 3. TAS: RELAX Specification for Unforeseen Environment related to the Response to Unforeseen Events Requirement. Personalization is indicated through reviews

The catalog can also be used when analysts have *not yet* identified which uncertainty or requirement to specify. In this case, the catalog is used as a source of inspiration. If it is not easy to identify the phase in which the uncertainty may occur, then the analysts can search for the name of the uncertainty. If the exact name is not available, they try to understand if there is a similar uncertainty looking at the 'Name' and 'Also Known As' fields. When no identical or similar uncertainty is found, then the catalog should be extended (see next section).

5 How to Evolve SURE!

This section explains the steps to adding new uncertainties to our SURE! catalog, alongside their respective RELAX requirements specification (see Fig. 4).

Identifying and Describing Uncertainties: Adding a new uncertainty in SURE! starts with its naming and classification. The name should be general and independent of any specific artifact. The classification consists of the phase

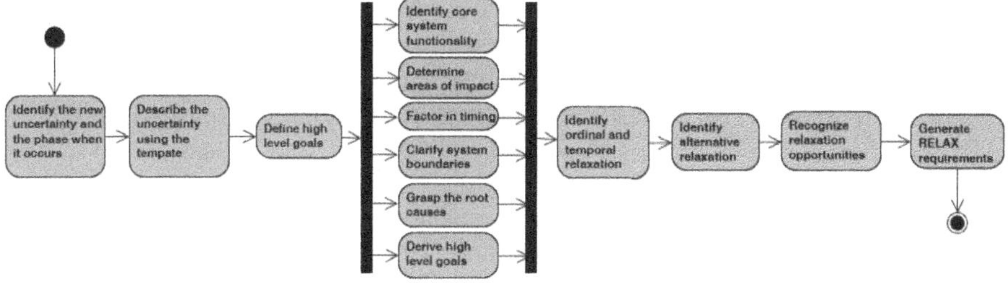

Fig. 4. The main steps to extend SURE!

identification in which the uncertainty may occur: requirements, design, and runtime. The uncertainty is further described using the revised template as in Table 1. Some of the fields are easier to compile (e.g., context, sample illustration, also known as) because they are explicitly required/mentioned in the artifact or they can be easily inferred, while others are more complex (e.g., impact, degree of severity, evaluation) because they are usually not addressed by the artifact. For example, only very few artifacts mention evaluation mechanisms.

Deriving RELAX Requirements for the New Uncertainty: In the next step, attention pivots to the translation of the uncertainty into requirements, formulated using RELAX. To compile the RELAXed requirements, our proposed approach follows five steps, which guide the translation of uncertainties, described using the common template, into relevant components of the RELAX language constructs: (1) define high-level goals, (2) identify temporal and ordinal relaxation, (3) identify alternative relaxation, (4) recognize relaxation opportunities, and (generate RELAX requirements specification.

6 Discussion and Next Steps

SURE! aims to become a reference for requirements specification for software systems dealing with uncertainties. Its definition has considered SAS artifacts, since this type of systems is designed to deals explicitly with uncertainties. However, its general feature makes it suitable to any type of system. Drawing a parallel to the well-known widely used GoF Design Pattern, SURE! supports the requirements elicitation and specification. We envision extending SURE! with an additional catalog that supports the design phases by covering strategies for mitigating uncertainties. Such strategies have been proposed in the past, notably in the form of goal-based approaches [1, 14–16], but without a clear link between the uncertainty being addressed, the related requirements and the mitigation strategies. Such link is important to bridge the gap between requirements and design, and eventually runtime, making it a useful tool for practitioners.

SURE! is an extensible catalog. Its current version is an initial one and we expect the community to contribute to its enrichment, both with other uncertainties and requirements and (potentially) with mitigation strategies as described above. We also aim to provide an online textual editor with syntax highlighting and auto-completion for supporting analysts in writing RELAX specifications.

Acknowledgement. This research is supported by ExtremeXP, a project co-funded by the European Union Horizon Programme under Grant Agreement No. 101093164.

References

1. Mahdavi-Hezavehi, S., Weyns, D., Avgeriou, P., Calinescu, R., Mirandola, R., Perez-Palacin, D.: Uncertainty in self-adaptive systems: a research community perspective. ACM Trans. Autonomous Adaptive Syst. **15**(4), 101–10 (2020),MahdavispsHezavehispsUncertainty 2020
2. Weyns, D.: An Introduction to Self-adaptive Systems: A Contemporary Software Engineering Perspective. IEEE Press, Wiley (2020)
3. Esfahani, N., Razavi, K., Malek, S.: Dealing with uncertainty in early software architecture. In: 20th ACM SIGSOFT Symposium on the Foundations of Software Engineering, p. 21. ACM (2012)
4. Lupafya, C.: A framework for managing uncertainty in software architecture. In: 13th European Conference on Software Architecture, pp. 71–74. ACM (2019)
5. Silva, K., Melegati, J., Silveira, F.F., Wang, X., Ferreira, M.G.V., Guerra, E.: Archhypo: managing software architecture uncertainty using hypotheses engineering. IEEE Trans. Software Eng. **51**(2), 430–448 (2025)
6. Ramirez, A.J., Jensen, A.C., Cheng, B.H.: A taxonomy of uncertainty for dynamically adaptive systems. In: 7th International Symposium on Software Engineering for Adaptive and Self-Managing Systems, pp. 99–108. IEEE (2012)
7. Whittle, J., Sawyer, P., Bencomo, N., Cheng, B.H., Bruel, J.-M.: Relax: a language to address uncertainty in self-adaptive systems requirement. Requirements Eng. **15**, 177–196 (2010)
8. Gerostathopoulos, I., Raibulet, C., Alberts, E.: Assessing self-adaptation strategies using cost-benefit analysis. In: 19th International Conference on Software Architecture Companion (ICSA-C), pp. 92–95 (2022)
9. Walker, W.E., et al.: Defining uncertainty: a conceptual basis for uncertainty management in model-based decision support. Integr. Assess. **4**(1), 5–17 (2003)
10. Perez-Palacin, D., Mirandola, R.: Uncertainties in the modeling of self-adaptive systems: A taxonomy and an example of availability evaluation. In: 5th ACM/SPEC International Conference on Performance Engineering, pp. 3–14 (2014)
11. Baresi, L. Pasquale, L., Spoletini, P.: Fuzzy goals for requirements-driven adaptation. In: 18th IEEE International Requirements Engineering Conference, pp. 125–134. IEEE (2010)
12. Van Lamsweerde, A., Darimont, R., Letier, E.: Managing conflicts in goal-driven requirements engineering. IEEE Transactions on Softw. Eng. **24**(11), 908–926 (1998)
13. Weyns,D., Calinescu, R.: Tele assistance: A self-adaptive service-based system exemplar. In: 10th International Symposium on Software Engineering for Adaptive and Self-Managing Systems, pp. 88–92 (2015)
14. Cámara, J., et al.: The uncertainty interaction problem in self-adaptive systems. Sw and Sys Modeling J. **21**(4), 1277–1294 (2022)

15. Calinescu, R., Mirandola, R., Perez-Palacin, D., Weyns, D.: Understanding uncertainty in self-adaptive systems. In: International Conference on Autonomic Computing and Self-Organizing Systems, pp. 242–251. IEEE (2020)
16. Solano, G.F., Caldas, R.D., Rodrigues, G.N., Vogel, T., Pelliccione, P.: Taming uncertainty in the assurance process of self-adaptive systems: a goal-oriented approach. In: 14th Intl. Symposium on Softw. Eng. for Adaptive and Self-Managing Systems, pp. 89–99. IEEE/ACM (2019)

Architecting Federated Learning Systems: A Requirement-Driven Approach

Luciano Baresi, Livia Lestingi(✉), and Iyad Wehbe

Politecnico di Milano, Piazza Leonardo Da Vinci 32, Milan 20133, Italy
{luciano.baresi,livia.lestingi,iyad.wehbe}@polimi.it

Abstract. The emerging Federated Learning (FL) paradigm offers significant advantages over the traditional centralized architecture of machine learning (ML) systems by reducing privacy risks and distributing computational load. However, the network topology (i.e., the number of available clients and their characteristics) has a critical impact on performance metrics. This work investigates how application-specific requirements can drive architectural choices and how such choices impact FL performance. Specifically, we present a requirement-driven reference architecture for FL applications. Using a standard benchmark, we empirically evaluate 20 architecture realizations under different boundary conditions. The effectiveness of each realization is assessed on the basis of the accuracy of the trained model and the wall clock time required to complete the training. By combining our experimental results with existing qualitative studies from the literature, we devise a guideline to help prospective users select the most suitable configuration based on their application-specific non-functional requirements.

Keywords: Federated Learning Architecture · Performance Analysis · Requirement-driven Design

1 Introduction

In Federated Learning (FL), unlike traditional centralized solutions, Machine Learning (ML) models are trained in a decentralized fashion on several *client* devices with a *server* acting as orchestrator and aggregator [15]. Figure 1 provides an overview of the FL process. Training occurs in rounds. At the beginning of a round, the server shares the global model parameters with clients to retrain fragments of the model locally. When training ends, the clients return the parameters of the model trained locally to the server. The server aggregates the local parameters, then updates and evaluates the global model. Learning terminates either when a fixed number of rounds is performed or when the global model fulfills set performance requirements, like a target level of accuracy.

FL exhibits significant advantages with respect to centralized training in terms of reducing the risk of privacy breaches and computation costs. Data used for training are only stored locally on clients and never shared with the server,

V. Andrikopoulos et al. (Eds.): ECSA 2025, LNCS 15929, pp. 224–239, 2026.
https://doi.org/10.1007/978-3-032-02138-0_15

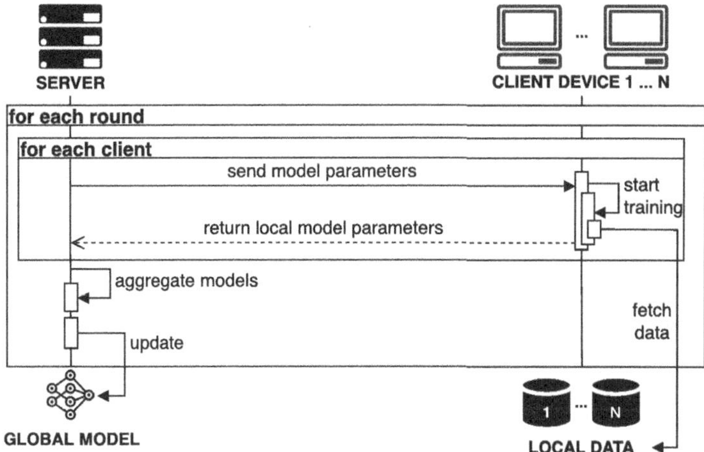

Fig. 1. Overview of the FL process.

which only has visibility over the model parameters. By doing so, the risk of data leaks is significantly reduced. Moreover, FL dilutes the computational load of training between clients rather than concentrating it on a single machine.

On the other hand, FL performance varies significantly with different setups (e.g., the number of clients and respective parameters for local training) and different boundary conditions, such as an unstable network slowing down communication between the server and the clients [9]. Another major challenge of FL applications comes from the management of data heterogeneity, that is, non-Identically Independently Distributed (IID training data from diverse and geographically distributed devices [1,9]. Moreover, previous studies show that, when selecting the set of active nodes for each round, while random selection remains a widely used solution, more sophisticated selection strategies can significantly improve performance [17]. Since nodes can be heterogeneous and provide different resources, hyperparameters defining the workload assigned to each node in each round must be tuned through configuration strategies.

The impact of architectural choices on FL performance has received little investigation in the literature, consisting mainly of qualitative studies [5,11,12]. This paper presents a reference architecture for FL that incorporates both node selection and configuration strategies. Specifically, we expand on this line of work with an empirical study of the cost effectiveness of all combinations of five state-of-the-art node selection strategies and four node configuration strategies under two different boundary conditions for a total of 40 evaluated settings.

Existing node selection and configuration algorithms are essentially driven by three factors: the characteristics of the local dataset, the loss function of the local model, and the training time on the clients [13]. The five selection and four configuration strategies selected for this study are such that the resulting analysis covers all factors. Concerning performance metrics, we rely on the accuracy of the global model at the end of each round and the wall-clock time necessary to complete a set number of rounds, which provides an overview of the cost-effectiveness of a FL solution.

The proposed architecture is structured to decouple the choice of the selection strategy from that of the configuration strategy and to have user-specified non-functional requirements drive both choices. By combining the qualitative analysis results available in the literature and the empirical results presented in this work, we outline some guidelines for prospective FL users to tailor their solution to the requirements of their specific application.

The paper is structured as follows. Section 2 outlines the preliminary concepts underlying the work, Sect. 3 presents the devised architectural solution, Sect. 4 reports on the empirical validation campaign, Sect. 5 surveys related work and Sect. 6 concludes the paper.

2 Preliminaries

The following section outlines the node selection and configuration strategies employed in our study. Specifically, we consider five strategies for dynamic node selection: *FedAvg*, *Dynamic Sampling*, and three variants of power-of-choice, *pow-d*, *cpow-d*, and *rpow-d*. We then consider four workload assigning techniques: *static*, *uniform*, Round Time (RT), and Equal Computation Time (ECT).

All strategies assume that N nodes are available in total and that FL terminates after a set number R of rounds. The subset of nodes selected for a round $i = 1 \dots R$ is referred to as $N_i \subseteq N$, where $|N_i|/N$ is the *sampling rate*. The local dataset of a node $k = 1 \dots |N_i|$ in round i is referred to as $D_{k,i}$ and has size $s_{k,i}$. Let $s = \sum_{k=1}^{|N_i|} s_{k,i}$ be the size of all the data used for the training in round i, $p_{k,i} = s_{k,i}/s$ is the fraction of the data assigned to node k in round i. The weights resulting from the training round i at node k are indicated as w_k^i (w^i indicates the aggregated parameters of the global model after round i).

2.1 Node Selection Strategies

Node selection strategies determine set N_i for each round. Our analysis covers FedAvg (the de-facto standard baseline, which is data-based), Dynamic Sampling (time-based), and three variants of Power of choice (loss-based).

In FedAvg, the training fraction of the nodes $|N_i|/N$ selected at each round is fixed and remains constant throughout the training [15]. At the end of a round, the server aggregates the parameters using a simple average weighted on the fraction of local data ($w^{i+1} = \sum_{k=1}^{|N_i|} p_{k,i} w_k^i$ holds).

In Dynamic Sampling, the subset of nodes $|N_i|/N$ selected in each round changes as learning progresses [7]. The technique exploits the fact that the accuracy of the global model tends to increase at each round, thus fewer nodes are necessary further down the line compared to at the beginning of the training. The sampling rate decreases with *decay coefficient* β ($|N_i| = |N_1|/e^{\beta i}$ holds).

For each node k and each round i of local training, the loss function $F(w_k^t)$ provides a performance metric complementary to precision (the best nodes to be chosen have the highest loss). Power-of-choice dynamically samples nodes based on their local losses to minimize global loss and achieve faster convergence by prioritizing those with a higher loss [3]. At the beginning of round $i + 1$, the server selects a set of candidate nodes with probability proportional to their $p_{k,i}$ (nodes with a larger dataset are more likely to be selected), evaluates their losses $F(w_k^i)$, and selects the active set with the nodes that perform best.

We analyze three variants of power-of-choice. Pow-d—the base variant—computes losses using the entire training dataset, entailing higher computational and communication costs. Cpow-d builds on the base variant by calculating losses in batches of the training dataset. Rpow-d skips the initial sampling by calculating the cumulative average loss through local iterations. For nodes that have never been selected, the values are set to ∞.

2.2 Node Configuration Strategies

Before starting a training round, configuration strategies tune the workload assigned to each node k in N_i, which is determined by hyperparameters such as the number of epochs $E_{k,i}$, the batch size $B_{k,i}$, and the fraction of samples $r_{k,i}$.

Configuration *Static* simply considers predetermined values, regardless of the characteristics of the nodes. Configuration *Uniform* slightly refines this by sampling parameters from preset uniform distributions, which can be configured to account for workload heterogeneity. Configuration *RT* assigns parameters proportionally to the computation power of each node, measured in iterations per second (IPS and indicated as IPS_k. ECT configuration assigns parameters based on IPS_k and a desired computation time T, specifically the epochs are calculated as $T \cdot IPS_k \cdot B/s_k \cdot r$, where B and r can be set to default values.

3 Requirement-Driven FL Architecture

The devised FL architecture, represented in Fig. 2, features three subsystems with several components that realize FL applications that adjust the configuration of the client network based on application-specific requirements round-by-round. The proposed solution expands on the well-established reference architecture presented by Lo et al. [11].

The three subsystems, **Server**, **Client**, and **Data Collector** are detailed in the following sections. Note that the original architecture in [11] also features a subsystem that deals with deploying the resulting global model at its target destination. Although essential in putting the trained model to use, the contributions of this work do not impact the deployment phase, which is, therefore, left out of the presentation for the sake of conciseness.

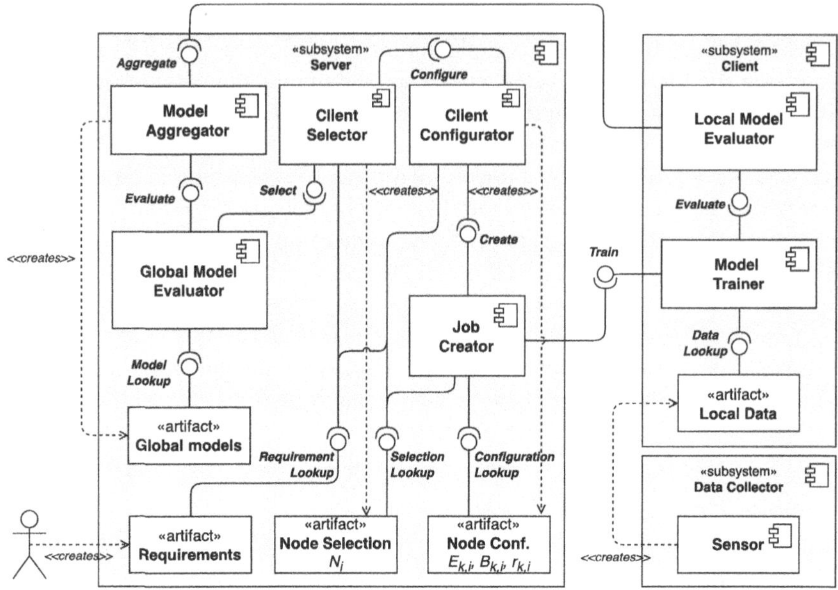

Fig. 2. Component Diagram of the proposed architectural solution.

Server. The **Server** subsystem is the core of the FL process, acting as both an aggregator and an orchestrator. It is responsible for managing the training cycle by selecting clients, configuring workloads, aggregating model updates, and evaluating performance.

According to Fig. 1, when local training ends, **Server** receives the parameters of the models trained by the clients. **Model Aggregator** applies a federated optimization technique, such as FedAvg, FedProx, or other aggregation mechanisms [16], to compute the global model for the next training round (stored and maintained as an artifact). This aggregation process ensures that knowledge is effectively distilled from distributed clients without requiring direct access to their raw data, preserving privacy. **Global Model Evaluator** then retrieves the newly created global model and evaluates it against a validation dataset.

A defining characteristic of this architecture is its ability to integrate user-specified requirements into the FL process. These requirements, stored as artifacts and retrieved through the *Requirement Lookup* interface, serve as a guide for multiple operational decisions. In its current stage of development, we assume that the requirements are established and specified by the prospective FL user and provided to the architecture as artifacts. Investigating the trade-offs among the different notations and languages available to express such requirements is currently out of the scope of this work.

Global Model Evaluator retrieves the user-specified requirements to look up the termination criterion and determine whether a new round of training is necessary. If the termination criterion is not met, the setup of the new round begins. Firstly, **Client Selector**, like the homonymous pattern [12], determines and stores the subset of nodes N_i for the new round through a selection strategy. Among the available options (see Sect. 2.1), **Client Selector** chooses the selection strategy that best fits the specific requirements.

The selection is strategically informed by the user-defined requirements, specifically the desired quality metrics of the FL application driving the requirement formulation. For example, a primary concern with metric "model performance" can be expressed as a non-functional requirement of the form "the resulting global model must have accuracy greater than a certain threshold". The considered quality metrics, listed in the following, are a subset of those considered in the study by Lo et al. [12] resulting from a systematic literature review of 231 papers on FL and 24 real-world applications:

- *Model Performance*: Accuracy of the resulting global model.
- *Scalability*: Capability of the system to maintain stable performance consistently even with an increasing number of clients.
- *Statistical Heterogeneity*: Differences in data distribution and quality among the clients.
- *System Heterogeneity*: Differences in computing, communication, and energy resources among the clients.
- *Accountability and Reliability*: Capability of the system to maintain stable performance even in the light of unexpected changes in its operating conditions and to keep its progress traceable by stakeholders.
- *Communication Efficiency*: Capability of the system to minimize communication costs and network overhead due to server-client interactions.
- *Computation Efficiency*: Capability of the system to minimize the computational power required to complete the training.

A possible guideline mapping requirements to selection strategies that this component can embed is a contribution of this work.

Once set N_i has been chosen, **Client Configurator** adjusts the workload of each node through a configuration strategy (see Sect. 2.2). The selection of the most suitable configuration strategy also derives from requirements and yields parameters $E_{k,i}$, $B_{k,i}$, $r_{k,i}$ for each node k in N_i. Note that the so-devised architecture supports the use of a different selection or configuration strategy for different rounds should requirements change while the training progresses.

Finally, **Job Creator** initiates the training job for each client according to the latest set of selected nodes and hyperparameters.

Client. Upon receiving the job from *Job Creator*, each client in the set N_i begins the training process locally through **Model Trainer** according to the set hyperparameters. To this end, the component retrieves the data collected for training, which, according to the core concept of FL, is stored locally on the client. When the problem at hand involves *multi-task* machine learning (for example, classifying language and spam-related features when training a spam filter), previous studies show that a multi-task **Model Trainer** leads to better performance in FL when non-IID data are present [2,8].

Table 1. Parameters selected for the experiments. Where both a default value and a range are reported, the latter is used by node configuration strategies involving sampling, such as uniform configuration.

Component	Description	Symbol	Default Value	Range
Node Selector	Total nodes	N	10	-
	Sampling rate	$\|N_i\|/N$	0.9	-
	Decay coefficient	β	0.1	-
Node Configurator	Epochs	$E_{k,i}$	4	$[1, 5]$
	Batch size	$B_{k,i}$	32	$[32, 128]$
	Fraction of samples	$r_{k,i}$	1.0	$[0.1, 0.8]$
	Desired computation time	T	30s	-
Job Creator	Model	-	CNN	-
	Training Dataset	-	cifar-10	-
	Degree of imbalance	α	$\{0.5, 100.0\}$	-
Model Trainer	Rounds	R	20	-
	Learning rate	η	0.001	-

When training is completed, **Local Model Evaluator** evaluates the performance of the trained model on a test dataset, and then shares the model parameters with the server (specifically, **Model Aggregator** to close the loop). The latter client-to-server communication step might be conditioned to set performance criteria that the model must meet to be shared with the server (otherwise, retraining might be necessary).

Data Collector. This subsystem is responsible for populating the datasets stored locally in each client and is used for training with **Sensor** readings. Given the domain-agnostic nature of the presented architecture, **Data Collector** is represented as a standalone subsystem with respect to *Client* but, when instantiating the architecture, they can be deployed on the same device. For example, an IoT system that receives data from distributed external sensors (which are, however, never shared with the server) and a mobile phone that uses pictures taken through the internal camera.

4 Experimental Validation

This section reports on the experimental campaign carried out to quantitatively assess how different realizations of the reference architecture presented in Sect. 3 impact FL. Specifically, experiments address the following questions:

- **RQ1.** How does each realization of the devised architecture, under different boundary conditions, impact the accuracy of FL-trained models?
- **RQ2.** How long does FL take to complete with the different realizations?

- **RQ3.** How do the different realizations impact the selected quality metrics underlying possible application-specific requirements?

The remainder of the section describes the setup of the experiments, the results obtained and lessons learned, and the threats to the validity and current limitations of this study.

4.1 Design of the Experiments

To address the reported research questions, the proposed architecture is implemented using the Python language. Experiments consist of applying FL with the different architecture realizations under analysis to a standard benchmark problem. The latter involves training a Convolutional Neural Network (CNN) on the cifar-10[1] training dataset, consisting of 10 equivalence classes. FL is performed in a simulation setting relying on the Flower[2] framework. All experiments are performed on a commodity machine equipped with an Apple M3 chip with 10 cores and 24 GB of memory.

The study involves realizations that differ in node selection and configuration strategies, of which, according to Sect. 2, five and four alternatives are considered, respectively. To simulate different boundary conditions depending on factors external to the FL architecture, experiments involve different degrees of training data heterogeneity. We employ the Dirichlet distribution to partition the data and replicate different data distributions [10,18], which is parametric in the degree of imbalance indicated as α. For this study, we use two different values of α (100.0 and 0.5), which correspond to low and high degrees of heterogeneity, respectively. This results in 20 architecture realizations, each evaluated under two different boundary conditions, for a total of 40 settings.

The parameters selected for the experiments are reported in Table 1. The set termination condition is to complete $R = 20$ rounds, which preliminary analyses show to be sufficient, with this benchmark, to reach an accuracy plateau. Local training is performed with a learning rate 0.001. All experiments involve a pool of $N = 10$ clients, of which 9 are selected at each round by selection strategies with a fixed sampling rate. The decay coefficient for dynamic sampling is set to $\beta = 0.1$. Concerning workload configuration, static configurators employ default values 4, 32, and 1.0 for epochs, batch size, and fraction of samples, respectively, while the uniform configurator draws samples from ranges $[1, 5]$, $[32, 128]$, and $[0.1, 0.8]$. ECT is set to have a desired computation time for each node of $T = 30$ s.

For each selected architecture variant, identified by a triple of node selection strategy, configuration strategy, and value of α, we repeat the experiment 5 times, for a total of 5×40 experiments. Repetitions differ for a random seed, resulting in a different partition of the dataset split between the nodes at the beginning of the process, while the other parameters do not change.

Concerning **RQ1**, the performance obtained with each realization is quantified through the accuracy of the global model at the end of the 20th round.

[1] https://www.cs.toronto.edu/~kriz/cifar.html.
[2] https://flower.ai.

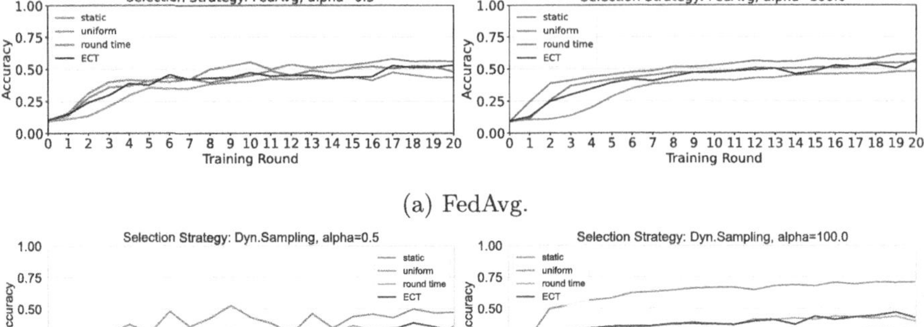

(a) FedAvg.

(b) Dynamic Sampling.

Fig. 3. Accuracy trends for architecture variants with random client selection and Dynamic Sampling (average among the 5 repetitions of each combination).

Specifically, we report the average between the five repetitions of each variant, indicated as $\overline{Acc}$. To address **RQ2**, we report the wall-clock time needed to complete each FL experiment (i.e., from the start to the end of the 20th round). For **RQ3**, we combine the quantitative results obtained with qualitative studies available in the literature to drive the design of the FL architecture solution based on application-specific requirements.

4.2 Results

Results for **RQ1** regarding the obtained performance metrics are reported in Table 2, Fig. 3, and Fig. 4.

Figure 3 and Fig. 4 show the global model accuracy obtained round-by-round for every pair of client selection and configuration strategies, with $\alpha = 0.5$ (plots on the left) and $\alpha = 100.0$ (plots on the right). Specifically, Fig. 3 and Fig. 4 report the average round-by-round accuracy between the 5 repetitions of every solution under analysis. Table 2 reports the confidence interval for the 5 repetitions of all configurations at the end of the 20th round (the final accuracy of the resulting global model). When $\alpha = 100.0$ holds (thus, in a low heterogeneity setting), Dynamic Sampling with a static configuration shows the best performance. Conversely, with non-IID data, pow-d with a static configuration leads to the best performance.

Inspecting the trends in Fig. 3 and Fig. 4, it is evident that, regardless of the configuration, having non-IID data (thus, with $\alpha = 0.5$) slows the convergence of the model training process. However, since it uses a decreasing number of nodes which alters the stability of the process, fluctuations are more prominent with Dynamic Sampling, given that the model is becoming more fragile to the so-called client-drift problem, especially with a static configuration, even though it results in the highest accuracy.

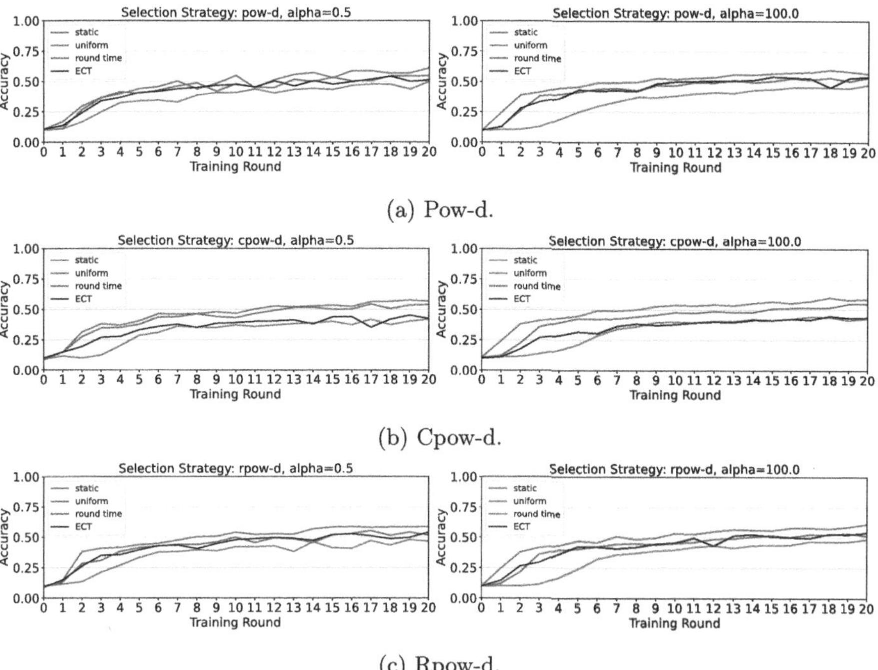

(a) Pow-d.

(b) Cpow-d.

(c) Rpow-d.

Fig. 4. Accuracy trends for architecture variants with power-of-choice selection strategies (average among the 5 repetitions of each solution under analysis).

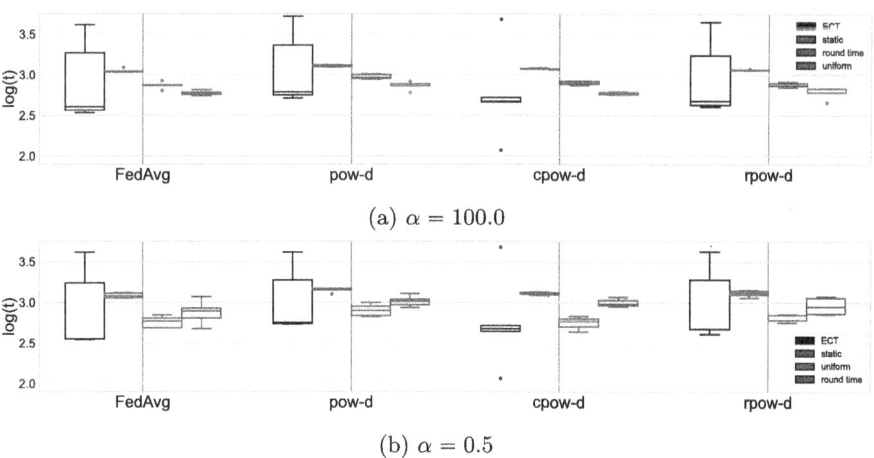

(a) $\alpha = 100.0$

(b) $\alpha = 0.5$

Fig. 5. Wall-clock time distributions ([min] and logarithmic scale) for all configurations under analysis.

Table 2. Values of $\overline{Acc}$ for all considered variants (mean and standard deviation among all repetitions). The best result per row is in bold, while the best result per column (and value of α) is underlined.

		Static	Uniform	RT	ECT
$\alpha = 100.0$	FedAvg	$\mathbf{0.62 \pm 0.02}$	0.48 ± 0.01	0.55 ± 0.01	0.57 ± 0.10
	Dyn. Sampling	$\mathbf{0.71 \pm 0.02}$	0.33 ± 0.02	0.40 ± 0.04	0.42 ± 0.04
	Pow-d	$\mathbf{0.57 \pm 0.04}$	0.48 ± 0.03	0.54 ± 0.03	0.54 ± 0.12
	Cpow-d	$\mathbf{0.59 \pm 0.03}$	0.43 ± 0.03	0.55 ± 0.02	0.44 ± 0.19
	Rpow-d	$\mathbf{0.61 \pm 0.01}$	0.49 ± 0.02	0.52 ± 0.03	0.54 ± 0.08
$\alpha = 0.5$	FedAvg	$\mathbf{0.56 \pm 0.04}$	0.44 ± 0.05	0.48 ± 0.05	0.53 ± 0.10
	Dyn. Sampling	$\mathbf{0.47 \pm 0.10}$	0.29 ± 0.03	0.37 ± 0.04	0.31 ± 0.13
	Pow-d	$\mathbf{0.61 \pm 0.05}$	0.50 ± 0.07	0.55 ± 0.06	0.51 ± 0.13
	Cpow-d	$\mathbf{0.57 \pm 0.03}$	0.42 ± 0.05	0.54 ± 0.03	0.43 ± 0.18
	Rpow-d	$\mathbf{0.59 \pm 0.03}$	0.47 ± 0.04	0.52 ± 0.06	0.54 ± 0.11

Table 3. Time to complete FL ([min]) with all considered variants (mean and standard deviation among all repetitions). The best result per row is in bold, while the best result per column (and value of α) is underlined.

		Static	Uniform	RT	ECT
$\alpha = 100.0$	FedAvg	18.8 ± 1.0	$\mathbf{9.9 \pm 0.6}$	12.3 ± 1.1	23.7 ± 24.5
	Dyn. Sampling	7.1 ± 0.1	$\mathbf{1.9 \pm 0.4}$	5.8 ± 0.2	5.3 ± 0.1
	Pow-d	21.7 ± 0.6	$\mathbf{12.3 \pm 1.3}$	15.9 ± 0.9	30.7 ± 30.3
	Cpow-d	19.8 ± 0.3	$\mathbf{9.9 \pm 0.3}$	13.4 ± 0.7	21.2 ± 29.4
	Rpow-d	19.3 ± 0.3	$\mathbf{10.4 \pm 1.4}$	12.7 ± 0.7	25.1 ± 26.2
$\alpha = 0.5$	FedAvg	20.3 ± 1.3	$\mathbf{9.7 \pm 1.4}$	13.1 ± 3.9	23.0 ± 24.4
	Dyn. Sampling	8.0 ± 1.5	$\mathbf{2.2 \pm 0.4}$	6.3 ± 0.2	6.3 ± 1.2
	Pow-d	23.7 ± 1.4	$\mathbf{13.5 \pm 2.1}$	17.4 ± 2.4	25.5 ± 23.2
	Cpow-d	21.6 ± 1.0	$\mathbf{9.5 \pm 1.7}$	16.9 ± 2.0	21.0 ± 29.2
	Rpow-d	21.8 ± 1.7	$\mathbf{11.1 \pm 1.0}$	15.7 ± 3.3	24.9 ± 24.5

RQ1 summary. Out of the 20 cases under analysis, Dynamic Sampling with a static configuration lead to the best performance with homogeneous data, while pow-d with a static configuration performs best with non-IID data.

Results on **RQ2** on the wall-clock time needed to complete the set FL experiments are reported in Fig. 5 and Table 3. Uniform consistently leads to shorter training times, with the minimum when combined with Dynamic Sampling, both with homogeneous and non-IID data. Finally, except for ECT when combined with random selection or power-of-choice variants, all configurations show a small standard deviation among the repetitions, thus exhibiting limited sensitivity to randomness. ECT explicitly attempts to assign each client a workload consistent with a desired computation time. Any mismatch (caused by differences in random seeds, data distribution, device performance, etc.) can make per-round timing fluctuate more than in strategies that do not aim to equalize times.

> **RQ2 summary.** Dynamic Sampling with a uniform configuration leads to the shortest training time both with homogeneous and non-IID data.

By combining these empirical results with existing studies in the literature, we map the configurations under analysis to the quality metrics in Sect. 3 to address **RQ3**. Specifically, Table 4, for each variant and quality metric, reports whether a positive, negative, or neutral impact is known from the literature or empirically observed in the experimental campaign. The analysis builds on the findings of [12] using a hybrid qualitative and quantitative approach to provide users with a guide to make architectural decisions driven by requirements.

Table 4. Mapping between the considered architecture variants and the quality metrics (building upon [12]): '+' (resp. '−') indicates that the variant positively (resp. negatively) impacts the metric, while an empty cell indicates that the impact is either not known or neutral.

	Model Performance	Scalability	Statistical Heterogeneity	System Heterogeneity	Accountability/ Reliability	Communication Efficiency	Computation Efficiency
FedAvg	−	−	−		+	−	−
Dyn. Sampling	+	+	−		−	+	+
Pow-d	+	−	+		+	−	−
Cpow-d	−	−	−		+	−	−
Rpow-d	−	−	−		+	−	−
Static	+	−	+	−	+		−
Uniform	−	−	−	−	+		+
RT	−	+	−	+	+		−
ECT	−	+	−	+	−		−

The tradeoff analysis resulting from our experimental campaign provides several key insights. First, regarding node selection strategies, Dynamic Sampling emerges as a compelling option when final model performance, as well as communication and computation efficiency, are primary concerns. This is due to the decreasing number of participating nodes as training progresses, which reduces communication overhead and computational requirements. However, Dynamic Sampling also introduces instability in the learning process. Since fewer nodes participate in later rounds, fluctuations in the convergence behavior become more evident, and the final performance may be highly sensitive to the number of training rounds. This variability must be carefully considered when selecting Dynamic Sampling for applications where stability is paramount.

For scenarios requiring accountability, reliability, and robust performance in the presence of non-IID data, power-of-choice variants, particularly pow-d, are preferable. Pow-d actively prioritizes nodes with higher local losses, accelerating convergence and improving global model performance in heterogeneous settings. However, this approach comes at the cost of increased computational and communication overhead, as selecting the most informative nodes requires additional steps compared to simpler strategies like FedAvg. The two modified versions of pow-d, namely cpow-d and rpow-d, exhibit slightly different tradeoffs. While they mitigate some computational inefficiencies, they still incur additional costs. Additionally, all three power-of-choice strategies exhibit reduced scalability due to the extra per-round computations required for loss-based selection.

With respect to configuration strategies, our analysis highlights a clear tradeoff between performance, efficiency, and adaptability. Static configuration results in the best model performance, as it ensures consistency in workload distribution across rounds, allowing for stable convergence. However, it does not account for differences in client resources, making it suboptimal in heterogeneous settings. Similarly, uniform configuration, while improving computational efficiency, does not optimize resource utilization across different nodes. This results in potential inefficiencies when dealing with diverse hardware and network capabilities.

For applications expected to be deployed in heterogeneous environments, RT and ECT constitute a more suitable alternative. RT tunes the workload based on the computational power of each node, ensuring a balanced distribution that maximizes overall system efficiency. This approach enhances scalability and the handling of system heterogeneity. However, it does require additional overhead to profile nodes and assign workloads accordingly. ECT adopts a similar approach but equalizes the computation time across nodes, which can be beneficial in balancing resource utilization but can also introduce variability in convergence rates, potentially leading to reduced accountability. The high variance in computation times may cause instability in the training process, making ECT a less reliable choice for applications requiring strict performance guarantees.

RQ3 summary. The analysis reinforces that, due to the absence of a global optimum, case-specific requirements should underpin the realization of the FL architecture. If stability and accountability are critical, pow-d and RT configurations are preferable, albeit at the cost of increased complexity. If efficiency is the primary concern, Dynamic Sampling combined with uniform configuration provides a streamlined approach with reduced communication and computation overhead. However, for scenarios requiring adaptability to heterogeneous infrastructures, RT and ECT provide the necessary flexibility while maintaining a balanced tradeoff between performance and efficiency.

4.3 Threats to Validity

To mitigate external validity threats and reduce the risk of obtaining results by chance, we repeat our experiments 5 times starting from 40 configurations. Preliminary evaluations show that the selected budget of clients and rounds is sufficient to achieve a plateau in accuracy when training a CNN with dataset cifar-10. However, further analyses with a different budget of clients and rounds and experiment parameters (e.g., different decay coefficients or uniform distribution ranges) are necessary to generalize the findings of this study.

Given the limited sample size (5 samples for each tested configuration), conclusions drawn relying on statistical tests (such as the Mann-Whitney U test [14])—that exhibit limited reliability with small sample sizes—may lack a solid ground. We instead base our conclusions on confidence intervals whose credibility does not change with sample size. Nevertheless, we acknowledge that a deeper study (i.e., with more repetitions) is necessary to properly address the inner randomness of the FL process and more conclusively assess the statistical significance of the described results.

5 Related Work

In recent years, several studies have examined FL from various architectural and methodological angles. This section surveys related work and explains how our work both builds on and extends the current state-of-the-art.

Previous studies analyze the FL paradigm from a software architecture perspective. Zhang et al. [19] compare four alternatives for system architectures of FL: centralized, hierarchical, regional, and decentralized and analyze their communication overhead, model evolution speed, and overall scalability. *FLRA* [11] is a pattern-oriented reference architecture for FL systems. They derive an end-to-end blueprint, covering phases like job creation, model deployment, and monitoring, by synthesizing both academic results and industrial best practices.

Lo et al. [12] and Di Martino et al. [5] build a catalog of architectural patterns tailored to FL ([5] specifically targets the healthcare setting), of which the Client Selector (also in the architecture presented in this work) is an example. Each pattern maps a specific stage in the FL model life cycle, providing a straightforward blueprint for practitioners. However, while their catalog offers important insights, it mainly serves as a reference for recurring design solutions.

Several studies benchmark FL performance under varying circumstances. Li et al. [9] provide a foundational survey on FL, addressing how constraints such as limited on-device resources, non-IID distributions, and user privacy shape the need for novel optimization schemes. Previous work also focuses specifically on node selection strategies [6,13], highlighting selection principles (e.g., data heterogeneity, hardware constraints), scheduling challenges, and research directions.

In summary, foundational studies on FL from a software architecture perspective [11,12] primarily consist of qualitative analyses of foundational literature in combination with industrial case studies. Our work represents a step forward in this area by contributing empirical evidence on how architectural decisions affect FL performance. The most recent contribution in this line of research, by Compagnucci et al. [4], selects, implements, and quantitatively compares four patterns from Lo's catalog [12] using the same benchmark adopted in our study. Their results highlight trade-offs in performance and computational efficiency. Our work complements theirs by focusing on alternative configuration choices for a single pattern—namely, the Client Selector—thus examining the problem at a finer level of granularity. Building on these results, our goal is to offer the community practical guidelines for making architectural decisions in FL systems, grounded in both qualitative insights and empirical evidence.

6 Conclusions

We present a requirement-driven approach to making architectural choices for FL that combines node selection strategies with workload configuration strategies. We empirically validated through experiments involving 20 different architecture variants in presence of uniform or non-IID data. Our findings provide insights into the trade-off between minimizing training time and achieving the highest accuracy induced by the different combinations of node selection and workload configuration strategies. Furthermore, we integrate these insights with existing qualitative studies to derive a possible guideline for FL users to make more informed choices based on their specific requirements.

While laying a foundation for a hybrid quantitative-qualitative approach to support designers, further work is necessary to consolidate the generalizability of the study (e.g., differently sized or more heterogeneous clusters of nodes or different termination conditions). Furthermore, we plan to extend the analysis to a wider range of external sources of uncertainty (e.g., missing nodes in the network due to loss of communication or clients with different privacy needs).

Acknowledgements. This work has been supported by project COBOL (CO mmunity-Based Organized Littering), funded by the MUR under the PRIN 2022 PNRR program (contract nr. P20224K9EK).

Data Availability Statement. All reported results and the code used to perform the experiments are available on Zenodo (https://zenodo.org/records/15103611).

References

1. Baresi, L., Dolci, T., Wehbe, I.: On assessing heterogeneity management solutions in federated learning systems. In: International Conference on Utility and Cloud Computing, pp. 517–522. IEEE (2024)
2. Caruana, R.: Multitask learning. Mach. Learn. **28**, 41–75 (1997)
3. Cho, Y.J., Wang, J., Joshi, G.: Towards understanding biased client selection in federated learning. In: International Conference on Artificial Intelligence and Statistics, pp. 10351–10375. PMLR (2022)
4. Compagnucci, I., Pinciroli, R., Trubiani, C.: Performance analysis of architectural patterns for federated learning systems. In: International Conference on Software Architecture. IEEE (2025)
5. Di Martino, B., Di Sivo, D., Esposito, A.: Architectural patterns for software design problem-solving in the implementation of federated learning structures within the e-health sector. In: Barolli, L. (ed.) Advanced Information Networking and Applications, pp. 347–356. Springer, Cham (2024). https://doi.org/10.1007/978-3-031-57931-8_34

6. Fu, L., Zhang, H., Gao, G., Zhang, M., Liu, X.: Client selection in federated learning: principles, challenges, and opportunities. IEEE Internet Things J. **10**(24), 21811–21819 (2023)
7. Ji, S., Jiang, W., Walid, A., Li, X.: Dynamic sampling and selective masking for communication-efficient federated learning. IEEE Intell. Syst. **37**(2), 27–34 (2021)
8. Kairouz, P., et al.: Advances and open problems in federated learning. Found. Trends® Mach. Learn. **14**(1–2), 1–210 (2021)
9. Li, T., Sahu, A.K., Talwalkar, A., Smith, V.: Federated learning: challenges, methods, and future directions. IEEE Signal Process. Mag. **37**(3), 50–60 (2020)
10. Li, X., Huang, K., Yang, W., Wang, S., Zhang, Z.: On the convergence of FedAvg on non-IID data. arXiv preprint arXiv:1907.02189 (2019)
11. Lo, S.K., Lu, Q., Paik, H.-Y., Zhu, L.: FLRA: a reference architecture for federated learning systems. In: Biffl, S., Navarro, E., Löwe, W., Sirjani, M., Mirandola, R., Weyns, D. (eds.) ECSA 2021. LNCS, vol. 12857, pp. 83–98. Springer, Cham (2021). https://doi.org/10.1007/978-3-030-86044-8_6
12. Lo, S.K., Lu, Q., Zhu, L., Paik, H.Y., Xu, X., Wang, C.: Architectural patterns for the design of federated learning systems. J. Syst. Softw. **191**, 111357 (2022)
13. Mayhoub, S., M. Shami, T.: A review of client selection methods in federated learning. Arch. Comput. Methods Eng. **31**(2), 1129–1152 (2024)
14. McKnight, P.E., Najab, J.: Mann-whitney U test. In: The Corsini Encyclopedia of Psychology, p. 1 (2010)
15. McMahan, B., Moore, E., Ramage, D., Hampson, S., Arcas, B.A.: Communication-efficient learning of deep networks from decentralized data. In: Artificial Intelligence and Statistics, pp. 1273–1282. PMLR (2017)
16. Qi, P., Chiaro, D., Guzzo, A., Ianni, M., Fortino, G., Piccialli, F.: Model aggregation techniques in federated learning: a comprehensive survey. Futur. Gener. Comput. Syst. **150**, 272–293 (2024)
17. Wu, H., Wang, P.: Node selection toward faster convergence for federated learning on non-IID data. IEEE Trans. Netw. Sci. Eng. **9**(5), 3099–3111 (2022)
18. Yu, H., Yang, S., Zhu, S.: Parallel restarted SGD with faster convergence and less communication: demystifying why model averaging works for deep learning. In: Proceedings of the AAAI Conference on Artificial Intelligence, vol. 33, pp. 5693–5700 (2019)
19. Zhang, H., Bosch, J., Olsson, H.H.: Federated learning systems: architecture alternatives. In: Asia-Pacific Software Engineering Conference (APSEC), pp. 385–394. IEEE (2020)

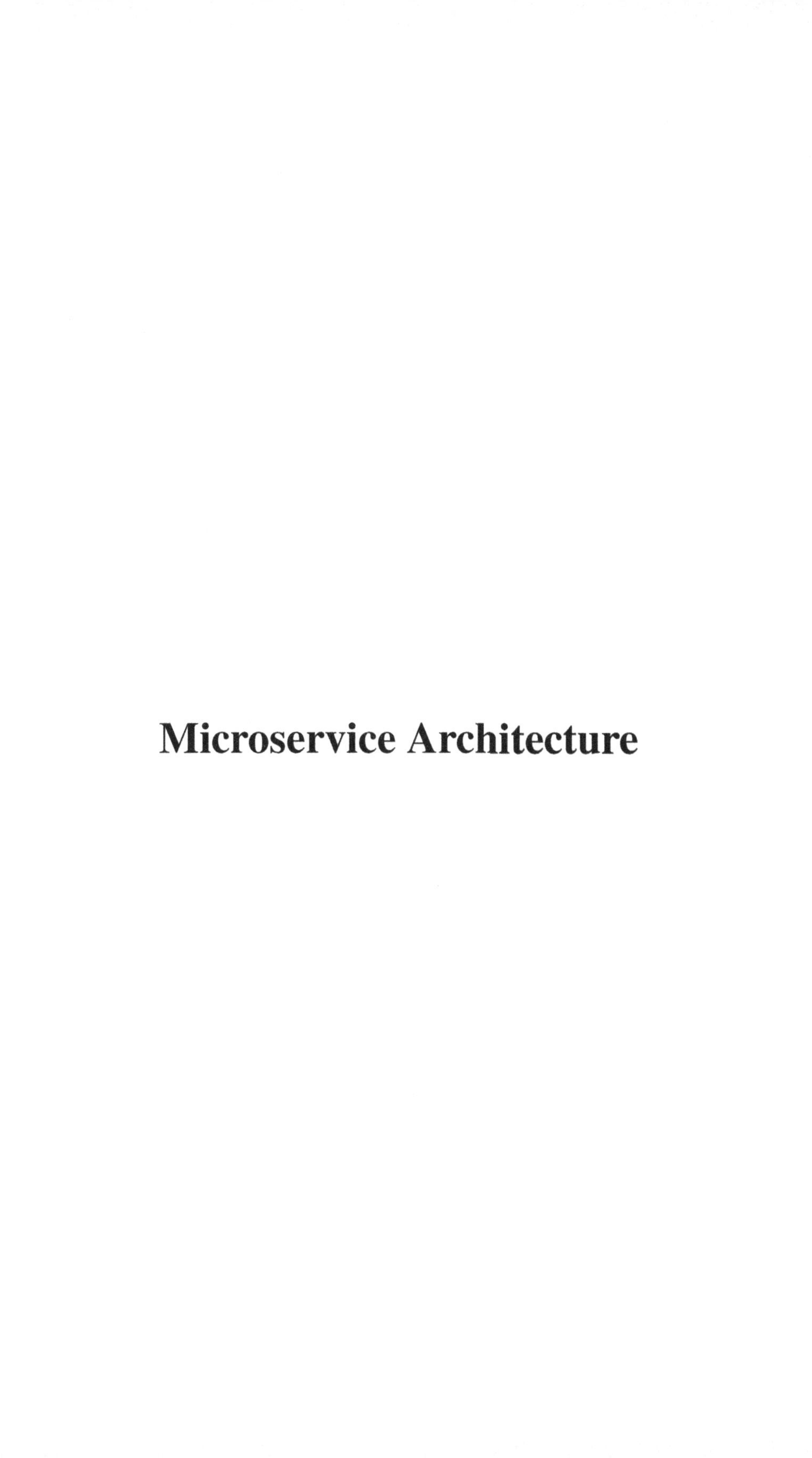

Microservice Architecture

Centrality Change Proneness: An Early Indicator of Microservice Architectural Degradation

Alexander Bakhtin(✉), Matteo Esposito, Valentina Lenarduzzi, and Davide Taibi

University of Oulu, Oulu, Finland
{alexander.bakhtin,matteo.esposito, valentina.lenarduzzi,davide.taibi}@oulu.fi

Abstract. Over the past decade, the wide adoption of Microservice Architecture has required the identification of various patterns and anti-patterns to prevent Microservice Architectural Degradation. Frequently, the systems are modelled as a network of connected services. Recently, the study of temporal networks has emerged as a way to describe and analyze evolving networks. Previous research has explored how software metrics such as size, complexity, and quality are related to microservice centrality in the architectural network. This study investigates whether *temporal* centrality metrics can provide insight into the early detection of architectural degradation by correlating or affecting software metrics. We reconstructed the architecture of 7 releases of an OSS microservice project with 42 services. For every service in every release, we computed the software and centrality metrics. From one of the latter, we derived a new metric, Centrality Change Proneness. We then explored the correlation between the metrics. We identified 7 size and 5 complexity metrics that have a consistent correlation with centrality, while Centrality Change Proneness did not affect the software metrics, thus providing yet another perspective and an early indicator of microservice architectural degradation.

Keywords: Microservices · Centrality · Temporal networks · Architectural Smells

1 Introduction

Over the past decade, the adoption of Microservice Architecture (MSA) has led to the identification of various architectural patterns and anti-patterns to prevent Microservice Architectural Degradation (MAD) [4,24]. Detecting such anti-patterns often involves modelling the microservice system (MSS) as a network of connected services [2]. Recently, Bakhtin et al. [5] proposed to consider network centrality as a new perspective on MSA since they found the centrality

V. Andrikopoulos et al. (Eds.): ECSA 2025, LNCS 15929, pp. 243–259, 2026.
https://doi.org/10.1007/978-3-032-02138-0_16

metrics to not be correlated with Software Metrics (SMs) such as size, complexity, and quality. However, they only analyzed one most recent version of the studied systems and MSA networks, without considering the data *temporally*.

In the field of network science, the study of temporal networks (TNs) has gained traction as a powerful way to model and analyze networks that evolve [29]. Such approaches can extend traditional centrality metrics into the temporal dimension, resulting in *temporal* centrality metrics (TCs, [17,20,29,33]). Such a temporal perspective has also sparked interest in software engineering research. For instance, Saarimäki et al. [25] highlight the importance of incorporating time as a critical yet underexplored dimension in software analysis.

Therefore, leveraging the promising results obtained by Bakhtin et al. [5], we extended their study by reconstructing the architecture and calculating SMs and TCs for seven releases of *train-ticket* OSS MSS benchmark. In this work, we studied the correlation of TCs and SMs temporally, as well as the ability of TC to affect SMs. Our results provided the following insights:

- we identified 7 size and 5 complexity metrics that have a consistent and strong correlation with TCs,
- we defined the Centrality Change Proneness (CCP) based on an existing TC, and
- CCP rank does not affect the SMs and thus offers a completely new perspective on the MSA and an early indicator for MAD.

Our results offer an example of using temporal centrality to track architectural trends in MSA. For practitioners, we introduce the CCP score as a means to identify potentially problematic services early. For researchers, our findings suggest exploring the relationship between code complexity and MSA, as well as investigating how centrality metrics can be leveraged to detect architectural anti-patterns such as Nano, Hublike, and Mega services.

Paper Structure: Section 2 summarizes the related works, Sect. 3 presents the Study Design, Sect. 4 presents the results of the emprical study and Sect. 5 provides a discussion of the outcomes, while Sect. 6 address the Threats to Validity of the study and Sect. 7 concludes the work. Additionally, the Online Appendix [6] contains the extended theoretical background of this work.

2 Related Work

Recent research endeavours have applied networks for the assessment of MSA and detection of MAD. For instance, Bakhtin et al. [4] carried out a literature review to identify which Microservice API patterns can be detected leveraging several techniques, including call graphs of the MSS. al Maruf et al. [2] used traces from Istio[1] service mesh to reconstruct the architecture of the *train-ticket* MSS and perform pattern and anti-pattern detection. Brandon et al. [9] also aggregated microservice communication obtained through dynamic analysis into

[1] https://istio.io/.

static networks and used network similarity measures to group the networks into correct and anomalous ones to perform root cause analysis. Chakraborty et al. [12] proposed to use instance-level monitoring data to build a causal graph of service monitoring metrics enriched by information about the system architecture.

Most applications of TNs to MSA currently rely on monitoring or tracing data obtained through dynamic analysis. For example, Angelo and Orazio [21] proposed a Kubernetes scheduler that takes into account among other things the dynamic TN of microservice communications to improve cluster allocation. Xu et al. [32] built a neural network that uses a TN of microservice traces as input to forecast system states. Chen et al. [13] defined a neural network with similar input to perform anomaly detection. Sun et al. [28] leveraged graph autoencoders to extract the architectural information from the TN of traces to perform root cause analysis. To our knowledge, this work is the first attempt to apply TNs to statically reconstructed microservice networks in the context of MAD.

Abufouda and Abukwaik [1] argued for properly adopting temporal network methods in Empirical Software Engineering. However, their review focused only on applications of TNs for developer collaboration networks as in, e.g., the work by Bakhtin et al. [8].

3 Empirical Study Design

We designed and conducted this empirical study following the guidelines by Wohlin et al. [31].

3.1 Goal, Research Questions, and Hypotheses

The **goal** of our study is to analyze how the **temporal centrality** of microservices *correlates* with software metrics such as size, complexity, and quality, and whether the **derived CCP score** *can affect* those metrics.

Therefore, we defined two **Research Questions (RQs)**:

> **RQ$_1$** Does microservice temporal centrality correlate with size, complexity, or quality metrics?

Since architectural degradation is, by definition, a temporal phenomenon, we are interested to see if the presence or lack of correlation is observed throughout the development process in the different releases of the system and describe the related trends. Previously, Bakhtin et al. [5] analyzed the correlation of size, complexity, and quality metrics with network centrality metrics across 24 MSS projects. They found that there is seldom a correlation between software and centrality metrics. However, the authors considered only one network snapshot per system and did not look into the temporal evolution of centrality. Thus, we aim to leverage *temporal* centrality metrics designed specifically for evolving networks [17,20,29,33]. Formally, to answer this research question, we conjecture and test the following **null** and **alternative** hypotheses:

$\boldsymbol{H}_{01}$ *There is no correlation between microservice temporal centrality and size metrics.*
$\boldsymbol{H}_{02}$ *There is no correlation between microservice temporal centrality and its code complexity.*
$\boldsymbol{H}_{03}$ *There is no correlation between microservice temporal centrality and quality metrics.*
$\boldsymbol{H}_{11}$ *Microservice temporal centrality and size metrics are correlated.*
$\boldsymbol{H}_{12}$ *Microservice temporal centrality and code complexity are correlated.*
$\boldsymbol{H}_{13}$ *Microservice temporal centrality and quality metrics are correlated.*

Apart from providing time-wise centrality metrics, one novel aspect that only temporal centrality analysis can provide is a score that indicates how likely a node is to vary its centrality in the temporal network based on historical observations. Taylor et al. [29] defined it as the First-Order Mover score (FOM).

We propose the **Centrality Change Proneness (CCP)** rank, which is obtained from the FOM score by assigning to each quartile of the FOM score a value on the ordinal scale `LOW`, `MEDIUM-LOW`, `MEDIUM-HIGH`, `HIGH`. To analyze this newly proposed rank in the context of MAD, we formulate:

RQ$_2$ Can the microservice Centrality Change Proneness affect size, complexity, or quality metrics?

Taylor et al. [29], who defined the FOM score, proposed to use it to rank the nodes in a temporal network. We hypothesize that observing the CCP rank of microservices can help identify negative (or positive) trends in the service's architecture, composition, or quality that contribute to MAD. Taylor et al. [29] analyzed TNs of university exchange in mathematics. The authors observed that Georgia Tech University had a high FOM score, and indeed, its centrality increased from 1965 to 1975. Using knowledge about the historical period represented by the network, the authors note that this university is known to have invested heavily in mathematical research during that period.

Formally, to assess the capabilities of CCP to affect the variance of the size, complexity, and quality metrics, we pose the following **null** and **alternative** hypotheses:

$\boldsymbol{H}_{04}$ *CCP of a microservice does not affect size metrics.*
$\boldsymbol{H}_{05}$ *CCP of a microservice does not affect complexity metrics.*
$\boldsymbol{H}_{06}$ *CCP of a microservice does not affect quality metrics.*
$\boldsymbol{H}_{07}$ *FOM score of a microservice does not correlate with the other temporal centrality metrics.*
$\boldsymbol{H}_{14}$ *CCP affects the size metrics with statistical significance.*
$\boldsymbol{H}_{15}$ *CCP affects complexity metrics with statistical significance.*
$\boldsymbol{H}_{16}$ *CCP affects quality metrics with statistical significance.*
$\boldsymbol{H}_{17}$ *FOM score of a microservice is correlated with the other temporal centrality metrics.*

3.2 Project Selection and Data Collection

In this section, we adopt the procedures and replication package from Bakhtin et al. [5] for data collection.

(1) Project selection. Bakhtin et al. [5] recently compiled a dataset of OSS MSS projects suitable for network analysis by reconstructing their architectures. From 125 GitHub Java Spring repositories, only 24 yielded reasonably complete architectures using the *Code2DFD* tool [26]. We focus on these 24 projects and examine their version and release history to identify candidates for temporal architectural analysis. Based on commit history, number of services, and discovered connections, we noticed that the *train-ticket* project [34][2] shows significant structural evolution [7]. From release `v0.0.1` to `v0.0.2`, developers removed the Register, Login, and SSO services, replacing them with User and Auth services. Between `v0.2.0` and `v1.0.0`, food-related services were restructured. This level of architectural change made *train-ticket* a suitable subject for temporal analysis. According to changelogs of other MSS from the dataset, updates were limited to dependencies or libraries and not architecture. Observing the architectural networks of these projects in different releases, we noticed that they are identical and thus unsuitable for temporal network analysis. Therefore, we selected *train-ticket* and analyzed its seven published releases.

(2) Reconstructing the Architecture and Temporal Network. Using the exact version of the *Code2DFD* tool [26] as in [5], we reconstructed and examined the architecture of each published release of *train-ticket* and merged them into a single TN capturing microservice interactions over time. Consistent with [5], we applied the same preprocessing steps:

(2.1) Retain only the largest weakly connected component. Due to false negatives in connection detection, reconstructed networks may contain unconnected components. We keep only the largest weakly connected component[3].

(2.2) Remove databases connected to a single service. Database nodes (e.g., `mysql`, `mongo`) represent infrastructure, not architecture, and typically have low centrality. Since their code is not part of the repository, we exclude any such database node connected to only one service, filtering out elements that follow the *one database per microservice* pattern[4,5] and avoid skewing the analysis.

(3) Computing Temporal Centrality. To consider the centrality in the temporal perspective, we selected four algorithms (more details in the Online Appendix [6]) as follows: Taylor et al. [29] (Taylor algorithm) extended the eigenvector centrality measure of a static network into the temporal domain by constructing a *supra-centrality matrix* of a temporal network by utilizing *centrality matrices* of the network snapshots and *inter-layer coupling* of nodes across

[2] https://github.com/FudanSELab/train-ticket/.

[3] https://mathworld.wolfram.com/WeaklyConnectedDigraph.html.

[4] https://www.baeldung.com/cs/microservices-db-design.

[5] https://microservices.io/patterns/data/database-per-service.html.

snapshots; Yin et al. [33] (Yin algorithm) modified the Taylor algorithm [29] by considering snapshot similarity as the inter-layer coupling measure for nodes; Liu et al. [20] (Liu algorithm) follow a similar approach as Yin et al. [33], but they also used the sum of node degrees to construct centrality matrices; Huang et al. [17] (Huang algorithm) modified the Taylor algorithm [29] by fitting an ARMA model (Auto-regressive Moving Average, [16]) to sequences of nodes' degrees to determine inter-layer coupling.

We implemented these algorithms in Python using the *numpy* library. Each algorithm produces several centrality metrics offering different perspectives: Joint, Conditional, Marginal Layer, and Marginal Node centralities. In addition, the Taylor algorithm provides the Time-Averaged Centrality and First-Order Mover (FOM) score, resulting in a total of 18 centrality metrics. Since the FOM score is computed over the entire temporal network (TN) and does not yield a time series, we extended the analysis by recalculating the FOM score and the corresponding CCP rank for each release. We accumulated the TN until each release, simulating how these metrics would evolve if the system were continuously analyzed throughout development.

(4) Computing Size, Complexity, and Quality Metrics. We retrieved and stored the source code of all seven *train-ticket* releases and run *Understand*, *JaSoMe*, and *SonarQube* tools on each version. Such tools produce metrics at the package level, so we manually mapped each package to its corresponding microservice based on its location in the project's directory structure [5]. This process was repeated for each release to account for structural changes like renaming and refactoring. Since microservices can span multiple packages, we aggregated package-level metrics into service-level ones using `Sum`, `Avg`, and `Max` as appropriate–ratios used only `Avg` and `Max`, while counts used all three. After filtering out incomplete data, our final dataset included 25 *Understand*, 55 *JaSoMe*, 19 *SonarQube*, and 18 temporal centrality metrics, computed for 43 microservices across 7 *train-ticket* releases–forming the basis for our analysis.

3.3 Data Analysis

In this section, we use the computed temporal centrality metrics from the architectural TN reconstructed with *Code2DFD*, size metrics from *Understand* and *JaSoMe*, complexity metrics from *JaSoMe* and *SonarQube*, and quality metrics from *SonarQube* tools for our analysis.

As described in Sect. 3.2, we aggregated package-level metrics to the service level using `Sum` (87 metrics), `Avg` (60), and `Max` (47), bringing the total number of unique software metrics to 196.

Temporal centralities were derived using only three out of four algorithms (Taylor, Liu, and Yin). We excluded the Huang algorithm due to its reliance on time series modelling across snapshots, which was unreliable given only seven snapshots. They are omitted from our analysis, but for completeness, we include them in our replication package [6].

Only a subset of services exhibit significant non-zero centrality metrics (Fig. 1). This is likely due to the small size of the network and the sparsity of its adjacency matrices. Notably, the services with non-zero values are indeed the more connected and central ones. We expect that larger industrial systems would mitigate these limitations. Additionally, as noted in Sect. 3.2, some services were introduced or removed partway through development, affecting their presence in the centrality analysis. Regarding MLC, all three algorithms resulted in a peak at release `v0.0.4` (Fig. 2), suggesting that services in this snapshot were collectively more central than in other releases.

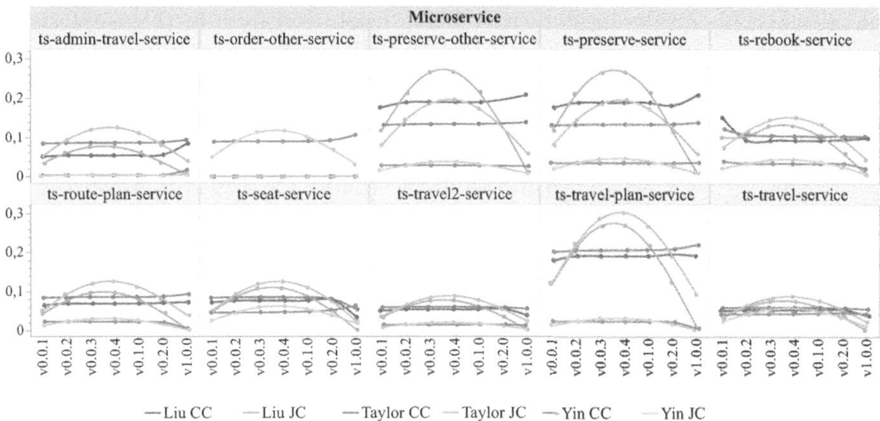

Fig. 1. Microservice Joint and Conditional centrality [29] trajectories as given by the three considered methods [20,29,33] across the releases

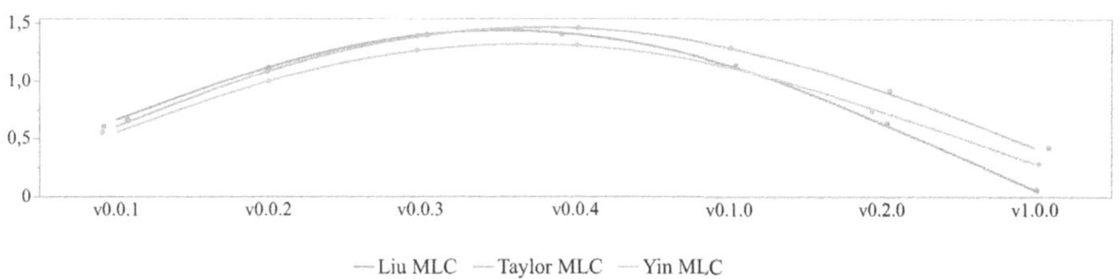

Fig. 2. Sum of the centralities of all microservices (MLC, [29]) for each release of *train-ticket*

Finally, to select the proper statistical test, we must assess the metrics' distribution [15]. To test the normality of the distribution of the data, we posed the following **null** and **alternative** hypotheses:

$\boldsymbol{H}_{0\mathcal{N}}$ The gathered metrics are normally distributed.
$\boldsymbol{H}_{1\mathcal{N}}$ The gathered metrics are *not* normally distributed.

We tested $\boldsymbol{H}_{0\mathcal{N}}$ using Anderson-Darling (AD) test [3]. AD tests whether data points are sampled from a specific probability distribution by evaluating the differences between the cumulative observed distribution and the hypothesized distribution, i.e., in this case, the normal distribution. Since we gathered metrics for seven releases of *train-ticket*, we tested the hypotheses on each metric for each release separately, resulting in 1072 hypothesis tests. We rejected 919 null hypotheses (Table 1), thus asserting that most of the gathered **metrics are not normally distributed**.

We excluded a metric if we could not reject the null hypothesis in at least one release. This results in 50 metrics being **excluded** from further analysis.

Table 1. Counts of rejected null hypotheses for Anderson-Darling Test

	Version	Rejected null hypotheses							Total
		`v0.0.1`	`v0.0.2`	`v0.0.3`	`v0.0.4`	`v0.1.0`	`v0.2.0`	`v1.0.0`	
Metric	Size	55	57	53	54	55	57	61	392
	Complexity	46	48	47	49	50	54	51	345
	Quality	25	27	25	28	28	27	22	182
	Total	126	132	125	131	133	138	134	919

To address $\mathbf{RQ_1}$, since the data do not follow a normal distribution, we choose Spearman's ρ [27] to test the correlation of different SMs with the TCs, instead of Pearson's test, which assumes normally distributed data [23]. The non-parametric test evaluates the monotonic relationship between variables, assessing whether a change in one variable leads to another, either in the same direction (positive correlation) or a different (negative correlation). To interpret ρ values, we adopt Dancey and Reidy's interpretation [14]. We computed the correlation of each SM with each TC in each release, which resulted in 11242 correlation tests. Finally, we adopted a stricter significance threshold of $\alpha = 0.01$ to balance between controlling Type I and Type II errors and maintaining statistical power while testing 11242 correlations. Due to the volume of pairwise correlation tests, the Bonferroni correction would result in a stricter threshold ($\alpha' = \frac{0.05}{11242} = 4.4 \cdot 10^{-6}$), deemed overly conservative for an exploratory study [18] leading to a substantial increase in the likelihood of Type II errors, i.e., potentially obscuring weaker but meaningful correlations.

To address $\mathbf{RQ_2}$, we converted the normalized FOM (Norm(FOM)) score computed for each release to CCP rank by considering the quartiles of the Norm(FOM) score, and we assigned to each microservice a CCP on the ordinal scale `LOW`, `MEDIUM-LOW`, `MEDIUM-HIGH`, `HIGH` based on the corresponding quartile. This provides us with a way to rank nodes that do not depend on a predetermined threshold but on the quartiles of the FOM score specific to each studied system. In our case, the quartiles resulted in values 0.054365, 0.098269, 0.156734, We applied the Wilcoxon signed-rank test (WT, [30]), a non-parametric statistical method designed to compare two related samples of paired data, to test the hypotheses $\boldsymbol{H}_{14}$-$\boldsymbol{H}_{16}$. The WT assigns signs based on the direction of the differences between paired observations and then sums the positive and negative ranks separately. The test statistic is defined as the lowest of the two sums. Similar to Spearman ρ, we use the Wilcoxon test because it does not assume a normal data distribution. In our case, the paired data are the CCP rank and the SMs. Since we tested each SM in each release, we performed 1022 hypothesis tests. To test $\boldsymbol{H}_{17}$, we also computed the Spearman ρ correlation of Norm(FOM) with all the other computed temporal centrality metrics.

Finally, we aimed to perform a time-series analysis of temporal centrality and software metrics. However, due to the small number of releases *train-ticket* has, all applicable time-series methods either failed to converge or converged to null values. We believe such an analysis would be relevant when considering a bigger system with a more extended development history and is one potential direction for future work stemming from the proposed temporal centrality approach.

4 Results

In this Section, we report the results of the empirical study.

4.1 Correlation of Centrality with Software Metrics (RQ$_1$)

We computed the Spearman ρ value for each SM and TC for each release, which provided 11242 hypotheses. We could reject the null hypothesis only in 2434 cases (Table 2). Hence, for the reminder analysis and discussion, we include only those metrics that show a **statistically significant correlation** with **at least one** centrality metric across **all releases** (Sect. 3.3), resulting in the inclusion of only 7 size and 5 complexity metrics, while all quality metrics were excluded.

Table 2. Counts of rejected null hypotheses for Spearman Rho correlation

	Version	Rejected null hypotheses							Total
		`v0.0.1`	`v0.0.2`	`v0.0.3`	`v0.0.4`	`v0.1.0`	`v0.2.0`	`v1.0.0`	
Metric	Size	258	272	267	165	158	114	74	1308
	Complexity	237	216	188	78	78	50	33	880
	Quality	75	42	21	35	29	23	21	246
	Total	570	530	476	278	265	187	128	2434

As for the **size** metrics, we tested a total of 5,159 hypotheses and were able to reject only 1,308 (Table 2). Applying our metric inclusion criterion, only 7 size metrics remained. Among these, all statistically significant correlations are positive and range from moderate to strong in strength (Fig. 3). For such metrics, we examined the trends in Spearman's ρ values across the different releases. We see that the Ratio of Private to Public Methods (RPPM) is not correlated significantly in the first three releases, while `CountStmtExe` (CSE) and `Sum(TLOC)` are not significantly correlated in the last four releases (Fig. 3). `CountDeclClass` (CDC) and `CountDeclMethodPrivate` (CDMP) are consistently positively correlated. Conversely, the first release, `v0.0.1`, differs from the others since it is the Taylor centrality metrics that fail to correlate with most software metrics rather than the other way around. We can conclude that **size metrics** are **not correlated** with temporal centrality.

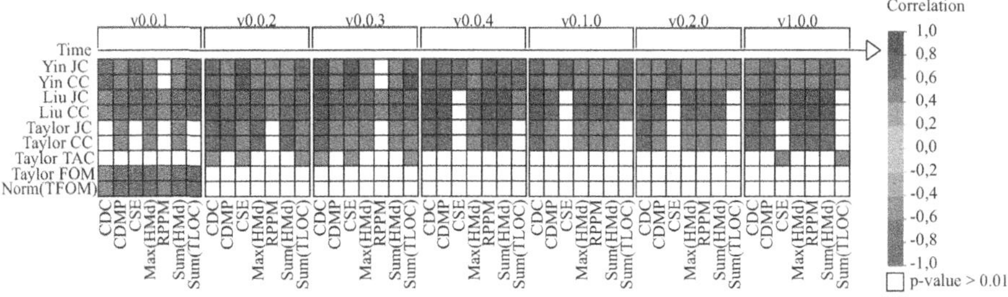

Fig. 3. Heat-map of correlation of microservice temporal centrality with size metrics across the releases

As for the **complexity** metrics, we tested a total of 4312 hypotheses but could only reject 808 (Table 2). We are only left with 5 metrics correlated with at least one centrality consistently (Fig. 4). Most correlations among the selected metrics are positive, while the correlation is strong to perfectly negative for `Max(SIX)` metric. `SIX` is the *specialization index* of the class from *JaSoMe* tool[6], defined as $\frac{DIT*NORM}{NOM}$, where `DIT` is Depth of the Inheritance Tree, `NORM` is Number of Overridden Methods, and `NOM` is the total Number of Methods.

The average of Cognitive Complexity (Avg(CC)) seems to be consistently positively correlated in all releases, while the absolute value of Cognitive Complexity (CC) loses and gains statistical significance intermittently.

We observe that Yin metrics always correlate with all the metrics, while other centralities are mostly not correlated with anything. Looking at the Spearman ρ values trends across the releases, we see that for complexity metrics, almost the same metrics show statistically significant correlations in all releases. The variations in statistical significance across releases are certainly spurious. Given that we could not reject most of the null hypotheses, we conclude that **complexity** metrics are generally **not correlated** with temporal centrality.

As for the **quality** metrics, we tested 1771 hypotheses and rejected only 246. According to our metric inclusion criterion, we could not select any metrics for further analysis and discussion since none were consistently correlated with the same centrality across the releases. We thus conclude that **quality** metrics are **not correlated** with temporal centrality.

[6] https://github.com/rodhilton/jasome/blob/master/README.md.

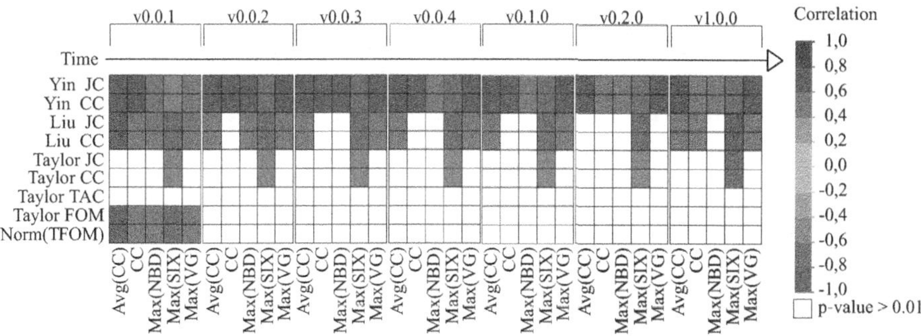

Fig. 4. Heat-map of correlation of microservice temporal centrality with complexity metrics across the releases

Overall, Microservice temporal centrality does ***not*** *correlate with size, complexity, nor quality metrics.*

4.2 Affect of CCP on Software Metrics (RQ$_2$)

As described in Sect. 3.3, we converted the FOM score to the CCP ordinal scale. Figure 5 shows the trajectories of CCP rank across releases for some microservices of *train-ticket* system (same as Fig. 1). We have tested the 1022 hypotheses of the WT and could only reject 71 (Table 3).

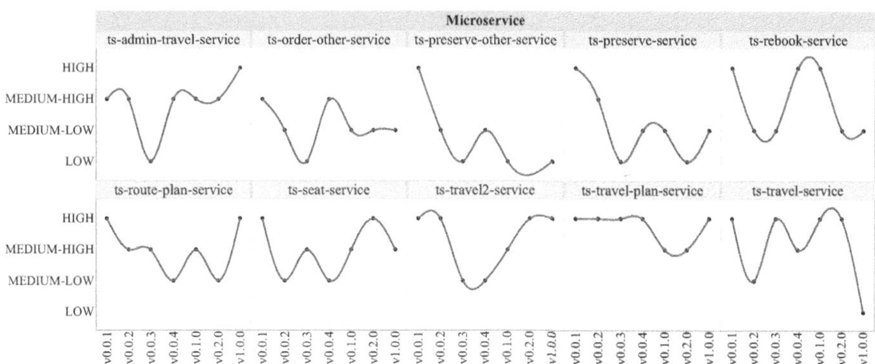

Fig. 5. Trajectories of CCP rank across the releases

We observe that most of the rejected hypotheses correspond to the first release. Notably, there is not a single SM that would be consistently affected by

CCP across all releases. There seems to be a spurious result for one size metric at the latest, seventh release (`Max(NSF)`). Essentially, the FOM and thus CCP scores are *undefined* for the very first release since the analysis performed by Taylor et al. [29] to derive the FOM score does not apply because then the TN consists of only one snapshot. Moreover, TAC and FOM were not correlated with SMs for most releases (RQ1, Figs. 3, 4). We can thus conclude that **CCP rank** does **not affect** the variance of **size, complexity, or quality** metrics as *the project matures.*

Table 3. Counts of rejected null hypotheses for Wilcoxon Test

	Version	Rejected null hypotheses							Total
		`v0.0.1`	`v0.0.2`	`v0.0.3`	`v0.0.4`	`v0.1.0`	`v0.2.0`	`v1.0.0`	
Metric	Size	35	0	0	0	0	0	1	36
	Complexity	28	0	0	0	0	0	0	28
	Quality	7	0	0	0	0	0	0	7
	Total	70	0	0	0	0	0	1	71

As for the correlation of normalized FOM with centrality, we only observed a statistically significant correlation for the first release but not subsequent ones (see Online Appendix [6]). As outlined earlier, FOM at the very first release is technically *undefined*, so we can conclude that overall, the **FOM score** and, thus, **CCP rank** are **not correlated** with **temporal centrality** and thus provide *a new perspective* on the evolution of the microservice architectural network.

All in all, Microservice Centrality Change Proneness does ***not*** *affect size, complexity, nor quality metrics.*

5 Discussion

Observing the trends over time, we notice a decreasing number of rejected correlation hypotheses (Table 2). This suggests that as the architecture matures and stabilizes, its structure and, thus, quality become increasingly decoupled from the properties of the individual microservices. After all, the architecture and its centrality are defined by an abstract graph, independent of the internal implementation of the services. **Consequently, with a stable architecture, each microservice in the MSA can vary in size, complexity, or quality based solely on how it is being developed.** This conclusion aligns with the observations of Shrikanth and Menzies [10] that "early bird" data, i.e., data from only a handful of the earliest commits of a project, has significant predictability for the quality of the project. Furthermore, this corroborates the result of Bakhtin et al. [5], where the authors showed a lack of correlation between centrality and SMs for the *latest* release of several MSS projects. Our temporal analysis shows that this indeed should have been the expected result.

Similarly, comparing the findings of Bakhtin et al. [5] and ours, we observe a strong negative correlation between `Max(SIX)` and centrality metrics in our analysis of complexity metrics. In their study, Bakhtin et al. [5] excluded the `Max(SIX)` aggregation due to its failure in the AD test, but reported that both `Avg(SIX)` and `Sum(SIX)` exhibited statistically significant strong negative correlations with degree centrality. Furthermore, they included additional complexity metrics such as `DIT` and `NORM`, which also showed moderate to strong negative correlations with degree, eigenvector, and closeness centrality scores. This consistent pattern suggests a future research direction - **investigate the relationship between microservices' class inheritance complexity and the quality of the resulting MSA network**, as characterized by centrality and other relevant network measures. However, since `Max(SIX)` reflects only the most complex class within a microservice, future empirical studies should consider aggregations such as `Avg` and `Sum`, which capture complexity across all constituent classes, to see if the most complex class alone or the overall complexity affect the architecture.

Furthermore, our results suggest that the proposed **CCP rank can provide a new perspective on MSA** alongside the temporal centrality trajectories, which would not require a pre-determined threshold. We see that, out of 10 services presented in Fig. 5, *ts-admin-travel-service*, *ts-rebook-service*, *ts-route-plan-service*, *ts-seat-service*, *ts-travel2-service*, *ts-travel-plan-service*, and *ts-travel-service* have their CCP rank as `MEDIUM-HIGH` or `HIGH` for most of the releases, which is corroborated by the fact that in Fig. 1, these services are continuously changing their centrality along a U-shaped curve. We realize that for this data set, the MLC trend of peaking around release `v0.0.4` due to apparent active development at that release overshadows all other trends, so all Joint Centralities also peak at the same release and do not show other trends, while the normalized Conditional Centralities stay mostly flat, indicating a stable architecture consistent with *train-ticket* being a benchmark demo app designed in advance. Release `v0.2.0` seems to be an inflection point, with centralities at the next release `v1.0.0` either rising or falling. This can be explained by the refactoring of food-related services performed while preparing that release. Since both FOM and CCP can be computed from the early releases of a project, and given our observation that centrality becomes increasingly decorrelated from software metrics in later stages, we argue that the **CCP rank can act as an *early degradation indicator* in MSA systems.** A microservice's tendency to significantly change its centrality in the network may indicate shifts in dependency structures, which could stem from flawed architectural decisions or an improper division of responsibilities. For example, as empirically validated by Palomba et al. [22], the presence of code smells can make the software components more change- and fault-prone. This insight is particularly valuable for practitioners as it offers a means to detect potentially problematic services early in the development lifecycle, enabling timely architectural adjustments.

Finally, as suggested by Bakhtin et al. [5], an important future research direction would be to explore how microservice centrality within an MSA, particularly temporal centrality, **can be leveraged to detect architectural anti-patterns** such as Nano, Hublike, or Mega services [11].

6 Threats to Validity

We discuss the threats to the validity of our study, following the guidelines defined by Wohlin et al. [31].

Construct Validity. Our design, including our choice of tools or data filtering, may affect our results. We used existing tools Understand, JaSoMe, and SonarQube for SMs computation with no adjustment. For TCs, we created our implementation of the considered algorithms, which might be subject to human error in understanding or implementing the algorithms. The studied network is small and sparse, which could have resulted in numerical instability and provided many zero values during the computation.

Internal Validity. The selection of projects to be studied can bias our results since we used a single OSS benchmark microservice project. We tried to replicate the process of Bakhtin et al. [5], so we were restricted by the projects they could successfully perform the analysis on. We tried to find all suitable projects for temporal analysis with evolving MSA, but our investigation determined *train-ticket* as the only suitable candidate. We hope that this study can eventually be replicated on a big industrial platform.

External Validity. Mining platforms like GitHub can bias the results, since its user base comprises contributors to open-source projects, potentially skewing findings toward this specific demographic. The focus on OSS constitutes a bias since it may not represent the industrial microservice-based systems since *train-ticket* is a benchmark app developed by researchers but nonetheless adopted widely in empirical studies on MSA. Our data collection process exhibits the same threats as in [5] - imperfect reconstruction with the Code2DFD tool and the necessity to keep only the weak connected component and filter databases.

Conclusion Validity. Some of the used temporal centrality methods connect nodes both to the past and to the future snapshots, thus potentially causing the flow of information in a way that is not causally possible [19,29], affecting our reasoning on centrality trends in MSA. Moreover, we correlated the JC and CC values computed for the temporal network at the latest release, while FOM values were computed incrementally by release.

7 Conclusion

Our work further supports the notion that network centrality provides new insight into microservice architecture [5]. We illustrated that temporal centrality becomes less and less related to software metrics as the MSA matures, indicating that the quality of implementation and architectural structure decorrelate over time and need to be evaluated separately.

For **researchers**, our findings open some promising paths. Future research should investigate whether and how centrality, specifically temporal algorithms, can serve as a smell for MSA anti-pattern detection such as Nano, Hub-like, or Mega services. Furthermore, our findings indicate that it is necessary to better understand the effect of internal code complexity on architectural topology and stability of microservice systems.

For **practitioners**, our proposed *Centrality Change Proneness* (CCP) ranking offers a lightweight, early-warning indicator of architectural volatility. Services that repetitively have high CCP rankings are most likely to undergo centrality changes, uncovering underlying responsibility misalignments or changing dependencies, i.e., a warning sign of architectural anti-patterns at an early point in time [10,22].

Acknowledgments. This work has been funded by the Research Council of Finland (grants n. 359861 and 349488 - MuFAno) and Business Finland (grant 6GSoft).

Data Availability Statement. All the background, scripts, and data used for analysis are available in our Online Appendix [6].

References

1. Abufouda, M., Abukwaik, H.: On using network science in mining developers collaboration in software engineering: a systematic literature review. Int. J. Data Mining Knowl. Manag. Process (IJDKP) **7**(5/6), 17–34 (2017)
2. Al Maruf, A., Bakhtin, A., Cerny, T., Taibi, D.: Using microservice telemetry data for system dynamic analysis. In: 2022 IEEE International Conference on Service-Oriented System Engineering (SOSE), pp. 29–38. IEEE (2022)
3. Anderson, T.W., Darling, D.A.: Asymptotic theory of certain “goodness of fit” criteria based on stochastic processes. Ann. Math. Stat. 193–212 (1952)
4. Bakhtin, A., Al Maruf, A., Cerny, T., Taibi, D.: Survey on tools and techniques detecting microservice API patterns. In: 2022 IEEE International Conference on Services Computing (SCC), pp. 31–38. IEEE (2022)
5. Bakhtin, A., Esposito, M., Lenarduzzi, V., Taibi, D.: Network centrality as a new perspective on microservice architecture. In: 2025 IEEE 22nd International Conference on Software Architecture (ICSA), pp. 72–83 (2025)
6. Bakhtin, A., Esposito, M., Lenarduzzi, V., Taibi, D.: Replication package and online appendix for “centrality change proneness: an early indicator of microservice architectural degradation” (2025). https://doi.org/10.5281/zenodo.15100706
7. Bakhtin, A., Esposito, M., Taibi, D.: Challenges in constructing temporal architecture networks for microservice systems. In: Arctic AI 2024 (2024)
8. Bakhtin, A., Li, X., Taibi, D.: Temporal community detection in developer collaboration networks of microservice projects. In: European Conference on Software Architecture, pp. 174–182. Springer, Cham (2024)

9. Álvaro Brandón, Solé, M., Huélamo, A., Solans, D., Pérez, M.S., Muntés-Mulero, V.: Graph-based root cause analysis for service-oriented and microservice architectures. J. Syst. Softw. **159**, 110432 (2020)
10. Shrikanth, N.C., Menzies, T.: Assessing the early bird heuristic (for predicting project quality). ACM Trans. Softw. Eng. Methodol. **32**(5) (2023)
11. Cerny, T., Abdelfattah, A.S., Al Maruf, A., Janes, A., Taibi, D.: Catalog and detection techniques of microservice anti-patterns and bad smells: a tertiary study. J. Syst. Softw. **206**, 111829 (2023)
12. Chakraborty, S., Garg, S., Agarwal, S., Chauhan, A., Saini, S.K.: Causil: causal graph for instance level microservice data. In: WWW 2023, pp. 2905–2915. Association for Computing Machinery, New York (2023)
13. Chen, J., et al.: Tracegra: a trace-based anomaly detection for microservice using graph deep learning. Comput. Commun. **204**, 109–117 (2023)
14. Dancey, C.: Statistics without maths for psychology. Prentice Hall (2007)
15. Falessi, D., Laureani, S.M., Çarka, J., Esposito, M., Costa, D.A.D.: Enhancing the defectiveness prediction of methods and classes via JIT. Empir. Softw. Eng. **28**(2), 37 (2023)
16. Hannan, E.J., Rissanen, J.: Recursive estimation of mixed autoregressive-moving average order. Biometrika **69**(1), 81–94 (1982)
17. Huang, Q., Zhao, C., Zhang, X., Wang, X., Yi, D.: Centrality measures in temporal networks with time series analysis. EPL (Europhys. Lett.) **118**(3), 36001 (2017)
18. Kim, J.H., Choi, I.: Choosing the level of significance: a decision-theoretic approach. Abacus **57**(1), 27–71 (2021)
19. Kumar, T., Narayanan, M., Ravindran, B.: Effect of inter-layer coupling on multilayer network centrality measures. J. Indian Inst. Sci. **99**(2), 237–246 (2019)
20. Liu, R., Zhang, S., Zhang, D., Zhang, X., Bao, X.: Node importance identification for temporal networks based on optimized supra-adjacency matrix. Entropy **24**(10), 1391 (2022)
21. Marchese, A., Tomarchio, O.: Evaluating microservices communication relationships for scheduling containers on kubernetes clusters. In: van Steen, M., Ferguson, D., Pahl, C. (eds.) CLOSER CLOSER 2022. CCIS, vol. 1845, pp. 45–65. Springer, Cham (2024). https://doi.org/10.1007/978-3-031-68165-3_3
22. Palomba, F., Bavota, G., Penta, M.D., Fasano, F., Oliveto, R., Lucia, A.D.: On the diffuseness and the impact on maintainability of code smells: a large scale empirical investigation. Empir. Softw. Eng. **23**(3), 1188–1221 (2018)
23. Pearson, K.: VII. note on regression and inheritance in the case of two parents. Proc. Roy. Soc. London **58**(347-352), 240–242 (1895)
24. Pigazzini, I., Fontana, F.A., Lenarduzzi, V., Taibi, D.: Towards microservice smells detection. In: Proceedings of the 3rd International Conference on Technical Debt, pp. 92–97 (2020)
25. Saarimäki, N., Moreschini, S., Lomio, F., Penaloza, R., Lenarduzzi, V.: Towards a robust approach to analyze time-dependent data in software engineering. In: 2022 SANER, pp. 36–40. IEEE (2022)
26. Schneider, S., Scandariato, R.: Automatic extraction of security-rich dataflow diagrams for microservice applications written in java. JSS (2023)
27. Spearman, C.: The proof and measurement of association between two things. Am. J. Psychol. **15**(1), 72–101 (1904)
28. Sun, Y., et al.: Interpretable failure localization for microservice systems based on graph autoencoder. ACM Trans. Softw. Eng. Methodol. **34**(2) (2025)

29. Taylor, D., Myers, S.A., Clauset, A., Porter, M.A., Mucha, P.J.: Eigenvector-based centrality measures for temporal networks. Multiscale Model. Simul. **15**(1), 537–574 (2017)
30. Wilcoxon, F.: Individual comparisons by ranking methods. Biom. Bull. **1**(6), 80 (1945)
31. Wohlin, C., Runeson, P., Höst, M., et al.: Experimentation in Software Engineering. Springer (2012)
32. Xu, Y., Ge, J., Tang, H., Ding, S., Li, T., Li, H.: System states forecasting of microservices with dynamic spatio-temporal data arXiv:2408.07894 (2024)
33. Yin, R.R., Guo, Q., Yang, J.N., Liu, J.G.: Inter-layer similarity-based eigenvector centrality measures for temporal networks. Physica A **512**, 165–173 (2018)
34. Zhou, X., Peng, X., Xie, T., Sun, J., Xu, C., Ji, C., Zhao, W.: Benchmarking microservice systems for software engineering research. In: Proceedings of the 40th International Conference on Software Engineering: Companion Proceedings, pp. 323–324 (2018)

A Comparative Analysis of Monolith vs Microservices Energy Consumption

Roberta Capuano(✉), Eoan O'Dea, and Henry Muccini

FrAmeLab, University of L'Aquila, L'Aquila, Italy
{roberta.capuano,henry.muccini}@univaq.it, eoan.odea@graduate.univaq.it

Abstract. As energy demands rise and sustainability becomes critical, Information and Communication Technology's energy footprint is increasingly monitored. In this context, software architecture may play a significant role in determining a system's energy consumption.

This study aims to evaluate and compare the energy consumption of monolithic and microservice-based software to understand their implications for sustainable software design. We applied a cohort study approach in a controlled experimental environment using two open-source Java applications—*PetClinic* and *TicketMonster*—each implemented in both monolithic and microservice versions. Three use cases, representing different workloads, were defined and executed 30 times each per version, resulting in 360 total runs. Server energy use was measured with Powerstat and analyzed using Welch's t-test.

Our findings show that microservices may consume less energy than their monolithic counterparts under medium and heavy loads. Specifically, *PetClinic* and *TicketMonster* showed energy reductions of 4.99% and 5.05%, respectively. Across all use cases and applications, microservices demonstrated an average energy saving of 5.02% compared to monoliths.

These results suggest that microservice architectures may offer improved energy efficiency in high-demand scenarios due to better resource utilization and modular execution. While the study is limited to controlled conditions and two case studies, it provides a foundation for further research on architectural decisions and sustainable software engineering practices.

Keywords: software architecture · energy efficiency · sustainable software

1 Introduction

Advancements in *Information and Communication Technology* (*ICT*) have greatly enhanced modern life but also driven a sharp increase in global energy consumption, which has tripled since 1980. Projections suggest energy demand will exceed supply by 2030 [1]. This trend highlights the need for energy-efficient software systems [2,3], especially as *ICT* accounts for 1.8% to 3.9% of *Global*

V. Andrikopoulos et al. (Eds.): ECSA 2025, LNCS 15929, pp. 260–275, 2026.
https://doi.org/10.1007/978-3-032-02138-0_17

Greenhouse Gas (*GHG*) emissions [4,5]. Sustainability is becoming a key focus in regulations and corporate strategy. Policies like the EU's Ecodesign for Sustainable Products Regulation [6] and the Corporate Sustainability Reporting Directive [7] now push organizations to assess and report the environmental impact of their digital infrastructure. Reflecting this shift, Gartner predicts that by 2027, 30% of large enterprises will include software sustainability in non-functional requirements, naming green software engineering a top trend for 2024 [21,22].

Although energy efficiency is not (yet) explicitly listed among the software quality standards that designers must evaluate during the design phase [12], research increasingly recognizes the architectural level as key to addressing energy-related concerns [13,14]. Decisions regarding system distribution or communication styles directly affect energy use [15], requiring architects to balance *Quality of Service* (*QoS*) and energy efficiency [25]. Selecting appropriate architectural development models is thus essential to meet non-functional requirements, including sustainability [9,10]. While architectural styles are known to influence attributes like latency, scalability, and reliability [15], their impact on software sustainability, particularly considering energy consumption, remains underexplored. This study addresses this gap by comparing the energy consumption of monolithic versus functionally equivalent microservice-based applications. This choice is driven by three main factors: (i) extensive prior work on migrating to microservices for better cohesion and coupling, with limited evaluation of resulting energy impacts; (ii) ongoing academic and industrial interest in migration both to [23,24] and from [16,17] microservices, and (iii) industry forecasts pointing to widespread adoption of microservices, with 74% of organizations already using them and 23% planning to adopt them [20].

By clarifying the sustainability implications of foundational architectural choices, this research establishes a necessary baseline for understanding energy behavior in software systems—one that can inform both immediate decisions and future investigations into finer architectural variations. Thus, the goal of this paper is to provide insights that can guide software architects in selecting architectural styles aligned with sustainability objectives. Thus, we aim to answer the following research question: *"How does microservice architecture compare to monolithic architecture in terms of energy consumption?"*. To answer this question, we established a controlled experimental environment using the *cohort protocol* [8,26,27] to measure the energy consumption of two open-source case studies: the *PetClinic* and *TicketMonster* applications, each implemented as functionally equivalent monolith and microservice applications. Three distinct use cases were defined for each application, executed over 30 iterations. A quantitative analysis employing *Welch's t-test* was conducted to evaluate their energy consumption, allowing for a systematic comparison of the two architectural styles. This quantitative analysis revealed statistically significant differences in energy consumption between a monolith and a microservice architecture, especially considering medium and heavy load use cases.

The rest of this paper is structured as follows: Sect. 2 presents the state-of-the-art in measuring the energy consumption of software applications. The implementation of the *cohort protocol* for the construction of the research methodology is reported in Sect. 3. Section 4 shows how the research methodology has been applied on the *PetClinic* and *TicketMonster* applications to perform the energy measurements. The results are analysed and discussed in Sect. 5. Section 6 discusses the threats to validity and the future works of our study. Finally, Sect. 7 concludes the paper.

2 Related Work

This section presents the state of the art on processes and tools for measuring the energy consumption of software, as well as the related work on the analysis of the energy efficiency of monoliths and microservices.

Software Energy Measurements Approaches: Various processes and tools have been proposed to assess software energy consumption. Ardito et al. [32] describes a four-phase method—goal definition, method selection, measurement, and analysis—to ensure reliable and comparable results. Mancebo et al. [33] propose an iterative process covering scope definition, environment setup, consumption measurement, and result analysis. Félix et al. [34] compare eleven approaches by architecture, granularity, and context. The *Green Software Measurement Model (GSMM)* [35] integrates existing methods, emphasizing stakeholder goals, method selection, realistic workloads, and broader data analysis. Cruz et al. [36,37] offer guidance on experimental setup and minimizing bias.

Measurement tools fall into hardware-based and hybrid methods [29]. Hardware tools (e.g., *Watts Up? Pro*, *Monsoon* [30]) provide accuracy but lack flexibility for cloud contexts. Hybrid approaches leverage counters and system metrics [31], often via tools like *PowerTop*[1], *PowerStat*[2], Intel's Energy Checker SDK[3], and Microsoft's *Joulemeter*[4]. Profilers like *cpufrequtils*[5], *Gnome/KDE monitors*[6], and language-specific tools such as *GNU gprof*[7], *ANTS Profiler* (.NET)[8], and *JProfiler* (Java)[9] track energy via resource usage.

Energy Measurements of Monoliths and Microservices: Recent research has increasingly examined the energy and performance implications of architectural patterns in cloud and microservices-based environments. Khomh et al. [38] explored cloud design patterns like *Local Sharding* and *Priority Queues*, revealing their potential to lower energy consumption, albeit with trade-offs in latency—highlighting the need for well-balanced configurations. A systematic review by

[1] https://wiki.archlinux.org/title/powertop.
[2] https://github.com/ColinIanKing/powerstat.
[3] https://www.intel.com/content/www/us/en/developer/tools/overview.html.
[4] https://research.microsoft.com/en-us/projects/joulemeter/.
[5] https://www.thinkwiki.org/wiki/How_to_use_cpufrequtils.
[6] https://apps.kde.org/en-gb/plasma-systemmonitor/.
[7] https://www.gnu.org/software/binutils/.
[8] https://www.red-gate.com/products/ants-performance-profiler/.
[9] https://www.ej-technologies.com/jprofiler.

Araújo et al. [1] compiles energy optimization strategies in microservices, emphasizing energy-aware architecture and identifying research gaps, especially around resource management. Zhao et al. [18] studied how microservice granularity affects energy and performance by comparing coarse-, medium-, and fine-grained versions of two systems under different workloads.

Several studies address energy efficiency in cloud computing. Procaccianti et al. [11] propose tactics such as continuous monitoring, self-adaptive systems, and cloud federation to improve energy usage by dynamically managing service deployment. The Elergy model presented by De Nardin et al. [40] builds on this by using predictive algorithms for proactive resource allocation, effectively reducing energy waste from over-provisioning. Beyond infrastructure-level strategies, developer-level decisions also play a key role. Jagroep et al. [13] highlight how choices in data structures and algorithms can influence energy usage, while Seo et al. [15] show that different communication styles (e.g., client-server vs. publish-subscribe) can lead to varying energy profiles.

Berry et al. [19] evaluate both monolith and microservice architectures under various replication setups, measuring energy using physical power meters on the entire machine. In contrast, we avoid confounding factors like scaling and isolate the architectural deployment model—comparing monoliths and microservices under fixed conditions, with server-only, software-based energy measurements.

Literature Findings: Current research and industry initiatives demonstrate a strong focus on developing methods and tools for measuring software energy consumption. Although energy efficiency is increasingly viewed as a critical quality attribute, limited attention has been given to its connection with software architecture models. Most studies have explored how aspects like developer choices, resource management, and self-adaptive mechanisms influence the energy efficiency of microservice-based systems. Despite some researchers proposing architectural patterns and tactics to reduce energy, to the best of our knowledge, only one of them directly compared the energy consumption of monolithic versus microservice architectures. However, the paper relies only on hardware-based energy measurement without dealing with confounding variables such as daemon processes. Our study fills this gap by empirically evaluating the energy consumption of applications built with both approaches.

3 Proposed Approach

This research analyses the energy consumption of monolithic and microservice architectures using a cohort study approach, as established in software engineering literature [8]. This method enables structured, time-based comparisons across groups [26, 41], allowing us to assess how architectural choices influence energy use under evolving workloads. By defining cohorts based on deployment model and observing them under consistent conditions, we can isolate architectural impact from other confounding factors—making this approach well-suited to analyzing long-term energy behavior.

Table 1. Client-Server Environment

	Host Server	Client Machine
Device	Dell XPS 13 7390	MacBook Pro
OS	Ubuntu Server 20.04 LTS	Mac OS Ventura 13.0.1
CPU	Intel Core i5, 4.1 GHz 4-Core	Intel Core i9, 2.3 GHz 8-Core
Memory	4 GB LPDDR3	16GB 2667 MHz DDR4

According to the *cohort protocol*, we define three types of variables: **independent**, **dependent**, and **confounding**. The **independent variable**—the factor believed to influence the outcome—is the *architectural development model* (monolith vs. microservices). The **dependent variable** is the software's *energy consumption*. **Confounding variables** are external factors that may bias this relationship. In our analysis, we control for confounders such as system environment, experiment timing, background processes, and resource usage.

3.1 Study Design

Cohort Selection: We define two cohorts, one for monolithic applications and one for their microservice counterparts. To reduce *confounding variables*, we applied inclusion criteria for project selection. We focus on open-source *GitHub* projects to support reproducibility. Each application must have both monolithic and microservice versions, use the same programming language (Java), and provide full-stack functionality (frontend, backend, and storage). Additionally, all applications must be deployable in containerized environments (e.g., *Docker*) to ensure consistency and isolation during experiments. We further restricted our selection to applications built with the widely adopted *Spring* ecosystem. Selected applications do not explicitly include sustainability or energy consumption as non-functional requirements, as not reported in their *README* files, ensuring their architectures were not pre-optimized for energy efficiency.

Experimental Setup: We conducted our experiments in a local environment to reduce *confounding variables*, avoiding noise from network latency and shared resources. A *client-server architecture* was used, with server and client hosted on separate machines as reported in Table 1, ensuring energy measurements—taken only on the server—were not affected by client-side activities. The server ran *Ubuntu Server 20.04 LTS*, chosen for its efficiency and reduced background process interference compared to desktop environments.

To understand system responses under realistic conditions, we chose three *use cases* to reflect the different operational loads. Each *use case* represents normal user or administrative actions, enabling us to capture how the system handles different demands. Thus, we define light, medium and heavy load *use cases* for each application. Each *use case* contains a frontend list of tasks and a selection of API requests to perform. Both of these are executed with 50 parallel

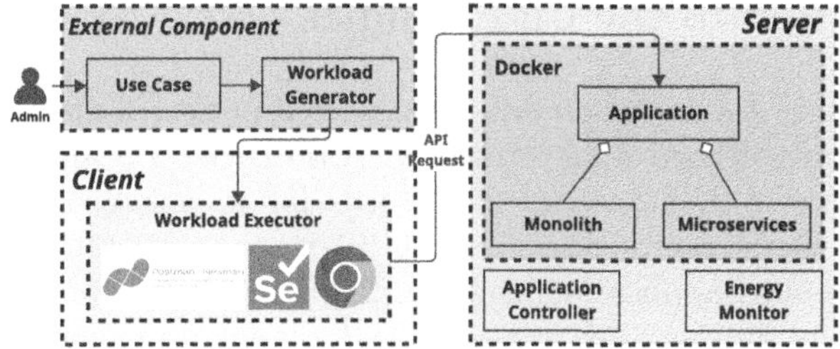

Fig. 1. Experimental Process.

instances to simulate concurrent user activity. More information about the *use cases* considered in our analysis is reported in Sect. 4.

Energy consumption was monitored using *Powerstat*, which captures system-wide power usage. We automated the experimental process with *bash scripts* to improve reproducibility and reduce human error. As shown in Fig. 1, the setup involved a *client*, *server*, and an *external component* that triggered the experiment by providing a *use case*. Each use case was processed by a workload generator and executed on the client using *Selenium*[10] for frontend interactions (via Chrome) and *Newman*[11] for API requests.

3.2 Data Collection, Analysis and Interpretation

In the following, we detail the approach used to collect energy consumption data during the experiment, obtaining accurate and representative measurements that capture the full spectrum of application behavior [15].

Energy data was collected on the server side at regular one-second intervals using *Powerstat*, allowing the experiment to capture both steady-state and transient phases [37]. Resulting in 393 samples taken per iteration per use case per architecture. To reduce the influence of fluctuations and outliers, two averaging techniques were applied. The first, *individual iteration averaging*, calculates the average energy consumption within each experiment iteration. The second, *multiple iteration averaging*, computes the overall average across all iterations to provide a representative value for each cohort. Each experiment was repeated 30 times per architecture per use case [36,49], totalling 60 runs per use case. Across 2 applications, 3 use cases and 2 architectures, this resulted in 360 independent runs. This repetition reduces random variability and improves result reliability. The three use cases were tested independently to capture energy behavior under varied workloads for both monolithic and microservice systems.

[10] https://www.selenium.dev/.
[11] https://github.com/postmanlabs/newman.

4 Application to the Case Studies

The application of the inclusion criteria reported in Sect. 3 allowed us to select two open-source software applications: *PetClinic* (*PC*)[12] and *TicketMonster* (*TM*)[13]. *PC* has 1.8K stars and 2.3K forks for its microservices version on GitHub, while the monolithic version has 497 stars and 906 forks. On the contrary, *TM* is an older application, counting 228 Stars and 463 forks for its monolithic implementation, and 28 Stars and 18 forks for its microservices counterpart. The replication package, linked in the data availability section of this paper, is available for study replicability.

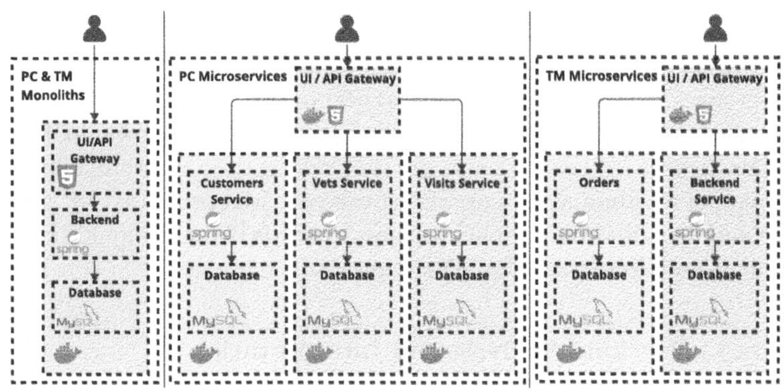

Fig. 2. Monolithic and Microservices Architectures - *PetClinic*

Both applications provide *CRUD*-related functionalities and include a comparable number of microservices. Notably, both adopt the widely used *Spring* ecosystem—used by 67% of developers according to a 2024 survey [43]—making them representative of real-world implementations.

Case Studies Description: *PetClinic* (PC) and *TicketMonster* (TM) are sample Java applications built using the *Spring* framework, showcasing how to develop database-driven systems with modern tools. Both use a common technology stack—*OpenJDK 11*, *Maven 3.8.4*, and *MySQL*—and implement core features such as data management and user interaction, making them suitable for exploring typical enterprise application patterns.

While they offer comparable levels of functionality, they differ in domain focus and technology integration. *PC* centers on managing *owners*, *pets*, *appointments*, and *veterinarians*, serving as a clean example of a typical business application. *TM*, on the other hand, focuses on *event management* and *ticket sales*. It contains

[12] https://github.com/spring-petclinic.

[13] https://github.com/ticket-monster-msa/monolith.

Table 2. Use Cases Descriptions and Complexity - *PetClinic* and *TicketMonster*

Application	Description	Complexity[c]
PetClinic	*UC1* - Users create a new owner, add a pet, and search by owner's last name.	10 GET
	UC2 - Users create a new owner, add four pets, and update two pet names.	5 POST, 5 DELETE
	UC3 - Users create a new vet and five appointments.	5 GET, 5 POST, 5 PUT, 5 DELETE
TicketMonster	*UC1* - Users browse events and purchase 25 tickets for one event.	10 GET
	UC2 - Users browse events and purchase 25 tickets across three events.	5 POST, 5 DELETE
	UC3 - Users create a new venue, category, performance, and event.	5 GET, 5 POST, 5 PUT, 5 DELETE

[c] Measured in terms of API Requests.

a database of pre-populated *events*, *event categories*, and *venues*, where users can purchase multiple tickets. It also demonstrates integration with *Red Hat* and *JBoss* technologies, running on *Wildfly 23.0.2*, and includes features such as an *administration panel* and a simulated *bot* for automated ticket purchases.

Architecture's Description: Figure 2 presents a side-by-side comparison of the monolithic and microservices architectures for both the *PC* and *TM* applications. The monolithic design, shared by both applications, follows a three-tier architecture comprising a UI/API Gateway, a Spring-based backend, and a MySQL database. In contrast, the microservices architectures decompose functionalities into independently deployable services, each encapsulated within its own Docker container and backed by a dedicated MySQL database. The *PC* microservices architecture consists of a UI/API Gateway and three domain-specific services: *Customers*, *Vets*, and *Visits*. The *TM* application, meanwhile, is structured into a UI/API Gateway, an *Orders Service*, and a *Backend Service*.

Code analysis highlights the differences in complexity between the architectural styles. The *PC* monolith comprises 122 files and 6,454 lines of code, whereas its microservices version spans 140 files and 14,532 lines. Similarly, the *TM* monolith contains 252 files and 44,210 lines of code, while its microservices counterpart includes 312 files and 48,484 lines. These differences reflect the added complexity and modularity introduced by transitioning to microservices.

Use Cases and Experiments Description: Table 2 summarizes the *PC* application's use cases, categorized by workload intensity: *Light Load* (UC1), *Medium Load* (UC2), and *Heavy Load* (UC3), based on the number and type of *API* requests. Each experiment, repeated 30 times per application and version, involved executing a single use case after a warm-up phase, with 50 parallel instances simulating user activity. This level of concurrency was empirically cho-

Table 3. Monitor Values in Joules across Iterations - *PetClinic*.

Use Case ID	Architecture	Iterations			Statistics		
		10	20	30	Min.	Max.	Avg.
UC1- Light Load	Monolith	93.98	107.50	86.89	86.39	108.22	97.42
UC1 - Light Load	Microservices	93.34	107.13	86.31	85.94	107.75	97.07
UC2 - Medium Load	Monolith	143.98	161.50	146.89	136.39	173.01	150.55
UC2- Medium Load	Microservices	135.62	153.13	138.52	128.02	164.64	142.01
UC3 - Heavy Load	Monolith	213.98	241.50	216.89	206.39	253.01	223.55
UC3 - Heavy Load	Microservices	193.98	221.50	196.89	186.39	233.01	203.55

Table 4. Monitor Values in Joules across Iterations - *TicketMonster*.

Use Case ID	Architecture	Iterations			Statistics		
		10	20	30	Min.	Max.	Avg.
UC1	Monolith	109.93	108.77	108.35	101.63	124.01	108.82
UC1	Microservices	109.82	108.67	108.25	101.54	123.89	108.71
UC2	Monolith	153.07	151.47	150.79	141.41	172.98	151.52
UC2	Microservices	144.05	142.52	142.03	133.26	162.29	142.60
UC3	Monolith	292.07	289.05	287.42	269.38	331.28	289.08
UC3	Microservices	271.00	268.18	266.87	250.21	306.66	268.24

sen for stable and consistent energy measurements. Though higher concurrency is common in production, our aim was controlled architectural comparison. All services ran as single instances, without replication or load balancing.

Use Cases Energy Analysis - PetClinic: Table 3 reports the energy consumption measured for each use case across different iterations (10, 20, and 30). In addition, the table reports the minimum, maximum and average energy consumption considering all the iterations. The energy consumption trends in *PC* reflect warming-up or stabilization effects during initial iterations. *UC3* consistently showed the highest energy consumption, followed by *UC2* and *UC1*. This pattern aligns with increased resource usage for more intensive tasks. For example, the average energy consumption for *UC3* reached 223.55 Joules (monolith) and 203.55 Joules (microservices), compared to 97.42 Joules (monolith) and 97.07 Joules (microservices) for *UC1*. Regardless of architectural development models, energy consumption increased proportionally with workload intensity, highlighting the positive correlation between workload and energy usage. Across all use cases, the *monolithic architecture consistently consumed more energy* than the microservices architecture.

Use Cases Energy Analysis - TicketMonster: Table 4 summarizes the measured values for all use cases and iterations of the *TM* application. To streamline the analysis, results at 10, 20, and 30 iterations are reported, with

Table 5. Energy Comparison: Monolith vs Microservices Architectures

Application	Architecture	Use Case ID	Use Case Avg.	Overall Avg.	Mono. and Micro. Avg.
TicketMonster	Monolith	*UC1*	108.82 J	183.14 J	170.15 J
		UC2	151.52 J		
		UC3	289.08 J		
PetClinic	Monolith	*UC1*	97.42 J	157.17 J	
		UC2	150.55 J		
		UC3	223.55 J		
TicketMonster	Microservices	*UC1*	108.71 J	173.18 J	160.36 J
		UC2	142.60 J		
		UC3	268.24 J		
PetClinic	Microservices	*UC1*	97.07 J	147.54 J	
		UC2	142.01 J		
		UC3	203.55 J		

minimum, maximum, and average values computed across all 30 iterations for a comprehensive overview. Energy consumption trends for the use cases (*UC1*, *UC2*, and *UC3*) and architecture development models (monolith and microservices) reveal a general decline during the initial iterations. This decrease suggests warming-up or stabilization effects in the application or underlying system. As anticipated, *UC3* consistently exhibited the highest energy consumption. In contrast, *UC1* and *UC2* required less energy, aligning with their reduced workload intensity.

While the limited sample size precludes definitive conclusions regarding architectural comparisons, the results suggest that microservices may generally consume slightly less energy than their monolithic counterpart across use cases and iterations under controlled conditions.

Commonalities in Variability. The recorded measurements show notable variability across iterations within the same *use case* and architecture. Such variability underscores the challenges in accurately measuring software energy consumption, influenced by background processes, hardware fluctuations, and limitations in measurement tools [45,46]. Additionally, the variability across iterations attributed patterns, even across use cases. We believe these peaks are due to the accumulation of memory usage and system resources over time, which can lead to brief spikes in processing demands as the system manages and releases cached data or garbage collection cycles [42].

5 Discussion

This section compares the results observed during the experiments on both the *PetClinic* (*PC*) and the *TicketMonster* (*TM*) applications. Thus, based on our quantitative analysis, we provide the answer to our research question. In addition, we discuss the threats to the validity of our study.

General Observations Comparing Both Case Studies: Table 5 presents the average energy consumption data (in Joules) for each use case, comparing the *Monolith* and *Microservices* architectures across the *PC* and *TM* applications. Analyzing the **impact of architecture** on the energy consumption, we observe that both applications exhibit a similar trend: *microservices architecture generally consumes less energy compared to the monolithic architecture.* The difference in energy consumption between architectures is more pronounced in the case of the *TM* application compared to *PC*. This may be due to *TM*'s more intensive runtime behavior, such as greater *CPU* or memory usage, which amplifies the benefits of microservice isolation.

While the trend holds, the difference in energy consumption between architectures is minor in the *PC* case study compared to *TM*. This suggests for more straightforward applications like *PC*, the overhead associated with microservices might be closer to the potential energy savings they offer.

Another essential aspect to be considered is the **impact of workload intensity**. In our analysis, both applications demonstrate increasing energy consumption with higher iteration numbers. This trend is likely due to the fluctuations in resource utilization and system behaviour, even under controlled experimental conditions. In addition, both applications exhibit **variability** in energy consumption across different iterations within each use case. More details about the factors impacting the variability of the results are detailed in Sect. 6.

Answer to the Research Question. To address the research question, *"How does microservice architecture compare to monolithic architecture in terms of energy consumption?"*, we conducted a statistical analysis comparing the energy consumption of monolithic and microservice versions of each application (*PC* and *TM*). For each use case, we applied *Welch's t-test* [47,48] to compare 30 independent observations of energy consumption per architecture, ensuring unequal variances and sample independence. Table 6 presents the test results reporting the t-statistic, p-value, effect size (Cohen's d) and the relative difference in energy consumption between architectures.

Table 6. *TicketMonster and PetClinic* - Welch's t-test Results with Effect Sizes

Application	Use Case	t-statistic	p-value	Effect Size (d)	% Diff.
TicketMonster	*UC1*	−0.094	0.925	$-0.024^{\dagger}$	−0.15%
	UC2	−6.019	$1.3 \times 10^{-7*}$	$-1.553^{\ddagger}$	−6.81%
	UC3	−7.056	$2.5 \times 10^{-9*}$	$-1.823^{\ddagger}$	−8.18%
PetClinic	*UC1*	−0.209	0.835	$-0.054^{\dagger}$	−0.36%
	UC2	−3.715	$4.6 \times 10^{-4*}$	$-0.959^{\ddagger}$	−5.67%
	UC3	−6.462	$2.3 \times 10^{-8*}$	$-1.669^{\ddagger}$	−8.95%

The results reveal statistically significant reductions in energy consumption for the microservice versions of both applications under medium (*UC2*) and high

(*UC3*) workloads. For example, *UC3* for *TM* version consumed 8.18% less energy than its monolithic counterpart ($p = 2.5 \times 10^{-9}$, $d = -1.823$), and *PC* showed an 8.95% reduction ($p = 2.3 \times 10^{-8}$, $d = -1.669$). These effect sizes indicate a strong practical difference. Conversely, with *UC1*, the observed differences were minimal and not statistically significant for either application.

On average across all use cases, the microservice versions consumed 4.99% (*PC*) and 5.05% (*TM*) less energy than the monolithic versions. These findings suggest that microservices, due to their modularity and potential for finer-grained resource scaling, can lead to improved energy efficiency [39], particularly under moderate to heavy workloads. However, these results are specific to the two applications studied and the experimental context, and generalizability is discussed in Sect. 6.

6 Threats to Validity

While this research provides valuable insights into the energy efficiency of microservices compared to monolithic architectures, several factors may affect the validity of our findings. We analyse these threats in terms of internal, external and construct validity.

Internal Validity: Our study examines two Spring-based applications, *PetClinic* (*PC*) and *TicketMonster* (*TM*), reflecting a significant share of real-world microservices (62% adoption among 440 practitioners [43]). To mitigate selection bias, we chose open-source applications and ensured reproducibility. Measurement errors from background processes or tool limitations were minimized through a rigorous methodology using well-established tools as reported in Sect. 3. To account for variability, we conducted 30 iterations per experiment.

External Validity: Generalizability is a key concern, as factors like programming languages and functionalities can influence energy consumption. Additionally, our controlled environment may not fully reflect real-world cloud deployments, where network latency, resource contention, and dynamic scaling play a role [13,15]. However, our focus was on comparing architectures rather than deployment environments. While further studies on diverse applications and operational settings are needed, our results provide a strong foundation for understanding the architectural impact on energy efficiency. The applications used in this study only contain two and three services, respectively, limiting the representativeness of real-world systems. While open-source microservice repositories exist [50,51], finding functionally equivalent monolithmicroservice pairs remains a significant constraint, which we acknowledge as a limitation in architectural scale and realism.

Construct Validity: The tools and metrics used for measuring energy consumption have inherent limitations and may not fully capture all aspects of energy usage. To mitigate this, we ensured proper calibration and conducted measurements under consistent and controlled conditions. Additionally, Several factors contribute to energy variability, including system fluctuations (e.g., hardware performance and background processes), measurement granularity (as *PowerStat* captures system-wide energy but not individual components in *Docker*), and application behaviour (e.g., *garbage collection* and *caching*). Recognizing these factors helps improve the reliability of our findings and provides a clearer understanding of energy consumption patterns. Additionally, this analysis was conducted at a system level and did not isolate the energy impact of individual components or services within each architecture. Future work could explore fine-grained profiling to identify energy hotspots within applications.

Conclusion Validity: Our conclusions are based on statistically significant results using Welch's t-test with 30 independent observations per group, reporting p-values and effect sizes. While assumptions like independence and sample consistency may influence validity, controlled conditions and consistent trends across applications support the reliability of our findings.

7 Conclusion

This study aimed to compare the energy efficiency of two architectural models: monolithic and microservice-based systems. We selected two open-source applications—*TicketMonster* (*TM*) and *PetClinic* (*PC*)—each with monolithic and microservice versions. Three use cases were defined per application to represent varying workloads, and each was executed 30 times per version, totalling 360 runs. Experiments were conducted in a controlled environment to reduce external variability. Statistical analysis using *Welch's t-test* revealed statistically significant differences in energy consumption between the two architectural models, particularly under medium and heavy loads. The microservice versions of *TM* and *PC* consumed 4.99% and 5.05% less energy, respectively, compared to their monolithic counterparts. These results suggest that microservices may offer improved energy efficiency.

While promising, these findings are based on two case studies in a controlled environment. Real-world factors like network latency and cloud scaling may affect energy use. Future work will explore microservice replication and scaling policies to better assess their impact on energy efficiency and refine the architectural comparison. Overall, this study underscores the potential of microservices for energy-efficient software design opening for further research on sustainable architectural choices.

Acknowledgments. This work was supported by the Italian PNRR MUR Centro Nazionale HPC, Big Data e Quantum Computing, Spoke9 - Digital Society & Smart Cities.

Data Availability Statement. The data that support the findings of this study are openly available on GitHub at https://github.com/eoanodea/energy-and-architectural-styles.

References

1. Araújo, G., et al.: Energy consumption in microservices architectures: a systematic literature review. IEEE Access **12**, 186710–186729 (2024)
2. Calero, C., Piattini, M. (eds.): Green in Software Engineering, vol. 3. Springer, Cham (2015)
3. Manotas, I., et al.: An empirical study of practitioners' perspectives on green software engineering. In: Proceedings of the 38th International Conference on Software Engineering, pp. 237–248 (2016)
4. Freitag, C., Berners-Lee, M., Widdicks, K., Knowles, B., Blair, G.S., Friday, A.: The real climate and transformative impact of ICT: a critique of estimates, trends, and regulations. Patterns **2**(9) (2021)
5. Cruz, L., Gutierrez, X.F., Martínez-Fernández, S.: Innovating for Tomorrow: The convergence of SE and Green AI. arXiv preprint arXiv:2406.18142 (2024)
6. European Commission: Ecodesign for Sustainable Products Regulation (2024). https://tinyurl.com/4e3ftach. Accessed 15 May 2025
7. European Commission: Corporate Sustainability Reporting Directive (2024). https://tinyurl.com/2s3py7ac. Accessed 15 May 2025
8. Saarimäki, N., Lenarduzzi, V., Vegas, S., Juristo, N., Taibi, D.: Cohort studies in software engineering: a vision of the future. In: Proceedings of the 14th ACM/IEEE International Symposium on Empirical Software Engineering and Measurement (ESEM), pp. 1–6 (2020)
9. Elahi, A., Babamir, S.M.: Evaluating software architectural styles based on quality features through hierarchical analysis and Fuzzy Integral (FAHP). In: 2015 7th Conference on Information and Knowledge Technology (IKT), Urmia, Iran, pp. 1–6 (2015). https://doi.org/10.1109/IKT.2015.7288800
10. Me, G., Calero, C., Lago, P.: Architectural patterns and quality attributes interaction. In: 2016 Qualitative Reasoning about Software Architectures (QRASA), Venice, Italy, pp. 27–36 (2016). https://doi.org/10.1109/QRASA.2016.10
11. Procaccianti, G., Lago, P., Bevini, S.: A systematic literature review on energy efficiency in cloud software architectures. Sustain. Comput. Inf. Syst. **7**, 2–10 (2015)
12. IEEE/ISO/IEC International Standard for Software, systems and enterprise–Architecture description. ISO/IEC/IEEE 42010:2022(E), pp. 1–74 (2022). https://doi.org/10.1109/IEEESTD.2022.9938446
13. Jagroep, E., van der Werf, J.M., Brinkkemper, S., Blom, L., van Vliet, R.: Extending software architecture views with an energy consumption perspective: a case study on resource consumption of enterprise software. Computing (2017)
14. Woods, E., Fairbanks, G.: The pragmatic architect evolves. IEEE Softw. **35**(6), 12–15 (2018)
15. Seo, C., Edwards, G., Malek, S., Medvidovic, N.: A framework for estimating the impact of a distributed software system's architectural style on its energy consumption. In: Seventh Working IEEE/IFIP Conference on Software Architecture (WICSA 2008), pp. 277–280. IEEE (2008)
16. Su, R., Li, X., Taibi, D.: Back to the Future: From Microservice to Monolith. arXiv preprint arXiv:2308.15281 (2023)
17. Su, R., Li, X., Taibi, D.: From microservice to monolith: a multivocal literature review. Electronics **13**(8), 1452 (2024)
18. Zhao, Y., De Matteis, T., Bogner, J.: How Does Microservice Granularity Impact Energy Consumption and Performance? A Controlled Experiment. arXiv preprint arXiv:2502.00482 (2025)

19. Berry, V., Castelltort, A., Lange, B., Teriihoania, J., Tibermacine, C., Trubiani, C.: Is it worth migrating a monolith to microservices? An experience report on performance, availability and energy usage. In: 2024 IEEE International Conference on Web Services (ICWS), pp. 944–954. IEEE (2024)
20. Gartner, Inc. Microservices Architecture: Have Engineering Organizations Found Success? Gartner Peer Community (2023). https://tinyurl.com/bdetfjwz
21. Gartner: Gartner Identifies the Top Five Strategic Technology Trends in Software Engineering for 2024 (2024). https://tinyurl.com/bdfs3jce. Accessed 15 May 2025
22. Gartner, Inc. Top Strategic Technology Trends for 2023: Sustainable Technology (2023). https://tinyurl.com/2bty9ph5
23. Taibi, D., Lenarduzzi, V., Pahl, C.: Processes, motivations, and issues for migrating to microservices architectures: an empirical investigation. IEEE Cloud Comput. **4**(5), 22–32 (2017)
24. Ponce, F., Márquez, G., Astudillo, H.: Migrating from monolithic architecture to microservices: a rapid review. In: 2019 38th International Conference of the Chilean Computer Science Society (SCCC), Concepcion, Chile, pp. 1–7 (2019). https://doi.org/10.1109/SCCC49216.2019.8966423
25. Stier, C., Koziolek, A., Groenda, H., Reussner, R.: Model-based energy efficiency analysis of software architectures. In: Weyns, D., Mirandola, R., Crnkovic, I. (eds.) ECSA 2015. LNCS, vol. 9278, pp. 221–238. Springer, Cham (2015). https://doi.org/10.1007/978-3-319-23727-5_18
26. Euser, A.M., Zoccali, C., Jager, K.J., Dekker, F.W.: Cohort studies: prospective versus retrospective. Nephron Clin. Pract. **113**(3), c214–c217 (2009)
27. Fucci, D., et al.: A longitudinal cohort study on the retainment of test-driven development. In: Proceedings of the 12th ACM/IEEE International Symposium on Empirical Software Engineering and Measurement, pp. 1–10 (2018)
28. Gupta, U., et al.: Chasing carbon: the elusive environmental footprint of computing. In: 2021 IEEE International Symposium on High-Performance Computer Architecture (HPCA), pp. 854–867. IEEE (2021)
29. Ghaleb, T.A.: Software energy measurement at different levels of granularity. In: 2019 International Conference on Computer and Information Sciences (ICCIS), pp. 1–6. IEEE (2019)
30. Kulikov, N., Yaitskaya, E., Shvedova, A., Zhalnin, V.: Power consumption meter for energy monitoring and debugging. In: Voinov, N., Schreck, T., Khan, S. (eds.) Proceedings of International Scientific Conference on Telecommunications, Computing and Control. SIST, vol. 220, pp. 499–511. Springer, Singapore (2021). https://doi.org/10.1007/978-981-33-6632-9_44
31. Wu, X., Taylor, V.: Utilizing hardware performance counters to model and optimize the energy and performance of large scale scientific applications on power-aware supercomputers. In: 2016 IEEE International Parallel and Distributed Processing Symposium Workshops (IPDPSW), Chicago, IL, USA, pp. 1180–1189 (2016). https://doi.org/10.1109/IPDPSW.2016.78
32. Ardito, L., Coppola, R., Morisio, M., Torchiano, M., Risi, M.: Methodological guidelines for measuring energy consumption of software applications. Sci. Program. (2019)
33. Mancebo, J., Garcia, F., Calero, C.: A process for analysing the energy efficiency of software. Inf. Softw. Technol. **134**, 106560 (2021)
34. Felix, R., Bockisch, C.: Survey of approaches for assessing software energy consumption. In: Proceedings of the 2nd ACM SIGPLAN International Workshop on Comprehension of Complex Systems (2017)

35. Guldner, A., et al.: Development and evaluation of a reference measurement model for assessing the resource and energy efficiency of software products and components—Green Software Measurement Model (GSMM). Future Gener. Comput. Syst. (2024)
36. Cruz, L.: Green Software Engineering Done Right: a Scientific Guide to Set Up Energy Efficiency Experiments (2021). https://tinyurl.com/4vs3ux79
37. Cruz, L.: Tools to Measure Software Energy Consumption from your Computer (2021). https://tinyurl.com/4t7v8zz2
38. Khomh, F., Abtahizadeh, S.A.: Understanding the impact of cloud patterns on performance and energy consumption. J. Syst. Softw. (2018)
39. Berry, V., Castelltort, A., Lange, B., Teriihoania, J., Tibermacine, C., Trubiani, C.: Is it worth migrating a monolith to microservices? An experience report on performance, availability and energy usage. In: 2024 IEEE International Conference on Web Services (ICWS), pp. 944–954. IEEE (2024)
40. De Nardin, I.F., da Rosa Righi, R., Lopes, T.R.L., da Costa, C.A., Yeom, H.Y., Köstler, H.: On revisiting energy and performance in microservices applications: a cloud elasticity-driven approach. Parallel Comput. **108**, 102858 (2021)
41. Szklo, M.: Population-based cohort studies. Epidemiol. Rev. **20**(1) (1998)
42. Shimchenko, M., Österlund, E., Wrigstad, T.: Scheduling Garbage Collection for Energy Efficiency on Asymmetric Multicore Processors. arXiv preprint arXiv:2403.02200 (2024)
43. Perforce Software, Inc. 2024 Java Developer Productivity Report - Success Page — JRebel & XRebel by Perforce (2024). https://tinyurl.com/bru3nmuy
44. Messina, A., Rizzo, R., Storniolo, P., Tripiciano, M., Urso, A.: The database-is-the-service pattern for microservice architectures. In: Renda, M.E., Bursa, M., Holzinger, A., Khuri, S. (eds.) ITBAM 2016. LNCS, vol. 9832, pp. 223–233. Springer, Cham (2016). https://doi.org/10.1007/978-3-319-43949-5_18
45. Georgiou, K., Xavier-de-Souza, S., Eder, K.: The IoT energy challenge: a software perspective. IEEE Embed. Syst. Lett. **10**(3), 53–56 (2017)
46. Lago, P.: Challenges and opportunities for sustainable software. In: 2015 IEEE/ACM 5th International Workshop on Product Line Approaches in Software Engineering, pp. 1–2. IEEE (2015)
47. Dybå, T., Kampenes, V.B., Sjøberg, D.I.: A systematic review of statistical power in software engineering experiments. Inf. Softw. Technol. **48**(8), 745–755 (2006)
48. Kitchenham, B., et al.: Robust statistical methods for empirical software engineering. Empir. Softw. Eng. **22**, 579–630 (2017)
49. Hogg, R.V., Tanis, E.A., Zimmerman, D.L.: Probability and Statistical Inference, vol. 993. Macmillan, New York (1977)
50. Amoroso d'Aragona, D., et al.: A dataset of microservices-based open-source projects. In: Proceedings of the 21st International Conference on Mining Software Repositories (2024)
51. Černý, T., Chy, M.S.H., Arju, M.A.R., Sooksatra, K., Abdelfattah, A.S., Lenarduzzi, V.: A multi-variant benchmark for microservice systems in software engineering research. In: Ampatzoglou, A., et al. (eds.) ECSA 2024. LNCS, vol. 14937, pp. 21–29. Springer, Cham (2024). https://doi.org/10.1007/978-3-031-71246-3_3

Data-Driven Understanding of Design Decisions in Pattern-Based Microservices Architecture

J. Andres Diaz-Pace[1(✉)], Catia Trubiani[2], and David Garlan[3]

[1] ISISTAN Research Institute, CONICET, UNICEN University, Tandil, Buenos Aires, Argentina
andres.diazpace@isistan.unicen.edu.ar
[2] Gran Sasso Science Institute, L'Aquila, Italy
catia.trubiani@gssi.it
[3] Software and Societal Systems Department, Carnegie Mellon University, Pittsburgh, PA, USA
garlan@cs.cmu.edu

Abstract. The adoption of architectural patterns has recently been assessed in relation to their impact on the performance of microservice-based applications. For example, offloading common functionalities of multiple microservices to a gateway may lead to a system response time improvement. However, for a given system requirement, e.g., the latency of services or the utilization of resources, the benefit of choosing an architectural pattern is not guaranteed. Therefore, it becomes important to collect data about the parameters that contribute to the effective use of patterns, thus understanding the relationships between design decisions and performance requirements. In this work, we propose a data-driven approach to assess the quantitative impact of design decisions for a given pattern on the achievement of performance tradeoffs. Our approach seeks to control the pattern parameters that cause variations, i.e., sensitivity, in performance tradeoffs. Starting from a dataset including parameters related to three microservices patterns (i.e., Gateway Offloading, Command and Query Responsibility Segregation, and Anti-corruption Layer) and their performance characteristics, we do apply machine learning techniques (i.e., PRIM and CART) to infer constraints on the parameter values. This is helpful to understand and reduce the performance sensitivity of pattern configurations. Our results support software architects in making informed decisions by providing insights on the parameters related to the behavior of microservices patterns.

Keywords: Data-driven Sensitivity Analysis · Design Decisions · Architectural Patterns · Microservices · Performance metrics

1 Introduction

Microservice-based applications have gained the attention of researchers and practitioners [6,28], and also the software architecture community has been

V. Andrikopoulos et al. (Eds.): ECSA 2025, LNCS 15929, pp. 276–293, 2026.
https://doi.org/10.1007/978-3-032-02138-0_18

attracted to pursue methodologies to support their successful development [1,17]. Although the adoption of patterns has a long history [13], their effective use and their impact on quality attributes are a more recent research trend [20,22].

Software architects developing microservice-based systems, especially in industry, have pointed out the need to quantitatively assess the effects of patterns on quality-based requirements [23]. For instance, focusing on performance-related characteristics such as system response time or resource utilization [11], it is important to understand how they lead to different tradeoffs depending on specific pattern configurations and related design assumptions.

To enable a quantitative analysis, a recent work [16] has shown that well-known microservices patterns can be modeled and evaluated through software performance engineering (SPE) techniques, e.g., queueing networks [10]. Interestingly, the SPE models show that the performance properties of the patterns are sensitive to design decisions and input parameters. Furthermore, the variability in the values of such parameters has an effect on the performance tradeoffs achievable by the patterns. These parameters might refer to environmental conditions (e.g., incoming request rate) or design decisions of the solution (e.g., implementing a software or hardware isolation mechanism for a certain pattern). This scenario raises the notion of *sensitivity* of a design decision (belonging to a pattern), and how to exploit parameter ranges that allow a system to achieve desired performance properties [25]. For instance, in a microservices pattern, the heterogeneity of requests and their frequencies may influence the design decision to achieve a good tradeoff targeting low utilization and fast response time [16].

Motivated by the scenario above, we delve into the variability of the parameters that characterize microservice-based architectural patterns, so that controlling such parameters can make the pattern behavior (or design model) less prone to performance variations. Our goal is to reduce the sensitivity of input parameters thus understanding the performance variation of patterns' configurations. We follow a data-driven approach to profile the space of configuration alternatives for a given model (e.g., a pattern), identify the most influential model parameters and performance tradeoffs, and run a sensitivity analysis with respect to the tradeoffs. Furthermore, given a target tradeoff (e.g., fast response time and average resource utilization), we provide a procedure that infers constraints on the parameter values to ensure that the tradeoff is met. To do so, we rely on machine learning (ML) techniques for scenario discovery, such as the patient rule induction method (PRIM) [7] and classification/regression trees (CART) [4].

We perform an evaluation by focusing on three microservice patterns [23]: (i) *Anti-corruption Layer*, (ii) *Command Query Responsibility Segregation*, and (iii) *Gateway Offloading*. We study the effects of input parameter variations on some performance metrics (i.e., response time and utilization), before and after applying parameter constraints. Our experimental results demonstrate that the proposed approach infers specific ranges of input parameter values for the microservices configuration that many times reduce its performance variations, thus, achieving the desired tradeoff. Our approach provides knowledge to software architects on performance sensitivity due to the identification of key parameters of a pattern model, thus supporting them in making informed decisions.

The remainder of the paper is organized as follows. Section 2 provides background knowledge on the adopted architectural patterns and ML algorithms. Section 3 describes the proposed methodology along with a motivating example that clarifies the goal of this paper. Section 4 briefly introduces the experimental setup, followed by the evaluation that is discussed in Sect. 5. Related work is presented in Sect. 6, thus positioning our contribution in the state-of-the-art approaches. Section 7 outlines concluding remarks and future work.

2 Background

This section provides knowledge on foundational concepts, discussing the characteristics of the selected microservices patterns and the adopted ML algorithms.

2.1 Architectural Patterns

From a performance-based perspective, the selected microservices patterns [19] include a set of relevant input parameters that have been evaluated in [16], and we got inspiration from these parameters to build our dataset for this work. It is worth remarking that the theoretical performance models presented in [16] have been validated through an extensive experimentation in [14] where there is evidence of a correspondence between real measurements of resource utilization and system response time with respect to model-based performance predictions, thus assessing the validity of the performance models and results.

Table 1 lists the parameters considered in one of the patterns we analyze. Note that there are some common parameters that are replicated for all patterns, such as the number of requests in the system (N), and the thinking time, i.e., the idle time before a new system request is issued (Z). Next, we explain the specific parameters of the three patterns.

Gateway Offloading (GO). The problem occurs when different services require the same functionality (e.g., encryption) in their pipeline, thus causing a backlog of requests. The solution involves offloading shared or specialized service functionalities to a gateway proxy that manages them more efficiently, thus preventing service slowdowns. The architectural diagram [19] consists of four main components: three services (i.e., `S1`, `S2`, and `S3`) and the gateway (i.e., `GW`) that hosts common services. Table 1 shows that the performance of this pattern is affected by the service times of all components, i.e., S_{GW}, S_{S1}, S_{S2}, and S_{S3}.

Command and Query Responsibility Segregation (CQRS). The problem originates from traditional architectures that query and update the same (software or hardware) resource. As a solution, operations that read data are segregated from operations that update data. This can be performed at the software level (i.e., read and write requests use separate interfaces, but they are located on the same machine), or at the hardware level (i.e., having two different machines).

Table 1. Gateway Offloading and its Performance-related Parameters

Pattern	Parameters	Description
GO	N	Total amount of requests in the system
	Z	Thinking time
	S_{GW}	Service time of GW component
	S_{S1}	Service time of service S_1
	S_{S2}	Service time of service S_2
	S_{S3}	Service time of service S_3

The architectural diagram [19] differs in case of a software or hardware solution. The former includes a database component (i.e., `DB`) only, whereas the latter has two database components (i.e., one for queries, `DB-read`, and one for updates, `DB-write`) that require synchronization. The pattern's performance is affected by the service times of the DB components (S_{DB}, $S_{DB-read}$, and $S_{DB-write}$), and by the time needed to synchronize read and write requests ($R \leftrightarrow W$).

Anti-Corruption Layer (ACL). The problem arises when an application leverages different systems for its operation, e.g., a (recently) migrated application needs to interact with a legacy system that makes use of technologies not compatible with the primary application. From a domain-driven design perspective, this pattern applies whenever it is necessary to isolate domain models, not only to set apart legacy systems. The solution introduces an adaptation layer that mediates the communication between a (modern) application and a legacy system. The architectural diagram [19] consists of three main components: two subsystems (i.e., `SS1` and `SS2`) and the anti-corruption layer (i.e., `ACL`) that acts as adapter and mediates the communications between the two subsystems. The pattern's performance is affected by the probability of invoking the ACL component ($Prob$), and by the service times of the three involved components, i.e., S_{SS1}, S_{ACL}, and S_{SS2}.

2.2 Scenario Discovery Algorithms

In the following, we briefly describe two algorithms for scenario discovery (SD) [5], which is a type of ML technique used for finding regions of interest in a highly-dimensional dataset containing inputs and outputs for a model.

PRIM (Patient Rule Induction Method). It is a bump-hunting algorithm [7] that searches for regions (bumps) in the input space with relatively high (or low) values for a target variable. In our dataset, this variable takes Boolean values depending on whether a performance requirement is met. PRIM describes the regions by simple rules, as they are rectangles called *boxes* in the input space. PRIM works by slowly reducing the data size by small amounts iteratively. First, candidate boxes are generated. Each box removes a data portion based on the levels of a single input variable. This stage is known as top-down peeling. Second, for each candidate box, the relative improvement in the number of outputs (i.e., performance metrics) inside the box is calculated, and the candidate box with the highest improvement is selected. Third, the data in the selected box replace the starting data, and the process is repeated. There is also a second stage, known as bottom-up pasting, which is the inverse of the peeling stage. The process ends based on stopping criteria (e.g., the current box is too small). PRIM seeks for regions having both a high density of positive instances (i.e., those satisfying the target property) and a good coverage of the space being analyzed.

CART (Classification And Regression Trees). It is a decision tree algorithm [4] that recursively splits the data into subsets based on the values of input variables, until creating a tree-like structure for predicting a target variable. Similarly to PRIM, we assume that the target variable is a Boolean property, and use CART to address a classification problem. CART creates a binary decision tree, in which nodes are split into sub-nodes based on a threshold value of an input variable. The root node is considered as the initial set and split into two subsets by considering the best input and threshold value. These subsets are split using the same logic. This process continues until the last pure subset is found in the tree or the maximum number of leaves is reached. Node splitting relies on the Gini impurity criterion [4], which measures the probability of misclassifying a random instance from a subset labeled according to the majority class. The lower the Gini impurity, the more pure a subset is. CART evaluates all possible splits and selects the one that best reduces the impurity of the subsets. Pruning is used to remove nodes that contribute little to classifier accuracy. In general, CART is faster than PRIM, although it might not identify the same rules for a dataset.

3 Approach

We propose a data-driven framework to support the architect's understanding of the outcomes of certain design decisions and assumptions on performance properties of a microservices pattern. In particular, we identify the pattern parameters that contribute the most to performance variability and infer constraints for those parameters to reduce the performance sensitivity, providing an envelope of (desired) pattern behavior. Our research goal is to establish a richer knowledge base for software architects. To this end, we provide project-specific evaluations by leveraging existing patterns along with their performance data.

Our framework is a processing pipeline as outlined in Fig. 1. The pipeline comprises four phases: pattern modeling, data collection, sensitivity assessment of pattern parameters, and inference of parameter constraints. Constraints are computed using either the PRIM or CART algorithms.

3.1 Processing Pipeline

The process begins with the specification (or model) of a pattern M. Our framework does not prescribe a specification formalism. The requirements for the pattern modeling are: an initial architecture (i.e., the model components and their connections), and the specification of parameters (e.g., the variability in the service time of a specific system resource). The model M must distinguish: (i) the available design decisions (i.e., input parameters), (ii) the variations for the parameters (i.e., the possible values to be assigned), and (iii) the performance metrics of interest (i.e., output results). Variability in the parameters (inputs) will be reflected in variability in the performance metrics (outputs).

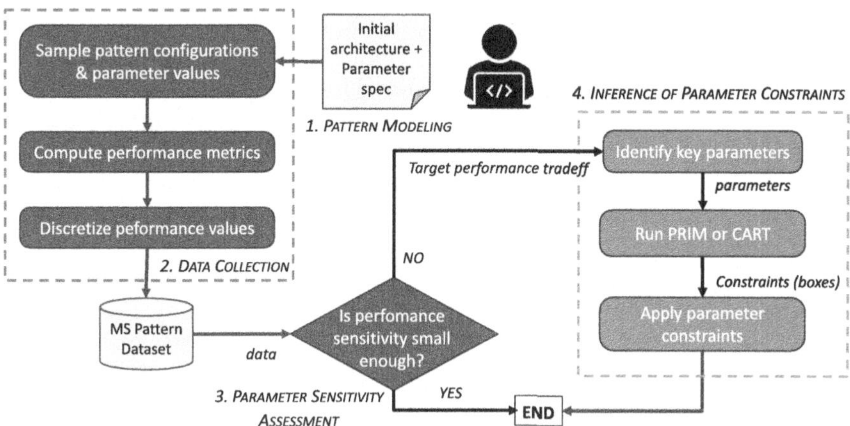

Fig. 1. Main phases of the proposed framework for analyzing and acting on the performance sensitivity of microservices patterns.

Once M is chosen, the data collection phase refers to the generation of alternative instances in terms of different pattern configurations and different parameter values for each configuration. These instances define the so-called *configuration space*. The number of instances to sample is determined by the architect. Each instance is evaluated by a performance model, which simulates how each pattern configuration behaves under given parameter values (e.g., different workload variations) and computes a set of metrics (e.g., response time, utilization). The metric values define the *quality-attribute space* for the configuration space.

To facilitate the treatment of the quality-attribute space, we apply a discretization procedure that bins the values for each performance metric according to an ordinal (or Likert) scale. For instance, for response time, we use a 3-point scale $<fast, average, slow>$ which converts the metric numeric values into categorical ones. In the general case, the architect can partition the quality-attribute space into more bins or even discretize it into arbitrary regions (e.g., below or above specific thresholds). Any instance is mapped to a label that results from the concatenation of the categorical values for the metrics. This way, the instances are grouped in the quality-attribute space according to the tradeoffs of their labels. These tradeoffs capture quality-attribute properties for performance sensitivity analysis. Both the configuration and the (discretized) quality-attribute spaces are stored in a dataset. It is worth remarking that decisions and input parameters co-exist in the generated data. This implies that a certain design decision (e.g., no-offloading) will be mapped to a region of the space (quadrant) when exposed to a certain workload, whereas it may belong to a different region when considering another workload intensity value.

In the third phase, called parameter sensitivity assessment, the software architect chooses a target tradeoff (e.g., $<average, fast>$ for utilization and response time, respectively) and determines whether the performance variability of the M configurations, with unconstrained decisions and parameters, is good enough for her preferences. This assessment can be made, for instance, by visually inspecting the quality-attribute. For example, the decision of offloading long services in Fig. 3 shows that the resulting architectural configurations can vary from $<low, fast>$ to $<low, slow>$. If the performance variability is too high, then parameter constraints must be imposed to reduce the pattern sensitivity.

Fourth, the constraint inference phase seeks to control for the uncertainty in the parameter values, and thus reduce the variability of the performance metrics. We rely on PRIM and CART for scenario discovery (SD). In our context, SD refers to the identification of conditions that cause a set of instances (for a target configuration) to satisfy a given property with a bound variability. For simplicity, these properties correspond to the regions defined by the quality-attribute labels. Nonetheless, other types of quality-attribute properties could be formulated. To reduce the number of parameters to be taken by SD algorithms, a sensitivity analysis filter can be applied so that only the most relevant parameters are processed by the SD algorithm. To this end, we implement a correlation analysis of the parameters with respect to the performance metrics, and retain those parameters with high correlation values. Finally, the architect can decide which the parameter constraints (called boxes) to apply to the pattern configurations.

3.2 Motivating Example

As an example of how our approach works, let us consider the *Gateway Offloading (GO)* pattern [16] introduced in Sect. 2.1. A *GO* instantiation for three services and two pipelines is illustrated in Fig. 2. In this example, let us assume a model with two request types, *request A* and *request B*, which need to be served by the system, one being executed by the first pipeline (*service1*) and another one being executed by the second pipeline (*service2* and *service3*). Let us also assume that the three microservices require the requests to be decrypted before executing them. When using the *GO* pattern, the encryption operation is deployed in the *gateway* component.

The *GO* performance depends on the operations being offloaded, as the time a request spends in the gateway to execute the offloaded operation is taken away from the other services. Thus, the offloading strategy becomes a *design decision* for the pattern. Based on [16], let us consider three alternatives for this decision, namely: *no offloading*, *offloading short operations* (e.g., those with execution times up to 5ms), or *offloading long operations* (e.g., execution times between 5ms and 10ms). As performance metrics, let us assume that architects

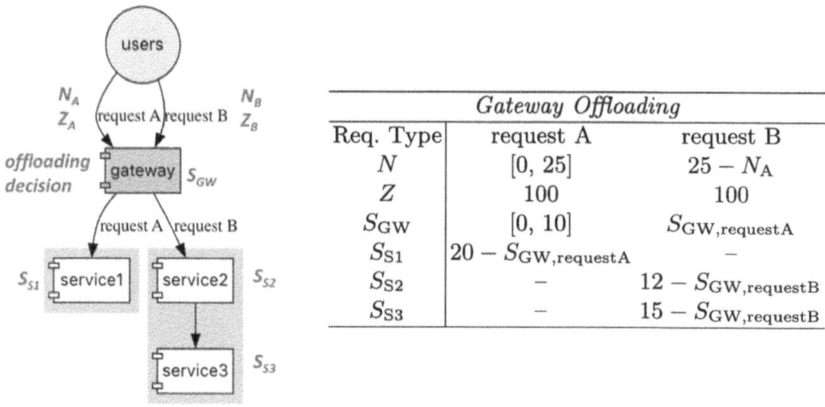

Gateway Offloading		
Req. Type	request A	request B
N	[0, 25]	$25 - N_{\mathrm{A}}$
Z	100	100
S_{GW}	[0, 10]	$S_{\mathrm{GW,requestA}}$
S_{S1}	$20 - S_{\mathrm{GW,requestA}}$	–
S_{S2}	–	$12 - S_{\mathrm{GW,requestB}}$
S_{S3}	–	$15 - S_{\mathrm{GW,requestB}}$

Fig. 2. Example of a *Gateway Offloading* pattern with performance parameters.

are interested in response time and utilization at the gateway. To estimate these metrics, the architect can make assumptions about the behavior of the gateway and microservices when processing requests, and also about the system environment. These *assumptions* are captured by parameters, such as the number of requests (N_A, N_B), the time before requests are issued (Z_A, and Z_B), and the execution times for each component (S_{GW}, S_{S1}, S_{S2} and S_{S3}). Based on these parameters, queuing networks (QNs) [10] can be applied to estimate performance metrics. By using the numerical values provided in [16] we can see that tradeoffs exist between utilization and response time for the three alternatives, as depicted in Fig. 3. For simplicity, we discretize the values for response time and utilization into three regions, each one exposing a feasible tradeoff category for the problem. In the general case, the quality-attribute space can be partitioned in multiple regions, depending on the variability of the metrics under analysis or the architect's needs.

A software architect might be interested in *GO* configurations with average or high utilization and average or fast response time. In the quality-attribute space in Fig. 3, we can see the performance variations in the configurations due to possible design decisions and assumptions. In this context, a design investigation for the architect is whether constraints can be imposed on the assumptions (or on the decisions) to reduce performance variability and thus, increase the chances that a pattern configuration fulfills a given tradeoff. This effort focuses on the *insensitivity* of a configuration, or a group of related configurations. In other words, our approach aims to understand how sensitive the performance of a configuration is to variations in its assumptions or design decisions. For instance, in the *GO* space in Fig. 3, the decision of off-loading short services seems to be mostly insensitive regarding the $<fast, average>$ tradeoff for utilization and response time, although it might deviate towards configurations with slower response time. The no-offloading decision shows a considerable sensitivity for the <$fast, low$> tradeoff, while off-loading long services is always insensitive around the <$fast, high$> tradeoff.

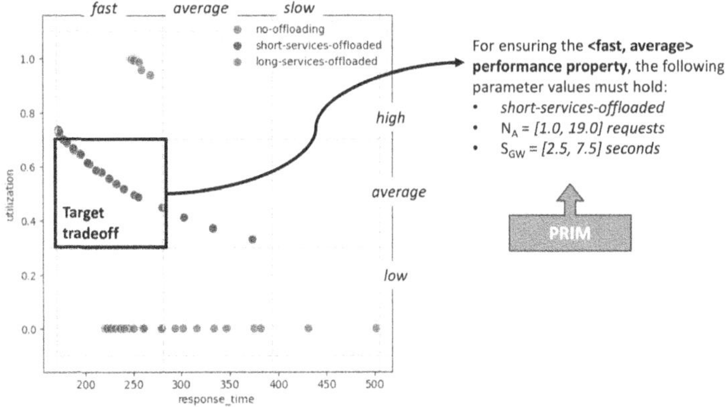

Fig. 3. Tradeoffs between response time and utilization for different configurations of the *Gateway Offloading* pattern. On the right, the constraints imposed (via PRIM) for reducing the sensitivity of achieving a target tradeoff are shown.

Let us consider that the architect wants to ensure both average utilization and fast response time as her target tradeoff. Thus, she needs to select an appropriate decision (e.g., off-loading short services) and also avoid deflections due to parameter variability. In particular, she can try to bound relevant parameters, such as N_A, N_B, S_{GW}, in such a way the *GO* configurations fall within the <$fast, average$> region. This effect can be achieved with $N_A = [1.0, 19.0]$ and $S_{GW} = [2.5, 7.5]$. These constraints express rules for controlling the parameter values. The architect can rely on these rules to understand the design decisions related to the behavior of the *GO* pattern. For instance, she can realize that the gateway service time S_{GW} is instrumental in the pattern performance, but also environmental factors play a role, e.g., the rate of incoming requests of *request A* (N_A) influences the pattern response. However, finding a set of constraints that ensure insensitive configurations with respect to a quality-attribute property is not straightforward. Here is where SD algorithms become useful.

4 Experimental Setup

We evaluate our approach by exercising it on three microservices patterns and computing different performance metrics for the pattern configurations. The experiments involve the patterns *Gateway Offloading (GO)*, *Command Query Responsibility Seggregation (CRQS)* and *Anticorruption Layer* (ACL), as modeled in [16]. We aim at addressing the following research questions:

- **RQ#1**: Which design decisions are more effective for satisfying a performance tradeoff?
- **RQ#2**: For a given design decision, how do PRIM and CART help to reduce sensitivity with respect to a performance tradeoff?

According to the processing pipeline of Fig. 1, we initially generate a dataset per pattern by executing its corresponding QN model and then visually inspect the distribution of the pattern configurations with respect to the tradeoffs. Two performance metrics are discretized into three equally-spaced ranges of values, leading to these tradeoff categories: *fast*, *average*, and *slow* for response time, and *high*, *average* and *low* for utilization. These results mainly target **RQ#1**.

For assessing the PRIM and CART algorithms, we split the pattern datasets into training and test sets (70/30) using stratification on the tradeoff labels, as typically done in ML. We remove outliers from the datasets via the z-score method ($z = 3$). We additionally perform a feature analysis via the F-statistic to retain the most relevant parameters (features) with respect to utilization and response time (targets). These parameters were later fed into the algorithms. In PRIM, we apply the algorithm on the training set for every combination of (feasible) tradeoff label and design decision, and record the parameter rules (boxes). In CART, we consider each design decision, as the resulting tree generates the parameter rules for all the tradeoff labels at once.

For answering **RQ#2**, all the boxes obtained from both algorithms are used for evaluation on the test set. To quantify the effects of imposing the parameter rules, we compute the percentage of configurations that satisfy each performance property (i.e., tradeoff label) before and after applying the boxes. We refer to this percentage as *density score*. We also analyze differences in the scores for the boxes generated by each algorithm to assess performance sensitivity improvements.

5 Evaluation

Figure 4 shows the distributions of quality-attribute tradeoffs for the different configurations. There are three alternative decisions for the *GO* pattern, two decisions for the *CQRS* pattern, and one decision for the *ACL* pattern. Each quadrant refers to a different performance requirement (for the corresponding pattern) involving a tradeoff between utilization and response time. As depicted in Fig. 4, not all the tradeoffs were feasible in our sampled architectural space.

Tradeoff Analysis of *GO* Pattern. Figure 4a shows that the decision of no-offloading always results in a low system utilization, and the response time can fluctuate between fast and slow depending on the parameter values. This scenario indicates that the architect should apply parameter constraints to ensure a good response time. In turn, the decision of offloading only long services always leads to a high utilization and an average response time, and thus seems to be an adequate decision for a reasonable performance (if a high utilization is not problematic for the system). When the goal is to optimize response time, the decision of offloading short services gives average-to-fast response time with an

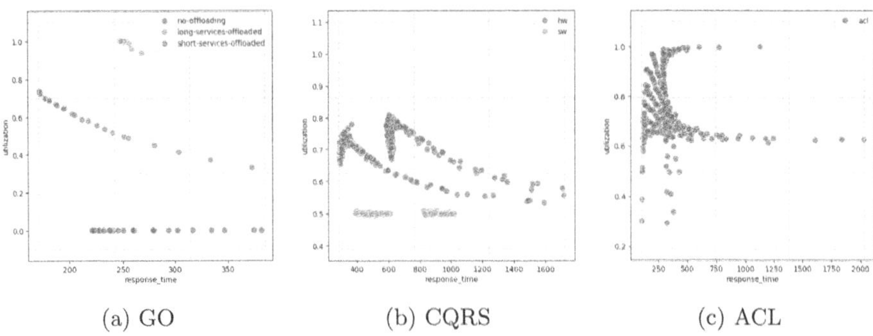

(a) GO (b) CQRS (c) ACL

Fig. 4. Distribution of configurations with respect to the performance tradeoffs.

average utilization. Nonetheless, parameter constraints are necessary to avoid deflections towards configurations with slow latency.

Tradeoff Analysis of *CQRS* Pattern. Figure 4b exhibits a similar trend as the *GO* pattern with respect to trading off average-to-low utilization and average-to-fast response time. If the software decision is chosen, the system utilization will be always low, and the architect could apply additional constraints to opt between an average or fast response time. The hardware decision is preferred for obtaining a high utilization, but the response time might degrade for some parameter values in the configurations. In this scenario, the architect should control for the parameter values to keep the response time fast or average (i.e., avoid the bottom-right quadrant).

Tradeoff Analysis of *ACL* Pattern. Figure 4c differs from the previous ones, since here all performance variations are due to parameter values. The best configurations have average-to-high utilization with mostly fast response time. However, deflections towards low utilization or slower response times are observed. To avoid those scenarios, the architect should apply appropriate constraints on the parameter values, especially on the frequency of despatching requests to the ACL component.

Summarizing, Fig. 4 visualizes the pros and cons of each microservice pattern, and how decisions could be taken to achieve specific performance tradeoffs, thus answering **RQ#1**. Furthermore, the analyses expose the sensitivity of certain pattern configurations, depending on the tradeoff targeted by the architect.

Based on the previous datasets, we ran PRIM and CART for the feasible configurations, design decisions, and tradeoffs, in order to obtain a spectrum of boxes and density scores. The results are summarized in Tables 2, 3, and 4. Performance tradeoff is represented by *response time* (fast, average, slow), and *utilization* (high, average, low). Please note that test sets represent the baselines, i.e., without applying any algorithm. PRIM and CART produce density score values after applying the boxes for different performance tradeoffs. The values are in bold (and green), underlined (and yellow) or framed (and red) to highlight whether the change was positive, marginal or negative, respectively, in terms of configurations meeting the target tradeoff after imposing the constraints.

Constraints for *GO* Pattern. After splitting the dataset (78 instances), we build the PRIM and CART models using the training set ($\approx$ 45 instances). Out of 8 possible parameters, N_A, N_B, and S_{GW} turned out to be the most relevant ones for performance sensitivity of the pattern in both algorithms. Table 2 summarizes the density metrics obtained from the experiments. The first block of rows (test set) shows the initial scores for different tradeoffs, in which the most prevalent tradeoffs ($<fast, low>$, $<average, high>$, $<fast, average>$) depend on the design decision implemented at the gateway. For instance, the first row in the table indicates that with no-offloading 50% of solutions belong to the $<fast, low>$ tradeoff, 30% falls in the $<average, low>$ quadrant, whereas 20% relates to the $<slow, low>$ tradeoff. When PRIM is applied, for instance, in the sixth row for the *SSO* decision and $<fast, high>$ as the target tradeoff, 100% of the constrained configurations belong to that tradeoff quadrant. The parameter constraints for this case are $N_A = [8.0, 12.0]$ and $S_{GW} = [2.5, 7.5]$. The constraints for all the cases are provided in the reproducibility package.

Both algorithms were able to effectively constraint certain parameters for ensuring the desirable tradeoffs of Fig. 4a, namely: $<fast, low>$ (no-offloading), $<fast, average>$ and $<fast, high>$ (short-services offloading). On one hand, PRIM was able to address more cases than CART, although it was not effective at improving all of them. On the other hand, the cases addressed by CART were limited but all of them were improved. CART outperformed PRIM for the $<fast, average>$ (1.00 versus 0.83 w.r.t. 0.67 as the initial score) and $<average, average>$ (0.33 versus 0.13 w.r.t. 0.11 as the initial score) targets under the decision of short-services offloading. PRIM did better than CART for the $<fast, high>$ target (1.0 versus 0.5 w.r.t. 0.11 as the initial score). The differences can be attributed to the internal working of the algorithms, which returned different parameter ranges even for the same targets. In CART, we observed that improving the $<average, average>$ and $<fast, high>$ targets (with short-services offloading) had a positive side-effect on the $<fast, average>$ target, which is the most prevalent tradeoff in the space.

Constraints for *CQRS* Pattern. The PRIM and CART models are built from the training set (382 instances) and their rules are applied to the test set (256 instances). The most prevalent tradeoffs are $<fast, average>$ for the hardware decision and $<fast, low>$ and $<average, low>$ for the software alternative. Coincidentally, both models identify the frequency of write requests in the database (*Z_write*) as the key parameter for performance sensitivity of the pattern. Furthermore, both models are in agreement suggesting a lower frequency for the parameter that relates to the writing requests.

Table 2. GO pattern's results. Decisions are: no-offloading (NO), short-services-ofloaded (SSO), long-services-ofloaded (LSO). Average is abbreviated with avg.

GO	*Decision*	*Performance tradeoff*	*fast, low*	*fast, avg*	*fast, high*	*avg, low*	*avg, avg*	*avg, high*	*slow, low*	*slow, avg*	*slow, high*
Test set	NO		**0.50**			**0.30**			**0.20**		
	LSO							**1.00**			
	SSO			**0.67**	**0.11**		**0.11**			**0.11**	
PRIM	SSO	*avg, avg*		0.75	0.12		0.13				
		fast, avg		**0.83**	0.17						
		fast, high			**1.00**						
		slow, avg					1.00			0.00	
	LSO	*avg, high*						1.00			
	NO	*avg, low*	0.83			0.17					
		fast, low	**1.00**								
		slow, low	0.50			0.30			0.20		
CART	SSO	*fast, high*		0.50	**0.50**						
		avg, avg		0.33			**0.33**			0.33	
		fast, avg		**1.00**							
	NO	*fast, low*	**1.00**								

Table 3. CQRS pattern's results. Decisions are: hardware separation (hw) and software separation (sw). Average is abbreviated with avg.

CQRS	*Decision*	*Performance tradeoff*	*fast, low*	*fast, avg*	*fast, high*	*avg, low*	*avg, avg*	*avg, high*	*slow, low*	*slow, avg*	*slow, high*
Test set	hw		0.04	**0.84**		0.02	**0.05**		**0.06**		
	sw		**0.44**			**0.56**					
PRIM	hw	*avg, avg*	0.17	0.43		0.03	**0.20**		0.17		
		avg, low	0.05	0.81		0.02	0.06		0.07		
		fast, avg		**1.00**							
		slow, low	0.22			0.11	0.11		**0.56**		
	sw	*avg, avg*	0.52			0.48	0.00				
		avg, low	0.46			0.54					
		fast, avg	0.41	0.00		0.59					
		slow, low	0.43			0.57			0.00		
CART	hw	*fast, avg*		**1.00**							
	sw	*fast, avg*	0.45	0.00		0.55					

Table 4. ACL pattern's results. Decision consists of the frequency of invoking the ACL component. Average is abbreviated with avg.

ACL	*Decision*	*Performance tradeoff*	*fast, low*	*fast, avg*	*fast, high*	*avg, low*	*avg, avg*	*avg, high*	*slow, low*	*slow, avg*	*slow, high*
Test set	acl		0.02	**0.48**	**0.39**		**0.09**	0.01		0.01	
PRIM	acl	*fast, avg*		**1.00**							
	acl	*fast, high*		0.04	**0.96**						
CART	acl	*fast, avg*		**0.73**			0.20			0.07	
	acl	*fast, high*		0.10	**0.87**			0.03			

As noted from the density metrics in Table 3, both PRIM and CART obtain maximal effectiveness at improving the $<fast, average>$ target, which is a desirable target with the hardware decision, according to Fig. 4b. CART is very limited and could not address other tradeoffs. However, PRIM successfully addresses the $<average, average>$ (0.2 w.r.t. 0.05 as the initial score) and $<slow, low>$ (0.56 w.r.t. 0.06 as the initial score) targets for the hardware decision, even when those tradeoffs are not prevalent in the dataset. This result highlights an interesting feature of PRIM that is not observed in CART, as it mostly detects prevalent tradeoffs.

Constraints for *ACL* Pattern. The pattern dataset was split (234 instances) in order to build the PRIM and CART models on the training set ($\approx$ 138 instances). The most prevalent tradeoffs are $<fast, average>$ and $<average, high>$, which are also desirable targets, according to Fig. 4c.

The corresponding rules are evaluated on the test set, and both yield gains in the density scores for the target tradeoffs above, with a slight score increment for PRIM over CART. The parameters N_A and N_B are shared by the two algorithms as being relevant for performance sensitivity, with more or less the same ranges of values. The reason is that these parameters relate to the workload of requests, thus affecting the performance metrics. However, PRIM also returned *p_A* as a relevant parameter, while CART returned *1- p_B* for the same role. These two parameters relate to the probability of invoking the ACL component that plays a key role for this pattern. In PRIM, the suggested ranges for *p_A* were below 0.5 for $<fast, average>$ and above 0.7 for $<fast, high>$. In CART instead the value range for *1- p_B* was below 0.5 for both tradeoffs.

Summarizing, these analysis results answer **RQ#2**. In general, the score improvements for all the patterns are most noticeable in those quality-attribute tradeoffs encompassing many configurations in the dataset, i.e., tradeoffs with a reasonable coverage of solutions in the space. Both PRIM and CART work well for certain under-represented tradeoffs for the *GO* and *CQRS* patterns.

6 Related Work

Microservices are increasingly popular due to their promises of agility, scalability, maintainability, and performance [8], which have even attracted major vendors, e.g., Netflix [21]. Recent studies have remarked on the importance of evaluating the performance of microservices, e.g., [1,6,28] to mention a few recent ones. In the following, we discuss the main approaches related to the aspects tackled in this paper, acknowledging that our selection of works is not exhaustive.

Performance Evaluation. Di Francesco et al. [18] collect 103 studies on microservice architectures, and performance is observed to grow in popularity and relevance among microservice quality attributes. Li et al. [11] review 72 studies and outline performance as one of critical attributes when designing a microservices application. Wijerathna et al. [24] show that performance is often evaluated during the latest stages of the development cycles, hence fixing issues becomes expensive, so it is instead preferable to incorporate performance-based knowledge from the architectural phase. All these studies highlight the importance of performance analysis in microservices architectures, thus endorsing our research.

Architectural Patterns. Khomh et al. [9] study a cloud-based application along with six design patterns that influence the system performance and energy consumption, but there is no sensitivity analysis in the derived findings. Akbulut et al. [2] evaluate the performance of three design patterns, and measurements reveal that the patterns perform better or worse depending on the different scenarios they are applied to. Amiri et al. [3] leverage the adoption of architectural patterns to explore performance and reliability tradeoffs. Ma et al. [12] present a correlation mechanism to detect cloud design patterns showing an anomalous performance behavior. Long et al. [15] assess the usage of one design pattern that aims to balance the incoming load of requests, thus showing a positive impact on the performance of a serverless application. Overall, these studies evaluate the impact of applying architectural patterns, but they do not quantitatively compare the design decisions along with the correlated sensitivity analysis, as we pursue in this paper.

Behavioral Robustness. The notion of sensitivity is related to robustness, as recently renewed by Zhang et al. [26]. Robustness is defined as the largest set of deviating environmental behaviors under which the system is capable of guaranteeing a desired property. This concept evolved into a robustification objective [27], i.e., how to improve the robustness of a design (while minimizing the cost of architectural changes) against potential deviations. A tool-based approach is proposed in [25] where repairs are synthesized from solving a multi-objective problem that minimizes the amount of behaviors and the costs of design modifications. Our research is motivated by controlling the possible deviations in design patterns' parameters with respect to performance properties. This is achieved through PRIM and CART that reduce the variability of parameters.

In summary, to the best of our knowledge, there are several approaches that investigated the performance behavior of pattern-based microservices architectures. Our novelty relies on inferring rules to support architects in understanding and controlling pattern variability while achieving performance tradeoffs.

7 Conclusion and Future Work

This paper proposes a data-driven analysis of architectural patterns applied in the context of microservices applications. Our results provide insights to software architects since they are informed on the key parameters that affect the adoption of architectural patterns and their impact on performance tradeoffs, thus contributing to the quantitative evaluation of microservices applications. In this work, we rely on Queuing Networks as analytical models for performance, since we exploit a publicly available dataset[1] that includes different parameter ranges and reports interesting performance variations and insights. However, we recall that our approach is not tied to any performance modeling formalism, its primary goal is to collect data about patterns and their performance indicators as the basis for sensitivity analysis and subsequent constraint inference.

As future work, we plan to analyze a larger set of architectural patterns and their combinations, even from different application domains, and to consider other quality indicators, such as reliability and security. We are interested in deriving design decisions with associated tradeoffs so that software architects have a wider understanding of the alternative decisions at their disposal. We also plan to assess the actual adoption of architectural patterns in industrial case studies, thus collecting further data to study the variability of pattern parameters.

Acknowledgments. We would like to thank the anonymous reviewers for their valuable feedback that was helpful to improve the quality of the paper. This work has been partially funded by the MUR-PRIN project 20228FT78M DREAM, MUR Department of Excellence 2023 - 2027 for GSSI, and PNRR ECS00000041 VITALITY. Also, the work has been partially supported by PICT-2021-00757 project, Argentina.

Data Availability Statement. We provide a reproducibility package with the scripts and datasets used in our experiments at: https://doi.org/10.5281/zenodo.15526563.

References

1. Ahmad, H., Treude, C., Wagner, M., Szabo, C.: Smart HPA: a resource-efficient horizontal pod auto-scaler for microservice architectures. In: 2024 IEEE 21st International Conference on Software Architecture (ICSA), Hyderabad, India, pp. 46–57 (2024). https://doi.org/10.1109/ICSA59870.2024.00013
2. Akbulut, A., Perros, H.G.: Performance analysis of microservice design patterns. IEEE Internet Comput. **23**(6), 19–27 (2019)

[1] https://zenodo.org/records/7524410.

3. Amiri, A., Zdun, U., Hoorn, A.V.: Modeling and empirical validation of reliability and performance trade-offs of dynamic routing in service- and cloud-based architectures. IEEE Trans. Serv. Comput. **15**(6), 3372–3386 (2021)
4. Breiman, L., Friedman, J.H., Olshen, R.A., Stone, C.J.: Classification and regression trees (1984)
5. Bryant, B.P., Lempert, R.J.: Thinking inside the box: a participatory, computer-assisted approach to scenario discovery. Technol. Forecast. Soc. Chang. **77**(1), 34–49 (2010)
6. Di, P., Liu, B., Gao, Y.: MicroFuzz: an efficient fuzzing framework for microservices. In: Proceedings of the International Conference on Software Engineering (ICSE) – Software Engineering in Practice Track (2024, to appear)
7. Friedman, J.H., Fisher, N.I.: Bump hunting in high-dimensional data. Stat. Comput. **9**(2), 123–143 (1999)
8. Jamshidi, P., Pahl, C., Mendonça, N.C., Lewis, J., Tilkov, S.: Microservices: the journey so far and challenges ahead. IEEE Softw. **35**(3), 24–35 (2018)
9. Khomh, F., Abtahizadeh, S.A.: Understanding the impact of cloud patterns on performance and energy consumption. J. Syst. Softw. **141**, 151–170 (2018)
10. Lazowska, E.D., Zahorjan, J., Graham, G.S., Sevcik, K.C.: Quantitative System Performance - Computer System Analysis Using Queueing Network Models. Prentice Hall (1984)
11. Li, S., et al.: Understanding and addressing quality attributes of microservices architecture: a systematic literature review. Inf. Softw. Technol. **131**, 106449 (2021)
12. Ma, M., Lin, W., Pan, D., Wang, P.: ServiceRank: root cause identification of anomaly in large-scale microservice architectures. IEEE Trans. Dependable Secure Comput. **19**(5), 3087–3100 (2022)
13. Martin, R.C.: Design principles and design patterns. Object Mentor **1**(34), 597 (2000)
14. Meijer, W., Trubiani, C., Aleti, A.: Experimental evaluation of architectural software performance design patterns in microservices. J. Syst. Softw. **218**, 112183 (2024)
15. Ngo, K.L., Mukherjee, J., Jiang, Z.M., Litoiu, M.: Evaluating the scalability and elasticity of function as a service platform. In: Proceedings of the International Conference on Performance Engineering (ICPE), pp. 117–124 (2022)
16. Pinciroli, R., Aleti, A., Trubiani, C.: Performance modeling and analysis of design patterns for microservice systems. In: Proceedings of the International Conference on Software Architecture (ICSA), pp. 35–46 (2023)
17. Quéval, P.J., Zdun, U.: Extracting the architecture of microservices: an approach for explainability and traceability. In: Proceedings of the European Conference on Software Architecture (ECSA), pp. 346–353 (2023)
18. Di Francesco, P., Lago, P., Malavolta, I.: Architecting with microservices: a systematic mapping study. J. Syst. Softw. **150**, 77–97 (2019)
19. Microsoft Learn: Cloud Design Patterns (2022). https://learn.microsoft.com/en-us/azure/architecture/patterns/. Accessed Apr 2024
20. Sousa, T.B., Ferreira, H.S., Correia, F.F.: A survey on the adoption of patterns for engineering software for the cloud. IEEE Trans. Software Eng. **48**(6), 2128–2140 (2022)
21. Thönes, J.: Microservices. IEEE Softw. **32**(1), 116 (2015)
22. Tundo, A., Mobilio, M., Riganelli, O., Mariani, L.: Monitoring probe deployment patterns for cloud-native applications: definition and empirical assessment. IEEE Trans. Serv. Comput. (2024)

23. Vale, G., Correia, F.F., Guerra, E.M., de Oliveira Rosa, T., Fritzsch, J., Bogner, J.: Designing microservice systems using patterns: an empirical study on quality trade-offs. In: Proceedings of the International Conference on Software Architecture (ICSA), pp. 69–79 (2022)
24. Wijerathna, L., Aleti, A., Bi, T., Tang, A.: Mining and relating design contexts and design patterns from stack overflow. Empir. Softw. Eng. **27**(1), 8:1–8:53 (2022)
25. Zhang, C., Dardik, I., Meira-Góes, R., Garlan, D., Kang, E.: Fortis: a tool for analysis and repair of robust software systems. In: Proceedings of the International Conference on Formal Methods in Computer-Aided Design (FMCAD), pp. 1–9 (2023)
26. Zhang, C., Garlan, D., Kang, E.: A behavioral notion of robustness for software systems. In: Proceedings of the Joint Meeting on European Software Engineering Conference and Symposium on the Foundations of Software Engineering (ESEC/FSE), pp. 1–12 (2020)
27. Zhang, C., Saluja, T., Meira-Góes, R., Bolton, M., Garlan, D., Kang, E.: Robustification of behavioral designs against environmental deviations. In: Proceedings of the International Conference on Software Engineering (ICSE), pp. 423–434 (2023)
28. Zhang, C., Dong, Z., Peng, X., Zhang, B., Chen, M.: Trace-based multi-dimensional root cause localization of performance issues in microservice systems. In: Proceedings of the International Conference on Software Engineering (ICSE), p. 894 (2024)

Software Architecture Practices, Perspectives and Evolution

Architectural Design Decisions and Best Practices for Fast and Efficient CI/CD Pipelines

Francesco Urdih[1,2](✉), Theodoros Theodoropoulos[1], and Uwe Zdun[1]

[1] Software Architecture Research Group, Faculty of Computer Science, University of Vienna, Vienna, Austria
{francesco.urdih,theodoros.theodoropoulos,uwe.zdun}@univie.ac.at
[2] Faculty of Computer Science, UniVie Doctoral School Computer Science DoCS, University of Vienna, Vienna, Austria

Abstract. Continuous Integration/Deployment (CI/CD) pipelines are critical for integrating developer changes and maintaining high-quality software deployments. The increasing frequency of commits and deployments places significant demands on CI/CD systems, requiring improved speed and efficiency. While numerous tools and techniques have been proposed to increase the velocity of CI/CD pipelines, there is a notable gap in architectural guidance for developers on key design decisions and best practices. To address this, we conducted a grey literature review using Straussian Grounded Theory to develop a UML-based model to guide software architects and developers in their decision-making. Our research focuses on identifying architectural design decisions (ADDs) and best practices as decision options that improve the speed and efficiency of CI/CD pipelines. The study analyses 38 sources, building a formal model comprising 6 ADDs and 30 best practices. This work contributes a structured, architecturally guided approach to optimizing CI/CD systems.

Keywords: CI/CD · Software Architecture · Design Decisions · Speed · Efficiency

1 Introduction

Continuous Integration and Continuous Deployment (CI/CD) [7] pipelines enable seamless integration of code changes, enhancing feedback speed and ensuring high-quality releases [1]. Speed and efficiency are crucial in CI/CD systems, as slow pipelines delay the development of new features [10] and overall deployments. With frequent commits and rapid releases becoming standard, the performance of CI/CD pipelines faces increasing pressure.

Several studies have proposed tools and techniques to enhance CI/CD performance [4,5,11]. However, there is no comprehensive approach guiding developers through the key architectural design decisions, available design options,

V. Andrikopoulos et al. (Eds.): ECSA 2025, LNCS 15929, pp. 297–305, 2026.
https://doi.org/10.1007/978-3-032-02138-0_19

and their interrelations. This lack of guidance is problematic as CI/CD pipelines and their surrounding systems have evolved into complex infrastructures critical for building, testing, and deploying software.

To address this, we conducted a grey literature (GL) study [6] using Straussian Grounded Theory (GT) [2] to formalize UML-based models guiding software architects in their decision-making. More formally, we investigated:

- **RQ1**: Which best practices are practitioners using to improve the speed and efficiency of CI/CD pipelines?
- **RQ2**: What are the relations between the identified best practices?
- **RQ3**: Which ADDs are related to improving performance in CI/CD systems, and how are the design options (i.e., the identified best practices) connected with the ADDs?

The primary contributions of this work are: **(1)** a grey literature study on CI/CD best practices for speed and efficiency, analyzing 38 sources in-depth; **(2)** a formal model containing 6 ADDs, and 30 best practices.

2 Methodology

Figure 1 summarizes the research approach used in this work. We applied Straussian Grounded Theory to analyze 38 grey literature[1] sources. GT is a systematic method that, through iterative analysis, enables theory discovery from empirical data. Stol et al. [8] discussed its application in Software Engineering and proposed domain-specific guidelines.

We used popular search engines (e.g., Google, Bing, DuckDuckGo) to collect sources, starting with queries like "speeding up CI/CD pipelines" and "CI/CD pipelines performance." Following GT's *theoretical sampling*, additional GL was added based on analysis of previous sources. We also employed *backward snowballing*—examining references in already selected sources. Literature collection ended upon reaching *theoretical saturation*, i.e., when new sources stopped contributing to the developed model. We excluded sources deemed irrelevant (e.g., only discussing CI/CD benefits/challenges), of poor quality (e.g., lacking discussion), or heavily promotional. Sources that only briefly mentioned their product were retained. All the sources can be found in the replication package [9].

In line with Straussian GT, our analysis involved *open*, *axial*, and *selective coding*, all performed manually. In open coding, data fragments (e.g., sentences) were assigned concepts. Axial coding linked these concepts. Selective coding then grouped them under a central category. While coding, we applied a key GT technique: *memoing*—writing notes/sketches to clarify concepts, categories, and relationships, and to support theory development. Memos aid in the GT practice of *constant comparison*—comparing existing and new data to refine theory. Since GT analysis begins before data collection ends, we analyzed sources as we found them. All memos can be found in the replication package [9].

[1] Grey literature [6] includes practitioner books, videos, blogs, presentations, etc.

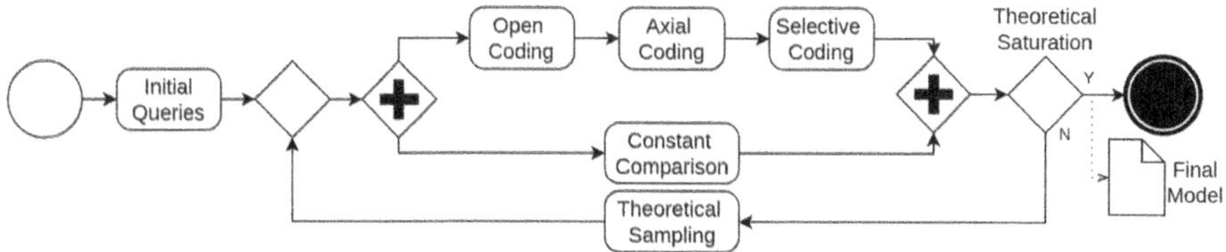

Fig. 1. The methodology applied in our paper.

Table 1. The best practices presented in this work, grouped by ADD and sorted by the number of mentions across grey sources.

Best Practice	Number of Mentions	Addresses Speed	Addresses Efficiency
Shared Across ADDs			
Pipeline Observability	20	✓	✓
ADD: Tasks Reduction			
Pipeline Asset Caching	22	✓	✓
Conditional Pipeline and Job Triggering	17	✓	✓
Interruptible Pipelines	9	✓	✓
Selective Testing	8	✓	✓
Incremental Build	5	✓	✓
Minimal Image Design	4	✓	✓
Mocked External Services	4	✓	✓
Asset Retention Policy	4		✓
Single Build	3		✓
ADD: Tasks and Resources Organization			
Task Parallelization	28	✓	
Task Splitting	16	✓	
Custom Runner Classes	13	✓	✓
CI/CD Architecture Scaling Strategy	11	✓	✓
Automatic Task Splitting	9	✓	
Manual Task Splitting	8	✓	
Pipeline Test Ordering	8		✓
Task Merging	3	✓	✓
ADDs: Conditional Triggering			
File Changes Condition	10	✓	✓
Job-Level Condition	9	✓	✓
Pipeline-Level Condition	9	✓	✓
Branch Condition	8	✓	✓
Trigger Type Condition	6	✓	✓
Commit Message Condition	3	✓	✓
ADD: Task Parallelization			
Intra-Pipeline Parallelism	24	✓	
Inter-Jobs Parallelism	19	✓	
Independent Jobs	13	✓	
Job Matrix	10	✓	
Inter-Pipelines Parallelism	5	✓	
Intra-Job Parallelism	4	✓	

To model the ADDs, we used the meta-model in the replication package [9]. Each design decision can involve multiple design option combinations. We highlighted especially beneficial ones using the <<*can be combined with*>> relation.

3 Architectural Design Decisions

This section presents the study results as an Architectural Design Decision model. Table 1 overviews all the decision options, as well as how many sources reference them. A detailed mapping (e.g., the degree to which a source mentions a practice) is included in the replication package [9]. Given the space restrictions, we included only one model's view in Fig. 2, leaving all the other views in the replication package [9].

ADD: Tasks Reduction. Improving the speed and efficiency of a CI/CD pipeline can be achieved by reducing the number of tasks, without compromising its core purpose, such as building, testing, and deploying applications. Figure 2 shows all related options. Notably, monitoring the pipeline, as promoted by the *Pipeline Observability* best practice, supports task reduction by revealing performance issues and bottlenecks.

One key option for this ADD is *Pipeline Asset Caching* [4], where assets (e.g., dependencies, build artifacts) are cached for reuse within the current and future pipeline runs. This reduces the need to re-download assets from external services or re-compute them locally (e.g., binary packages), thus saving time and resources. However, cache management (e.g., restoring or validating cache data) has a performance overhead. Among other things, defining a *Retention Strategy* is crucial to choosing how long assets are kept before deletion. Three other options depend on cached assets: *Single Build*, *Incremental Build*, and *Selective Testing*. In the build phase, *Single Build* improves efficiency by building the application once, caching the result, and reusing it in subsequent jobs instead of rebuilding. *Incremental Build* further improves performance by saving build results and rebuilding only components (and their dependencies) affected by a commit—especially useful with frequent commits. Similarly, *Selective Testing* [5] reduces testing time by running tests only on files impacted by a commit, often leveraging cached code coverage data. Given the importance of testing for ensuring correctness, reliability, and performance, skipping tests may be an anti-pattern if the version reaches production. The best practice *Conditional Pipeline and Job Triggering* can help avoid this by running the pipeline or specific jobs based on custom conditions, adding flexibility. In addition to *Selective Testing*, *Interruptible Pipelines* can also benefit from *Conditional Triggering*. *Interruptible Pipelines* suggests stopping a pipeline if a new commit is pushed to the same branch, reducing workload. One example combines these: run all tests without interruption in the `main` or `master` branches, but run change-affected tests and allow interruptions on others.

The seven design options discussed so far can be applied to any existing pipeline, with many possible combinations. In contrast, two additional options may not always be applicable: *Mocked External Services* and *Minimal Image Design*. The former involves using mock-ups instead of real tools or services during tests, saving time and resources. The latter reduces container images to the essentials (e.g., via multi-stage builds), lowering the time and resources needed to build and pull images in subsequent jobs.

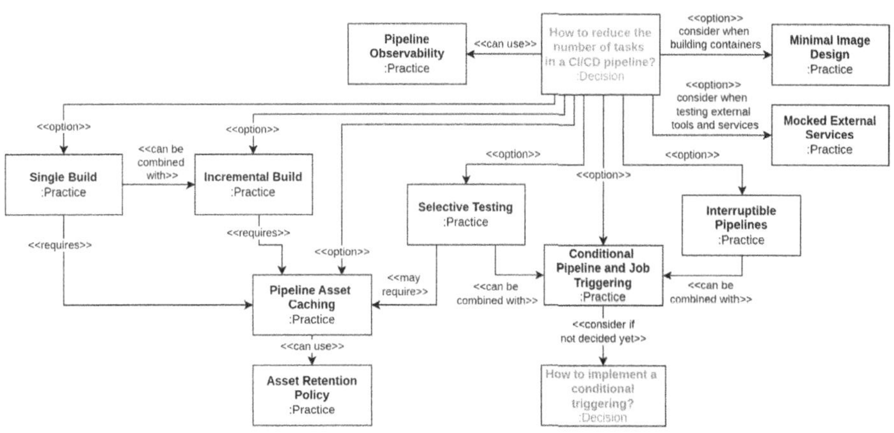

Fig. 2. Decision for reducing the number of tasks in a CI/CD pipeline.

ADD: Tasks and Resources Organization. Organizing tasks and resources effectively can accelerate a CI/CD pipeline. This ADD includes eight design options: two focused on resources (*Custom Runner Classes* and *CI/CD Architecture Scaling Strategy*), five on tasks (*Pipeline Task Ordering*, *Task Merging*, *Task Splitting*, and its two variants), and one on both (*Task Parallelization*). *Custom Runner Classes* suggests using runner types with different specs (e.g., memory, CPU) for tasks with distinct resource needs. *CI/CD Architecture Scaling Strategy* adjusts system resources by scaling them based on workload.

Task Parallelization boosts throughput by increasing task concurrency. More on it is detailed in the corresponding ADD, presented below. *Task Parallelization* is especially effective when paired with *Task Splitting*, the practice of dividing large tasks—manually or automatically—into smaller jobs or workflows. This option depends on parallelization to enhance performance. Note that each executed job has a starting cost (e.g., loading a container image). For this reason, when too many small jobs are present, *Task Merging* should be applied to combine them. Finally, *Pipeline Test Ordering* aims to reduce wasted computation (if the pipeline fails) by sequencing tests wisely: running resource-intensive ones (e.g., end-to-end tests) only after initial checks (e.g., linting, unit tests).

ADDs: Conditional Triggering. We previously introduced *Conditional Pipeline and Job Triggering* as a way to reduce tasks in a CI/CD pipeline. In the grey literature, we found several applications of this practice and identified three ADDs with six decision options. Architects must first decide where to apply conditions: at the *pipeline level* or *job level*. The former determines whether to trigger the entire pipeline, while the latter targets specific jobs, offering greater flexibility. Both approaches were common in practitioner sources and can be used together. After selecting the condition granularity, the next step is choosing the triggering rules. The most frequent is based on committed *File Changes*, but

Trigger Type and *Branch* are also widely used. Finally, *Commit Message* content can serve as a trigger, though this rule is prone to human error (e.g., typos, forgetfulness) and should be applied with caution.

ADD: Task Parallelization. The most frequently mentioned practice in the examined sources is *Task Parallelization*. Thus, we modeled an ADD on how to apply it. We identified six design options, four of which are variants. Parallelism can be achieved by running multiple pipelines (*Inter-Pipeline Parallelism*) or within a single pipeline (*Intra-Pipeline Parallelism*). The latter is more widely cited in the grey literature, likely because not all CI/CD tools support defining multiple workflows per repository. Within a pipeline, parallelism can occur inside a job using multiple threads (*Intra-Job Parallelism*) or by executing several jobs concurrently (*Inter-Jobs Parallelism*). The latter includes two variants: *Independent Jobs* and *Job Matrix*. *Independent Jobs* are widely used, as CI/CD systems automatically run jobs in parallel if no explicit dependencies exist. This practice can also support *Manual Task Splitting*. *Job Matrixes* enable automatic task distribution across workers and offer better maintainability than *Independent Jobs*, though they are unsuitable when tasks are highly interdependent or require strict sequencing.

4 Discussion

RQ1. Table 1 summarizes 30 best practices for improving CI/CD pipeline speed and efficiency, identified through analysis of 38 practitioner sources. These practices span various areas of CI/CD pipelines, including task parallelization, asset caching, and job/workflow triggering. Nine practices are particularly frequent, mentioned in at least one-third of the sources: *Task Parallelization*, *Pipeline Asset Caching*, *Pipeline Observability*, *Conditional Pipeline and Job Triggering*, *Task Splitting*, *Custom Runner Classes*, and three more related to *Task Parallelization*. Notably, several of the practices present multiple variants.

RQ2. We found several connections between best practices, including: *<<require>>* from *Incremental Build* to *Pipeline Asset Caching*, *<<can use>>* from *Pipeline Asset Caching* to *Asset Retention Policy*, *<<has variant>>* from *Inter-Jobs Parallelism* to *Independent Jobs*, and *<<can be combined with>>* from *Job Matrix* to *Automatic Task Splitting*. The *<<can be combined with>>* relation reflects only the most effective combinations, not all possibilities. A key insight is the central role of *Pipeline Observability*. While it does not directly improve speed or efficiency, it enables the adoption of many other practices. This was noted in over half (20 of 38) of the grey literature sources.

RQ3. We identified 6 architectural design decisions, each associated with multiple best practices. Not all options are universally applicable; for instance, *Minimal Image Design* can reduce enacted tasks only when containers are built in the pipeline. Furthermore, as highlighted for RQ2, some design options depend on others to function or are more effective when combined. Finally, we also discovered a <<*can use*>> relation linking the ADDs to *Pipeline Observability*.

5 Threats to Validity

Construct Validity. The construct validity of this study is influenced by the use of GL and GT, both of which pose potential risks. Grey literature varies in quality and credibility, but prior research supports its value in capturing practitioner perspectives [6]. We addressed issues by systematically selecting and analyzing 38 sources. For Grounded Theory, threats stem from the complexity and potential inconsistencies in its application. Stol et al. [8] identify essential steps—coding, memoing, and theoretical saturation—which we rigorously followed to ensure methodological rigor.

Internal Validity. This study faces two main threats: selection bias in GL and researcher bias in modeling ADDs. Selection bias could cause the omission of relevant sources. We mitigated this by using theoretical saturation as the stopping criterion, halting model development only when new sources added no design options. As shown in the replication package [9], no new options appeared after `S11`, yet 27 additional sources were included for robustness. Design options were included only if mentioned in at least three sources—all but three options met this after analyzing half of the sources. More details are in the replication package. Researcher bias in modeling ADDs is another threat. While unavoidable, we minimized it through independent reviews of each ADD.

External Validity. A key threat to external validity is generalizability. To address this, we analyzed both technology-agnostic and technology-specific sources (spanning seven CI/CD tools), as detailed in the replication package [9]. This diversity enhances external validity, though applicability to less conventional setups may still be limited.

6 Related Work

Certain best practices presented in our work have already been analyzed in other studies. Gallaba et al. [4] proposed a framework to automatically cache dependencies across pipeline runs based on system calls. Memon et al. [5] presented a technique to apply *Selective Testing* by reversing the dependencies of the files modified in a commit. Although these works propose tools to help use the studied practice, their application is limited to that single practice.

Other works have studied more than one practice proposed in our study. Yin et al. [11] have cataloged practices to reduce tasks in pipelines, mining 7795 open-source repositories. Their findings present several practices related to *Conditional Pipeline and Job Triggering*. Contrary to our work, their paper focuses on one specific technology and provides only one class of practices. Additionally, Duvall et al. [3] mentioned in their book on Continuous Integration some techniques to improve the pipelines, such as: *Task Parallelization*, *Mocked External Services*, *Pipeline Observability*, *Pipeline Test Ordering*.

None of these works proposes formal models incorporating design decisions, decision options, and their relationships regarding speed and efficiency for CI/CD pipelines. To the best of our knowledge, no current work does that. In addition, despite the benefits of GL to analyze practitioners' views [6], none of the listed studies systematically utilized these knowledge sources.

7 Conclusions and Future Work

In this study, we used Straussian GT to analyze 38 GL sources focused on improving CI/CD pipeline speed and efficiency. Our findings are summarized in a model comprising ADDs, decision options, and their relationships. We aimed to answer three research questions. In RQ1, we identified 30 best practices for enhancing CI/CD workflows. For RQ2, we linked these practices, specifying possible, required, and variant combinations. In RQ3, we uncovered 6 ADDs along with their corresponding design options. Practitioners can apply the proposed model to better understand CI/CD pipeline best practices for performance or to revise existing architectures. Finally, our model can serve as a starting point for future extensions and validations of the proposed best practices.

Acknowledgments. This research was funded in whole or in part by the Austrian Science Fund (FWF) project CQ4CD, Grant-DOI: 10.55776/I6510. For open access purposes, the authors have applied a CC BY public copyright license to any author accepted manuscript version arising from this submission.

Data Availability Statement. All artifacts produced in this study are available in the replication package [9], including the memos from the coding phase and tables summarizing our findings. We used the *Wayback Machine* to archive each grey source indefinitely and included both the original and archived links.

References

1. Chen, L.: Continuous delivery: huge benefits, but challenges too. IEEE Softw. **32**(2), 50–54 (2015)
2. Corbin, J., Strauss, A.: Basics of Qualitative Research: Techniques and Procedures for Developing Grounded Theory. Sage publications, Thousand Oaks (2014)
3. Duvall, P.M., Matyas, S., Glover, A.: Continuous Integration: Improving Software Quality and Reducing Risk. Pearson Education, Boston (2007)
4. Gallaba, K., Ewart, J., Junqueira, Y., Mcintosh, S.: Accelerating continuous integration by caching environments and inferring dependencies. IEEE Trans. Softw. Eng. **48**(6), 2040–2052 (2020)

5. Memon, A., et al.: Taming google-scale continuous testing. In: 2017 IEEE/ACM 39th International Conference on Software Engineering: Software Engineering in Practice Track (ICSE-SEIP), pp. 233–242. IEEE (2017)
6. Rainer, A., Williams, A.: Using blog-like documents to investigate software practice: benefits, challenges, and research directions. J. Softw. Evol. Process **31**(11), e2197 (2019)
7. Shahin, M., Babar, M.A., Zhu, L.: Continuous integration, delivery and deployment: a systematic review on approaches, tools, challenges and practices. IEEE Access **5**, 3909–3943 (2017)
8. Stol, K.J., Ralph, P., Fitzgerald, B.: Grounded theory in software engineering research: a critical review and guidelines. In: Proceedings of the 38th International Conference on Software Engineering, pp. 120–131 (2016)
9. Urdih, F., Theodoropoulos, T., Zdun, U.: ADDs and best practices for fast and efficient CI/CD pipelines (2025). https://doi.org/10.5281/zenodo.15639753
10. Widder, D.G., Hilton, M., Kästner, C., Vasilescu, B.: A conceptual replication of continuous integration pain points in the context of travis ci. In: Proceedings of the 2019 27th ACM Joint Meeting on European Software Engineering Conference and Symposium on the Foundations of Software Engineering, pp. 647–658 (2019)
11. Yin, M., Kashiwa, Y., Gallaba, K., Alfadel, M., Kamei, Y., McIntosh, S.: Developer-applied accelerations in continuous integration: a detection approach and catalog of patterns. In: Proceedings of the 39th IEEE/ACM International Conference on Automated Software Engineering, pp. 1655–1666 (2024)

From Lab to Market: Architectural Evolution in Open Source Transition

Sven Thielen[1(✉)], Björn Salgert[2], and Thomas Franz[2]

[1] Niederrhein University of Applied Sciences, Krefeld, Germany
sven.thielen@hs-niederrhein.de

[2] University of Applied Sciences Düsseldorf, Düsseldorf, Germany
{bjoern.salgert,thomas.franz}@hs-duesseldorf.de

Abstract. Commercializing research results in the form of software products is a common exploitation path that drives innovation and also targets economic goals. This research provides insights on the relation of software architecture evolution with respect to the commercialization of academic open source software. Using a mixed-methods study of JackTrip, a real-time networked audio software transitioning from academia to commercial use, we i) assessed its structural decay via static analysis of 19 historical versions (2015–2022) and ii) investigated potential reasons via developer interviews. The static analysis reveals escalating architectural smells and dependency volatility despite optimistic metrics, coinciding with pandemic-era commercialization. Interviews highlight tensions between legacy constraints and modernization efforts, leading to workarounds that complicate maintainability. Hybrid governance struggles to balance the mix of contributors and commercialization goals, while documentation gaps impede onboarding and refactoring. Our findings underscore erosion risks for academically rooted OSS: real-time constraints, rapid undocumented growth, and interdisciplinary contributions amplify technical debt. JackTrip exemplifies trade-offs between innovation and sustainability in dual academic-commercial settings, offering insights into erosion drivers in such projects. This work calls for deeper research on managing architectural sustainability in interdisciplinary OSS.

Keywords: Architectural Erosion · Open Source Software (OSS) · Hybrid Governance · Real-Time Systems · Software Archipelago · Cathedral-Bazaar Model

1 Introduction

Architectural erosion, the gradual decay of a system's structural integrity, is a serious risk for sustainable software [11]. This paper presents research on erosion in an open source software (OSS) project that originated in academia and transitioned to commercial use. Academic environments promote domain-specific optimizations (e.g., low-latency audio streaming), whereas commercialization

V. Andrikopoulos et al. (Eds.): ECSA 2025, LNCS 15929, pp. 306–322, 2026.
https://doi.org/10.1007/978-3-032-02138-0_20

prioritizes maintainability and scalability. This tension is amplified in real-time contexts with performance-critical design decisions that establish technical debt. Despite increased research on erosion phenomena [1,10,11], the dynamics of hybrid academic-commercial projects remain understudied, particularly those with interdisciplinary contributors and undocumented growth phases.

We address this through a longitudinal case study of JackTrip, a 25-year-old Stanford-originated OSS for networked music performance (NMP) commercialized during the COVID-19 pandemic. JackTrip's evolution is characterized by real-time audio constraints, hybrid governance, and shifting stakeholder priorities. We investigate:

RQ1: What structural trends indicate architectural erosion in an academically-originated OSS project (like JackTrip) transitioning to commercial use?

RQ2: How do academic research environments and specialized domains (e.g., low-latency audio streaming of JackTrip) influence erosion?

RQ3: How do governance transitions in hybrid academic-commercial models (exemplified by JackTrip's transition) contribute to erosion causes?

Using Laser et al.'s "software archipelago" paradigm [7] and Raymond's cathedral-bazaar dichotomy [16], we analyze JackTrip's fragmentation and protocol legacy constraints represent systemic risks in academically rooted OSS. Our mixed-methods approach improves empirical understanding of erosion in hybrid governance environments balancing innovation with sustainability, while also suggesting additional research on interdisciplinarity and academic-commercial governance in OSS projects.

2 Related Work

Architectural Erosion in OSS: Li et al. [11] systematically mapped erosion causes and symptoms, highlighting a gap in empirical studies of real-world projects. Our case study addresses this gap through a mixed-methods analysis of JackTrip's 25-year evolution. According to Baabad et al. [1], erosion can manifest as accumulating architectural smells (e.g., dependency cycles), which increase in JackTrip's architectural evolution (see Sect. 5.1). They identify rushed evolution, recurring changes, and lack of developer awareness as primary causes. We consider their findings in developer interviews while remaining open to other explanations. Li et al. [10] further highlight erosion's dual impact on runtime and design-time quality, urging deeper empirical investigation. Our longitudinal code analysis and developer interviews support this argument.

Academic Software Challenges: Academic OSS projects face unique erosion risks. Laser et al. [7] describe how "software archipelagos" emerge from proof-of-concept tools and evolve into large long-lived academic tool suites under "publish or perish" constraints. This pattern reoccurs in JackTrip's academic development drivers, architectural challenges, and latency-driven trade-offs (Sect. 5.2, Theme 3–6). Carlin et al. [3] critique undervaluation of software as research output, while

Robillard & Robillard [17] and Liu et al. [12] identify systemic weaknesses in academic software (e.g., ad hoc practices, poor documentation). We discover the context of documentation gaps and identify contributors who acquire software engineering practices during their engagement.

OSS Participation and Documentation: Coelho et al. [5] observe that OSS contributors voluntarily enagage in projects to enhance them for personal needs. This is consistent with JackTrip's "computer musician" culture (Sect. 5.2, Theme 7), which eventually turns users into developers. Their findings on documentation's role in sustaining participation align with Migliorini et al. [13], who note sparse architectural views in OSS projects, particularly post-inception. Our study extends these insights by examining how documentation gaps hinder contributor onboarding and refactoring (Sect. 5.2, Theme 5).

3 Methodology

This explanatory single-case study employs a mixed-methods approach [18] to investigate erosion in JackTrip, selected as a critical case (introduced in Sect. 4). JackTrip's 25-year evolution addresses RQ1 (structural trends via static analysis), RQ2 (domain constraints via interviews), and RQ3 (governance via contributor narratives). Figure 1 illustrates our workflow and employed methods. The static code analysis has been conducted before the semi-structured interviews, in order to gather knowledge about JackTrips architecture to support the discussion within the interviews. To avoid a bias of the interviewer, a structured protocol methodology [18] has been implementented (see Sect. 3.2).

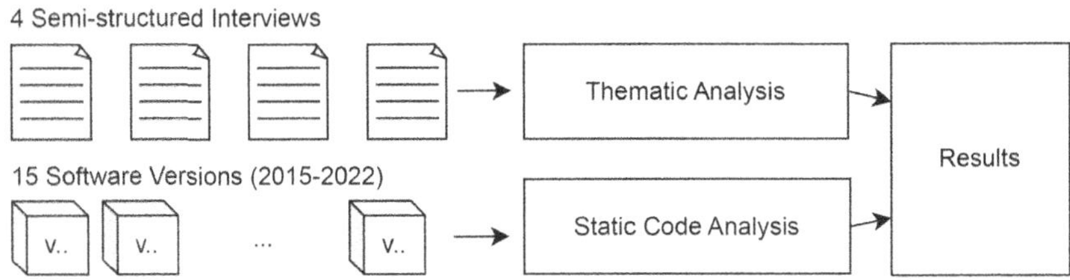

Fig. 1. Methods overview

JackTrip's status as an *extreme yet representative case* [18] is further justified by the absence of comparable longitudinal studies on hybrid academic-commercial OSS, and its role as a living laboratory for architectural tension between artistic as well as research goals (e.g., low-latency optimizations) and commercial maintainability. Section 4 details contextual factors, while Sect. 5 reports static analysis results and interview themes, which are discussed in Sect. 6.

3.1 Software Architecture Analysis

RQ1 is addressed by a software architecture recovery and analysis on 19 historical versions (v1.1–1.6.8) from JackTrip's public repository[1], selected to observe its commercialization while retaining a reference point in its early evolution. Figure 2 illustrates the release timeline from 2015 to 2022. Architectural views were recovered using ARCADE Core[2], a reimplementation of ARCADE under active development, and metric reliability was validated through pilot testing on three early versions (v1.1, v1.3.0, v1.4.0).

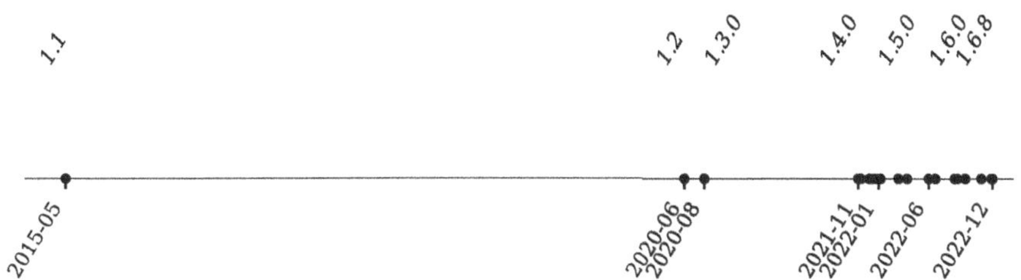

Fig. 2. Release timeline from JackTrip v1.1 to v1.6.8. Dates shown as Year-Month.

Dependency-based smells (dependency cycles, link overload [8]) were prioritized as potential indicators of erosion, though we acknowledge these trends correlate with rather than definitively prove architectural decay. We utilized a pre-release of ARCADE Core providing a number of relevant metrics: Architecture-to-Architecture (a2a), Cluster Coverage (cvg) [9], BasicMQ, TurboMQ [14] and Architectural Instability [9]. For transparency reasons, we also report intra-connectivity (cohesion) and inter-connectivity (coupling) used to calculate the BasicMQ and TurboMQ metrics. While our analysis utilized three architecture recovery methods (ACDC, ARC, PKG), this paper focuses on views generated by the algorithm for comprehension-driven clustering (ACDC) [19] due to space limitations. The full results are archived for reproducibility (Sect. 7).

3.2 Semi-structured Interviews

To complement RQ1's quantitative findings, we conducted semi-structured interviews with four key contributors representing distinct stakeholder roles: an academic founder (IE1, 2000–present), a hobbyist contributor (IE2, 2019–present), a professional stakeholder (IE3, 2020–present), and a hybrid contributor (IE4, 2020present) who started contributing as a hobby and was involved in the early stage of commercialization.

Interviews followed a structured protocol [18] comprising four phases: introduction, admission questions, primary discussion, and retrospective. Sessions

[1] https://github.com/jacktrip/jacktrip.

[2] https://github.com/usc-softarch/arcade_core.

ranged from 37 to 55 min, with duration varying based on participants' depth of elaboration. Each interview began with an alignment on software architecture and erosion definitions. Admission questions explored temporal engagement and organizational challenges, as well as specifics on tooling and infrastructure observed in the project's documentation.

Primary discussions targeted RQ2 and RQ3 through open-ended probes across five dimensions: technical-artistic tradeoffs, domain adaptations, development speed changes, error patterns, and temporal pressures. Participants were asked to describe the consideration of design principles in developer discussions, as well as to retrospectively analyze maintainability-impacting decisions, and imagine a hypothetical redesign. Interviewers used spontaneous or follow-up questions based on engagement and adaptively changed question order while documenting emergent assumptions.

The interviews were transcribed using OpenAI Whisper[3], manually corrected against recordings, and validated by participants. Pseudonymized transcripts underwent thematic analysis [2] with quality assurance checks. Triangulation with findings from static code analysis supported theme refinement.

4 Case Overview

This section contextualizes JackTrip's erosion analysis through its real-time audio domain constraints, 25-year evolutionary trajectory, hybrid academic-commercial stakeholder ecosystem, and documentation practices.

4.1 Dual-Use Domain: Performances and Network Acoustics

JackTrip originated from Stanford's SoundWIRE group to study network acoustics and enable networked music performances (NMPs) by streaming uncompressed, low-latency audio over UDP. Musical signals, sent as discrete packets, face network issues like jitter and packet loss, which the human ear perceives as distortions in pitch or timbre. JackTrip maintains performance quality by buffering and inserting silence to mask these disruptions.

Concurrently, it repurposes network links as virtual resonators using the Karplus-Strong synthesis algorithm (later replaced by Freeverb implemented in Faust). Variations in latency "plucked" the network like a string, producing detuned harmonic effects. This turned technical challenges such as packet loss into artistic features, making JackTrip both a research tool and a performance medium [4].

4.2 Architectural Evolution: Framework Integration and Scalability

JackTrip's architecture developed in three phases. Initially, it used a modular plugin design with CommonC++, threads, and sockets for audio streaming, supplemented by the Qt framework and Synthesis Tool-Kit. In 2009, it integrated

[3] https://github.com/openai/whisper.

the Jack Audio Connection Kit (JACK)[4], which provided consistent low-latency processing through real-time scheduling and fixed buffer sizes, improving multi-core CPU use and Mac OS X support. By 2010, rising demand for multi-location concerts led to a hub mode or "multi-client concurrent server" design, coordinating sessions over TCP and assigning UDP ports dynamically to control, route and mix an arbitrary number of client audio channels [6].

4.3 Stakeholder Ecosystem

Stanford's Center for Computer Research in Music and Acoustics (CCRMA), founded in the 1960s, blends music and technology innovations such as FM synthesis (used in Yamaha's DX7) and Linux audio optimizations. These advances fostered communities like "Planet CCRMA" and nstitutionalized a "multivocality" approach—treating coding and composition as iterative, creative practices. Under its current director, this ethos drives projects like JackTrip [15].

JackTrip's shift from academic project to production infrastructure accelerated during COVID-19 pandemic due to increased demand for internet-based NMPs. Community-driven enhancements by about 22 documented volunteer developers included adding a GUI via QJackTrip[5]. In 2020, the nonprofit JackTrip Foundation formed to maintain the core OSS, alongside JackTrip Labs commercial services. JackTrip Labs offers cloud-hosted "Virtual Studio" subscriptions using preconfigured hub servers for easy session setup.

4.4 Documentation Structure and Evolutionary Traces

JackTrip's documentation provides user guides and compiling instructions, alongside historical source code migration notes. JACK remains the preferred audio backend, though RtAudio[6] provides a cross-platform alternative labeled "not fully functional." The changelog marks key milestones: introduction of the hub mode in version 1.1, IPv6 support in 1.2, an "optional GUI from QJackTrip" in 1.4.0, and integration of the Virtual Studio alongside the classic QJackTrip GUI plus "clode cleanup and maintenance" efforts in 1.6.0.

5 Results

Building on the trade-offs shaped by latency-critical design described above, this section presents our mixed-methods findings: static code analysis reveals structural decay patterns (RQ1), and developer interviews elucidate academic-commercial tensions and domain constraints (RQ2, RQ3).

[4] https://jackaudio.org.
[5] https://www.psi-borg.org/other-dev.html.
[6] https://github.com/thestk/rtaudio.

5.1 Static Code Analysis

Figure 3 compares the system architectures of JackTrip v1.1 and v1.6.8. The ACDC based visualizations illustrate the introduction of clusters and dependencies. Clusters (e.g., body files with associated header files) are named by their filenames, including the relative path, and represented by circles, while lines with arrowheads point to dependencies.

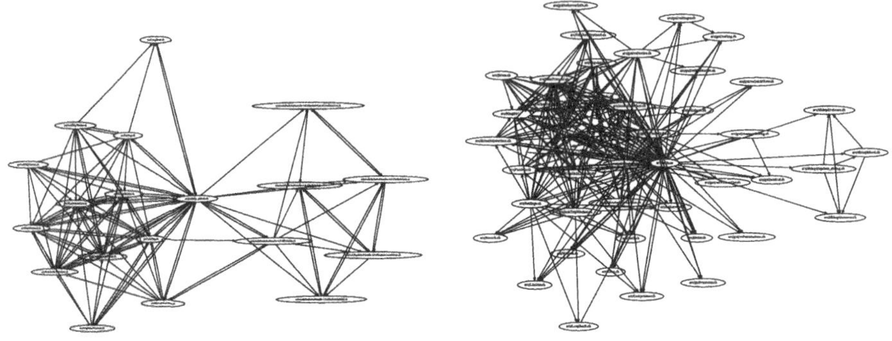

Fig. 3. Visualization of JackTrip's architecture in v1.1 (left) and v1.6.8 (right).

Version 1.6.0 introduces the `src/gui/virtualstudio.c` cluster and multiple `src/gui/vs*`-prefixed clusters indicating a Virtual Studio feature relation. While initial dependencies are localized, subsequent versions (1.6.1–1.6.8) distribute dependencies to other clusters. Other `src/gui/*` clusters see no dispersion of dependencies throughout the evolution. The `src/jacktrip_globals.c` cluster exhibits volatile dependency patterns in early versions, peaking at 13 external dependencies (v1.2) before sharply declining to a single self-referential header in version 1.3.0. Similarly, `src/Settings.c` accumulates four external dependencies in versions 1.1 to 1.2, which is reduced (self-referential header) in the following release. The `src/jacktrip_globals.c` cluster centralizes dependencies in early versions (1.1–1.2) (Fig. 3, left). In version 1.3.0, this characteristic transitions to the `src/jacktrip_main.c` cluster, and in v1.4.0, the dependency epicenter is designated as `src/main.ss` subsystem. This subsystem serves as architectural core for subsequent versions, as shown in v1.6.8 (Fig. 3, right).

Architectural metrics and dependency smells for the illustrated JackTrip versions are presented in Table 1. Most significantly, link overload (LO) smells increase from 1 (v1.1) to 11 (v1.6.8), while dependency cycles (DC) decrease from 2 to 1 post-v1.3.0. New LO smells are introduced with specific releases (v1.3.0, v1.4.0, v1.6.0, and v1.6.2), and remain present in between. Although dependency cycle (DC) smells decrease to one, from version 1.1 onwards this single cycle involves an increasing number of clusters, including `src/Settings.c` since the beginning. Moreover, clusters entering the cycle persist in all subsequent versions.

Table 1. Architectural metrics and smells for JackTrip versions 1.1–1.6.8 (2015–2022) using ACDC recovery, as described in Sect. 3.1.

Release Date	Ver	a2a	cvg	Intra Conn	Inter Conn	Basic MQ	Turbo MQ	Arch Inst	DC	LO
2015-05-27	1.1	–	–	0.23	0.06	0.17	0.17	0.56	2	1
2020-06-07	1.2	92.76	89.47	0.27	0.06	0.17	0.17	0.56	2	1
2020-08-05	1.3.0	57.64	57.90	0.24	0.07	0.17	0.16	0.58	1	2
2021-11-02	1.4.0	83.22	95.24	0.24	0.06	0.18	0.16	0.53	1	5
2021-11-11	1.4.1	100	100	0.24	0.06	0.18	0.16	0.53	1	5
2021-12-05	1.4.2	98.43	100	0.24	0.06	0.19	0.17	0.52	1	5
2021-12-19	1.4.3	100	100	0.24	0.06	0.19	0.17	0.52	1	5
2022-01-03	1.5.0	100	100	0.24	0.06	0.19	0.17	0.52	1	5
2022-01-07	1.5.1	100	100	0.24	0.06	0.19	0.17	0.52	1	5
2022-03-02	1.5.2	97.53	96.43	0.24	0.06	0.19	0.17	0.52	1	5
2022-03-28	1.5.3	100	100	0.24	0.06	0.19	0.17	0.52	1	5
2022-06-01	1.6.0	90.25	100	0.24	0.04	0.20	0.18	0.47	1	8
2022-06-21	1.6.1	100	100	0.24	0.04	0.20	0.18	0.47	1	8
2022-08-17	1.6.2	93.59	100	0.25	0.04	0.21	0.19	0.44	1	11
2022-08-23	1.6.3	100	100	0.25	0.04	0.21	0.19	0.44	1	11
2022-09-16	1.6.4	98.03	100	0.24	0.03	0.21	0.20	0.44	1	11
2022-11-02	1.6.6	95.69	100	0.24	0.03	0.21	0.19	0.44	1	11
2022-12-02	1.6.7	97.69	100	0.24	0.03	0.22	0.20	0.42	1	11
2022-12-06	1.6.8	100	100	0.24	0.03	0.22	0.20	0.42	1	11

Architectural instability decreases from 0.56 (v1.1) to 0.42 (v1.6.8). It gradually increases from 0.56 in version 1.1 to 0.58 in version 1.3.0 before dropping to 0.53 in the following release. A minor reduction to 0.52 occurs with the release of version 1.4.2 and lasts until 1.5.3. With that release, architectural instability decreases in three steps to the final value of 0.42 in version 1.6.8. Architecture-to-architecture (a2a) and cluster coverage (cvg) align to 100% post-2021, supporting the trend toward stability. The architectures and clusters of version 1.3.0 deviate significantly from 1.2. Other versions exhibit similarities over 90%. While cvg only drops below 100% for version 1.5.2, the a2a metric has a stronger correlation to the specific versions where architectural instability decreases and new LO smells are introduced.

BasicMQ (0.17–0.22) and TurboMQ (0.16–0.20) remain low but consistent throughout the evolution, with a modest increasing trend. Their trends also correlate with the aforementioned metrics. However, BasicMQ remains stable while TurboMQ decreases in version 1.3.0. This is inconsistent with the findings for a2a, cvg, and architectural instability. After initially increasing from v1.1 to v1.2, intra-connectivity (cohesion) at approximately 0.24 remains stable through v1.3.0. Inter-connectivity (coupling) declines from 0.06 to 0.03 in three steps.

Though version 1.3.0 peaks at 0.07, the release of v1.4.0 decreases the value back to 0.06, version 1.6.0 to 0.04, and version 1.6.4 to a final value of 0.03.

5.2 Thematic Analysis of Interviews

Thematic analysis of developer interviews, as described in Sect. 3, reveals seven interrelated themes shaping JackTrip's architectural trajectory.

Theme 1: Phases of Accelerated Evolution. Interviewees observe fluctuating evolution speeds, with accelerated development during the COVID-19 pandemic in 2020. Interviewee 1 (IE1) describes JackTrip's evolution as occurring in five distinct "waves": (1) 2000–2004 saw foundational research and academic experimentation; (2) 2004–2009 focused on core development via rewrites using JACK and Qt; (3) 2010 marked stabilization of core technology for practical deployment; (4) 2011–2019 involved refining a mature codebase for applications like teleconcerts; and (5) 2020 onward prioritized GUI development, commercialization, and usability. IE1 frames the OSS-commercial project relationship as a synergistic "tandem thing."

Interviewee 3 (IE3) corroborates rapid post-2020 evolution through retrospection and quantitative analysis of code changes. Interviewee 2 (IE2) identifies a second acceleration tied to JackTrip Labs' (see Sect. 4.3) involvement, which shifted focus toward client experience—a transition some contributors found challenging. Interviewee 4 (IE4), however, downplays JackTrip Labs' impact on broader OSS contributions.

Theme 2: Governance Ambiguity and Hybrid Development. IE4 highlights early governance ambiguity between JackTrip Labs and the OSS project, leading to rapid but unstable codebase evolution. Contributors frequently committed changes without coordination, creating technical debt (e.g., outdated code requiring refactoring). Synchronization risks escalated due to disproportionate commits from full-time commercial developers versus external voluntary contributors, occasionally causing a broken release. Recent process refinements (e.g., shorter commit cycles and increased pull requests) have mitigated merge conflicts and manual fixes.

IE3 underscores the commercial team's systematic bug resolution, including automated safeguards like package signature checks developed after analyzing improper signings ("mental postmortem"). IE1 contextualizes early instability (pre-2011) within limited collaboration: prior to 2004, a single-maintainer workflow without version control or code review hindered bug detection and resolution.

Theme 3: Development Drivers and Organizational Dynamics. JackTrip's evolution is driven by external events (e.g., conferences, demonstrations like NAMM[7]), transient pandemic-induced demand, and academic milestones (PhD deadlines, research cycles). IE3's participation, for instance, stemmed from his desire to support a large virtual choir (40200 users) during the pandemic, where JackTrip's latency and scalability met critical requirements. IE1 emphasizes volunteer passion as a catalyst, noting how new ideas spark momentum—"when the ball gets rolling"—influencing JackTrip Labs' project management.

Time pressure, termed by IE3 as "the overriding factor for everything," shapes JackTrip Labs' operations: bug fixes, customer demands, and resource coordination impact feature prioritization. Scrum workflows help manage workloads, though IE3 notes teams require three months to stabilize. Contrastingly, OSS development lacks formal planning. IE2 highlights transient engagement patterns typical in OSS, where contributors address single features or hobbyist maintenance (e.g., CI tasks) before departing.

Theme 4: Technical Debt and Architectural Challenges. Usability barriers persisted until IE4's QJackTrip GUI integration. IE2 highlights growing complexity in settings management following GUI integration, as JackTrip's CLI origins require dual handling. This "double management," alongside feature accretion without deprecation, complicates code navigation and forces adaptations to legacy design choices. IE1 contextualizes early technological shifts, such as rewrites adopting JACK and Qt, as drivers of both innovation and debt.

Architectural divergence amplifies challenges. IE3 notes that JackTrip Labs' opportunity to build modern microservices contrasts with high coupling via Qt's signals and slots in the OSS codebase. IE4 confirms architectural discussions on cohesion occurred in developer meetings, while IE2 critiques entangled cross-platform code—exemplified by OS-specific macros scattered across modules. He advocates a shared library approach, aligning with interviewees' consensus to decouple core protocol logic from application layers (client/server and CLI/GUI).

Modernization barriers persist: IE3 criticizes reliance on Qt over modern C++ standards, while IE1's HackTrip prototype, a rebuilt hub client using RtAudio and Qt 6, demonstrates alternatives. IE3 views such efforts as potential foundations for incremental refactoring, bridging JackTrip Labs' best practices and legacy constraints of the OSS.

Theme 5: Protocol Limitations and Redesign Proposals. IE2 identifies protocol extensibility constraints, citing the lack of a version indicator or feature negotiation in the header. He proposes a versioned protocol with dedicated channels (e.g., OSC, MIDI) in addition to the audio signal.

IE4 attributes limitations to early technological trade-offs: the original protocol's minimal header and small packet size prioritized speed in low-bandwidth eras but now hinder extensions (e.g., exit codes to distinguish intentional terminations from dropped connections). IE4 also addressed legacy workarounds, such as non-compliant port-binding for IPv4—an "ingenious" solution that failed

[7] https://www.namm.org.

with IPv6 adoption—and emphasizes backward compatibility needs. He proposes revising JackTrip's protocol specification.

Despite consensus on redesign, hesitancy persists. IE3 links this to insufficient technical documentation, which complicates onboarding and fuels uncertainty about systemic overhaul. Resolution requires balancing modernization with legacy support, yet gaps in architectural clarity stall progress.

Theme 6: Latency-Driven Trade-Offs. JackTrip's hub mode exemplifies specialized design for networked music performances (NMPs), contrasting with video streaming's broader use cases. The server aggregates and mixes client audio streams in real-time, demanding high bandwidth and processing power. IE1 highlights geolocated Virtual Studio rooms (Sect. 4.3) as an example of this architecture.

IE4 describes how early decisions were shaped by internet latency constraints: developers prioritized local audio processing (e.g., via JACK, then state-of-the-art), embedding low-latency principles that later conflicted with usability needs. To accommodate non-technical users, JackTrip Labs now sacrifices some efficiency, leveraging improved internet infrastructure. IE4 notes that early reliance on frameworks like JACK and Qt—due to the absence of dedicated audio toolkits—further entrenched technical debt, while modern redesigns seek to balance legacy priorities with accessibility.

Theme 7: Interdisciplinary Synergy. JackTrip's core mission is to replicate in-person musical collaboration. This drives its integration of music technology trends (IE3) alongside niche innovations like third-order ambisonics and wide-area reverberation research (IE1, IE2). IE4 underscores tensions in balancing accessibility with specialization: while JackTrip Labs' Virtual Studio rooms simplify server management for paid users, they introduce operational and codebase complexity. Academic users, however, often bypass third-party dependencies by leveraging institutional infrastructure.

IE1 stresses collaborative design between engineers and musicians, framing contributors as "computer musicians" who blend technical and artistic expertise to evaluate features. This interdisciplinary ethos underpins JackTrip's evolution, even as JackTrip Labs prioritizes usability for non-specialists—a reflection of its dual identity as both research tool and commercial product.

6 Discussion

JackTrip's architecture reflects its academic roots, domain-specific constraints, and hybrid governance. We discuss these findings in relation to our research questions and outline directions for further study.

6.1 RQ1: Structural Symptoms of Erosion in Academic OSS

Static code analysis uncovers progressive architectural decay in JackTrip through smells despite metrics indicating stability trends (Table 1). The a2a and cvg metrics decrease significantly in version 1.3.0, released during the pandemic. This indicates substantial architectural changes corroborated by increased instability and LO smells, while DC smells decrease. These trends align with developers' perceptions of rapid pandemic-era evolution (Sect. 5.2, Theme 1).

While later versions improved modularity (BasicMQ and TurboMQ constantly increased post-v1.4.0), new smells were introduced during commercialization. BasicMQ's positivity (cohesion > coupling) in JackTrip suggests baseline encapsulation. TurboMQ's intra-/inter-connectivity ratio, constrained by design where typical systems score 0.05–0.33 (per ARCADE Core's author), aligns with norms. JackTrip's fundamental inter-connectivity and intra-connectivity metrics indicate sufficient encapsulation (components use internal resources effectively while minimizing external dependencies).

LO smells increase (8 to 11) between v1.6.0 and v1.6.8, correlating with JackTrip Labs' Virtual Studio additions. The core cluster `src/gui/virtualstudio.c` becomes entangled in link overload proliferation and a persistent DC smell (Sect. 5.1). These trends align with Baabad et al.'s observation that architectural smells accumulate invisibly during rapid evolution [1]. Further research may explain whether and why other academic OSS must sacrifice modularity for domain-specific optimizations, as seen in JackTrip's latency-critical design (Sect. 5.2, Theme 6).

6.2 RQ2: Academic Environment and Domain Constraints

While erosion patterns in long-term projects are not unique to JackTrip, its academic-commercial transition intensified erosion risks. The IPv4-based protocol, designed during early internet experimentation (Sect. 5.2, Theme 5), complicated IPv6 adoption and extensibility. JackTrip's early development (2000–2004) aligns more closely with the cathedral model, where a single researcher iterated on prototypes without version control (Sect. 5.2, Theme 2), prioritizing latency optimizations. Transitioning to a more open, bazaar-like model brought benefits but also challenges in managing the growing complexity of the codebase. Raymond's emphasis on modularity in successful bazaar-style projects [16] is particularly relevant here, as JackTrip struggles with monolithic structure and the desire to move core technology into a library. Strict latency requirements (Sect. 4.1) introduced dependencies later deemed technical debt (Sect. 5.2, Theme 4). Interdisciplinarity—where contributors blend music and engineering expertise (Sect. 5.2, Theme 7)—fueled creativity and rapid prototyping but could not account for architectural integrity, corroborating Robillard & Robillard's [17] critique of ad hoc academic practices.

As Laser et al.'s archipelago model [7] illustrates, JackTrip risks evolving through isolated "islands" addressing distinct needs (e.g., internet reverberation, Virtual Studio) and different use cases without cohesive integration. This potential fragmentation, traceable in architectural visualizations (Fig. 3), reflects challenges reconciling academic experimentation with commercial maintainability. During commercialization, contributors like IE4 (hobbyist-turned-developer) and JackTrip Labs prioritized feature additions (Sect. 5.2, Theme 3) evolving semi-independently from the OSS codebase. While Raymond's "release early, release often" principle accelerated innovation [16], it induced fragmentation and reimplementation—evident in HackTrip (Sect. 5.2, Theme 4), a modern rewrite diverging from the main codebase in terms of client/server separation. The archipelago model thus reframes cathedral-bazaar dynamics, illustrating how academic-commercial hybrids potentially face erosion.

6.3 RQ3: Erosion Drivers in Hybrid Governance

JackTrip reveals three potential causes for erosion while highlighting academic-project nuances. First, its developer community presents a unique mix of contributors with varying levels of erosion awareness: professional developers, academic researchers, and hobbyists. Contributors often need musical and engineering expertise (Sect. 5.2, Theme 7), creating a diverse but potentially inexperienced developer base. While some contributors engage short-term for specific features, others maintain long-term involvement (Sect. 5.2, Theme 3) regulating commercial objectives (e.g., JackTrip Labs) or eventually become involved in its commercialization. Personal-need-driven engagement overlaps with the findings of Coelho et al. [5], while unawareness of architectural principles and strategies is known to be a presumable erosion cause [1].

Second, JackTrip Labs' modern practices (e.g., microservices, recent C++ standard) clash with OSS legacy dependencies (e.g., Qt signals/slots, JACK audio backend) in the codebase. This induces architectural fragmentation, as seen in the visualization of Virtual Studio clusters (e.g., `src/gui/vs*`) and the surge of LO smells (Table 1), mirroring Laser et al.'s archipelago model of independently evolving "islands" [7]. JackTrip exemplifies the erosion risks from protocol implementation lacking formal specifications. Designed for IPv4 and minimal latency (Sect. 4.1), it lacked versioning/extensibility mechanisms, forcing workarounds (Sect. 5.2, Theme 5) for backward compatibility. This was critical for maintaining user trust but complicated modernization needs (e.g., IPv6 adoption). IE2's proposal for a versioned protocol addresses this but requires spec documentation of the existing protocol. HackTrip's redesign offers progress (Sect. 5.2, Theme 4). However, its academic origins risk repeating past mistakes (e.g., latency prioritization, documentation gaps).

Third, JackTrip's contributor base—spanning CCRMA researchers, hobbyists, and JackTrip Labs engineers—reflects a "multivocal" culture blending art and engineering (Sect. 4.3). While fostering innovation (e.g., ambisonic support), it tends to complicate architectural oversight. IE1's "computer musicians" concept (Sect. 5.2, Theme 7) may be susceptible to invite contributors prioritizing domain-specific optimizations and neglecting formal software engineering training. IE4's GUI introduction improved usability but complicated settings management characterized by its CLI-era approach (Sect. 5.2, Theme 4). JackTrip Labs'

Scrum process model improved organization from the commercial side (Sect. 5.2, Theme 3) but could not fully mitigate legacy decisions, highlighting the need for hybrid governance models in academic-commercial OSS. Furthermore, tensions of interdisciplinary contribution seem to be understudied and requires further investigation.

6.4 Architectural Lessons for Hybrid OSS

Protocol Design for Extensibility. JackTrip's IPv4-centric protocol, created under early internet constraints, became a legacy challenge. Contributors suggested adding version negotiation headers and dedicated feature channels (e.g., OSC/MIDI) to future-proof such systems. Retrofitting these mechanisms, as seen in IE4's workarounds, was costly and error-prone, highlighting the importance of forward-compatible protocol specifications.

Decoupling Core Logic from Frameworks. Tight integration of latency-sensitive audio logic with frameworks like Qt/JACK slowed modernization. Isolating core logic into standalone libraries and separate client applications like the HackTrip prototype, protects key code from client-side and commercial feature changes. Governance models should enforce modular boundaries to limit fragmentation and allow steady refactoring.

Hybrid Governance Boundaries. Coordination gaps between commercial and OSS contributors increased instability during development. Clear module ownership—separating commercial features from core OSS—with harmonized CI/CD (e.g., automated testing) can reduce merge conflicts and foster collaboration, as seen in more current JackTrip releases.

Aligning Refactoring with Academic Cycles. Legacy dependencies and rapid, pandemic-driven development led to technical debt. Synchronizing refactoring with academic milestones (e.g., PhD completions, grant cycles) ensures knowledge transfer before contributor turnover, maintaining architectural integrity as priorities shift.

6.5 Threats to Validity

This study acknowledges potential threats to validity using the framework by Runeson et al. [18], which operationalizes validity categories for case study research.

Construct validity risks arise from potential mismatches between operationalized metrics and theoretical concepts. For instance, documentation gaps in JackTrip's evolution could compromise data completeness. To mitigate this, we triangulated findings across the recovery methods in static code analysis and interviews. We acknowledge the value of methodological comparisons and metrics based on multiple recovery methods but defer this to future work.

Internal validity concerns include environmental influences on the case. We minimized this by analyzing code versions released prior to the study and using semi-structured interviews with predefined questions to reduce researcher bias.

External validity limitations stem from the single-case design, which limits generalizability. While JackTrip's context is unique, its hybrid academic-commercial dynamics offer transferable insights for OSS projects balancing specialized domain requirements (e.g., real-time systems) with broad usability goals. Generalization to other sectors requires further validation.

Reliability risks involve replicability due to evolving tools (e.g., using a ARCADE Core's pre-release) and researcher subjectivity in qualitative coding. We addressed this by documenting our analysis steps and publishing datasets.

7 Conclusion and Outlook

This longitudinal study advances understanding of architectural erosion in hybrid academic-commercial OSS, revealing how real-time domain constraints and multivocal contributors amplify risks. Static code analysis showed structural decay through LO smells and dependency volatility, while interviews identified erosion drivers: rapid pandemic-era feature accretion, undocumented protocol evolution, and divergent contributor practices. JackTrip's technical debt exemplifies risks when academically rooted systems transition to commercial settings.

These findings emphasize the need for architectural foresight and adaptive governance models balancing innovation and sustainability in dual-identity OSS projects with interdisciplinary contributors. To address documentation gaps, we propose adopting Architectural Decision Records to formalize protocol constraints and refactoring rationale (e.g., IPv6 adoption). Automated API documentation tools (e.g., Doxygen) integrated into CI/CD pipelines could synchronize code changes with developer-facing documentation, reducing inconsistencies. Contributor onboarding should prioritize documentation continuity.

The study particularly highlights challenges in interdisciplinary OSS where domain experts are susceptible to lack architectural training. We advocate research into pragmatic architectural practices for non-professional contributors to improve maturity in application-domain-focused projects. While JackTrip serves as primary evidence, comparative studies of other academic-commercial OSS could generalize findings. Future work may quantify how governance shifts (cathedral to bazaar or vice versa) affect technical debt accumulation, assess economic trade-offs between viability and refactoring, and ethnographically examine how multivocal contributors navigate architectural risks. [8]

Acknowledgments. We extend our sincere gratitude to the JackTrip community—its contributors, users, and JackTrip Labs—for their openness and collaboration throughout this research. Special thanks to Chris Chafe at Stanford University's CCRMA for fostering an environment where interdisciplinary tools thrive. This work relied critically on the ARCADE Core toolset revitalized by Marcelo Schmitt Laser. Marcelo's expertise and responsiveness enabled robust analysis of JackTrip's structural trends.

[8] https://zenodo.org/records/15519470.

Data Availability. We acknowledge open data and share the graphs, metrics and smells data of our static code analysis alongside pseudonymized interview transcripts via Zenodo.

Disclosure of Interests. The authors have no competing interests to declare.

References

1. Baabad, A., Zulzalil, H.B., Hassan, S., Baharom, S.B.: Software architecture degradation in open source software: a systematic literature review. IEEE Access **8**, 173681–173709 (2020). https://doi.org/10.1109/ACCESS.2020.3024671
2. Braun, V., Clarke, V.: Thematic analysis. In: APA Handbook of Research Methods in Psychology, Vol 2: Research Designs: Quantitative, Qualitative, Neuropsychological, and Biological, pp. 57–71. American Psychological Association, Washington (2012). https://doi.org/10.1037/13620-004
3. Carlin, D., Rainer, A., Wilson, D.: Where is all the research software? An analysis of software in UK academic repositories. PeerJ Comput. Sci. **9**, e1546 (2023). https://doi.org/10.7717/peerj-cs.1546
4. Chafe, C.: I am streaming in a room. Front. Digit. Humanit. **5** (2018). https://doi.org/10.3389/fdigh.2018.00027
5. Coelho, J., Valente, M.T., Silva, L.L., Hora, A.: Why we engage in floss: answers from core developers. In: Proceedings of the 11th International Workshop on Cooperative and Human Aspects of Software Engineering, CHASE '18, pp. 114–121. Association for Computing Machinery, New York (2018). https://doi.org/10.1145/3195836.3195848
6. Cáceres, J.P., Chafe, C.: JackTrip/SoundWIRE meets server farm. Comput. Music. J. **34**(3), 29–34 (2010). https://doi.org/10.1162/COMJ_a_00001
7. Laser, M.S., Minh Le, D., Garcia, J., Medvidović, N.: Architectural archipelagos: technical debt in long-lived software research platforms. In: 2021 IEEE/ACM International Conference on Technical Debt (TechDebt), pp. 94–98 (2021). https://doi.org/10.1109/TechDebt52882.2021.00019
8. Le, D., Link, D., Shahbazian, A., Zhao, Y., Mattmann, C., Medvidović, N.: Toward a Classification Framework for Software Architectural Smells. Technical report, University Southern California (2017). https://api.semanticscholar.org/CorpusID:204748461
9. Le, D.M., Carrillo, C., Capilla, R., Medvidovic, N.: Relating architectural decay and sustainability of software systems. In: 2016 13th Working IEEE/IFIP Conference on Software Architecture (WICSA), pp. 178–181 (2016). https://doi.org/10.1109/WICSA.2016.15
10. Li, R., Liang, P., Soliman, M., Avgeriou, P.: Understanding architecture erosion: the practitioners' perceptive. In: 2021 IEEE/ACM 29th International Conference on Program Comprehension (ICPC), pp. 311–322 (2021). https://doi.org/10.1109/ICPC52881.2021.00037
11. Li, R., Liang, P., Soliman, M., Avgeriou, P.: Understanding software architecture erosion: a systematic mapping study. J. Softw.: Evol. Process **34**(3), e2423 (2022). https://doi.org/10.1002/smr.2423
12. Liu, D., Xu, S., Brockmeyer, M.: Investigation on academic research software development. In: 2008 International Conference on Computer Science and Software Engineering, vol. 2, pp. 626–630 (2008). https://doi.org/10.1109/CSSE.2008.1400

13. Migliorini, S., Verdecchia, R., Malavolta, I., Lago, P., Vicario, E.: Architectural views: the state of practice in open-source software projects. In: Software Architecture, pp. 396–415. Springer, Cham (2024). https://doi.org/10.1007/978-3-031-70797-1_27
14. Mitchell, B., Mancoridis, S.: On the automatic modularization of software systems using the bunch tool. IEEE Trans. Softw. Eng. **32**(3), 193–208 (2006). https://doi.org/10.1109/TSE.2006.31
15. Nelson, A.J.: The Sound of Innovation: Stanford and the Computer Music Revolution. The MIT Press, Cambridge (2015). https://doi.org/10.7551/mitpress/10086.001.0001
16. Raymond, E.: The cathedral and the bazaar. Knowl. Technol. Policy **12**(3), 23–49 (1999). https://doi.org/10.1007/S12130-999-1026-0
17. Robillard, P.N., Robillard, M.: Improving academic software engineering projects: a comparative study of academic and industry projects. Ann. Softw. Eng. **6**(1–4), 343–363 (1999). https://doi.org/10.1023/A:1018925902814
18. Runeson, P., Höst, M., Rainer, A., Regnell, B.: Case Study Research in Software Engineering. John Wiley & Sons, Ltd., Hoboken (2012).https://doi.org/10.1002/9781118181034
19. Tzerpos, V., Holt, R.: ACCD: an algorithm for comprehension-driven clustering. In: Proceedings Seventh Working Conference on Reverse Engineering, pp. 258–267 (2000). https://doi.org/10.1109/WCRE.2000.891477

How Do Practitioners Perceive the Relevance of Software Architecture Research?

Everton Cavalcante[1(✉)], Elisa Yumi Nakagawa[2], Rick Kazman[3], and Thais Batista[1]

[1] Federal University of Rio Grande do Norte, Natal, Brazil
everton.cavalcante@ufrn.br

[2] University of São Paulo, São Carlos, Brazil
elisa@icmc.usp.br

[3] University of Hawaii, Honolulu, HI, USA
kazman@hawaii.edu

Abstract. Despite significant advances in Software Architecture (SA) research over the past three decades, questions remain about its impact on industry practices. This study examines how practitioners perceive the relevance of SA research by conducting interviews with 12 experienced professionals who evaluated 96 papers published at the European Conference on Software Architecture (ECSA) over the last decade. Most of the interviewed practitioners rated SA research as necessary due to its potential application in solving practical issues in practice. However, criticisms included a lack of generalizability, limited added value beyond existing tools and practices, and an overemphasis on context-specific solutions. These findings emphasize the need for research that is both applicable and adaptable to diverse industrial contexts, thereby enhancing the practical value and impact of SA research.

Keywords: Software Architecture · Industry · Research impact

1 Introduction

Software Architecture (SA) plays a critical role in the design, development, and maintenance of robust software-intensive systems. Besides influencing fundamental decisions about the system's structure, behavior, and quality attributes, SA can serve various purposes throughout the life cycle of these systems, including documentation and communication of design decisions, quality attribute analysis, code generation, guidance for maintainers, and many others [1]. Since SA became an established discipline in the 1990s, researchers have proposed numerous approaches, tools, and methodologies to support architecture design and evaluation. However, considerable uncertainty remains about how these research contributions are perceived and adopted in industrial practice.

V. Andrikopoulos et al. (Eds.): ECSA 2025, LNCS 15929, pp. 323–331, 2026.
https://doi.org/10.1007/978-3-032-02138-0_21

The broader field of Software Engineering (SE) has long been concerned about the disconnect between academic research and practical application [2,6]. To investigate this issue, Lo et al. [7] conducted a study to assess the relevance of research based on an evaluation of papers published in leading SE conferences, including the International Conference on Software Engineering (ICSE), the Symposium on the Foundations of Software Engineering (FSE), and the joint with the European Software Engineering Conference (ESEC/FSE). Carver et al. [4] replicated the study with other practitioners, examining papers from the International Symposium on Empirical Software Engineering and Measurement (ESEM), while Franch et al. [5] did the same for papers from ICSE, ESEC/FSE, ESEM, the IEEE Requirements Engineering Conference (RE), and the International Working Conference on Requirements Engineering: Foundation for Software Quality (REFSQ). These studies found that, while many research outputs are considered valuable, their practical adoption has been limited. Still, investigations into SA research from a practitioner's perspective remain scarce [8].

This paper presents the results of a study examining how practitioners evaluate the relevance of SA research. Through structured interviews with 12 experienced practitioners, we explored the perceived value of the SA research reported in 96 peer-reviewed papers published at the European Conference on Software Architecture (ECSA), one of the most important conferences on SA, between 2015 and 2024. Our results contribute to an understanding of how the industry receives SA research and offer some insights for making SA research even more impactful and accessible.

The remainder of this paper is structured as follows. Section 2 describes the study design. Section 3 presents the obtained results. Section 4 elaborates on the study findings. Section 5 discusses threats to the validity of our study. Section 6 brings final remarks.

2 Study Design

This section outlines the study design, which replicates the previous ones for SE [4,5,7] but specifically focuses on SA. We made the dataset, data collection instrument, and study data available in a replication package (see the Data Availability statement at the end of this paper).

Goal and Research Question. The primary goal of this study was to explore the relevance of SA research as perceived by practitioners. We did not aim to assess the impact of specific scientific contributions in SA but rather the overall relevance of the research to practice, which may help to identify disconnects between academia and industry. We formulated the following research question: *How do practitioners perceive the relevance of SA research?*

Dataset. To ensure the study focused on high-quality SA research, we selected papers published in ECSA, an important conference dedicated to the field,[1] between 2015 and 2024. We considered full papers published in the *Research Track* and *Industry Track* or similar, excluding short papers (e.g., emerging work and position papers) and those related to SA education and training. We compiled a set of $N = 143$ papers, and we randomly selected 96 of them for evaluation. We retrieved the full text of all the papers from the ECSA proceedings available online from the SpringerLink[2] digital library. Our replication package lists the papers, which are identified as P1, P2, ..., PN.

Rather than asking participants to read the papers in full or abstracts varying in terms of quality, writing style, and length (which could influence the participant's evaluation), we followed the work by Franch et al. [5] and synthesized one-sentence summaries for the papers using the following structure: *A [type of study or contribution] for [purpose] to [benefit expected to practice]*. For example:

> *A semi-automatic approach for detecting antipatterns in Java code-based systems to support developers in identifying and resolving those affecting legacy code.* (P120)

To improve reliability and control, we manually created the summaries using the authors' words extracted from the abstract of each paper whenever possible. Moreover, we did not include explicit names of approaches, frameworks, tools, or companies to reduce bias in the evaluation. When the abstract did not contain enough detailed information, we referred to the introduction and conclusion sections to clarify the paper's content. This approach helped us maintain consistency in the information participants used for their evaluations.

Data Collection. We collected data through semi-structured interviews via videoconference, with each interview lasting approximately 20 min. As this study replicates previous surveys, we used the same questions for data collection. However, we chose to conduct interviews instead of administering questionnaires to gather deeper insights from practitioners. Our replication package includes the script with the interview questions as part of the study protocol.

To ensure that the interviews would not take up too much of the participants' time, each participant was randomly assigned eight paper summaries to evaluate. We asked participants to rate each as *essential*, *important*, *unimportant*, or *irrelevant*. Following each rating, we invited them to elaborate on their assessment, providing qualitative justifications that offered deeper insight into their reasoning. In total, 96 unique papers were evaluated in the interviews, with no participants evaluating the same papers as a means to expand the corpus of analysis. Our replication package contains the collected data, organized into a spreadsheet.

---

[1] Our future work will expand the analysis to papers published in the IEEE International Conference on Software Architecture (ICSA).

[2] https://link.springer.com.

Participant Sampling and Ethical Considerations. We adhered to national and international regulations governing research involving human beings, as well as the procedures for collecting and processing their data. Before conducting our study, we obtained approval from an institutional ethics review board (IRB).[3]

We recruited participants by sending email invitations through our contact networks. Our inclusion criteria required participants to be working in software development within a company or conducting research directly related to the industry. Twelve practitioners agreed to participate. Before each interview began, we informed participants that their involvement was voluntary and asked for their consent to record and transcribe the interviews.

Data Analysis. We qualitatively analyzed the data collected in the interviews using thematic analysis [3] on the transcripts that we produced from the interview recordings. After reading the transcripts, we generated codes and combinations based on excerpts from the text through an inductive coding process. Our replication package includes the data collected during the interviews, annotated with the identified codes and themes.

3 Results

This section presents the results of our study. Section 3.1 gives a demographic overview of participants. Section 3.2 examines the practitioners' perceptions of SA research.

3.1 Demographics

Experience and Education. Participants have diverse experience levels in SA, ranging from two to 18 years, with an average of seven years (median of five years). One-third hold a university degree in Computer Science or a related field, while approximately two-fifths hold advanced degrees, such as a Master's or PhD.

Role and Involvement. All participants engage in SA, with seven responsible for architecting activities and five contributing to them. While about a third identify as software architects, almost half of the respondents (five) are software developers, indicating that some organizations assign architect-like responsibilities to developers across various team sizes.

[3] The study received ethical approval in Brazil under Certificate of Ethical Approval (CAAE) number 85724625.0.0000.5537. The approval status can be verified via the Brazilian National Research Ethics platform (*Plataforma Brasil*): http://plataformabrasil.saude.gov.br.

Context. Participants work in teams of varying sizes, with half in large teams (10–49 members) and a third in medium teams (5–10 members). They represent five countries: seven from Brazil, two from Spain, and one each from Germany, Ireland, and the Netherlands.

3.2 Practitioner Perceptions on the Relevance of SA Research

Most participants in our study (72%) assessed SA research positively, with more than a quarter rating it as essential, despite a significant number of papers (28%) being rated negatively. Figure 1 depicts the codes regarding positive and negative feedback from participants arising from the qualitative analysis of the answers they provided. Note that these codes are not mutually exclusive, as multiple codes emerged from the participants' speech.

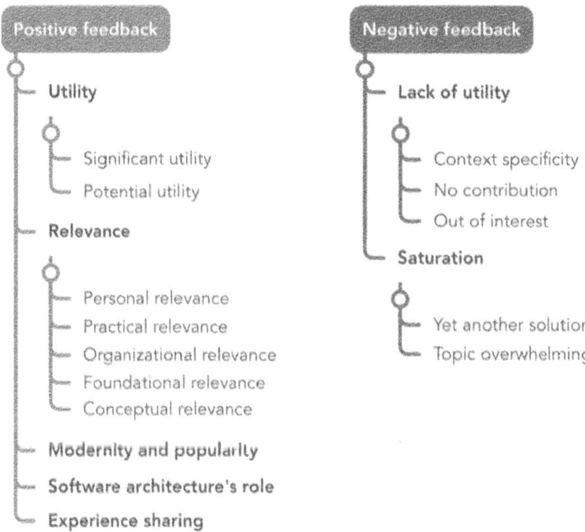

Fig. 1. Codes for positive and negative feedback regarding the relevance of SA research from the point of view of practitioners.

Positive Feedback. Positive perceptions were most frequently associated with research demonstrating practical *utility*. Participants viewed the research utility as *significant* when they were confident that it addresses an actual problem or challenge in the respondent's workplace or in practice in general. To a minor degree, the research has *potential* utility if it could be applied to some extent in practice, including specific contexts, but the respondent is not entirely sure about that. We identified 20 occurrences of utility from participants, with 11 indicating significant utility and nine indicating potential utility. An instance of significant utility comes from participant I2:

> "This one is essential because my team and I use this kind of study as a basis to define everything we adopt in the industry. [...] That is, we can directly use results from this kind of research to support decisions and practices we use in the company." [I2-P21][4]

Relevance encompasses aspects of the research's impact on practice, particularly regarding the addressed problem or proposed solution. We identified five dimensions: (i) the research is meaningful from a practitioner's *personal* perspective; (ii) it has *practical* relevance and applicability in other contexts; (iii) it can positively influence teamwork and dynamics within an *organization*; (iv) it offers results that may serve as a *foundation* for further developments; and (v) it helps clarify *conceptual* issues for stakeholders like software architects and developers. The codes for these dimensions were the most frequent, with 41 occurrences, particularly *practical relevance* (23) and *organizational relevance* (nine).

Modernity and popularity refers to research focused on contemporary topics like microservices, the Internet of Things (IoT), blockchain, and sustainability. In our sample of 96 papers, 14 (14.6%) addressed microservices, with six positive feedback instances highlighting challenges in migrating monoliths to this architecture and the potential role of SA in easing these issues.

Experience sharing was also valued as positive it allows practitioners and organizations to learn from successful cases. The following quote from a participant highlights the importance of experience reports on SA:

> "It is usually good to take a step back, see what other companies in the same industry, in similar industries, are doing; I think it is important. The relevance is also due to this sharing of experiences." [I3-P49]

Negative Feedback. We identified three key reasons participants provided for the perceived *lack of utility* of research in practice. *Context specificity* refers to research tailored to narrow contexts, hindering broader application. Research is deemed to offer *no contribution* when it fails to address real problems in the participants' workplace. *Out of interest* highlights the industry's focus on more pressing needs over specific research topics. We noted 20 instances of lack of utility as negative feedback, with half related to context-narrowed research.

Additionally, *saturation* describes limited research contributions due to the existence of other solutions already used in the industry. *Yet another solution* implies that research must demonstrate its value over current methods. *Topic overwhelming* indicates that research on widely addressed topics is less likely to be adopted by industry.

Summary of findings. Practitioners perceive SA research as relevant to practice but note instances of limited contributions and a lack of interest in the industry,

[4] The tuple [Ix-Py] means participant Ix evaluating paper Py.

suggesting a disconnect between research and practice. In addition, the specificity of many solutions in the papers limits the generalizability of the research results.

4 Discussion

Our findings suggest that SA research is valued by practitioners when it demonstrates straightforward utility, addresses recognized problems, and aligns with prevailing technologies and practices. Participants appreciated work that could be readily applied or adapted within their organizational contexts.

Another significant insight is the evolving role of software architects. Most participants identified primarily as software developers and yet reported engaging in SA tasks, such as architectural decision-making and evaluation. This observation suggests that SA research should be designed to support a broader spectrum of software professionals, not just formally designated architects.

Finally, we noticed that the most prominent barrier to perceived relevance was context specificity, as Franch et al. [5] observed earlier as well. Although we acknowledge that tailored solutions arising from research are essential for tackling specific issues in the industry, research that is too closely tied to its context may be seen as less important due to the challenges in applying it to different environments. Therefore, SA research should strive for a balance between addressing specific issues and offering insights that can be generalized or adapted across settings.

5 Threats to Validity

External Validity. The threats to the external validity of our study concern the representation of the SA research landscape and participant recruitment. We focused on ECSA papers, which is a conference known for its high quality, even though ICSA could also serve as a valuable source. We could have considered other SE conferences (e.g., ICSE), but we deemed that a conference specifically targeting SA, such as ECSA, could offer a more targeted representation of the research in this area. Although we have followed the same methodology as prior studies and agreed that using conference papers provides timeliness and original research contributions, we are aware that not every industry-relevant research on SA appears in conference papers. Further work can strengthen our results by including other sources.

The representativeness of the participants also affects the external validity of our study. Even though we obtained a high response rate (70.59%) for the interview invitations, the small number of participants ($n = 12$) from a few countries (five) limits the generalizability of our results. Our future work can increase both the sample size and geographical diversity, as well as include varied practitioner roles, considering that most of our participants were software developers or architects.

Internal Validity. The main threat to the internal validity of our study stems from using summaries rather than full papers or abstracts, which may introduce bias. We aimed to standardize summaries using a template as Franch et al. [5] did and attempted to minimize bias by extracting words from the original papers.

Construct Validity. As a threat to the construct validity of our study, participants' understanding of "relevance" may lead to inconsistencies. Moreover, misunderstandings of some terms in summaries, even though derived directly from the original papers, could affect ratings. The semi-structured interviews we conducted helped clarify these concerns without introducing bias.

6 Conclusion

This paper examines the relevance of SA research from a practitioner's perspective through a survey of 12 experienced practitioners who evaluated summaries of 96 papers published in ECSA. Our goal was to assess their perceptions regarding the applicability of these research findings to real-world issues and situations. While participants generally found SA research relevant, they noted instances where the study did not address real-world challenges and lacked industry interest. They also pointed out that the specific nature of many solutions limits broader applicability, highlighting a disconnect between research and practical use.

When considering the factors influencing practitioners' perceptions, practitioners tended to favor research that demonstrates direct utility in their daily work over traditional academic metrics. To enhance the adoption of research findings in practice, SA researchers should focus on developing solutions that tackle real-world problems and provide immediate practical value, thereby fostering a more collaborative and impactful research ecosystem.

Acknowledgments. This study was partially financed by the Brazilian National Council for Scientific and Technological (CNPq) and São Paulo Research Foundation (FAPESP), grants 2023/00488-5 and 2024/00329-7.

Data Availability. The study data can be found in the replication package available online at https://doi.org/10.5281/zenodo.14993301

Disclosure of Interests. The authors have no competing interests to declare relevant to this article's content.

References

1. Bass, L., Clements, P., Kazman, R.: Software Architecture in Practice, 4th edn. Addison-Wesley Professional, Boston (2021)
2. Beecham, S., O'Leary, P., Baker, S., Richardson, I., Noll, J.: Making Software Engineering research relevant. Computer **47**(4), 80–83 (2014). https://doi.org/10.1109/mc.2014.92

3. Braun, V., Clarke, V.: Using thematic analysis in Psychology. Qual. Res. Psychol. **3**(2), 77–101 (2006). https://doi.org/10.1191/1478088706qp063oa
4. Carver, J.C., Dieste, O., Kraft, N.A., Lo, D., Zimmermann, T.: How practitioners perceive the relevance of ESEM research. In: 10th ACM/IEEE International Symposium on Empirical Software Engineering and Measurement (ESEM), pp. 1–10 (2016). https://doi.org/10.1145/2961111.2962597
5. Franch, X., et al.: How do practitioners perceive the relevance of Requirements Engineering research? IEEE Trans. Softw. Eng. **48**(6), 1947–1964 (2022). https://doi.org/10.1109/TSE.2020.3042747
6. Garousi, V., Borg, M., Oivo, M.: Practical relevance of software engineering research: synthesizing the community's voice. Empir. Softw. Eng. **25**(3), 1687–1754 (2020). https://doi.org/10.1007/s10664-020-09803-0
7. Lo, D., Nagappan, N., Zimmermann, T.: How practitioners perceive the relevance of Software Engineering research. In: 10th Joint Meeting on Foundations of Software Engineering (FSE), pp. 415–425 (2015). https://doi.org/10.1145/2786805.2786809
8. Wan, Z., Zhang, Y., Xia, X., Jiang, Y., Lo, D.: Software architecture in practice: challenges and opportunities. In: 31st ACM Joint European Software Engineering Conference and Symposium on the Foundations of Software Engineering (ESEC/FSE), pp. 1457–1469 (2023). https://doi.org/10.1145/3611643.3616367

Towards Legal Knowledge Transfer Based on Software Architecture

Nicolas Boltz[1(✉)], Janne Wagner[2], Leonie Sterz[1], Oliver Raabe[1], and Christopher Gerking[1]

[1] Karlsruhe Institute of Technology (KIT), Karlsruhe, Germany
{nicolas.boltz,leonie.sterz,oliver.raabe,christopher.gerking}@kit.edu
[2] University of Bamberg, Bamberg, Germany
janne.wagner@stud.uni-bamberg.de

Abstract. More and more legal norms directly target software-based systems. Although these norms often require some form of legal assessment, such as the data protection impact assessments mandated by the General Data Protection Regulation, they are usually conducted in separated steps before or after development. As legal norms translate to requirements of the system to be developed, they have a profound influence on the software design and architecture, which makes subsequent changes cost intensive. Therefore, it should be ensured that software architects are provided with knowledge that supports them in designing legally compliant systems. In this paper, we derive challenges for legal knowledge transfer and discuss how we address them. As an initial approach, we define a metamodel for structured legal comments and present a first attempt to automatically annotate them within data flow diagrams. The approach is demonstrated with an example system in a real-world legal context, illustrating why supported knowledge transfer is necessary.

1 Introduction

Legal norms such as the EU General Data Protection Regulation (GDPR) and the AI Act increasingly refer to software-based systems and also contain more and more specific technical requirements. These legal provisions translate into requirements and significantly influence the software architecture. Yet, software development and legal assessments are often separate steps, as seen with data protection impact assessments mandated by the GDPR. Legal issues arising from implementation details may go unnoticed and, if identified at all, are typically discovered later in the development process, thereby increasing the costs of addressing such problems [5].

To meet legal requirements appropriately and take suitable measures where necessary, a software architect would need not only expertise in their domain but also significant knowledge or guidance of the specific legal domain in which

J. Wagner—The research was conducted when the author was with KIT.

V. Andrikopoulos et al. (Eds.): ECSA 2025, LNCS 15929, pp. 332–340, 2026.
https://doi.org/10.1007/978-3-032-02138-0_22

the system under development operates. However, current research indicates that technical experts often lack legal knowledge and understanding, e.g., about privacy and data protection [3,10,17]. A potential reason for this—and a major obstacle when dealing with the legal domain from a technical perspective—is the different levels of abstraction and the differences in terminology and methodology [18]. Without guidance, it is particularly challenging for non-legal experts to fully understand and implement what is required by legal norms. Consequently, the successful development of legally compliant software systems requires the interaction of both technical and legal experts. In practice, however, this collaboration between both domains proves difficult [18]. Existing approaches often remain within the technical domain and apply technologies, such as machine learning and natural language processing, to certain areas of law [1,8,19,20], or aim to support and automate work based on legal practice [13]. Facilitating the transfer of knowledge from the legal domain to educate the technical domain, e.g., software architects, is a largely overlooked field of research.

With this objective in mind, this paper presents an initial concept for the systematic creation and provision of *legal comments*—structured and comprehensible legal notes for software architects derived from legal sources. The purpose of *legal comments* is to explain different aspects of the legal nature that apply to a given software architecture element, thereby indicating points in the software architecture that require special attention. The proposed approach does not intend to replace collaboration with legal experts but complements it. The transfer of legal knowledge generally aims to simplify the collaboration between legal experts and software architects by enabling the latter to develop a stronger foundational understanding and awareness of the legal aspects of the software system. In addition, it is desirable to educate architects about legal issues so that they can ask legal experts questions that arise on their own initiative.

To consider the views of both domains when developing the concept, this paper is the product of interdisciplinary work between researchers in software engineering, legal informatics, and data protection law, reflected in the author list. As our contribution, we propose a metamodel for legal comments derived from general legal methodology. Based on the metamodel, we provide a web-based, community-driven platform for creating and evolving legal comments. As an initial effort, we supply a sample catalog of comments for the definitions and principles of the GDPR. We further describe an early approach to automatically annotate legal comments to elements within data flow diagrams (DFDs) as a way to indicate points in the architecture that require special attention.

2 Concept

In our concept, we aim to assist software architects during the design phase, as well as in further development and audits, by helping them understand the legal framework and enabling informed design decisions. We aim to achieve this by providing fine-grained legal comments that offer detailed, context-specific information and recommendations for action concerning elements in data flow diagrams (DFDs). However, the level of detail in the comments is critical, as there is a risk of overwhelming software architects with too much information, which again discourages them from engaging with the general topic.

DFDs are a widely used way of representing software architecture and are already frequently used to evaluate various aspects of information security of software architectures [15,16,22], including privacy and data protection [2,4]. Our approach focuses on the extended DFD syntax of Seifermann *et al.* [16] and Boltz *et al.* [6]. The extension adds labels that represent additional semantic information and can either be determined as a characteristic of a node or data flowing between nodes, such as specifying user roles or data sensitivity.

In this section, we first provide a structure for comments by defining a legal comment metamodel derived from legal methodology. We further describe our initial approach to annotating legal comment instances to DFD elements and how we aim to present these comments in an accessible way to software architects. To this end, we also present our web-based community platform that enables the creation and refinement of meaningful comments and also serves as a way to access additional information to comments.

2.1 Legal Comment Metamodel

Our proposed legal comment metamodel is inspired by legal methodology. Most legislative texts are written in abstract and generalized language to apply to as many real-life cases as possible. In addition, the use of undefined or not conclusively defined legal terms allows for a broad scope of interpretation. Courts and legal experts interpret and concretize laws when applying them to concrete systems and contexts, following a specific methodology. In European and German law, this involves analyzing the wording, system, purpose, and history of the norm. These interpretations and concretizations are documented in legal literature, for example, in so-called commentaries, which systematically explain laws paragraph by paragraph or article by article.

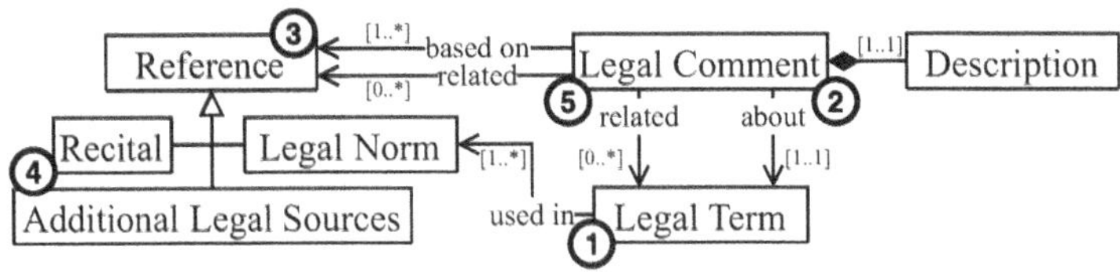

Fig. 1. Structure of legal comments as metamodel.

For our metamodel, *Legal Terms* that might require explanation are extracted from the *Legal Norm* they are *used in* (1). Each *Legal Comment* is *about* one *Legal Term* and contains a *Description* (2) that captures all relevant information about the corresponding *Legal Term* as a natural language text. As the description is not merely a rephrasing of a legal norm but might combine information of interpretations and concretizations, a *Legal Comment* is *based on* different *References* (3). As an initial selection, references in our metamodel can be other *Legal*

Norms, *Recitals*, or generally *Additional Legal Sources* (4), such as the aforementioned commentaries. These references are not meant to be citations but serve to point to the primary source of information used. Furthermore, the description of *Legal Comments* may include other terms that are considered potentially unfamiliar. These terms should be defined in separate *Legal Comments* to avoid overloading descriptions with information. To this end, *Legal Comments* refer to *related Legal Terms* or *References* (5). *Related References* that are not the base of the comment can also be added as guidance for interested software architects to gain a deeper understanding of the general legal domain and further legal knowledge on their own. The resulting metamodel is shown in Fig. 1.

2.2 Community Platform

Similar to existing collaborative approaches [9,11], we developed a community-driven platform for creating and refining legal comments, ensuring adaptability to legal changes, and improving cross-domain communication. The platform provides a web-based front-end for viewing, creating, and refining legal comments and persists comments as issues in GitHub using a predefined textual format. By default, GitHub issues provide a discussion section, which community members can use to comment on and discuss legal comments. The platform is currently still under active development but is already available online[1] and provided as part of our data set (see Sect. 6). As a first effort and starting point, we have created an initial set of 16 individual legal comments for the legal terms of the definitions and general principles of the GDPR. The legal comments were compiled in interdisciplinary discourse by the authors during multiple sessions to ensure that the descriptions are not only correct regarding their legal content and structure but also understandable for people outside the legal domain.

2.3 Annotation

To use legal comments, we propose an annotation algorithm that automatically associates legal comments with nodes in DFDs. We utilize the data flow analysis (DFA) approach of Boltz *et al.* [6] to identify DFD nodes with labels that indicate that a certain legal comment is relevant. The DFA approach uses *data flow queries* defined in a natural language DSL to check the DFD and provide a set of nodes that satisfy the query. On our community platform, we have included the option to add such queries to legal comments. We did not explicitly add data flow queries as a first-class element, as we wanted our metamodel to be independent of the software architecture representation and annotation logic.

To annotate the legal comments to a DFD, we iterate over all legal comments that are currently relevant to the system under development. The selection of legal comments that need to be considered still depends on the legal expert. Using the queries added to a legal comment by either a legal expert or a software architect, we fetch all nodes that should be annotated with the comment. A

[1] https://model-based-data-protection-assessments.github.io/LegalComments/.

simple annotation model defines a relationship between legal comments and DFD nodes. As we also want to present legal comments to software architects in an accessible way, we add the annotations to the concrete DFD syntax of the tooling provided by Boltz *et al.* [6]. For our initial approach, we add a textual representation of the legal comment, consisting of the legal term, description, and references as tooltips to the annotated nodes.

It needs to be made clear that this is only an initial approach. Handling multiple annotated legal comments for one node so that they continue to be comprehensible and understandable remains a challenge. Also, including comments of a broader legal scope might require more elaborate approaches specific to the system context, e.g., other software architecture representations.

3 Evaluation

For our preliminary evaluation, we aim to show the feasibility of our proposed legal comments and annotation approach by applying it to an abstract representation of a real-world smart mobility system. The evaluation scenario involves a vehicle communicating with a roadside unit (RSU). By choosing a system in the context of automated data processing in the mobility domain, we also aim to highlight the importance of legal knowledge transfer in general. Figure 2 (left) shows a schematic representation of the system. It is comprised of a vehicle that broadcasts data via V2X (Vehicle-to-Everything) communication to an RSU. The RSU receives this information, notifies a traffic signal, and relays relevant data to a local transport agency. As the system described is a traffic system for traffic management, it is subject to legal regulations in road traffic law, such as the *German Road Traffic Act*[2] (StVG). However, as personal data is potentially being processed, the GDPR also applies.

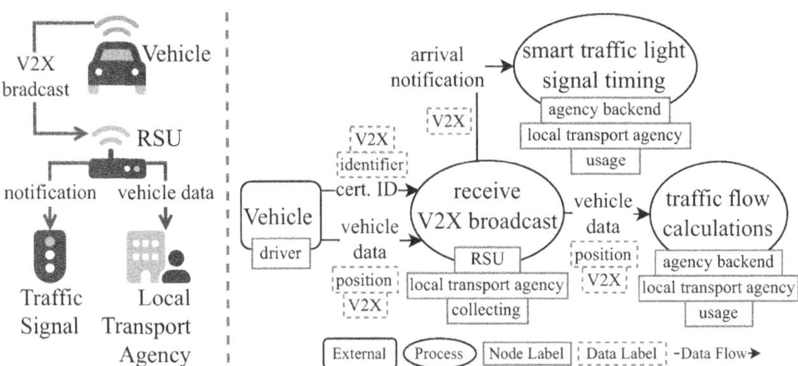

Fig. 2. Evaluation scenario as schematic interactions of participants (left) and DFD with indicated label annotations (right).

[2] https://www.gesetze-im-internet.de/englisch_stvg/.

A DFD representation of our example is shown on the right of Fig. 2. Here, the data transmitted by the vehicle and RSU is explained in more detail using DFD labels. The RSU receives the broadcasted *vehicle data* containing, among others, an identifier in the form of a *certificate ID* as well as the *vehicle position*. The RSU simply informs the traffic light about the vehicle's arrival, whereas the vehicle data containing the position is relayed to the local transport agency. By omitting the *certificate ID* after the first processing step, the data is considered sufficiently anonymized according to Paragraph 63e) of the StVG. The GDPR, however, specifies more stringent requirements regarding when data is anonymous. In the described system, a person could, for example, be identified without the certificate ID using the position information.

This legally challenging situation originates from disparate definitions of when data in the context of automated data processing in V2X communication is anonymized, i.e., the natural person who is the subject of the data is no longer *identifiable*. For the architect to be able to design the system in compliance with data protection law and, if necessary, obtain legal advice beforehand, the architect must be informed about the requirements for anonymization and potential contradictions in the law.

To annotate a clarifying legal comment, we define a data flow query. For the described mobility system, we need to identify DFD nodes that represent the *collection* of *V2X* data that contains some information that is a direct *identifier* of the data subject. Using the corresponding labels of the DFD, we define the following query:

Data with label *V2X* and *identifier*
flows to
Node with label *collecting*

The query returns the *receive V2X broadcast* node to be annotated with the legal comment of *Identifiability (StVG)*. Figure 3 shows the annotated legal comment as a tooltip.

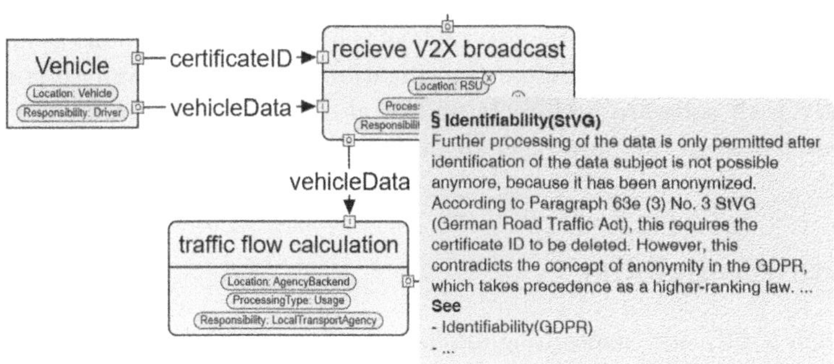

Fig. 3. Legal comment for *Identifiability (StVG)* annotated to a node of the evaluation scenario, shown as a tooltip.

4 Related Work

With regard to the intersection of law and computer science, existing approaches apply technologies, such as machine learning and natural language processing, to certain areas of law [1,8,19,20] to automate parts of or support legal practice. Other approaches within the field of software architecture and design-time modeling define model-based representations of laws [21], define law-focused extensions of software architecture representations [6,18], and/or design-time analyses of legal concepts [2,4,7,13]. Pedroza *et al.* [12] define a model-based concept that aims to provide guidance for system design aimed at software engineers who are not knowledgeable in law. However, they primarily focus on concepts of the GDPR and do not focus on the transfer of legal knowledge, but more on conveying best practices in conceptualization and implementation.

5 Conclusion

In this paper, we have presented our concept for architecture-based legal knowledge transfer. We propose enabling informed design decisions through legal comments that can provide detailed, context-specific information and recommendations regarding software architecture elements. We have proposed a legal comment metamodel as a structure for legal comments and a community platform for creating legal comments. We also presented an annotation algorithm based on DFDs to provide legal comments to software architects. As a preliminary evaluation, we applied our concept to a real-world scenario in the context of smart mobility systems and highlighted the importance of legal knowledge transfer.

For future work, we aim to expand our legal comment catalog to cover additional laws such as the EU NIS2 directive, AI Act, and traffic law, focusing on the automotive domain due to its strong use of model-based approaches. Also, DFDs, while useful and widely applied, are rarely sufficient as a standalone representation of software architecture or require to be enriched with other domain-specific information. To ensure broader applicability, our idea could be extended to other architectural description languages, such as the UML[3], the Palladio Component Model [14], or the Vehicle Signal Specification[4]. Lastly, we aim to conduct a user study with software architects and legal experts to evaluate the usability and effectiveness of our approach in design-time modeling and runtime audit scenarios.

6 Data Availability

We provide a data set[5] containing all code artifacts of our metamodel and community platform. We also provide instances of our GDPR legal comments and evaluation scenario for reproduction.

---

[3] https://www.omg.org/spec/UML.
[4] https://covesa.github.io/vehicle_signal_specification/.
[5] https://doi.org/10.5281/zenodo.15100380.

Acknowledgment. This work was funded by the Topic Engineering Secure Systems of the Helmholtz Association (HGF) and supported by KASTEL Security Research Labs, Karlsruhe.

References

1. Abualhaija, S., Ceci, M., et al.: AI-enabled regulatory change analysis of legal requirements. In: RE, pp. 5–17 (2024)
2. Ahmadian, A.S., Strüber, D., et al.: Supporting privacy impact assessment by model-based privacy analysis. In: SAC, pp. 1467–1474 (2018)
3. Alhazmi, A., Arachchilage, N.A.G.: I'm all ears! Listening to software developers on putting GDPR principles into software development practice. Pers. Ubiq. Comput. **25**(5), 879–892 (2021)
4. Alshareef, H., Tuma, K., et al.: Precise analysis of purpose limitation in Data Flow Diagrams. In: ARES, pp. 1–11 (2022)
5. Boehm, B., Basili, V.: Top 10 list [software development]. Computer **34**(1), 135–137 (2001)
6. Boltz, N., Hahner, S., et al.: An extensible framework for architecture-based data flow analysis for information security. In: ECSA, pp. 342–358 (2023)
7. Boltz, N., Sterz, L., et al.: A model-based framework for simplified collaboration of legal and software experts in data protection assessments. INFORMATIK (2022)
8. Breaux, T.D., Vail, M.W., Anton, A.I.: Towards regulatory compliance: extracting rights and obligations to align requirements with regulations. In: RE, pp. 49–58 (2006)
9. Colesky, M., Caiza, J.C.: A system of privacy patterns for informing users: creating a pattern system. In: EuroPLoP, pp. 1–11 (2018)
10. Hadar, I., Hasson, T., et al.: Privacy by designers: software developers' privacy mindset. Empir. Softw. Eng. (2018)
11. Hahner, S., Niehues, N., et al.: ARC3N: a collaborative uncertainty catalog to address the awareness problem of model-based confidentiality analysis. In: MODELS-C, pp. 640–644 (2024)
12. Pedroza, G., Muntés-Mulero, V., et al.: A model-based approach to realize privacy and data protection by design. In: S&P Workshops, pp. 332–339 (2021)
13. Pullonen, P., Tom, J., Matulevičius, R., Toots, A.: Privacy-enhanced BPMN: enabling data privacy analysis in business processes models. Softw. Syst. Model. **18**(6), 3235–3264 (2019)
14. Reussner, R.H., Becker, S., et al.: Modeling and Simulating Software Architectures: The Palladio Approach. MIT Press, Cambridge (2016)
15. Schneider, S., Özen, T., et al.: microSecEnD: a dataset of security-enriched dataflow diagrams for microservice applications. In: MSR, pp. 125–129 (2023)
16. Seifermann, S., Heinrich, R., et al.: Detecting violations of access control and information flow policies in data flow diagrams. JSS **184**, 111138 (2022)
17. Senarath, A., Arachchilage, N.A.: Why developers cannot embed privacy into software systems? An empirical investigation. In: EASE, pp. 211–216 (2018)
18. Sion, L., Dewitte, P., et al.: An architectural view for data protection by design. In: ICSA, pp. 11–20 (2019)
19. Sleimi, A., Sannier, N., et al.: An automated framework for the extraction of semantic legal metadata from legal texts. Empir. Softw. Eng. (2021)

20. Torre, D., Abualhaija, S., et al.: An AI-assisted approach for checking the completeness of privacy policies against GDPR. In: RE, pp. 136–146 (2020)
21. Torre, D., Alferez, M., et al.: Modeling data protection and privacy: application and experience with GDPR. Softw. Syst. Model. **20**, 2071–2087 (2021)
22. Tuma, K., Scandariato, R., Balliu, M.: Flaws in flows: unveiling design flaws via information flow analysis. In: ICSA, pp. 191–200 (2019)

Industry Papers

WebAssembly with wasi-nn for Edge Machine Learning Inference: Experiences and Lessons Learned

Joshua Bachmeier[1(✉)], Vladimir Yussupov[2], Jörg Henß[1], and Heiko Koziolek[2]

[1] FZI Research Center for Information Technology, Karlsruhe, Germany
{bachmeier,henss}@fzi.de
[2] ABB AG Corporate Research Center Germany, Mannheim, Germany
{vladimir.yussupov,heiko.koziolek}@de.abb.com

Abstract. In industrial automation, machine learning (ML) is used to analyze sensor data for predictive maintenance or process optimization. To reduce latency and protect intellectual property, it is preferred for selected inference tasks to be run on small edge clusters instead of the cloud. Ideally, such tasks should be implemented as portable, hardware-agnostic software and executed in a secure environment to handle untrusted 3rd-party software. A potential solution is to bundle the machine learning model execution in machine-neutral WebAssembly code. The novel wasi-nn API proposal enables efficient execution of ML inference tasks from within a WebAssembly sandbox using a vendor-neutral interface. In this work, we show how these technologies can be applied to provide a solution to this challenge. We analyze existing wasi-nn implementations and design a generic architecture for "isolated inference at the edge" with a prototype implemented in Rust. We find that the wasi-nn ecosystem is still immature and native libraries are often required, which impairs the desired portability. Due to the use of native libraries by wasi-nn implementations, the performance overhead of execution in WebAssembly is insignificant. Finally, we discuss alternatives, e.g., creating custom host APIs or compiling ML frameworks to WebAssembly.

Keywords: Machine Learning · Inference · Edge Computing · WebAssembly · wasi-nn

1 Introduction

Internet of Things (IoT) edge computing has grown substantially in recent years and now covers many industrial scenarios [7]. Besides interfacing with cloud backends, process production plants, factories, or smart buildings now often utilize edge computing for directly executing ML workloads. In industrial automation, edge clusters collect sensor data for temperature, pressure, flow, level, and speed, to analyze the resulting time series data for opportunities regarding predictive

V. Andrikopoulos et al. (Eds.): ECSA 2025, LNCS 15929, pp. 343–359, 2026.
https://doi.org/10.1007/978-3-032-02138-0_23

maintenance or optimized production [10]. Being concerned with low latency or availability of cloud backends [12], or issues regarding information security and intellectual property (IP), many industrial production operators favor running ML inference tasks locally on small edge clusters.

These operators often favor running edge software on already available hardware, prompting the edge software providers to create hardware-agnostic services. Targeting machine-neutral WebAssembly (Wasm) binary code from high-level programming languages can provide portability across CPU architectures. The Wasm system interface (WASI) provides a standardized way for Wasm modules to access system-level APIs for file I/O, networking, or multithreading when running outside of a browser. A WASI proposal called `wasi-nn` provides a standardized, vendor-neutral interface to load and execute ML models in Wasm modules. While there are already Wasm runtimes supporting `wasi-nn`, the proposal is not finalized, and the implementations remain experimental.

There are multiple works on Edge ML systems (e.g., TensorFlow Lite, Pytorch Mobile, or TinyML) [7], implying trade-offs between cloud and edge inference, as well as hybrid approaches. Researchers have benchmarked ML inference frameworks on mobile devices [11,15], but these did not include ML inference based on `wasi-nn`. Khelifa et al. [8] have conducted a case study of Wasm runtimes for AI applications on the edge and briefly discussed `wasi-nn` but did not use it.

Under the observation that performing isolated ML inference on the edge using Wasm and `wasi-nn` is still an open problem we formulate the following research questions:

1. Can WebAssembly and the `wasi-nn` proposal with their current implementations be used for performing isolated ML inference tasks on edge devices?
2. What is the performance overhead of `wasi-nn` compared to directly using general-purpose ML frameworks such as ONNX?

To answer these questions, we provide an experience report that analyzes the current state of `wasi-nn` and its available implementations in Wasm runtimes. To assess the maturity of the underlying toolchain, we implemented an exemplary ML component in Rust that is compiled into Wasm with WASI interfaces to load a publicly available time-series model into Wasmtime with ONNX support and starts the model inference. We chose Wasmtime because it has the most mature implementation of `wasi-nn`. To analyze the performance overhead, we compared using the ONNX C-runtime directly against using it through `wasi-nn`.

We found that Wasm and the Wasm component model are potentially well-suited for the intended use case of portable edge ML inference, but that existing `wasi-nn` implementations only offer GPU acceleration for OpenVINO and WinML. The model formats ONNX or OpenVINO with their portable runtimes could be good candidates to provide unified ML runtimes to industrial IoT users. Since Wasm workloads are natively supported in (lightweight) Kubernetes [9], using respective components could conveniently leverage container orchestration. In our experiments, however, we encountered several problems during conversion of models due to unsupported operations and tensor shape mismatches.

The ecosystem around WASI and `wasi-nn` is still young, with tools and libraries remaining in an experimental stage.

This paper is structured as follows. We first provide an introduction to Wasm and its use for ML inference in Sect. 2. We analyze related work for AI/ML applications on edge devices in Sect. 3 and compare the available implementations of `wasi-nn` in Sect. 4. In Sect. 5 we propose an architecture supporting our approach and introduce a prototypical implementation. We discuss lessons learned and generalize them for a broader audience in Sect. 6. Finally, we conclude the experience report in Sect. 8 and sketch future work.

2 Background

This section briefly discusses WebAssembly, its application scenarios and, specifically, its use for machine learning inference at the edge.

2.1 WebAssembly and Its Applicability to Industrial IoT

WebAssembly (Wasm) [14] is a portable binary instruction format originally designed for efficient and safe execution of non-JavaScript code in browsers. With the advent of multiple standalone Wasm runtimes [16] such as Wasmtime[1] and Wasmedge[2], it also became possible to deploy Wasm to embedded devices, in the cloud, or at the edge. Additionally, WebAssembly System Interface (WASI) [4] is a set of Wasm-native, runtime-independent Application Programming Interfaces (APIs) that aim to improve interaction between Wasm code and outside world by enabling, e.g., Wasm modules to access the file system of the underlying host in a uniform fashion. WASI proposals include interfaces for working with file system and system time [3].

While the core Wasm specification focuses on the semantics of *Wasm modules* and their interoperability using primitive data types, the Wasm Component Model [1] was introduced to address the lack of standard mechanisms for exchanging complex data types and composition of Wasm modules using well-established concepts from component-based engineering [2]. Essentially, a Wasm component wraps a Wasm module together with an interface definition describing what functionalities and data types a component depends on and exposes to clients. This enables Wasm components and their compositions to interoperate independently of language-specific implementations and paves the way for implementing polyglot applications with Wasm.

Efficiency, portability, and security guarantees of Wasm are well-suited for industrial IoT scenarios, e.g., portable processing of large amounts of sensitive sensor data directly on constrained edge devices. As legacy code can often be

---

[1] Wasmtime GitHub repository: https://github.com/bytecodealliance/wasmtime.

[2] WasmEdge runtime: https://wasmedge.org.

[3] List of currently active WASI proposals: https://github.com/WebAssembly/WASI/blob/main/Proposals.md.

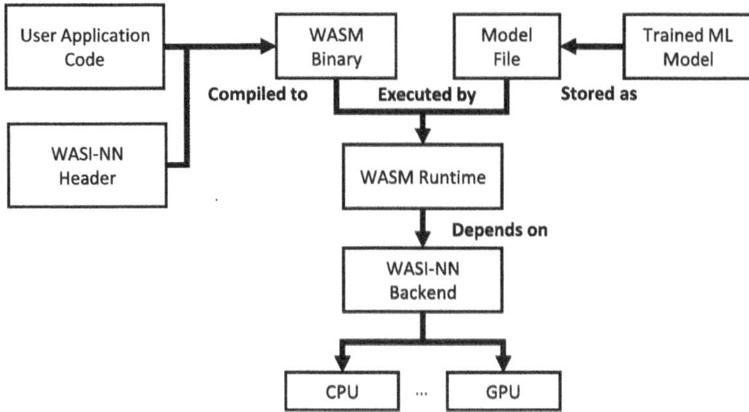

Fig. 1. Conceptual Architecture for ML Inference with wasi-nn

compiled into Wasm, industrial IoT scenarios can employ Wasm in context of systems integration [13]. The trade-off between portability and performance makes Wasm also useful for edge offloading use cases [6] as also highlighted in multiple research publications that explore the applicability of Wasm for edge-based computation scenarios [16].

2.2 Machine Learning Inference at the Edge Using Wasi-Nn

As discussed in Sect. 2.1, WASI provides necessary means for Wasm binaries to interact with the outside world. For performing ML inference tasks with Wasm, the WASI proposal `wasi-nn`[4] introduces a generic interface that abstracts from the technical details of ML inference framework implementations. The main design goals of `wasi-nn` are (i) to enable using existing model formats such as ONNX as-is and (ii) support accessing heterogeneous ML capabilities of host programs from Wasm code in a uniform manner. This enables using existing models in Wasm and running them with the best possible acceleration option available on the compute node that hosts a Wasm runtime in a portable fashion.

Figure 1 depicts the core building blocks required for running ML inference tasks at the edge using Wasm and `wasi-nn`[5]. The User Application Code and `wasi-nn` Header consitute a Wasm-based application for running ML inference with respect to a Trained ML Model that is stored as a Model File of specific format, e.g., ONNX or OpenVINO. To actually run such Wasm-based user applications, a Wasm Runtime is required that supports the respective `wasi-nn` Backends, e.g., PyTorch, ONNX, or OpenVINO. In its turn, the `wasi-nn` backend enables using the specific hardware acceleration options available at host, e.g., CPUs or GPUs.

[4] wasi-nn proposal: https://github.com/WebAssembly/wasi-nn.

[5] The figure is based on https://www.w3.org/2020/06/machine-learning-workshop/talks/introducing_wasi_nn.html.

3 Related Work

Jouini et al. [7] provide a survey of ML frameworks, applications, and research directions in edge computing. Besides on-device and cloud intelligence, authors discuss *edge intelligence* with ML inference running on edge servers.

APIs. There exist different APIs for Edge ML Inference. The ONNX Runtime[6] provides a cross-platform ML inference engine that executes models in the Open Neural Network Exchange Format (ONNX). It supports different hardware accelerators (e.g.,. NVIDIA GPUs, Intel CPUs, or ARM devices) without changing the loaded models. It differs from `wasi-nn`, since it mandates a specific model format, but it can be triggered by a Wasm runtime implementing `wasi-nn`. The automation company Beckhoff provides an ML Inference Engine, which accepts ONNX models, for their PC-based PLC control runtime TwinCAT3[7].

LiteRT, formerly TensorFlow Lite[8], is Google's lightweight ML inference library for mobile and IoT devices that accepts TensorFlow models and supports different platforms (Android, iOS, Linux, microcontrollers). TensorFlow Lite includes a delegate mechanism that lets developers delegate ML inference to specialized hardware or APIs. This allows it to abstract from vendor-specific accelerators, but it is also built around a specific model format. The Android-specific Neural Networks API (NNAPI)[9] is a C API designed to accelerate ML inference on mobile devices by abstracting hardware accelerators.

Other APIs are WinML and DirectML (tied to Windows), ARM NN SDK (tied to ARM devices), Intel's OpenVINO Toolkit (tied to Intel hardware), Apple's Core ML (tied to Apple hardware), and WebNN (specifically for web applications). Compared to these, `wasi-nn` stands out as model-agnostic and minimal.

Academic Studies. Besides these APIs, there are also numerous academic studies on ML inference APIs and WebAssembly. A case study similar to our work was conducted by Khelifa et al. [8]. The authors examine the feasibility and performance of Wasm runtimes for deploying ML inference on edge devices. They also discussed the `wasi-nn` extension and noted that the current Wasmtime implementation only supported the OpenVINO backend targeting Intel CPUs.

There are also several benchmarking studies for ML inference, which do not involve Wasm runtimes. Zhang et al. [15] benchmark TensorFlow Lite, PyTorch Mobile, Caffe2, MNN, and SNPE on 15 models across 10 smartphones and found that no single library outperforms others on all models and hardware. Luo et al. [11] introduce AIoTBench for evaluating ML frameworks on mobile devices.

[6] ONNX runtime website: https://onnxruntime.ai/.

[7] TwinCAT3 product site: https://www.beckhoff.com/en-en/products/automation/twincat/tfxxxx-twincat-3-functions/tf3xxx-measurement/tf3800.html.

[8] LiteRT website: https://ai.google.dev/edge/litert.

[9] NNAPI Guide: https://developer.android.com/ndk/guides/neuralnetworks.

Table 1. Model format support across different Wasm runtimes

Model format	Wasmtime	WasmEdge	WAMR
OpenVINO	✓	✓	✓
ONNX	✓ [1]	× [2]	×
pyTorch	✓ [1]	✓	×
TensorFlow	×	× [2]	×
TensorFlow Lite	×	✓	✓
WinML	✓ [3]	×	×
ggml (llama.cpp)	×	✓	✓
ChatTTS	×	✓	×
MLX	×	✓	×
Neuralspeed	×	× [2]	×
Piper	×	✓	×
Whisper	×	✓	×

[1] optional
[2] stubs prepared
[3] only on Windows

Their results show, for example, that different phones have varying degrees of support for certain frameworks and that no single framework is best in all cases.

Our study is most closely related to the experience report by Khelifa et al. [8], but provides specific results on the `wasi-nn` implementations of different Wasm runtimes, which the previous study did not provide.

4 Current Implementations

Currently, three main implementations of `wasi-nn` bindings are available as open source projects: Wasmtime and the WebAssembly Micro Runtime (WAMR) hosted by the Bytecode Alliance, and WasmEdge being an official sandbox project of the CNCF. Moreover, to assess the maturity of these bindings, we investigated the available support of ML frameworks and support of `wasi-nn` features. As support for `wasi-nn` is still considered experimental, all three runtimes require custom builds to enable `wasi-nn` support. All implementations make use of the system-wide C bindings to run ML tasks, thus, making portability dependent on the availability of frameworks on the used system architecture and os. Usually not all ML frameworks are supported as default options, as frameworks have to be installed manually in the system before.

As Table 1 shows, only OpenVINO is available in all three implementations while pyTorch and TensorFlow Lite are available in two out of three. Especially WasmEdge has support for model(-family) specific inference backends like Llama.cpp or Piper and Whisper used for speech input/output. The bindings provide only limited support for using GPUs and TPUs mostly depending on the availability of non-standard built libraries and hindering out-of-the-box use.

5 Prototype

To validate the feasibility of using Wasm and `wasi-nn` for custom inference tasks at the edge and illustrate the shortcomings, we designed and implemented a prototype. For this example, we use a simple PatchTST model that was trained on temperature data for realizing the timeseries forecasting part of the prototype.

5.1 Requirements and Design Considerations

With the goal to enable users of an edge offering to execute custom ML inference workloads on the edge nodes while ensuring the security and integrity of the edge node itself, we formulate the following informal requirements:

1. Users of the edge offering can provide *portable components* that bundle the inference task to be run on the edge device.
2. The component is executed in *isolation* from the remaining edge device.
3. The component receives a window of data points, e.g., industrial *time series* data, and produces an *inference result* such as a forecast or a classification.
4. The component must handle *conversion of data points* to a tensor format appropriate for the model and must *interpret* the resulting tensor.

Furthermore, the performance overhead of the solution should be small. Ideally, multiple different model formats and programming languages are supported.

While the use of WebAssembly or `wasi-nn` is not listed as a requirement (solutions employing different systems could also be applicable to the envisioned use case), the focus of this study lies on judging the usage of WebAssembly and `wasi-nn` for these requirements, hence this prototype utilizes these technologies. Nevertheless, we consider alternative approaches in Sect. 6.3.

5.2 Architecture

The prototype realizes a simple service architecture, as shown in Fig. 2: A data stream handler receives data from industrial installations and provides individual data points collected into data windows via a REST interface to the service. The service is a WebAssembly runtime (in our case, Wasmtime), which runs a single Wasm component that employs the WASI-HTTP system interface. Internally, the component is made up of two parts: an in-house framework maintained by the industry automation company and the core component made by the user.

The core component can be called a *wrapper*, as it wraps up the execution of the actual ML model. Its purpose as such is twofold: Firstly, it normalizes and scales the input data and converts them into a tensor of a shape that is suitable to the model being run. Secondly, it interprets the resulting tensor produced by the model and formats it in a useful way that can be returned to the data stream handler. These two tasks are specific to the concrete model to be executed and, therefore, this functionality must be provided by the user.

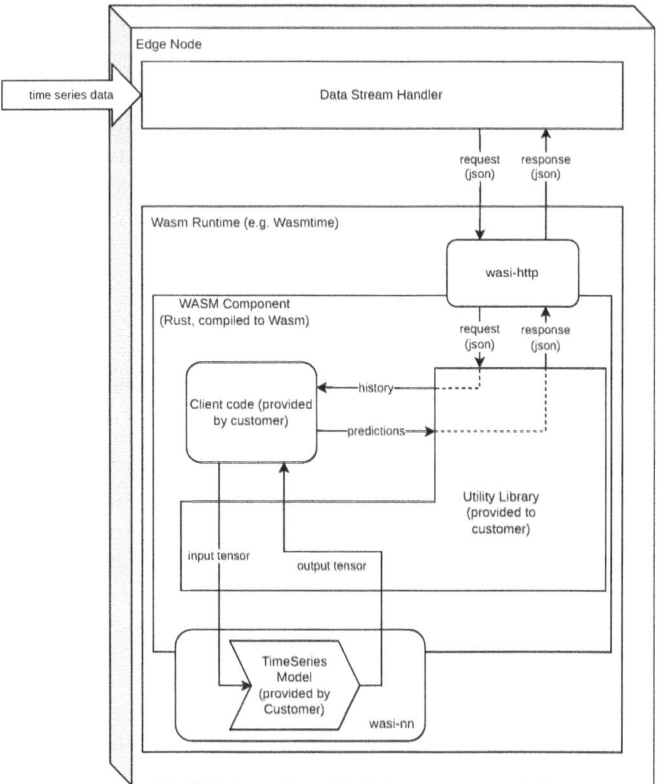

Fig. 2. Design of the Prototype

Several aspects of implementing such wrappers are made easier by a utility library or a framework. Since the interfaces provided by `wasi-nn` and WASI HTTP are low-level, the library provides some utilities and layers on top of the system interfaces that are more straightforward to use. It also takes care of parsing the contents of HTTP requests and constructing HTTP responses for the wrapper. If required, it could also provide a caching buffer to collect data points into data windows, in case the environment does not provide a time-series of sufficient length as context or only single-point samples. Moreover, it can store the necessary configuration parameters for the pre- and post-processing steps.

Within the requirements and restrictions outlined in Sect. 5.1, there are multiple possible approaches. For example, the utility library could be a distinct WASI compoment, which would allow the client code to be written in any language, at the cost of a more complex architecture. During development of this prototype, we considered multiple designs. A detailed discussion of these is out of the scope of this paper.

5.3 Prototype Implementation

The prototype is implemented in Rust, which can be compiled to WebAssembly and has support for WASI. Bindgen tooling for WIT, the specification language for the interfaces in the component model, is readily available and experimental solutions for building Wasm components out of Rust crates are available. Most existing Rust libraries in the public Rust crate registry can be seamlessly compiled to Wasm if they do not use shared libraries or advanced operating system interfaces. For example, even a big crate such as serde can be compiled to Wasm without any additional considerations, while openvino-rs, which employs the OpenVINO C API installed on the host system, cannot be compiled as the shared library that it links to is not available within the Wasm runtime.

The prototype implements the presented architecture and as such, is separated into two parts: The library and the actual component. The component includes the library as a regular Rust-dependency and can then be compiled to a WebAssembly component, which can be run in a suitable Wasm runtime (as is discussed in Sect. 4, currently only Wasmtime). Our implementation is publicly available on GitHub[10].

6 Lessons Learned

During this study, we encountered several issues that hinder adoption of our approach. Firstly, the ecosystem around WebAssembly, the component model, and `wasi-nn` is experimental and fast-changing. Breaking changes, incomplete feature support in implementations, and outdated documentation and guides are to be expected. Furthermore, implementations and APIs are fairly minimal at this point, so many helper functionality that is standard in most ML framework, e.g. for converting data to tensors and back, is still missing in the `wasi-nn` ecosystem, resulting in more required boilerplate code.

This can be partially mitigated by providing an in-house framework, as in our prototype. While these problems factor into a decision on whether to use this approach, we will focus our discussion on more fundamental issues. One of the goals of wrapping ML workloads in Wasm components is to achieve platform independence: Once compiled to Wasm, a component could be run on many different edge environments, provided a sufficiently feature-complete Wasm runtime. However, we found that support for model formats (e.g. ONNX or OpenVINO) in the runtimes is usually accomplished by linking to the official, native libraries of the model format. Because of this, supporting different model formats usually requires the availability of multiple, often large, shared libraries, which is not always the case in edge environments.

A natural use case for machine learning at the edge is online-training / refining the model on the edge device with real-world data. As of now, the `wasi-nn` proposal only supports inference, while API level support for model training is

[10] Prototype component: https://github.com/joshuabach/wasi-nn-edge-demo Prototype library: https://github.com/joshuabach/wasi-nn-edge-demo-lib.

not on the horizon, let alone implementation support for it. This idea has been discussed within the community[11] but it is so far out of scope for the proposal.

Modern timeseries forecasting models, like PatchTST or TSMixer, as required in the industrial automation domain, predominantly utilize transformer-based architectures. During our investigation into the deployment of these models, we encountered several challenges. Specifically, when converting existing models to ONNX or OpenVino formats, we observed the presence of unsupported operators within the neural network graphs. This hinders the conversion and adoption of existing models as special model patches have to be created that work around these limitations. Moreover, most forecasting models, as stated before, are relying on library functions for input and output (de)normalization, thus it is necessary to store and apply a distinct pre- and post-processing routine when using pre-trained models.

6.1 Performance

An initial comparison of `wasi-nn` performance was done by Deislabs in 2021 using an experimental ONNX implementation for `wasi-nn`[12]. They compared the ONNX C-runtime against tract[13], a Rust-based (feature limited) ONNX runtime that can even be cross-compiled to Wasm. Deislabs compared both tract and the ONNX runtime using native and `wasi-nn` interfaces against Tract running as Wasm and found only a moderate performance impact of 10–20% when using the `wasi-nn` interface compared to 280–360% running Tract in Wasmtime. In our replicated experiment, we benchmarked the ONNX C-runtime using Rust against Wasm interfacing using `wasi-nn`. Our benchmark is based on the official ONNX SqueezeNet 1.1 model and performs either 1, 10 or 100 inference iterations. The results are shown in Table 2.

Table 2. Benchmark results for 100 iterations SqueezeNet

Benchmark	Time (mean $\pm\sigma$)
onnxruntime rust (single threaded)	971.2 ms ± 8.1 ms
onnxruntime rust (default threading)	519.5 ms ± 15.6 ms
wasmtime wasi-nn onnx	765.8 ms ± 40.5 ms
tract rust	1.629 s ± 0.042 s
wasmtime wasi-nn tract	1.829 s ± 0.026 s
wasmtime tract as Wasm	14.875 s ± 0.100 s

We measured a decrease in performance by 50 to 70% when comparing the `wasi-nn` version against the multi-threaded (default) ONNX runtime. The single

[11] Wasi-nn online-learning issue: https://github.com/WebAssembly/wasi-nn/issues/6.

[12] Deislabs wasi-nn ONNX evaluation: https://github.com/deislabs/wasi-nn-onnx.

[13] Tract library: https://lib.rs/crates/tract-onnx.

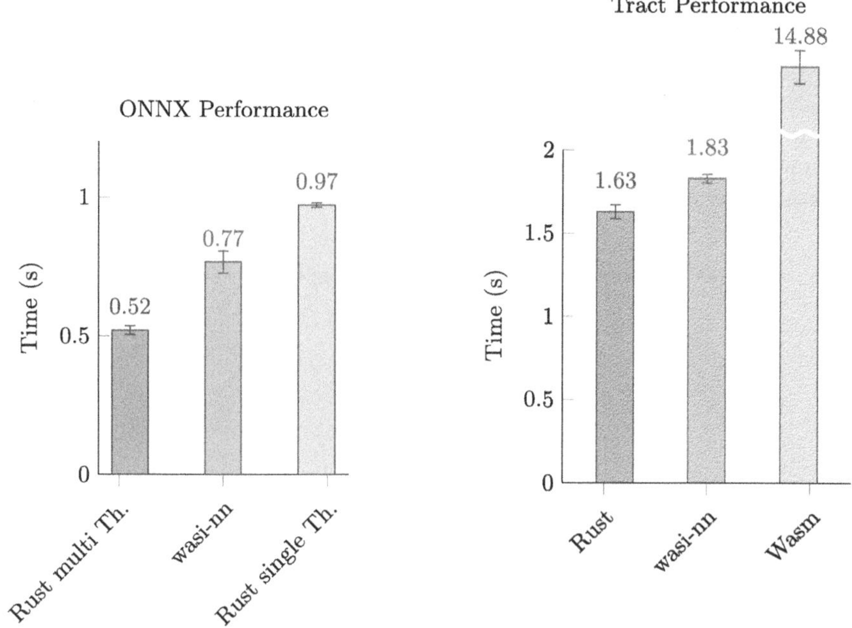

Fig. 3. ONNX and tract comparison

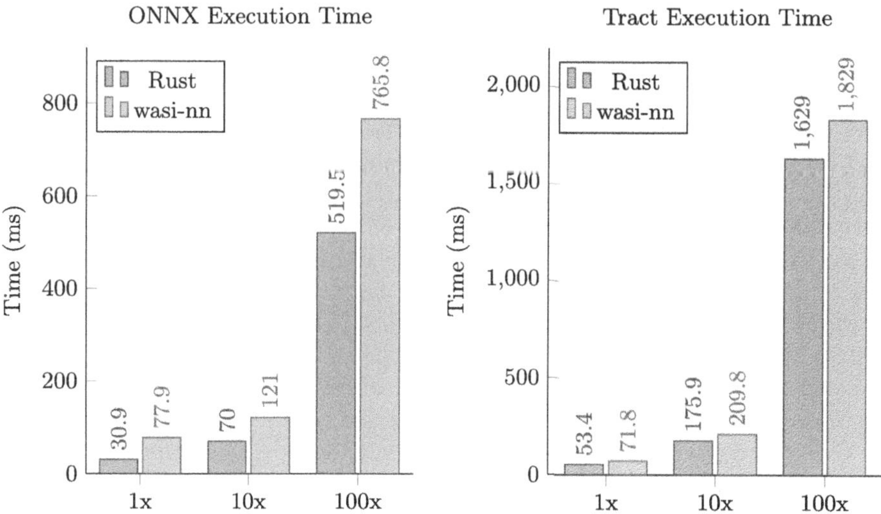

Fig. 4. ONNX and tract scaling

threaded ONNX runtime was, however, still slower, showing that the wasmtime `wasi-nn` implementation is also running ONNX multi-threaded. This is seen in the graph *ONNX Performance* of Fig. 3.

The inclusion of tract (version 0.21.11) in wasmtime has the advantage that no external frameworks are necessary for ML inference, as everything is included in the wasmtime runnable. The performance impact of this is shown in the graph *Tract Performance* of Fig. 3. Overall, the tract enabled version of wasmtime ran slower by a factor of two to three and `wasi-nn` only slightly decreased its performance. Using tract cross-compiled to Wasm took about 8 times longer when compared to the `wasi-nn` version, making it rather unfeasible.

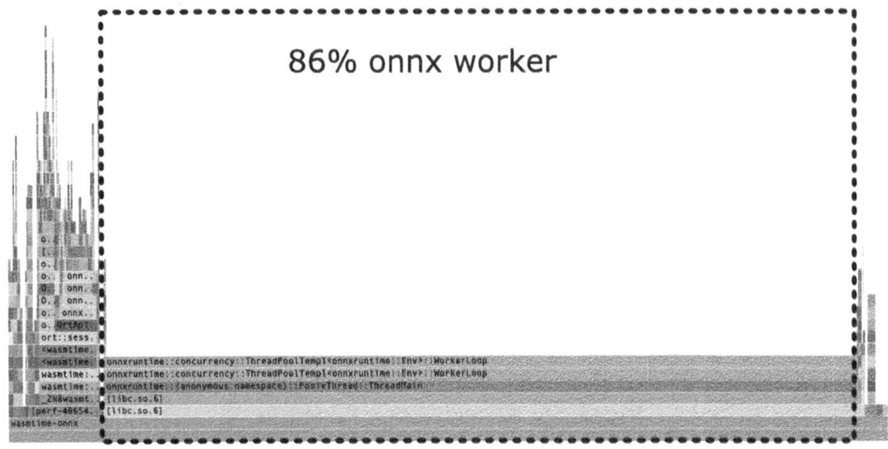

Fig. 5. Flame chart showing the time spent in ONNX runtime vs. wasm runtime

To determine the static overhead (i.e. the time spent setting up the runtime etc.) of `wasi-nn`, the execution time of running a single inference task can be compared to the time for running multiple inference tasks in the same benchmark. These results are shown in Fig. 4. Based on our results we conclude that using ONNX via `wasi-nn` has a static overhead of 40 to 45 ms and a dynamic overhead of 2.5 to 5.1 ms per invocations. For tract we can assume a static overhead of about 15 ms and dynamic overhead of 2 to 3.4 ms. All overheads include both the overhead of using just-in-time-compiled WebAssembly instead of ahead-of-time-compiled Rust and the cost of using the `wasi-nn` interface via the Wasmtime module system.

We conducted several additional experiments to assess the performance of the `wasi-nn` interface in its current state. As discussed before, all `wasi-nn` implementations we reviewed use the native C-bindings for running ML tasks. Therefore, the performance of the actual inference tasks should not differ from native execution. We analyzed several `wasi-nn` examples using `perf` and Wasmtime.

When visualized as flame graphs [5] we could identify the Wasmtime module cache as one source of performance overheads, especially when running single inference tasks. Figure 5 shows a flame chart (a time sorted flame graph) that shows a typical `wasi-nn` execution where the c-based ONNX workers account for 86% of runtime while model preparation (8.5%) and result postprocessing (2.5%) have minor influence. In this case, the remaining 3% are related to the wasmtime startup and module cache. This seems contradictory to the 10–20% impact measured before, however, this percentage represents the CPU time vs. the wall-clock time measured before due to multi-threaded execution in ONNX.

6.2 Usability

In spite of the problems presented here, there are clear benefits to the considered approach. With WebAssembly, there is a new option for isolation. Compared to established approaches like containerization or even full virtualization, a WebAssembly runtime is much more lightweight. Compared with other virtual-machine-based languages, such as Java, WebAssembly runtimes are smaller and more popular source languages have first-class support.

Even container runtimes like crun are adding support for running WebAssembly payloads in managed environments. The WASI component model enables developers to compose functionality even across languages. With `wasi-nn` there is a way to move execution of the main workload out of the slower Wasm environment onto faster native execution.

So for use cases where there is some flexibility in the edge execution environment (to ensure proper model support), both performance and the level of isolation are important and implementing a somewhat experimental technology is acceptable, the approach is applicable and well-suited.

6.3 Alternative Approaches

Having discussed the disadvantages and scope of the use cases for which this approach is applicable, some alternatives can be considered:

Directly using native ML libraries is not an option, as these cannot be accessed from within the Wasm sandbox. However, it could be an option to develop a custom host API that can be used from within the Wasm runtime to run inference tasks on the host side utilizing the native libraries. This approach is similar to how `wasi-nn` itself is implemented, but the in-house API could be less generic than `wasi-nn`. Implementing this would be a major development effort but opens up a lot of flexibility as the API can be tailored exactly to the specific use case. It would also forgo the need to arrange with the unstable nature of the specifications, at least to some degree.

Another option might be to compile the ML frameworks themselves to Wasm. This can be achieved by implementing a model engine in a language than can be compiled to Wasm. For example, the inference engine *tract*, which can read and evaluate ONNX models, is implemented entirely in Rust and can be compiled to native Wasm. Although theoretically possible, it is unclear whether this is feasible for specific model engines. Even then, the performance overhead is prohibitively high compared to running the model natively. This is aggravated by the fact that `wasi-nn` currently does not support ML hardware acceleration.

Another option might be to forgo WebAssembly completely and use a classical software container approach, such as Docker. This would allow using native machine learning libraries and tooling with minimal effort. This approach, however, requires target platform specific code and increases the size of deployable units. For example for Docker this means the customer has to provide a full Docker/Linux image, instead of just a Wasm module and a model file.

7 Threats to Validity

This section discusses relevant threats to validity [3] and the corresponding mitigation measures we applied to address these threats.

Conclusion Validity. The accuracy of conclusions may be affected by different maturity of Wasm and `wasi-nn` toolchains and availability of ML libraries for different programming languages and toolchains. To address this risk, prior to selecting a technology stack for proof-of-concept implementation, the maturity of existing `wasi-nn` implementations was assessed with respect to support for `wasi-nn` and the Wasm component model as this combination provides the most straightforward way to modularize, compose, and execute Wasm-based ML inference tasks. Rust and Wasmtime, were, therefore, chosen to assess the feasibility of using Wasm and `wasi-nn` for engineering and running ML inference tasks at the edge. As this research was neither designed as a comprehensive technology comparison nor performance evaluation research, the experiments were not conducted on diverse edge hardware.

Internal Validity. To address the selection bias with respect to available `wasi-nn` implementations, different search sources were used to identify `wasi-nn` implementations including GitHub search, official WASI and `wasi-nn` documentation, as well as standard web search engines. The search for available implementations was also separately conducted by two researchers. Other risks that may affect assessment outcomes include (i) version difference and (ii) inconsistent configuration across tools.

To accommodate for these risks, the versions and configurations for the experiments were fixed and a version control system was used for better transparency and traceability.

Construct Validity. Example risks in this category include the choice of (i) performance metrics that may not capture all quality aspects of ML inference at the edge, as well as (ii) the benchmarked opensource inference model that may not accurately represent the complexity of real-world industrial automation scenarios.

It is worth emphasizing that the completeness of performance evaluation and choice of ML models were not in the scope of this work. Therefore, the proof-of-concept implementation focused on a common industrial use case of processing timeseries data and validated the feasibility of using Wasm and `wasi-nn` from the implementation and performance point of view.

External Validity. Our results may not generalize to other kinds of ML model architectures or edge computing workloads. Furthermore, the results may not be easily reproduced on future framework versions or emerging edge hardware due to breaking changes.

All of these risks are further mitigated by our prototype being thoroughly documented and released under an open source license, which enables further evaluation, analysis and variation of our results.

8 Conclusion

In this study, we evaluated the usability of WebAssembly combined with the `wasi-nn` proposal as a driver for isolated ML inference tasks on edge computing devices. We found that this fairly novel technological ecosystem is still quite immature but already usable (research question 1). As part of an in-house framework for *isolated inference at the edge* it can be part of a productive solution.

We found that Rust support for WebAssembly, including the component model, while technically only officially supported at "Tier 2"[14], is stable and can be used without issues. The `std`-library and most crates can be seamlessly used when targeting Wasm, unless they link to native shared libraries. The only caveat is sometimes outdated online resources, for example regarding the relatively recent support of the component model.

It achieves good isolation of the workload execution with only minimal performance overhead (research question 2) and WebAssembly as a common denominator offers a high degree of flexibility regarding soft factors, such as the choice of programming language for the customer. Major drawbacks are missing support for online training and the lack of true platform-independence, due to the dependency on native machine learning model engines in most runtimes.

We only did a minimal performance evaluation comparing `wasi-nn`, native execution and pure Wasm exeuction with a small sample size. This already provided some insights, but to further asses the usability of `wasi-nn`, we recommend a more comprehensive performance evaluation of our approach, including comparison of different models and runtimes. Another angle of interest not focused on in this study is the security of our approach. While the WebAssembly virtual machine runs the guest code in isolation, we did not analyze the strength and limitations of this isolation explicitly, nor did we evaluate the concrete Wasm runtimes with regard to security. This is especially relevant since `wasi-nn` in itself is an interface that runs code on the host system, therefore constituting a possible escape path from the isolation which should be analyzed.

For now, the proposed solution is a promising technology for software architects and industrial automation providers looking to develop next-generation

[14] Target Tier Policy: https://doc.rust-lang.org/nightly/rustc/target-tier-policy.html.

offerings for data analysis and predictive maintenance. To become a stable product, more work and research is required: The continued development and adoption of the `wasi-nn` proposal needs to be further advanced and stabilized. We identified alternative approaches to `wasi-nn`, some based on WebAssembly, but also using more classical setups. The viability and drawbacks of these should be further evaluated via more detailed analysis and development of suitable prototypes.

References

1. Bytecode Alliance Foundation: The WebAssembly Component Model (2025). https://component-model.bytecodealliance.org
2. Crnkovic, I., Sentilles, S., Vulgarakis, A., Chaudron, M.R.V.: A classification framework for software component models. IEEE Trans. Softw. Eng. **37**(5), 593–615 (2011). https://doi.org/10.1109/TSE.2010.83
3. Feldt, R., Magazinius, A.: Validity threats in empirical software engineering research-an initial survey. In: Seke, pp. 374–379 (2010)
4. Gohman, D., et al.: WebAssembly System Interface (2025). https://doi.org/10.5281/ZENODO.4323446
5. Gregg, B.: The flame graph. Commun. ACM **59**(6), 48–57 (2016). https://doi.org/10.1145/2909476
6. Hoque, M.N., Harras, K.A.: Webassembly for edge computing: potential and challenges. IEEE Commun. Stand. Mag. **6**(4), 68–73 (2022). https://doi.org/10.1109/MCOMSTD.0001.2000068
7. Jouini, O., Sethom, K., Namoun, A., Aljohani, N., Alanazi, M.H., Alanazi, M.N.: A survey of machine learning in edge computing: techniques, frameworks, applications, issues, and research directions. Technologies **12**(6), 81 (2024). https://doi.org/10.3390/technologies12060081
8. Khelifa, S.E., Bagaa, M., Ouameur, M.A., Ksentini, A.: Case study of webassembly runtimes for AI applications on the edge. In: Global Information Infrastructure and Networking Symposium, GIIS 2024, Dubai, United Arab Emirates, 19–21 February 2024, pp. 1–6. IEEE (2024).https://doi.org/10.1109/GIIS59465.2024.10449907
9. Koziolek, H., Eskandani, N.: Lightweight kubernetes distributions: a performance comparison of microk8s, k3s, k0s, and microshift. In: Proceedings of the 2023 ACM/SPEC International Conference on Performance Engineering, ICPE 2023, Coimbra, Portugal, 15–19 April 2023, pp. 17–29. ACM (2023).https://doi.org/10.1145/3578244.3583737
10. Koziolek, H., Grüner, S., Rückert, J.: A comparison of MQTT brokers for distributed IoT edge computing. In: Jansen, A., Malavolta, I., Muccini, H., Ozkaya, I., Zimmermann, O. (eds.) ECSA 2020. LNCS, vol. 12292, pp. 352–368. Springer, Cham (2020). https://doi.org/10.1007/978-3-030-58923-3_23
11. Luo, C., He, X., Zhan, J., Wang, L., Gao, W., Dai, J.: Comparison and benchmarking of AI models and frameworks on mobile devices. CoRR (2020). https://arxiv.org/abs/2005.05085
12. Qiu, T., Chi, J., Zhou, X., Ning, Z., Atiquzzaman, M., Wu, D.O.: Edge computing in industrial internet of things: architecture, advances and challenges. IEEE Commun. Surv. Tutor. **22**(4), 2462–2488 (2020). https://doi.org/10.1109/COMST.2020.3009103

13. Ray, P.P.: An overview of webassembly for IoT: background, tools, state-of-the-art, challenges, and future directions. Future Internet **15**(8), 275 (2023). https://doi.org/10.3390/FI15080275
14. World Wide Web Consortium (W3C): WebAssembly Core Specification (2024). https://www.w3.org/TR/wasm-core-2
15. Zhang, Q., et al.: A comprehensive benchmark of deep learning libraries on mobile devices. In: WWW '22: The ACM Web Conference 2022, Virtual Event, Lyon, France, 25–29 April 2022, pp. 3298–3307. ACM (2022).https://doi.org/10.1145/3485447.3512148
16. Zhang, Y., Liu, M., Wang, H., Ma, Y., Huang, G., Liu, X.: Research on webassembly runtimes: a survey. CoRR (2024). https://doi.org/10.48550/ARXIV.2404.12621

Software Architecture for a Robust, Multithreaded, Realtime, Control System Used on an Adaptive Racecar

Harry George Direen[1](✉), Randal Hugh Direen[1], George York[2], James Edward Direen[1], Vernon Joseph Brabec[3], and Shanjay Kailayanathan[4]

[1] DireenTech Inc., Colorado Springs, CO 80921, USA
{hdireen,rdireen,jdireen}@direentech.com
[2] US Air Force Academy, Colorado Springs, CO, USA
george.york@afacademy.af.edu
[3] GeoEdge LLC, Livermore, CA, USA
[4] Axcessiom Technologies Inc., Oshawa, ON, Canada
shanjay@axcessiom.ca

Abstract. The software architecture for a robust, multithreaded control system as used in an adaptive racecar is covered. A racecar was adapted so it can be driven by a person with quadriplegia by head control only. The car is steered by the driver turning his/her head left and right. A sip-n-puff system is used for controlling the throttle and brake. The control software was further adapted to tie in a patient's brain implant to augment the control of the car. The primary focus is on the software architecture that was developed for autonomous control of unmanned aerial vehicles and used in the racecar.

Keywords: Software Architecture · Multithreaded · Realtime · Robust · Control System · Racecar · Publish Subscribe Messages · Message Queues · Adaptive Racecar

1 Introduction

The adaptive racecar has roots in work we were doing with cadets at the US Air Force Academy on various adaptive technologies sponsored by a non-profit group called FalconWorks. Through FalconWorks we were introduced to Dr. Falci, a neurosurgeon at Craig Hospital in Denver Colorado who works with patients with spinal cord injuries. One patient had been a racecar driver and wanted to get back behind the wheel of a racecar. Dr. Falci had contacts with Furniture Row Racing (FRR) in Denver who donated a NASCAR racecar along with some funding to adapt the racecar so that a person with quadriplegia (paralyzed from the neck down) can drive the car using head controls. Dr. Falci asked if we would take on the challenge of adapting the car, which began the project. In further work with the University of Miami Miller School of Medicine the car control system was adapted to tie in a patient's brain implant to augment the control of

V. Andrikopoulos et al. (Eds.): ECSA 2025, LNCS 15929, pp. 360–366, 2026.
https://doi.org/10.1007/978-3-032-02138-0_24

the racecar (BCI – Brain Computer Interface). A couple of YouTube videos show the system in operation [1, 2]. Details of the adaptive racecar can be found in the paper: "Head-Controlled Racecar for Quadriplegics"[3].

Some of the authors were also working under research grants at the US Airforce Academy [4–6] to autonomously control unmanned aerial vehicles. The software systems and architecture we developed for autonomous control of UAV's was a natural fit and starting point for the racecar's control software. The software architecture designed for UAV control takes advantage of modern, multicore processor computers, such as the NVIDIA Jetson embedded computers [7], to reliably handle simultaneous, real-time tasks and image processing. The software architecture works on standard operating systems such as Linux, iOS, and Windows.

2 Adaptive Racecar Design

The adaptive racecar is an actual NASCAR cup car with an 850 hp engine capable of running at full track speeds. Furniture Row Racing provided the car and modified the car to add doors so that a paralyzed person can get in and out. The person driving the car under head control sits in the passenger seat of the car with an instrumented helmet on. The car is steered by the driver turning their head left and right. Throttle and brake are controlled using a sip-n-puff system. Blowing or providing pressure into the sip-n-puff tube is translated into throttle control. Sucking on the tube backs off the throttle and then applies the brake. For the version of the car using a BCI (brain computer interface), the BCI system was tied to the throttle control so that the driver had to think throttle on, to get the car to go and increase speed. A safety driver sits in the car's driver's seat and can take control of the car at any time. Safety is a very high concern with the system. A summary of the racecar control system is provided here. A more detailed description is given in the paper: "Head-Controlled Racecar for Quadriplegics" [3].

A block diagram of the car's control system is given below (Fig. 1).

To measure head orientation for steering purposes, we used gyroscopes located on the helmet and on the car in combination with a camera and image processing.

For steering, we used a DCE Motorsport's EPAS (Electric Power-Assist Steering) Pro Race system [8].

Two Kar-tech linear actuators [9] are used for controlling the throttle and brake. The actuators are CAN bus controlled from the system's control computer.

An Origin Instruments Breeze™ Sip and Puff module [10] was used to allow the driver to control throttle and brake.

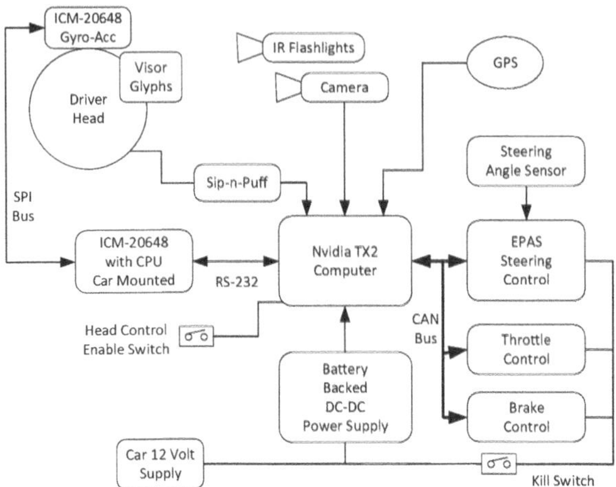

Fig. 1. Racecar Control System

3 Rabit Multi-threaded Management System

A multi-threaded management system, named Rabit, was originally developed under research grants at the US Airforce Academy [4–6] and used to autonomously control unmanned aerial vehicles. At the time the authors developed Rabit, the research group was using single-board computers running either Linux or Windows on the UAVs so Rabit was designed to be used in that environment. Since we were not using a real-time operating system, Rabit was designed to provide similar features.

The Rabit Multi-threaded Management System is a system composed of managers or tasks that run on separate threads, and a messaging system to safely communicate between the managers. Publish-subscribe messages along with message queues are used to communicate between managers in a thread safe way. For those familiar with ROS (Robot Operating System [11]) a Rabit Manager corresponds loosely with a ROS Task. One of the key differences between ROS and Rabit is that Rabit runs as a single multi-threaded process where each manager runs on a separate thread. In ROS each Task is a separate operating system process. The roots of Rabit (originally denoted HOPS) began in 2010 which as I understand was the timeframe the first versions of ROS were released. The authors of Rabit were not aware of ROS at that time.

Running Rabit in a single process as a multithreaded system allows efficient message passing due the shared memory space. Messages and data can be shared via memory copies and pointer passing rather than brokering messages between operating system processes. This can be critical for timing and when large data structures like images are moved around.

Rabit source code is open source and freely available on GitHub. There is a C++ version [12] and a.NET C# version [13]. Additional documentation covering Rabit's operation is included with the source code.

4 Racecar Software Architecture

Figure 2 shows the primary control software architecture. Each blue rectangle represents a Rabit manager. The light blue arrows represent Rabit message queues. The orange arrows represent publish-subscribe messages used for primary control. There are a wide range of publish-subscribe messages (indicated by unconnected arrows) used in the system which are impossible to show without cluttering the diagram.

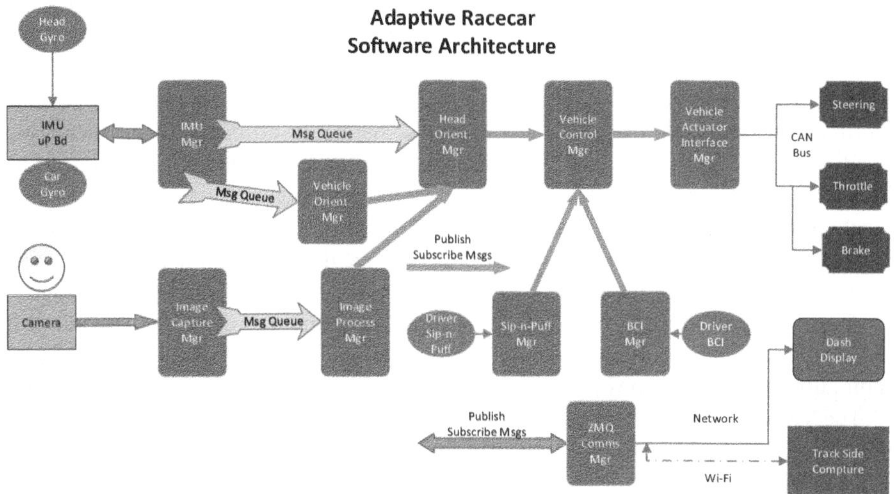

Fig. 2. Racecar Software Architecture

The following is a brief description of the different managers' responsibilities. It is beyond the scope of this paper to provide a full description of the racecar's control software.

The IMU (Inertial Measurement Unit) microprocessor board has on-board and off-board accelerometer gyroscope sensors. The on-board sensors are used for the car's orientation and the off-board sensors are used for the head orientation. The TX2 computer communicates with the IMU uP board over an RS-232 interface. A Rabit manager is dedicated to communicating with the IMU uP board. The Rabit manager is responsible for parsing and formatting the accelerometer and gyroscope data from the on-board and off-board sensor sets and then sending the data over Rabit queues to the Head Orientation Manger and the Vehicle Orientation Manager. Rabit message queues were used to ensure that sensor data samples are not lost or skipped. The Head and Vehicle Orientation Managers make use of Rabit's Message Queue event system. They are woken from a sleep state whenever a sensor data message is inserted into their respective queue.

The Vehicle Orientation Manager receives the car accelerometer and gyroscope data. The manager integrates the gyroscope data to generate an estimated car orientation. This car/vehicle orientation estimate is published in a Rabit message making it available to other managers, especially the Head Orientation Manager. The Head Orientation

Manager just needs and makes use of the latest vehicle orientation estimate so a Rabit publish-subscribe message works well for this case.

The Image Capture Manager is responsible for capturing images from the webcam (camera). The manager puts the image in an OpenCV matrix format. The manager also tags each image with metadata and encapsulates the image and metadata into a Rabit message. The message is sent to the Image processing manager over a Rabit message queue.

The Image Processing Manager is for determining an absolute head orientation relative to the car based upon each image that it receives. The Manager generates a Rabit message containing the head orientation information and posts the message as a Rabit publish-subscribe message.

The Head Orientation Manager receives the head accelerometer and gyroscope data. The manager integrates the gyroscope data to generate an estimated head orientation based upon the gyroscope data. This manager is also responsible for combining the vehicle orientation estimate with the head orientation to obtain a gyroscope-based head orientation relative to the car. This head orientation estimate is combined in a Kalman filter with the image-based head orientation to generate the head orientation used to steer the car. This final head orientation is published in a Rabit publish-subscribe message.

A sip-and-puff manager is responsible for reading the data from the sip-and-puff module. This data is processed into a -100 to $+100$ percent range and published in a Rabit publish-subscribe message.

The Vehicle Control Manager is responsible for the overall control of the car's steering, throttle and brake control. The Vehicle control manager publishes Rabit messages used by the Vehicle Actuator Manager who sends CAN messages to the car's Steering, Throttle and Brake actuators.

An external interface communication manager uses ZeroMQ [14] with Google Protocol Buffer messages [15] to communicate with an external computer and for communicating with a separate display located on the car's dashboard. The external computer monitor is a Windows based monitor program which allows real-time monitoring of the racecar system on a track-side computer over a Wi-Fi interface. The system display process is a separate Python program which displays operational head orientation information, sip-and-puff information, and status information.

An optional BCI (Brain Computer Interface) manager is used to communicate with a driver's BCI system. This was implemented for one specific driver that had a brain implant. The BCI system picked up a signal indicating a hand open or close thought event. A Rabit message is published indicating the hand open or close thought event.

5 Conclusions

The Rabit multithreaded, event driven, software framework works in the adaptive racecar, UAV autonomous control systems, and several other products we have developed. Three of the authors (Harry, Randy, and James Direen) have driven the car using head control, at times over 100 mph. Paralyzed US Army veterans drove the car under head control at over 125 mph. We are working with Axcessiom Technologies [17] in the development of their driver assistance system that uses facial gestures to activate vehicle functions, such as windshield wipers and turn signals, so that drivers with disabilities who require the use of hand controls can gain confidence and independence on the road.

Acknowledgments. Racecar adaptation was done in conjunction with Falci Adaptive Motorsports: https://falcimotorsports.com. Furniture Row Race team in Denver Colorado donated the car, expertise and money to support the project. Pikes Peak International Raceway and Joe Garone provide racetrack facilities, racecar drivers and tremendous help and support with the project. Duncan Steward and FalconWorks for kickstarting the program: https://www.facebook.com/FalconWorksOutreach.

Data Availability. Rabit source code is available in C++ and.NET C# versions on GitHub [3, 4]. The source code for the adaptive racecar can be obtained on GitHub [16] and Figshare DOI: https://doi.org/10.6084/m9.figshare.29043392.

Disclosure of Interests. Dr. Harry Direen and Dr. Randal Direen worked on the development of Rabit under the guidance of Dr. George York, as part of multiple research grants at the US Air Force Academy [4–6].

Disclaimer. *The views expressed in this article, book, or presentation are those of the authors and do not necessarily reflect the official policy or position of the United States Air Force Academy, the Air Force, the Department of Defense, or the U.S. Government.* Approved for public release: distribution unlimited.

References

1. Smart driving cars summit (2019). https://www.youtube.com/watch?v=8VZEUsgyoas
2. Falci adaptive motorsports: innovate 78. https://www.youtube.com/watch?v=hLZX7vdy3S4&t=64s
3. Direen, H.G., Direen, R.H., Direen, J.E.: Head-controlled racecar for quadriplegics. In: 2020 American Control Conference (ACC), Denver, CO, USA, pp. 262–267 (2020). https://doi.org/10.23919/ACC45564.2020.9147433
4. US air force academy UAS research center. https://www.usafa.edu/research/research-centers/center-unmanned-aircraft-systems/
5. General Purpose Graphics Processing Units (GPGPUs) Accelerated Processing in Unmanned Aerial Vehicles, BAA-USAFA-2009-1, Agreement No.: FA7000-15-2-0002, March 2015 to March 2018
6. Counter UAS using Small UAVs Equipped with high performance NVIDIA Jetson Nano Computers, Agreement No.: FA7000-19-2-0037, Sept. 2019 to Sept. 2022
7. NVIDIA Jetson embedded computing. https://www.nvidia.com/en-us/autonomous-machines/embedded-systems
8. DCE motorsport's EPAS. http://www.dcemotorsport.com/Home/EPAS
9. Kar-tech linear actuator. https://kar-tech.com/servo-linear-actuator.html
10. Origin instruments Breeze^{TM} sip and puff. https://orin.com/access/sip_puff/
11. ROS – Robot Operating System. ros.org
12. Rabit C++. https://github.com/rdireen/rabitcpp
13. Rabit C#. https://github.com/rdireen/rabitcsharp
14. ZeroMQ. https://zeromq.org/

15. Protobuf. https://protobuf.dev/
16. Adaptive racecar control software. https://github.com/wavelet55/AdpativeRacecarControlSoftware
17. Axcessiom technologies. https://axcessiom.ca/#/

Asynchronous Interoperability Description and Authentication: Addressing Challenges in a Webhook-Based Event-Driven Architecture

Jean-Philippe Gouigoux[1], Dalila Tamzalit[2](✉), and Khaoula Jbari[2]

[1] Salvia Developpement, Paris, France
Dalila.Tamzalit@univ-nantes.fr
[2] UMR 6004, Nantes Université, École Centrale Nantes, CNRS, LS2N, 44000 Nantes, France

Abstract. Despite adopting a contract-first, standardized API best practice approach, Salvia Development, a software publisher in the real estate sector, encountered difficulties in maintaining synchronous, point-to-point interoperability with its 1,200 customers. The increasing complexity, lack of reactivity and agility, hindered its ability to meet its customers' evolving needs and to target new markets. In response, an asynchronous interoperability architectural style based on events was envisaged, leveraging an Event-Driven Architecture (EDA) implemented with webhooks. However, existing interoperability standards or software solutions such as OpenID Connect, JSON Web Token, MOM, ETL or OpenAPI, are not adapted for asynchronous interoperability needs in event description standardization and secure exchanges. This paper presents the initial findings from a collaborative effort with Nantes Université to address these issues. The first result is the establishment of interoperability between Salvia's software, called SPO, and several CRM editors, by standardizing event and payload descriptions. The second result is the authentication and authorization of webhook callbacks by proposing a novel way of establishing authorization for callbacks without the need for a user account or even identification.

Keywords: Asynchronous Interoperability · Even-Driven Architecture · Authentication · Secure callbacks · Webhook

1 Introduction

In modern software development, as the complexity of software systems and their number increase, the ability to communicate and work together harmoniously has become ever more essential. This concept, known as *interoperability* [20], and more precisely *technical interoperability* [18], is the ability of software systems to cooperate despite their heterogeneity. Technical interoperability is achieved through integration, generally via HTTPS(S), for web applications.

V. Andrikopoulos et al. (Eds.): ECSA 2025, LNCS 15929, pp. 367–377, 2026.
https://doi.org/10.1007/978-3-032-02138-0_25

Synchronous interoperability implies real-time interactions with an external system [6]. *Asynchronous interoperability*, conversely, implies interactions over an extended period of time. Thus, a given system can send and receive events independently, without the need for real-time synchronization.

Salvia Développement[1] and its six sister Business Units (BU) are publishers and integrators of business solutions for the property and local public sector. They design, integrate and operate a range of Line-Of-Business software applications on the real estate domain. To expose its software applications, Salvia adopted a synchronous contract-first, standardized API approach. Despite this best practice, the company encountered difficulties in maintaining interoperability using a Point-to-Point mode [4], leading to tight coupling between Salvia's software application and its customers' systems. The customers expressed 1) a need for quicker data updates than nightly refreshes and 2) a need for bandwidth economy, as only a few percents of the data would change in a given workday. The solution was to adopt an asynchronous interoperability to dynamically respond to changes and expose only data modifications. This was partly achieved through the implementation of an event-driven architecture (EDA) [12] using webhooks [2]. This technology was chosen because of its lightweight style and also because it was already used by major web players like Github. However, its adoption was hindered since existing standards and tools for interoperability are not adequate for managing asynchronous interoperability in the description, subscription and secure data exchange. This paper presents a novel approach to address these issues, and in particular improve the security of subscription.

After this introduction, the paper is organized as follows: Sect. 2 presents the context of moving from a synchronous point-to-point interoperability to an asynchronous one based on EDA and webhooks. Section 3 identifies the challenges faced while adopting asynchronous interoperability by exposing the two main problems. Section 4 presents the proposed approach and discusses its limitations while Sect. 5 presents the state of the art before concluding and presenting our future works in Sect. 6.

2 General Context

The SPO[2] application of Salvia Développement is central to managing real estate project data, serving as an indispensable tool in the life-cycle of property development. This application is adept at handling various aspects of real estate projects, from searching for suitable land to the intricate planning of financial elements. It enables thorough management of subsidy budgets, construction costs, and sales budgeting, offering a comprehensive view of each project's financial viability. A significant part of the SPO application's functionality involves managing data for individual real estate lots. As each project progresses, the application tracks crucial milestones and updates. When a construction phase is completed, SPO should communicate this information as soon as it occurs to their concerned

[1] https://www.salviadeveloppement.fr/.

[2] "*SPO: Salvia Pilotage des Opérations*" meaning "*Salvia Operations Management*".

clients. However, rather than pushing it when the changes occur, SPO uses a synchronous Point-to-Point interoperability [4] which is not reactive. In addition of this lack of reactivity, it represents a direct and dedicated connection and tight coupling between SPO and each system of its 1,200 customers, with up to 1,500 requests for data transfer per day.

To find an appropriate solution enhancing interoperability, a preliminary feasibility study[3] has been conducted to compare different other integration approaches than the Point-to-Point one, with the objective to reduce the bandwidth and ensure real-time notifications: Hub & Spoke [13], Service-Oriented Architecture (SOA) [7] and Event-driven architecture (EDA) [12]. This last architectural style has been selected. In fact, EDA allows to trigger actions through event generation in response to given identified changes. Systems that want to be notified in real-time when the event is triggered, must subscribe to it beforehand to be notified when the event occurs. EDA makes systems able to communicate only when needed rather than continuously checking for updates or needing direct integrations between them, like currently in SPO. With regard to its practical implementation, the EDA architectural style can be implemented by combining various technologies, like event streaming platforms, message brokers, stream processing frameworks, API gateways... In the current context, webhooks have been chosen [2] for their lightweight feature. However, despite their advantages, Salvia encountered issues when attempting to adopt the EDA and webhooks efficiently, as detailed in the following section.

3 Problem Statement

The two main issues Salvia encountered to adopt efficiently for SPO an asynchronous interoperability leaning on the EDA coupled to webhooks are: a lack of standards for event description and subscription and issues of securing data exchanges. Before exploring the raised problems in more detail, we first establish necessary definitions to facilitate a comprehensive reading.

3.1 Definitions

As the vocabulary and expression are not (yet) standardized for asynchronous interoperability, there is often confusion between the words and concepts. We propose the following definitions that we will lean on:

- *Trigger:* human action (generally via an API) on a business entity raising an event.
- *Event:* description of business context changes, with the performed action on a given business entity. An event is exposed by a third-party.
- *Subscription:* action asking to be informed of the occurrence of an event.

[3] This study was conducted as part of another project that is outside the scope of this paper.

- *Callback:* mechanism enabling the event-subscribing third-party to provide the stream, generally an URL, to be called by the event-exhibiting third-party, generally an API.
- *Webhook:* mechanism allowing an API to send real-time data to the event-subscribed third-party as soon as an event occurs.
- *Payload:* content of the callback, describing the event and associated context information.
- *Publication:* action of issuing callbacks.

3.2 Lack of Description and Subscription Standards

Cloud interoperability needs and gains to rely on practice standardization to allows enterprises to go beyond the constraints of distinct and heterogeneous cloud ecosystems. As a proof, synchronous interoperability is well-established, leaning on standards like XML, JSON, HTTP and all the associated RFCs from IEEE, IETF, W3C, OASIS and many other organizations. OpenAPI is the norm for API description. REST principles are also a de facto standard and security relies on a stable foundation constituted with OAuth, JWT, OpenID Connect, SCIM, etc. Nowadays, APIs are well-understood and well-used. However, for asynchronous interoperability, the design of events and the necessary delivery infrastructure that complement the APIs is still challenging. Current norms and software solutions (like HTTP status codes, OpenID Connect, OpenAPI, JSON Web Token, MOM, ETL etc.) are not adequate for managing asynchronous interoperability in the description, subscription and secure data exchange. As the subscription phase is synchronous, usual aspects of synchronous APIs apply as well. However, the actual difference lies in the subscription mechanism that links the subscription phase with the publication one which is asynchronous for sending event-triggered callbacks. When looking at OpenAPI, there is a very limited grammar, at least in its current version 3.1.0., to describe this mechanism. While the norm defines a webhook attribute, it does not say anything about retrieving the list of events, describing their payload, how to specify the registration address, what the payload should contain (event identifier, time, etc.). It does not expose any parameter, neither to specify a condition on the emission of a callback based on the entity that triggers the event, nor to describe the requested payload. As current norms, standards and tools are not sufficient to address asynchronous description and publication needs, *the first main problem we address is how to fill the gap of the lack of standardization in description and subscription for asynchronous interoperability.*

3.3 Security Access Issues with Webhooks

The second issue is the lack of secure data exchanges due to the use of webhooks. In contrary to brokers and middleware that present a high degree of industry-wide trust in their use, webhooks, while representing the appropriate lightweight solution for Salvia, are not trusted third parties. Therefore, it is necessary to find a solution that secures asynchronous interoperability. Security in interoperability leans on three key aspects: *Identification*, *Authentication* and *Authorization* [17]. Authentication and authorization is almost fully standardized in the domain of synchronous calls, including the use of external Identification and Authorization Management (IAM) software [15]. These three key security aspects are mature for synchronous interoperability. However, security with webhooks has not reached this maturity, especially for the authentication.

In fact, subscribing to an event requires the provision of an URL, called an *endpoint* [19], to receive notifications when the event occurs. This represents a potential security vulnerability if the URL is leaked. This is due to the asynchronous nature of the callback: the client is authenticated when she subscribes but she is potentially no more authenticated when the event occurs or her rights changed. It is essential to reassure clients that the callback will be authentic and not compromised by a potential URL leak and aligned with client's authorizations. This highlights the importance of authentication ("*how do I prove who I am?*") and authorization ("*I only get what I'm entitled to*") in an asynchronous interoperability. Currently, the following practices are generally used to address authentication needs:

- A subscription by providing an *URL* without rights management: if the URL leaks, security is compromised and the client may receive fraudulent callbacks.
- A subscription using a *security token* [5]: while the duration of an access token is usually very limited (a few minutes), the synchronous nature of this call makes it easy for the emitter to use its ID token, generally a JWT token [8] to generate another access token and call the command another time.

However, these authentication mechanisms are not well adapted for the use of webhooks. It is important to note that webhooks, due to their asynchronous nature, are exclusively used between systems and applications. Callbacks are thus automated and sent to a system, not to a human as it is the case with classical APIs. Consequently, it is not possible to predict when callbacks will be triggered. Additionally, it is not feasible to manage a potential expiration date or the consequences of such an event. This has brought companies to adapt authentication mechanisms for the callbacks as follows:

- The most obvious way to counteract the expiration date is to increase the lifespan of the JWT token. Most IAM applications allow the increase of this parameter, but only to a certain point as this would weaken security and go against the *principle of least privilege* that ensures to access only the information and resources that are necessary for its legitimate purpose [16].
- Many companies use IP-filtering and/or ClientCertificate/Mutual TLS protocol to implement exchange security and partially avoid the limitation in time, but in all cases, certificates still have to be renewed.
- A more sophisticated approach is to share a secret between the servers that participate in the events-based requests [9]. A Hash-based Message Authentication Code added to the HTTP headers is closer to the webhooks operation,

as it applies to the messages themselves and not to the whole "pipe" but it only acts at the very broad level of data transportation.

We consider thus that previously presented types of authentication and their observed adaptations are not well-suited to webhooks-based asynchronous interoperability. *The second main problem we address is how to ensure authentication in a highly secure manner while easily ensuring the principle of least privilege for asynchronous interoperability.*

4 Approach

Our approach proposes firstly a standardization for description and subscription to event and secondly a fully automatic solution to ensure a high degree of security, without time constraints and facilitates compliance with the principle of least privilege.

4.1 Description and Subscription

This first contribution aims to pose a first attempt of standardizing the description of event type and the payload. Salvia will identify all event types and describe them following the contract, as illustrated in Fig. 1.


```
{ "eventId": "763745378537547",
  "eventDate": "2025-03-12:04:34:12Z+02:00",
  "eventType": {
      "entityType": "urn:salvia:operation:lots",
      "eventAction": "PATCH" },
  "target": "/api/operations/lots/2364" }
```


Fig. 1. An Event callback following a standardized contract.

eventID is a unique identifier that is used for unique execution even if a retry policy is activated (concept of unique delivery). *eventDate* can be used by the receiver as a business value date in order to reach eventual consistency. *eventType* has been standardized using the URI norm, as well as the standard RFC for HTTP verbs to represent the kind of action on the entity. There should be an alignment between this verb and the verb used for an API call in the hypothesis the business event comes from such a call, even if it is not automatic. Indeed, if an entity is created (via the POST operation), the granular event will be about its creation (via POST also). Finally, the *target* attribute points to the entity concerned by the event, and is of course a standardized URL. This information is used in order for the event receiver to come back to the emitter and ask for more information. Though the roundtrip takes more time, it is essential that the event payload does not contain any possibly confidential data. This a good practice to only send the URL of the instance and let the authorization process run anew against the next request. Of course, as standardization is of uttermost important, this content has been created by uniformizing many existing practices, and described through a JSON-formatted, OpenAPI-based file. This standardization of the contract implies also that all the other players, mainly the clients, are invited to respect it. The main benefit is, by "standardizing" this contract, this will ease the subscription phase in a smooth way, avoiding to fall back on Point-to-Point connectors.

4.2 Security Access: Identification, Authentication, Authorization

To address the limitation that the authorization of a webhook callback is linked to the authentication of the sender, our approach authorizes the callback without any reference to authentication nor even identification of the sender. We designed an authorization method based on a subscription-based unique identifier, that does not even needs a JWT token. Each client's subscription is accompanied by a generated *Universally Unique Identifier* (UUID) [10][4]. Each specific need of an event and its related information will have its own subscription and will have its own callback and thus its own UUID. This generated UUID becomes a *shared secret* [3] between the server and the client's system, ensuring trust for only the identified perimeter. The steps are depicted in Fig. 2 and explained after.

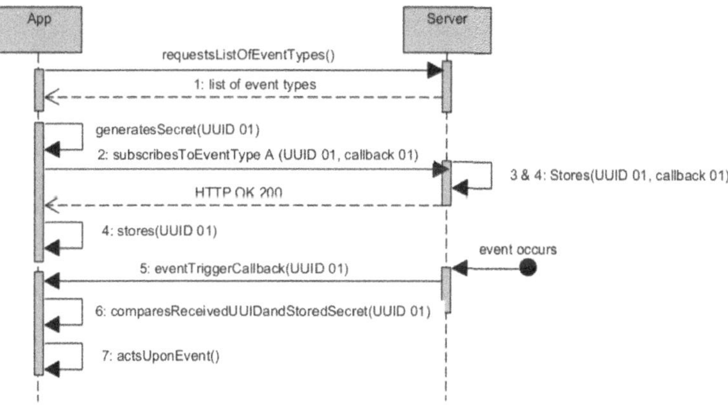

Fig. 2. Security access: Identification, Authentication, Authorization.

1. The server provides a list of events it can trigger;
2. The client generates a subscription identifier and subscribes to a given event, with filters if they are supported;

[4] The term Globally Unique Identifier (GUID) is also used, mostly in Microsoft systems.

3. The server stores the webhook definition, and of course the callback URL provided by the client;
4. The client and the server store the unique identifier, which is the *shared secret*;
5. The server is responsible to reach the callback URL when an event occurs. It is only in charge with putting the unique subscription identifier in the HTTP request;
6. The client compares the identifier coming in to the ones it has generated;
7. It then takes decision to handle the event content.

Communications must of course be encrypted to protect this secret since it is the only coupling, but, even if it is disclosed, the impact is limited to the sole subscription, since there is no user associated with the connection. This method has a great advantage of providing authorization without needing user identification neither authentication. If a compromise happens, only the channel is at risk, and not the complete identity of the user account. Another advantage of the approach that we have experienced is the level of compartmentalization it allows. Indeed, identifiers can be freely defined by the subscriber to distinguish between types of events, or even filters on these events, without any dependency on the server other than it storing the secret with the subscription options. Revocation is eased by the fact that the client as well as the server are able to cancel a given channel of communication without jeopardizing the other ones. Each of them is completely independent for revoking the link since they both store the identifier generated and removing it is enough to block any further exchange.

4.3 Discussion

One of the obvious drawbacks in the proposed solution is the need to store many UUIDs on both side of the events exchanges. This results in 1) additional server space used, though this is negligible due to the limited size of a UUID, 2) time in UUID generation, again not a real problem as GUID V7 implementation are now very fast, and 3) risk of loss of subscription if the data were to be lost, which can prove a real problem if applications rely on the server to secure their subscription. Another point of discussion is the actual security improvement associated to the solution. Indeed, there is no major confidentiality improvement in the exchange of a secret if its format does not change (the chosen UUID could be an HMAC signature, or even a certificate). The risk is only reduced by the division of perimeter in case a UUID is leaked (reduction of attack surface), which means that 1) it only provides a clear additional level of security if subscriptions are numerous, and 2) the risk is not reduced in the case the storage of secrets itself is compromised. On these two points, we expect that first uses in production and return of experience from the pilot customer and the pilot integration partner will provide for additional experience and allow for insights on these potential drawbacks and limitations.

5 State Of The Art

Despite thorough literature searches, we have not found works addressing new solutions for securing webhooks for asynchronous interoperability. Works leaning on middleware, broker or router, like [1] leaning on AMQP and MQTT, are out of scope since this solution is not envisaged in this work (see Sect. 2). Some research works propose securing asynchronous interactions, but these primarily rely on identity management, in contrast to our work that do not rely on identity or authentication. The work that aligns most closely with our concerns is the one of Dixit&al [5]. They address the need of securing asynchronous interaction challenges encountered in Business-to-Business and SaaS environments by leaning on webhooks. They secure identity management by extending the System for Cross-Domain Identity Management (SCIM) standard protocol. Some other works are further from our approach, like Xiong&al that propose a cross-domain identity management system based on the concept of the Decentralized Identifier standard [21]. Other interesting research works address specifically asynchronous interoperability but they focus on formalizing the common asynchronous authentication problem [11,14]. Finally, even if the blockchain domain uses the notion of *shared secret*, we did not consider dedicated works since their feature of non-repudiation without a trusted third is rarely needed for events.

6 Conclusion and Future Works

This paper presents a novel solution to respond to a lack of standards for event description and subscription and for secure exchanges of asynchronous interoperability of an EDA implemented with webhooks. The first contribution is to propose a standardized contract to describe event type and lean on it for event subscription. It provides a consensual description of an event type that all partners must respect, in order to facilitate subscriptions to event. The second contribution proposes a novel approach to secure data exchange by using a shared secret during the subscription avoiding the need of authentication during callbacks. This ensures total anonymity, with no time limit and offering an adjustable perimeter granularity for subscription. Tests remain to be realized and production-based experiments is still in progress. For confidentiality reasons against Salvia competitors, we cannot provide more detailed examples about designing and testing the solution. However, the first deployments have proven to be easy to create, owing to the excellent decoupling this enables. Additional subjects are currently addressed, in particular around including an expiration date in the subscription for security reasons. The idea is to add an account for identification of the subsequent operations on the client, without needing authentication. This account will not be attached to a real user, but would help in tracing historical changes in the events receiver for aim of analysis. This approach is so promising that we are crafting a proposal to extend the OpenAPI 3.1.0 standard. This last includes a section on webhooks but is currently silent about the callbacks authentication and authorization issues of asynchronous interoperability. We also aim to include event-type definition, filtering and reduction of the bandwidth by additional filtering of the payload. Reduction of the payload is also a future work, needing to strike the right balance between confidentiality (like no GDPR-related personal data in the callback) and efficiency. Once the complete grammar additions have been tested with the beta customers and improved, for the hoped-for improvements to reach public state, we will be able to give more details. In addition, we aim to refine our authentication strategies, assess their integration with new technologies, and bolster their scalability and security, essential for responsiveness, adaptability, efficiency and security, meeting the evolving demands of complex digital ecosystems.

References

1. Basig, L., Lazzaretti, F.: Reliable Messaging Using the CloudEvents Router. Ph.D. thesis, OST Ostschweizer Fachhochschule (2021)
2. Biehl, M.: Webhooks–Events for RESTful APIs, vol. 4. API-University Press (2017)
3. Brassard, G., Salvail, L.: Secret-key reconciliation by public discussion. In: Helleseth, T. (ed.) EUROCRYPT 1993. LNCS, vol. 765, pp. 410–423. Springer, Heidelberg (1994). https://doi.org/10.1007/3-540-48285-7_35
4. Briggs, T.L., Baum, S.J., Thomas, T.M.: Interoperability framework. J. Ship Prod. **21**(02), 99–107 (2005)
5. Dixit, S., Jangid, J.: Asynchronous scim profile for security event tokens. J. Comput. Anal. Appl. **33**(6) (2024)
6. Ellis, C.A., Gibbs, S.J., Rein, G.: Groupware: some issues and experiences. Commun. ACM **34**(1), 39–58 (1991)
7. Erl, T.: SOA Design Patterns. Pearson Education, Boston (2008)
8. Jones, M., Bradley, J., Sakimura, N.: Json web token (jwt). Technical report (2015)
9. Karnin, E., Greene, J., Hellman, M.: On secret sharing systems. IEEE Trans. Inf. Theory **29**(1), 35–41 (1983)
10. Leach, P., Mealling, M., Salz, R.: A universally unique identifier (uuid) urn namespace. Technical report (2005)
11. Maram, D., Kelkar, M., Eyal, I.: Interactive multi-credential authentication. In: Proceedings of the 2024 on ACM SIGSAC, pp. 408–422 (2024)
12. Michelson, B.M.: Event-driven architecture overview. Patricia Seybold Group **2**(12), 10–1571 (2006)
13. Miller, F.P., Vandome, A.F., McBrewster, J.: Enterprise Service Bus. Alpha Press (2009)
14. Mouallem, M., Eyal, I.: Asynchronous authentication. In: Proceedings of the 2024 on ACM SIGSAC, pp. 3257–3271 (2024)
15. Olabanji, S., Olaniyi, O., Adigwe, C., Okunleye, O., Oladoyinbo, T.: Ai for identity and access management (iam) in the cloud: exploring the potential of artificial intelligence to improve user authentication, authorization, and access control within cloud-based systems. In: Authorization, and Access Control within Cloud-Based Systems, 25 January 2024(2024)
16. Saltzer, J.H., Schroeder, M.D.: The protection of information in computer systems. Proc. IEEE **63**(9), 1278–1308 (1975)
17. Schneier, B.: Identification, authentication, and authorization. In: Beyond Fear: Thinking Sensibly About Security in an Uncertain World, pp. 181–206 (2003)
18. Van Der Veer, H., Wiles, A.: Achieving technical interoperability. European telecommunications standards institute (2008)

19. Waxman, B.M.: Routing of multipoint connections. IEEE J. Sel. Areas Commun. **6**(9), 1617–1622 (1988)
20. Wegner, P.: Interoperability. ACM Comput. Surv. (CSUR) **28**(1), 285–287 (1996)
21. Xiong, Y., Yao, S., Li, P.: D2cdim: did-based decentralized cross-domain identity management with privacy-preservation and sybil-resistance. In: International Symposium on Emerging Information Security and Applications, pp. 191–208. Springer, Heidelberg (2022). https://doi.org/10.1007/978-3-031-23098-1_12

Variant Management Impact on Architectural Maintainability in Embedded Systems – A Case Study

Bengt Haraldsson[1,2] and Miroslaw Staron[1(✉)]

[1] Chalmers University of Technology, University of Gothenburg, Gothenburg, Sweden
[2] Scania CV AB, Södertälje, Sweden
bengt.haraldsson@scania.com

Abstract. Context: The heavy vehicles market need of new software functions is increasing, which means that the embedded systems in vehicles are growing in size and complexity. To stay competitive, OEMs must develop multiple vehicle models with the same embedded systems, which requires variant management for proper behavior in different configurations. **Objective**: We explore how different solutions to variant management impact the architectural maintainability of embedded systems. We study compile-time and build-time solutions w.r.t. their complexity. **Methods**: We conduct a case study at Scania CV AB, an OEM in the heavy vehicle segment. Two large embedded systems controlling complex hardware were chosen as units of analysis. **Results**: We found that the use of software product lines greatly decreased the complexity of system components. However, other customization approaches were found to increase the component complexities in the studied systems. Dependencies between components were analyzed and we found evidence of increased component coupling as a result of splitting components in a layered architecture approach, reducing the complexity within a component, but trading it with higher complexity on an architectural level. **Conclusions**: These findings suggest that variant management approaches, while enhancing customization, affects maintainability. We found that the importance of balancing variant flexibility with architectural simplicity is key to mitigate long-term maintenance challenges. There seems to be a total amount of complexity that cannot be reduced, only moved around, and the key issue for developers and architects is to understand how to find a balance.

Keywords: Automotive · Embedded Systems · Variant Management · Maintainability

1 Introduction

Embedded systems in the automotive industry have grown significantly in size and complexity [14], leading to increased effort to achieve maintainability as

Supported by Vinnova, Scania CV AB, and Software Center.

V. Andrikopoulos et al. (Eds.): ECSA 2025, LNCS 15929, pp. 378–388, 2026.
https://doi.org/10.1007/978-3-032-02138-0_26

defined by ISO/IEC 25010:2023 [4]. Given that up to 70% of the total lifetime development cost are maintenance costs [6], it becomes imperative for industry actors to understand how to maximize embedded system maintainability.

System architecture can impact maintainability effort [8], and depending on how successful the system's structure becomes, maintenance activities can be fast and efficient or intricate and costly. One source of complexity in embedded systems development is the ability to control slightly different mechatronic hardware, for example, different engines, gearboxes, or sensors [2,10] with variants of the same system. There are different ways of solving the problem of variant management, but so far little research has been done to understand how this impacts maintainability from an architectural perspective. For this reason, we conduct a case study at an original equipment manufacturer (OEM) in the heavy vehicle segment to investigate how different approaches to variant management impact the architectural maintainability of embedded systems. When conducting our study, we follow the guidelines prescribed by Runeson and Höst [13].

We guide our research with the following questions:

- **RQ1**: Which variant management strategies lead to higher component complexity?
- **RQ2**: How do different variant management strategies affect the structural properties (such as modularity and coupling) of the embedded system?

We combine analysis of variability management strategies on code level and architecture level with qualitative data from developers to understand how different strategies for variant management affect the architectural maintainability effort.

The rest of this paper is structured as follows. Section 2 introduces theory and previous work relevant for the study. Section 3 describes how this research is designed and the case context. Section 4 presents the results, and Sect. 5 discusses and relates them to the literature. Finally, Sect. 6 presents the conclusions from the study.

2 Background and Related Work

Three areas are important for our study: 1) concepts and metrics of software maintainability, 2) variant management, and 3) architectural patters for managing software variability.

Research has extensively explored ways to quantify maintainability to help predict maintenance efforts throughout a system's lifecycle [6]. Commonly used metrics include McCabe Cyclomatic Complexity, which assesses code complexity, and object-oriented metrics such as Li and Henry's measure that evaluate the relationship between objects [6].

Despite numerous proposed metrics, there is still limited empirical evidence drawn from industry contexts, as highlighted by Malhotra and Lata [6] and Elmidaoui et al. [1].

Embedded automotive systems require managing variability due to differences in hardware, customer requirements, and installation conditions [2,10]. Variant management is often approached through Software Product Lines (SPLs), which allow multiple products to share common components while supporting unique customer needs [2,10]. One significant challenge identified is creating variability models for existing product lines, especially when integrating mechatronic hardware [3,7]. Additionally, the "clone-and-own" strategy, where existing code is copied and modified independently for new variants, is frequently discussed as an alternative approach. Although it simplifies initial development, this practice can lead to redundancy and maintainability issues over time [2].

Beyond SPLs, variant management is also accomplished through compile-time and run-time configurations. Compile-time strategies involve preprocessor directives and conditional compilation, whereas run-time strategies depend on configurable parameters defined in external files [2].

Software architecture significantly impacts system maintainability [8]. Mari and Eila [8] highlight that the level of modularization in a component-based system directly influences maintainability, as independent modules minimize propagation of changes.

3 Methodology

We follow the exploratory case study methodology prescribed by Runeson and Höst [13].

Components with different variant management strategies were identified and compared to evaluate the impact on maintainability effort using the evaluation metrics: 1) Cyclomatic complexity. 2) Cohesion and coupling (measured using fan-in, fan-out).

The following steps were taken during quantitative system-data collection:

1. Three software product line versions were chosen from two systems, and component source code files gathered to construct a valid (and buildable) system variant.
2. Component average and maximum complexity was calculated on function level using the Lizard Code Complexity calculator[1] Python package.
3. Functional dependencies were collected by parsing the system with the LLVM compiler[2] and analyzing function calls. Both fan-in and fan-out calls were considered.
4. Outliers were detected, both in terms of complexity and dependencies, and the files and components identified by outlier functions were analyzed.

We complemented the quantitative code and architecture measurements with qualitative data to triangulate our data collection [13]. The qualitative data was collected from developer interviews, gathering all mentions of variant management and performing thematic analysis on these excerpts. The developers in the

[1] https://github.com/terryyin/lizard.

[2] https://llvm.org/.

study were chosen for their long experience working with embedded systems in general, and the systems under study in particular. We interviewed five developers who were chosen from around 200 developers after recommendations from the line management responsible for the two systems. More information about the developers can be found in Table 1.

Table 1. Developer years of experience and role.

Developer	Current system	Total	System	Role
1A	7	23	A	Senior developer and advisor
2A	16	20	A	Senior developer and architect
3A	12	12	A	Developer
1B	6	6	B	Developer
2B	7	18	B	Senior developer

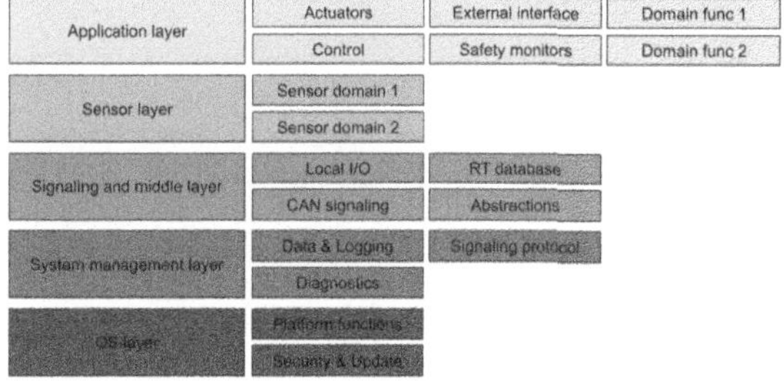

Fig. 1. Illustration of the layered architecture of the studied systems.

3.1 Case Description

Scania CV AB is a Swedish OEM with a high degree of internally developed software systems. In this context, the two systems that form *units under study* [13] are two real-time embedded control systems that control complex mechatronic hardware. The hardware (ECU) for these systems and their firmware, or base software, is supplied by Tier 1 suppliers. Software, including the operating system and middleware, is developed in-house.

The units of analysis in the case are two embedded control systems, detailed in Table 2. Architecturally, the systems can be described as a mix of a layered architecture and a component-based real-time architecture. Each component is a collection of source files (.c- and .h-files) that form a cohesive functional grouping, e.g., controlling some mechatronic hardware or monitoring the status of a hardware via sensor input. The systems are divided into layers, and the layers into different domains. The components then reside in the domains. Figure 1 shows the layers and abstracted domains (not revealing actual implementation details).

Variant management is implemented in different ways, where the three main strategies are:

- **Stragedy A**: Single-component across product lines. Compile-time configuration based on pre-processor directives. Customized further with parametrization and calibration.
- **Strategy B**: Separate component variants are created for one or more product lines. This means that a number of .h and .c files that make up the main functionality of the component will have versions with the same name, but different content. Customized further with parametrization and calibration, similar to "clone-and-own" [2].
- **Strategy C**: Hybrid set-up where separate variants are created, but a large portion of functionality remains common over product lines.

The different customization steps used in the case organization are illustrated in Fig. 2

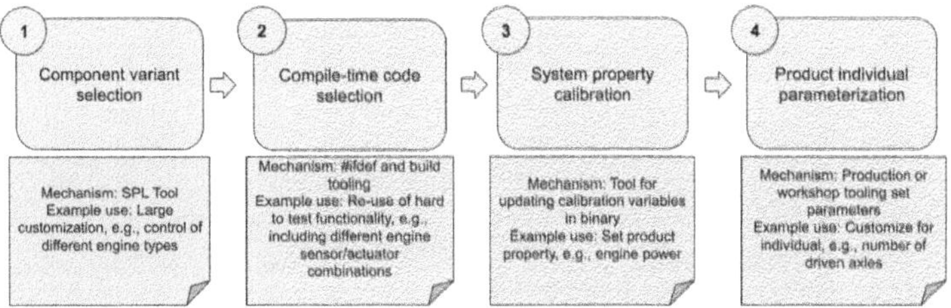

Fig. 2. Possible steps (and their order) used when creating system variants.

Table 2. Details on units of analysis. Systems A and B.

System	# components	Approx. # files	Approx. # LOC
A	58	2,000	500,000
B	121	3,000	800,000

4 Results

The results presented here were collected from parsing and statically analyzing source code files grouped in components and collecting the data from the analysis. The function with maximum complexity for each component was analyzed manually to understand the reason for the complexity score. Furthermore, developer interviews were transcribed and thematically analyzed.

4.1 Quantitative Results for RQ1: Complexity Analysis

The analysis of impact on complexity from variant management strategies shows that the dominant strategy for the Application layer is strategy B, followed by strategy C. Keeping control of complex hardware as separate or largely separate variants is beneficial. The same goes for sensor control and monitoring in the Sensor layer. Signaling & Middleware as well as System management layers, on the other hand, seem to be more susceptible to keeping common components over multiple product lines. The OS-API is mostly header files with low complexity. The distribution is shown in Fig. 3.

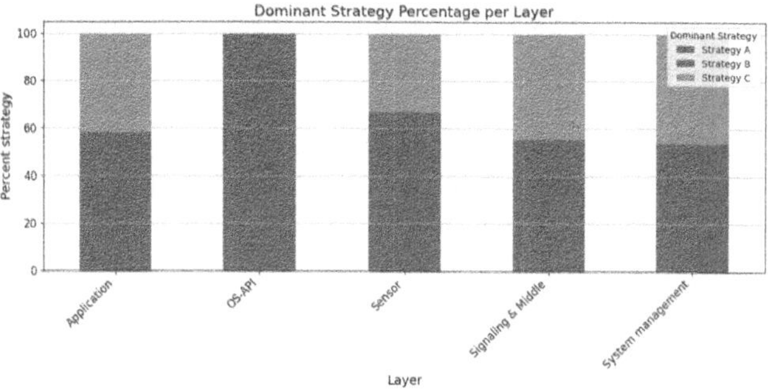

Fig. 3. Figure showing percentage of strategy used per layer in the architecture.

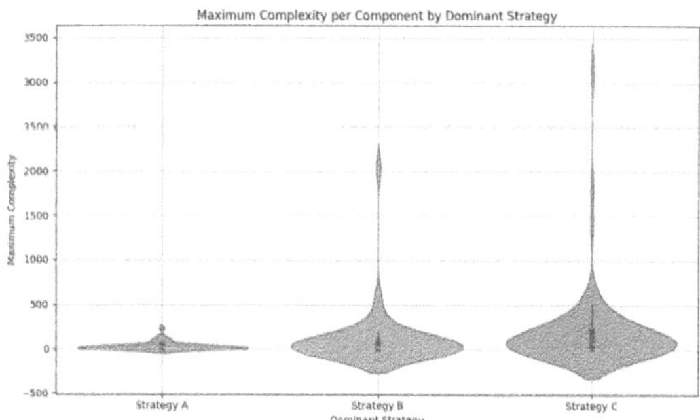

Fig. 4. Figure showing the distribution of maximum complexity per component grouped by dominant strategy.

Figure 4 shows the distribution of maximum complexity per component grouped by dominant strategy (A, B, or C). Strategy A is narrow and short with most values clustered near the bottom, meaning that strategy A leads to a low and consistent complexity. Strategy B is taller with wider distribution, and it peaks at quite a high value, meaning that strategy B has more variation in complexity and higher complexity. Strategy C stretches over a wider range and has the highest peak, meaning it is the least consistent and has the highest complexity.

4.2 Quantitative Results for RQ2: Coupling and Cohesion Analysis

Fan-in and fan-out were calculated between components. Cohesion was calculated as:

$$\text{cohesion}(C) = \frac{\text{number of calls within component C}}{\text{total calls made by C}} \tag{1}$$

The distributions are collected in Fig. 5, and show that: 1) Fan-in has a higher and taller distribution for Strategy A, and to some extent for Strategy C, suggesting that the common cross-product line files are highly dependent upon other components. 2) Fan-out is more evenly spread, but components using Strategy C generally tend to have higher and more varied dependency on other components. 3) Cohesion is highest in components using Strategy A, although it seems possible to achieve high cohesion employing all strategies.

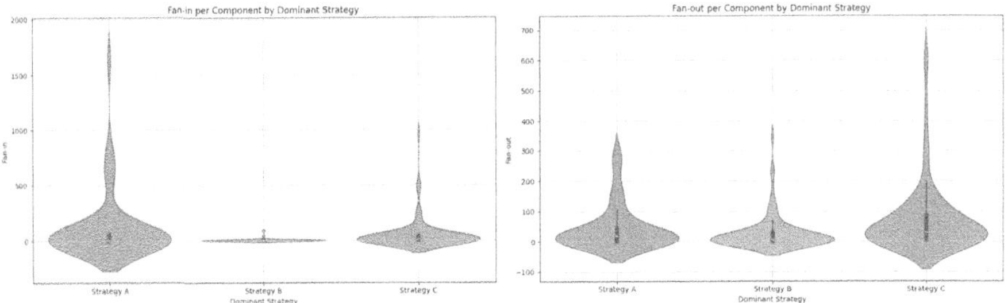

(a) Distribution of fan-in per component grouped by dominant strategy.

(b) Distribution of fan-out per component grouped by dominant strategy.

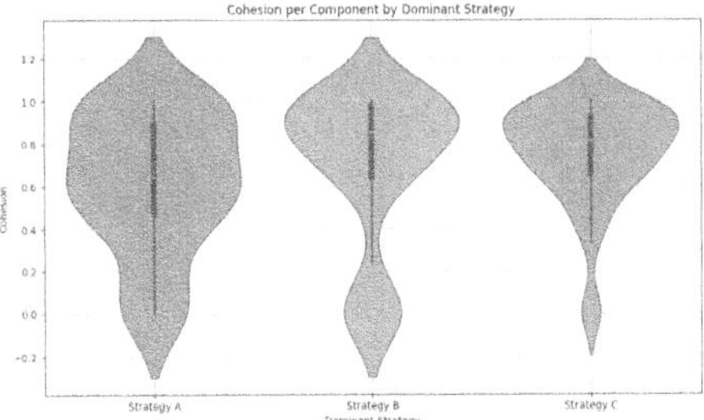

(c) Distribution of cohesion per component grouped by dominant strategy.

Fig. 5. Results from structural analysis.

It is also important to note that Strategy A led to lower complexity and higher cohesion.

4.3 Qualitative Results from Developer Interviews

The developer interviews were scanned for all mentions of variant management, and thematic analysis was performed. The following themes were found:

Increasing Amount of Variants: Across multiple developers' accounts, a recurring issue is the rapid growth of variants, often driven by hardware differences. **RQ1 Link**: This directly increased component complexity. When too many variants coexist, developers face more dependencies, more if/else logic, and overall parts that are harder to maintain. **RQ2 Link**: The structural property most impacted is coupling—many variants create interdependencies across code, intensifying the risk that a change in one branch breaks another.

Variant Strategy Impact on Architecture: Interviewees describe a range of variant-handling strategies confirming strategies A, B, and C. **RQ1 Link**: Inconsistent use of these strategies can increase complexity. **RQ2 Link**: (1) Splitting code into separate modules can maintain clarity. However, too many modules may fragment the architecture. (2) Some strategies preserve common interfaces; others rely on shared logic with many if/else statements.

Increased Testing Effort: Multiple interviewees highlight that the more variants there are, the more tests must be run to ensure no unintended side effects in another variant. **RQ1 Link**: As the number of variants grows, the maintenance/testing effort grows, indirectly adding to "complexity" (complex to confirm correctness across variants). **RQ2 Link**: Testing overhead can push teams to keep code more unified (to reduce test permutations), but that can increase code complexity.

Organizational Complexity: Developers repeatedly mention that deadlines, legacy integration, and a "high project pace" reduce the time available to restructure code for better long-term maintainability. **RQ1 Link**: Lack of time to refactor or unify variant-handling leads to growth in complexity over time. **RQ2 Link**: Work with structural properties is prioritized lower than feature delivery to multiple product lines quickly.

Summarizing Qualitative Answers to Research Questions

(1) High modularity arises when each variant that differs substantially is properly isolated (one developer notes that "If the code is so different, create a separate variant"), and truly common aspects are kept in shared modules with clean interfaces.
(2) Low coupling is easier to maintain when these boundaries are well-established and tested. However, partial overlap between variants can create hidden couplings if not carefully managed.

5 Discussion

In this study we investigated how different variant management strategies influence both the complexity of individual components and the structural properties of the overall software architecture.

We identified a trade-off between customization and manageable complexity. Strategies B and C generally had higher and Strategy A lower and more consistent complexity. As also seen in the literature, complex hardware control was a major contributor to high complexity scores [3], leading to the use of Strategy B. However, as the interviews revealed, Strategy A can lead to an abundance of conditional statements and an eventual surge in the testing overhead. This leads to the conclusion that there seems to be a total amount of complexity that cannot be reduced, only moved around.

The structural analysis of fan-in, fan-out, and cohesion indicated that common modules used across multiple variants tend to see high fan-in. At the same time, developers highlighted how "splitting modules into too many specialized variants" can increase the effort of maintaining them, particularly if large segments of functionality remain partially shared (Strategy C). These observations underscore the nuanced effect of variant management on traditional quality attributes like coupling and cohesion [8,11].

A key insight emerging from the interviews is that no single variant strategy works perfectly in all scenarios. Instead, an optimal approach may be to apply the strategies selectively, e.g., separate modules for drastically different hardware, but maintain well-defined shared interfaces for truly common functionality. This aligns with literature on software product line practices [2].

Validity: The following threats to validity have been identified:

Construct Validity. This study uses cyclomatic complexity and function-call analysis (fan-in, fan-out) as proxies for maintainability. While these metrics are widely adopted in software engineering [6], they might not capture all aspects related to maintainability. We triangulated metric-based analysis with qualitative insights from developer interviews to mitigate this. **Internal Validity**. Internal validity could be threatened by other factors that influence component complexity or structural properties. For instance, certain components are inherently more complex because they implement control of complex hardware. We addressed this by examining multiple components across two embedded systems and cross-referencing complexity measures with developer interviews. **External Validity**. This case study was conducted at a single OEM in the heavy-vehicle segment, so generalizing the findings to other organizations or domains may be limited. However, many automotive and embedded contexts face similar variant management challenges [2,10].

Overall, we have taken measures to reduce threats to validity by combining multiple data sources and following established case study protocols [13].

6 Conclusions

This study showed that different strategies for variant management affect embedded systems' complexity and structural properties. Overall, if a system's task is complex (such as controlling complex hardware), there are ways of balancing complexity, structural coupling, and cohesion so that they become manageable in their context. For example, creating completely separate variants of a component will make the complexity of the code more manageable, moving some of the complexity to testing effort and building system complexity.

Future research could replicate our methodology across different companies or product lines, comparing how domain-specific constraints (e.g., safety standards, hardware diversity) impact architectural maintainability outcomes.

References

1. Elmidaoui, S., Cheikhi, L., Idri, A., Abran, A.: Empirical studies on software product maintainability prediction: a systematic mapping and review. E-Informatica Softw. Eng. J. **13**(1), 141–202 (2019)
2. Eklund, U., Gustavsson, H.: Architecting automotive product lines: industrial practice. Sci. Comput. Program. **78**(12), 2347–2359 (2013). https://doi.org/10.1016/j.scico.2012.06.008
3. Fischer, S., Linsbauer, L., Lopez-Herrejon, R.E., Egyed, A., Ramler, R.: Bridging the gap between software variability and system variant management: experiences from an industrial machinery product line. In: 2015 41st Euromicro Conference on Software Engineering and Advanced Applications, pp. 402–409 (2015). https://doi.org/10.1109/SEAA.2015.57
4. ISO/IEC 25010:2023 (2023). https://www.iso.org/obp/ui#iso:std:iso-iec:25010:ed-2:v1:en. Accessed 28 May 2024
5. Jin, W., Zhong, D., Cai, Y., Kazman, R., Liu, T.: Evaluating the impact of possible dependencies on architecture-level maintainability. IEEE Trans. Softw. Eng. **49**(3), 1064–1085 (2023). https://doi.org/10.1109/TSE.2022.3171288
6. Malhotra, R., Lata, K.: A systematic literature review on empirical studies towards prediction of software maintainability. Soft. Comput. **24**(21), 16655–16677 (2020). https://doi.org/10.1007/s00500-020-05005-4
7. Manz, C., Stupperich, M., Reichert, M.: Towards integrated variant management in global software engineering: an experience report. In: 2013 IEEE 8th International Conference on Global Software Engineering, pp. 168–172 (2013). https://doi.org/10.1109/ICGSE.2013.29
8. Mari, M., Eila, N.: The impact of maintainability on component-based software systems. In: 2003 Proceedings 29th Euromicro Conference, pp. 25–32 (2003). https://doi.org/10.1109/EURMIC.2003.1231563
9. Mo, R., Cai, Y., Kazman, R., Xiao, L., Feng, Q.: Architecture anti-patterns: automatically detectable violations of design principles. IEEE Trans. Softw. Eng. **47**(5), 1008–1028 (2019)
10. Pal, M., Dommeti, K.D., KK, P.: Software product line architecture strategy to develop large scale products with conflicting customer requirements. In: 2024 IEEE 21st International Conference on Software Architecture Companion (ICSA-C), ICSA-C, pp. 48–53 (2024). https://doi.org/10.1109/ICSA-C63560.2024.00014

11. Rachow, P.: Refactoring decision support for developers and architects based on architectural impact. In: 2019 IEEE International Conference on Software Architecture Companion (ICSA-C), pp. 262–266 (2019). https://doi.org/10.1109/ICSA-C.2019.00054
12. Rahmati, Z., Tanhaei, M.: Ensuring software maintainability at software architecture level using architectural patterns. AUT J. Math. Comput. **2**(1), 81–102 (2021)
13. Runeson, P., Höst, M.: Guidelines for conducting and reporting case study research in software engineering. Empir. Softw. Eng. **14**(2), 131–164 (2009)
14. Automotive Software Architectures. Springer, Cham (2021). https://doi.org/10.1007/978-3-030-65939-4_9

AI-Driven Machine Learning Architecture for Scalable Irrigation Detection in Precision Agriculture: A Case Study with CropX

Jakub Ozimek[1], Matan Yakobovich[1], Henk-Jan Hoving[2], and Andrea Capiluppi[1(✉)]

[1] Department of Computing Science, University of Groningen, Groningen, The Netherlands
a.capiluppi@rug.nl

[2] CropX Europe, Groningen, The Netherlands

Abstract. Agriculture is a significant contributor to global water consumption, making the optimization of irrigation practices essential for sustainability. CropX, an agritech startup, seeks to automate irrigation event detection using large-scale Volumetric Water Content (VWC) data from IoT sensors. Ensuring scalability and accuracy is vital for decision-making within CropX's farm management system.

This paper describes the development of scalable machine learning (ML) models to automate irrigation detection in large, unbalanced datasets. We discuss the architectural patterns and software design decisions that enable these models to be effectively deployed within an AI-driven system, emphasizing MLOps and CI/CD practices. Multiple ML models were tested, including statistical methods (ARIMA, Kalman Filter), anomaly detection techniques (Isolation Forest), and ensemble approaches. These were evaluated using performance metrics such as F1 score, precision, and recall. Additionally, we highlight the role of human-in-the-loop strategies in refining model predictions, showcasing the interaction between agronomists and AI-driven recommendations.

Our contribution includes an analysis of the software architecture used for deploying ML models, focusing on microservices, data pipelines, and scalable cloud-based solutions. We illustrate how this system integrates with existing farm management platforms and discuss its implications for future AI-based agent systems in precision agriculture.

The ensemble models achieved superior performance, significantly improving the F1 score compared to individual models. Their integration into CropX's infrastructure has enhanced irrigation event detection while optimizing resource usage. In addition, a robust software architecture will support continuous integration and model evolution, ensuring system scalability.

Keywords: Machine learning · time series analysis · anomaly detection · precision agricolture · sensorless prediction

V. Andrikopoulos et al. (Eds.): ECSA 2025, LNCS 15929, pp. 389–405, 2026.
https://doi.org/10.1007/978-3-032-02138-0_27

1 Introduction

Water stress is a critical global issue, particularly in agriculture, which is responsible for a significant portion of water consumption [28]. The need for more efficient water management strategies has driven the adoption of precision irrigation technologies, with the goal of optimizing resource use while maintaining or improving crop yields. In this context, CropX, an agritech startup, offers digital farming solutions, including a farm management system that relies heavily on accurate irrigation event detection. Manual labelling of the VWC data gathered from IoT-enabled sensors is impractical due to the scale, automated machine learning (ML) models need to be developed to handle this task.

Machine learning has become integral to modern agriculture, addressing challenges such as crop yield prediction, anomaly detection and resource optimisation [7,23]. In particular, ML models have been successfully employed for detecting anomalies in time-series data, including irrigation events and sensor faults, by leveraging deep learning, ensemble methods and statistical models [2,13]. However, the application of these models to large, unbalanced datasets in real-world agricultural settings remains challenging, particularly in ensuring scalability and robustness across diverse environments [24]. Current methods often struggle to maintain accuracy and efficiency when applied to large-scale data, underscoring the need for scalable solutions that can operate effectively in diverse agricultural contexts. This paper not only evaluates machine learning models for irrigation detection but also explores how these models fit within a broader software architecture, utilizing architectural patterns that ensure reliability and scalability.

Water management systems, including precision irrigation, have also benefited from advances in sensor technology and ML-driven analysis [9,25]. Soil moisture measurement plays a crucial role in these systems, with soil moisture sensors and remote sensing technologies helping to optimise irrigation scheduling and conserve water [27,30]. Despite the promise of these technologies, challenges remain in terms of scalability, cost and technological adoption, particularly for widespread use in agriculture [20].

The main challenge addressed in this work is the development of scalable, accurate machine learning models to automate the detection of irrigation events from VWC data. CropX's vast dataset presents both an opportunity and a challenge: while the data can provide valuable insights for improving agricultural efficiency, manual labelling of such large datasets is not feasible. This project aims to develop ML models that can handle the complexity of time-series agricultural data, while ensuring the scalability and integration of these models into CropX's broader farm management system.

The contributions of this paper are twofold:

1. An evaluation of statistical, anomaly detection and machine learning models for detecting irrigation events in large, unbalanced time-series datasets. This includes models such as ARIMA, Kalman Filter, Isolation Forest and ensemble methods like XGBoost.

2. An analysis of the software engineering practices required to integrate these models into CropX's real-time decision support system. We focus on system architecture, continuous integration and data management strategies to ensure scalability, reliability and maintainability of the solution.

The remainder of this paper is organised as follows: Sect. 2 provides an overview of related work on machine learning in agriculture, focusing on anomaly detection and precision irrigation systems. Section 3 outlines the methodology, including data pre-processing, model selection and implementation. Section 4 presents the results of the models, discussing their performance in the context of irrigation detection. Section 5 examines the software engineering aspects of integrating the models into CropX's system. Finally, Sect. 6 discusses the threats to validity and how we plan to mitigate each, while Sect. 7 concludes the paper and suggests directions for future research.

2 Related Work

The integration of AI in software development is expanding, with applications across various stages of the SDLC [4,11]. AI-powered CI/CD is emerging as a key approach for automating software delivery [16]. While offering efficiency improvements, AI integration also presents challenges, particularly within Agile methodologies [6]. AI is being applied to automate routine tasks, analyze datasets, and enhance productivity [3]. However, integrating AI governance into the SDLC remains complex [12]. Research at Microsoft highlights challenges in AI-based software development, such as managing data and customizing models [1]. Additionally, developing continuous AI pipelines introduces challenges in data handling, model training, and system operations [26].

Our work addresses gaps in scalability and integration in AI-driven agricultural applications, particularly for irrigation event detection. While prior research explored AI in agriculture, we focus on large-scale datasets and ML-based solutions for irrigation management. Our contributions enhance scalability and ensure real-time deployment, supporting agricultural decision-making while addressing challenges in precision agriculture.

Below, we discuss ML applications in agriculture, focusing on anomaly detection and crop yield prediction (2), as well as precision irrigation and water management, emphasizing sensor technologies and ML-driven optimization (2).

Machine Learning in Agriculture - ML is integral to precision agriculture, improving crop management, livestock care, and resource optimization. ML models aid in crop yield prediction, disease detection, and soil analysis by leveraging sensor and weather data [7,23]. These models enhance agricultural efficiency and sustainability [14]. Crop yield forecasting, using historical and environmental data, offers improved accuracy over traditional methods [15].

Anomaly detection plays a crucial role in monitoring irrigation events, sensor faults, and crop behavior. Time series analysis, deep learning, and ensemble methods are widely used for anomaly detection [2,13]. Integrating these techniques into agricultural monitoring improves farm productivity by enabling early issue detection [18]. However, challenges persist in building scalable models for diverse environments [24].

Our study advances this field by implementing scalable ML models designed for large, unbalanced agricultural datasets. Using anomaly detection, statistical, and ensemble methods (e.g., Isolation Forest, ARIMA), we enhance model generalization for real-world conditions.

Precision Irrigation and Water Management - Water conservation is a major agricultural concern, with precision irrigation technologies optimizing resource use while sustaining yields [25]. ML-driven systems, integrated with IoT and remote sensing, enable site-specific irrigation based on real-time soil and plant data [8,9]. Advanced irrigation techniques, such as drip and sprinkler systems, achieve significant water savings [22]. However, economic and technological barriers hinder widespread adoption [20].

Soil moisture measurement is crucial for efficient irrigation. Advances in sensor and remote sensing technologies have improved accuracy, contributing to water conservation and crop yield optimization. Soil moisture sensors can reduce water use significantly while maintaining productivity [27]. Remote sensing offers broad coverage but is limited to surface moisture, whereas sensors provide subsurface data [29]. Future research aims to develop high-precision, cost-effective sensors for optimized irrigation [21,30].

Our work builds upon these advancements by integrating ML models with IoT-enabled sensors in real-time production environments. By leveraging MLOps and CI/CD practices, we ensure scalable and adaptive solutions for precision irrigation at scale.

3 Methodology

3.1 Site Selection and Description

The research project was carried out in collaboration with CropX[1], an international agritech startup focused on providing digital farming solutions. CropX's core mission is to enhance farm management practices through the development of tools that monitor and optimise irrigation, fertiliser usage and other agricultural inputs. Central to CropX's solution is its farm management system, which collects and analyses soil moisture and irrigation data from sensors installed in various locations worldwide. These insights are used to assist farmers in improving resource efficiency and ensuring sustainable agricultural practices. Figure 1 shows how CropX integrates soil data, sensors and software solutions containing ML models[2].

[1] https://cropx.com/.

[2] System architecture taken from https://aws.amazon.com/solutions/case-studies/cropx-case-study/.

For the purposes of this study, data from CropX's sensor network was utilised. The sensors monitor VWC in real-time, enabling accurate tracking of irrigation events. CropX operates across multiple global locations and the datasets provided included information from fields with different environmental and soil conditions. The diversity in site characteristics allowed for the development and testing of machine learning models that can generalise across different farming conditions.

In addition to working with the data, the project was embedded within CropX's existing software ecosystem. This required the integration of machine learning models into CropX's larger farm management platform, ensuring compatibility and smooth interaction with their existing infrastructure. We worked closely with the company's software engineer, following standard industry practices and adhering to CropX's development methodologies. This collaboration allowed to develop AI solutions within a real-world production environment, contributing to CropX's active systems.

Moreover, the project involved handling large-scale sensor data, requiring efficient data engineering practices to ensure that the models could function reliably and in real-time. On the other hand, our task was to optimise data ingestion pipelines, and to ensure that the ML models were capable of processing and predicting events across different farming locations globally. This large-scale data management was essential to ensure the models could be deployed effectively within CropX's operational systems.

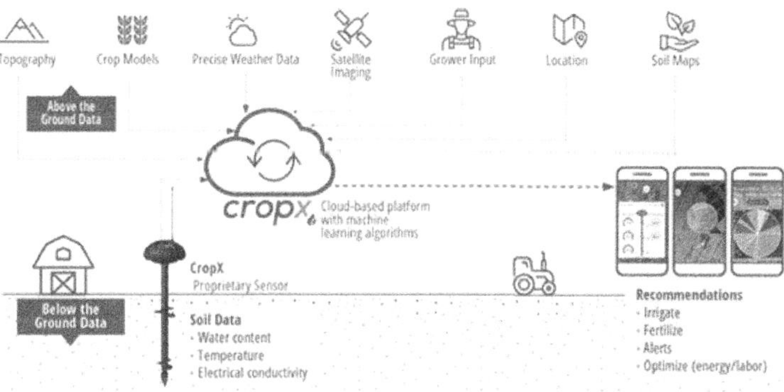

Fig. 1. CropX integration of sensors, ML and software solutions

The collaboration between CropX and the University of XYZ represents an important intersection of industry and academic research aimed at solving key challenges in modern agriculture. The integration of AI and software engineering practices within a commercial setting, with real-world data and industry tools, emphasised the practical application of the research outcomes.

3.2 Datasets

In the context of this case study, CropX provided two main categories of datasets: labeled and unlabeled. Both datasets were delivered in CSV format, containing columns such as 'field node ID', 'timestamp UTC', 'height' and volumetric water content ('VWC'). The labeled dataset included an additional 'label' column, representing the likelihood of an irrigation event occurring[3]. The core structure of the datasets is summarised in Table 1.

The *labeled* dataset contained approximately 400,000 rows and about 2,000 labeled irrigation events. In contrast, the *unlabeled* datasets were substantially larger, containing a combined 10 million rows: this difference alone highlighted the need for scalable machine learning solutions.

3.3 Architectural Design

To ensure the scalability of CropX's ML-powered irrigation detection, we designed a modular, cloud-based microservices architecture. Each component is responsible for specific tasks, including data ingestion, anomaly detection, and decision support. The architecture follows event-driven principles to facilitate real-time processing of sensor data.

Key architectural patterns include:

- **Event-driven architecture:** Ensures that new sensor readings trigger anomaly detection in real-time.
- **Microservices-based deployment:** Allows for independent scaling of different components, such as the prediction engine and data pipeline.
- **CI/CD integration:** Automates model deployment, validation, and rollback strategies for continuous updates.
- **Human-in-the-loop interaction:** Provides agronomists with an interface to validate and refine model predictions, incorporating domain expertise into the AI workflow.

Table 1. Dataset Columns

Column	Type	Description
field node ID	Integer	ID of the field node where the measurement was taken
timestamp UTC	DateTime	Time of the measurement
height	Integer	Depth at which the measurement was taken (inches)
VWC	Float	Volumetric Water Content
label	Float	Likelihood of an irrigation event (labeled dataset only)

[3] This label was only available in the smaller, labeled dataset.

3.4 Model Selection

The process of model selection involved evaluating a variety of statistical, machine learning and clustering models based on their ability to detect anomalies in the context of time-series soil moisture data. The dataset included large-scale, unbalanced data, posing a challenge for many algorithms. The models tested were chosen based on their previous performance in similar contexts, with the primary goal of optimising for F1 score (Table 2).

Table 2. Overview of models considered for anomaly detection

Model Type	Models Considered
Statistical Models	Moving Average, ARIMA, Kalman Filter
Change Point Detection	Binary Segmentation
Classical Machine Learning	OCSVM, Isolation Forest, IFASD, LOF, XGBoost
Clustering	DBSCAN

Initially, two statistical models (*Moving Average* and *Kalman Filter*) were selected for their simplicity and success in handling time-series data. In addition, the ARIMA model (AutoRegressive Integrated Moving Average) was also tested [5]: since it has been particularly effective in time-series anomaly detection, and in diverse contexts ([17,19,31].

The *Kalman Filter* was chosen for its ability to handle noisy data through recursive filtering. It works by updating estimates of the state variables over time based on new data and its associated noise.

The *Isolation Forest* model was included due to its robust anomaly detection capabilities in high-dimensional data. It constructs isolation trees where anomalies are identified by short average path lengths. An enhanced version, *Isolation Forest ASD*, was also considered due to its ability to process streaming data through sliding windows.

During the initial trials, certain models were set aside. The *One-Class Support Vector Machine* (OCSVM) and *Local Outlier Factor* (LOF) models exhibited poor performance when dealing with the unbalanced nature of the dataset, particularly in detecting irrigation events with high accuracy. As such, they were not pursued further in this study. Also synthetic oversampling techniques (such as SMOTE) were considered to further enhance minority class performance in irrigation detection, but only considered as future work.

Finally, supervised models like *XGBoost* and *DBSCAN* were tested. Despite being a supervised learning model, *XGBoost* was selected for a proof-of-concept due to its efficiency in handling large datasets and proven track record in machine learning competitions. However, due to the lack of extensive labeled data, it was not prioritised for further exploration. *DBSCAN* was used as it does not require predefined cluster counts and performed well in clustering-based anomaly detection.

3.5 Evaluation Metrics

The evaluation of the models was based primarily on binary classification metrics, as anomaly detection in this context is a binary problem: either an irrigation event is detected or not. The following metrics were used to assess model performance:

- **F1 Score:** The harmonic mean of precision and recall, representing the balance between false positives and false negatives.
- **Precision:** The ratio of correctly predicted irrigation events to the total number of detected events.
- **Recall:** The ratio of detected events to the total number of actual irrigation events in the ground truth.
- **False Positive Rate (FPR):** The proportion of non-irrigation events incorrectly classified as irrigation events.
- **False Negative Rate (FNR):** The proportion of irrigation events that were not detected by the model.

The F1 score was used as the primary metric for model comparison due to its ability to balance precision and recall. Each model's performance was evaluated by tuning hyperparameters such as contamination rate (for Isolation Forest) and window size (for Moving Average). Confusion matrices were generated to calculate the aforementioned metrics.

3.6 Testing Procedure

The model testing followed a structured flow, where each model was implemented in Python and tested using a unified procedure. The following steps summarise the testing flow:

1. Implement the model in Python.
2. Adjust hyperparameters.
3. Test performance using the chosen metrics.
4. Repeat steps 2 and 3 until optimal parameters are found.
5. Conclude the testing process.

4 Results

The models were evaluated using a cross-validation approach, ensuring that the results were not biased by any single subset of the data. The results of the machine learning models applied to CropX's irrigation event detection system are summarised in Table 3. The evaluation focused on key performance metrics including F1 score, precision, recall, false positive rate (FPR), and false negative rate (FNR).

- **Moving Average (MA)**: The MA model performed well in cases where the data had *minimal variance*. However, its simplicity made it unsuitable for more diverse datasets with higher variability. It was easy to implement but lacked robustness in detecting anomalies in more complex scenarios.
- **ARIMA**: This model, while powerful for time series forecasting, struggled with anomaly detection for the irrigation dataset. ARIMA's reliance on stationary data required transformations, which made it less flexible for detecting irregular irrigation events.
- **Kalman Filter**: The Kalman Filter showed promising results by effectively combining noisy data streams and smoothing them. However, its F1 score (0.436) indicated limited success in detecting irrigation events, and further optimisation of noise parameters would be needed for better accuracy.
- **Binary Segmentation (BinSeg)**: This change point detection model yielded the best results for univariate time series. With an F1 score of 0.517, it effectively identified shifts in water content. The penalty value of 4 provided the optimal performance, reducing both false positives and false negatives.
- **Isolation Forest (IF)**: Isolation Forest excelled in anomaly detection due to its simplicity and computational efficiency. Its performance improved as parameters such as contamination level and number of trees were optimised. It was particularly effective at detecting irrigation anomalies with minimal adjustments.
- **Isolation Forest ASD (IFASD)**: A variant of Isolation Forest, IFASD introduced sliding windows to enhance performance with streaming data. It improved on the original model in handling time series data, but further testing with optimal parameter configurations was recommended.
- **DBSCAN**: This density-based clustering model detected anomalies by identifying noise points. While novel in agricultural anomaly detection, it struggled with parameter tuning (e.g., neighbourhood radius and minimum points). Results indicated it was less effective than other models tested for irrigation event detection.

4.1 XGBoost

Due to the limited availability of labeled data, XGBoost was implemented only as a proof of concept. Since acquiring labelled data was a challenge, we created pseudo-labelled data through an interpolation process to simulate the presence of real labels. This allowed us to apply XGBoost to predict irrigation events based on the available volumetric water content data.

The model was tested with different hyperparameters (tree depth, learning rate, and the number of boosting rounds) in an effort to optimise its performance. The results demonstrated that XGBoost offered promising outcomes, especially in terms of a low false positive rate compared to other models evaluated.

Although we concluded that XGBoost showed potential in this context, the proof of concept was merely an initial step. Further testing with a comprehensive, fully labelled dataset would be necessary to avoid overfitting and to validate the model's robustness in detecting irrigation events. While the initial results were encouraging, future research would need to focus on obtaining and utilising more extensive labelled data to fully exploit the benefits of the XGBoost model.

4.2 Ensemble Model

The best F1 scores were achieved with an ensemble model which combined the top-performing models (Isolation Forest, MA and ARIMA), as well as the less performing ones. We used two approaches to determine the weights to be used in the ensemble: the first was based on each of the models weighing the same (thus, with a weight of $\frac{1}{7}$).

In the second approach, each model got assigned weight based on their corresponding highest F1 score: each weight was calculated as the fraction of the model's F1 score by the sum of F1 scores. In addition, two models (DBSCAN and KF) showed better performance in the ensemble than in the individual runs: for DBSCAN, the best individual performance was achieved with an eps value of 0.007, but ab eps value of 0.01 produced better overall results within the ensemble model. A similar pattern was observed with the Kalman filter: it performed best on its own with a measurement noise value of 0.4, but within the ensemble, a noise value of 1 yielded better performance.

A table representing highest F1 scores, and the resulting weights, is presented below, Table 4.

Fixed Weights. In the fixed-weight configuration, each model contributed equally to the ensemble's decision-making process. The threshold for anomaly detection was varied, and the best performance was achieved with a threshold value of 0.5, yielding an F1 score of 0.716. This threshold value effectively

Table 3. Performance of Models with Best Parameters and Error Rates (False Positive Rate and False Negative Rate)

Model	Parameters	F1	Precision	Recall	FPR	FNR
MA	Window size (30), Threshold (3)	0.641	0.639	0.690	0.043	0.332
ARIMA	Threshold (4), Feature choice (vwc_diff)	0.668	0.697	0.707	0.039	0.338
KF	Threshold factor (1.5), Observation noise (0.4)	0.436	0.457	0.468	0.543	0.532
BiSeg	Penalty (4), Feature choice (vwc)	0.517	0.524	0.574	0.051	0.446
IF	Feature choice (vwc_diff_pct), Contamination (0.009), Bootstrapping (yes), Estimators (100)	0.639	0.650	0.625	0.18	0.38
IFASD	Sliding window (2000), Step size (200)	0.655	0.787	0.593	0.013	0.463
DBSCAN	eps (0.007), Min Samples (10)	0.450	0.478	0.491	0.522	0.509
XGBoost	Max Tree Depth, Feature choice (vwc)	0.678	0.720	0.650	0.10	0.34
Ensemble (fixed weights)	Model weights ($\frac{1}{7}$ for each), Threshold (0.5)	0.716	0.749	0.708	0.023	0.324
Ensemble (variable weights)	Model weights (variable), Threshold (0.8)	0.723	0.738	0.737	0.025	0.305

Table 4. Highest F1 scores and resulting weights for the models in the ensemble.

Model	F1 score	Calculated weight
MA	0.641	0.16
ARIMA	0.668	0.17
KF	0.420	0.11
BinSeg	0.517	0.13
IF	0.639	0.16
IFASD	0.655	0.17
DBSCAN	0.420	0.11

required a majority of models (four out of seven) to agree on an anomaly detection for it to be flagged. Precision increased to 0.749, while recall balanced at 0.708, demonstrating strong performance in anomaly detection, particularly in minimising false positives.

Variable Weights. For the variable-weight configuration, each model was assigned a weight proportional to its highest F1 score. This approach further refined the ensemble by prioritising models with better performance. The highest F1 score obtained with variable weights was 0.723, with a threshold value of 0.8. Precision increased significantly to 0.738, though recall decreased slightly to 0.737. This approach enhanced precision while slightly sacrificing recall, suggesting that a trade-off exists between the two metrics depending on the application requirements.

Overall, the ensemble model provided superior performance compared to any individual model, with the highest F1 score achieved when using variable weights and an anomaly detection threshold of 0.8.

The ensemble model's superior performance confirms the value of integrating multiple machine learning techniques for irrigation detection. Its balance between precision and recall, along with the low false positive rate, makes it an ideal candidate for real-time irrigation management systems. This finding aligns with earlier studies [7,14], who also emphasised the importance of ensemble methods for improving accuracy in agricultural machine learning applications.

5 Discussion

Integrating machine learning models into production, such as CropX's farm management system, requires robust software engineering practices for scalability, reliability, and maintainability. This section explores key challenges and solutions.

System Architecture - CropX's irrigation detection system integrates real-time data ingestion from IoT-enabled soil moisture sensors with ML-based anomaly detection (see Fig. 1). ML applications in agriculture must handle large, streaming datasets [14,23], necessitating a scalable, distributed architecture. CropX addresses this by enabling real-time processing and inference, ensuring minimal latency. The system's ability to scale horizontally by adding nodes aligns with best practices in precision agriculture [7,25], allowing adaptation to increasing data volumes. Scalability and flexibility remain critical for agricultural technologies evolving in diverse conditions [24].

Data Management - Effective data management is vital for irrigation detection, where sensor data can be noisy and incomplete. Data preprocessing and feature engineering are essential to maintaining ML model performance [14,30]. CropX employs an automated pipeline for real-time data cleaning and preprocessing, imputing missing values and computing features like soil moisture change rates. Similar preprocessing strategies are used in precision irrigation to optimize water usage [27,29]. Automation ensures consistent, high-quality input data, addressing challenges of sensor failures and noisy readings, as seen in other IoT-integrated agricultural systems [9,20].

Continuous Integration and Deployment (CI/CD) - Deploying ML models in production requires continuous updates to adapt to changing conditions [24]. CropX applies MLOps practices to automate deployment and monitoring via CI/CD pipelines, as follows:

- *Model versioning and experimentation*: CropX version-control's models and data to enable structured experimentation before deployment. This is crucial for irrigation detection, where models must adapt to seasonal variations and sensor behaviors [2,13].
- *Automated deployment and monitoring*: Trained models are deployed automatically, ensuring updates meet performance benchmarks. Similar practices are found in other ML-driven agricultural systems, where automated deployment is necessary to handle field variability [10,15]. Continuous monitoring detects performance degradation, enabling timely corrective actions, a best practice in MLOps for dynamic environments.
- *Retraining* Retraining schedules are usually monitored based on seasonal patterns and data drift metrics. Drift detection techniques (such as feature monitoring) are also planned to ensure long-term model reliability.

Maintainability and System Evolution - Modularity and maintainability enable seamless integration of new models and system evolution. Flexibility in ML-driven agricultural systems is critical for adapting to changing environmental conditions and practices [14,25]. CropX's modular design allows updates without disrupting the entire system, ensuring adaptability to new crop management or irrigation needs. As precision irrigation technologies advance, with improved sensors and remote sensing methods [21,30], CropX's infrastructure supports integration of emerging sensor types and data sources, further enhancing irrigation detection.

6 Threats to Validity

In this section we report the threats to internal, external, construct and conclusion validity. Internal validity refers to the degree to which the observed results are due to the variables of interest and not confounding factors. External validity concerns the generalisability of the study's findings to other contexts. Construct validity addresses the degree to which the study accurately measures the concepts it intends to measure. Conclusion validity refers to the reliability of the relationship between the treatment and the outcome (in our study, between the machine learning models and the irrigation event detection).

6.1 Internal Validity

In this study, one potential threat arises from the pre-processing steps applied to the Volumetric Water Content (VWC) data. Since the dataset contains millions of rows, the balance and cleaning of this large-scale data might introduce biases. For instance, incorrect handling of missing data or outliers could skew the model's performance metrics. Additionally, the hyperparameter tuning process, particularly for ensemble methods, might inadvertently favour certain models over others, leading to overfitting in the dataset.

Mitigation: To reduce this risk, a systematic and transparent data pre-processing pipeline was established, with clear documentation of how missing data, outliers and noise are handled. Cross-validation techniques such as k-fold cross-validation should be applied to prevent overfitting, ensuring that models generalise well to unseen data. Sensitivity analysis could be employed to assess the influence of pre-processing decisions on the model's performance.

6.2 External Validity

The data used in this study were sourced from the sensors deployed by CropX in specific agricultural environments. Although the fields vary in soil type and environmental conditions, the generalisability of the models to different crops, climates, or geographic regions remains uncertain. The models may perform differently when applied to datasets with diverse agricultural practices or where irrigation systems vary significantly, such as in regions with different water management strategies or sensor technologies.

Mitigation: To enhance external validity, first the models should be tested on additional datasets from various agricultural contexts, including different geographic regions, crops and irrigation systems. Second, it would help to conduct field trials in new environments in order to identify limitations and refine the models for broader applications. Third, incorporating multimodal data such as weather information or crop type could improve the model's adaptability across diverse scenarios. Finally, future research should involve testing the system on additional datasets from diverse climates, irrigation systems, and crop types to generalize the findings.

6.3 Construct Validity

In this case, irrigation event detection relies on machine learning models identifying changes in VWC levels. A threat to construct validity arises from the assumption that these changes directly reflect irrigation events. In practice, other factors such as man-made irrigation, soil type, or sensor malfunction could affect VWC readings, potentially leading to false positives or negatives in the model's outputs. The labelled dataset, although extensive, may also introduce bias if the labelling process is not perfectly aligned with actual irrigation events.

Mitigation: To mitigate this threat, the model's output was cross-referenced with additional data sources, such as rainfall records or farmer-reported irrigation logs, to distinguish irrigation events from environmental factors. In future, the labelled data could be enhanced through semi-supervised learning, using a combination of expert knowledge and automated labelling tools to reduce human bias in the labelling process. Regular audits of sensor functionality would also help ensure data quality and accuracy.

6.4 Conclusion Validity

The key metrics used, such as F1 score, precision and recall, provide a robust foundation for evaluating model performance. However, given the unbalanced nature of the dataset and the relatively small number of labelled irrigation events, the results may overestimate the models' capabilities. Additionally, the ensemble approach, which combines several models, may mask poor performance from individual models, leading to an overly optimistic interpretation of the overall accuracy.

Mitigation: To ensure conclusion validity, more attention should be given to evaluating the model's performance on minority classes (irrigation events), potentially through oversampling techniques or generating synthetic data to address class imbalance. Using alternative metrics like the Matthews Correlation Coefficient (MCC) can also offer a more nuanced evaluation of performance. Lastly, transparency in reporting the performance of individual models within the ensemble would ensure that any limitations of individual techniques are not obscured by the overall ensemble performance.

7 Conclusion

In this paper, we presented the integration of machine learning models into CropX's farm management system, specifically designed for scalable irrigation event detection based on large-scale Volumetric Water Content (VWC) data from IoT-enabled sensors. The work addressed key software engineering challenges, including the need for scalability, robust data management and continuous integration and deployment (CI/CD) processes, all of which are critical for deploying AI systems in production environments.

The ensemble model, which combined anomaly detection and time-series models, demonstrated superior performance for detecting irrigation events, achieving a high F1 score while maintaining low false positive rates. This success highlights the potential of machine learning models to significantly improve water management in precision agriculture, where real-time analysis and timely interventions are crucial. Our solution provided a sound foundation for real-world applications, particularly in agriculture, where the deployment of AI systems must be reliable and scalable.

By adopting modern software engineering practices, including modular system design and automated model deployment through MLOps pipelines, CropX has been able to ensure that its machine learning models can be continuously updated and monitored in real time, allowing for adaptive and reliable irrigation management. Additionally, the system's ability to handle large-scale sensor data in a distributed manner ensures that it can scale as CropX's network of sensors and customers grows.

While this study demonstrates promising results, several areas for further research were identified to enhance CropX's irrigation detection system: i) Incorporating *weather* and *climate data* could improve irrigation predictions, accounting for factors like evaporation and seasonal water availability; ii) incorporating *weather* and *satellite data* could also enhance irrigation event differentiation from natural water inputs, providing more robust predictions; iii) exploring *deep learning models*, such as recurrent neural networks (RNNs) or LSTMs, could capture more complex temporal patterns in VWC data, improving prediction accuracy; iv) the system's framework could be adapted for other agricultural tasks, such as crop health monitoring, pest detection, or yield prediction, enhancing the platform's value.

Data Availability. The data associated with this study are publicly available online in the replication package available at https://anonymous.4open.science/r/CropX-42E8/README.md

References

1. Amershi, S., et al.: Software engineering for machine learning: a case study. In: 2019 IEEE/ACM 41st International Conference on Software Engineering: Software Engineering in Practice (ICSE-SEIP), IEEE (2019)
2. Avolio, C., Tricomi, A., Zavagli, M., De Vendictis, L., Volpe, F., Costantini, M.: Automatic detection of anomalous time trends from satellite image series to support agricultural monitoring. In: 2021 IEEE International Geoscience and Remote Sensing Symposium IGARSS. IEEE (2021)
3. Barenkamp, M., Rebstadt, J., Thomas, O.: Applications of AI in classical software engineering. AI Perspect. **2**(1) (2020)
4. Sorte, B.W., Joshi, P.P., Jagtap, V.: Use of artificial intelligence in software development life cycle: a state of the art review (2015)
5. Box, G.E., Jenkins, G.M., Reinsel, G.C., Ljung, G.M.: Time Series Analysis: Forecasting and Control. John Wiley & Sons, Hoboken (2015)
6. Cabrero-Daniel, B.: Ai for Agile development: a Meta-Analysis (2023). arXiv.org

7. Deepa, R., Sivasamy, A., Selvam, S.: Optimising agricultural practices with machine learning: a comprehensive review. Int. J. Agric. Innov. Technol. Globalisation **3**(4), 354–369 (2023)
8. Evans, R.G., Sadler, E.J.: Methods and technologies to improve efficiency of water use. Water Res. Res. **44**(7) (2008)
9. Gundim, A.D.S., Melo, V.G.M.L.D., Coelho, R.D., Silva, J.P.D., Rocha, M.P.A.D., França, A.C.F., Conceição, A.M.P.D.: Precision irrigation trends and perspectives: a review. Ciência Rural **53**(8) (2023)
10. Gupta, S.K., et al.: Anamoly detection in very large scale system using big data. In: 2022 International Conference on Knowledge Engineering and Communication Systems (ICKES), pp. 1–6. IEEE (2022). arxiv:2112:14663
11. Kulkarni, R.H., Padmanabham, P.: Integration of artificial intelligence activities in software development processes and measuring effectiveness of integration. IET Softw. **11**(1), 18–26 (2017)
12. Laato, S., Birkstedt, T., Mäantymäki, M., Minkkinen, M., Mikkonen, T.: Ai governance in the system development life cycle. In: Proceedings of the 1st International Conference on AI Engineering: Software Engineering for AI, vol. 2, pp. 113–123. ACM (2022)
13. Leon-Lopez, K.M., Mouret, F., Arguello, H., Tourneret, J.Y.: Anomaly detection and classification in multispectral time series based on hidden markov models. IEEE Trans. Geosci. Remote Sens. **60**, 1–11 (2022)
14. Liakos, K., Busato, P., Moshou, D., Pearson, S., Bochtis, D.: Machine learning in agriculture: a review. Sensors **18**(8), 2674 (2018)
15. Salokhe, M.R.: Machine learning: applications in agriculture (crop yield prediction, diease and pest detection). Int. J. Adv. Res. Sci. Commun. Technol., 592–597 (2023)
16. Mohammed, A.S., Saddi, V.R., Gopal, S.K., Dhanasekaran, S., Naruka, M.S.: Ai-Driven Continuous Integration and Continuous Deployment in Software Engineering. In: 2024 2nd International Conference on Disruptive Technologies (ICDT), vol. 4, pp. 531–536. IEEE (2024)
17. Moschini, G., Houssou, R., Bovay, J., Robert-Nicoud, S.: Anomaly and fraud detection in credit card transactions using the ARIMA model. In: The 7th International Conference on Time Series and Forecasting, vol. 8, p. 56. MDPI (2021)
18. Moso, J.C., Cormier, S., de Runz, C., Fouchal, H., Wandeto, J.M.: Anomaly detection on data streams for smart agriculture. Agriculture **11**(11), 1083 (2021)
19. Pena, E.H.M., de Assis, M.V.O., Proenca, M.L.: Anomaly detection using forecasting methods ARIMA and HWDS. In: 2013 32nd International Conference of the Chilean Computer Science Society (SCCC), IEEE (2013)
20. Preite, L., Solari, F., Vignali, G.: Technologies to optimize the water consumption in agriculture: a systematic review. Sustainability **15**(7), 5975 (2023)
21. Munoth, P., Goyal, R., Tiwari, K.: Sensor based irrigation system: a review (2018)
22. Rastogi, M., et al.: advancing water conservation techniques in agriculture for sustainable resource management: a review. J. Geography Environ. Earth Sci. Int. **28**(3), 41–53 (2024)
23. Sharma, A., Jain, A., Gupta, P., Chowdary, V.: Machine learning applications for precision agriculture: a comprehensive review. IEEE Access **9**, 4843–4873 (2021)
24. Shaukat, K., et al.: A review of time-series anomaly detection techniques: a step to future perspectives. In: Arai, K. (ed.) FICC 2021. AISC, vol. 1363, pp. 865–877. Springer, Cham (2021). https://doi.org/10.1007/978-3-030-73100-7_60

25. Jog, S., Bhole, J., Gaikwad, A., Modi, A., Jadhav, C.: The green revolution 2.0: weather forecasting and precision irrigation reshaping crop yield enhancement. Int. J. Sci. Res. Sci. Eng. Technol. 83–89 (2023)
26. Steidl, M., Felderer, M., Ramler, R.: The pipeline for the continuous development of artificial intelligence models–current state of research and practice. J. Syst. Softw. **199**, 111615 (2023)
27. Touil, S., et al.: A review on smart irrigation management strategies and their effect on water savings and crop yield. Irrigat. Drainage **71**(5), 1396–1416 (2022)
28. UNESCO, et al.: The United Nations world water development report 2021: valuing water. United Nations (2021)
29. Vereecken, H., Huisman, J.A., Bogena, H., Vanderborght, J., Vrugt, J.A., Hopmans, J.W.: On the value of soil moisture measurements in vadose zone hydrology: a review. Water Res. Res. **44**(4) (2008)
30. Yu, L., et al.: Review of research progress on soil moisture sensor technology. Int. J. Agric. Biol. Eng. **14**(3), 32–42 (2021)
31. Zare Moayedi, H., Masnadi-Shirazi, M.: ARIMA model for network traffic prediction and anomaly detection. In: 2008 International Symposium on Information Technology. IEEE (2008)

Correction to: Software Architecture

Vasilios Andrikopoulos, Cesare Pautasso, Nour Ali, Jacopo Soldani, and Xiwei Xu

Correction to: V. Andrikopoulos et al. (Eds.): *Software Architecture*, LNCS 15929, https://doi.org/10.1007/978-3-032-02138-0

The original version of frontmatter was inadvertently published with the incorrect, which have now been corrected. The corrections to the book have been updated with the changes.

The updated version of this book can be found at https://doi.org/10.1007/978-3-032-02138-0

V. Andrikopoulos et al. (Eds.): ECSA 2025, LNCS 15929, p. C1, 2026.
https://doi.org/10.1007/978-3-032-02138-0_28

Author Index

A

Abdelmukaram, Osman 214
Abdelsalam, Kamel M. K. 99
Amalfitano, Domenico 73
Arts, Rowan 20
Ashraf, Elia 99

B

Bachmeier, Joshua 343
Bakhtin, Alexander 243
Baresi, Luciano 224
Batista, Thais 323
Becker, Steffen 181
Bhatt, Hiya 38
Biswas, Shaunak 38
Bochicchio, Matteo 90
Boltz, Nicolas 332
Brabec, Vernon Joseph 360

C

Capiluppi, Andrea 389
Capuano, Roberta 260
Cavalcante, Everton 323

D

De Luca, Marco 73
de Oliveira, Glauber Queiroz 116
Di Nucci, Dario 20
Diaz-Pace, J. Andres 276
Direen, Harry George 360
Direen, James Edward 360
Direen, Randal Hugh 360

E

Eisenreich, Tobias 144
Esposito, Matteo 243

F

Fasolino, Anna Rita 73
Ferreira, Renato Cordeiro 20
Fontana, Francesca Arcelli 90
Franz, Thomas 306

G

Garlan, David 276
Gerking, Christopher 332
Gerostathopoulos, Ilias 214
Gouigoux, Jean-Philippe 367

H

Haraldsson, Bengt 378
Heck, Petra 3
Henß, Jörg 343
Hoving, Henk-Jan 389

J

Jbari, Khaoula 367

K

Kailayanathan, Shanjay 360
Kazman, Rick 20, 323
Keim, Jan 99
Koziolek, Heiko 343
Kugele, Stefan 161
Kumara, Indika 20

L

Lenarduzzi, Valentina 243
Lestingi, Livia 224

M

Mata, Núria 161
Mauser, Lucas 144
Mendonça, Nabor C. 116
Motsios, Angelos 127
Muccini, Henry 260

N

Nakagawa, Elisa Yumi 323
Nedvědický, Pavel 144

V. Andrikopoulos et al. (Eds.): ECSA 2025, LNCS 15929, pp. 407–408, 2026.
https://doi.org/10.1007/978-3-032-02138-0

O
O'Dea, Eoan 260
Okumus, Fazli Faruk 161
Ozimek, Jakub 389

P
Peeters, Manon 3
Pelliccione, Patrizio 73

R
Raabe, Oliver 332
Raibulet, Claudia 214
Rakhunathan, Srinivasan 38
Reisis, Dionysios 127
Riegler, Michael 197

S
Salfeld, Maike 161
Salgert, Björn 306
Sametinger, Johannes 197
Santilli, Tiziano 73
Schweizer, Markus 161
Snoeren, Jacco 3
Sodhi, Balwinder 59
Sofat, Aashna 59
Soliman, Mohamed 99
Stadler, Marco 197
Staron, Miroslaw 378
Sterz, Leonie 332
Stieß, Sarah 181
Straub, Raphael 181

T
Taibi, Davide 243
Tamburri, Damian Andrew 20
Tamzalit, Dalila 367
Tessa, Claudio 90
Theodoropoulos, Theodoros 297
Thielen, Sven 306
Tichy, Matthias 181
Trubiani, Catia 276
Tsagkaropoulos, Alexandros 127
Tsigkanos, Christos 127

U
Urdih, Francesco 297

V
Vaidhyanathan, Karthik 38
van den Heuvel, Willem-Jan 20
Vasilakis, Christoforos 127
Venkatesh, Ashwin Prasad Shivarpatna 99
Veracx, Merel 3
Vierhauser, Michael 197

W
Waghubinger, Daniel 197
Wagner, Janne 332
Wagner, Stefan 144
Wäschle, Moritz 144
Wehbe, Iyad 224

Y
Yakobovich, Matan 389
York, George 360
Yussupov, Vladimir 343

Z
Zacchi, João-Vitor 161
Zdun, Uwe 297
Zimmermann, Eva 144

The manufacturer's authorised representative in the EU is Springer Nature Customer Service Centre GmbH, Europaplatz 3, 69115 Heidelberg, Germany. If you have any concerns regarding our products, please contact ProductSafety@springernature.com

Printed and bound by CPI Group (UK) Ltd, Croydon, CR0 4YY
28/04/2026
02098524-0007